Introduction to Scholastic Theology

INTRODUCTION TO

Scholastic Theology

Ulrich G. Leinsle

Translated by Michael J. Miller

The Catholic University of America Press
Washington, D.C.

Originally published in 1995 in German as Ulrich G. Leinsle,
Einführung in die scholastische Theologie
(Paderborn: Verlag Ferdinand Schöningh).

The paper used in this publication meets the minimum requirements
of American National Standards for Information Science—
Permanence of Paper for Printed Library Materials,
ANSI Z39.48-1984.
∞

Library of Congress Cataloging-in-Publication Data
Leinsle, Ulrich Gottfried.
[Einführung in die scholastische Theologie. English]
Introduction to scholastic theology / Ulrich G. Leinsle ;
Translated by Michael J. Miller.
p. cm.
Includes bibliographical references and index.
ISBN 978-0-8132-1792-5 (pbk. : alk. paper)
1. Scholasticism—History. I. Title.
B839.L4513 2010
230.09—dc22 2010028748

Contents

Abbreviations

Abbreviations for editions of complete works are noted during the discussion of the individual authors.

Periodicals and Series

ABG	Archiv für Begriffsgeschichte. Bonn.
AFP	Archivum Fratrum Praedicatorum. Rome.
AFrH	Archivum Franciscanum Historicum. Firenze [Florence].
AHD	Archives d'histoire doctrinale et littéraire du moyen âge. Paris.
AHSI	Archivum Historicum Societatis Iesu. Rome.
AnPraem	Analecta Praemonstratensia. Averbode.
ATG	Archivo teologico Granadino. Granada.
BGPh(Th)MA	Beiträge zur Geschichte der Philosophie (und Theologie) des Mittelalters. Münster.
CollFr	Collectanea Franciscana. Rome.
CUP	Chartularium Universitatis Parisiensis. Ed. by Heinrich Denifle. 4 vols. Paris 1889–1897.
EThL	Ephemerides theologicae Lovanienses. Leuven/Louvain.
FStud	Franziskanische Studien. Münster.
FZPhTh	Freiburger Zeitschrift für Philosophie und Theologie. Fribourg.
HDG	Handbuch der Dogmengeschichte. Ed. by Michael Schmaus. Freiburg im Breisgau.
HDThG	Handbuch der Dogmen- und Theologiegeschichte. Ed. by Carl Andresen. Göttingen.
HJ	Historisches Jahrbuch (der Görresgesellschaft). Munich.

HPBL	Historisch-politische Blätter für das katholische Deutschland. Munich.
HZ	Historische Zeitschrift. Munich.
MS	Mediaeval Studies. Toronto.
QuD	Quaestiones Disputatae. Freiburg im Breisgau.
RBen	Revue bénédictine de critique, d'histoire et de littérature religieuses. Maredsous.
RÉAug	Revue des études augustiniennes. Paris.
RechAug	Recherches augustinennes. Paris.
RGST	Reformationsgeschichtliche Studien und Texte. Münster.
RMAL	Revue du Moyen-âge latin. Strasbourg.
RSR	Recherches de science religieuse. Paris.
RThAM	Recherches de théologie ancienne et médiévale. Leuven/Louvain.
RThom	Revue thomiste. Paris.
SMGB	Studien und Mitteilungen zur Geschichte des Benediktinerordens und seiner Zweige. Munich.
SSL	Spicilegium sacrum Lovaniense. Leuven/Louvain.
StudLeib	Studia Leibnitiana. Wiesbaden.
ThPQ	Theologisch-Praktische Quartalschrift. Linz.
VIEG	Veröffentlichungen des Instituts für Europäische Geschichte Mainz. Wiesbaden.
WiWei	Wissenschaft und Weisheit. Düsseldorf.
ZKG	Zeitschrift für Kirchengeschichte. Stuttgart.
ZKTh	Zeitschrift für katholische Theologie. Innsbruck.

Introduction to Scholastic Theology

Introduction: What Is Scholastic Theology?

An introduction to Scholastic theology is in the first place an ambiguous undertaking, especially if it is to be done by a philosopher. It approaches its object from outside, so to speak. Its goal is to accompany the reader until he can move about without this introduction. But in what field should he be able to move about? In Scholastic theology, you will answer. Therefore the first question to ask is: "What is Scholastic theology?"

The whole purpose of this volume is to answer that question, and to do so only in a rudimentary way, in the form of an introduction. Therefore it is understood not as a question about the oft-invoked "essence" of Scholasticism, but rather—straightforwardly in an introduction—as a phenomenological or semantic question: What (sorts of things) do we signify with the term "Scholastic theology"? These may be quite dissimilar phenomena which admit of no univocal concept.[1] The characterization of a discipline as "Scholastic" seems initially and unproblematically to hark back to a use of the term "scholastic" that can be described as "pedagogical" and should be treated with well-founded suspicion. That is why it is necessary to survey the history of the concept "Scholastic theology," whereby "theology" is regarded as being specified by the adjective "Scholastic." At the same time we must stake out the boundaries within which this introduction will range.[2]

1 On the history of the concept "Scholasticism"

Derived from "σχολή" (leisure, ease, spare time, but also leisure devoted to the sciences, e.g., an instructor's lecture), we encounter "σχολαστικός"

1. The question is framed in a similar way in Schönberger, *Scholastik*, 15–19.

2. See especially the comprehensive study by Quinto, *Scholastica*; see also Schmidinger's article "Scholastik," *HWP* 8:1332–42; Schmidinger, "'Scholastik' und 'Neuscholastik'" and the bibliography cited therein.

for the first time in a philosophical context in the *Politics* of Aristotle (384–322 BC). It signifies a freely chosen activity which is performed for its own sake, and ultimately θεωρία as an expression of σχολή, the pursuit of what is essential unencumbered by the immediate requirements of living.[3] Aristotle's disciple Theophrast (372/369–288/285 BC) uses "σχολαστικός" in this sense to describe himself: he is someone who lives for θεωρία.[4] "Βίος θηωρητικός" for Chrysippus (281/277–208/204 BC) is synonymous with "βίος σχολαστικός" as a term for the way of life proper to the philosopher alone.[5] Through the organization of "schools of philosophers," "σχολή" or *"schola"* becomes in Cicero's time (106–43 BC) a term for everything concerned with the business of schooling: the place, the instruction, but also the [ideological] alignment of the school.[6] A *scholasticus,* accordingly, is anyone who has to do with the school, and in a broader sense an educated man *(eruditus, literatus, sapiens),* but especially the rhetorician (*rhetor,* first century BC) and the learned legal counselor (third century AD).[7]

This linguistic usage is essentially preserved in Christian antiquity also. We find *"scholasticus"* (sometimes in the superlative) especially as a mark of distinguished learning and erudition and as a term for rhetoricians, advocates and officials.[8] As late as the Merovingian period it is the customary title for a civil servant, whereas from the Carolingian period on it also designates the head of a cathedral, municipal, or monastic school.[9] In any case *scholasticus* is not found in the early and High Middle Ages as a (self-) description of a particular kind of theology, but rather as a description of persons, books, or a manner of speaking or teaching *(scholastice loquentes, scholasticae disputationes),* whereby "scholastic" can simply mean "learned," but also "academic" [*schulmässig,* sometimes implying dependence on a school of thought]. With reference to the education of his day, Haimo of Auxerre († ca. 855) defines *"scholastice"* as *"philosophice sive dialectice."*[10] In the twelfth century *scholasticus* serves in monastic circles (admittedly in very few instances) to character-

3. Aristotle, *Politics* 1313 b, 2–3; 1322 b, 38–39; 1341 a, 18–19; see also *Nicomachaean Ethics* 1177 b, 22.

4. Diogenes Laertios, *Vitae philosophorum* V, 37, ed. H. S. Long, vol. 1 (Oxford, 1965), 215.

5. Plutarch, *Moralia* 1033 c, ed. M. Pohlenz and R. Westmann (Leipzig, 1959), 6:2–3.

6. Cicero, *Tusculanae disputationes* 1.7–8, ed. K. Büchner (Zürich-Stuttgart, 1966), 8–9; 1.113 (114–15); 2.6 (146–47); 3.81 (270–71); 5.25 (278–79).

7. See Du Cange, *Glossarium mediae et infimae latinitatis* (Paris, 1883–1887), 6:350 (Papias); Sueton, *De grammaticis et rhetoribus* 30, ed. G. Burgudi (Leipzig, 1963), 4. *Theodosiani Libri* XVI, 8.10.2, ed. Th. Mommsen—P. M. Meyer (Berlin, 1905), 405. Claus, *Ho Scholastikós,* 20ff., 150ff.

8. See Manser, "Die mittelalterliche Scholastik"; Claus, *Scholastikós,* 95–125.

9. See Schmidinger, "Scholastik," 1334.

10. See Landgraf, "Zum Begriff der Scholastik," 488.

ize the methods and persons of the municipal or cathedral schools.[11] Even the title *Historia scholastica* by Petrus Comestor (ca. 1100–ca. 1179) indicates nothing more than the fact that the work was a popular medieval textbook.

"Scholastic" as a description of medieval philosophy and theology is a modern term. Erasmus of Rotterdam (1466–1536) and Martin Luther (1483–1546) explicitly contrast their positions with those of "scholastic" theology and philosophy, which they see embodied in the three late medieval schools *(sectae)* of the Thomists, the Scotists, and the Nominalists. "Scholasticism" takes on negative connotations and implies reverence for Aristotle, barbaric Latin, hair-splitting, sophistry, useless logical disputations and pastoral barrenness.[12] Luther's *Disputatio contra scholasticam theologiam* (1517) distances itself from a particular sort of theology, which besides the aforementioned evils is characterized by its Aristotelianism (especially the *Metaphysics*) and the overemphasis on man's capability as opposed to the grace of God which alone is effective *(sola gratia)*.[13] In view of this clear dissociation of Luther and the humanist disdain for Scholastic "barbarism," the early Protestant school cannot be described as Scholasticism. Moreover the initial Protestant altercations with Aristotelian metaphysics are conducted in a humanistic and not a Scholastic spirit. Thus in 1598 Rudolf Goclenius (1547–1628) publishes an *Isagoge in Peripateticorum et Scholasticorum Primam Philosophiam, quae dici consuevit Metaphysica*.[14] Later Christoph Scheibler (1589–1655) describes *"Theologia scholastica"* as a "strange sort of theology, as it is pursued by the noble professors at the great schools and other schools. In which nothing else is to be found but what they had to discuss most ingeniously *pro* and *contra*." In contrast, correct theology is entirely "directed *ad praxin* [toward practical formation] or at training."[15]

The rejection of Scholastic theology expounded here, however, could not prevent the establishment, influenced by the newly incorporated metaphysics of Catholic (and especially Spanish) Scholasticism, of a sort of Scholasticism in the Protestant schools as well, although it soon met with resistance from within those ranks.[16] The undifferentiated use of *scholasticus*

11. See Chenu, *La théologie au douzième siècle*, 325; Leclercq, *Wissenschaft und Gottverlangen*, 11.

12. See Dalfen, *Erasmus von Rotterdam*; Quinto, *Scholastica*, 133–41; Schmidinger, "'Scholastik' und 'Neuscholastik,'" 36–38.

13. WA 1, 224–28; see also the *Römerbrief-Vorlesungen* [Lectures on the Letter to the Romans] dated 1515–1516: WA 56, 273, 296, 312, 337, 354; Quinto, *Scholastica*, 208–15.

14. Frankfurt, 1598; see also Leinsle, *Ding*, 175–88.

15. Ch. Scheibler, *Aurifodina theologica* (Leipzig, 1727^2), A3ff. ; Leinsle, *Ding*, 324.

16. Especially Jakob Thomasius, "Historia variae fortunae, quam Metaphysica experta est," in Thomasius, *Erotemata Metaphysica* (Leipzig, 1670); see also Leinsle, *Reformversuche*, 141–46.

even as late as the seventeenth century is illustrated by the early Aristotelian scholar Christian Dreier (1610–1688), who contrasted his own philosophy with the interpretation of Aristotle proposed by *"Scholastici et Jesuitae,"* calling the former *"scholastica speculatio"* as opposed to *"praxis civica."*[17] The term "Scholasticism" is fraught with even more negative connotations in Enlightenment philosophy, which since the days of Christian Thomasius (1655–1728) saw in the "pedantic philosophy" of the "Papist monks and friars" nothing but a prejudiced doctrine beholden to the authority of the "dark," unenlightened centuries of yore.[18]

In contrast, the so-called Second Scholasticism or Baroque Scholasticism at the Catholic universities and religious houses of study at the turn of the eighteenth century consciously regarded itself as the continuation and renewal of medieval philosophy and theology.[19] Precisely in the expression *"theologia scholastica,"* however, "scholastic" acquires a new meaning. As distinguished from so-called positive theology (exegesis, casuistry, canon law), it designates *"theologia speculativa"* (systematic theology), which is carried out methodically first in the *Commentary on The Sentences of Peter Lombard,* and later in the *Summa Theologiae* of Thomas Aquinas or in the treatises of a *cursus theologicus.*[20]

"Scholasticism" thus signifies, from both the outsider's and the insider's perspective in the sixteenth to eighteenth centuries, medieval, and early modern philosophy and theology, especially at Catholic (but sometimes also at Protestant) universities and upper schools until the Enlightenment.[21] The Enlightenment claimed to have prevailed over it. The Catholic renewal of Scholastic (especially Thomistic) philosophy and theology in direct opposition to the Enlightenment in the nineteenth century is therefore described as Neoscholasticism. Although the term "Neo-Scholastic" originally had a political emphasis within the context of the Ultramontane movement, it eventually appears, thanks to the legitimacy bestowed on it by the encyclical *Aeterni Patris* dated August 4, 1879, as the name selected by philosophers, theologians, and periodicals themselves to make clear their

17. Ch. Dreier, *Sapientia seu Philosophia prima* (Königsberg, 1644), a2^{v}; see also Leinsle, *Reformversuche,* 128–34.

18. Ch. Thomasius, *Einleitung zur Hof-Philosophie* (Frankfurt/Leipzig, 1710), 39f. ; see also Leinsle, *Reformversuche,* 162–67. This theme continued to be influential down to the time of Hegel, see Schmidinger, "'Scholastik' und 'Neuscholastik,'" 42–43.

19. See Giacon, *La seconda scolastica;* Leinsle, "Scholastik," 54–69.

20. See Quinto, *Scholastica,* 238–95; Schmidinger, "'Scholastik' und 'Neuscholastik,'" 44; Lang, *Loci theologici,* 28; Tshibangu, *Théologie positive.*

21. See Leinsle, "Scholastik," 54–56.

ecclesiastical alignment.[22] Yet Neoscholasticism, like Baroque Scholasticism, is not just a repetition of the Middle Ages, but at least partially an application of Scholastic methods and teachings to new questions, which are nevertheless treated along the same lines as the old authorities and methodologies. Scholasticism (in most cases restricted to Thomism) thereby becomes a normative standard of philosophy and theology.

2 Attempts at a definition

"What-is-it" questions are not uncommonly understood to be questions calling for a definition. So it happened that in Neoscholasticism there were attempts to define the essence of the normative standard "Scholasticism" and thus to delineate a theoretical paradigm for the academic discipline.[23] These attempts at a definition should be critiqued in terms of their presuppositions and their historical suitability.

As early as 1909 the historian Martin Grabmann advocated a concept of Scholasticism informed by the Scholastic method: "The Scholastic method intends to gain as much insight as possible into the contents of the faith through the application of reason and philosophy to the truths of revelation, so as [1] to bring supernatural truth closer to the human mind which reflects on it, [2] to make possible a systematic, organically structured general presentation of the truth about salvation, and [3] to be able answer reasonably the objections raised against the contents of revelation."[24] This influential definition of the term, nevertheless, is both too broad and too narrow. It restricts Scholasticism to theology. However, since specialists have demonstrated that the methods of decisive importance for medieval theology were developed in jurisprudence and medicine, in some cases within Islam, "Scholasticism" can no longer be restricted to theology alone.[25] To explain and defend the rationality of the contents of revelation, moreover, is not an independent method but rather a concern that can be pursued by different methods. The narrowing of the Scholastic method to this concern leads Grabmann to conclude that theologians who apply the technique of

22. See Schmidinger, "'Scholastik' und 'Neuscholastik,'" 48–52.

23. Quinto stages a debate between the *"pars destruens"* (De Wulf, Grabmann, etc.) and the *"pars construens"* (De Rijk, Wieland), *Scholastica* 330–87; Schönberger offers a good overview and at the same time a critique of these attempts in *Scholastik,* 20–40; see also Schmidinger, "'Scholastik' und 'Neuscholastik,'" 46–47.

24. Grabmann, *Geschichte* 1:36–37; see also Quinto, *Scholastica,* 339–49.

25. See Koch, "Von der Bildung der Antike"; Madiski, "Scholastic Method."

Scholastic theology but do not share this concern (e.g., heretics) cannot be deemed "Scholastic theologians."

Grabmann's handy definition, furthermore, is a critical response to a tradition of Neoscholastic attempted definitions which, in contrast to a purely historical delimitation of Scholasticism as the science taught at medieval schools,[26] tried to find a *substantial formal component* of Scholasticism. Maurice de Wulf regards as Scholastics those thinkers who from the twelfth century until the late Middle Ages formed an "overwhelming majority," displayed unity in a great number of basic ideas and achieved a great and substantial *synthesis* of fundamental Western beliefs.[27] This substantial unity in doctrinal beliefs again restricts Scholasticism to medieval theology and harmonizes the doctrinal conflicts that were present; according to this view, any irreconcilable doctrinal tendencies, especially in the late Middle Ages, can only be classified as "anti-Scholasticism" or as the disintegration of the (High) Scholastic synthesis.[28] The temporal limit "until the late Middle Ages" is at a loss to account for the phenomenon of a Second Scholasticism. De Wulf's desire to define the contents of Scholasticism is shared by Clemens Baeumker, who in any case assumes only a "common property" of a formal and substantial sort: receptivity, submission to authority, preeminence of tradition over the work of the individual, conformity to a school.[29] Fernand Van Steenberghen takes up an intermediate position between de Wulf and Baeumker by insisting, over and above the more formal common features, on the "foundational doctrines" as a "sort of common basis upon which the great masters of the thirteenth century constructed their philosophical buildings in various styles out of more or less dissimilar materials."[30] In this passage expressly applies to the thirteenth century only, so that other epochs of Scholastic teaching are left out of consideration.

We encounter a more *historical-phenomenological* delimitation, which should be read at the same time, however, as a critique of the attempts at a substantial definition, in the writings of Gallus Manser (1866–1950), who understands "Scholasticism" to mean everything that was taught at me-

26. Thus, Manser, "Scholastik," 321–28.

27. De Wulf, *Geschichte der mittelalterlichen Philosophie,* 81–84; concerning the critique: Schönberger, *Scholastik,* 20–21; Quinto, *Scholastica,* 330–39.

28. Starting with Mandonnet, Siger de Brabant. In light of the critique of this concept, de Wulf later repudiated it; for an author who retains the division but with different emphases, see Schmidt, "Scholastik."

29. Baeumker, "Christliche Philosophie," 339–43.

30. Van Steenberghen, *Philosophie im 13. Jahrhundert,* 500; see also Quinto, *Scholastica,* 402–3.

dieval schools.[31] Bernhard Geyer is similarly cautious with regard to the term Scholasticism, which in his opinion has the shortcomings of all historical abstractions and is in essence "practically worthless." At best one can mention several characteristics of Scholastic philosophy: a close relation between philosophy and theology, dependence on ancient philosophy, especially Aristotle's, and a particular "Scholastic" method.[32] Josef Pieper, following Hegel, attempts to understand Scholasticism as the process by which the "barbarian" peoples assimilated the educational heritage of pagan and Christian antiquity, as "a scholarly undertaking on a vast scale that was carried on for several centuries."[33] This definition of course fits some aspects of early and high Scholasticism, but certainly not late and Baroque Scholasticism. Finally, Wolfgang Kluxen defines "Scholasticism" in the primary sense as "the medieval form of 'science' in general"; for "all theoretical knowledge assumes the form of rational knowledge, becomes *scientia.*"[34] But basically that makes the term "Scholasticism" superfluous, because it only underscores the scientific character of the philosophy and theology taught in the schools during the Middle Ages.

This term is fraught with so many misunderstandings that even the field of medieval studies today largely dispenses with it. "The concept of Scholasticism has ceased to be a theme of medieval studies."[35] Instead of a Scholasticism that has been over-defined as a theoretical uniformity, Kurt Flasch recommends acknowledging only a methodical and terminological continuity.[36] This methodical, academic form for the Scholastic theology and philosophy of the Middle Ages and the early modern period, as viewed by outsiders (especially by its opponents), reduces the tradition to a construct that can be more easily countered once it has been labeled.

As we can see, however, this name appears to admit of no univocal application.[37] On the other hand, the label Scholastic, as an *initial distinction* can be used not only against later opponents but also with reference to contemporary theological phenomena (monastic spirituality, epistolary

31. Manser, "Scholastik," 321–23.

32. *Ueberwegs Grundriss der Geschichte der Philosophie,* vol. 2: *Die patristische und scholastische Philosophie,* ed. B. Geyer (Berlin, 1928[11]), 141–43; on this concept compare Quinto, *Scholastica,* 351.

33. Pieper, *Scholastik,* 28, 48–52.

34. Kluxen, "Thomas von Aquin," 181.

35. Schönberger, *Scholastik,* 36; see especially Flasch, *Einführung in die Philosophie des Mittelalters,* 38.

36. Flasch, *Geschichte der Philosophie,* 2:29; see also Schönberger, *Scholastik,* 36–37.

37. See Schönberger, *Scholastik,* 41–51.

literature, mysticism). Thus Bonaventure already distinguishes the *"disciplina scholastica,"* as a theoretical teaching that is suited to *"audiendo solum"* ["hearing only"], from a *"disciplina monastica"* in which one must be trained by *"observando"* ["by observing it"].[38] Scholastic theology is distinguished from other forms; indeed, the universities went so far as to appoint professors to separate chairs for Scholastic (= speculative, systematic) theology and positive theology in the seventeenth century.[39] This did not cause Scholasticism to be "a particular entity with a specialized literature . . . , its claim to predominance never entirely unchallenged"; it was that already in the Middle Ages, as Wolfgang Kluxen correctly observes.[40] In this distinguishing function (from within and without) with regard to other forms of theology (in the Middle Ages as well) I see also therefore along with Rolf Schönberger the possibility that the Scholastic forms of theology can be described without necessarily presupposing a univocal concept of Scholasticism.[41] It is beside the point that the Scholastic method (or methods) was not actually developed in theology but was also used in law, philosophy, and medicine. This only shows that, from the perspective of that time, it was a matter of scientific method, by which theology also was guided. Thus Lambert Marie de Rijk, too, regards "Scholasticism" as a collective, not generic term for that scientific activity, especially philosophy and theology, that follows a particular method, which in turn is characterized by a particular system of teachings and concepts, distinctions, propositional analyses [*Satzanalysen*], logical techniques, and rules of debate.[42] One could therefore say: the development and application of these methods *creates and distinguishes* Scholastic theology as a scientific or academic theology, and thus as a particular undertaking, from other sorts of theology.

That doesn't bring us any farther, though, unless this method can be defined or reconstructed in detail. Statements by medieval theologians about their method are rare, however; systematic treatises *De methodo* are not

38. Bonaventure, *Collationes in Hexaemeron* II.3, in *Opera omnia,* ed. Quaracchi (1882–1902), 5:337a; see also Quinto, *Scholastica,* 81–87.

39. See, for example, *Die Matrikel der Universität Innsbruck,* vol. 2, *Matricula theologica,* part 1, ed. J. Kollmann (Innsbruck, 1965), lvi; see also Leinsle, *Studium im Kloster,* 95–97.

40. Kluxen, "Thomas," 181.

41. See Schönberger, *Scholastik,* 45: *"Scholastik* [. . .] *läßt sich wohl nur durch eine Kombination von einzelnen Beschreibungen, aber nicht durch eine definitorische Formel fassen."* ["Scholasticism . . . can probably be understood only through a combination of individual descriptions but not through a formulaic definition."]

42. De Rijk, *La philosophie au moyen âge,* 20–21. Concerning the critique, see Schönberger, *Scholastik,* 49–50.

commonly found until the sixteenth century, and again these treatises on logic typically apply generally to the scientific method that must be used in all disciplines if they intend to be considered sciences.[43] Thus the statement that Scholasticism is a "method without a 'discourse'" can hold true only for parts of medieval Scholasticism but not for the modern offshoots.[44] It's just that this *"discours de la méthode"* [methodological discourse] is treated not in the specialized discipline in question but rather generally in the study of Logic for all the disciplines. Here of course we should distinguish the scientific method, as it is established for instance in the *Posterior Analytics* of Aristotle, from the form of presentation and the teaching technique, so that even within this methodological concept of "Scholasticism" differentiations again take effect, which show that the Scholastic method, too, is not a uniform construct but rather a complex methodological paradigm with shifting techniques, presuppositions, manners of representation and standards of rationality. Common to them all, however, is their orientation to a standard of scientific rigor (which in each case is determined by the times). If we want to understand what Scholastic theology means in a particular era, we must therefore above all study the underlying concept of science.[45] For that concept determines the methods to be applied, and these in turn determine the form in which the related discipline is handed down orally and in writing. Therefore the characterization of a discipline as Scholastic can be made comprehensible only in terms of the scientific criteria and techniques of the Middle Ages and of the early modern period.

3 Characteristics

If a definition of the essence of Scholasticism is not possible, then at least a few characteristics should be listed to make the object in question—Scholastic theology in the Middle Ages and the early modern period—more accessible. An initial characteristic is its *academic character* [*Schulmässigkeit,* a term that sometimes implies *dependence on a school of thought*], in contrast to forms of free, spiritual or monastic theologizing. Thus Jean Leclercq has suggested speaking about a "theology of the schools" instead of about "Scholastic theology."[46] But new problems crop up here. In the me-

43. See Ashworth, *Language and Logic;* Leinsle, *Ding,* 452–59.

44. Schönberger, *Scholastik,* 50. The general discourse, however, should be expected after the general acceptance of the *Posterior Analytics* in logic.

45. This has been carried out in an exemplary way by Schrimpf, "Bausteine."

46. Leclercq, "Renewal of Theology," 72.

dieval school system there were various types of schools at which theology was taught: monastic schools, cathedral and municipal schools, and later religious houses of studies, general houses of study, and universities.[47] Among the monastic schools a further distinction must be made between internal schools for the choir monks and the schools for the externs (people living in the world). One suspects that these different schools with their different students represent in each case a different theology. Thus Anselm of Canterbury, who since Grabmann has been considered "the father of Scholasticism," was a monk in Bec at the time when he wrote his most important works. If one restricts "Scholastic theology" to the nonmonastic schools, then Anselm is not a Scholastic. On the other hand, a typical Scholastic like Abelard was from time to time a monk and an abbot and was conversant with the forms of monastic theology.[48] Moreover in the twelfth century we are dealing with a strongly person-centered scholarly education, which was acquainted not only with a school *in* Laon but with a school *of* Laon, a school of Abelard or a Porretan school (at various locations). Here, at the latest, Scholastic theology in the sense of "the theology of the schools" dissolves into more than one.[49]

Likewise a definition of Scholastic theology by means of a standard of scientific rigor or rationality, as Wolfgang Kluxen and Gangolf Schrimpf have suggested, seems to be insufficiently precise as a uniform criterion.[50] For even in the patristic period we find rational proof of the faith and scientific theology with methods that are basically Scholastic (*quaestiones et responsiones,* commentary),[51] since even Grabmann can speak about the "Scholasticism of the late Greek patristic era."[52] However the concept of science and the standard of rationality change, as Schrimpf demonstrates in an exemplary fashion, not only between the ninth and the twelfth century (Scotus Eriugena and Abelard) but even more with the reception of the *Posterior Analytics* of Aristotle and in the early modern debate on method. Yet presumably the factor that characterizes the Scholastic form of theology as an academic, scientific and rational penetration of the deposit of faith, with a special technique and form of presentation that distinguish it from other

47. See Leclercq, *Wissenschaft;* Koch, *Artes liberales.*

48. See Stock, *The Implications of Literacy,* 525.

49. See Leclercq, "Renewal," 72–74, in which he nevertheless insists that generally in the twelfth c. there were two kinds of theology (monastic and Scholastic).

50. See Schrimpf, "Bausteine," 2–3; 24–25.

51. See especially Studer, *Schola Christiana,* 126–31.

52. Grabmann, *Geschichte,* 1:92.

forms, is found precisely in the reception of the current concept of science in the theological schools [of a given era]. What distinguishes medieval and early modern Scholasticism, then, is in each case the contemporary standard of rationality and scientific rigor that is not shared by other historical periods, whereas the fundamental effort to study the deposit of faith in an academic, scientific and rational way will always be the indispensable concern of any theology.[53]

It is beside the point, initially, that these standards are not the property of theology but are received [from other disciplines]. "Scholastic" procedures are not restricted to the Western theology of the Middle Ages, as we have seen.[54] Thus Abelard's *Sic-et-Non* method, which some consider to be typical of early Scholastic theology, can also be found in the writings of Patriarch Photius of Constantinople († ca. 891) as well as in the works of the canonists Bernold of Constance († ca. 1100) and Ivo of Chartres († ca. 1165).[55] George Madiski was able to show, furthermore, that the Aristotelian or high Scholastic method, along with the elements of *Sic-et-Non, lectio,* and *disputatio* already had their "natural habitat" in Islamic law around a century earlier.[56] The structure of the *Summa Theologiae* of Thomas Aquinas is by no means his special property, but rather an instructional system that was used widely in the Arab world as well.[57] Even Photius' acquaintance with the *Sic-et-Non* might have been due to Arabic influence.[58] More remarkable, as matters stand, is the acceptance of these basically nontheological methods and standards for use in theology. In each instance they change the self-understanding of theology in the schools and universities. They lead to conflicts and debates with the opponents of these methods, who see in them nothing but "frivolous innovations" of pagan origin which will dilute the wine of God's word and destroy the simple faith.[59]

Thus it seems most likely that synchronic [*zeitbedingte*] methods and scientific standards were what gave rise to Scholastic theology. Bernhard Geyer has already recommended this way of proceeding: "The easiest way to gain insight into the nature of Scholastic theology is to start by examin-

53. On this subject see the impressive remarks of Pope Benedict XVI in "The Regensburg Academic Lecture": Benedict XVI, "Faith, Reason and the University: Memories and Reflections," in *Origins* 36/16 (Sept. 28, 2006): 248–52.

54. See especially Studer, *Schola Christiana,* 83–135.

55. Grabmann, *Geschichte* 1:113, 234–39, 242–46.

56. Madiski, "Method," 648ff.

57. Ibid., 651–57.

58. Ibid., 568–69.

59. See, for example, Petrus Damiani, *De sancta simplicitate scientiae inflanti opponenda* (PL 145, 695–704).

ing its form of presentation and method."[60] As to its method, however, this theology is "reflection on the text,"[61] whether individual books of the Bible, the *Opuscula sacra* of Boethius, Pseudo-Dionysius, or later the *Quatuor libri sententiarum* of Peter Lombard and finally the *Summa Theologiae* of Aquinas.[62] Because of the form of instruction in the schools, theology, like philosophy, is mainly interpretation, commentary on normative texts, whether as a gloss, a literal commentary, paraphrase, or commentary in questions. The text sparks questions *(quaestiones),* which are then discussed further in separate treatises or, at the universities from the thirteenth century on, in a *disputatio.*[63] Theology is conducted in (to some extent ritualized) questions and answers. A fundamental clarification of the truth is expected, especially where the authorities seem to contradict one another. Initially, therefore, the most important instrument is logic. But there are inquiries into many things that pertain to neither the monk who is interested in his salvation nor the simple believer.[64] This inquiry, however, which seemingly stops at nothing, is characteristic of Scholastic theology as a rational, scientific theology, but also exposes it to the charge that it is only an "inclination to formulate arguments without a serious problem."[65]

4 Scholastic theology

If we are to define "Scholasticism" or "theology" in the Middle Ages, we cannot start from today's concepts. In the patristic era the concept of theology covered a broad spectrum of themes and approaches, including Christian doctrine as a whole but also and especially *"theologia triparta"* made up of poetic, political, and philosophical theology.[66] The semantic fixation of *theologia* upon the present understanding of the term came about together with the development of a professional, academic, "scholastic" theology in the twelfth century.[67] Yet besides this term, other much more widely-used

60. Geyer, "Begriff," 113.

61. Schönberger, *Scholastik,* 83.

62. See especially Häring, "Commentary and Hermeneutics."

63. See Schönberger, *Scholastik,* 52–80; on patristics, see Studer, *Schola Christiana,* 126–35.

64. See Schönberger, *Scholastik,* 55–58.

65. K. R. Popper, *Objektive Erkenntnis* (Hamburg, 1984), 32.

66. See Studer, *Schola Christiana,* 12–13.

67. See Geyer, "Facultas theologica," 138–45; Enders, "Zur Bedeutung"; Leppin, *Theologie im Mittelalter,* 54, speaks not unfairly about "the beginning of a process of professionalizing the academic world view" [von einer "beginnende(n) Professionalisierung der akademischen Weltwahrnehmung"].

expressions appear, such as *"divinitas," "sacra lectio," "sacra pagina," "divina pagina," "doctrina sacrae scripturae." Theologia* and *theologi* seem to be used generally for theological science and the corresponding educational system only in university terminology from 1200 on.[68] But since it is a foreign word, even then it is rarely found even in the writings of theologians, and the older expressions *sacra pagina* and *sacra doctrina* are maintained until Thomas Aquinas.[69] It is striking that the development of a uniform, handy designation clearly went hand in hand with the development of a corresponding self-consciousness of the proponents of scientific theology in the schools and universities. This was probably the result of interaction with the other *facultates.* Theology's own claim to be a science had to be demonstrated, among other reasons because of the position of the *docentes in theologica facultate* at the universities and in society.[70]

But this could best be achieved by complying with the generally recognized scientific standards. In that way theology proved at the same time to be a *rational* enterprise. To begin with it is a conjecture that the development of the name *theologia* was accompanied by a different understanding of rationality in matters of faith, for instance, as opposed to the *"intellectus fidei"* that Anselm of Canterbury had sought. This becomes evident in the application of the Aristotelian concept of science to theology and in the new questions that subsequently arise: whether a scientific theology is necessary at all, in what sense theology is a science in the strict Aristotelian sense, whether it has a theoretical or a practical character, etc.[71] As a scientific, rational enterprise Scholastic theology is supported by the conviction that it is possible by the corresponding methods to find truth *in theologicis* [in theological matters] as well, especially the truth of theological propositions (*sententiae* [German *Sätze*]). This leads especially in the fourteenth century to the discussion of individual theological statements (sometimes apparently detached from their systematic context) with regard to their truth value.[72] What to outsiders appears to be pointless quibbling about terminology and phraseology is driven by this rational impulse to secure the truth in theology by scientific methods.[73]

68. For examples, ibid., 141–43.

69. *S.Th.* I q.1: *"De sacra doctrina, qualis sit et ad quae se extendat."* For a contrasting view, see II/II q.1 a.5 ad 2: *"Unde etiam theologia scientia est."*

70. See *CUP* I n.32 (I, 91).

71. See Geyer, "Facultas theologica," 144.

72. See Hoffmann, "Satz," 298–313.

73. See O. Schwemmer, *Philosophie der Praxis* (Frankfurt, 1980), 93: *"Die mittelalterliche Scho-*

The difference between theology and faith, which is a constituent of the former, becomes even more accentuated, the less the questions discussed in theology have to do with the practical problems in the lives of believers; for "the habit of questioning has a theoretical character in the strict sense,"[74] even when theology is understood as a practical science (as in Bonaventure and Duns Scotus). Of course immediately practical and political questions are also discussed in the schools, sometimes heatedly (poverty, begging, usury, charging interest, tithes, etc.), but they alone do not abolish the discrepancy between school and life that seems to be a constitutive element of Scholastic theology.[75] This theology is directed first of all to the teacher or student who is involved in the business of education, whether in the form of *lectio, disputatio,* or the Scholastic sermon.

Another difference, however, between theology and the Church's Magisterium, is articulated through the rationalization, scientific adaptation, and adoption of nontheological, philosophical modes of argumentation. This gives rise to the phenomenon of learned heresies (as distinct from popular heresies) and the *Lehrzuchtverfahren,* the trial of the theologian in which a finding of heterodoxy would cost him his professorship.[76] This can lead to an opposition between "Scholastic" and "ecclesiastical," as noted for instance by Gerhoh of Reichersberg († ca. 1169): the schools in France are irreconcilable with the Roman Church because of their undisciplined inquiries.[77] Not infrequently the wandering scholars and masters who did not lead a well-ordered life in a monastery but lived more or less without supervision in a foreign city were regarded with mistrust because they lacked the comportment befitting men of the Church.[78]

The fact that we retain the expression "Scholastic theology" in spite of the abovementioned problems has its basis precisely in the development of medieval theology. That is why we understand Scholastic theology not as a

---

lastik kann man geradezu als eine fast totale Herrschaft des Sprachsystems über alle anderen Orientierungs-, Reaktions- und Interaktionssysteme ansehen. Das dialektisch nach allen Seiten hin abgesicherte Argument, das jeweils beweist, was nur sein kann und was jedenfalls nicht sein darf, reicht aus, um Wahrheit und Wissen zu garantieren." ["Medieval Scholasticism can be regarded as an almost total dominion of the linguistic system over all other systems of orientation, reaction, and interaction. The argument that has been tested and proved on every side proving in each instance what must be and what cannot be, is sufficient to guarantee truth and knowledge."]

74. Schönberger, *Scholastik,* 63.

75. For further discussion see Flasch, *Einführung,* 38; Schönberger, *Scholastik,* 64–68.

76. See esp. Fichtenau, *Ketzer und Professoren.*

77. Ibid., 254–55.

78. Ibid., 245–57.

defining, univocal term, but rather as a collective name for the theology that was developed along various lines in medieval schools and universities and to some extent was still pursued or renewed in the early modern period. The characteristics that distinguish it from contemporary forms of theology (epistolary literature, monastic treatises, spirituality, mysticism) are the methods accepted in these schools for use in theology: commentary on an authoritative text, *lectio, disputatio,* and *praedicatio,* taking into account the changing standards of rationality and concept of science in the individual eras. But since these standards and concepts, like the methods themselves, are part of a development, Scholastic theology should not be understood either as a uniform structure, the essence of which can be summed up in a definition. Instead its history can only be reconstructed genetically. Nor should this lead to a genetic definition but rather, within the framework of an introduction, merely to an independent understanding of the inquiries, methods, and results of Scholastic theology in the Middle Ages and the early modern period. This will be accomplished by alternating survey chapters with the description of central problems in the respective historical periods. In these contexts the individual theologians will be introduced along with their solutions. Therefore this volume does not offer a comprehensive presentation of the history of theology or dogma. Nor can it evaluate the individual theologians in terms of their achievements.[79] An appropriate understanding of Scholastic theology could, though, also help to overcome many prejudices against "ivory-tower Scholasticism," for example, the idea that a Scholastic is nothing but a theologian who "under pressure from a past that is deemed authoritative vainly attempts with outdated methods to illuminate an outdated matter, without any lively understanding of present-day problems."[80]

79. For that purpose we refer the reader to the well-known standard works, especially the *Handbuch der Dogmengeschichte* (*HDG*) and *Handbuch der Dogmen- und Theologiegeschichte* (*HDThG*). Good surveys are offered in Evans, ed., *Medieval Theologians;* Köpf, ed., *Theologen des Mittelalters;* Leppin, *Theologie im Mittelalter.*

80. G. Krüger, *Das Dogma von der Dreieinigkeit und Gottmenschheit* (Tübingen, 1905), 259; cited in Grabmann, *Methode* 1:1.

1 How Did Scholastic Theology Come About?

Since an unequivocal definition of "Scholasticism" does not seem possible, we are left with the option of describing the development in intellectual history that led to the characteristic features of western Scholastic theology in the Middle Ages and the early modern era. The extent to which the conventional subdivision into pre-, early, high and later Scholasticism is useful would have to be demonstrated in this context by documenting paradigm shifts, that is, changes in methodological and thematic issues.

1 Patristic themes and methods

Medieval theology is not an absolutely new beginning: extensive areas of it owe much to the thematic and methodological precedents from the patristic period. Therefore the most important components of this patristic heritage must be presented at least briefly in order to understand better the achievement of medieval theologians.

1.1 Philosophy and theology

The "Scholastic" theology of the Middle Ages was not the first to develop in close contact and dialogue with philosophy. This was already true of the "scientific theology" of the patristic era.[1] Likewise, we are familiar with acceptance of pagan παιδεία by Christians since the days of Paul, and also with the rejection thereof in the name of the folly of the Cross (see 1 Cor 1:18–21; Acts 17:19–34). In particular the school of Alexandria (Clement [† ca. 215], Origen [† 253]) tried to recast all the Greek philosophical modes of thought into theology, yet it was aware of the difference between the "barbaric phi-

1. See, among other studies, Stockmeier, *Glaube und Kultur*, 120–37; Studer, *Schola Christiana*, 170–94; Kobusch, *Christliche Philosophie*, 26–57.

losophy" of Christianity and the richly differentiated Hellenistic culture of its day. Greek philosophy is not necessary for salvation, but it is for a deeper understanding of what is believed: "However, just as we declare it possible to be a believer without any knowledge of the art of writing, so too we agree that one cannot possibly understand the teachings contained in the faith without learning. For the ability to accept correct teachings and to reject the others comes not simply from faith, but only from faith that is based on knowledge."[2] Faith, then, needs rational justification of its content *(fides quae)* and of the assent given by the believer *(fides qua)*. Now this rational justification, which is supposed to lead to an understanding of the content of the faith, takes place with the help of the intellectual methods and philosophical precedents of the era in question. For Christianity in late antiquity, this implies philosophy. The philosophy of the Greeks, however, seemed to Clement [of Alexandria] to have been surpassed by Christ. "Since the Word Himself has come to us from heaven, we need not, I reckon, go any more in search of human learning to Athens and the rest of Greece.... For if we have as our teacher Him that filled the universe, ... the whole world, with Athens and Greece, has already become the domain of the Word."[3] This priority of the Christian message over pagan philosophy is a constituent element of every Christian theology, if it is not to be relativized as an arbitrary philosophy of religion or worldview. What is relativized instead is philosophy: it becomes a propaedeutic or preparatory instruction for the faith insight and for theology as well, and thus its claim to be the independent way of salvation for the educated men of late antiquity is denied.

Yet this optimistic equilibrium between pagan philosophy and Christian revelation in a scientific theology is not shared by all. Tertullian († after 213) speaks in a different language: "What indeed has Athens to do with Jerusalem? What concord is there between the Academy and the Church?... Our instruction comes from 'the porch of Solomon,' who had himself taught that 'the Lord should be sought in simplicity of heart.' ... We want no [wise sophistry] after possessing Christ Jesus, no inquisition after enjoying the Gospel! With our faith, we desire no further belief. For this is our primary faith, that there is nothing which we ought to believe besides."[4]

2. Clement of Alexandria, *Stromateis* I 35, 2.

3. Clement of Alexandria, *Exhortation to the Heathen* [*Protreptikos*] XI 112, 1. The surpassing knowledge of Christ was essential to the Church Fathers, a point emphasized especially by Studer, *Schola Christiana*, 151–70.

4. Tertullian, *Praescriptio haereticorum* [*The Prescription against Heretics*] 7 (PL 2, 23–24).

Through this retreat to faith alone, however, Christians in the cultured and philosophically trained world of late antiquity became liable to the accusation that they were irrational and uneducated; Celsus (around 178 AD), for example, ascribes to the Christians the following maxim: "Do not examine, but believe! . . . Your faith will save you! . . . The wisdom of this life is bad, but foolishness is a good thing!"[5] The reasons for rejecting philosophy soon become set pieces of argumentation: Philosophy offers only ingenious, formal erudition without any practical benefit for everyday life; the schools of philosophy disagree; the lives of philosophers do not correspond to what they teach; philosophy is the source of all heresies; moreover it is restricted to an elite, whereas Christianity is addressed to the uneducated and the illiterate as well. Then there are the individual doctrines of the philosophers' schools that contradict Christianity.[6] All this seems to suggest that Christianity is incompatible with pagan philosophy, which is fundamentally entangled in error: "So, then, where is there any likeness between the Christian and the philosopher? between the disciple of Greece and of heaven? between the man whose object is fame, and whose object is [salvation]? between the talker and the doer? . . . between the friend and the foe of error? between one who corrupts the truth, and one who restores and teaches it? between its thief and its custodian?"[7] Yet in these antitheses there is also a subliminal admission that the Christian theologian is dependent on a set of skills, if he is to perform his service as a restorer and interpreter of truth and an enemy of error. But where is this skill set to be obtained, if not from education, including the philosophy of the day? Indeed, philosophy is employed at the very least in the erudite attack on a theology that works with philosophical methods.

A pragmatic rejection of philosophy is found in many circles of early Christian monasticism, which understood itself to be a "philosophy" committed to a definite way of life (asceticism).[8] Thus Eusebius († 339) relates that Origen "restrained himself as much as possible by a most philosophic life, sometimes by the discipline of fasting, again by limited time for sleep. And in his zeal he never lay upon a bed, but upon the ground. . . . By giving

5. Origen, *Contra Celsum* I, 9, 11–13 (SChr 132,98).

6. See the article by H. Görgemanns, "Philosophie: Griechische Patristik," in *HWP* 7:617; Studer, *Schola Christiana*, 154–56; Kobusch, *Christliche Philosophie*, 41–50: "Das Christentum–Platonismus für das Volk."

7. Tertullian, *Apologeticum* [*Apology*] 47, 1–8 (CCh SL 1, 163, 1–164, 32).

8. See Studer, *Schola Christiana*, 13–14, Kobusch, *Christliche Philosophie*, 34–40.

such evidences of a philosophic life to those who saw him, he aroused many of his pupils to similar zeal."[9] The philosophy of the monks was reduced to asceticism, and so any concern with education (παιδεία) beyond the simple faith seemed to them reprehensible. Athanasius († 373) quotes the Father of monasticism, Anthony (251–356) as saying: "To those who have the in-working through faith, demonstrative argument is needless, or even superfluous. For what we know through faith this you attempt to prove through words. . . . So the inworking through faith is better and stronger than your professional arguments."[10] The appearance of heresies made the monks suspicious of scientific theology also, as the disputes over Origen showed. Sweeping judgments condemning philosophy and theology at the same time were not uncommon.[11]

When the step is taken from simple faith to theology, this happens even in the patristic period through the addition of rational reflection, or as Bonaventure (1217/8–1274) would later put it, *"per additionem rationis."*[12] Of course *ratio* in theology takes on a particular form in every age. For the Church of the patristic period it was pagan and to some extent Gnostic philosophy, from which standard lines of argumentation were adopted. The positive or negative value of such theology, however, is measured according to the Church Fathers by the positive or negative value of the philosophy that is applied and rendered theologically fruitful. On the one side stands Origen: "It is, in agreement with the spirit of Christianity, of much more importance to give our assent to doctrines upon grounds of reason and wisdom than on that of faith merely."[13] The contrary position is represented again by Tertullian when he warns against mixing faith and philosophy in a diluted theology that reflects "the dignity of Plato, or the vigour of Zeno, or the equanimity of Aristotle, or the stupidity of Epicurus, or the sadness of Heraclitus, or the madness of Empedocles," depending on the school that is followed. Instead Christians have the duty to restore truth in its purity, to purge the clear blue sky of the clouds of philosophy and thus of all heresy.[14] For philosophy is the soil that produces all erroneous doctrines, against which simple faith seems to be charmed because it knows nothing about them: "It is better for you to

9. Eusebius, *Church History* VI, 3, 9.
10. Athanasius, *Vita Antonii* 77 (PG 26, 951A).
11. See Stockmeier, *Glaube und Kultur,* 132–33.
12. Bonaventura, Sent. prooem. q.1 concl. (I, 7b).
13. Origenes, *Contra Celsum* I, 13.
14. Tertullian, *De anima* 3, 2–3. (CCh SL 2, 785, 11–24).

remain in ignorance, lest you should come to know what you ought not."[15] But how should the Christian discriminate then among various teachings? How is he to confront heresies effectively when they break out, and argue against them? How is he supposed to find his way when differences come to light even in the sacred Scriptures that have been accepted authoritatively? Without the methods of question and answer *(quaestiones et responsiones,* ζητήματα) that were expertly developed by the Alexandrine school, without the combination of scriptural and rational arguments *(probationes),* without the philological, philosophical, and in some cases allegorical commentary on an authoritative text which was customary in the philosophical schools of late antiquity also, no progress can be made.[16] But with that we have taken the step from faith to a theology which now understands itself to be scientific and is guided by contemporary standards of rationality.

1.2 *Auctoritas* and *ratio*

Behind the multilayered relation between philosophy and theology there is a pair of concepts that would become decisive for Scholastic theology but had already developed initially in the patristic period: *auctoritas* and *ratio. Auctoritas* in a Christian context implies both the quotable literary authority of the Bible and of the early Church Fathers and also the official authority of God and of the Church leadership.[17] In both cases the *auctoritas* is not infrequently justified by its age, just as the normative character of the earliest period of Christianity, in connection with the *priscus mos* [venerable custom] of Roman law, was one of the predominant intellectual paradigms of late antiquity and of the Middle Ages.[18] This justification of ecclesiastical customs solely because of their age was countered already in the writings of Cyprian of Carthage († 258) with the demand for reason: "Neither must we prescribe this from custom, but overcome opposite custom by reason." Even more explicitly: "[C]ustom without truth is the antiquity of error."[19] Reason as the test of a truth claim appears here in the first place as an appeal against a traditional justification of ecclesiastical customs, yet it is not to be restricted to that role; for the truth claim demanded by reason becomes a definitive motif of all theology as a rational enterprise.

15. Tertullian, *Praescriptio haereticorum* 14, 2 (CCh SL 1, 198, 6–7).
16. Concerning these methods, see especially Studer, *Schola Christiana,* 171, 201–4.
17. See the article "Autorität," in *HWPh* 1:723–30; Studer, *Schola Christiana,* 230–65.
18. See Stockmeier, *Glaube und Kultur,* 227–35.
19. Cyprian, ep. 71, 3 (CSEL 3, 2, 773); ep. 74, 9 (806–7).

Augustine (354–430) deserves credit for having been the first to think through comprehensively, and in a way that decisively shaped Scholastic theology, the relation between *auctoritas* and *ratio.* In his thought this relation cannot be reduced to a simple formula. Not the least important influence on his perspective was Alexandrinian theology with its deliberate inclusion of philosophy.[20] As early as his stay in Cassiciacum, Augustine clearly enunciated the insufficiency of mere *auctoritas* for an educated man: The *"auctoritas majorum"* ["authority of the ancestors"] is restricted to that of the wise, yet even with them only the *"rationes"* ["reasonable arguments"] should count.[21] On the other hand he is indebted to the *auctoritas* of sacred Scripture for overcoming his skepticism.[22] In those passages in Augustine's writings where he reflects on the mutual relationship of the two, it is less a conflict between reason and authority than a demand for the reasonable justification of authority, as in Cyprian's works. One conflict that can occur, at any rate, is the clash of divine *auctoritas* with arrogant human reason *(praesumptio, astutia).*[23] In contrast, *"vera ratio,"* that reason which has confirmed its truth claim in the light of divine truth as well, is in agreement with the latter. This applies also to the authority of the Holy Bible, but not to scriptural exegesis, which always remains a human, fallible, and risky undertaking.[24] Moreover, *auctoritas* is temporally and logically prior to *ratio.* This is justified theologically with regard to divine *auctoritas* as an act of grace, as a demand upon faith and a preparation for *ratio: "auctoritas fidem flagitat et rationi praeparat hominem."*[25] This is why human knowledge can advance from *auctoritas* to *ratio,* from faith to insight into what is believed. Now this step is no longer an act of intellectual arrogance but rather a requirement for a truly reasonable life; for someone who remains obligated to authority alone does not reach the goal of human life, of the *"beata vita,"* since he does not arrive at knowledge of the truth but rather stops at faith. But to Augustine—at least in Cassiciacum—stopping at faith is something for people who are too lazy, too stupid, or too preoccupied for the sciences.[26]

Yet the path to *ratio* does not start at every sort of faith, since the histori-

20. See the groundbreaking study by Lütcke, *Auctoritas,* esp. 34–46, 182–95.

21. Augustinus, C. Ac. I, 3, 7–8. (CChr SL 29, 6–8); for possible sources, see Lütcke, *Auctoritas,* 36–38.

22. See Lütcke, *Auctoritas,* 84–88.

23. See, for example, Augustinus, ep. 102, 14 (CSEL 34, 555–57).

24. See Augustinus, ep. 143, 7 (CSEL 44, 257).

25. Augustinus, vera rel. 24, 45 (CCh SL 32, 215, 4–5).

26. Augustinus, de ord. I, 5, 15 (CCh SL 29, 115, 37–41); II, 9, 26–27 (121–23); C. Ac. II, 20, 43 (60, 16–61, 24).

cal record is for Augustine an object of faith only, but not of *ratio.* Above and beyond the test of the credibility of the report, historical facts are the object of faith alone.[27] On the other hand, intelligible facts (e.g., of mathematics and other disciplines) can only be examined rationally. Finally, objects *"de divinis rebus"* ["concerning godly things"] are believed first, but then they may under certain circumstances provide the basis for a rational insight as well.[28] This, however, is only sometimes the case, and it presupposes a moral purification. Even the facts of salvation history are not immediately the object of rational insight; rather, through our faith in them we arrive at an insight into the timeless, intelligible truths *(aeterna)* about God that are contained in scriptural statements concerning salvation history.[29] The step from *credere* to *intellegere* [from believing to understanding] therefore has a temporal component but also a thematic component. Here, too, reason is again concerned about the truth of the theological statement (or of the proposition to be believed authoritatively) that has been made intelligible: *"Tunc agnoscemus quam vera nobis credenda imperata sint."* ["Then we will recognize how true those things are that we are commanded to believe."][30] The insight of reason corroborates the authority, not in simply accepting it, but rather on the basis of the truth that has been recognized.

Even the faith that temporally precedes the *intellegere* is for Augustine not an irrational faith; therefore authority as such also refers to *ratio.* For the believer, too, must render an account about whom he believes *(cui sit credendum)* and therefore examine the authority with regard to its credibility. There is no other way for this to happen, however, than through rational arguments.[31] On the other hand, finite reason *(quantulacunque ratio)* inevitably runs up against its limits and recognizes therein the necessity and usefulness of faith.[32] Finally, faith in the authority hermeneutically presupposes an understanding of the words of that authority and thus a preliminary understanding of the object of faith that does not come from the faith itself.[33] Rational justification of the faith authority and rational penetration of the content of the faith, when they are institutionalized, make up the chief components of theology.

27. Augustinus, div. quaest. 48 (CCh SL 44A, 75); C. epist. fund. 12, 15 (CSEL 51, 1, 208–9).
28. Augustinus, div. quaest. 48 (CCh SL 44A, 75, 7–10).
29. Augustinus, ag. christ. 15 (CSEL 41, 118, 17–21).
30. Augustinus, quant. an. 76 (CSEL 89, 224, 11–12).
31. Augustinus, vera rel. 45 (CCh SL 32, 215, 4–8).
32. Augustinus, ep. 120, 3 (CSEL 34, 707, 2–5).
33. Augustinus, En. in Ps. 118, 18, 3 (CCh SL 40, 1720–1); see Duchrow, *Sprachverständnis,* 106–7.

For Augustine, this *auctoritas* is now, after Christ's divine authority, the continuation thereof *par excellence* in the *"auctoritas scripturae"* ["authority of Scripture"], as he repeatedly emphasized from 392 on.[34] Yet here too, being personally affected by the word of God is contrasted with the hermeneutic-theological approach to Scripture, which defuses scandalous passages by means of contemporary allegorizing and thus responds to the *"verbi auctoritas"* ["authority of the word"] with its own interpretation: that it is only a matter of a *"figurata locutio"* ["figurative speech"].[35] On the other hand the correct exegesis is actually a part of the authoritative character of Scripture; for Augustine it is a true book in terms of (natural) science as well. One proviso: If a sentence in the Bible were clearly false in the literal sense, it would have to be interpreted in some other way. All sources of errors in the codex or in the translation should be assessed in advance.[36] The problem of possible contradictions in the Bible itself, which was a major concern of the patristic authors and a favorite point of attack on the part of the "unbelievers," prompted Augustine to resolve these alleged contradictions in an exemplary way in *De consensus evangelistarum.* Agreement and harmonization are the order of the day here, since there must not be any contradictions in a book having divine authority, neither within the book itself nor in comparison to extra-biblical truths.

If *ratio* is at the service of biblical *auctoritas* as a matter of principle, then the Church's teaching authority in the service of the truth also appears as an "external hermeneutic principle" and "guardian of true exegesis."[37] Consequently for people today the Church's authority is sufficient cause to believe the authority of Scripture, as Augustine put it in the famous saying: *"Ego vero evangelio non crederem, nisi me catholicae ecclesiae commoveret auctoritas"* ["Indeed, I would not believe the Gospel if the authority of the Catholic Church did not move me to do so."][38] Justifying this authority of the Church is again the task of *ratio,* especially in debating with pagans and heretics—a task that is admirably taken up in *De moribus Ecclesiae Catholicae et de moribus Manichaeorum.* The *ratio auctoritatis* attempts to prove that acceptance of the authority and obedience to it is an act of reason or at least a reasonable activity. Augustine sums up this program of theologi-

34. Augustinus, duab. anim. 9 (CSEL 25, 1, 61, 20); see Lütcke, *Auctoritas,* 128–36.
35. Augustinus, doct. chr. III, 15 (CCh SL 32, 87, 19–22).
36. Augustinus, ep. 82, 3 (CSEL 34, 354, 2–22); see ep. 143, 7 (CSEL 44, 258, 2–9).
37. Lütcke, *Auctoritas,* 144.
38. Augustinus, c. ep. fund. 5 (CSEL 25, 1, 197, 22–23); see util. cred. 31 (ibid., 38–40).

cal investigation in the alternative: proof of the truth of the contents of the faith or proof of the authoritative position of the one who demands that we believe this content.[39] Despite this basically harmonizing tendency, it must not be overlooked that *ratio* has a critical potential as well, which in certain circumstances can endanger the position of the *auctoritas.* Therefore theology is always an adventure of critical reason in the presence of the claim of divine, biblical and ecclesiastical authority.

1.3 Augustine's program of Christian education and theology

Of incalculable importance for Scholastic theology is not only Augustine's nuanced synthesis of *ratio* and *auctoritas,* but also the equilibrium that he strikes between pagan education, concentrated in the *artes liberales,* and Christian faith.[40] The seven liberal arts (grammar, rhetoric, logic, arithmetic, geometry, astronomy, music) are regarded initially as a propaedeutic to philosophy.[41] In them the essential knowledge of the educated man of late antiquity is codified. The arts supply the philosopher with arguments and examples. At the same time they offer a preliminary exercise of the mind as a preparation for the abstract truths of philosophy.[42] Thus during his early philosophical period, the value of the *artes* was quite well defined for Augustine.

From a theological perspective, this role as a propaedeutic to philosophy can no longer suffice. When Augustine sets about describing Christian education in his work *De doctrina christiana* (388–97), he is well aware of the long struggle over the legitimacy of pagan παιδεία within the framework of Christianity. For Augustine it is justified inasmuch as it is enlisted in the service of religious purposes: *"tibi serviat quidquid utile puer didici, tibi serviat quod loquor et scribo et numero"* ["May anything useful I learned as a boy serve Thee; may that which I say and write and reckon serve Thee"].[43] A worldly education that does not lend itself to being ordered to this religious objective is stigmatized as a useless and sinful *"curiositas."*[44] With regard to

39. Augustinus, c. ep. fund. 14 (211–12). Listed as possible arguments: the professional and moral qualifications of the person invested with authority, miracles, the fulfillment of prophecies, and more generally: the success, age, and continuous tradition of the authority, recognition of the authority even among opponents. See Lütcke, *Auctoritas,* 166–76.

40. See esp. Marrou, *Augustinus,* 163–392; Studer, *Schola Christiana,* 102–3, 149.

41. On the varying divisions of the *artes* in Augustine's writings, see Ferrarino, "Quadruvium," 359–64.

42. Augustinus, de ord. I, 2, 3 (CCh SL 29, 90, 1–17); see Leinsle, "Weltordnung," 369–77.

43. Augustinus, conf. I, 15, 24 (CCh SL 27, 23, 7–8).

44. Ibid., X, 35, 54–57 (ibid., 184–86); see Marrou, *Augustinus,* 296–97.

man's eternal destiny, an education in the liberal arts contributes nothing unless it is used as a path to God. Therefore caution is required also when themes from pagan education are placed at the service of Christian theology, so that "the demon of art" does not thereby insinuate itself again into Christian education.[45]

The philosophical outline of a *"studium sapientiae"* ["study of wisdom"], as set forth in Cassiciacum in *De ordine,* is less decisive for medieval theology than the theological purpose to which profane education is put in *De doctrina christiana.* On the one hand the bishop of Hippo adheres to philosophy as a path to God, yet he places it in the Christian context of faith, so that it becomes *"sapientia christiana."*[46] An indispensable condition for this, however, is the study of the *artes;* besides this education there is no other way by which one can reach *sapientia.*[47] If the way of *sapientia* were the only way, then only a few would arrive at theology. Augustine himself traveled that path. The bishop of Hippo now realizes that in addition to this sapiential type of theology another type is necessary, which makes it possible to employ the arts and sciences directly in the service of the faith. Augustine now terms this latter type *scientia:*

> not indeed so as to attribute to this knowledge [*scientia*] everything whatever that can be known by man about things human, wherein there is exceeding much of empty vanity and mischievous curiosity, but only those things by which that most wholesome faith, which leads to true blessedness, is begotten, nourished, defended, strengthened; and in this knowledge most of the faithful are not strong, however exceeding strong in the faith itself. For it is one thing to know only what man ought to believe in order to attain to a blessed life, which must needs be an eternal one; but another to know in what way this belief itself may both help the pious, and be defended against the impious, which last the apostle [1 Cor 12:8] seems to call by the special name of knowledge.[48]

The task of this theological knowledge, therefore, according to Augustine, is to beget, nourish, defend, and strengthen the faith, to present it to believers and to defend it against unbelievers. This outlines the *ecclesiastical aims* of a theology that is supposed, on the one hand to prepare for the faith, and on the other hand to justify it and to communicate it in catechesis. The

45. See Augustinus, conf. V, 3, 4 (CCh SL 27, 59, 26–38); doct. chr. IV, 14, 30–31 (CCh SL 32, 137–39); Marrou, *Augustinus,* 296–97.

46. See Augustinus, ep. 218 (CSEL 57, 426); ep. 155 (CSEL 44, 430–34).

47. Augustinus, de ord. 2, 18, 47 (CCh SL 29, 132–33).

48. Augustinus, de trin. 14, 3 (CCh SL 50A, 424, 56–67); see Augustinus, doct. chr. 2, 7, 9–11 (CCh SL 32, 36–38).

basis for this program of theology is therefore the study of sacred Scripture: The *"divinarum scripturarum studiosus"* undertakes the study of this *scientia.*[49] Yet even as early as Augustine, theology cannot be reduced to exegesis: besides plainly exegetical works, which in any case are repeatedly interrupted by speculative questions, there are dogmatic and polemical treatments and elementary summaries of the substance of the faith.[50] This corresponds exactly to the stated ecclesiastical aims of the theological *scientia.*

Within this framework, the old pagan education can be justified in an officially Christian society only by reasons from the Bible and in the service thereof. Whatever useful things can be found in it are either to be found in the Bible also or else to be used in interpreting it. The value of profane education is thereby drastically relativized: only as a resource or auxiliary discipline to theology does it have any justification in the Christian world of education.[51] Augustine thereby aligns himself with the conciliatory tendency among the Church Fathers in the debate about *παιδεία*. His achievement consists of *De doctrina christiana* but above all in the fact that he outlined a plan of studies and an examination of theological methods for the *"divinarum scripturarum tractator et doctor"* ["one who commented on and taught the sacred Scriptures"].[52] Naturally the linguistic subjects of the *Trivium,* especially grammar and rhetoric, seemed particularly important for the theologian. To Latin grammar was added the knowledge of foreign languages, primarily Greek and Hebrew. Yet Augustine associates with grammar the exact sciences: history, geography, natural history, and the mechanical arts. These are followed by rhetoric and dialectic (logic) as instruction in the formal laws of right thinking and science. The so-called *Quadrivium* of mathematical arts (arithmetic, geometry, music, and astronomy, which Augustine sometimes calls celestial mechanics) make the transition to philosophy, which is pursued here essentially as doxography: a selective overview of the teachings of the pagan philosophers, insofar as they agree with the Christian faith.[53] Augustine adopts to a great extent the curriculum of the schools of his day and now places it as a whole at the service of the interpretation of divine revelation. He modifies several subjects, however, and thereby gives rise to those problematic areas that then led to debates

49. Augustinus, doct.chr. 2, 7, 10 (CCh SL 32, 37, 15).
50. For example, Enchiridion (CCh SL 46, 21–114), de fide et symbolo (CSEL 41, 1–32).
51. Augustinus, doct. chr. 2, 42, 43 (CCh SL 32, 76–77).
52. Ibid., 4, 4, 6 (119, 1); see Augustinus, prooem. 4–9 (2–6).
53. Ibid., 2, 40, 60 (73–74).

in nascent Scholasticism. It makes sense to supplement the languages with Hebrew, but it is surprising that he excludes the ancient classics from this curriculum. By no means does the former rhetorician intend to present this propaedeutic education as an end in itself. It is no longer a question of the slow, thorough training of the mind for the philosophical ascent to God, as we still find in *De ordine,* but rather of a set of lessons that can be used in theological work and are to be learned as soon as possible, *"ut non sit necesse christiano in multis propter pauca laborare"* ["so that the Christian need not labor over many things for the sake of a few"].[54] Abbreviation, an emphasis on the rudiments and elementary instruction are therefore the order of the day. Brief manuals, compendia, and lexicons are recommended. Such books were prized and composed in late antiquity by both Christian and non-Christian educators.[55]

The goal of the curriculum in *De doctrina christiana* is clearly the interpretation of the Bible, which in Augustine's view is the principal way in which theology is carried on as a science. Here, too, he basically applies the procedures of the ancient schools to a new text: *lectio, emendatio, enarratio.* Not included, however, is the aesthetic *iudicium* in the reading of the classics; for the Bible is not a work of art whose aesthetic value is at issue.[56] From this grammatical perspective Augustine then moves to the theological-systematic perspective, especially in discussing the topical-hermeneutic rules of Tyconius (before 383), which are to be read as keys for understanding Scripture and as means for constructing a theological system, even though Augustine recognizes that they are inadequate.[57] In contrast Augustine takes as his basis a hermeneutic system governed by a quartet of concepts: *res, signum, uti,* and *frui:* Christian doctrine as a whole is divided, like any science, into *res* [topics, matter] and *signa* [signs]. The written word itself is a sign *par excellence.* The things signified thereby, however, are meant either to be used *(uti)* or to be enjoyed in a godly manner *(frui).*[58] This division therefore is by no means exclusively theological; Augustine explicitly assumes it for every *"doctrina."*

54. Ibid., 2, 39, 59 (73, 30–31).

55. See Marrou, *Augustinus,* 347–48; Studer, *Schola Christiana,* 177–78.

56. See Marrou, *Augustinus,* 356.

57. Augustinus, doct. chr. 3, 42–37, 56 (CCh SL 32, 102–16); Tyconius, Liber de septem regulis (PL 18, 15–66; critical edition: F. C. Burkitt, *The Book of Rules of Tyconius* [Cambridge, 1894, reprinted 1967], "Texts and Studies 3, 1": *de domino et eius corpore; de domini corpore bipertito; de promissis et lege; de specie et genere; de temporibus; de recapitulatione; de diabolo et eius corpore* [On the Lord and His Body; on the bipartite Body of the Lord; on the promises and the Law; on species and genus; on times; on recapitulation; on the devil and his body].

58. Augustinus, doct. chr. 1, 2, 2 (CCh SL 32, 7, 1–8, 20); see Grillmeier, "Symbolum," 156–64.

Therefore the *"doctrina christiana"* also has to follow these general rules. Only by filling in this general schema does Augustine produce one that is specifically theological, a basic outline of systematic theology with which Augustine prefaces his work.[59] The goal is God, who is the sole object of the *frui,* from which all the rest is elaborated: Christ as Incarnate Wisdom of God and Redeemer, and his Body, the Church. At the same time, these are the eternal, unchangeable truths that are supposed to be learned from Scripture by means of the profane education.

1.4 Systematic and axiomatic theology: Boethius

Whereas Augustine's concept of theology as a whole was basically the scientific interpretation of sacred Scripture, the "last Roman," who is also called the "first Scholastic," A. M. S. Boethius († 524) followed another path in his *Opuscula sacra* (ca. 512–521), which were extremely influential and often commented on during the Middle Ages.[60] Stylistically these five short works are occasional compositions, some of them letters that aim at answering a very specific question, for example, "How the Trinity is One God and not three gods" (treatise 1, *De Trinitate*), "Whether Father, Son and Holy Spirit are affirmed about the Godhead substantially" (treatise 2), and "How substances can be good in what they are, although they cannot be substantial Good" (treatise 3, *De hebdomadibus*).[61] The philosophy to which Boethius is consciously indebted is Neoplatonism, in connection however with the thought of Aristotle, some of whose works on logic Boethius translated (the so-called *Logica vetus:* The Categories, *De interpretatione*). The purpose is to treat theological questions using new terminology and philosophical methods in a way that can be described as rational-argumentative.[62]

The basis for his argumentation in these Trinitarian debates is no longer Scripture alone, but rather the already formulated *"sententia"* ["thinking"] of

59. Augustinus, doct. chr. I, 5, 5–21, 19 (CCh SL 32, 9–16).

60. See Schrimpf, *Axiomenschrift;* A. M. S. Boethius, *Die Theologischen Traktate,* translated, with Introduction and notes by Michael Elsässer (PhB 397) (Hamburg, 1988), vi.

61. See Lambert, "Nouveaux éléments." Stylistic studies show the close connections between treatises 1, 2, and 5, whereas *De hebdomadibus* is stylistically closer to the Commentaries on Aristotle and *De fide catholica* appears to be rather disparate in its style.

62. Boethius, de trin. prol. (ed. Elsässer 3, 1–4): *"Investigatam diutissime quaestionem* [. . .] *formatam rationibus litterisque mandatam offerendam vobis communicandamque curavi."* ["I have carefully investigated this question at great length, framed it with reasonable arguments and committed it to writing so as to offer and communicate it to you."] Ibid., (3, 16–18): *"Idcirco stilum brevitate contraho et ex intimis sumpta philosophiae disciplinis novorum verborum significationibus velo. . . ."* ["For that purpose I aim at a concise style and clothe the matters taken from the most profound disciplines of philosophy in new terminology. . . ."] For the sources, see esp. Micaelli, *Studi;* Micaelli, *Dio.*

the Catholic Church, which is to be supported and defended now with philosophical methods.[63] To that end Boethius presents an explicit justification of his theological approach in a review, along Aristotelian lines, of the methods and fields of the theoretical sciences, natural science, mathematics and theology: *"In naturalibus igitur rationabiliter, in mathematicis disciplinaliter, in divinis intellectualiter versari oportebit."* ["It will be necessary, therefore, to proceed reasonably in matters of natural science, systematically in mathematics, and intellectually in godly matters."][64] We proceed "intellectually," however, when we adhere strictly to logic and metaphysics and refrain from all misleading figurative expressions about theology. Boethius does not outline a comprehensive theological system but rather develops his method chiefly with reference to doctrine about God and the Trinity. In medieval commentaries on this work, therefore, special attention is always paid to his theological epistemology and methodology.

The third theological work, *De hebdomadibus,* becomes very important for early and high Scholasticism. The method that Boethius uses here is the axiomatic method common in mathematics since Euclid (ca. 295 BC), which is applied now, though, to the realm of metaphysical theology. Again this is not something specifically theological but rather a general, scientific way of proceeding: *"Ut igitur in mathematica fieri solet ceterisque etiam disciplinis, praeposui terminos regulasque, quibus cuncta quae sequuntur efficiam."* ["Therefore, as is usually done in mathematics and also in other disciplines, I present first the terms and rules, from which I will prove all that follows."][65] Here this treatment, which begins with definitions and axioms, is explicitly characterized as a scientific procedure. From the axioms—self-evident propositions that are accepted by everyone without further proofs—all the consequences are then to be derived according to the rules of logic. They are now the basis for the entire discourse, which in keeping with the questions framed in this work, is a metaphysical-theological discourse. It concerns the goodness of creatures, which they cannot have in and of themselves. No wonder this rigorous approach repeatedly stimulated theologians to proceed likewise in their fields (e.g., Alan of Lille [ca. 1120–1202]).[66] Most notably the schools of St. Victor, Chartres, and the circle of Gilbert Porreta († 1154) devoted attention to the *Opuscula sacra.* The whole

63. Boethius, de trin. c.1 (ed. Elsässer 4, 6–7).
64. Ibid., c.2 (8, 16–18).
65. Boethius, De hebd. (34, 14–16); see Dreyer, *More mathematicorum,* 100–106.
66. See below, section 2.8.

work is constructed out of nine axioms, the first of which defines generally what a *"communis animi conceptio"* is (a "common concept of the mind," the κοιναί ἤννοιαι of the Stoic-Neoplatonic tradition). In the axiomatic method, however, everything depends on the axioms and the correct logical derivation of the conclusions. The goal is proof. Boethius' short treatise, therefore, along with *De Trinitate,* became an important medieval textbook but at the same time a model of the method of theological proof.

This method is applied directly to theology in the treatise *De fide catholica,* which offers a brief summary of the fundamental tenets of the faith, whereby the doctrine on the Trinity again constitutes the *"arx religionis nostrae"* ["fortress of our faith"].[67] The Trinitarian doctrine is then explicitly related to the Bible, which presents all this to our faith: *"Haec autem ut credantur vetus ac nova informat instructio."* ["The Old and the New Law, moreover, propose that these things should be believed."][68] Their authority is the bond that holds the whole Church together.[69] Finally, treatise 5, *Contra Eutychen et Nestorium* had great influence on the further development of theological terminology, for example, the concept of "person." In this work Boethius tries to set forth and prove Catholic teaching about the two natures in Christ. Here, too, in keeping with the axiomatic method, he attributes heresy to an ignorance of the initial postulates, combined with the arrogance of false knowledge.[70] Examining presuppositions and above all defining the terms used (*natura, persona,* etc.) is therefore the indispensable task of theology if it is to avoid errors.

The wide-ranging influence of Boethius as "schoolmaster of the Middle Ages" developed out of the peculiar character of his writings. The clearest evidence of this is the tradition of direct commentary on his philosophical and theological works.[71] A second type of influence was the adoption of the axioms from *De hebdomadibus,* which we encounter substantially more often than direct commentary. One can say the same about the terminology of *De Trinitate* and *Contra Eutychen* in Trinitarian doctrine and Christology.[72] Finally and least often we find the composition of distinct theological works in the axiomatic method borrowed from Boethius, which neverthe-

67. Boethius, De fide cath. (ed. Elsässer 46, 8–10; 48, 31).
68. Ibid. (46, 29–48, 30).
69. Ibid. (62, 258–63).
70. Boethius, Contra Eut. (ibid., 66, 30.41–42).
71. See Häring, "Commentary of Gilbert of Poitiers"; Häring, *Commentaries on Boethius;* Green-Pedersen, *Topics.*
72. See Schrimpf, *Axiomenschrift,* 148–49.

less, precisely as a scientific method for theology, prescribes an unmistakable standard of rationality.

1.5 Collections of sentences: Isidore of Seville

Whereas Augustine recommended manuals, compendia, and lexicons as resources for theological science, it was only a matter of time until such works were composed for the discipline of theology itself. A model of this genre is the three-volume collection of *Sententiae* by Isidore of Seville (ca. 560–633), which furthermore, because of his grammatical, exegetical, and encyclopedic works, especially the *Differentiae* and the *Etymologiae* (= *Origines*), became the universal reference work of the Middle Ages.[73] Isidore was not alone in his attempt at a theological synthesis, which essentially refers to the teachings of the patristic period. Earlier Prosper of Aquitaine (ca. 390–after 455) collected in his *Sententiarum ex operibus S. Augustini delibatarum Liber* 392 sentences from Augustine's writings and put them into a new context, which admittedly is still not very systematic. Fulgentius of Ruspe (467–532) proceeds more systematically in his little book *De fide ad Petrum*, which influenced systematic theology in the Middle Ages.[74]

In dissemination and influence, however, these two authors are surpassed by Isidore's *Sentences*, which in book 1 present an outline of dogmatic theology, in book 2 the doctrine on virtues and in book 3 the doctrine on vices. The organization of the dogmatic section is still relatively topical but already anticipates the theological systematization of the Middle Ages: like Augustine in *De doctrina christiana*, Isidore starts with God as the *"summum bonum"* ["supreme good"]. The attributes of God are discussed (chs. 1–3), and then the fact that he can be known from the beauty of creation (chs. 4–5); as a transition to the teaching on creation there is a treatise on eternity and time (chs. 6–7). The doctrine about creatures is presented in a treatise about the world (ch. 8), evil (ch. 9), angels (ch. 10), man (ch. 11), his soul (ch. 12), and senses (ch. 13). Next comes doctrine about Christ (ch. 14), the Holy Spirit (ch. 15), the Church, heresies and pagans (chs. 16–17), the Old Testament Law (ch. 18), for the interpretation of which the seven rules of Tyconius are again applied (ch. 19),[75] about the difference between the testaments (ch. 20), the Creed and prayer (ch. 21), Baptism and Eucharist (ch. 22), martyrdom and miracles (chs. 23–24), and about the Antichrist and his miracles (ch. 25). This

73. See especially Fontaine, *Isidore de Séville;* Cazier, *Isidore de Séville.*
74. See Grillmeier, "Fulgentius von Ruspe."
75. See Cazier, "Tyconius."

leads to the treatise on eschatology (chs. 26–30): the resurrection, judgment, hell and its punishments, and eternal happiness.[76]

Not only Isidore's theological system but also his method of working already exhibits clear features of medieval Scholasticism. The writings of the classic authors of antiquity but also those of ecclesiastical writers already formed a very copious library. As is still the case today in academic work, the first task is therefore that of selecting sources and making excerpts. It testifies to the level of Isidore's scholarship, however, that he states this method as such and attempts, usually in the prologue of his works, to justify it within the framework of a *captatio benevolentiae* [rhetorical device to gain the reader's good will]. He expressly describes his approach as a *culling of flowers* on different meadows; the result, he says, is therefore in the first place a *florilegium* (anthology): *"veterum ecclesiasticorum sententias congregantes, veluti ex diversis pratis flores lectos ad manum fecimus."* ["By gathering the sentences of the old ecclesiastical writers, we have made them readily available like flowers selected from various meadows."] The guiding principle for the selection is abbreviation: *"et pauca de multis breviter perstringentes"* ["touching briefly upon a few things out of many"], so that even *"fastidiosi lectores"* ["readers who are difficult to please"] will not be scared away by too voluminous a work. Yet with mere excerpts and summaries a scientific work is only just begun (which is true today also). Next comes one's own achievement, which in Isidore's view consists of two phases: addition and modification: *"pleraque etiam adjicientes, vel aliqua ex parte mutantes"* ["adding many things also, or changing them in some respect"].[77] Therefore if we want to emphasize the author's own achievement or opinion, we will have to pay attention not only to which sentences he cites, but above all to what he himself adds, leaves out or changes. When Isidore describes his own method also as bringing out goods from a treasury *(depromere)* or as gathering flowers *(deflorare),* he is by no means inventing a new method but is employing one that was cultivated in the literature of late antiquity.[78] Here again, therefore, the method of working is not exclusively theological but rather has been borrowed from the profane science of late antiquity. This work calls for a large library, on the one hand, and on the other hand for a good memory as well: *"veteris lectionis recordatio."* Memory is not infallible, however, and so many errors are mixed in with passages that are cited ex-

76. See Cazier, *Isidore de Séville,* 77–81.
77. Isidor, quaest. in Gen., praef. (PL 83, 207b); see Fontaine, *Isidore de Séville,* 763–84.
78. For illustrations, see Fontaine, *Isidore de Séville,* 767–68.

actly.[79] Such errors are not infrequently characteristic, since they may reveal the author's intended interpretation or purpose.

The resulting textbook is not exactly original or stylistically elegant, but it is clear and short: *"conpendiosa brevitas"* ["comprehensive brevity"] is called for, not the verbosity of late classical rhetoric: *"prolix enim et occulta taedet oratio; brevis et aperta delectat."* ["Long-winded and obscure oratory is tiresome; brief, clear speech is delightful."][80] Recognizing the author's own achievement is not always easy; it lies in the arrangement of the excerpts, in the additions, omissions and changes, which can be detected only through comparison with the sources. The compiler, after all, does not make them explicitly but rather sweeps his tracks. Therefore the work as a whole, for instance the *Sententiae,* is not just like a mosaic in which available stones are merely placed alongside one another according to a definite plan. Isidore does not stop at mere doxography (a review of the authors' opinions), but rather makes out of the patristic sentences a whole *(cento)* consisting of related parts, as Gregory the Great had done before him in an exemplary way in his *Moralia.*

A justification of the overall plan, for instance of the *Sententiae* or even the *Etymologiae,* is still lacking in Isidore. Thus the very first book of the *Sententiae* exhibits an arrangement leading from the doctrine on God to eschatology; the structure of the Christology and Pneumatology, however, is puzzling, as are the individual chapters in the teaching about the Church and her institutions. The division here is predominantly associative and topical; moreover the *Sententiae* are not introduced by a *Praefatio* in which the author might have justified his intention and method. In this form and with this structure, nevertheless, the *Sententiae* of Isidore become, along with Augustine, Fulgentius of Ruspe, and Gennadius of Marseille († 492/505), a model text for the theology of the early Middle Ages, which will likewise refrain at first from justifying its theological method and systematization.[81]

2 Scholastic theology: Methods and presentation

The simplest way to arrive at an understanding of Scholastic theology is by starting from its academic form. Although the rudiments of its methods and presentational forms are anticipated in the patristic era, in the schools

79. For illustrations, see Fontaine, *Isidore de Séville,* 780.

80. Isidor, quaest. in Gen., praef.3 (PL 83, 208b); orig. 13, praef. 1–4, ed. W. M. Lindsay (Oxford 1911).

81. See Grillmeier, "Symbolum," 164–69.

of the tenth through twelfth centuries they are developed in a way that becomes typical for Scholasticism.

2.1 Development of the schools, curriculum, and the liberal arts

The school is the homestead of Scholastic theology and the soil in which it thrived. Theology signifies here an academic discipline, even when the word for it was nonexistent. Theology did gain admission to the schools, yet not everywhere and not always in the same way. Therefore we should take a preliminary look at the development of the school system and the course of education until around 1200.

One characteristic of the so-called Carolingian Reform was the organization of schooling in imperial circles with a marked reliance on the educational heritage of late antiquity.[82] Because of competition with Constantinople, the capital of the eastern Roman Empire, among other reasons, the value of education was recognized, at least for a small clientele from the upper classes.[83] The era, however, had no educational heritage of its own to offer. So they were guided by the curriculum of late antiquity, as established by Augustine, Boethius, and Cassiodorus (ca. 480–after 580): The *artes liberales* again became the common property of "education" and a propaedeutic for theology, for a career in the service of the ruler or the Church. The institutions responsible for this new education were on the one hand the court of Charlemagne (768–814) at the Palatine school, and on the other hand churches and monasteries. Tours, Laon, Corbie, Ferrières, Fulda, Reichenau, and St. Gallen deserve special mention in this regard. This laid the foundation for very different types of schools:[84]

1. *Public schools* in governmental, commercial, and population centers: The Palatine school of Charlemagne was initially considered to be such. Later this role was taken over by the public city schools, which had a long tradition, especially in Italy. The curriculum—usually under ecclesiastical supervision—was by no means aimed at the training of clerics, but rather was meant to provide a broad preparatory education.
2. *Cathedral schools* under the direction of a *scholasticus*. These, too, were not really devoted to theology but were in the first place preparatory schools for higher service in the clergy, the sciences and professions, or

82. See Marenbon, *From the Circle of Alcuin.*
83. See Flasch, *Einführung,* 18–24.
84. For an initial overview, see Evans, *Old Arts,* 8–15; Evans, *Philosophy and Theology.*

in the empire. Yet in these very schools theology very quickly made itself at home and found a privileged place.[85]

3. *Personal schools* were centered on a teacher of philosophy or theology. This type reached its full flowering in the twelfth century. Sometimes it began with a teaching position at a city or cathedral school, for example, in Laon. However, the site could change frequently, as in the case of Abelard (1079–1142): the school is wherever the teacher is.[86]
4. *Monastery schools for externs:* Ever since monasteries took on educational duties, their schools were accessible to those who lived outside the monastic community. The instruction was often first-rate, which assured them of influence similar to that of the cathedral schools, until they diminished in importance as a result of competition with the city schools and universities.
5. *Monastery schools for interns:* These provided the literary, monastic and theological education for future members of the religious order itself. The theology offered therein was often clearly aimed at (and restricted to) the requirements of monastic life.
6. *Schools for special disciplines,* for example, for law (Bologna) and medicine (Salerno); these became customary especially in Italy. At such schools theology was unimportant. On the other hand, even these schools contributed to the development of those methods that, being scholastic (and therefore scientific), went on to have an effect on theology.[87]

"Scholastic theology" therefore is not uniformly related to one type of school, but rather to a process of teaching and learning that distinguishes it from other forms of theologizing. Theology is an academic subject that presupposes, however, a previous education, as Augustine authoritatively described it for this era. Neither theology nor the preparatory education is initially an end in itself in the operation of the school, for the students intend to complete their education and leave the school. Therefore the new schools recognize that the trend in late antiquity toward the compendium, the lexicon and rudimentary education is suitable for their situation, and so they adopt these elements. So it is once again the *artes liberales* through which the profane knowledge of late antiquity is handed on to the early Middle Ages. Alcuin (730/35–804) relates this knowledge *instrumentally*

85. Concerning the German schools, see Sturlese, *Deutsche Philosophie.*
86. See Leclercq, "Renewal," 72–73.
87. See Madiski, "Scholastic Method"; Kantorowicz, "Quaestiones disputatae."

to sacred Scripture, which he considers the quintessence of theology, for it alone contains true, divine knowledge about man and the world.[88] What was taught at Carolingian and post-Carolingian schools often amounted to more than a modest curriculum. Consider that it served primarily to instruct future officials and clerics in reading and writing, the rudiments of Latin and the simplest forms of reckoning (sometimes on the fingers) so as to calculate the date of Easter. Comprehensive instruction in all the *artes* is described as late as Lupus of Ferrières († 862) as a pious wish and a mere fable: *"hoc tempore fabula tantum est."*[89] The "curriculum" may have existed, but the actual execution usually looked quite different. In individual cases, however, depending on the teacher and the students, the offerings could be of very high quality. On the other hand, many schools limited themselves according to Alcuin's program to elementary instruction, without really applying these skills then to sacred Scripture and thus pursuing theology.[90] Since Alcuin's time, the fact that the truth about the world and about man can be found in sacred Scripture is as much a commonplace as the merely instrumental status of the *artes.* This rules out the possibility of a conflict between philosophy that is part of the liberal arts and theology; for one either draws on those resources or else sets them aside. One does not dispute with them as though they were dialogue partners with equal rights.

The relationship between philosophy and theology is also described within the framework of this course of education. For Alcuin the seven liberal arts are *"septem philosophiae gradus"* ["seven degrees of philosophy"]: they therefore constitute philosophy as a whole but are at the same time understood as a propaedeutic *"ad culmina sanctarum Scripturarum"* ["leading up to the summits of sacred Scripture"].[91] Even Duns Scotus Eriugena changed nothing in this curriculum, which describes the available profane knowledge as *philosophia* and while teaching the liberal arts has theology in view: "Understood as the quintessence of science, which had already been brought to its conclusion in the ancient world, they are supposed to guarantee reliable access to and development of that totality of truth which Sacred Scripture contains."[92] In this context the pursuit of philosophy also means initially the pursuit of instruction in the *artes,* as exemplified by the intro-

88. Alcuin, *Disputatio de vera philosophia* (= Dialectica) (PL 101, 854A); see Schrimpf, *Eriugena,* 28–35.

89. Letter from Lupus of Ferrières to Einhard (MGH Epist. VI, 8).

90. See Alcuin, Disp. de vera phil. (PL 101, 853A. 854A).

91. Ibid. (853–54); see Werner, "Meliores viae sophiae."

92. Schrimpf, *Eriugena,* 35.

duction to the manual by Martianus Capella, *De nuptiis Mercurii et Philologiae* (ca. 430), which contains within the framework of a late classical fictional narrative a compendium of seven compendia of the *artes liberales,* and thus can serve as a substitute for the individual writings of Cassiodorus and Boethius.[93] Philosophy as that is understood today was offered as part of the *Trivium,* especially in the study of dialectic, which if necessary drew upon those sections of Aristotle's *Logic* that had been translated by Boethius, Porphyry's (ca. 233–ca. 305) *Isagoge* to the Categories, and the logical writings of Boethius himself. Introductory philosophical questions, the division of the sciences, and the justification of the liberal arts were treated under that heading also. In these discussions of the classification of the sciences it became clear, however, that the seven *artes* could not be harmonized so easily with the Platonic, the Stoic, or the Aristotelian division of philosophy.[94]

The twelfth century is characterized by the expansion of the philosophical-propaedeutic course of studies, albeit formally still within the framework of the *artes.* Interest in treating questions of natural philosophy, metaphysics, and ethics did not yet go beyond these parameters. Apart from the works of Boethius *(De hebdomadibus* and *De consolatio)* and parts of the Platonic dialogue *Timaeus,* however, comprehensive sources for this purpose were not available. Moreover this education did not provide any specialized training, but rather the general scientific skills needed to address the questions of the individual specialties (law, medicine, theology). Augustine had already included architecture and medicine among the arts.[95] Besides the old *artes* Isidor lists two new sciences: law and medicine. In places like twelfth-century Paris where special schools for the liberal arts are founded, these are always merely a preparation for the higher studies that even the *magistri* of these schools take up after a brief stint of teaching. This is true of the theologians also. They too—both students and masters—come from these schools; most often the latter have taught for some time in the *artes* as well, but not too long: *"non est consenescendum in artibus"* ["one should not grow old in the arts"].[96] The "introduction to scientific work" that was learned in them, however, continues to have decisive importance for the pursuit and methodology of higher studies; the most important in the case of theology are the "trivial" verbal arts of grammar and dialectic.

93. Ibid., 37–48.
94. See Van Steenberghen, *Philosophie,* 55–66; Evans, *Arts,* 15–19.
95. See Ferrarino, "Quadruvium."
96. See Van Steenberghen, *Philosophie,* 81–82.

But is it permissible to set about the study of God's word with such profane methods or "arts"? The conflict that had played itself out in early Christianity between pagan παιδεία and Christian revelation now appears in a different form: does the word of the Bible obey the rules of grammar? May we approach the mystery of faith with logical methods? Shouldn't we live the Gospel instead of picking it apart philologically (grammatically) and philosophically (dialectically)? If so, what is the purpose of the long time of preparation in profane arts that are of no use for salvation and only promote arrogance and the academic idleness of the masters and scholars?

In applying grammar, theology occupies itself with the analysis of biblical passages, while systematic theology gives preferential treatment to the study of the words and names that we use in theological statements about God. After an introduction, Praepositinus of Cremona († 1210) begins his *Summa, "Qui producit ventos"* with the programmatic statement: *"E vocabulis quae de Deo dicuntur incipiamus"* ["Let us begin with the words that are predicated of God"].[97] Theology becomes a grammar of speech about God, which is supposed to obey the laws of reasonable discourse.

Besides grammar, dialectic is the principal instrument of theology. Since Augustine's day, dialectic is that discipline which determines the truth of reasonable argumentation and its conformity to the rules. It decides whether propositions are formally correct and free from contradictions. That is why Scholastic theology appears in the form of a determination of the truth value of statements that are introduced (not only in the works of Praepositinus) by the expressions: *"quaeritur de hac (propositione) . . ."* ["the question is asked about this proposition . . ."], *"utrum concedendum sit . . ."* ["whether it should be granted . . ."], *"an dici debeat . . ."* ["or whether it should be said . . ."].[98] In the Letters of St. Paul correct or incorrect syllogisms are identified, or else the ideas therein are put into syllogistic form.[99] This, however, attributes to a formal and, what is worse, profane discipline the competency to decide in matters of theology and faith. This very soon gives rise to a protest, which in the history of philosophy is known under the heading of "dialecticians and anti-dialecticians."[100] Yet even the so-called anti-dialecticians certainly acknowledge in most cases a purely instrumental service rendered by the *artes,* which is that much easier to do because they are looking at a philosophy

97. Praepositinus of Cremona, *Summa "Qui producit ventos"* I, 1, 1: ed. Angelini, *Ortodossia,* 187, 1.

98. See Angelini, *Ortodossia,* 31–32.

99. For example, Lanfranc of Bec, Comm in 2 Cor 3:10–15 (PL 150, 225–26); see Sigebert von Gembloux, De scriptoribus ecclesiasticis c.155 (PL 160, 582).

100. See, for example, Evans, *Arts,* 57–90.

that is restricted to instrumental disciplines (grammar, logic). Peter Damian (1007–1072), too, who is usually cited as a proponent of the "ancillary understanding" of philosophy, speaks generally in his work *De divina omnipotentia* about that *"humanae artis peritia"* ["skill in human art"], which in discussing *"sacra eloquia"* ["sacred words"] must not arrogate to itself the *"jus magisterii"* ["right of mastery, of teaching authority"] but should perform services for her mistress *"velut ancilla"* ["as her handmaid"]. For human art itself is fallible and cannot arrive at the truth without the guidance of the divine word.[101] The substantial truth claim of the word of God thus withstands the rational test of truth by human reason.

2.2 Instructional procedure

Theology as an academic discipline is connected with the instructional procedure in the school. The latter is carried out in an interdisciplinary way, first in the *lectio* [reading] of a text that is regarded as authoritative, for example, a book of the Bible, a passage from the Church Fathers, or the classical authors (Martianus Capella, Donatus, Cicero, Boethius, Pseudo-Dionysius). *Lectio* means first of all commenting on a section-by-section reading of a text, a method that reached its apogee in the schools of the twelfth century. In many respects it resembles contemporary exegetical lectures or the reading of texts as a seminar exercise. Yet the format that was to be followed makes clear both the Scholastic, medieval character of this procedure and also its rationality. The *"authentica,"* the actual words of the reading itself, are contrasted with one's own words and those of one's contemporaries, which were called the *"magistralia."*[102] The *lectio* is therefore the privileged place where *auctoritas* and *ratio* come up for discussion.

The basic form of the *lectio* is divided into five phases:[103]

1. The *accessus ad auctores:* introductory questions such as authorship of the book, the literary genre, time of composition, place in the systematic context, the division or outline of the entire book, the usefulness to the reader, etc. are considered here.
2. The *littera:* the authentic text is presented aloud in sections. In most written commentaries this is omitted. Only the first few words *(lemmata)* of the corresponding section are noted.

101. Petrus Damiani, De divina omnipotentia, c.5 (PL 145, 595–622).
102. See Chenu, *Théologie,* 351–65.
103. See Rentsch, "Kultur," 75–76. Rentsch, however, omits no.1!

3. The *divisio textus:* the section of the text under discussion is divided thematically into smaller subsections, sometimes down to the level of individual sentences or clauses.
4. The *expositio:* the thematic presentation of the doctrinal content of the individual section or sentence while confronting it with earlier and contemporary opinions. A prerequisite for this is an explanation of terms and distinctions among their meanings. They are sometimes listed alphabetically in the *distinctiones* literature.[104] One cannot always affirm that the authoritative text is true in the literal sense; one then resorts to the technique of *exponere reverenter:* One pays the necessary respect to the authority (e.g., the biblical text) by looking for a good meaning of the text, by advocating another opinion—objectively but by making distinctions, for instance in linguistic usage or meaning.
5. The *dubia:* after the presentation of the text, the instructor brings up and answers questions that refer either to the text itself or follow from it thematically. This is the *"Sitz im (Schul-)Leben"* ["the (academic) experiential setting"] for the development of a second literary genre in the scholastic enterprise: the *quaestio.*

As the conclusion of the *lectio,* however, the *quaestio* is the privileged place for the question of truth. By answering it in his *conclusio* or *sententia,* the master decides also as to the truth of theological propositions. Thus factual questions are assumed to be answerable.[105] Originally it was most often a matter of harmonizing discrepancies between authorities. Given the many different opinions, this is increasingly replaced by the question about the truth of a matter. Wherever the decisive method is logical-rational examination, optimism prevails that the truth can be found, even in the multiplicity of opinions. Scholastic questions are therefore not skeptical but rather sometimes curious-sounding questions; for one can ask about anything, especially in schools where the *quaestio* has become independent of the *lectio* method and is a separate pedagogical device. The *magister* does not always have an answer. Odo of Ourscamp († after 1171), for example, postponed his answer once to the next day.[106] At first questions are not posed according to a fixed rule or system, but rather as they come up, as in the ancient

104. See especially with regard to scriptural commentary Rouse & Rouse, "Statim invenire."

105. Concerning the following "characteristics of Scholastic inquiry," see Schönberger, *Scholastik,* 53–80.

106. Grabmann, *Methode,* 2:26.

quaestiones et responsiones or in a modern question-and-answer session.[107] The simplest answers, naturally, are references to authorities with whom the master agrees.

The results of the *quaestiones* are summarized in literary form at first in similarly miscellaneous collections of questions, which quite often contain material by different and sometimes anonymous authors.[108] Sometimes scholars looked through the scriptural commentaries of the *magistri* for *quaestiones* and excerpted them, for example, in the case of Robert of Melun († 1167) and Richard of St. Victor († 1173). The place of many questions in the outline of systematic theology became clear in this way.

Already in the patristic era there was theological questioning, precisely about biblical passages. Often perplexed confreres or preachers are the ones posing the questions; we have vivid examples of this in Augustine's explanation of several questions about the Letter to the Romans.[109] This mode of instruction has its source in the dialogical, dialectical questions of antiquity. We are well acquainted with medieval disputation of questions in connection with the *lectio* from the ninth century on. At first it does not seem to have been a disputation with assigned roles, but rather a simple inquiry, especially in the case of contradictory authorities, which were perhaps followed by an equally simple answer by the teacher. Probably that was how it was usually done in the school of Anselm of Laon († 1117). We then encounter fully developed *quaestiones* with *pro* and *contra* around the mid-twelfth century in the works of Odo of Ourscamp, who was a student of Anselm of Laon and Abelard. Even in these early examples some of the more difficult passages from Scripture are explained by extended questions. The logical methods for this are provided initially within the framework of the *dialectica* in the *artes liberales;* Haimo of Halberstadt († 853), too, distinguishes between a simple, random disputation and *liberaliter disputare,* which presupposes the methods of the *artes liberales.*[110] A strictly logical *disputatio in forma* (in syllogistic form) is possible only after the general acceptance of the *Logica nova* (especially the *Topica* and the *Sophistici elenchi*): John of Salisbury († 1180) maintains that without these, one does not dispute "artistically" but haphazardly.[111] The great disputations became a field of intel-

107. See Studer, *Schola Christiana,* 128–29.
108. See Landgraf, *Einführung,* 40–42.
109. CSEL 84; see Studer, *Schola Christiana,* 201–3.
110. Landgraf, *Einführung,* 41.
111. John of Salisbury, *Metalogicon* l.3 c.10 (PL 199, 910).

lectual activity in the thirteenth and fourteenth centuries; they were dependent on the university organization. Among these academic events we must distinguish between the ordinary disputations that took place weekly or biweekly, and the solemn *Disputationes de quolibet,* which were not customary until the latter half of the thirteenth century and were held twice year, before Christmas and Easter. Here any theological question at all could be brought up. Therefore the *Quodlibeta,* the literary outcome of these disputations, are important documents of that time.[112]

Thomas Aquinas (1225–1274) carefully presents the simplest form of disputed questions in his textbook for beginners, the *Summa Theologiae,* although he first warns about the conventional welter of arguments and questions.[113] Thomas divides the individual question first into *articuli,* the structure of which corresponds to the general scheme of the *quaestio.*

1. Posing of the question: *Quaeritur, utrum (an)* . . . [It is asked whether . . .] This really is a question, not just a thesis that is to be proved in the following lines. The precise manner in which the question is phrased already contributes much to the answer. This answer is open, however, and not already decided by the formulation.
2. Arguments
   a) *videtur quod sic/quod non:* [It seems that it is / that it is not . . .] Arguments for a possible answer are given (in Thomas' works only a few): Scripture, the Church Fathers *(auctoritates)* and reasonable arguments *(rationes);*
   b) *sed contra:* [But on the other hand . . .] Arguments for the opposite answer (Thomas usually gives only one). Since the question is open, we are not dealing here with proponents or opponents of a thesis, but rather with alternatives that are to be discussed rationally; each alternative must be in principle non-contradictory and possible.
3. Response: *Respondeo dicendum. . . .* [I reply by saying . . .] The *conclusio,* which is often given sententiously in a single sentence, is the place where the question is resolved, the place for the actual teaching of the *magister,* who attains therein his highest authority. For his task is the *determinatio magistralis* [magisterial decision], whereas the presentation of the arguments and sometimes also their analysis along the lines of the given *conclusio* was usually a matter for the *baccalaurei* [bachelors of arts]. The

112. See Van Steenberghen, *Philosophie,* 83.
113. Thomas Aquinas, S.Th. I, 1, Prol., Marietti edition (Turin-Rom, 1952).

answer given is justified by means of the arguments presented in step 2 or with new arguments of the *magister.*

4. The analysis of the arguments from step 2 along the lines of the given *conclusio: Ad primum (etc.) dicendum . . .* [concerning the first argument, it should be said . . .]. The *solutio* usually provides important amplifications of the *conclusio* in dealing with the arguments, which are by no means rejected wholesale as arguments of opponents, but rather are discussed in detail.

This basic pattern is followed to a great extent in the thirteenth century, although it is greatly elaborated in the *quaestiones disputatae de quolibet.* The proliferation of Scholastic opinions on a given question causes the *quaestiones* scheme in late Scholasticism (e.g., in William of Ockham [ca. 1285–1347]) to appear more complex and tortuous, because here the individual *opiniones* are discussed in depth, whereas the few introductory arguments hardly carry weight any more.[114]

2.3 The Bible and Scholastic theology

Until well into the thirteenth century theology consists of lengthy passages of biblical exegesis. "*Theologia*" and "*sacra pagina*" or "*divina pagina*" are to a great extent synonymous until Thomas Aquinas.[115] Sacred Scripture is the preeminent object of academic *lectio,* which should be distinguished carefully from the *lectio divina* of monastic spirituality.[116] Whereas the latter involves the personal study and assimilation of the scriptural passage for the sake of the spiritual life, the academic *lectio* makes available the entire toolkit of procedures for interpreting a literary text, first and foremost the criteria of the *artes liberales,* especially grammar and dialectic. For the explanation of the content, the *florilegia* from the writings of the Church Fathers are indispensable. These explanations were added to the authentic text orally at first, then in writing as well in the form of glosses: a procedure that was familiar from legal scholarship. Similarly, the textbooks used in teaching the liberal arts were glossed, for example, works by Boethius, Martianus Capella, Donatus, and Priscianus.[117] Depending on the positioning of the glosses in the manuscript, we distinguish between interlinear and

114. The schema is described in Rentsch, "Kultur," 88–89.

115. See Geyer, "Facultas theologica," 141–43.

116. See Leclercq, *Wissenschaft,* 84–86.

117. See Smalley, *Study,* 46–66; for additional information and corrections, see Bertola, "Glossa ordinaria"; also Holtz, "Rôle des Commentaires."

marginal glosses. Interlinear glosses usually add explanations of individual words, while marginal glosses add more extensive comments (usually patristic *sententiae*) on individual verses or passages. Thus we find a wealth of literature in gloss form from the time of Berengar of Tours († 1088), and then in the circle that included Bruno the Carthusian († 1101) and in the school of Anselm of Laon. From the end of the ninth century on, the prevailing method is a combination of interlinear and marginal gloss.

The most widely diffused and therefore the most important gloss in early Scholasticism still contains riddles for scholars today: the *Glossa ordinaria,* which in later Scripture commentaries is presupposed as an initial gloss and sometimes acquires an authoritative character as "the Gloss" pure and simple.[118] The *magister* therefore relies on the *Glossator.* The *Glossa ordinaria* is a collective work, which came to include material by various authors. The earliest parts (on the books of Wisdom and Sirach) were written by Walafried Strabo († 894). Evidently the *Glossa ordinaria* assumed its final form in the school of Laon (Anselm, Radulfus [† 1131/33], Gilbertus Universalis [† 1334]); nevertheless the attribution of individual parts to a particular author is uncertain. E. Bertola's attribution of the *parva glossatura* to Anselm of Laon, the *media glossatura* to Gilbertus Universalis, and the *magna glossatura* to Peter Lombard (ca. 1095–1160) is plausible as far as the chronological sequence is concerned, but not proven. Again, the authoritative status of a gloss as a "Scholastic gloss" is not limited to works about the Bible and thus about theology. We can trace the same development with respect to the topical and theological writings of Boethius.[119] The *Glossa ordinaria* provides for every book in the Bible an introduction, for which Jerome (340/50–419/20) usually acts as godfather, and then in connection with the individual verses a more or less concise scholarly *apparatus* made up of patristic and medieval sources (that are later called *expositores* as opposed to the *glossator* or the *ordinator glos[a]e* himself). The *expositores* range from the Church Fathers through the Venerable Bede (672/73–735), Walafried Strabo, Paschasius Radbertus (ca. 790–ca. 859), Duns Scotus Eriugena († ca. 880), via Haimo of Halberstadt, Lanfranc of Bec (ca. 1010–1089), Hrabanus Maurus (780–856), and Berengar down to the commentaries of the school of Laon and Gilbertus Universalis.[120]

To a great extent the glosses continue to follow the so-called *catena*

118. See Bertola, "Glossa ordinaria"; Swanson, "Glossa Ordinaria."
119. See Schrimpf, *Axiomenschrift;* Green-Pedersen, *Topics.*
120. See Smalley, *Study,* 66.

technique, which we still find in the *Catena aurea* of Thomas Aquinas. This method, again, is not limited to scriptural commentary, but can be found in "systematic" works also as late as the twelfth century.[121] The most important patristic passages on a verse from Scripture are cited (and in systematic or polemical works, of course, the relevant scriptural passages as well). The citations are reconciled with one another as to their content, while discrepancies and various possible interpretations are indicated. Thus it is a procedure that still owes much to *auctoritas,* while *ratio* limits itself to selecting and discriminating among the authorities, weighing their importance and arranging them accordingly. These very features made the gloss a reference work and textbook whose value and influence could hardly be exaggerated. Indeed, the scholar found immediately for every passage the most important and advanced teachings and thus was spared the trouble of studying the sources himself. Out of this *Glossa,* at the service of further commentary but also of preaching, grew a wealth of literature consisting of *distinctiones, allegoriae,* or *adnotationes* on individual words or passages.[122]

These glosses became important—not only in the field of law—precisely where the literal text was difficult to understand or (in law) impossible to obey. Glossing a text in such cases often meant mitigating, adapting, explaining, and thus reinterpreting it. Against this background we can see why Francis of Assisi (1181/82–1226), for example, stipulated in his testament that his Rule must be followed *"sine glossa,"* that is, to the letter and without relaxation or adaptation.[123] *"Glossa"* increasingly has the connotation of *"falsitas"* and is therefore replaced, for instance, by Thomas Gascoigne (1403–1458) in the fifteenth century with *"expositio communis."*[124] Yet the gloss could also become a problem for theological instruction itself: it immediately provided the interpretation, so that as a result one could bypass the text itself. Robert of Melun (ca. 1100–1167) clearly points out the dangers of such a "gloss theology": the mere recitation of glosses without further investigation, and instead questions that allegedly probe deeply but are only based on ignorance of the books of the Bible, for instance, whether Ezra lived before or after Moses. In Robert's opinion this reverses the order of teaching: secondary literature is put in the first place, the text is neglected

121. See, for example, Schrimpf, *Eriugena,* 85–86.

122. See Häring, "Commentary," 177–78.

123. Ibid., 182–85; Francis of Assisi, *Testamentum, Opuscula S. Francisci,* L. Lemmens, ed. (Quaracchi, 1904), 79.

124. See Smalley, *Study,* 271.

and all the effort is devoted to the *"studium glosularum."* The *"intelligentia textus"* ["understanding of the text"], the *"sententia"* ["thought, meaning"], however, does not depend on the study of glosses per se. The purpose of studying sacred Scripture is precisely to understand the text, to elaborate the *sententia,* and not to know the right section of the Gloss: *"Non enim ille bene legit, qui quod scriptura sentit diligenter non exponit."* ["He does not read well who does not explain diligently what Scripture means."][125] It does no good merely to recite from glosses, which after all say only what others have said about a passage. A gloss has no authority of its own above and beyond the authority of the Fathers who are cited. Therefore it is miserable ignorance and damnable stubbornness to think that one has obliged oneself *"quasi sacramento"* ["as if by an oath"] to recite from the glosses.[126]

The process of finding the *sententia* of biblical passages sparks questions, which are then further elaborated in the form of a *quaestio* and put into written form in the *Scriptural commentaries.*[127] The procedure follows the general pattern of *lectio* or *disputatio.* Whereas at first it was only a few individual questions, for example in the works of Gerard of Csanád († 1046), in the school of Laon the number increased appreciably, until in the *glossatura magna* we find the genre of a commentary in *quaestiones.* We have an example by Robert of Melun from the period 1145–1155 entitled *Questiones de Epistolis Pauli.*[128] This is no accident, because for him the *quaestio* and not the gloss is the right instrument with which to discover the *sententia* of the text. Later the questions were sometimes detached from the commentary and circulated independently: thus the genre of the commentary in *quaestiones* came about. Yet they are still related to the Bible, they are still *quaestiones de divina pagina.*[129] A division of labor in the organization of the thirteenth-century university appeared here: The *baccalaureus biblicus* lectured on a sort of "fundamental exegesis" with the assistance of the Gloss; the *magister,* in contrast, expounded the meaning *(sententia)* by means of *quaestiones.* In these the text itself can often be disregarded—in the manu-

125. Robert of Melun, *Sententiae,* "praefatio," in *Œuvres de Robert de Melun,* ed. R. M. Martin, vol. III, 1 (Louvain, 1947), 11, 28–12, 1; see Grabmann, *Methode,* 2:342–46.

126. Robert of Melun, *Sent. praef.,* vol. III, 1: 24, 17–29; see Grabmann, *Methode,* 2:348–49.

127. For an indispensable inventory of medieval scriptural commentaries, see Stegmüller, *Repertorium Biblicum,* 11 volumes in all.

128. Robert de Melun, *Questiones de Epistolis Pauli,* in *Œuvres,* ed. R. M. Martin, vol. II (Louvain, 1938); see Smalley, *Study,* 66–82.

129. Robert de Melun, *Questiones de divina pagina,* in *Œuvres,* ed. R. M. Martin, vol. I (Louvain, 1932).

script version as well—and be replaced by a systematic arrangement of the questions. The transition from biblical *lectio* to systematic theology should be seen precisely in this gradual detachment of the *quaestiones* and the *sententia* arrived at therein from the biblical text.[130] Biblical exegesis *(divina pagina)* and systematic presentation *(fides catholica)* are nevertheless still united in one work.[131] It was not always a commentary directly on the biblical text, though: Zacharias Chrysopolitanus bases his *In unum ex quatuor* (written between 1140 and 1145) on the harmony of the Gospels by Ammonios of Alexandria, which he uses as an outline for what is essentially a *catena* of passages from the Church Fathers and contemporary *magistri.*[132]

Many Scholastic scriptural commentaries are extant not in a copy *(ordinatio)* composed by the *magister* himself, but only in transcripts *(reportationes)* written down by students; these versions may or may not have been revised and therefore not infrequently contain discrepancies or disagreements; because of these errors and misunderstandings they should be used with caution.[133] Not all the books of the Bible were annotated in the schools with the same zeal and partiality. The Psalms, the Pauline Letters and Genesis 1 were among the biblical texts most commented on in the early twelfth century. In contrast, there was essentially nothing written about the rest of the Pentateuch and the historical books of the OT, the prophets, or even the Gospels and the Acts of the Apostles.[134] In 1121 or 1123, when Abelard tried to hold a *lectio* on Ezekiel in Laon, this was forbidden as something unusual.[135] Soon scholars noticed also the errors and uncertainties in the biblical text [i.e., the Vulgate] on which the commentary was based. Hebrew was for the most part unknown. Stephen Harding (1059–1134) and the early Cistercians, especially Nikolaus Manjacoria († ca. 1145), however, with the help of Jews, worked on a corrected version of the [Latin] OT text so as to restore the *"hebraica veritas."*[136]

Scriptural interpretation flourished in a particular way in the school of the Canons Regular of St. Victor in Paris, where the tradition of monastic spirituality *(lectio divina)* was combined with that of Scholastic exegesis.

130. See Smalley, *Study,* 75–81.

131. See Bliemetzrieder, "Anselme de Laon," 480.

132. PL 186, 11–619; see van den Eynde, "Magistri"; Evans, "Zachary of Besançon."

133. See Smalley, *Study,* 200–1.

134. See Geerlings, "Commentaires patristiques," esp. 208–11; Studer, *Schola Christiana,* 206–8, 293–94.

135. Abaelard, *Historia calamitatum* 202–36, ed. J. Monfrin (Paris, 1959), 69–70.

136. See Smalley, *Study,* 79–80.

Hugh of St. Victor († 1141) wrote numerous works "occasioned" by the Bible, which became important precisely because they combined spiritual interpretation with Scholastic instruction. Besides the *Notul[a]e ad litteram* [Brief notes on the literal sense] for the historical books of the OT, there are homilies on Ecclesiastes, a threefold exegesis of the Lamentations, commentaries on the Magnificat and the Our Father, etc.[137] The latter works, like those of Richard of St. Victor, offer a spiritual, mystical, scriptural exegesis that presupposes the doctrine of the fourfold meaning of Scripture. In contrast, Andrew of St. Victor († 1174) should probably be described as the most important literal exegete of the twelfth century—so much so that even at Isaiah 7:14 he presents only the Jewish interpretation, which prompted Richard to write an *Invectio . . . contra Andream socium suum super illud Ecce virgo concipiet* ["Invective against Andrew his confrere concerning the passage 'Behold, a virgin shall conceive'"].[138] Andrew also kept in contact with Jewish exegetes.[139]

At the Parisian schools of theology in the second half of the twelfth century, *sacra pagina* was advocated primarily by three figures of paramount importance: Petrus Comestor, Petrus Cantor († 1197) and Stephen Langton (who remained in Paris until 1206; † 1228). They no longer expounded individual passages or books from the Bible, but rather explained all of sacred Scripture comprehensively, usually for a moral purpose. It was noted about Stephen Langton: *"Totam scripturam* primus medullitus et moraliter *cepit exponere"* ["He was *the first* to begin to explain all of Scripture *in a thoroughgoing and moral way*"].[140] Only occasionally does the commentary still follow the method of glossing individual passages. Then there is a basic introduction to the Bible, the *Historia scholastica* by Petrus Comestor, which provides a survey of the biblical books and of history from the creation of the world to the death of the apostles. The possibilities for spiritual exegesis are always indicated precisely, as Hugh of St. Victor had demanded in his *Didascalicon.* As Zacharias Chrysopolitanus had done, Petrus Cantor too first presents the biblical texts in a harmonization that is then glossed, so that the whole work is described also as *Verbum abbreviatum.* For the purposes of spiritual exegesis he offers in his *Summa Abel* an alphabetically arranged

137. PL 175.

138. MS Paris, BN lat. 13432, f.65–83. See Häring, "Commentary," 193.

139. See Smalley, *Study,* 145–56; Berndt, *André de Saint Victor.*

140. *Catalogus virorum illustrium* 27, ed. N. Häring, "Two Catalogues of Medieval Authors," in *Franciscan Studies* 26 (1966): 201; see Quinto, *Stefano Langton,* 1–42.

lexicon of possibilities for exegesis, grouped under individual headings (beginning with *Abel*). The theory of exegesis is investigated in writings such as *De difficultatibus Sacr[a]e Scripture* and *De Tropis loquendi.*

The Scholastic interpretation of the Bible, which includes a variety of approaches, presupposes the theory that Scripture has more than one meaning or sense. Very important proponents of this theory of the fourfold sense of Scripture were Hugh of St. Victor with his *Didascalicon,* Petrus Cantor, and last but not least in the thirteenth century Bonvanture's prologue to the *Breviloquium;* the latter two are also in the Victorine tradition.[141] The senses of Scripture are not just exegetical methods; for Hugh they are disciplines which together produce the *sacra doctrina.* Therefore the theologian in the Middle Ages had to be well versed in all these areas, from literal exegesis to the mystical-spiritual interpretation. Although the emphasis may depend on the individual author and the field in which he worked (school, monastery, parish), the literal sense usually predominates. The doctrine of the fourfold sense of Scripture was practically canonized and handed down in the oft-cited mnemonic verse by Augustine of Dacia († 1281):

> *Littera gesta docet, quid credas allegoria,*
> *moralis quid agas, quo tendas anagogia.*[142]

The foundation for the spiritual interpretation is the *littera* or the *historia.* Without it a spiritual interpretation goes astray as a matter of principle. There is no question about the historicity of divine revelation in the biblical books. Thus Hugh recommends beginning with a careful *lectio* of the historical books of the Bible. The *littera* is, so to speak, the alphabet that the theologian has to learn first. He who proceeds otherwise acquires knowledge like that of a donkey.[143] For an understanding of the historical sense, history and geography should be applied, besides the linguistic disciplines.

Upon this foundation, then, the building of the spiritual interpretation is constructed; *allegory* is the first step. Allegorical interpretation, which was already common in reading classical authors in the schools of antiquity, found a home especially in Alexandrian exegesis. It concerns initially

141. See esp. de Lubac, *Exégèse médiévale* [*Medieval Exegesis*]; Chenu, "Théologie symbolique"; Smalley, *Study,* 242–63.

142. "The literal sense teaches what happened; what you should believe—the allegorical; the moral (= tropological) sense—what you ought to do; what you should strive for—the anagogical." See Châtillon, "Vocabulaire," 17–18.

143. See Hugh of St. Victor, *Didascalicon* VI, 3, ed. Ch. H. Buttimer (Washington, 1939), 114, 9–10: *"quorum scientia formae asini similis est. noli huiusmodi imitari."*

an overall interpretation of Scripture in relating the OT to the NT as the "prophetic prefiguration" or "type" of the latter.[144] In OT words, figures and events, components of the NT event involving Christ and the Church are discerned. Allegory occurs as verbal allegory (words that have a meaning other than the literal sense), but also as *"allegoria facti"*: events and figures "mean" something else above and beyond the historical context. There are many methods, some of which are handed down in fixed patterns; the images and metaphors used are generally intended to reveal something hidden, to open up a new dimension of understanding.[145] This is true also for biblical numbers, for which precise rules were handed down from the days of Augustine. Unfamiliarity with numbers is an obstacle to the allegorical and mystical understanding of many scriptural passages, he maintains explicitly in *De doctrina christiana*.[146] The technique of number allegory is developed in the twelfth century in precise rules: for example, the analogy between number and what is numbered, the interpretation of numbers as sums of terms or products of factors, affinities, and types of numbers based on their composition, but also the meaning of the symbolic numbers themselves (4, 7, 12, etc.).[147]

The moral or *tropological* sense derives from Scripture rules for Christian living and its virtues, either for the Church as a whole or for the individual person. This kind of interpretation, which passes from *"factum"* to *"faciendum"* [from what has been done to what should be done], reaches its apogee in the moral-pastoral scriptural exegesis of Petrus Cantor and Stephen Langton, sometimes mixed with clear criticism of conditions in the Church. The basic models for this interpretation are the pastoral rules and the *Moralia in Job* by Gregory the Great († 604).[148]

The mystical or *anagogical* sense is by no means the exclusive province of contemplative circles; rather it is one of the forms of exegesis even in non-monastic schools. The anagogical sense points on the one hand to the Second Coming of Christ at the end of the ages, but on the other hand to the mystical anticipation thereof in the individual soul and its ascent to heavenly glory. Anagogy as the goal of the spiritual interpretation of Scripture can be more or less closely connected with allegory or tropology; it

144. Dohmen, "Schriftsinn."

145. See esp. Spitz, *Metaphorik* and the discussion there of individual images and metaphors.

146. Augustinus, doct. chr. II, 16, 25 (Cch SL 32, 50, 52–53).

147. Basic presentation in Meyer / Suntrup, *Lexikon der mittelalterlichen Zahlenbedeutungen*; see also Hellgardt, *Zahlenkomposition*; *idem*, "Zahlenallegorese."

148. See Smalley, *Study*, 242–63; Baldwin, *Masters*.

usually cannot do without a foundation in the allegorical interpretation of Scripture.[149]

In works entitled *Distinctiones* and *Allegoriae* the possibile interpretations of individual words or objects are then set down as though in a lexicon, whereby types are developed: "Jerusalem" means literally the city in Israel, allegorically the Church, tropologically the human soul, and anagogically the heavenly Jerusalem in glory.[150] Individual Scripture passages for a particular interpretation can also be listed under a keyword: for example, it is possible to interpret "bed" allegorically as sacred Scripture (Song of Songs 1:16), tropologically as contemplation (Luke 17:34), conscience (Psalm 6:6) or carnal desire (Amos 6:4), anagogically for eternal punishment (Job 17:13) and eternal happiness (Luke 11:7).[151] The danger of such allegorical-symbolic interpretation lay in neglect of the text itself in its literal sense, even for the *"doctrina fidei."* Thomas Aquinas clear-sightedly insists instead on the primacy of the *littera:* Only from the literal sense can a valid theological argument be obtained, not from an allegorical interpretation.[152]

Nevertheless it would not do justice to medieval biblical studies if one were to see only the symbolic-spiritual interpretation. Indeed in St. Victor and in the Parisian schools flourishing centers of literal exegesis developed under Andrew of St. Victor († 1175), Herbert of Bosham († 1186), Petrus Comestor, and others. [153] Andrew of St. Victor limits himself exclusively to the *historia.* The other senses of Scripture are of as little interest to him as Scholastic theological questions, insofar as they are not immediately related to an understanding of the *littera.* He consults Jewish exegetes and compares the text of the Vulgate with the Hebrew wording. The interpretation of the Church Fathers is measured accordingly and quite often criticized.[154] Strongly influenced by Andrew was Herbert of Bosham, who claimed to be the first to expound the *Hebraica* [Hebrew version] after the example of Jerome.[155] He does not venture to soar on the pinions of a difficult spiritual interpretation but rather is determined to keep his feet on the ground and elaborate only the meaning of the *littera.*

149. See Adamus Scotus, *Ad viros religiosos: quatorze sermons d'Adam Scot,* ed. F. Petit (Tongerlo, 1934), 28 and 94.

150. See Dohmen, "Schriftsinn," 20.

151. See Smalley, *Study,* 247; Bataillon, "Instruments de travail"; Bataillon, "Intermédiaires."

152. Thomas Aquinas, *S.Th.* I q.1 a.10 ad 1 (I,9).

153. See Smalley, *Study,* 112–242. For the works of Andrew of St. Victor, see: *CCh CM* 53.

154. See Berndt, *André de Saint Victor.*

155. See Smalley, *Study,* 186–95; see also by the same author "Commentary."

This study of the *littera* broadens theologically through the influence of the *Historia scholastica* by Petrus Comestor, which Stephen Langton deemed as influential as the *Liber Sententiarum* of Peter Lombard. Taking it as his model, Peter of Poitiers (ca. 1130–1205) wrote his *Compendium Historiae in Genealogia Christi,* in which he gives an outline of biblical history from Adam to Christ in the form of a genealogical tree of Christ.[156] These works were the basic bibliography for the "Introduction to the Bible" course that the *baccalaurei biblici* at a thirteenth-century university had to teach. The format of this instruction has come down to us in several manuscripts from the turn of the thirteenth century: in the prologue the purpose of the *lectio* was formulated; then Jerome's prologue to the book in question was read. The text was read through line by line; in a later development, students would bring their own copies and annotate them. In addition the glosses were always read. They were named after their initial words and ranked according to the weight of the authority: Augustine, Bede, etc.; next difficulties from the glosses were presented.[157] Once the *littera cum glosis* of a passage had been read through, the lecturer went back to the beginning and started the allegorical interpretation. For that purpose, however, the text as such had to be established first and, if necessary, corrected, since punctuation marks were not used in the manuscripts; consequently individual words could belong to either the previous or the following sentence. Furthermore there was no standard division into chapters, much less a numbering of the verses. Instead the book was usually divided into *tituli* (meaning units), which were listed at the beginning like a table of contents. In Paris, at least, no standard division of the Bible into chapters and verses developed until the thirteenth century. The divisions, punctuations, and corrections were compiled, especially in the thirteenth century, in so-called *correctoria.* Stephen Langton's corrections and divisions of the biblical text became influential. But even an obviously faulty text could provide support for a particular spiritual interpretation.[158] Around this time likewise the first concordances appear; unlike the reference works that we have today, these contained parallel passages compiled by Stephen Langton, among others, based on the glosses.[159]

Preaching flourished in the thirteenth century, thanks in part to the ar-

156. See Moore, *Peter of Poitiers,* 118–22.

157. E.g., in Stephen Langton: Smalley, *Study,* 216–19.

158. Ibid., 220–23.

159. Ibid., 241.

rival of the mendicant orders in the university cities. The *postilla* became very important in this development. (The term comes from the expression *post illa verba* [after these words], that is, the explanation following the scriptural verse or passage.) In this form of commentary explanations were added to the biblical text that had been divided into meaning units *(loci),* whereas by then the term *glossa* referred only to the interlinear and marginal glosses. It is remarkable how closely the early mendicants followed the spiritual interpretation of Scripture by the Victorine school, while continuing also their study of the literal sense. Clearly the tradition of *lectio divina* was adopted in the Dominican and Franciscan Orders, and to that end they fell back on the tried and true assistance of Hugh of St. Victor, for instance. At the same time they distinguished their Scripture studies from the speculative theology of the *magistri* who were secular clerics. The prime example is the influential *Postilla super totam bibliam* by the Dominican Hugh of St. Cher († 1263) and his collaborators (ca. 1235). He sees in the disciples who plucked ears of grain on the Sabbath (Mark 2:23) the *"fratres studentes"* ["student friars"] in their *"studium scripturarum"* ["study of the Scriptures"]; the Pharisees who forbade them to do so are of course the theologians, who in turn are to be divided into two groups, the *"morales"* (probably in the tradition of the Parisian schools of moral theology, which included Cantor, Langton, Philipp the Chancellor [† 1236]), and the *"questioniste"* (the strict Scholastics). The *"moralistae"* say, "It is not good to incorporate so many *quaestiones* into theology." The *"questionist[a]e"* say: "It is not good to invent so many moral interpretations." The bottom line, per Hugh: *"et quilibet reprehendit quod nescit."*[160] Hugh's *Postilla* became the most important supplement to the *Glossa ordinaria,* for example in the works of Bonaventure and Albert the Great († 1280) and at Oxford. His importance was eclipsed in the early modern period (especially for preachers on account of the various moral "practical applications") by the Franciscan Nicholas of Lyra († 1349).

This cordoning off of biblical theology from Scholastic theology is clearly indicated also by the differentiated linguistic usage in the thirteenth century. Until then *"sacra pagina"* had meant both the biblical books and theology as a whole. In reference to the Bible itself the term is now increasingly replaced by *"Scriptura"* or *"Biblia,"* so that the *"magister in sacra pagina"* is not necessarily (just) an exegete, but also a systematic theologian. Now

160. "And each finds fault with what he does not know." Hugh of St. Cher, *Postilla in Bibliam* (Paris, 1530–1545), VI f. 86; see Smalley, *Study,* 269. Supplementary remarks at ibid., XIII.

the business of the instructor is no longer *sacram paginam glossare* [to gloss the sacred text] but rather *Scripturam postillare* [to comment on Scripture]. For examples of the latter we should mention the scriptural commentaries of Thomas Aquinas and Bonaventure. In Paris (unlike at Oxford) the *postilla* generally presents only a few questions concerning systematic theology and mostly *quaestiones* that refer only to the text.[161]

2.4 Collections of sentences and Summas

Besides Scripture-based biblical theology, the twelfth-century schools saw the development of a systematic theology that presented its findings in the form of systematically arranged collections of sentences and summas.[162] We are acquainted with their patristic models, Prosper of Aquitaine and especially Isidore of Seville. In the linguistic usage of biblical theology, *"sententia"* means the (deeper) meaning or doctrinal content of a Scripture passage. This matter was raised in the *lectio* or *quaestio* and then pinned down. Next come the "sentences" of the Church Fathers and of contemporaries, which were collected in the glosses. Independent collections of sentences sometimes show already in the title that they are anthologies of statements, questions, solutions, and theses of other scholars: *"Sententi[a]e a magistro Untolfo collect[a]e," "Sententi[a]e Augustini a magistro Anshelme conjunct[a]e."*[163] Even the compiler of the most important volume of sentences, Peter Lombard, is described by contemporaries not as an author but rather as a *"collector sententiarum."* The *"flores patrum"* ["flowers of the Church Fathers," i.e., sayings collected in *florilegia*] are then also described as *"sententiae."* These collections, however, are still intended as systematic introductions to the study of sacred Scripture, after the model of Augustine's *De doctrina christiana.* This is made clear even in the titles: *Sententie divine pagine, Sententie divinitatis.* In the course of a disputation *"sententia"* then means also the master's authoritative solution to a question, or else one position that is contrasted with another.[164]

Later on systematic collections of sentences, especially introductory works, are not infrequently referred to as *Summae,* and smaller introductory

161. Smalley, *Study,* 271–77.

162. See Grabmann, *Methode,* 2:21–24.

163. The most important Early Scholastic collections of sentences are listed in Landgraf, *Einführung,* 35–39.

164. Grabmann, *Methode,* 2:23, maintains that this meaning does not occur until the thirteenth century; it is already attested, however, in Vivianus of Prémontré (ca. 1140): see Leinsle, *Vivianus* 7*, 7–8: *"alterius quorum sententie vos consensum tribuisse fortasse recolitis"* ["perhaps you recall that you had agreed with the *sententia* = opinion of someone else among them"].

textbooks as *Summulae.*[165] Robert of Melun defines the *Summa* as *"singulorum brevis comprehensio"* ["a brief compendium of individual facts"]. Honorius of Autun († ca. 1137) calls his world chronology *Summa totius.* Abelard describes his *Introductio* to theology as *"aliquam sacrae eruditionis summam quasi divinae scripturae introductionem"* and thus indicates precisely the purpose of such a "basic course": an introduction to the study of sacred Scripture, which is still the chief object of theology.[166] Nevertheless the introductory courses become more and more voluminous. Even Hugh of St. Victor calls his not exactly little work, *De sacramentis christianae fidei,* a *"brevem quandam summam omnium."*[167] Then in the late twelfth century *"summa"* becomes the term for a theological introductory and reference work in general, which often is arranged alphabetically as well, like the *Summa qu[a]e dicitur Abel* by Peter Cantor, but also for basic moral-ascetical manuals, like the summas *de vitiis et virtutibus* [on vices and virtues], for catechetical outlines, collections of sermons, homiletics handbooks, compilations of cases heard in the confessional, liturgical manuals, and last but not least in the form of *summulae logicales* for introductory books on logic. Around 1200 *summa* refers to the systematic summary of an academic subject, which has far surpassed the little introductory textbook and the technique of compiling sentences.[168] Thomas Aquinas, however, meant his *Summa* of theology to be understood again as a textbook for beginners.

Collecting and systematically arranging sentences, nevertheless, involves some fundamental methodological problems that are hardly noticeable when one simply reads or uses such collections, which are usually quite dry. If sentences by several authors are to be compiled under one keyword, the basic prerequisite is that they not be contradictory, even though they are worded so as to make different statements. *"Diversa, non adversa,"* was the slogan by which one tried to resolve this difficulty: Whereas the authors say different things, they do not contradict each other, but rather complement one another meaningfully and, taken as a whole, correspond to the truth.[169] This was already the classical principle used in the patristic era to arrive at a *"consensus evangelistarum"* ["agreement among the Gospel writers"] in places where they are obviously divergent.[170] What the *"consensus evangelistarum"*

165. For linguistic usage in antiquity, see Studer, *Schola Christiana,* 130.
166. PL 178, 979.
167. "a brief summary, so to speak, of all [the Sacraments]"; PL 176, 183.
168. Particular illustrations can be found in Grabmann, *Methode,* 2:23–24.
169. See Leinsle, *Vivianus,* 50–52.
170. See de Lubac, "Diversi."

was for the patristic era, is for the twelfth century the agreement of patristic authorities and contemporary teachings. In this regard early Scholasticism usually harks back to the same principle: The Church Fathers do say different but not conflicting things.[171] Above and beyond patristic passages, the principle is then applied to the apparently contradictory sentences of contemporaries or of a single author.[172] For, as Robert of Melun explains, in one author we find a conciseness that makes him difficult to understand, in another verbosity and furthermore a different arrangement of the material in each; yet through the principle of harmonization, *"diversa, non adversa,"* out of all this a scholar can produce *"unum sententiarum excellentissimum corpus"* ["one quite outstanding body of *sententiae*"].[173] The technique of *"exponere reverenter"* ["explaining reverently"] or *"pie interpretari"* [interpreting piously] is conducive to this effort. When authorities conflict, at least one must be interpreted in such a way as to make the contradiction appear avoidable.[174] Thus Hugh of St. Victor assumes on principle that the declarative [or indicative] form [of an argument] is just another means of investigating the thesis in question and should not be immediately understood as the author's thesis.[175]

One scholar who does not share this optimism about the possibility of harmonizing authorities is Abelard. After all, Augustine in his *Retractiones* took into account the fact that *"diversa et inter se adversa"* could be found in his own works.[176] Early scholars in canon law in particular had to assess the possibility of contradictory precepts. They developed the method of *"sic et non"* ["yes and no"] in order to produce a *"concordantia canonum"* ["concordance of canons"].[177] Abelard admits in the very first sentence of his *Sic et Non* that in the wealth of patristic sources there can be *"non solum ab invicem diversa, verum etiam invicem adversa"* ["not only different but also conflicting things"].[178] In that case one cannot simply impute falsity to the one side, but rather must carefully and methodically examine the origin and meaning of the sentences: Is the work in question authentic? Is it possible that the author retracted an opinion? Have linguistic usage and the meaning

171. See de Ghellinck, *Mouvement,* 481–82, 517–23.
172. E.g., in Bernard of Clairvaux, Cant. 81, 11 (ed. Leclercq III, 291).
173. Robert of Melun, Sent., praef. (ed. Martin III, 1, 46–47).
174. See Chenu, *Théologie,* 364–65.
175. Hugh of St. Victor, De sacramentis I, 1, 2 (PL 176, 187).
176. Augustinus, Retr., prol.2 (CSEL 36, 9).
177. See de Ghellinck, *Mouvement,* 472–81; Grabmann, *Methode,* 2:199–221.
178. Abaelard, *Sic et Non,* prol (PL 178, 1339); see Leinsle, *Vivianus,* 53–55.

of the words been maintained or have they changed? The historical-critical examination here is accompanied therefore by linguistic criticism. If the difficulty cannot be resolved even by all these means, then the weight of authority is the deciding factor. The logical consistency of the rational edifice must be preserved, however.

Due to the methodical character of the collections of sentences and early summas, the peculiar manner and doctrine of each work can be discerned only through a careful investigation of the working method and technique of compilation. The precise combination, selection and arrangement of the excerpted material, along with the linguistic treatment of previously formed sentences, allow the scholar to identify the personal achievement of the *"collector sententiarum."*[179] Verbal fidelity is often less important than the functional modification of the texts, because editorial reworking is a more decisive factor than verbatim repetition for the coherence and consistence of the theory being presented and indicates more clearly the compiler's own thinking and his acceptance, rejection or criticism of a sentence. The passages written by the compiler himself are part of this editorial activity also, since they go beyond the merely mosaic-like work of putting sentences together.[180]

Differences are clearly noticeable even in the doctrinal function of direct quotations. In the school of Laon the verbatim citation is replaced by an independent formulation of the substantial content, of the "Patristic idea."[181] The scriptural verses cited in the patristic passage often disappear along with it. Later collections of sentences then make use of the earlier ones as a matter of course and sometimes arbitrarily (Hugh of St. Victor). Divisions, examples but also revised patristic passages are taken from them and again reshaped. Many collections of sentences practically found and come to define a school, for example, the *Sententie Anselmi* for the school of Laon. In the *Sententiae Berolinenses* a patristic citation is turned into a question, which the author himself then answers along Augustinian lines with a *"dicimus."*[182] In contrast, Vivianus of Prémontré, for example, is still working much more simply around 1140. In his writings the most important means of harmonization is still omission, especially when he copies out one source

179. See esp. Weisweiler, "Sententiae Anselmi," Weisweiler, "Sententiae Berolinenses"; Weisweiler, "Arbeitsmethode."

180. See Leinsle, *Vivianus,* 55–90.

181. Weisweiler, "Sententiae Anselmi," 232.

182. See Weisweiler, "Sententiae Berolinenses," 356.

at length and summarizes. His own editorial activity here is minimal; it is evident occasionally in a change of *"ergo"* to *"igitur"* on in supplements to individual words. Not infrequently with his summarization technique, the long discussions of the source are cited only as theses or *sententiae,* whereas the biblical foundation and all the rhetorical trimmings are left out.[183] Naturally, the function of a citation is changed most often in passages where only the gist is quoted. Texts are regrouped in a new systematic framework and acquire new functions: What was an answer in the source becomes a question; what was a premise there becomes a thesis; cautious formulations are adopted apodictically; the logical structure of the source text is sometimes completely unraveled; occasionally texts from several sources are so interwoven that a hybrid text results. Sentences by contemporaries are usually introduced by a *"quidam"* ["a certain person"] who then has to be identified. Passages by the compiler himself connect the quotations, hold the text together through cross references (which may themselves be quoted again) and not insignificantly deal with the sources by thematically classifying, explaining, modifying, accepting, or rejecting the sentence under consideration.

Since collections of sentences in early Scholasticism are still understood to be at the service of scriptural interpretation but at the same time are regarded as systematic works, we should pay special attention to the function of citations from Scripture in this incipient "systematic theology." By way of example the following functions should be mentioned:

1. Foundation of thematic exegesis.
2. A stylistic device resulting from spiritual exegesis (especially in monastic circles and treatises).[184]
3. Biblical introduction of a theological term, for example, *"libertas a peccato"* by referring to 2 Cor 3:7 and Rom 6:20–22.
4. Biblical characterization of persons, things and times, for example, *"sancti homines"* supported by Rom 6:14 and Luke 10:42.
5. A type of argument *("auctoritas").*[185]

Already in the school of Anselm of Laon, *"authentica"* and *"magistralia,"* patristic authority and the master's sentence *("definitiones magistrales"* and

183. For examples, see Leinsle, *Vivianus,* 61–62.
184. See Leclercq, *Wissenschaft,* 83–102.
185. See Leinsle, *Vivianus,* 95–101.

"dicta magistralia") appear side by side with equal right. More and more often the teachings of the Church Fathers are dealt with only in the context of discussion with the *magistri.* Now it is not uncommon for the latter to be presented right at the beginning of the collection. Thus the collection *Liber Pancrisis* begins with the list of authors from whose works the sentences and questions were taken: Augustine, Jerome, Ambrose, Gregory the Great, Isidore, Bede, and then the *"moderni magistri,"* the contemporaries follow: William of Champeaux († 1122), Ivo of Chartres († 1116), Anselm, and Radulfus of Laon.[186] The *Deflorationes* of Werner of St. Blasien († 1174) still distinguish precisely the *"authentica doctrina Patrum"* ["authentic teaching of the Fathers"] (Gregory, Hilary of Poitiers, Augustine, Isidore, Jerome, Bede, Remigius) and the others *"qui modernis temporibus catholici atque orthodoxi magistri fuere"* ["who have been Catholic and Orthodox masters in modern times"] (e.g., Zacharias Chrysopolitanus, Hugh of St. Victor, Honorius of Autun). Werner fittingly describes his own work as *"syntagmatizare,"* arranging systematically, so that the result is *"un florilège sagement classé"* ["a wisely ordered florilegium"].[187] Sentences of the Fathers and the masters alike were then used above all in questions and disputations, which in the late twelfth and early thirteenth century were also written down in the form of summas. Eventually the collections of sentences themselves, especially those of Peter Lombard, soon became in turn the object of *abbreviationes* and glosses, in which the masters gave their opinions on the new subject matter.[188]

2.5 Theological systematization

What is accomplished in the collections of sentence and summas is not only the assimilation of *auctoritas* by means of *ratio,* but also the arrangement of the material that has been handed down into a theological framework. This outline itself is again dependent on patristic sources, especially on Augustine, and yet it is elaborated differently in the individual schools of the twelfth century. Theological systematization takes place through this process.[189] According to the classification of H. Cloes we can distinguish three basic types of systematic theology, which, however, do not often ap-

186. See Chenu, *Théologie,* 358.

187. PL 157, 726; see Glorieux, "Werner de Saint-Blaise."

188. See Landgraf, *Einführung,* 43–47.

189. See the groundbreaking study by Cloes, "Systématisation"; see also Grillmeier, "Symbolum."

pear in the purest form: a biblical type that examines salvation history, a logical type that studies concepts, and a systematic theology that is a mixture of both forms.[190]

We already find a systematic biblical theology dealing with salvation history in the school of Anselm of Laon. After a short presentation of the doctrine about God, he makes the transition to the creation of the world, of angels and of men. For the doctrine on redemption *("regeneratio et reparatio")*, salvation history offers a chronological scheme consisting of the time of the natural and the written (OT) law and the time of grace.[191] The sacraments are then more or less explicitly classified under the time of grace. Yet the *Sententiae Atrebatenses,* for example, place Christology before the scheme of the three eras in salvation history, which are thereby interpreted as a comprehensive salvific event in Christ.[192]

Hugh of St. Victor, too, structures his systematic masterpiece *De sacramentis* along the lines of salvation history, centered at any rate on man. Theology has to describe why man was created and as what, how he fell and was restored.[193] The entire treatise on God is subsumed under the first question, whereas the angelology, for example, causes some difficulties in this outline. The anthropocentric approach, however, is soon replaced by the basic schema of *"opus conditionis"* (book 1) and *"opus restaurationis"* (book 2: Christ and the sacraments until the end of the ages). Since the *"opus restaurationis"* is defined as *"Incarnatio Verbi cum omnibus sacramentis suis,"* the treatise on the sacraments can easily be incorporated here in the *"opus restaurationis."*[194] Yet the discussion of simony, vows, virtues, and vices also is squeezed into the teaching on sacraments.

Extremely influential for medieval systematic theology were the four books of *Sentences* by Peter Lombard. The *"Magister sententiarum,"* however, does not organize his work around salvation history alone, but rather initially cites in the prologue the Augustinian scheme of *"res—signum, uti—frui"* from *De doctrina christiana.* This seems at first to be a perfectly logical conceptual arrangement. In fact, however, this scheme "goes nowhere" and the Lombard's structure is essentially determined by Hugh of St. Victor.

190. Cloes, "Systématisation," 287.

191. *Sententie Anselmi, Anselm von Laons systematische Sentenzen,* ed. F. Bliemetzrieder, in *BGPhMA* 37/2–3 (Münster 1919): 78–79.

192. Ed. O. Lottin, *Les Sententie Artebatenses,* in *RThAM* 10 (1938): 218.

193. Hugh of St. Victor, de sacramentis l.1 p.1 c.30 (PL 176, 205–6).

194. Ibid., l.1 prol. c.2 (183 B).

Book 1 deals *"De mysterio Trinitatis,"* which is associated with the *"res quibus fruendum est"* ["things that are to be enjoyed"]; yet, as in the later books, the division in the prologue is no longer applied. In book 2, which deals with creatures *("nunc ad considerationem creaturarum accedamus"),* Hugh's anthropocentric schema is explicitly adopted.[195] Book 3 then treats the Incarnation but, as the prologue to this book makes clear, under the heading of *"reparatio": "sic enim ratio ordinis postulat"* ["for that is what the arrangement demands"].[196] As with Hugh, the sacraments that are presented in book 4 also belong to the *"reparatio."* Not until the prologue to book 4 is the Augustinian distinction of *"res—signa; uti—frui"* applied again, since the sacraments as *"signa"* are particularly conducive to this treatment. Thus the discussion of the *"res"* is followed immediately by that of the *"signa."*[197] Then, however, the eschatology in part 2 of book 4 does not fit into this arrangement; on the other hand, in the structure organized according to salvation history it easily found its place in the *"reparatio,"* although Peter Lombard does not demonstrate this in greater detail either.

In contrast, we find a really thoroughgoing logical-conceptual schema in Abelard and his school. The approach resembles that of Augustine's *Enchiridion* but it is not simply borrowed. Whereas in that work Augustine uses the three supernatural virtues *(fides—spes—caritas)* as constructive elements in the system, Abelard bases his structure on *"fides—caritas—sacramentum."*[198] The *Theologia Scholarium* regards the *"humanae salutis summa"* ["perfection of human salvation"] as consisting of these three matters.[199] Faith is directed on the one hand to the very nature of the Deity, and on the other hand to the *"divina beneficia"* and all the *"dispensationes"* and *"ordinationes"* of God, as they are expressed in the creeds of the apostles and Church Fathers.[200] The presentation of *"fides"* itself begins therefore with the doctrine on God and the Trinity. In contrast, a consideration of God's gracious acts certainly can follow the course of salvation history, as that is expressed in the creeds. The Incarnation, too, is one of the *"beneficia"* and

195. Petrus Lombardus, *Sententiae in IV libris distinctae,* 2 vols., numbered 4 and 5 in the series *Spicilegium Bonaventurianum* (Grottaferrata 1971/81), l.2 prol. (4:329.6), l.2 d.16 c.1 (4:406.3–5).

196. Ibid., l.3 prol. (5:1, 3–15).

197. Ibid., l.4 prol. (5:231, 3–5); on the Augustinian tradition see Fuchs, *Zeichen und Wissen,* 33–45, 75–77.

198. Abelard's early "theologies" *(Theologia "Summi boni"* and *Theologia christiana)* do not come into consideration here, since they only offer treatises on God and the Trinity.

199. Abaelard, *Theologia Scholarium* I, 1 (CCh CM 13, 318, 1–2).

200. Ibid., I, 17 (326, 206–10).

"ordinationes" of God. In his *Sic et Non* Abelard modifies this schema so that the sequence runs *"fides—sacramentum—caritas"*; consequently the treatise on the sacraments immediately follows the one on faith, and moral theology is not dealt with until part 3 under the heading of *"caritas."* This now becomes the decisive structure for most collections of sentences by the school of Abelard. The *Epitome Hermanni* and the *Sententiae Florianenses* still follow the first schema, while the *Sententiae Parisienses,* Magister Roland († 1181) and Omnebene († 1185) follow the second. The *Epitome* clearly places the transition from the Incarnation to the Sacraments under the heading of the *"beneficia"*: the Incarnation is the *"summum beneficium"* ["supreme benefit"], as is generally taught; but the sacraments too are God's *"beneficia"* and accordingly should really be part of book 1 on the faith, or at least be closely connected with it.[201] Thus *"caritas"* as "moral theology" seems even more distinctly separated from "dogmatic theology."

The structure typical for Abelard can be presented schematically as follows, according to his *Sic et Non:*

1. *Fides*
    - 1.1 Treatise on God
        - 1.1.1 The Trinity
        - 1.1.2 The Attributes of God
    - 1.2 *Beneficia Dei*
        - 1.2.1 Treatise on Creation
            - 1.2.1.1 The Angels
            - 1.2.1.2 Man
        - 1.2.2 The Incarnation
        - 1.2.3 Mary and the Apostles (the Church)
2. *Sacramentum*
    - 2.1 Baptism
    - 2.2 Eucharist
    - 2.3 Matrimony
3. *Caritas*
    - 3.1 Love
    - 3.2 Good Works
    - 3.3 Sin

201. See *Epitome theologiae christianae* c. 38 (PL 178, 1738 C); contrast *Sententiae Florianenses,* ed. Ostlender, 14.

Whereas there had already been logical problems of classification in the schemata organized along the lines of salvation history, and historical arrangements of material within the conceptual schemata, in the mid-twelfth century several influential mixed forms developed. One such schema is presented by the *Summa Sententiarum,* which was compiled around 1135–40 under the influence of Hugh of St. Victor.[202] The first part, as with Abelard, is devoted to a presentation of the faith; indeed, it even uses Abelard's "summa formula": *"Tria sunt in quibus humanae salutis summa consistit,"* ["There are three things in which the perfection of human salvation consists,"] but now according to the schema *"mysterium divinitatis—sacramentum incarnationis,"* in which we can see again Hugh's influence. The editor of the *Summa Sententiarum* deals with Abelard much as Peter Lombard had dealt with the Augustinian schema. He steers the plan toward salvation history: After the treatise on God he regards the part on *"fides"* as being already concluded and then turns to creation, man, the fall, and the restoration (redemption), down to the *"remedia sacramentorum"* after the model of Hugh of St. Victor.[203] The sacraments themselves are treated according to the schema of the three eras or "Laws" in salvation history.

A different sort of mixed form is found in the *Sententiae divinitatis* from the Porretan school.[204] These sentences begin immediately with the doctrine of creation and then proceed to the creation of man, *"praetermisso angelorum tractatu"* ["omitting the treatise on the angels"]. Man is considered (1) in his creation according to the image and likeness of God, (2) in the state of freedom from sin, (3) in his fall, and (4) in his restoration. Here again there is tangible evidence of the influence of Laon and St. Victor.[205] In part 4 the Incarnation and the treatise on the sacraments (means of the *"reparatio"*) are presented. Only then does the *Tractatus de divinitate et Trinitate* follow. The transition indicates the overall connection: "*Diximus, qualiter ipse homo factus est, vidimus etiam quomodo per peccatum cecidit a* cognitione divinitatis, *et qualiter reparatus. Modo videamus* de ipsa divinitate et Trinitate." ["We have said how man himself was made, and we also saw how he fell through sin from *the knowledge of Divinity,* and how he was restored.

202. PL 176, 41–154; as to the dating, see Leinsle, *Vivianus,* 37–39; see also A. Grillmeier, "Fulgentius von Ruspe."

203. *Summa Sententiarum* tr. 2 c.1 (PL 176, 79 C); tr.3 c.2 (91 A); tr.4 c.1 (117 A).

204. Ed. B. Geyer, *Die "Sententiae divinitatis": Ein Sentenzenbuch der Gilbertischen Schule* (*BGPhMA* 7, 2–3) (Münster, 1909).

205. Sent. div., tr.1 (ed. Geyer 8*); tr.2 (ibid., 18).

Now let us see *about Divinity itself and the Trinity*."][206] This would be, then, a schema that ascends by way of salvation history (creation, fall, redemption) to the knowledge of God *(cognitio divinitatis)* as the goal of man and of theology. Right knowledge of God, however, is possibly only after the restoration of fallen man. Hence the position of the treatise on God and the Trinity at the conclusion of the *Sententiae divinitatis.*

The compiler of the *Ysagoge in theologiam,* from the broader school of Abelard, bases his work on a different schema of ascent.[207] He divides his collection into treatises on *"natura humana," "natura angelica"* and *"natura divina."* Human nature is presented in books 1 and 2 in terms of creation, body, and soul (including the faculties and virtues). The treatise on virtues is followed by the treatise on merit, grace and freedom, Paradise, and the prelapsarian state. The doctrine of the fall is likewise developed strictly in conceptual terms in the questions, *"quid sit malum, quid peccatum, quid vicium."* ["What is evil? What is sin? What is vice?"] The treatise on redemption adheres to the schema *"bona—mala—remedia malorum"* ["goods—evils—remedies of evils"], whereby the means of salvation are subdivided again according to the eras in salvation history.[208] The means of salvation in the era of grace consist partly of the Incarnation and sufferings of Christ, partly of the acraments. The author then attempts to develop his angelology (book 3) exactly in parallel to the first two books. Therefore with regard to the angels as well he follows the schema of creation, fall, and restoration (in this case: *confirmatio bonorum,* confirmation of the good angels [in their allegiance]). The discussions, however, are substantially shorter.[209] The treatise on God has a strongly epistemological accent: the ways of knowing God are presented, then the three divine attributes (power, wisdom, will), and finally the testimonies of the prophets and philosophers are considered.

The *Sentences* of Magister Roland (Bandinelli), composed around 1150, owe more to Abelard.[210] He adopts the schema *"fides—sacramentum—caritas,"* only to house within it much material from salvation history. The sub-

206. Sent. div. tr.4 (ibid., 155*); Cloes merely traces the schema of the Sent. div. back to a simple thematic arrangement.

207. *Écrits théologiques de l'école d'Abélard: Textes inédits,* ed. A. Langraf (SSL 14) (Louvain, 1934), 63–285.

208. Ibid., 130.

209. Ibid., 220: *"Brevem igitur de homine disputacionem brevior de arcana spirituum natura et summo Deo sequatur distinctio."* ["Let this brief argumentation about man, therefore, be followed by a briefer distinction between the secret nature of the spirits and the Supreme God."]

210. *Die Sentenzen Rolands nachmals Papstes Alexander III.,* ed. A. Gietl (Freiburg, 1891).

division of the treatise on *fides* into the doctrine about God and his *"beneficia,"* however, is replaced by the division into the doctrine on Divinity and an exposition of His works. The latter, however, include the angels, the creation of the world and of man, his fall, and the restoration, which is accomplished during the three eras of salvation history. Thus Roland clearly shows that he, like the *Summa Sententiarum,* is dependent on Hugh of St. Victor. In Roland's presentation, however, the third era of salvation history *(tempus gratiae)* overlaps with Abelard's second topic: *"sacramentum."* Thus he now wishes to treat that part of the faith (topic 1, *fides*) that pertains to the liberation and redemption of man, *"cuius quidem in sacramentis consistit redemptio"* ["whose redemption, indeed, is established in the sacraments"].[211] The difficulties of striking an equilibrium between the salvation-history schema and a conceptual organization are clear here, as they often are in the treatment of the sacraments, which on the one hand are means of redemption and on the other hand objects of faith.

2.6 Treatise and letter

Besides the literary forms that emerged directly from the academic enterprise (scriptural commentaries, collections of sentences, and summas), we find two freer genres, which nevertheless are important for the development of theology precisely in early Scholasticism: the free treatise (sometimes in dialogue form) and the letter. Both had originated in antiquity, not uncommonly from written or oral inquiries.[212] However, unlike Scholastic writings, which usually can be identified with a teaching position, the authenticity of such writings is more difficult to prove. It often happens that works by "lesser" masters are attributed to more important ones so as to ascribe greater influence to them.[213] Especially in circles of monks and canons regular, the monograph treatise (often conducted in dialogue form) was a favorite, for example, many works by Bernard of Clairvaux (ca. 1090–1153) or Aelred of Rievaulx (1110–1167).[214] The most important testimonials to this genre are perhaps the writings of Anselm of Canterbury (1033–1109), among them dialogues such as *De grammatico, de veritate, de libero arbitrio,* monographs such as the *Monologion* and *Proslogion, Cur Deus homo,* etc. We have a *Dialogus inter philosophum, judaeum et christianum* by Abelard. In these works one usually finds few immediate signs of academic activity. In-

211. Ibid., 154–55.
212. See Studer, *Schola Christiana.*
213. See Leinsle, "Hugo von St. Viktor."
214. See Leclercq, *Wissenschaft,* 171–212.

stead they often sparkle with a polished style, which in the dry atmosphere of collections of sentences, commentaries and summas can usually find a place only in the prologue.

Treatises often come about in response to inquiries or at the insistence of confreres, friends, or high-ranking personages. In such cases the treatise may become a letter as a result of the dedicatory epistle prefacing it, as of yore in many of Augustine's writings, which reply to very specific inquiries.[215] Precedents for the lofty epistolary style, which in the "epistolary treatises" is often sustained only in the dedication, could be found in Cicero and Seneca, but also in Augustine and Jerome. The models and rules of a good epistolary style are summarized in the *ars dictaminis*.[216] We find that the *ars dictaminis* and anthologies of letters flourish anew precisely at the beginning of the twelfth century.[217] Rhetorical figures of speech therefore define the style and the genre of theological letters also, which should be noted when interpreting them: "Someone who takes a medieval text seriously does not have to take all its formulations literally."[218]

Both letter and treatise not infrequently refer to contemporary controversies, of a Scholastic sort as well, and therefore contribute significantly to the clarification of theological questions and to the development and dissemination of theological doctrine.[219] They sometimes belong also to the genre of polemical literature, in which the author makes a personal effort to persuade his correspondent, who has taken up the opposite position; thus Adelmann of Lüttich († ca. 1061) exhorts Berengar of Tours to renounce his teaching on the Eucharist, which he regards as heretical.[220] Especially in monastic circles, such letters are *open* letters; the author counts on the fact that they will be read widely. Therefore, precisely because of their public character, letters often assume the form of a thematic treatment, for example, the *Epistola de buccella Judae data et de veritate Dominici corporis*, in which Guibert of Nogent (1053–1124) disputes Berengar's teaching and debates the question, whether Judas received the Eucharist at the Last Supper.[221] Such particular questions are characteristic of the theological episto-

215. E.g., Augustinus, quaest. ad Simpl. (CCh SL 44, 1).

216. See Leclercq, "Genre épistolaire," 63–70.

217. See the groundbreaking study, Ott, *Briefliteratur.*

218. Leclercq, *Wissenschaft,* 204.

219. See Leinsle, *Vivianus,* 42–44; the occasion here was the debate between Bernard of Clairvaux and Abelard around the time of the Synod of Sens (1140).

220. PL 143, 1289–96.

221. PL 156, 527–38.

lary literature of the twelfth century. A glance in Ludwig Ott's groundbreaking work shows, for example, the following problems treated in the writings of Walter of Mortaigne († 1174): the efficacy and effect of baptism by heretics, the manner of the divine omnipresence, Christ's sadness and agony, the legal effects of betrothal, the effects of vows in marital law, particular points in the doctrine about grace, the degrees of *caritas,* and knowledge in Christ's soul. Hugh of St. Victor expresses in a similar way his thinking about the will of Christ, Mary's virginity, but also about exegetical questions and the interpretation of particular passages, for example, the visit of Peter and John to the tomb (John 20:3–10). In letters, too, as in academic activity, individual theological formulas are examined with regard to their justification, for example, the Christological formula *"assumptus homo est Deus"* ["the man assumed (in the Incarnation) is God"] by Walter of Mortaigne or the statement *"Pater Spiritu Sancto diligit Filium"* ["The Father loves the Son by the Holy Spirit"] by Richard of St. Victor.

The method used in such theological epistolary treatises can certainly be characterized as Scholastic, embedded in the effort to edify the correspondent or to instruct him theologically. Moreover the excerpts and *florilegia* that had been collected from patristic writings and later authors offered a wealth of material for this purpose. Writers liked to compile points and convey them to the addressee in the form of handy treatises.[222] Even with lesser minds we find a simple procedure of compilation whereby they simply write out a "great source" in abbreviated form and conflate it with another consistent one. Thus Vivianus of Prémontré (ca. 1140) uses a relatively simply technique, which he terms a *"harmonia,"* to compile for the Dean and Master Gerhard of St. Quentin (attested to 1108–1138) his *Tractatus de libero arbitrio,* composed of lines from Bernard of Clairvaux and the *Summa Sententiarum.*[223] This and similar treatises usually have a specific occasion and purpose, which is a criterion for testing them historically and with regard to their authenticity. In this instance, for example, Gerard of St. Quentin had once proved, along with Vivianus, to be a follower of Bernard and an opponent of Abelard; this treatise was written in order to develop their position more emphatically and to distinguish it. Naturally here, as elsewhere, it is asserted that this is not supposed to make the correspondent any wiser (see Proverbs 1:5), since he is already well enough versed in these matters.

222. Concerning Richard of St. Victor's *"excerptiones"* see, for example, Ott, *Briefliteratur,* 651–57.
223. See Leinsle, *Vivianus,* 55–103.

Such formulaic modesty is a stylistic device and should be evaluated accordingly. Soon we find entire collections of letters by individual or various authors in which the attribution is often dubious and therefore should be tested in each case. Last but not least, such collections of letters can serve in turn, stylistically and thematically, as an influential source of further epistolary literature.

2.7 The Scholastic sermon

Petrus Cantor lists *lectio, disputatio,* and *praedicatio* [preaching] as the components of the study of sacred Scripture. *Lectio* lays the foundation, *disputatio* erects the walls, and *praedicatio* finishes the roof of the spiritual building.[224] The Scholastic sermon, one of the tasks of the *magistri,* is therefore formally and substantially an important element in the development and dissemination of Scholastic theology. Especially in the case of university sermons, this is not the least important method of grappling with current problems.[225]

Like theology in general, the homiletic teaching of the Middle Ages, set forth in the *Artes Praedicandi,*[226] was profoundly influenced by Augustine. In *De doctrina christiana,* after explaining the Christian course of education and the methods of scriptural interpretation, he gives an outline of Christian rhetoric, which adopts much from the rhetoric of Cicero and antiquity. The pastoral orientation of the sermon is more strongly accentuated in the much-utilized *Regula pastoralis* by Gregory the Great.[227] Early Scholastic homiletic teachings and examples (mostly from monastic circles) contribute other elements that are somewhat typically Scholastic.[228] The possibilities for interpretation according to the fourfold sense of Scripture are of course developed; thus Guibert of Nogent sees in the four senses the four wheels on which *sacra pagina* as a whole moves.[229] Alan of Lille already sees the sermon as a field on which *ratio* and *auctoritas* contend. For him the sermon signifies the highest (seventh) degree of perfection; it presupposes *confessio, oratio, gratiarum actio, perscrutatio scripturarum, inquisitio a maiore,* and *expositio scripturae* [profession of faith, prayer, thanksgiving, careful in-

224. Petrus Cantor, Verbum abbreviatum c.1 (PL 205, 25); see Smalley, *Study,* 208.

225. See Davy, *Sermons univeritaires;* Bataillon, "Crises"; Zier, "Sermons"; Bériou, "Sermons latins."

226. A basic reference is Charland, *Artes Praedicandi.*

227. See Roth, *Predigttheorie.*

228. See Leclercq, *Wissenschaft,* 189–201.

229. Guibert von Nogent, Quo ordine sermo fieri debeat (PL 156, 26 C).

vestigation of Scripture, consulting a more learned scholar, and the exposition of Scripture].[230] It should have the following structure: (1) *Auctoritas* (scriptural text), (2) *Captatio benevolentiae* [plea for the listeners' benevolence], (3) Interpretation of the text while citing further Scripture passages and authorities in support of one's arguments and thus "producing considerable excitement in the public and then calming it," (4) Exemplification.[231]

Whereas this schema is still essentially bound up with the rhetoric of antiquity, as it was handed down within the framework of the *artes,* the structure of the learned sermon changes significantly in the thirteenth century. Then, too, there was a new audience for the Latin sermon, which was zealously cultivated in the university cities especially by the mendicant orders that had just taken up residence there. The *Artes Praedicandi* list detailed rules for the learned *sermo.*[232] The university *sermo,* unlike the freer popular sermon, has the following structure:

1. The *thema* of the sermon is announced. This is a sentence *(dictum aliquod authenticum)* from sacred Scripture (e.g., taken from the readings for the day) that serves as the thematic foundation for the sermon.[233] Besides this there is also the custom, especially in the popular sermon, of explaining the whole Gospel (without stating a theme) in the form of a homily or a *postilla.*[234]
2. Next comes the *prothema,* another Scripture passage, the subject of an introductory discourse, which may be long or short and which is supposed to prepare the listeners to hear aright; the *prothema* is concluded with a *prayer.* Since the *prothema* leads the listener to the sermon, it should be regarded as something of a preached "popular homily," as J. B. Schneyer has concluded from his exemplary study of such *prothemata.*[235]
3. Once the listener is well disposed, the *introitus* follows, the introduction of the theme, which is mentioned again (also for the sake of latecomers). The *inventio* of the theme usually applies sacred Scripture and the Church Fathers, but on the other hand the Aristotelian rules of *"ars inveniendi,"* of thematic arrangements, quotations from philosophers or

230. Alanus ab Insulis, Summa de Arte Praedicatoria (PL 210, 111 B).

231. Roth, *Predigttheorie,* 40.

232. Ibid., 32–86; Charland, *Artes Praedicandi,* 109–226, including a detailed description of the structure of a sermon.

233. E.g., Thomas Waleys, *De modo componendi sermones,* c.2, in ed. Charland, *Artes Praedicandi,* 341.

234. See Charland, *Artes Praedicandi,* 112–13.

235. Schneyer, *Unterweisung.*

common proverbs, which are now supposed to lead the listener to the theme itself. But the theme can be introduced through a logical argument also, whereby the truth thereof and the necessity of discussing it can be demonstrated expressly.

4. The theme must then be subdivided in the *divisio.* Usually the words of the theme that are relevant to the further division of the sermon are emphasized. Here we should distinguish between the division of the text *(divisio)* that is usually done in the *lectio* also, and the *distinctio,* the subdivision of a theme according to its various aspects (e.g., love: love of God and love of neighbor). A multiplicity of meanings in one or more of the senses of Scripture can also be decisive for the division. The preacher has a wealth of material available, some of it already arranged alphabetically, in the *Distinctiones* and *Allegoriae.*[236] The art of structuring a Scholastic *sermo* is evident precisely in the correct division of the theme.
5. The division of the theme results in the division of the sermon in the *partium declaratio,* called *clavis* for short. This offers the key to understanding the *sermo* and proves the sufficiency of the division with regard to the various points. Naturally, for this proof one again uses concurring authorities, which may provide points for further *subdivisiones.* Usually a repeated threefold pattern develops, which is elaborated in *divisiones* and *subdivisiones* and gives the sermon the appearance of a tree that branches out extensively.[237]
6. Now, at last, the preacher can start the exposition of his theme, the *dilatatio.* Not all the parts of the division are always elaborated with the same thoroughness. In typical university sermons we find here, too, *auctoritas, ratio,* and *exempla* combined in each section. The use of authorities follows fixed rules of *allegatio* or citation [*Verbindung*]. They serve, for example, to elucidate an analogy, to mediate a difference, to define, interpret, describe, specify, modify, corroborate, subdivide, or supplement.[238] The *ratio* is required when explaining terms, but also when independently compiling and evaluating authorities, when including an etymology or the various hermeneutical possibilities in the fourfold interpretation of Scripture, when proving the truth of the articles of faith symbolically contained in the Scripture passage and stating the conditions and qualities of such an interpretation. Finally, the *exemplum* is chiefly supposed

236. See Rouse/Rouse, "Statim invenire."
237. E.g., Charland, *Artes Praedicandi,* illustration on title page.
238. Ibid., 196–98.

to underscore the affective and practical aim of the sermon.[239] Then there are several other stylistic devices for the embellishment *(ornatus)* of the discourse, which are systematized in detail. Thus Robert of Basevorn (ca. 1322) lists twenty-two stylistic devices for the university sermon in Oxford alone, among them the correct transition *(digressio, transitus)* to the next section of the *divisio,* artistic parallels, and balance among the sections, etc.[240]

7. After the long, skillful exposition, the preacher summarizes the main idea in a sentence or phrase in the *unitio,* which can also be a citation from an authoritative text.
8. The *clausio* or conclusion of the sermon is a short prayer, either a petition or a doxology, addressed to God.

Thematically the *sermones* are important in two respects: (1) they offer plenty of material for those who study the history of the times, and (2) they provide a usually critical insight into the state of affairs at the university and in society. The Parisian university sermons for the crucial year 1230–1231, edited by M. M. Davy, shed light on university and theological activity as well as on conditions in the Church and society. The accumulation of benefices, nepotism, simony, heresies and councils, the lifestyles and duties of prelates, clerics and professed religious, the lives of the social classes, and their relations with one another are oft-recurring subjects of the sermon.[241] On the other hand, however, there are developments within theology that are not the object of a disputation in the lecture hall but rather are addressed in the pulpit, especially the entrance of pagan Greek philosophy in the form of Aristotle into theology, which is a major concern in university sermons as late as Bonaventure's *Collationes in Hexaemeron* (1273).[242] It is pointed out repeatedly that the roles of *"domina"* ("mistress," theology) and *"pedissequa"* ("attendant, handmaid," philosophy) must not be interchanged, that the gold of theology cannot be replaced by the brass of Aristotle. The mingling of the two disciplines is an oft-recurring theme. Thanks to the rhetorical devices, the conservative cast of the theologians usually comes across more strongly in these moralizing sermons than in the business of the *lectio* and *disputatio* itself.[243] Possibly many a *magister* spoke his mind more clearly

239. See Bataillon, "Similitudines"; Bataillon, "Images."
240. Ibid., 212–18.
241. See Davy, *Sermons universitaires,* 82–119.
242. See Van Steenberghen, *Philosophie,* 212–31.
243. Examples in Davy, *Sermons universitaires,* 84–88.

from the unassailable position of the pulpit than he would have done in a *disputatio,* in which one has to expect objections at any moment.

The significance of the *sermones* was clearly recognized even in their day, as medieval collections of *sermones* demonstrate.[244] From early Scholasticism, moreover, we have collections by authors whose other works have largely been consigned to obscurity. Not infrequently the preacher's allegiance to a school becomes clearly evident, for instance the Porretanism of Radulphus Ardens († 1200) and Abelard's teaching on grace in others, whereas Martin of Léon († 1221) cites continuous passages from the *Sentences* of Peter Lombard.[245] Sermons, too, are at first collected individually (often as *reportationes*) and copied, and sometimes further edited, and thus crop up in the collections at the most unexpected places.[246]

The polished preaching technique of the university sermons, however, elicited criticism, not least in circles of monks and canons regular. The early Franciscans, too, distanced themselves from it at first and cultivated the popular sermon *"sine distinctionum clavibus"* [without the academic hair-splitting].[247] We find a distinct reaction to it also in the Life (written between 1260 and 1275) of the Premonstratensian Abbot Siard of Mariengaarde in Friesland, who ruled from 1164 to 1175.[248] It does indeed seem odd to apply Scholastic methods of preaching to a popular sermon for the proverbially doltish farmers of Friesland. The Scholastic extravagance could very well defeat the purpose of the sermon, that is, the proclamation of the faith. "Thus the entrance of Scholastic methods of instruction and disputation into the sermon, that is, definition and division, arguing, exemplifying and challenging, could appeal at best to the masters and students."[249] The biographer contrasts Siard's manner of preaching and that of the *"moderni."* The heavenly gift of preaching has been replaced by a long, inflated *sermo* consisting of many well-distinguished sections, which is of no use but only makes a splendid appearance.[250] The biographer consistently objects also to ownership of the *"libri et sermones modernorum"* ["books and sermons

244. Schneyer, *Repertorium,* 11 vols., is an indispensable inventory.

245. See Landgraf, *Einführung,* 47–48. Concerning the infiltration of philosophical terminology into the learned sermon, see L.-J. Bataillon, "L'emploi."

246. See Bataillon, "Sermons rédigés, sermons réportés (XIIIe siècle)," in *Prédication,* Art. III, 69–86.

247. See Bataillon, "Predicazione," 691–94.

248. See Leinsle, "Aristoteles."

249. Schneyer, *Geschichte,* 180.

250. *Vita Siardi* c.17, ed. H. Lambooij / J. A. Mol in *Vitae Abbatum Orti Sancte Marie. Vijf abtenlevens van het klooster Mariëngaarde in Friesland* (Hilversum / Leuuwarden, 2001), 306–8.

of the moderns"] for preaching in the parishes: his contemporaries just wanted to assemble a long *sermo* by heaping up biblical "authorities," citing chapter and verse, so as to prove themselves as *magistri.*[251] Once again the logic *("doctrina sophistica")* of Aristotle is to blame, which leads only to turmoil and disputes but not to peace of soul.[252] The *sermones* of the Scholastics are of no use to the listeners, since the latter pay attention exclusively to the *"modus procedendi,"* to the particular *divisiones,* and *distinctiones* but not to their own sins and negligence. People then recommend the *sermo* to others on account of its structure, its *"distinctio membrorum,"* but not for its content, which should serve to edify the listener.[253]

251. *Vita Siardi* c.12 (294–96), c.3 (258).

252. Ibid., c.17 (308, 16–18). See Absalon von Springiersbach, Sermo IV (PL 211, 27): *"Non regnat spiritus Christi, ubi dominatur spiritus Aristotelis."* ["The spirit of Christ does not reign where the spirit of Aristotle rules."]

253. *Vita Siardi* c.17 (308, 8–10).

2 The Self-Concept of Early Scholastic Theologies

At the same time as the development and general acceptance of Scholastic scientific methods in theology, the schools of the eleventh and twelfth centuries witnessed the elaboration of the themes of theology and the theoretical justification of it as a scientific discipline. Since a comprehensive history of theology or of the dogma cannot be offered within the parameters of this introduction,[1] we should at least point out the self-concept of the theological approaches, which were quite diverse.[2] This will make it clear that so-called early Scholastic theology is found only in a multiplicity of schools and theologies. Moreover the fact that their understanding of theology, relying on criteria for science and rationality, was quite often expressed in conflicts is not a superficial feature resulting from the schoolmasters' love of disputation, but rather is an essential part of theology as a Scholastic inquiry.

1 Freedom from contradiction and theological truth: Duns Scotus Eriugena

One focal point for the articulation of the early medieval understanding of theology was the controversy over the doctrine of predestination started by Gottschalk [Godescalc], a monk from Fulda and later from Orbais († 869), in which all the leading theologians of the day became involved. Gottschalk's teaching about *"gemina praedestinatio"* ["twin predestination"] stated, briefly, that from all eternity, in a single act of justice and mercy, God divided mankind into the damned and the elect, so that the destiny of the

1. For the history of dogma and theology, see esp. *HDG* and *HDThG;* for a detailed study see Landgraf, *Dogmengeschichte der Frühscholastik;* for the theology of the human act and ethics, see Lottin, *Psychologie;* for an overview see also Evans, ed., *Medieval Theologians* and Leppin, *Theologie.*

2. Concerning the problem of an historical "self-concept," see, for example, Borgolte, "Selbstverständnis."

individual human being is determined before birth. Hence redemption in Christ did not take place for all men. Baptism and membership in the Church are prerequisites for election, but not all the baptized are chosen. Moreover man's will is not free but wicked; grace alone working in the elect ensures that they do not give in or agree to evil and concupiscence. The good that man does, however, is not his work, but the work of God's grace.[3] Gottschalk's teaching, inspired by Augustine's doctrine of predestination and based on God's immutability, is logically consistent and well thought out. Yet it has dangerous consequences: man cannot change his eternal destiny by his own action. In the opinion of some contemporaries, this aided and abetted fatalism or immorality.

Gottschalk's scientific method still followed what his Abbot Hrabanus Maurus had taught in the Carolingian schools. This essentially consisted of a *catena* technique of noncontradictory sentences from the Church Fathers, underpinning a definite doctrine.[4] With the proof from authority and consistent definition, however, the apparatus of theology had already been exhausted. Therefore the standard of rationality was essentially considered to be the *dialectica* of the *artes liberales* and the proper use of the proof from authority. In Gottschalk's judgment, his teaching on predestination satisfied this criterion, whereas the Church's did not.

The official Church reaction to Gottschalk's teaching in the condemnations by the Synods of Mainz (848) and Quierzy (849) is less important to us here than the theological grappling with "the Gottschalk case."[5] In the judgments requested by Bishop Hinkmar of Rheims († 882) and King Charles the Bald (823–877), Prudentius of Troyes († 861), Lupus of Ferrières († 862), and Ratramnus of Corbie († after 868) unanimously indicate that Gottschalk's teaching on predestination agrees with that of Augustine and consequently should be a good Catholic position. In doing so the judges follow precisely the conventional scientific method that Gottschalk himself employs: logical consistency and the proof from authority ensure the truth of a theological teaching. In this case, therefore, methodically proven truth is opposed to an official ecclesiastical condemnation of the same teaching that is based mainly on practical religious considerations.

A further judgment that Hinkmar of Rheims ordered Duns Scotus Eri-

3. *Œuvres théologiques et grammaticales de Godescalc d'Orbais,* ed. D. C. Lambot (Louvain, 1945); see also Schrimpf, *Scottus Eriugena,* 74–79; Otten, "Carolingian Theology," 76–80.

4. See Jolivet, *Godescalc d'Orbais,* 161–84.

5. Schrimpf, *Johannes Scottus,* 77–78.

ugena († ca. 880) to make was supposed to set new standards for theology.[6] Scotus first offers a short doctrine on theological method, which is of fundamental importance. To him the proof from authority alone no longer seems sufficient, especially since a development can be traced in Augustine's works in his treatment of the question of predestination. That is why the formal foundation for a theological finding of truth is logic, as the *"ars disputatoria,"* the rules of which must be followed here. Logic, however, is synonymous with truth. *"Ratiocinatio"* is the term that sums up this effort, in direct contrast to mere rhetoric.[7] Theology as a scientific study is thus clearly distinguished, in its methods and purpose, from the rhetoric of ecclesiastical preaching. The right key to theology, albeit only a wooden one according to Augustine, is logic.[8] Scotus finds the method of theology, like that of every *"piae perfectaeque doctrinae"* ["conscientious and complete teaching"], in *philosophia,* which in Scotus' writings can generally be translated as "science."[9] Consistently, immediate reference is made therefore to "profane" methods, namely general scientific or philosophical methods, whereby "philosophy" denotes above all the whole field of the *artes.* Along with Augustine, however, "true religion" is then equated with true science/philosophy as a striving for truth:

> For if, according to St. Augustine, "it is believed and taught . . . that science, i.e., scientific striving for wisdom is nothing other than religion, inasmuch as those whose teachings we do not approve do not participate in the Sacraments together with us either," then what else does it mean to pursue science but *to elucidate the rules of the true religion,* through which the highest and noblest cause of all, God, is humbly honored and tracked down in a reasonable way? Therefore it follows that true science is true religion and conversely true religion is true science.[10]

These ideas, which essentially rely on the early Augustine, clearly set a task for theology: it must explain scientifically the rules of true religion. Therefore there can be no contradiction between true religion and true philosophy/science. Religion, too, is defined as a bit of reasonable praxis: in it knowledge about God is pursued in a reasonable manner; but only in theology are the rules of this praxis examined with respect to their truth. *"Regula"*

6. Johannes Scotus Eriugena, *De praedestinatione* (CCh CM 50).
7. Ibid., 1.2–3 (6.31–8.75); see also Scottus Eriugena, *Praef.* (3.30–4.36).
8. Ibid., *Praef.* (4.50–52).
9. Ibid., 1.1 (5.4–18); see also Schrimpf, *Scottus Eriugena,* 89.
10. Scottus Eriugena, *Praed.* 1.1 (5.9–18); see also Augustine, *De vera rel.* 5.8 (CCh SL 32, 187). German translation in Schrimpf, *Scottus Eriugena,* 89 (Herv. UGL).

in this context designates first of all the laws of logic and the other liberal arts, the "rules of right reason," and then in keeping with them the rules of true religion also.[11] These rules are not just theoretical truths, but also laws with practical significance. The elucidation of the rules takes place according to the scientific method in four steps; for every science is made up of four main parts or methods: division, definition, proof, and recapitulation [*Rückführung* = reduction to a simple formula]. A given whole is logically divided up into its parts and the units are defined. Then what is still implicitly contained in these statements is made clear by means of syllogistic proof, and finally everything is restated in terms of a single scientific foundation.[12] There should be recourse to these four procedures in solving each and every *quaestio,* and not just to the proof from authority. Logical correctness, that is, demonstrability, is to a great extent identified with truth in the works of Duns Scotus; moreover in his view ontic realities can also be expressed adequately in logically correct propositions.[13]

In the theological application of this method an erroneous teaching can be refuted "with true arguments" and with the authority of the Church Fathers, or else "refuted first with divine authority and then demolished according to the rules of reason which possesses the truth."[14] The first methodical step is therefore scriptural proof, then the second consists of applying the abovementioned scientific methods. In [official] judgments about predestination, therefore, it is first established that Gottschalk's teaching is contradictory; then the Church's teaching is demonstrated to be in itself free from contradiction and compatible with the teaching about man's free will. Only then can the proof from authority begin, so that the following sequence results: Scripture—*ratio*—*auctoritas.* The meaning of authoritative passages, however, is to be expounded according to all the rules of grammar and semantics; for the authority is nothing other than the truth discovered by reason, and an authority can never claim more than that. If a Church Father settles a question, this is only for the benefit of posterity.[15]

Scotus' concept of theology as a scientific, rational explanation of the

11. See Scottus Eriugena, *Praed.* 1.1–4 (5–9).

12. The four methods are adopted in Scottus Eriugena, *Periphyseon* V, 360–70 (CCh CM 145, 14).

13. See Schrimpf, *Scottus Eriugena,* 94.

14. Scottus Eriugena, *Praed.* 1.2 (7.42–44); 1.4 (9.105–7).

15. Scottus Eriugena, *Periph.* I, 3056–59 (CCh CM 161, 98): *"Nil enim aliud videtur mihi esse vera auctoritas nisi verae rationis virtute reperta veritas et a sanctis patribus ob posteritatis utilitatem litteris commendata."* ["True authority seems to me to be nothing other than the truth discovered by virtue of true reason and set down in writing by the holy Fathers for the benefit of posterity."]

rules of Christian religion was not in keeping with the times or the Carolingian educational system, as was demonstrated by the negative reactions of his student Prudentius, of the Bishop of Troyes († 861) and of Florus of Lyons († ca. 860). In Prudentius' view, the use of logic is one of the *"prophanae novitates"* ["profane novelties"] that had already been rejected in 1 Timothy 6:20. Florus, on the other hand, contrasts Scotus' scientific procedure with the *"ordo pietatis"* ["order of godliness"], that attributes to divine authority and sacred Scripture the additional role of judging as to the truth value of worldly books.[16]

2 Faith seeking understanding: Anselm of Canterbury

An eleventh-century theological controversy of similar dimensions can serve as the background for the understanding of theology formulated by the "Father of Scholasticism," Anselm of Canterbury (1033–1109), which is often taken to be normative for all of Scholasticism.[17] The dispute about the Last Supper in the debate with Berengar of Tours († 1088) unites and then again divides leading theologians in a discussion during which even the self-concept of theology becomes controversial.[18] Berengar's struggle to understand the words of consecration by means of logic arrives, unlike vulgar opinions, at the solution that *"fidei et intellectui"* ["to faith and the intellect"] bread and wine through transubstantiation become the Body and Blood of Christ, which are enjoyed by the faithful in a spiritual way, while bread and wine remain for the senses.[19] Berengar essentially justifies his teaching according to the method of Duns Scotus, giving to *ratio* (which is identified with truth) clear priority over *auctoritas*.[20] Yet by no means does Berengar renounce the proof from authority; rather, he depicts his teaching as being in harmony with Ambrose and Augustine. On account of insufficient logical *"perspicuitas,"* however, he declares null and void the oath that he swore to uphold the official formulation of the doctrine on the Eucharist in 1059.[21]

16. Prudentius, *De praedestinatione contra Joannem Scotum* (PL 115.1009–1336), Florus, *Adversus Joannis Scotti erroneas definitiones liber* (PL 119.101–250).

17. The "normative" view is taken especially by Grabmann, *Methode,* 258–340.

18. See Holopainen, *Dialectic,* 44–118; Gibson, "Berengar of Tours," 61–68; Cantin, "La 'raison'"; Schrimpf, "Bausteine," 9–16.

19. Berengar, *Purgatoria epistola contra Almannum,* in *Lanfranc et Bérenger: La controverse eucharistique du XIe siècle,* J. de Montclos (Leuven, 1971), 531–38; Berengar, *De sacra coena adversus Lanfrancum,* ed. W. H. Beekenkamp (Den Haag, 1941).

20. Berengar, *Sacr. coen.* 35.47–48, 52.

21. Ibid., 13; see also Hödl, "Confessio Berengarii."

Moreover according to Berengar it is not up to synods but rather to the theologian, the *"eruditus fidelis"* to present clearly (i.e., by means of logic), to the extent possible for our knowledge in this [earthly] condition, what a *"regula fidei"* ["rule of faith"] implies and what it excludes. Logical comprehension is by no means a profanation of the sacrament.[22] In the debate with his opponents Berengar makes it clear that theology cannot and must not do without the laws of logic: "As thinking beings we cannot renounce the laws of thought. One does not honor God by disowning the human mind, the rules of which are formulated in logic and grammar. Man as a thinking being is the image of God. He must not relinquish this dignity. Respect for the laws of thought has its own religious significance."[23]

Among the many writings in the controversy over Berengar, the contrary interpretation by Lanfranc of Bec deserves special attention with regard to its concept of theology and its method.[24] Lanfranc, the most important logician of his day, advocates in theology the unequivocal primacy of *auctoritas* over *ratio;* for faith, too, precedes rational comprehension. Faith is meritorious, while reason is not. Even Paul rejected logical endeavors where the faith is concerned (1 Timothy 6:20). Lanfranc himself tries to conceal as much as possible the involvement of logic in theology by presenting the consensus of authorities and grouping them according to their importance. The consensus and unanimity of the teaching are assumed, however, and must be preserved. The debate about the Eucharist thereby becomes at the same time a debate about the correct method for theology. Thus in 1059 there are discussions in Rome not only about the Eucharist, but also *"de eminentia rationis"* ["on the excellence of reason"] and *"de immunitate auctoritatis"* ["on the immunity, i.e., incontrovertible character of authority"].[25]

Anselm of Canterbury's fundamental answer concerning the task and method of theology should be viewed against the background of the Berengar controversy. His formula, *"fides quaerens intellectum"* ["faith seeking understanding"] caused him to become the "Father of Scholasticism."[26] The arguments that he developed in his influential works, *Monologion, Proslogion,* and *Cur Deus homo* are methodically presented in his *Epistola de in-*

22. Berengar, *Sacr. coen.* 3.47–48, 89–90.

23. Flasch, *Einführung,* 45.

24. Lanfranc, De corpore et sanguine domini contra Berengarium Turonensem (PL 150.407–442); see also Cantin, "Ratio"; Holopainen, *Dialectic,* 77–118.

25. Berengar, *Sacr. coen.* 18.

26. See Grabmann, *Methode,* 1:258–340.

carnatione Verbi.[27] As it was for Lanfranc, faith is the first thing for Anselm; he expressly adopts Augustine's motto, *"Credo, ut intelligam."* ["I believe so that I might understand."] To try to support the faith with logical, scientific reasons would be to secure Olympus against vibrations from human footsteps by cordoning it off. For faith is ultimately a grace given by God. On the other hand it is certainly in the interest of the believer to explain the faith and to make it comprehensible with the methods of scientific reason. This effort proceeds along two lines: the believer can gain insight into the intelligibility of the faith and he can thereby at the same time reply to objections and questions that arise as he probes the deposit of faith. For Anselm the monk and bishop, however, theology as the path to understanding the faith is always inserted into and ordered to the praxis of the life of faith. In thus viewing and securing the faith, however, one should not proceed from the formulations of sacred Scripture that have been accepted as authoritative, but rather from the interpretation of the doctrine of the faith given by the Church Fathers, as it has been elaborated from a systematic perspective. Yet even the Fathers themselves are not always unanimous and require interpretation. The task of safeguarding the unity of the faith in interpreting Scripture and the Fathers belongs to the pope. *Auctoritas* in the strict sense, therefore, is no longer a passage from Scripture or the Fathers, but rather a carefully formulated article of the *"fides christiana."*[28] The articles of faith form the *"regula veritatis"* ["rule of truth"], and therefore also the norm for an interpretation of the world that claims to be true. The task of *ratio* in this context is to strive for insight into the intelligibility and the coherence of what is believed through an ever deeper penetration into it. Of course contradictory interpretations may very well be ruled out thereby; the faith, nonetheless, remains superior in principle to *ratio.*

Even though the *auctoritas* of faith and of the Church has precedence over *ratio,* it still invariably relies on reason to develop an understanding of the faith. Anselm's own approach can be described in a no less influential and misunderstood motto than *"sola ratione"* ["by reason alone"].[29] The status of *ratio* is by all means maintained: *"ratio . . . et princeps et judex debet*

27. *Anselmi Cantuariensis Opera Omnia,* ed. F. S. Schmitt, vol. 2 (Rome, 1940; reprinted Stuttgart, 1968), 3–35; see also Schrimpf, "Bausteine," 16–19; Kienzler, *Glauben,* 25–157; Holopainen, *Dialectic,* 119–55; Gemeinhardt, "Theologische Methode."

28. Anselm, *Ep. de inc. verb.* (ed. Schmitt II, 5–8).

29. Anselm, *Monol. prooem* (ed. Schmitt I, 8.18–20); Anselm, *Prosl. prooem* (ed. Schmitt I, 93.2–4); in this passage, however, he writes *"sola cogitatione"*; Kienzler, *Glauben,* 28–33, argues that the expression is always *"sola ratione."*

omnium esse quae sunt in homine." ["Reason . . . must be the ruler and judge of everything that there is in man."][30] This *ratio,* however, is no longer just logic that is to be used purely as an instrument; in Anselm's writings it is expanded by an analysis, inspired mainly by Augustine and Boethius, of philosophical and in particular metaphysical concepts: substance, person, *libertas, veritas, rectitudo* [righteousness]. It is not logical consistency alone that now decides as to the correctness of one's understanding of the faith; one now strives for such an understanding with metaphysical methods. Only such an understanding offers the *"rationes necessariae"* ["necessary reasons"] that should enable theology to make the mystery of the Trinity intelligible in a binding way even to human understanding. This insight is never so complete as to eliminate faith; Anselm describes it instead as *"aliquatenus"* ["to a certain degree"]. Yet reason can arrive in just this way at insights that can be recognized as true without the foundation of the faith and therefore are to be accepted by the unbeliever as well, for example, it can arrive at the knowledge of God's existence, as the famous argument from the *Proslogion* is supposed to show. On the other hand, the inability to grasp something with the understanding or to make it intelligible is no reason for faith to reject it also. In this case *ratio* is by no means the judge of *fides.* Instead such an arrangement is morally ruled out as *"praesumptio."*[31]

If reason tried to debate in theology whether something in the Church's doctrine of the faith was not true *(quomodo non sit),* that demand of reason would be unjustified; the best remedy against such presumption is to refer to the humility with which one must first accept what the Church believes and professes. Only then can a Christian ask *(quaerere,* not *disputare), "quomodo sit"* ["how it is"]. Therefore theology can only offer insight into the How of what is believed, but can neither call into question nor substantiate the faith as a whole. Within the framework of his monastic, Augustinian understanding of theology, Anselm also points out that the prerequisite for a correct understanding of the faith is *"soliditas fidei"* ["firmness of faith"], acquired through *"sapientiae et morum gravitas"* ["wisdom and serious comportment"].[32] Theology without the practice of the faith is therefore not possible. Theology is necessary, however, because reference to the authority of the Church Fathers alone cannot suffice. With that, Anselm clearly distances himself from all those who think that the recitation of patristic

30. Anselm, *Ep. de inc. verb.* 1 (II, 10.1–2).
31. Ibid., 1 (II, 4.5; 6.6).
32. Ibid., 1 (II, 6.5–7.4).

sentences is already theology. In particular Anselm gives five reasons for the need to probe the faith *personally* and rationally, but at the same time he marks out the insuperable limits of this endeavor:

1. Life is short, and the Fathers could not say everything about the truths of the faith.
2. The *"veritatis ratio"* can never be fully exhausted by the human mind.
3. Christ bestows his gifts of grace on his Church until the end of time, and therefore he also grants progress in knowing these things.
4. Scripture itself invites us to investigate the faith, while clearly giving precedence to faith: *"Nisi credideritis, non intelligetis"* (Isaiah 7:9, Vulgate). ["Unless you believe, you shall not understand."]
5. Understanding the faith is a path leading from faith to the beatific vision of God as the goal of our life.[33]

3 Systematic treatment of patristic sentences: The school of Laon

Whereas the creative work of Anselm of Canterbury is carried out in the literary forms of treatise, dialogue, and letter, which are typical for monastic culture, we encounter the academic form of theology unmistakably in the school of Laon. Glosses and collections of sentences are the characteristic writings of this school. Not everything that is reputed to be by the principal of the school, Anselm (ca. 1050–1117), and his brother Radulfus († 1131/33) is authentic, as the definitive works by F. Bliemetzrieder, H. Weisweiler, and O. Lottin have shown.[34] Literarily speaking, too, these are academic productions, often different reworkings of the same source. The foundation was, first, Anselm's oral instruction, which attracted the scholars and churchmen of his day: John of Tours (ca. 1120), Adam Parvipontanus († before 1159), Gilbertus Universalis († 1134), Alberic of Rheims († 1141), but also Norbert of Xanten († 1134), who was prevented, however, by the monastic zealot Drogo († 1137), then Prior of St. Nikasius in Rheims, from attending Anselm's lectures on the Psalms.[35]

We search in vain for a theory of theology in the collections of sentences

33. Anselm, *Cur Deus homo* (II, 40.2–12).

34. Landgraf, *Einführung*, 55–62, lists collections of sentences; see also Bliemetzrieder, *Anselm von Laon;* Weisweiler, *Schrifttum;* Lottin, *Psychologie,* vol. 5.

35. *Vita S. Norberti* A (MHG SS 12, 678); see also Grauwen, *Norbert,* 42.82. Concerning Drogo: Leclercq, "Drogon."

from the school of Laon. We can discover it only by reading between the lines or by inferring it from their methods. The most striking thing initially in these collections of sentences, which in part are organized quite loosely or thematically, is the strictly patristic orientation, especially the reliance on Augustine. The sentences are used to resolve questions that either remain individual questions or else are put into a larger systematic context. Stereotypically they begin with *Quaeritur, Quaeritur etiam, Potest quaeri,* etc. ["It is asked," ". . . also," "It may be asked"].[36] Theology here is an *interrogative discipline.* The central themes are the Trinity, the doctrine of original sin, Christology, and the sacraments. Sometime we also find that sentences are taken from biblical glosses and collected in independent anthologies (e.g., the collection *Deus hominem fecit perfectum*) or reworked thematically (e.g., the collection *Dubitatur a quibusdam*).[37] The questions often go into great detail and show the downright rational approach of this school, for instance to Christology and the doctrine of redemption: Why didn't redemption occur earlier? Why not by a single word instead of through God's *kenosis* or self-emptying? Did God the Son take on flesh so as to deceive the devil? Why didn't the devil save Christ from death [i.e., thwart the redemption] when he recognized his divinity after the betrayal by Judas? Why were only men saved and not the angels? Why did God take on human nature but not angelic nature? Canonical questions are often mixed in with teaching on the sacraments, for instance with regard to the validity of consecration by a priest who is unworthy, excommunicated, or removed from the clerical state. The teaching on Penance usually deals at length with the measure of satisfaction and the magnitude of the sin.[38]

Answers to these questions are expected in the first place from the Church Fathers, above all from Augustine. This orientation toward the past is a characteristic feature of the school of Anselm of Laon, along with its relatively simple technique of compiling sentences and its initial efforts to systematize theology. Obviously there is little demand here for dialectical [logical] skill, nor for Anselm of Canterbury's metaphysical analysis of theological concepts. He did not become a fixture in this school but is mentioned only in passing. Instead Anselm and Radulfus apparently still adhere to the method of Lanfranc in his debate with Berengar: assigning weight to the authorities in such a way that the use of logic becomes un-

36. See Weisweiler, *Schrifttum,* 260–379.
37. Ibid., 292–311, 314–57.
38. Ibid., 276–81.

necessary or imperceptible. In contrast to the monograph tradition, of which Anselm of Canterbury is a part, the school of Laon tries to elucidate an overall theological context—naturally while citing the Church Fathers. One additional step in the general systematization is the thorough elaboration of an individual treatise, for example, on matrimony or simony. The patristic sentences, however, are already clearly accompanied by sentences by contemporaries, cited at least as *"quidam"* ["some authors"], while the distinctive technique of the *magister* in his manner of posing questions and of selecting, ranking and reconciling the sentences is evident in continuous series of new summas. These make use of the older works of the school, often as patterns.[39] The teacher usually expands them by inserting his own points, of course while citing patristic material (sometime whole *florilegia*), which in turn is often taken from another collection of the school. Weisweiler therefore speaks about the "additive method of the School."[40] The intention of an author and especially his theological system can be discerned precisely from his manner of interweaving the "ready-made" parts and his own additions. The justification of the individual teachings is supposed to be improved by new sentences, or else an unmethodical system should be replaced by a better one. "Nothing schematic, therefore, but everything living and most vivaciously alive, albeit often in detail work, which nonetheless reveals more clearly their love for the new method and for the material being treated."[41]

Most importantly, in the school of Laon we can observe the transition from exegesis to systematic theology. Anselm's contribution to the *Glossa ordinaria* has already been mentioned. His exegetical activity related to the *lectio* provided the material for the first systematic collections of sentences on individual questions, in typical fashion, for example, in his letter on the Eucharist entitled *"'Calix' id est potus sanguinis Christi,"* which in turn was included within larger collections of sentences.[42] A biblical-patristic character and a systematic theological approach are therefore the principal features of the first medieval theological school that merits the name.

This is directly connected, however, with the conservatism of this school, which is already quite evident in its choice of methods. We have a pertinent document that gives us an insight into the standpoint of Anselm

39. Weisweiler, "Arbeitsmethode."

40. Weisweiler, *Schrifttum*, 243; 239–43.

41. Ibid., 251.

42. Ibid., 190–204. [The title means "'Chalice,' that is, the drink of Christ's Blood."]

of Laon: his letter to Abbot Heribrand of St. Laurentius monastery in Lüttich.[43] In the very first sentence Anselm warns against trying to answer the questions at hand about God's good will and the evil in the world *"in pugnis verborum"* ["in battles of words"] rather than *"in sententia."* Two methods of theology are plainly indicated here: his own method of compiling sentences, which harks back to patristic material, and the dialecticians' "battles of words," which are immediately dismissed (with biblical arguments, of course) as childish. On the other hand, it is up to men to debate the correct meaning of individual passages. Anselm claims that this is part of his work and the work of his school. Others disagree, opining that they can pursue theology by logical and grammatical means: *"Haec non attendentes, quidam maxime inflati nomine scientiae, sensus Patrum ignorantes, languerunt, ut ait Apostolus, circa quaestiones et pugnas verborum."* ["Disregarding these things, some who are greatly puffed up in the name of science, while ignorant of the understanding of the Fathers, have grown faint, as the Apostle says, with questions and battles of words."] Specifically, Anselm accuses his opponents of childish behavior, arrogance in the name of science, unfamiliarity with the mind of the Fathers, a disordered and ultimately self-destructive desire to discuss questions and joust verbally. After this disqualification of other methods comes the methodical motto of the compilation method: *"diversa, non adversa."* The Fathers say different but not contradictory things. Therefore patristic passages must be sorted, interpreted, and arranged harmoniously: *"Sententiae quidem omnium catholicorum diversae, sed non adversae, in unam concurrunt convenientiam."* ["The different but noncontradictory sentences of all Catholic authors, moreover, meet in one agreement."] The goal of compilation is denoted by the word *"convenientia,"* and in the writings of Vivianus of Prémontré by *"armonia."* The methodical outlook and approach are identical.[44] Hopes are pinned on the possibility of harmonization, not on logical or grammatical investigations. For what matters is the *sententia,* the meaning, not the verbal formulation. Admittedly, there can be differences in wording that sound like *"contrarietates et pugnae"* ["oppositions and conflicts"]. Now there are typical reactions to these battles of words: those of little faith are horrified, but for combative theologians it is a parade ground, on which the presumptuous fight at length. In all the commotion the *"probati"* ["experts"] are excluded, whereas they can show, when all the

43. Edited by Lottin in *Psychologie,* 5:175–78.
44. See Leinsle, *Vivianus,* 50–52.

others fail, that it is not a matter of contradictions but rather of a real harmony among apparent dissonances. These *"probati"* are clearly the leading authorities for one's own school.

Thus the writings of Anselm of Laon exhibit neither a dialectical effort to interpret the patristic sentence nor—in contrast to Anselm of Canterbury—a specifically metaphysical interest. The main interest is rather moral and practical, in exegesis also, even when the questions become quite subtle, for instance in the doctrine on original sin and sacramental theology (e.g., whether Christ's Body which was given to the disciples at the Last Supper was capable of suffering).[45] The fact that such a conservative school became so widely influential at the beginning of the twelfth century and at the same time was prohibited as an innovation sheds considerable light on the ecclesiastical mentality of the time and shows, on the other hand, what an exceptional phenomenon the philosophical and theological thought of Anselm of Canterbury was. Not least important is the fact that the methods and writings of the school of Laon could be applied fruitfully in monastic circles and among canons regular for their *lectio divina.* This ensured that these works—circulated in manuscript form—would have a wide appeal. For their works handed down to later generations the treasure of patristic thought in a ready-made, systematic and harmonized form. Theology as the interpretation of sacred Scripture with reference to patristic material became a matter for *"probati"* in the setting of ecclesiastical schools: Who would not want to be one of them?

4 Theology as wisdom and way of life: Hugh of St. Victor († 1141)

Another school that was strongly influenced by the compilations of sentences from the school of Laon was the school of St. Victor in Paris, where since the days of William of Champeaux († 1122), its first teacher of theology, academic theology was combined with the cloistered life of the reformed canons regular. This synthesis crystallized remarkably in Hugh of St. Victor's understanding of theology.[46] Hugh's high esteem for the Scriptures and the Fathers connects him with the school of Laon, yet he plainly

45. See Lottin, *Psychologie,* 5.443–44.

46. See esp. Ernst, *Gewissheit des Glaubens;* [authentic works by Hugh], 287–92; Berndt, "Hugo von St. Viktor"; Sicard, *Hugues de Saint-Victor.* On the school itself and the older literature, see Landgraf, *Einführung,* 73–79.

uses patristic material much more freely and reworks it more independently than the works of Laon.[47] Theology as the interpretation of sacred Scripture is at the latter's service in his opinion also; at any rate it alone can fathom the truth and depth of sacred Scripture. That is why theology is by no means superfluous. Since its method of teaching and of presentation is to a great extent identical with that of secular disciplines, its distinctive features are now sought in its contents: theology's *materia* and *modus tractandi* [method of treating] must be defined.[48]

The object of sacred Scripture and thus of theology consists of "the works of man's restoration" *(opera restaurationis hominis)*. Consequently, theology is basically teaching about the redemption of mankind. It is possible to comprehend the *"opus restaurationis,"* however, only in terms of the *"opus conditionis."* Through this work of creation, what did not exist came to be; through the work of redemption, what had been lost was made better. "Therefore the work of creation consists in the creation of the world with all its elements; the work of restoration consists in the Incarnation of the Word with all his sacraments, which preceded it from the beginning of the world or follow after it until the end of the world."[49] The reality of creation, however, is primarily the object of "secular writings," which are summarized in philosophy. The *"opera restaurationis"* are reserved for the sacred Scriptures and constitute a *"dignior et sublimior materia"* ["more worthy and sublime matter"].[50] The reality of creation is treated in sacred Scripture, on the other hand, in a way that is only propaedeutic and dispositive, for sacred Scripture "could not show adequately how man was restored if it did not show first how he fell; nevertheless it could not show his fall adequately if it did not first explain how he had been established by God; but in order to show how man was first established, the foundation and creation of the whole world had to be presented, because the world was created for man's sake. His soul, indeed, was created for God's sake, and his body for the sake of his soul, and the world for the sake of the human body, so that the soul might be subject to God, the body to the soul and the world to his body."[51] Theocentricity and anthropocentricity are combined in this concept of a theology that intends to be primarily a doctrine of man's redemption. Conflict between philosophy and theology is avoided as long as no contradictions appear be-

47. Weisweiler, "Arbeitsmethode."
48. Hugo, *De sacr., prol.1* (PL 176.183 A); see also Hugo, *De script.* (PL 175.11 A).
49. *De sacr.,* prol.1 (PL 176.183 AB).
50. *De sacr.,* prol.2 (183 C).
51. *De sacr.,* prol.3 (184 B).

tween the biblical and the philosophical interpretation of the reality of creation. Nevertheless philosophy is not thereby relegated to a merely instrumental function, but rather its own field of inquiry is reserved for it; it has to cultivate this field with its own methods—ultimately, however, within the context of a comprehensive theological interpretation of the world. The matter (the general field) of theology, too, is attuned to man in salvation history as a whole: "First, therefore, it describes its matter in the fact that man was created and destined, then his misery in guilt and punishment, then restoration and mercy in the knowledge of truth and love of virtue; finally man's home and joy in blessedness."[52]

Hugh not only delimits the field that is the object of theology, distinguishing it from secular science, but also provides a doctrine of theological method as distinct from the philosophical disciplines, which he investigated as to their method and value in his *Didascalicon.* Like theology, the secular sciences *(artes),* too, are teleologically defined with man as their end and are understood as a propaedeutic of salvation. Their goal is the restoration of the likeness to God in us, for the degree of one's conformity with God corresponds to the degree of one's wisdom.[53] The path to this goal of man's striving for knowledge leads, however, by way of the *"studium sapientiae"* ["study of wisdom"], philosophy. For Hugh, however, philosophical wisdom is at the same time the divine wisdom of the Creator.[54] That is why the secular *artes* as a whole are at the service of *lectio* of sacred Scripture. Now within the framework of this philosophy there is already a theology; since it is a philosophical and thus a secular science, it is the *"theologia mundana"* as opposed to the *"theologia divina." "Theologia mundana"* tries to know God by way of creatures, through the *"simulacrum naturae"* ["likeness of nature"], whereas the *"simulacrum gratiae"* ["likeness of grace"], that is, the *"opus restaurationis"* in the Incarnation and the sacraments, remains the exclusive province of *"theo-*

52. Ibid. (184 C).

53. Hugo, *Didasc.* II, 1 (ed. Buttimer 23.17–19): *"hoc ergo omnes artes agunt, hoc intendunt, ut divina similitudo in nobis reparetur, quae nobis forma est, Deo natura, cui quanto magis conformamur tanto magis sapimus."* ["Therefore this is what all the arts accomplish and intend: that the divine likeness—which is for us a form, but for God his nature—might be restored in us; for the more we are conformed to it, the wiser we are."] See also Hugo, *Didascalicon de Studio legendi / Studienbuch,* trans. and intro. by Thilo Offergeld (Fontes Christiani 27) (Freiburg, 1997), "Einleitung" [Introduction], 68–79.

54. Ibid., II, 1 (ed. Buttimer 23.20–21); see also "Epitome Dindimi in philosophiam," ed. R. Baron, *Traditio* 11 (1955): 91–148, citation at 146: *"Finis enim omnis philosophiae agnitio est summi boni, quod in solo rerum omnium factore situm est."* ["The end of all philosophy is the knowledge of the supreme good, which is situated in the sole maker of all things."]

logia divina."[55] Thus Hugh allows a purely philosophical theology to make its appearance. As a fundamentally fallible reflection on the *"opus conditionis,"* it is bound up with the whole of theological wisdom, which is developed only in the reflections of sacred Scripture and acquires its certainty therein. When worldly theology sets itself up as an absolute and tries to do without ties to scriptural reflection on salvation history, it becomes an erroneous "wisdom of this world" as opposed to the wisdom (or folly) of God.[56]

Also corresponding to the sapiential character of Victorine theology within the framework of a community of canons regular is the *"modus tractandi"* ["method of treatment"] foreseen by Hugh. Natural predispositions, study and one's way of life must come together in a good Augustinian spirit in order to achieve the type of theologian suited to this school.[57] Therefore we are by no means dealing merely with a school or university curriculum. Rather, theology and one's way of life are very closely connected. Along with Bernard of Chartres († 1124/30), Hugh regards humility above all, zeal in questioning and researching, a tranquil life, silence and self-examination, poverty, and residence abroad as components of the *disciplina* of study:

> *Mens humilis, studium quaerendi, vita quieta*
> *Scrutinium tacitum, paupertas, terra aliena*
> *Haec reserare solent multis obscura legendi.*[58]
>
> [These things are wont to unlock for many people the secrets of reading.]

Anyone who approaches sacred Scripture with this attitude sees in it the perfection and surpassing of all worldly knowledge. The interpretation of sacred Scripture is gained by way of *lectio* and *meditatio,* the independent and also spiritual assimilation of the scriptural passage according to what Hugh regards as its threefold sense: historical, allegorical, and tropological. History and allegory promote man's knowledge; tropology his *"mores"* or morals; both sides must come to an agreement again in *"sapientia"* ["wisdom"].[59] For Hugh, too, theology consists essentially in the right manner and order of reading sacred Scripture, and therefore everything depends on

55. Hugo, *In hierarchiam caelestem* I, 1 (PL 175.925 D).

56. Ibid. (923B–928B).

57. Hugo, *Didasc.* III, 6 (ed. Buttimer 57.6); see also the introduction to Hugo, *Studienbuch,* ed. Offergeld, 68–69.

58. Ibid. III, 12 (ed. Buttimer 61.11–14); taken from Bernhard of Chartres; see also Lacroix, "Hugues de Saint-Victor."

59. Hugo, *Didasc.* V, 2.6 (ed. Buttimer 95.15–17; 104.21–22).

that for theology and the theologian: the path proceeds via *lectio* and *meditatio* to *oratio*, prayer, and from there to *contemplatio*. The knowledge that is gained along this path is not an end in itself, but rather as a matter of principle is at the service of the faith: to confirm the believer himself in the faith, to give an account of it and to hand it on to those who are less learned are the goals, and not *curiositas*, knowledge for the sake of knowledge or one's own vanity, which Augustine had already ruled out.[60]

The center of theology and sacred Scripture is the work of redemption in Jesus Christ. Since the knowledge of him is central, the allegorical interpretation is considered to have the greatest importance. But since I can interpret signs as such only if I already know the thing signified, in allegorical interpretation the NT should be read before the OT; for "divine Scripture as a whole is one single book and that one book is Christ, because divine Scripture as a whole speaks about Christ and divine Scripture as a whole is fulfilled in Christ, and when we read Scripture we strive, by knowing his deeds, words and commandments, to obtain the grace to do what he commanded and to receive what he promised."[61] The historical sense of Scripture, however, is the foundation for this spiritual-theological investigation, in the service of which all worldly sciences are also enlisted. With that Hugh has already formulated as a program what is then carried out in exegetical detail by Andrew of St. Victor. Here, too, theology is bound up with questioning *(studium quaerendi)*. This questioning about man and his redemption, however, is more than a merely academic custom; in keeping with the Augustinian tradition,[62] it is bound up with a way of life and ordered to a goal, both of which point beyond school to the praxis of the life of faith.

5 Theology as linguistic criticism: Peter Abelard

The sapiential, harmonious approach of Hugh is quite different from the program and form of theology in the writings of Abelard (1079–1142).[63] For him, as in the school of Laon, the object of theology consists of articles of faith formulated on the basis of the *"sacra pagina"*; the goal is the rational justification thereof, sometimes referred to as *"intelligentia."* The method is

60. Ibid., V, 10 (ed. Buttimer 111.5–112.5).

61. Hugo, *De arca Noe morali* II, 8 (PL 176.642 CD).

62. See Studer on *Augustinus De Trinitate*, 73–78.

63. See esp. Cottiaux, "Conception de la théologie"; Jolivet, *Arts du langage;* Niggli, "Philosophischer Scharfsinn."

the one commonly used in the schools: glosses, commentaries, but also the method of systematic *theologia* employing all available logical and philosophical means. Although for a time he was a monk and an abbot, Abelard moved in intellectual circles in Paris in which the students require only *"humanas et philosophicas rationes"* for theological truths and stake everything on *"intelligentia"* but not on the inscrutable wording of the Bible. They are unwilling to believe anything that they have not already comprehended and consider it ridiculous to preach incomprehensible things.[64] Therefore Abelard sets himself the task of developing *"intelligentia"* with human, philosophical arguments precisely on the basis of the authoritative scriptural text; in other words, to reveal its hidden meaning and to test its truth value not only through a series of patristic citations or through spiritual exegesis, but through rational examination. This examination therefore refers to the *"scriptum"* (the wording) and the *"sententia"* (the teaching).[65] This method, unlike Hugh's, is not typically theological but is valid generally *"in omni disciplina."* The decisive criterion here is *ratio,* which leads to a decision, if not always to certainty. For Abelard, however, the *ratio* referred to here is embodied in the *artes* of the Trivium, especially in dialectic.

Theology therefore is primarily the argumentative, linguistic, and logical examination of authoritative texts; it treats *"de scripto"* ["what is written"] along the lines of an exegesis of the *sacra pagina.* Abelard understands works of systematic theology—insofar as they are not participating in current debates—as introductions to the study of sacred Scripture *(divinae scripturae introductio).*[66] The argumentation must have at least probability in its favor and must not contradict the faith itself.[67] Therefore the arguments are drawn chiefly from philosophy and the realm of *"similitudines"* (analogies, especially in the doctrine of the Trinity). Thus the *magister* himself must first understand what he "is reading," that is, what he is presenting to the scholars in the *lectio.* The theological truths must not only be recited but understood and scientifically interpreted *(intellegi ac disseri).*[68] For this purpose there are both scriptural commentaries and systematic works *(Theologia Summi Boni, Theologia Christiana, Theologia Scholarium = Introductio in*

64. Abaelard, *Hist. cal.,* ed. J. Monfrin (Paris, 1967), 82, 690–83, 701.

65. Abaelard, *Dialogus inter Philosophum, Judaeum et Christianum,* ed. R. Thomas (Stuttgart–Bad Cannstatt, 1970), 97.1478–85.

66. Abaelard, *Theologia Scholarium, praef.* 1 (CCh CM 13.313.1–3).

67. Ibid., II, 18 (414.243–44): *"saltem aliquid verisimile atque humanae rationi vicinum, nec sacrae fidei contrarium proponere."*

68. Ibid., II, 56 (435.885–436.894).

Theologiam). The works of commentary, first and foremost the Commentary on the Letter to the Romans, work their way through the *scriptum* to the *sententia,* whereas the systematic works start with the logical, rational explication of the *sententia* itself.[69]

This becomes very clear in Abelard's first systematic presentation of theology, which however includes only the doctrine on the Trinity: in the *Theologia Summi Boni* (so named after its initial words; it is also called the *Tractatus de unitate et trinitate divina* [*Treatise on the divine unity and trinity*]), written in 1120.[70] Here Abelard makes the widest use thus far of the philosophy that consists mainly of Boethius and the *logica vetus.* He relates the philosophical concept of the highest good *(summum bonum)* to the Christian, Trinitarian God. In Abelard's view this is justified by Christ himself, the "Lord of the faith," who gave three different names to this same god of philosophy. Accordingly it is clear also that to a great extent the argumentation proceeds philosophically and that philosophical studies, especially of dialectic, are expressly demanded of the reader.[71] Whereas in exegetical and later systematic works the quotation of Scripture passages has the final probative force, that is not the case in this context; here further justification by *ratio* is required. Even here, however, Abelard remains faithful to the linguistic component of theology: the *Theologia Summi Boni* is intended as a rational investigation of what Christ accomplished in giving the god of philosophy the names Father, Son, and Spirit. The fact that this theology nevertheless does not lack a foundation in practical living (Abelard wrote the treatise as a monk) explains the repeated reference to the praise of God, which corresponds to the monastic tradition. In the teaching about the Holy Spirit, Plato's doctrine of the world soul (which is familiar from Macrobius and Boethius) is discussed extensively. The decisive feature in either case, however, is the explanation in terms of the philosophical categories of substance and accidents, person, etc.

Abelard clearly distinguishes his position, however, from that of the pseudo-dialecticians as well; they do not use their knowledge to interpret Scripture correctly but rather place it at the service of attacks against the faith and thus of the Antichrist.[72] That is no reason, however, to condemn

69. Editions: CCh CM 11–13; *Expositio in Epistolam ad Romanos: Römerbriefkommentar,* trans. and intro. by Rolf Peppermüller (Fontes Christiani 26/1–3) (Freiburg, 2000).

70. CCh CM 13.1–201: Abaelard, *Theologia Summi Boni,* trans. and ed. by U. Niggli (PhB 395) (Hamburg, 1989), with an extensive introduction; see also Nielsen, "Peter Abelard," 107–14.

71. Abaelard, *Theol. Summi Boni* III, 5.100 (CCh CM 13.201.1360–63).

72. Ibid., II, 1–4 (114.1–115.35).

dialectic and its application in theology; only its misuse leads to sophistry. What is bad is not the science but its misuse. Abelard decisively opposes "those untrammeled and wild combatants" who "through the one horn of their pride fight even against the Creator" and have "raised their voice against heaven."[73] Yet he himself makes very extensive use of dialectic and philosophy, on the basis of the faith, of course; at the beginning he presents briefly the content of the faith as *"totius disputationis thema et summa fidei"* ["the subject of all disputation and summary of the faith"], so as then to discuss the individual questions in a strictly rational way and to answer objections.[74] To a great extent the procedure here too is linguistic criticism and metaphysical analysis, as the questions and distinctions of the second book make clear: Why the divine substance is simple and formless; the distinction of Divine Persons, six meanings of *"idem"* and *"diversum"* ["same" and "different"]; meanings of "person," etc. In this way Abelard develops the fundamental question of theology: whether and how it is possible to apply human expressions to God. Nor does it do any good for the opponent in the disputation to say that he does not want to go into words and meanings but rather to keep to the truth of the meaning. He must nevertheless make clear what *"genitus"* ["begotten"] means, so as then to see that *"genitus"* and *"ingenitus"* ["unbegotten"] are designations of Persons in the Trinity. For Abelard, *"verba catholica"* ["Catholic words"] must be added to *"sana intelligentia"* ["sound understanding"].[75] The basis for this is chapter 1 of *Peri hermeneias* on the correspondence of word, concept, and thing.

This apparatus of semantic and logical analysis is used aptly so as to answer the objections of opponents; there are many of them, however, especially in Trinitarian matters. For Abelard too, nevertheless, theological questions are not verbal battles but rather objective inquiries [*Sachfragen*]. One must speak correctly about the object, however, with words that are employed *"ad placitum hominum"* ["for human purposes"]. There can be agreement about objective inquiries, therefore, only through agreement about the generally accepted meanings of the terms being used.[76] In this way one can reply for example to objections to the concept of substance with reference to the Trinity, to the status of the Divine Persons or to the

73. Ibid., II, 13 (118.125–119.128).

74. Ibid., II, 1 (123–29).

75. Ibid., III, 2.84 (194.1142–57); III, 1.33 (171.412–26).

76. Abaelard, *Sermo in Ann. Virginis,* ed. V. Cousin, in *Petri Abaelardi Opera* (Hildesheim, reprint 1970), 1:356–57.

questions of whether there is a real difference in God or how a Trinity of Persons is possible without real multiplicity.

In Abelard's writings the defense of the faith is followed by the positive step: the *amplificatio,* which is done *"verisimilibus et honestissimis rationibus"* ["by means of probable and most worthy reasons"].[77] Abelard sees clearly that many theological arguments are not compelling. Anselm of Canterbury's *"rationes necessariae"* are expressly retracted. The divine nature is ultimately incomprehensible; that is why a strict proof in this regard is often impossible. Language itself is metaphorical *(translata);* the trios by which the relations among the Three Divine Persons are explained are only *"similitudines"* (comparisons, analogies). When it is a question of proving a matter as it is in itself, however, standard linguistic usage with unambiguous meaning is required.[78] Abelard views the *"rationes honestae,"* however, as having higher value than mere *"necessitas."* Such reasonable arguments are expressed by the terms *"oportet," "convenit,"* or *"melius"* ["it is proper, fitting, better"]. The reasonableness of the divine relations and operations is thereby underscored, without strictly proving their necessity. Thus, for example, the unicity of God is proved from his functions as Creator and designer [*Ordner*] of the world, and it is demonstrated that this is far more conducive to God's honor than the premise of several gods.[79] Therefore it is a matter of arguments from reason and from appropriateness, which often have moral premises. When it is possible and necessary, however, for example in a debate with opponents or in resolving apparent contradictions between undeniable theological truths, the whole apparatus of dialectic must be applied so as to arrive at the *"amplificatio fidei"* ["fuller explanation of the faith"]. Here rational argument is at the service of the faith, even though some of Abelard's teachings were rejected as heretical.[80]

6 The metaphysical grammar of discourse about God: Gilbert Porreta

What Abelard sought and found above all in dialectic, his younger contemporary Gilbert Porreta (Gilbert de la Porrée, G. of Poitiers [† 1154]) and the Porretan school named after him found in grammar and in the works of

77. Abaelard, *Theologia Christiana* V, 1 (CCh CM 12.347.8).
78. Abaelard, *Theol. Summi Boni* III, 2 (194.1145–68).
79. Abaelard, *Theologia Christiana* V, 9–16 (350–54).
80. On Abelard's school see Luscombe, *School.*

Boethius: the scientific apparatus of theology.[81] For it must be shown now that theology is a science as Boethius understood it. Boethius' definition of the object of this science, which is dependent on Aristotle, applies in the first place however to philosophical theology: it deals with unmoved, abstract, and immaterial objects and therefore belongs to the field of purely intellectual knowledge. By virtue of its object, however, theological knowledge has greater truth than truths about the created world, which is subject to change.[82] For Christian theology, the path of knowledge leads from faith to the truth that is known, but not from the knowledge to faith. Supernatural faith is the prerequisite of theology. For the whole life of the unbeliever is sin, and there can be no good—understandably, given Gilbert's [Neo]platonism—without the greatest good.[83] That is why faith as a grace is understood, following Augustine, as enlightenment by God. Yet not all Christians receive in faith the same knowledge of God. For there are the *"animales"* or *"parvuli"* ["little ones"] and the *"spirituales"* or *"perfecti."* The former believe only the fundamental truths of Christianity, without even arriving at an initial insight into these truths *"in speculo et aenigmate"* [see 1 Cor 13:12].[84] The latter, in contrast, attain an understanding of the faith *"suppositionibus rationum,"* that presupposes rational arguments. Theology as opposed to simple faith comes about therefore precisely through the *"expositio rationum,"* the explanation of the reasonable arguments for the truths of faith. Of course it is not necessary for salvation; this can be attained by simple believers also.[85]

Yet even theology itself is not just a rational effort but ultimately a gift of the Holy Spirit, so that theology is really *"spiritualis"* only when it submits to the Holy Spirit.[86] For in the final analysis it is He himself who is at work in His gifts. Theology is therefore not a science like any other, but rather a spiritual knowledge of the truths of faith brought about by the Holy Spirit. To be sure, it happens by adducing reasonable arguments for the truths of faith. Since God himself on the one hand is the highest truth and on the

81. See esp. Van Elswijk, *Gilbert Porreta;* Nielsen, *Theology;* on the authenticity of his works, 40–46; for his concept of theology: Gilbert Porreta, *Commentarius in Boethii Opuscula sacra,* ed. N. M. Häring (ST 13) (Toronto, 1966). On his literary output and school: Landgraf, *Einführung,* 79–92.

82. Gilbert, *Comm. Boeth.,* 85.1–6, 86.10.

83. Gilbert, *Comm. in Ep. Pauli* (British Museum, London Cod.) add. 11.853–54.151r (cited by Nielsen, *Theology,* 116): *"doceo non, ut cognoscentes credant, sed ut credentes cognoscant de praedictis veritatem."* ["I teach not so that those who know might believe, but rather so that believers might know the truth of what is proclaimed."] See ibid., f.47v (Nielsen, *Theology,* 119).

84. Ibid., f.57r (Nielsen, *Theology,* 124).

85. Ibid., f.170r.85r (Nielsen, *Theology,* 125).

86. Ibid., f. 55r.63v (Nielsen, *Theology,* 126).

other hand produces the gift of theological knowledge, no conflict can arise here in the first place between faith and dialectic, as one finds in Berengar and Abelard. Theology has a *"veritas secundum pietatem"* ["truth in keeping with piety/devotion"], unlike the truth of grammar and dialectic. It is deposited in sacred Scripture and is useful for eternal salvation, whereas the secular sciences are useful only for temporal pleasures.[87] The task of theology, therefore, consists of the explicit knowledge of the faith so as to help instruct simple believers. They must also and particularly be enlightened as to the invalidity of the authority of heretics. Especially useful for this purpose is the logical analysis of the heretics' arguments, which often draw false conclusions from true premises. If the heretics say something right about God, it is only by chance.[88] Some pagan philosophers, in contrast, have attained a knowledge of God *"per naturalem rationem"* ["by natural reason"], but still not without God's help. They did not arrive at a knowledge of the Trinity and the Incarnation, though.[89] A knowledge that is used *"praeter rationem,"* however, in other words, not for the praise of God, which is the goal of theology, is useless.[90]

Philosophical knowledge of the world, moreover, cannot arrive at the ultimate necessity of its reasons and *regulae,* but can only support them by habit. Philosophical sentences have only a *"consuetudini accommodata necessitas"* ["necessity that befits custom"]. Only theology can make clear (metaphysically) the real causal connection, even where those philosophers who attribute absolute truth to their own sentences discover contradictions, for example, in the virgin birth.[91] An absolute truth of philosophical knowledge separated from theology is thus denied in principle. Knowledge of nature relies on the path from custom and induction and in its very methods cannot come into conflict with theology.[92] Theologically correct knowledge of nature, in contrast, must proceed from faith and from that point of departure arrive at theology, where, unlike philosophy, *"veri nominis atque absoluta necessitas"* ["a necessity truly so called and absolute"] rules: *"In his enim non cognoscentes credimus, sed credentes cognoscimus."* ["For we do not believe in these things by knowing them, but rather know by believing."][93] Accordingly, however, the correct knowledge of nature, like theology as a

87. Ibid., f.160r (Nielsen, *Theology,* 128).
88. Gilbert, *Comm. Boeth.* 235.57; 61.16; 161.9ff.; 234.51.
89. Gilbert, *Comm. in Ep. Pauli* f.6v–7r; f.139v–140r (Nielsen, Theology, 130).
90. Ibid., f.69r (Nielsen, *Theology,* 131).
91. Ibid., f.57v.140v (Nielsen, *Theology,* 136).
92. Gilbert, *Comm. Boeth.* 164.38; 323.61.
93. Ibid., 164.42.

whole, is also a gift and work of the Holy Spirit and is included in the *"catholica fides"* that becomes the starting point for the philosophical explanation of the world as well.[94] A conflict between right philosophy—which is now no longer restricted to instrumental logic but has become an explanation of nature—and theology is contradictory to the highest degree: it would be a contradiction in God himself.

Theology takes place methodically by presupposing the *"rationes."* As in every science one must distinguish here between the reasons proper to each discipline *(rationes propriae)* and the (thematically metaphysical) reasons common to all sciences *(rationes communes),* as they are summarized axiomatically by Boethius in *De hebdomadibus.* Gilbert understands *rationes communes* to include the a priori truths of logic and truths that have interdisciplinary validity (sometimes also in a figurative sense, e.g., *rationes naturales* in theology).[95] One must refer to these general rules (or rules taken from other sciences) especially when theology's own business comes to an end because there are no terms available to express it properly.[96] This raises again therefore the question of the justification and singularity of theological discourse, now under the aspect of a metaphysically founded grammar of discourse about God. Thus for instance *"esse"* [the verb "to be"] in the sentence *"Deus est"* means something other than in the sentence *"corpus est"* or *"homo est."* In theology *"esse"* is a proper name of God; in reference to creatures it does not express their own being but rather connotes their dependence upon God.[97] The same goes for *"bonum"* ["good"]. The grammar here, then, is founded upon a metaphysics that is profoundly influence by Boethius and Neoplatonism: God is the being of all created things, which thereby depend on him for their existence and goodness.[98]

For Gilbert this dependence guarantees the universal correspondence *(proportio)* between God and creature, the eternal and the temporal, which in turn justifies his application of arguments from the natural sciences (philosophy) in theology.[99] Gilbert is acutely aware of the metaphorical and linguistic character of theological discourse and knowledge. Theological truths, especially the doctrine of the Trinity, are almost ineffable *(vix dici*

94. Ibid., 164.48ff.

95. Ibid., 294.90; 191.6; 115.14ff.

96. Ibid., 136.26: *"dum scilicet, quod cogitamus, propriae significationis verbis explanare non possumus."* ["Namely, when we cannot explain what we are thinking in words that signify it properly."]

97. Ibid., 188; see also Van Elswijk, *Gilbert Porreta,* 252–60.

98. Gilbert, *Comm. Boeth.* 180.51.273.

99. Ibid., 87.

potest). Our concepts do not adequately correspond to their theological object. That is why the first question must always concern the exact meaning of the words in their own native science and the metaphysical-grammatical rules for transposing them for use in theology. It must always remain clear that we are dealing with figurative language, on the basis of a *"proportio communis,"* even and precisely when sacred Scripture itself makes use of such terms.[100] Theology becomes the doctrine of the *"nomina divina"* ["divine names"], which then must be standardized in their exact theological meaning: it becomes a scientific regulation of language, which then tries to encompass the whole doctrine of the faith argumentatively; it becomes *"argumentis probata fides catholica"* ["the Catholic faith proved by arguments"].[101]

The theology of Gilbert and the Porretan school is less euphoric in its use of dialectic than Abelard's; on the other hand it lacks the sapiential and spiritual character of the Victorines: it is instead the development of the linguistic side of discourse about God, carried out in textual studies, especially in commentary on sacred Scripture and Boethius. The authority of the Fathers of the Church remains unquestioned. The extent to which patristic arguments were valued is demonstrated by their research in the Greek Fathers down to Byzantium so as to corroborate their own controversial teaching on the Trinity.[102] Yet in this school authority is outranked by *ratio,* which is supposed to attain its goal in theology (the science superior to philosophy): *"veri nominis atque absoluta necessitas"* ["a necessity truly so called and absolute"] as the hallmark of the supreme science.

7 The textbook: The *Sentences* of Peter Lombard

The influence of one twelfth-century work of systematic theology outlasted that of all the others: the *Sententiae in IV libros distinctae* by Peter Lombard († 1160).[103] Various factors contributed to this phenomenon. Supplied with annotations and glosses early on, the *Sentences* enjoyed wide circulation from the early thirteenth century.[104] As is usual with textbooks,

100. Ibid., 57; Gilbert, *Comm. in Ep. Pauli* f.164v (Nielsen, *Theology,* 135, n. 77).

101. Gilbert, *Comm. Boeth.* 342.

102. See Häring, *Zwettler Summe,* 7; Sturlese, *Philosophie,* 143–56.

103. Critical edition: *Petrus Lombardus, Sententiae in IV libris distinctae* (Spicilegium Bonaventurianum 4/5) (Grottaferrata 1971/81). On the work and its influence see esp. I, 1 Prolegomena. Concerning Peter Lombard's theology as a whole: Colish, *Peter Lombard.*

104. See Lottin, "Premier commentaire," 64–71; Landgraf, "Drei Zweige"; Landgraf, "Sentenzenglossen"; for an overview, see Landgraf, *Einführung,* 93–109.

excerpts and abridgments are produced for use in school.[105] Thanks to the organization of the universities, a two-year lecture on Lombard, who is called the *Magister* for short, became obligatory for every *baccalaureus sententiarius* if he wanted to complete a master's degree. From then on commentaries on the *Sentences* were the most important sources of systematic theology, and this remained the case well into the sixteenth century. Then Alexander of Hales († 1245), even while functioning as *Magister actu regens* (1223–1227) still based his ordinary lectures not on a biblical text, as was the custom, but on the *Sentences* of Peter Lombard: a procedure that would set an academic precedent.[106] Yet initially the prospects of this theology were by no means that splendid; for like Gilbert and Abelard, Peter Lombard too had to endure the accusation of heresy.[107] However, the later bishop of Paris was expressly named by the Fourth Lateran Council (1215) as the source of orthodox teaching.[108] Besides the *Sentences* the most important extant works by Lombard are remarkable glosses on the Psalms and the Letters of St. Paul.

If we look at the work of the *"Magister Sententiarum,"* his great influence on future generations may at first seem surprising. It is by no means a very original or stylistically impressive work. It is very much in keeping with the summas of sentences compiled by followers of the school of Abelard and St. Victor. In the prologue the Lombard clearly states that he intended his work, written 1155–1158, to continue in the line of the early Scholastic collections of sentences. It is composed *"ex testimoniis veritatis in aeternum fundatis"* ["of testimonies of truth that are well-founded for all eternity"] and contains *"majorum exempla doctrinamque"* ["the examples and teachings of our ancestors"], in other words, it is not so much his own teaching as that of the Fathers that the reader finds in this supposedly little work. This should make it unnecessary to consult the numerous works of the Fathers individually: abbreviation and substitution as an encyclopedic principle for theology are clearly evident here.[109] But that also states precisely the purpose of this future textbook: to become the sole foundation for theology and to replace all other books (eventually even the Bible in coursework). The material, how-

105. Details in Landgraf, *Einführung*, 96–98.

106. See Petrus Lombardus, *Sent.* I, 1.117*–18; an indispensable reference work with regard to commentaries on the *Sentences* is Stegmüller, *Repertorium commentariorum*.

107. See de Ghellinck, *Mouvement*, 250–67.

108. DH No. 804.

109. Petrus Lombardus, *Sent.*, prol. n. 4f (I, 2.4.14–26).

ever, is quoted from the Fathers, who are immediately set up as authorities, and what the *Magister* himself says in addition should never stray *"a paternis limitibus"* ["from within the patristic boundaries"]. The immediate goal of the work is to explain the Catholic faith against all errors and heresies, as emphasized in the prologue, which as a whole is strongly apologetic.[110]

The Lombard's collection of sentences is a systematic collection; as we have seen, it is not organized exclusively along the lines of salvation history, nor is its basic schema purely conceptual; rather, it is a mixed form incorporating both possibilities. This very feature would fructify the theological work of the subsequent era: striking a balance between the biblical narrative approach and the claim to pursue systematic theology. In this the Lombard relies above all on the *Summa Sententiarum,* which for its part stands midway between Hugh of St. Victor and Abelard. Hugh's *De sacramentis* and Abelard's *Theologia Scholarium* and the *Summa Sententiarum* are Peter Lombard's immediate sources, as well as Ivo of Chartres and the *Decretum Gratiani.* In executing the plan, the *Magister* also cites his own glosses on the Pauline Letters and the Psalms and the *Glossa ordinaria.*[111] Augustine leads the patristic citations with approximately 950 passages. He is cited twice as often as all the other Church Fathers combined.[112] Especially remarkable among the Eastern Fathers of the Church is the early use of John Damascene († ca. 750); Pope Eugene III (1145–1153) had his work *De fide orthodoxa* translated into Latin by Burgundio of Pisa.[113]

The Lombard's theology as a whole, too, stands somewhere between Hugh of St. Victor and Abelard. He had studied in both schools before he became *magister* and *canonicus* at Notre Dame. He has the logical acuity of Abelard but in many instances also criticizes his position and takes up a contrasting one.[114] His logical training is already clear now in his theological system, which does not follow Abelard's schema *"fides—caritas—sacramentum"* but rather Augustine's schema of *"res—signa"* or *"uti—frui."* By repeatedly going through the contents of the OT and NT, the *Magister* produces the divisions of this schema. This outline still refers to Scripture itself, the *"forma praescripta in doctrina"* ["the prescribed form in (matters of) doctrine"], which exists prior to systematic speculation *("speculatio studiosa atque modesta").*[115] The decisive thing, at any rate, is that devising a system

110. Ibid. (4.15–20).
111. Ibid., Prolegomenon (1.1.118*–122*).
112. See Baltzer, *Sentenzen,* 2–12.
113. Colish, *Peter Lombard,* 22.
114. See Luscombe, *School,* 261–80.
115. Petrus Lombardus, *I Sent.* d.1 c.1 n.1f (I, 55.5–23).

and thus theology is a human activity. Systematic theology has not yet been completely separated from scriptural exegesis; that is precisely what would occur then as a result of commentaries on the *Sentences* of Peter Lombard.

Balance, caution, and a somewhat conservative approach characterize the Lombard's understanding of thology and his individual treatises as well. Already in the prologue he cites Hilary at length in opposition to those "sons of unbelief" who do not subject their intentions to *ratio* nor busy themselves with the *studium doctrinae* but try to support their dreams with words of wisdom. They do not follow the *"ratio veri"* ["reason of what is true"] but rather the *"ratio placiti"* ["reason of what is pleasing"]: their question and the basis for their arguments is not what is true, but rather whether it suits them. That is why their goal is not the defense of truth but rather their own notions; they want to teach these instead of the truth, adapting their doctrine to their desires. The Lombard evidently sees in his own time the same things that Hilary rebuked in his day: the debate between the solid presentation of theological truth and the defense of one's own ideas.[116] There is no need to underscore the fact that the *Magister* advocates the explanation of objective truth. It is remarkable, however, that with this citation he imputes moral defects to his opponents, yet emphasizes at the same time that an orientation to reason and continual study are apt to lead to the *"intelligentia veritatis"* ["understanding of truth"]. By no means, therefore, does he rebuke his opponents for studying too much and placing their trust in reason; rather, he is diagnosing a deficiency, or a wrong use of it.

Accordingly, the method of theology is first of all the clear, reasonable presentation of Church doctrine; the Lombard makes this point by quoting a methodological reflection on the doctrine of the Trinity from the works of Fulgentius of Ruspe (as cited by Augustine).[117] The first consideration is scriptural authority, *"auctoritates sanctarum Scripturarum."* From these texts one must prove *(demonstrandum)* what the Church's deposit of faith is. The contents of the faith are not to be proved by rational arguments, but rather to be corroborated by scriptural proof, *"utrum ita se fides habeat"* ["whether the faith understands itself thus"]. Only in the second step does *ratio* come into play, and with a clearly polemical tendency: the *"garruli ratiocinatores"* ["long-winded reasoners"] are accused of both ignorance and conceit; one must confront them with their own methods: arguments from reason and

116. *Sent.* prol. n.3 (3.16–4.10).

117. *I Sent* d.2 c.3 (I, 63.9–17): *"Quis ordo servandus sit cum de Trinitate agitur."* ["What order is to be preserved when it is a question of the Trinity."] See also de Ghellinck, *Mouvement,* 229–49.

"similitudines" (analogies), thus along the lines of an Abelard or a Gilbert. Yet the *Magister* himself specifies attributes for both of these methods of proof that are quite significant: a passage written by the Lombard states that the arguments from reason must be Catholic and the analogies must fit! Only in this way can one satisfy the opponents' philosophical demands. The *"mansueti"* [literally: "those who have been tamed"], in contrast, will be more perfectly instructed about the contents of the faith in this way; those who still cannot find what they are seeking, though, should sooner complain about their state of mind than about the truth or the systematic presentation of theology. Thus the methodological standard that is applied here to theology is just as clear as its strictly ecclesiastical character: founded on the ultimate authority of sacred Scripture, theology has to explain the contents of the faith in arguments from reason that are proven to be Catholic and in fitting analogies, in such manner that believers are led to a deeper understanding, whereas opponents will have no excuse left but their inability to understand it.

This programmatic statement in the middle of a dry textbook calls for theology, according to the understanding of the time, to be a scientific justification of the Church's faith (*"de ea quae est in nobis fide* [...] *rationem reddere"* ["to give a reason for that faith which is ours"]).[118] Uniting scientific rigor (still viewed here in the tension between *auctoritas* and *ratio*) and ecclesial character now becomes the program of a theology of the *via media* ["middle path"], which is based substantially on Peter Lombard and paves the way for him to enter into the curriculum of the thirteenth-century universities.[119]

8 Axiomatic theology

The attempts to establish theology as a science in the strict sense lead to the adoption of general scientific procedures in theology. This development is advanced the farthest in the thoroughgoing axiomatic approach to theology in the works of Alan of Lille [Alanus ab Insulis] (ca. 1120–1202) and Nicholas of Amiens. The two scholars take different models of the axiomatic method, however: Alan follows Boethius, *De hebdomadibus,* while Nicholas bases his work on Euclid.[120]

118. Concerning this medieval reading of 1 Peter 3:15 as a program for theology, see de Ghellinck, *Mouvement,* 279–84.

119. Ibid., 267–77.

120. See Evans, "Axiomatic Method," 36–52; Dreyer, *More mathematicorum,* 142–70.

The *Regulae de sacra theologia* by Alan of Lille highlight from the very start the connection with the secular sciences: All sciences have at their own foundation certain *regulae* [rules], which also indicate the limits of the science in question; the *regulae* go by different names: in logic they are *maximae* (namely, *sententiae*), in rhetoric—*loci communes,* in ethics—general principles, in physics—aphorisms, in arithmetic—*porismata,* etc. Like all other sciences, theology too as the *"supercaelestis scientia"* has its foundational rules or axioms.[121] These are per se of higher rank than those of all the other sciences, but they are also more difficult to discover. With Gilbert Porreta, Alan attributes absolute and irrefutable necessity *(necessitas absoluta et irrefragabilis)* to the theological axioms in contrast to the foundations of the natural sciences, which are based only upon the customary course of nature.[122] It is not easy, however, to find theological axioms or to formulate them correctly. Someone who follows only the natural sciences will necessarily perceive them as riddles *(aenigmata)* or paradoxes, which seem to be illogical and are difficult to grasp. In fact Alan's *regulae* include quite paradoxical formulas, for example, "Only the monad [*monas*] is Alpha and Omega without Alpha and Omega" (rule 5), "God is the intelligible sphere whose midpoint is everywhere and whose circumference is nowhere" (rule 7). They are also described as *emblemata* (e.g., the image of the sphere) or *entymemata,* whereas Boethius calls them *hebdomades* (according to Alan equal in *dignitas* to the *axioma*). Because of their difficulty, however, they are not to be expected of beginners, but rather demand an audience that is already experienced in theology.[123] The axiomatic presentation of theology, therefore, is not a didactic method of handing it on, but rather the scientific proof of logical consistency and necessity, and incidentally also the proof of the scientific character of theology.

The axioms of theology, however, are for Alan unambiguously metaphysical propositions, the most general and fundamental of which reads: *"Monas est, qua quaelibet res est una,"* ["A monad is that by which any thing is one,"] whereby the *"supercaelestis unitas"* by definition means God and at the same time the strongly Neoplatonic provenance of this (Boethian) metaphysics is made clear. It is required that these first propositions be unprovable and self-evident, so that everyone agrees with them immediately

121. Alanus ab Insulis, Regulae de sacra theologia, prol. (PL 210.621 AB); see also Chenu, "Un essai"; see also Glorieux, "Somme"; Dreyer, *More mathematicorum,* 142–62.

122. Alanus ab Insulis, Regulae, prol. (621 C–622 A).

123. Ibid. (623 B).

upon hearing them. Yet the decisive thing is not people's agreement, since many theological axioms are widely known (e.g., that there must be one single principle for all things), while other strictly metaphysical propositions (e.g., that for everything that is utterly simple, being and essence are identical) are known only to a few. The foundational axioms of the *Regulae,* however, are of the latter sort. The Trinity is brought in at the third rule, "The Monad begets a Monad and turns the ardor (of love) back upon itself" (rule 3).[124] Even the abovecited rules show that in Alan's system not all the rules are unprovable axioms of the same order; instead the later ones are supposed to be derived from the earlier ones, which he does accomplish in the first steps. On the other hand, the constant logical deduction becomes difficult in the case of facts from salvation history such as the Incarnation. It is "substantiated" in rule 99 based on the threefold status of man, his *thesis* (original natural and rational state), from which he can "stand out" *(exstasis)* in two directions: upward to God in his *apotheosis* and downward to the beasts in his *hypothesis.* Now since the latter occurs, God leaves his status of *apotheosis* and empties himself to the point of *hypothesis.*[125] Finally, relatively simple dogmatic statements, for example, concerning Christ's agony (rule 105) are quoted and explained as axioms too.[126] Precisely in this section and in his teaching on the sacraments, where his approach is more like that of a conventional summa, Alan's attempt shows how difficult it is to harmonize a metaphysical system of axioms and a biblical "fact" from salvation history or the historical institutions of the Church in such a way as to construct a thoroughly demonstrative science from those elements.

That is exactly what Nicholas of Amiens claims to do in the title of his work *Ars fidei Catholicae,* which was written between 1187 and 1197: give a technically correct presentation of the Catholic faith.[127] Here technically correct means according to Euclid's rules for the axiomatic method, which were originally laid down for geometry. Already in the twelfth century, then, we are dealing with a *Theologia more geometrico demonstrata,* at least accord-

124. Ibid., reg.1–3 (623 A–625 A).

125. Ibid., reg. 99 (673 C–674 A). The three statuses lead to the derivation of two sorts of theology *(supercaelestis* or *apothetica* and *subcaelestis* or *hypothetica)* and of a *"naturalis philosophia quae circa terrena vertitur"* ["natural philosophy which deals with earthly things"] in the summa *"Quoniam homines"* I n.2: ed. Glorieux, "Somme," 121.

126. Alanus, Regulae, reg. 105 (677 C).

127. Edition: M. Dreyer, *Nikolaus von Amiens: Ars fidei catholiciae—Ein Beispielwerk axiomatischer Methode* (*BGPhThMA,* n.s., 37) (Münster, 1993); see also Dreyer, *More mathematicorum,* 162–70.

ing to the plan. Axioms, definitions *(descriptiones)* and postulates *(petitiones)* are the basic scaffolding with which Nicholas begins his presentation (book 1: doctrine on God and the Trinity; book 2: creation of the world, the angels and men, freedom; book 3: Incarnation and redemption; book 4: the sacraments; book 5: eschatology). The definitions of cause, substance, matter, form, quality, accident, distinction and what is distinguished, movement, actuality, name and verb, number, are generally valid for all the parts (definitions are occasionally supplied subsequently in the later books). The three postulates say:

1. The cause of everything composite is the composer.
2. With reference to causes, an infinite regression is ruled out.
3. To the qualities of the causes of what is created, which themselves are not caused, belong their effects as well; thus for example God's goodness is declared on the basis of its causality and effect.[128]

Then there are seven additional generally valid axioms *(communes conceptiones)*:

1. Everything has being from that cause which brought its cause into being.
2. Every cause is temporally prior to and of a higher rank than what is caused by it.
3. Something is not at the same time prior, nobler or higher than itself.
4. If someone greater owns someone lesser, then the lesser is bound to place himself and all that he has in the service of the honor and the will of the greater.
5. Anyone who commits injustice deserves the greater punishment, the higher the rank of the one who was wronged.
6. Reparation is to be measured according to the rank of the one against whom a sin is committed.
7. What is heard moves the soul intensely, but what one has seen moves it most intensely.[129]

As one might easily suppose, the first three axioms pertain to the doctrine about God and creation, while the satisfaction theory of Anselm of Canterbury, for example, can be derived from axioms 4–6 and the doctrine of the sacraments follows from axiom 7. In contrast to the axiomatic system

128. Nikolaus of Amiens, *Ars* (ed. Dreyer 77.15–79.4).
129. Ibid. (ed. Dreyer 79.5–18).

of Alan of Lille, however, Nicholas carries out the logical deduction thoroughly, stating the axioms, definitions and postulates used in each case. Usually the proof concludes with: *"Et sic patet propositum,"* that is, the formerly unproven proposition that was merely assumed to be true has now been proved from the postulates. These postulates, however, are of a quite different sort. Not one of them is genuinely theological; axioms 1–3 are metaphysical propositions from the (Platonist) doctrine of causes, axioms 4–6 are rules of justice in medieval society, and finally, axiom 7 can most readily be appealed to as a generalized experience from everyday life. Whereas these axioms are valid for all the books, in the later books the necessary definitions are given explicitly, for instance the definitions of good, evil, useful, love, justice, merit, demerit, humility, mercy, glory, grace, and satisfaction for sin in book 2, and the definitions of sermon, sacrament, Baptism, Eucharist, Matrimony, Penance, the consecration of basilicas, anointing with chrism and oil, and Church in book 4. The axioms are applied to the theological questions, which are thus developed terminologically, but this gives rise precisely to the *"ars catholicae fidei"* ["art of the Catholic faith"]. For every technically correct presentation consists of definitions, distinctions, and propositions, which in a rigorous, logical sequence prove the propositions that are assumed hypothetically.[130] This method of *"probabiles fidei nostrae rationes"* ["plausible reasons for our faith"], becomes necessary however for Nicholas' apologetic purpose of providing an exposition of the faith that can lead Muslims, Jews, and heretics to the faith also, although it cannot ultimately prove the faith and thereby replace it.[131]

Nicholas, unlike Alan, cites not only metaphysical axioms but also principles of social justice and even of everyday experience, and his point of departure is Euclid's universal method instead of Boethius' Neoplatonic metaphysics; in this way he is spared the methodological gaps that Alan has to tolerate when he introduces salvation history and sacramental theology into his axiomatic system. The nontheological axioms of this theology, however, reveal the full significance of Nicholas of Amiens' undertaking: it is not about a technically correct exposition of theology as a learned, quasi-mathematical game or the reduction of faith to proved knowledge; instead

130. Ibid. (ed. Dreyer 77.13–15): *"Nempe editionem hanc artem fidei catholicae merito appello. In modum enim artis composita diffinitiones, divisiones continet, et propositiones artificioso processu propositum comprobantes."* ["Certainly, I call this exposition the art of the Catholic faith, and rightly so. For it is composed in the manner of an art and contains definitions and divisions and propositions that prove what is proposed by a skillful/systematic process."]

131. Ibid. (ed. Dreyer 76. 5–22).

it is about the scientific proof of the rationality of the contents of the faith, on the basis of metaphysics, social philosophy, and everyday experience.

9 Towards a standard theological language

In the late twelfth century theologians begin to sketch syntheses of the existing schools that join together the linguistic-grammatical, logical, biblical, metaphysical, and partially axiomatic approaches. Typical of these are the influential systematic works of Peter of Poitiers (ca. 1130–1205) and Praepositinus of Cremona (ca. 1150–1210).

Peter of Poitiers was a student of Peter Lombard and taught in Paris from 1167 to 1193. His most important work consists of the *Sententiarum libri quinque,* written before 1170/76.[132] If we compare the two collections of sentences, however, the striking difference is immediately apparent: besides traditional sentences, Peter of Poitiers discusses at great length the suitability of theological terms, sometimes new vocabulary that he himself introduces. Thus the affirmation of God's existence is immediately followed by a linguistic-critical reflection on distinguishing the words that are predicated of God and on their modes of expression (book 1, chapter 2). This systematic exposition in five books (Trinity, The Fall, Restoration through virtues, Restoration through the Incarnation, and Restoration through the Sacraments) is still understood as an introduction to sacred Scripture. It intends to present the *"disputabilia sacre pagine"* ["debatable points of Sacred Scripture"] in an orderly way *("in serie")* for beginners. The effort to systematize and the question technique are combined with a clear awareness of the linguistic execution of theology [*des sprachlichen Vollzugs von Theologie*].[133] In doing so Peter is undertaking a *"modesta inquisitio,"* thus indicating that he wishes to avoid all useless or ridiculous questions that are not genuinely theological.[134]

His method is first and foremost to make precise linguistic-logical distinctions, as is the heritage of the schools of Abelard and of the Porretans:

132. *Sententiae Petri Pictaviensis,* ed. Philip S. Moore and Marthe Doulong, vol. 1 (Publications in Medieval Studies 7) (Notre Dame, Ind., 1961); vol. 2 (Publications in Medieval Studies 11) (Notre Dame, Ind., 1950). See Moore, *Works.* This Petrus Pictaviensis should be distinguished from the Porretan who taught in Vienna, Magister Petrus, who is sometimes identified as the author of the "Zwettler Summa," and from a canon regular of St. Victor by the same name; see also Häring, *Zwettler Summe,* 3; Landgraf, *Einführung,* 105–9. Sturlese, *Philosophie,* 145–56.

133. See Petrus Pictaviensis, *Sent.* prol. (I, 1.15–2.35).

134. Ibid., Introduction XII*.

"Distingue, distinguenda est h[a]ec, non est danda sine distinctione," etc., we read again and again, especially where conflicting authorities must be harmonized. The first thing that a theologian has to learn, therefore, before tackling sacred Scripture, is a precise theological terminology, a standard theological language one might say, for without it one cannot understand anything at all about theological questions, in Peter's opinion. *"Nam ignorata virtute nominum et verborum, necesse est nihil eorum intelligi, quae hoc inquirantur."* ["For if one has overlooked the force of the nouns and verbs, then one will inevitably understand nothing of what is being sought thereby."][135] Thus immediately in the second chapter of book 1 he distinguishes nine word types or ways of using terms with reference to God:[136]

1. Designations of essence: *essentia, divinitas* [essence, divinity];
2. Designations of essence but sometimes also of Persons: *potentia, sapientia, bonitas* [power, wisdom, goodness];
3. Expressions of relation without reference: *simile, aequale* [like, equal];
4. Expressions of relation with reference: *pater, filius* [Father, Son];
5. Collective expressions for all the Persons together: *Trinitas.*
6. Expressions of relations involving all the Persons with respect to creatures: Creator, *Dominus* [Lord].
7. Expressions of temporal relations involving individual Persons with respect to creatures: *missus* [the One sent];
8. Temporal expressions of a non-relational sort: *Incarnatus, humanatus* [the One who was made flesh, became man];
9. Metaphorical expressions: *agnus, leo, character* [Lamb, Lion, character or spiritual mark (in sacramental theology)].

Making linguistic and terminological distinctions is combined in Peter's work with a didactic method that attaches great importance to precision and transparency. All nine word types are illustrated. Furthermore he has his students prepare schematic drawings *(figura)* that are also included in his work.[137]

A similar concept of theology forms the basis of the summa *"Qui producit ventos"* by Praepositinus of Cremona, who taught in Paris at the same

135. Ibid., PL 211.981 C.

136. Ibid., I, 2 (I, 11.25–43).

137. Ibid., I, 15 (I, 153) concerning predestination and reprobation; I, 22 (I, 193) on distinguishing among the Persons of the Trinity; I, 30 (I, 240) on the relation of the procession of the Holy Spirit from the Father and the Son; Alberich of Trois-Fontaines testifies that this didactic method was apparently an exceptional phenomenon: Introduction, xxi.

time as Peter of Poitiers and Alan of Lille and succeeded the former as chancellor of Paris. His approach is even closer than Peter's to the axiomatic method of Alan and the linguistic logic of the Porretan school; he begins the first book of his summa fully aware of the necessity for neat terminology: *"E vocabulis igitur qu[a]e de Deo dicuntur incipiamus."* ["Let us begin therefore with the terms that are predicated of God."][138] In contrast to Peter, Praepositinus now presents in detail the grammatical and syntactical rules that are supposed to make precise discourse about the relations in God possible. We are dealing therefore with the sketch of a theological grammar. First the required or available words are classified:

1. Words that are spoken without reference to time (*"ab aeterno,"* e.g., *Deus bonus, Deus justus*),
2. Words that are spoken with a temporal connotation (*"ex tempore,"* e.g., *Creator, refugium, Dominus*),
3. Words that are spoke about all three Persons and each one individually (e.g., *Deus*),
4. Words that are spoken about all three Persons together, but not about each individually (e.g., *Trinitas*),
5. Words that are spoken only about two Persons (e.g., *principium Spiritus Sancti* [the principle from which the Holy Spirit proceeds]),
6. Words that are spoken about only one Person (e.g., *Pater, Filius, Spiritus Sanctus*),
7. As for their grammatical classification, they are *nomina* ("names" = nouns and adjectives), verbs and participles.
8. In the case of the adjectives, it should also be considered whether they connote a division (e.g., *unus* [one]) or not (e.g., *bonus* [good]), whether they are single predicates (e.g., *aeternus*) or relational expressions (e.g., *coaeternus, coaequalis*) with reference to another Person or a third party (e.g., *prescius* [prescient]).[139]

Detailed rules for this vocabulary are now stated that define the meaning of a given term in theological usage:

1. All words that are spoken referentially about all three Persons and each one individually designate the divine essence, except for adjectives that connote a division.

138. Präpositinus, *Summa "Qui producit ventos"* I, 1 (ed. Angelini, *Ortodossia,* 197.1).
139. Ibid., (199.2–16).

2. Verbs, participles, and adjectives that connote a relation of Persons to one another are predicated in the plural of the three Persons together (e.g., *potentes omnia* [able to do all things], *coaeterni).*
3. Nouns that designate the divine essence are predicated in the singular of the three Persons (e.g., *Deus*).
4. Adjectives that express no relation of one Person to another have the same meaning when they are predicated in the plural of the three Persons (e.g., *"Pater et Filius et Spiritus Sanctus sunt aeterni"* [". . . are eternal"]).
5. In connection with Persons, adjectives that connote a division (e.g., *unus, aliquis, distinctus* [one, someone, distinct]) connote (in the [Latin] masculine or feminine gender) a distinction (e.g., *"Pater est unus, Filius est alius, Pater et Filius sunt duo"* ["The Father is one, the Son is another, the Father and the Son are two"]). In connection with nouns that designate the divine essence, they also designate the essence (e.g., *"Pater est unus Deus, Pater et Filius sunt una essentia"* ["The Father is one God; the Father and the Son are one essence"]); in the neuter gender they likewise designate the essence (e.g., *"Pater et Filius sunt unum"* ["The Father and the Son are one"]).
6. The noun *"persona"* designates the distinction, answers the question *"quid tres?"* ["three what?"] and in the plural is used collectively for all three Persons.[140]

The rules are not laid down here according to the axiomatic method, however, but rather emerge from a sometimes tedious disputation of the pro and con of patristic authorities and contemporary opinions, whereby the author is clearly aware of the constant possibility of false conclusions based on imprecise word usage *(fallaciae).*[141] Such terminological work presupposes, however, a previous knowledge about the contents of the faith as it is proposed by the Church. The object of discussion for theology is not that but rather the adequacy of human discourse in explaining it. A logical analysis of Praepositinus' procedure shows that the contents of the faith as formulated by the Church (whenever possible in standard language) can be expressed as axioms and in that form are the precondition for the whole discussion about the adequacy of the formulation. For example, the fundamental axioms for the doctrine of the Trinity are:[142]

140. Summary with citations: Angelini, *Ortodossia,* 21.

141. On the influence of the *Sophistici Elenchi* and on the beginnings of the *Logica Modernorum,* Angelini, *Ortodossia,* 108.

142. Ibid., 35, for synopsis.

1. The Father (Son, Holy Ghost) is God.
2. Father, Son, and Holy God are one God.
3. Father, Son, and Holy Ghost are three Persons.
4. The essence is Person (Father, Son, and Holy Spirit). [*Das Wesen ist Person . . .*]
5. God is (by his essence), is mighty (through his might), etc.
6. God is simple, eternal, unchanging, perfect, etc.
7. God is his essence, his might, etc.
8. The Father begets the Son; the Son is begotten by the Father; the Father and the Son breathe forth the Holy Spirit; the Holy Spirit proceeds from the Father and the Son.
9. The Father gives being to the Son by begetting; the Father and the Son give being to the Holy Spirit by breathing forth.
10. The Father is fatherhood *(paternitas),* and so on for the other Persons.

Thus Praepositinus does not stop at a vague axiomatic approach consisting of propositions that are not further reducible, but rather seeks to work out the necessary terminological precision for the axioms and all the statements derived from them. This procedure distinguishes his writings from the axiomatic method of Alan of Lille and Nicholas of Amiens. Now conclusions are drawn from axioms that are really theological. Theology has become a specialized science that intends to be sure of itself. Praepositinus is concerned not primarily with a metaphysical or rational-experiential justification of theology, but rather with its activity as an academic, scientific and ecclesial discipline: How can we produce a linguistically precise, correct, consistent, and at the same time ecclesiastically accepted theology by means of speculative grammar and the Aristotelian logic that is now widespread (especially using the *Topics* and the *Sophistici Elenchi*)?[143]

10 Scholastic and monastic theology

The development of "academic" theology in the schools of the twelfth century, which had already reached the stage of self-assurance with Praepositinus, was accompanied by theological currents that have been mentioned only incidentally thus far and since the study by J. Leclercq have been grouped under the general heading of "monastic theology."[144] While

143. Ibid., 107–11; Kobusch, "Grammatica speculativa."

144. See esp. Leclercq, *Wissenschaft,* and his extensive bibliography; for the contrast see also Quinto, *Scholastica,* 52–56.

it is correct to assume that the twelfth-century monastic orders and reform movements had an independent theological tradition, it is an oversimplification to contrast monastic and Scholastic theology. For Anselm of Canterbury was a monk, as was Abelard for a time; Hugh of St. Victor was a reformed canon regular; Alan of Lille, one of the most clearly defined Scholastics, became a Cistercian. On the other hand, figures such as Bernard of Clairvaux, Peter Damian, Rupert of Deutz (1075/80–1129/30) and Gerhoh of Reichersberg certainly were not part of the movement of genuine Scholastic theology but rather grappled with it more or less competently.

The cloistered life and life at institutions of higher education were different and to some extent incompatible, and not just in the twelfth century. Yet a Benedictine monastery was understood to be precisely a "school for the service of the Lord" *(dominici schola servitii),* certainly a school where in-depth study of the faith is embedded in a personal search for God and collective action for the praise of God.[145] The monastic school for interns is also included in this way of life and is thus clearly distinguished from the city or cathedral school that is populated by nonresident teachers and scholars. The Premonstratensian Philip of Harvengt († 1183), who himself had a Scholastic education, is one witness who mentions liturgy, prayer, silence, weeping, and *lectio divina* as the basic elements of cloistered life as opposed to the "tumult of secular schooling" (Laon and Paris being the prime examples).[146] Petrus Comestor sharply contrasts the *"claustrales,"* who devote themselves more to prayer than to *lectio* (in the technical sense), with the *"scholares,"* who spend all their time on *lectio* and have little left for prayer.[147]

Naturally it is easy, from the superior vantage point of one's own piety, to complain about or inveigh against the uselessness of Scholastic, academic theology and to rate *"sancta simplicitas"* higher than worldly *"curiositas."*[148] Nevertheless, what differentiates the two ways of life and the sorts of theologizing connected with them are the purpose, the methods and the oral and literary forms of their respective theologies. In monastic theology the purpose is to advance personally in the faith, to edify others, who often share the same way of life, or to defend against false teachings or harmful influences. Therefore in his scriptural exegesis Bernard of Clairvaux relates monastic theology to his own *experience* and thereby differentiates it from technical, scientific exegesis:

145. *Regula Benedicti,* Prologue 45 (CSEL 75.8).
146. Philipp von Harvengt, *Ep.* 7 (PL 203.58).
147. Petrus Comestor, *Sermo* IX (PL 198.1747).
148. See, for example, Petrus Damiani, *De sancta simplicitate* (PL 145.695–703).

As for us, we wish to proceed with caution and simplicity in commenting on these mystical and holy words. Let us conduct ourselves as does sacred Scripture, which interprets the wisdom hidden in the mystery with words that are our own; when it speaks to us about God, it depicts him with the help of our own feelings and sentiments. Scripture makes the invisible and hidden reality of God, which is of such exalted worth, accessible to the human mind, as though in vessels of little value that are taken from the reality known to us through the senses.[149]

The ordering of theology to cloistered life, liturgy, and prayer[150] makes the cloistered schools the home of symbolic-experiential scriptural exegesis, as it is practiced preeminently in the school of St. Victor but also in the poems that Alan of Lille wrote in the monastic tradition. Indeed, stylistic elegance and poetry are found in the cloisters and not in Scholastic collections of sentences: the poetic works of wandering scholars (and *magistri*) cannot be compared with it.[151] Again, the allegorical, tropological, and anagogical interpretation of Scripture (sometimes apart from Scholastic schemata) is cultivated above all in the tradition of the cloistered schools, and this gives rise to a *"théologie symbolique."*[152] The monastic tradition of spiritual exegesis and scholastic learning interpenetrate in the best examples of this genre, which often refer to the symbolism even in the title: for example, Richard of St. Victor's *Benjamin major* and *Benjamin minor;* Hugh of St. Victor's *De arca Noe morali* and *De arca Noe mystica.* Such works often originate from the *collationes,* spiritual-ascetical lectures for the confreres or conversations with them. Hugh, for example, shows them in the story of Noah's ark the whole structure of the Church, Christ, and the spiritual life. The ark moreover is depicted or construed in a downright symbolic way as a *figura* (image for meditation); in much the same way Adam of Dryburgh (Adamus Scotus, † 1212) paints a panorama of the whole world.[153] Among the Victorines in particular, however, the symbolic interpretation always has its foundation in the exact interpretation of the literal sense *(littera).* Since every part in the *figura* is important for the symbolic reading, this leads to questions and different interpretations, for example, in the treatise *De tri-*

149. Bernard of Clairvaux, *Super Cant.* 74.2 (*S. Bernardi Opera.* II, Roma, 1958, 240.16–22).

150. Bernard of Clairvaux, *De consid.* V, 32 (III, 493.24–25): *"at orando forte quam disputando dignius quaeritur et invenitur facilius."* ["But He is sought more worthily and found more easily by praying hard than by debating."]

151. See Leclercq, *Wissenschaft,* 260–75.

152. See esp. Chenu, *Théologie au XII,* 159–209.

153. Hugh of St. Victor, *De arca Noe mystica* (PL 176, 681–684); Adamus Scotus, *De tripartito tabernaculo* p. 2 (PL 198, 683–744); see also Sicard, *Diagrammes.* A remarkable reaction to Hugh is expressed in Smalley, *Study,* 96: "Oh yes! we think of the Kindergarten."

partito tabernaculo by the Premonstratensian Adamus Scotus in response to an extremely detailed inquiry from John of Kelso (ca. 1175) concerning Exodus 25–27, for example about the location and significance of the sixth tent curtain (Exodus 26:9) or of the bronze grating or network at the altar (Exodus 27:4).[154]

Remarkably, the historical sense that appears here is strongly connected with monastic theology. Whereas the theologians of the cathedral and state schools generally do not develop much of a sense of history, the historical foundations of the way of life in a specific cloister always provide an incentive to grapple with one's own past.[155] Out of historiography (e.g., monastic chronicles), however, develops an interpretation of history or a theology of history, as is evident in Otto of Freising († 1153), for instance. Historiography, too, becomes a means of theological edification and self-examination; this is clearly the case with the Cluniac abbot Petrus Venerabilis († 1156), who in the prologue to *De miraculis* becomes angry "about the indifference of many people who distinguish themselves by their knowledge, love of literature and eloquence yet are too lazy to leave to their posterity written records of the wonderful works that the Almighty accomplishes again and again on earth to strengthen his Church."[156] Thus historiography is ordered to the Church, the praise of God and mutual edification, whether in the form of hagiography (which sometimes assumes the form of an ascetical sermon on the subject of a saintly figure),[157] or in the form of a monastic, ecclesiastical, or secular chronicle. Such documents exhibit all possible combinations of theological intention, critical sense and belief in miracles, sometimes even in the defense of manifestly material interests.[158] Replaceable parts, like the sentences of the *magistri,* are carried over from one saint's life to the next, which in some instances is composed for a definite purpose, for instance to achieve the exaltation of the relics or canonization.[159]

Monastic theology most often regards itself in its existential setting as superior to Scholastic theology. Authors, including Bernard of Clairvaux, are fond of differentiating their work from Scholasticism by citing Jerome's remark that the monk has the *"officium lugendi"* ["duty of mourning"] and

154. PL 198.609–792; see also Chenu, *Théologie au XII,* 192–96; Leinsle, "Charitati militare," 9–10.
155. See Leclercq, *Wissenschaft,* 174–89.
156. Petrus Venerabilis, *De miraculis,* prol. (PL 189.907).
157. See, for example, the *Vita Siardi* (ed. Lamboij and Mol, *Vitae Abbatum,* 242–349; 43–51).
158. Examples in Leclercq, *Wissenschaft,* 179–82.
159. Examples in Leclercq, *Wissenschaft,* 186–87; Heffernan, *Sacred Biography.*

not the *"officium docendi"* ["duty of teaching"].[160] The excesses of the Scholastic enterprise and the personal conduct of *magistri* and *scholares* could provide welcome grounds for pious aloofness, as when Stephen of Tournai (1135–1203) wrote to the Pope: "The students are no longer interested in anything but what is new. The *magistri,* who loved their reputation above all else, compose new summas every day and new theological works that please the listeners and deceive them, as though the writings of the Fathers who explained sacred Scripture were not enough."[161] If one must pursue theology, then it should not be as a science with the methods of dialectic terminology (*"profanae vocum novitates,"* 1 Tim 6:20), for that does not edify but only leads to pride (*"scientia inflat,"* 1 Cor 8:1). With such passages from the Bible people in many circles believed that they were armed against the Scholastic enterprise.[162] Yet the rejection of all Scholastic, academic theology is neither a universal nor a necessary characteristic of "monastic" or cloistered theology. The addition of religious community life, however, makes the theology advocated here an existential-experiential theology, a kind of wisdom (e.g., in the school of St. Victor) that can then be contrasted with mere science, as Bernard of Clairvaux programmatically maintains: "There (in the schools) we hear what wisdom teaches; here we receive it into ourselves. There we are taught, here—deeply moved. Instruction produces knowledgeable men, whereas association [in religious life] produces wise men. . . . There one arrives at wisdom; here one penetrates into it."[163]

11 Learned heresy

From Gottschalk via Berengar down to Gilbert Porreta and Peter Lombard we encounter again and again in the history of theology the accusation of heresy. Scholastic theology and heresy—contrary to all later protestations—seem to be very closely connected. In contrast to the popular religious movements and heresies of the twelfth century, we are dealing here with a learned, academically trained departure from the norm of Church

160. Hieronymus, *Contra Vigilantium* 15 (PL 23.351); Bernard of Clairvaux, *Sup. Cant.* 64.3 (II, 168.3–4); *Ep.* 89 (VII, 236.3–4).

161. Stephen of Tournai, *Ep.* 251 (PL 211.517).

162. See, for example, Petrus Damiani, *De sancta simplicitate scientiae inflanti anteponenda* (PL 145.695).

163. Bernard of Clairvaux, *Sup. Cant.* 23.14 (I, 147.22–148.13).

doctrine.[164] Proceedings against teachers are therefore different from those against popular heresies. The mistrust with which ecclesiastical and cloistered circles viewed the free schools and the theology pursued in them provided a fertile soil for the suspicion of heresy: "Contrary to hallowed precepts, they debate about the incomprehensible Godhead; flesh and blood argue with many words and without reverence about the Incarnation of the Word. They divide up the indivisible Trinity and demonstrate the differences within it. There are already as many errors as doctors, as many teachings as listeners, as many blasphemies as public places." So Stephen of Tournai, Abbot of Mont Ste. Geneviève in Paris, to Pope Innocent III (1198–1216).[165] On the other hand, the learned heresies (e.g., of Abelard and Gilbert Porreta) are not uncommonly accused of being esoteric doctrines.[166] A lack of understanding of Scholastic terminology or of the Porretan "standard language" and methods in broad sectors of the Church further contributed to the suspicion of heresy.

As this early Scholastic theology was taking shape, we observe at the same time the development of a formal and juridically exact concept of heresy.[167] The background for this was the Gregorian reform along with the development of the papal primacy of jurisdiction. In this trend the concept of heresy, as found for instance in Gerhoh of Reichersberg and Peter Damian, applies only in a very restricted way to the learned heresy; above all it is a disciplinary measure aimed at departures from the *"Romana ecclesia": "hereticum esse constat qui Romane ecclesie non concordat,"* ["Anyone who does not agree with the Roman Church is recognized as a heretic,"] as Gregory VII put it (1073–1085).[168] This formula can then be applied to doctrinal deviations if one assumes that the Roman Church has always preserved the true faith; for unlike schism, heresy does not rend Church unity but rather the truth.[169] Only in this version can the reforming papacy's concept of heresy be applied to deviations in speculative theology, as Gerhoh's battle against Abelard and Gilbert's students proves. For him as a reformed canon regular,

164. See Fichtenau, *Ketzer;* Grundmann, *Religiöse Bewegungen;* Lambert, *Medieval Heresy;* Angenendt, *Religiosität,* 192–201.

165. *CUP* I, 48 n. 48.

166. See Abaelard, *Confessio fidei,* ed. Ch. S. Burnett, *Medieval Studies* 48 (1986): 132; Gaufred of Auxerre, Contra Capitula Gilberti c.1 (PL 185.595).

167. See esp. Lourdeaux and Verhelst, eds., *Concept of Hersesy;* Hageneder, *Häresiebegriff.*

168. Register of Gregory VIII (*MGH* Epist/4, VII, 25); see also Classen, *Häresiebegriff,* 31–32.

169. Thus Gerhoch von Reichersberg, *Liber de laude fidei,* (*Opera inedita,* Rom 1955/56, 1.254); von Reichersberg, *De investigatione Antichristi* I, 53 (MGH lib 3, 359–60); see also Beinert, *Kirche,* 368–80.

Scholasticism *(scholastice)* is the antithesis of ecclesiastical discipline *(ecclesiastice)*, with which doctrine is bound up. The *"scholae in Francia"* are the cradles of heresy and therefore contrary to the *"ecclesia Romana."*[170]

Bernard uses a substantially more interesting argument, from a formal perspective, in his polemic against Abelard and Gilbert.[171] On the one hand Bernard accuses Abelard of innovating in matters of faith: he says that a new faith is being set forth, that Abelard regards his *"novitates"* as superior to the faith and the doctrine of the Catholic Fathers; in short, that he is proclaiming a *"nova haeresis."*[172] This innovation is unmasked, however, as an old error, which goes back to the well-known heresies of the patristic era: Arianism in the doctrine on the Trinity, Pelagianism in the doctrine on grace, and Nestorianism in Christology.[173] This makes clear also the final judgment with which Bernard intervenes with Pope Innocent II (1130–1143) against Abelard: Whatever he says, deep down he is a heretic.[174] Heresy, though, is not simply an error in matters of faith that fallible human beings might make, but rather the adherence to error and the defense of it, after it has been pointed out that it is an error. Heresy therefore is not just a matter of the intellect but above all a matter of the will.[175] In Bernard's view this is precisely the case with Abelard, who despite the condemnation in Soissons in 1121 has not desisted from his errors but keeps producing new ones and arousing those that were sleeping concealed among the general public and thus is endangering the faith of the simple people.[176] Gilbert too is accused of innovation in the form of a distorted and obscure interpretation of the Trinity with which the Catholic Church cannot possibly agree.[177]

It is also typical of the twelfth century that the attacks against real and alleged heresies of the *magistri* originate with individual ecclesiastics. The papacy, at this stage in the development of its claim to universal jurisdic-

170. Gerhoch, *Dialogus* (MGH lib 3.227.235).

171. See Leclercq, *L'hérésie,* 12–26.

172. Bernard of Clairvaux, *Ep.* 190.26 (VIII, 38.16); 189.2–3 (VIII, 13–14); 192 (VIII, 43, 17–19); 190.2 (VIII, 18.25); 330 (VIII, 267.11–12).

173. Bernard of Clairvaux, *Ep.* 192 (VIII, 44.4–6): *"Cum de Trinitate loquitur, sapit Arium; cum de gratia, sapit Pelagium; cum de persona Christi, sapit Nestorium."* ["When he speaks of the Trinity, it smacks of Arius . . ."]. See *Ep.* 330–32 (VIII, 266–272); 336 (VIII, 276.1–4); 338.2 (VIII, 278.12–15).

174. Bernard of Clairvaux, *Ep.* 331 (VIII, 269.11–12): *"Monachum se exterius, haereticum interius ostendit."* ["He makes an outward show of being a monk, but inside he proves to be a heretic."]

175. Bernard of Clairvaux, *Ep.* 193 (VIII, 45.7–8): *"haereticum se probans, non tam in errore quam in pertinacia et defensione erroris."* [". . . proving that he is a heretic not so much in his error as in his obstinacy and defense of error."]

176. Bernard of Clairvaux, *Ep.* 331 (VIII, 269.15–270.4).

177. Bernard of Clairvaux, *Sup. Cant.* 80, 6–8 (II, 281–83).

tion, reacts only to accusations and very slowly. Trials of theologians are at first a local affair.[178] The Gottschalk case was still treated as a purely disciplinary matter. He was flogged in the presence of the Synod in Mainz in 848 and thrown into prison, where he nevertheless continued his theological work. The controversy with Berengar of Tours followed the procedures of synodal heresy trials, although even at that early date the reform papacy clearly participated. The synods or councils that passed judgment however were local ecclesiastical assemblies in Rome and Vercelli in 1050, in Paris (1050), in Tours (1054) and again in Rome (1059 and 1079). At the Lenten synod in Rome in 1059 it was explicitly noted that they had followed the procedure foreseen by the Council of Ephesus for the renunciation of heresy: Berengar must retract his erroneous teaching, affirm and subscribe to the creed that is presented to him and consign his writings to the fire by his own hand in the presence of the assembly.[179]

The proceeding against Abelard in Soissons in 1121 still followed essentially this same pattern: Abelard handed over his *Theologia Summi Boni* to the cardinal legate Cuno of Preneste (who served in that capacity from 1111–1121), who forwarded it to the Bishop of Rheims, who had jurisdiction. The latter had his theological advisors examine it. We have only Abelard's own account of this procedure, but the evident inability of the Church leadership to debate with highly educated *magistri* ultimately prompted the Church authorities to resort to the old disciplinary measures, as in the proceeding against Berengar.[180] In contrast, Bernard of Clairvaux and William of St. Thierry († 1148/49) prepared for the Synod of Sens (1140) with accusations against Abelard in letters and lists of errors.[181] Already in advance of the synodal proceeding Abelard objected to it in an *Apologia* and a *Confessio fidei*. The assembly in Sens was originally planned by Abelard as a debate with Bernard in the presence of other *magistri*. At the instigation of Bernard, however, it was to become a condemnation of a list of "errors" by the bishops of France. Abelard protested against this repurposing of a debate, appealed to Rome, left the synod and set out for the Eternal City. The interventions of his opponents were faster, however, and thus Innocent II condemned Abelard's teachings as a whole, imposed perpetual silence upon

178. See esp. Miethke, "Theologenprozesse."

179. See Bernold of St. Blasien, *De veritate*, ed. R. B. C. Huygens, "Bérenger de Tours, Lanfranc et Berold de Constance," *Sacris Erudiri* 16 (1965): 355–403, citation at 380.

180. Abaelard, *Historia Calamitatum*, ed. Monfrin, 82–89.

181. *Capitula haeresum Petri Abaelardi* (PL 182.1049–54); for further lists see Miethke, *Theologenprozesse*, 98, n. 60.

him, sentenced him to monastic house arrest and ordered his books to be burned. Given the haste of the proceeding and Abelard's later reconciliation with Rome, probably arranged by Petrus Venerabilis, it is not possible to say with certainty which teachings in particular were condemned.[182] Finally, the influence of the papacy was more clearly evident in the proceeding against Gilbert Porreta in the papal consistory at Rheims in 1148. The mere fact that Gilbert had a number of folio volumes containing patristic writings brought into the assembly room made it clear that a theological and not a disciplinary settlement of the dispute was called for. Contrary to Bernard's intervention, the consistory pronounced no unequivocal condemnation of Gilbert, but merely condemned an anonymous mediocre student work and had it torn to pieces.[183]

The exclusively local significance of the trials of theologians, the excessive demands upon the Church leadership in theological matters, but also the simplifying effect of polemics and "publicity" ensured that the effects of such condemnations would be relatively minor. Abelard's teachings were circulated precisely by means of the lists of errors.[184] One characteristic of theologian trials in the following period, however, would be to examine prepared lists of errors rather than the original writings. The consistory in Rheims was a prime example of a condemnation of "auditors' transcripts," and Gilbert's influence and the importance of his school were enhanced rather than diminished by it.

182. On the proceeding: Miethke, "Theologenprozesse," 96–102.
183. Ibid., 103–13.
184. See Luscombe, *School*, 103–42.

3 Theology as a Science at the University

Whereas twelfth-century theology was essentially characterized by the multiplicity of schools, the organization of the universities around the year 1200 and the widespread acceptance of the strict Aristotelian concept of science set forth in the *Posterior Analytics* placed theology as a body of knowledge in a new sociological and theoretical context: it had to maintain its place as a science within the university organization. Traditionally this passage of theology from an academic discipline to a university science is described as the transition from early to high Scholasticism.

1 The university as the home of theology

The university's understanding of its nature and mission and theology's claim to be a science were mutually dependent as they evolved. Therefore we will look first at the development of the first universities, their teaching activity, and the presentational forms that resulted from it.

1.1 University organization, teaching activity, and presentational forms

The early thirteenth century is characterized by the organization of a new scientific institution, the university.[1] Chronologically this began with the organizational forms of the Italian schools of Bologna and Salerno, which of course specialized in law or medicine respectively. Of paramount importance for theology was the corporate organization first of the *magistri* and later of the *scholares* in the various Parisian schools. We find the beginnings of this in the final decades of the twelfth century. Decisive steps in

1. On the history of the university see esp. Rashdall, *Universities;* Leff, *Paris;* Weijers, *Terminologie.*

this process included: the granting to the *magister* of authorization to teach (*licentia docendi*), dealing with the chancellor as the official ecclesiastical authority and with the city government of Paris as the municipal authority, the royal privilege of Philip II (1180–1233) dating back to 1200, and finally the university statutes of Chancellor Robert of Courson/Courçon (†1219) from the year 1215. Disputes, unrest, and strikes marked the development of the university in Paris in its struggle for independence from ecclesiastical oversight. For the University of Paris was still strongly influenced by the tradition of the cathedral school of Notre Dame, which (unlike Oxford) was ruled by a Church-appointed chancellor.[2] In contrast, at the end of the twelfth century in Oxford, located at a considerable distance from the see of the bishop of Lincoln who had jurisdiction, the various abbey schools gave rise to a *studium generale,* which in 1214 received papal approval from Innocent III.[3]

The university now defined the educational career of the future theologian also.[4] The student who enrolled in one of the "nations" [*nationes*] (in Paris there were four, in Oxford—three) at around the age of fifteen had to complete first the philosophical education institutionalized in the *facultas artium* [faculty of the arts] before he could be promoted to the "higher" faculties (theology, law, medicine). The relation between philosophy and theology was thus fixed also by the university: without philosophy no theology. After six years the scholar could become a *baccalaureus artium* [Bachelor of Arts]. As such he lectured on the classical texts under the direction of the *magister,* and upon concluding this *practicum* he obtained the *licentia docendi,* provided that he had reached the age of twenty-one. After what was usually a very short stint of teaching in philosophy he could then begin the study of theology (minimum age seventeen), and it took seven (later six) years to earn the baccalaureate.[5] The *baccalaureus biblicus* (minimum age twenty-five), after a solemn *principium* or *introitus,* lectured cursorily on the books of the Bible for one or more years as a *cursor.* Then as a *baccalaureus sententiarius* he spent two years under the supervision of a *magister* explaining the *Sentences* of Peter Lombard. With that he was a *baccalaureus formatus.* As such he had to participate in lectures and disputations and give

2. See Gabriel, "Conflict."

3. On the significant differences from the Parisian model (in the collegiate system, among other respects), see Leff, *Paris,* 75–115.

4. See Van Steenberghen, *Philosophie,* 81–83.

5. See Glorieux, "L'enseignement," and the bibliography therein.

sermons for four years in order to qualify as a *Magister* of Theology. After an examination of his university accomplishments by the *magistri* the *licentia docendi* was then conferred upon him, and after an evening disputation *(vesperies),* a commendatory speech on sacred Scripture and another disputation in the *Aula Episcopi* ("bishop's hall," hence called the *aulica*), as well as a disputation with four *magistri,* he was solemnly declared a *Magister;* as such he himself decided a disputation for the first time and now had to resolve the questions posed in the previous disputations explicitly in terms of his position *(resumptum).* The permanent exercise of his faculty to teach did not automatically go with the title. Therefore a *magister* who was actually a student teacher for a year in Paris was called a *magister actu regens.*[6]

As was already the case in the schools of the twelfth century, the forms of instruction were the *lectio, disputatio,* and *praedicatio* [reading, debate, sermon], which now, however, underwent institutional and formal developments. The *lectio* was still the central duty of the *magister,* especially the interpretation of the *sacra pagina,* that is, of a book from the Bible. These biblical lectures by the *magistri* became increasingly rare, though, over the course of the thirteenth century. Alexander of Hales lectured for the first time in Paris, even as a *magister,* on the *Sentences,* which in the course of training was actually the daily task of the *sententiarius.* The resulting *Commentaries on the Sentences* were, particularly after the *magistri* began to lecture on the *Sentences,* the most personal and most important Scholastic works that clarify the doctrinal development beyond the Lombard. As opposed to the auditor's transcript *(reportatio),* the lecture on the *Sentences* was then not infrequently published in a special *ordinatio* [outline of subjects treated] of the *magister* (or else as his own *scriptum*). In contrast, the cursory reading by the *baccalaureus biblicus* or *cursor* can be best compared to a sort of introductory lecture or "fundamental exegesis." In addition there were repetitions (sometimes called *collationes,* a term that can also mean spiritual talks, however).[7]

As a result of the institutionalization, similar variations arose in the area of the *disputatio,* especially the distinction between the ordinary disputation and the *disputatio de quolibet* [on an arbitrary subject]. The ordinary disputation was a matter for a *magister actu regens* in his school and his students. It took place in the afternoon between the canonical hours of none

6. See Glorieux, *Répertoire.*

7. Methodologically important is the precise investigation by Oliva, *Débuts,* 210–13, 225–52.

and vespers. The following morning the *magister* then held the sole lecture of the day. Students of other *magistri* could participate in such a disputation. *Baccalaurei* are obliged to do so a few times. In order to be a *sententiarius,* one must have collaborated at least twice as a respondent, once for a *magister* of another nation. The *baccalaureus formatus* himself could preside over a *quaestio tentativa* (as opposed to the *quaestio ordinaria* of the *magister*). Out of this orderly disputation developed the literary genre of the *quaestiones disputatae* (e.g., the *Q. d. de veritate* of Thomas Aquinas).

The *disputatio de quolibet* (also called *disputatio extraordinaria, quodlibetalis, quodlibetica*) reached its prime in the thirteenth century.[8] It originated institutionally around the time of the debates of 1229–1231 and at first was found chiefly in the schools of the mendicant orders. Usually during these solemn biannual disputations between fifteen and twenty questions were posed (although occasionally there were as many as thirty-four). The disputation was conducted in two steps: the discussion of the questions (the actual *disputatio*) on the first day and the *determinatio* of the *magister* on the next *dies legibilis* [day on which a lecture could be held]. Because of the free choice of questions, the *quaestiones de quolibet* always shed light on the pressing questions at the university and in society, but often too they discussed questions that sound purely "Scholastic," for example, in the *Quodlibets* of Henry of Ghent (ca. 1217–1293): whether the Holy Spirit would be distinguished from the Son by some relation if he did not proceed from him (V, 9 of 1280), or whether there is any temporal succession in eternity (V, 13). Many *magistri* made the *quodlibet* almost the main component of their literary activity (e.g., Henry of Ghent, Godfrey of Fontaines). In the late thirteenth and early fourteenth centuries, however, the main burden of work in the *quaestio de quolibet* was transferred to the *baccalaurei,* so that the disputations increasingly acquired an educational function and thereby diminished in theological value. At the same time there were also disputations of a more private sort, of which the *Sorbonica* at the Collège de Sorbonne in Paris was the most remarkable, since it assumed a permanent place in the curriculum.

We have already referred to the theological significance of the university sermons.[9] The sermon, which was attended by the members of the *universitas* as a community of ecclesial life, became the task of the *magistri* and

8. See Glorieux, *Littérature quodlibétique.*
9. See *Supra,* 1.2.7.

was firmly anchored in the program of formation, especially at the inaugural ceremonies for a new *magister* or *baccalaureus*. Furthermore the chancellor, too, had the right to speak during such ceremonies and to deliver a solemn discourse.

Besides these "major" literary forms in the university culture we find the minor ones, which were usually more common: collections of questions for the purposes of examination, indices *(margaritae)*, *florilegia*, college notebooks, concordances and abbreviations, which were substantially based on the technique of the twelfth century.[10]

1.2 The mendicant orders at the universities

At first glance it may seem paradoxical that the new religious orders—the Dominicans and the Franciscans, communities which were committed to renewing the Church in the spirit of the Gospel—became a part of this rigid, self-assured university organization that was usually striving for autonomy from the ecclesiastical authorities.[11] Yet precisely in the university cities this new "evangelical" movement found enthusiastic followers among the students and—remarkably—among the *magistri*. A conflict with the faculty of theology, which was staffed mainly by high-ranking secular clerics, was of course unavoidable. For the new orders brought with them to the university not only their own way of life and a strongly Bible-oriented tradition of teaching, but also a pronounced ecclesial sense. Moreover, they were directly subject to the pope and were regarded as his envoys to the university.

The Order of Preachers set out very early on the road to Paris, in keeping with its goal of training friars to preach and to debate, especially with the heretics in southern France. The first friars already arrived in Paris in 1217, and from 1218 on the university granted them residency in St. Jacques. Of course, the juridical questions about the corporate status of the local community remained unresolved at first. The place in question was a "House of Studies" sponsored by the univeristy, where university professors taught as well, for instance the "founder" of St. Jacques, John of Barastre († before 1240). We find similar circumstances in Oxford, where the first Dominicans took up residence in 1221.

The first Friars Minor came to Paris probably in the same year as the Dominicans, initially without any academic ambitions. Yet through their

10. See Grabmann, "Methoden"; Grabmann, "Hilfsmittel."
11. See esp. Berg, *Armut und Wissenschaft*.

intensive preaching activity and their way of life they soon gained influence in university circles. At first the Franciscans had no teacher of their own in their convent; by 1231, however, there is evidence that Haymo of Faversham († 1243/44) was lecturing the Friars Minor on the Bible as a *cursor.*[12] In Oxford, where the Franciscans settled in 1224, the highly regarded Chancellor Robert Grosseteste (ca. 1168–1253) held lectures for them from around 1230 on. Moreover, at the express wish of their Provincial, Agnellus of Pisa (1194–1232), the Friars Minor attended instructions at the university.[13]

The studies of the mendicant orders entered a new phase as a result of the entrance of university *magistri* into the orders, or else through the acquisition of the *licentia docendi* by the friars. During the disturbances at the university in 1229–1231 (a strike, the departure of *magistri* and *scholares* from Paris after the death of several students in altercations), the Dominicans succeeded (1229) in obtaining the *licentia docendi* for Roland of Cremona († ca. 1259). Already before he entered the order he had been a professor of philosophy in Bologna. His successor in Paris was Hugh of St. Cher († 1263), who had entered the order in 1225 as a bachelor of theology and a doctor of canon law. The Dominicans acquired a second professorial chair in Paris through the entrance of the *magister actu regens* John of Saint Gilles (ca. 1180–after 1258) in 1230. This was the situation for the Franciscans after the entrance of the *magister actu regens* Alexander of Hales, who consequently continued his lecturing in the convent of the Friars Minor.

The faculty of theology apparently took note of these admissions to the orders without raising major objections. Yet just the fact that the mendicants remained in Paris during the years 1229–1231 caused displeasure over their "uncorporate behavior."[14] A similar incident in 1253, however, led to a crisis in the secular clergy's opposition to the mendicants with the so-called Mendicant Conflict, in which not only the rights of the mendicant orders at the university were at stake, but increasingly the theological legitimacy of this way of life in an urban, university culture as well.[15]

Meanwhile other orders, too (e.g., the Cistercians and Praemonstratensians) had founded colleges in Paris (in order to eliminate the influence of the secular clergy on their young men in formation, among other reasons), and so in 1252 the existence of a college and the possession of the *licentia*

12. Ibid., 106.
13. See Little, "Franciscan School."
14. See Köhn, "Monastisches Bildungsideal," 30.
15. Glorieux, "Le conflit." For the pre-history, see Glorieux, "Les années."

docendi were made conditions for the acceptance of consecrated religious into the corporation of *magistri.* At the same time the professorial chairs for the religious were limited to one per order, which is why both Thomas Aquinas and Bonaventure were at first denied acceptance.[16] When the mendicants did not join the university strike of 1253 and refused to take the oath to uphold the new statutes, they were expelled from the corporation of *magistri* and excommunicated. Only through the repeated intervention of Pope Alexander IV (1254–1261) was the Mendicant Conflict concluded juridically in favor of the new orders, while the literary feud, especially in the debate of Thomas Aquinas and Bonaventure with William of Saint Amour († 1272) and Gerard of Abbéville († 1272), continued and increasingly became a disagreement over first principles. This also led to a growing influence of papal power in university activities; a case in point was the declaration of the Cardinal Legate Benedetto Gaetani (later Pope Boniface VIII [ruled 1294–1303]) in the year 1290:

> We command by virtue of due obedience that in the future no *magister* shall preach, debate, or privately or publicly state his opinion about the privilege [of the mendicants], under penalty of dismissal from office and the loss of benefice. The privilege of the mendicant friars shall remain in force, and whoever has any doubt about it should ask the Pope for clarification. Truly, I say to you, before the Roman Curia would withdraw this privilege from the mendicant friars it would sooner destroy the University of Paris.

The university's reacion was now unequivocal: "And the *universitas magistrorum* bowed its head, accepted the apostolic blessing and went home."[17] In contrast, the matter developed more harmoniously at first in Oxford. Here, though, with the appointment of Thomas of York († ca. 1260) as *Magister* in 1253, there were difficulties because of the fact that the Franciscans normally dispensed with the study of the *artes.* On the other hand, major conflicts arose in Oxford in the years 1311–1317 with regard to the obligation to lecture on the *Sentences* for a year before studying the Bible, which contradicted the custom of the mendicant orders in Oxford.[18]

1.3 Biblical or systematic theology?

The conflict over lecturing on the *Sentences* that played itself out publicly in Oxford in 1313–1317 was significant as a matter of principle: what

16. CUP I n. 200 (I, 226–27).

17. See Miethke, "Papst, Ortsbischof."

18. See Leff, *Paris,* 103–6.

should have priority in university theology, the *Sentences* or the Bible? The mendicants advocated a clear preference for the Bible from the very start. Once again, therefore, it was a question of the precedence of biblical or systematic theology. Thanks to the teaching of Robert Grosseteste, among others, theology at Oxford had an unmistakably biblical emphasis. Grosseteste plainly stands in the same tradition of moral-pastoral exegesis as Stephen Langton, for instance, since Thomas Eccleston describes his teaching with the Franciscans as *"tam in quaestionibus quam praedicationi congruis subtilibus moralitatibus"* ["both in questions and in subtle matters of morality suitable for preaching"].[19] Grosseteste is not part of the Parisian tradition of systematic theology, but rather applies himself to the Bible and the Church Fathers from a background of philosophy and natural science. Tellingly, the only twelfth-century "Scholastic" on his "reading list" was Hugh of St. Victor.[20] Grosseteste draws his theology mainly from Augustine and Gregory the Great, and was influenced philosophically by Seneca in particular, which only underscores the tropological-moral character of his scriptural exegesis.[21] For Grosseteste the Bible and theology (as *sacra pagina*) are still one. Later as bishop of Lincoln and chancellor of the University he still addresses the *magistri* of Oxford in clear terms and warns them against departing from this tradition. The books of the OT and the NT must remain the foundation for the edifice of theology. The morning hours are devoted to explaining them in the *lectiones ordinariae,* as was also the custom among the *magistri* in Paris.[22]

The staunch representative of the Oxford biblical tradition in Oxford, however, was the Franciscan Roger Bacon (ca. 1220–after 1292).[23] Even in his *Compendium studii theologiae* (after 1290) he still emphasized that the real concern of theologians is *"circa textum sacrum sciendum"* ["understanding the sacred text"]. Yet for fifty years scholars had been dealing chiefly with questions, as was evident from their treatises and enormous summas. In his view, however, these questions were really of a philosophical nature *"tam in substantia quam in modo"* ["both in substance and in method"].[24]

19. *Tractatus Fr. Thomae Eccleston De adventu Fratrum Minorum in Anglia,* ed. A. G. Little (Paris, 1909), 60; see also Little, "Franciscan School," 807.

20. See Southern, *Robert Grosseteste,* 187.

21. Ibid., 195, see the list: 3,000 citations from Augustine, 1,257 from Gregory the Great; Seneca leads the philosophers with 333 as opposed to Aristotle with only 68.

22. *Roberti Grosseteste Epistolae,* ed. H. R. Lund (Rolls Series, 1861), 346–47; see also Smalley, *Study,* 276–77.

23. On his life and work, see Hackett, "Roger Bacon."

24. Roger Bacon, *Compendium of the Study of Theology,* edition and translation with introduc-

Therefore compiling theological questions was in principle a betrayal of theology as scriptural exegesis. In his *Opus Minus* (1266/67) he had already severely attacked as *"peccatum"* ["a sin"] the usual Parisian practice of theological study, namely that a single summa of a *magister,* the Lombard's *Liber Sententiarum,* was preferred to the text that really should be interpreted in the theological faculty, sacred Scripture. The whole reputation of a theologian consisted then of his interpretation of the Lombard, and everyone thought that he had to write a commentary weighing as much as a horse. Once someone had lectured on the *Sentences* he felt that he was already a master of theology, although he had scarcely heard anything of his real *textus* yet. The *baccalaureus biblicus,* however, is subordinate to the *sententiarius.* The *sententiarius* has the best hours for his lectures, an assistant and a lecture hall at the religious house. The biblical scholar, however, has nothing and must go to the *sententiarius* to beg for his hours. The *sententiarius* even debates and is already considered to be a *magister.* The biblical scholar cannot debate. So it has been in Bologna and elsewhere. Bottom line: *"quod est absurdum"* ["this is absurd," i.e., a *reductio ad absurdum,* proving the falsity of the premises from the logical conclusion]. Subordinating sacred Scripture to the *Sentences,* moreover, contradicts an old faculty regulation. Every other faculty interprets only the authentic text. For if you really know and have understood the text exactly, you have learned everything that there is to learn in that faculty. Indeed, that is what the authentic text was made for. All the more reason that this should be the case in theology, for here the authentic text comes from the mouth of God and of the saints. The Church Fathers interpreted only the biblical text. That was the practice of the early teachers of theology, namely Robert Grosseteste and Adam Marsh († ca. 1259), the first teachers of the Franciscans at Oxford. Alexander of Hales, however, Bacon's Parisian confrere, was the first to lecture on the *Sentences* instead of the Bible, and from then on this abuse became established in the Franciscan Order as well. It would have been much better to lecture on the *Historia scholastica* by Petrus Comestor, as had been the custom earlier, for the latter work is essentially closer to theology (as *sacra pagina*) than the *Liber Sententiarum.* That is why Bacon advocated reinstating the *Historia scholastica* and abandoning the many questions that no longer have any relation to the sacred text. Instead, text-related questions should be posed. Now it is true, however, that

tion and notes by Thomas S. Maloney, [Studien und Texte zur Geistesgeschichte des Mittelalters 20], (Leiden, 1988), part 2, prologue, page 48; see also Bérubé, "Dialog," 111–12.

while the biblical scholars lecture on the text in a cursory fashion, they do not explain it, since they don't debate questions, whereas the theologians in their questions are really just pursuing philosophy. Yet the theological questions in the summas and sentences must be verified by the biblical text.[25] Then, too, the text commonly used in Paris is corrupted, the literal sense is often understood incorrectly and therefore the spiritual sense of Scripture is likewise wrong or dubious. Furthermore jurists, even if they don't have the faintest idea of canon law, are more highly esteemed in the Church than biblical scholars and attain ecclesiastical honors more quickly.[26] This biblical reaction to the situation in Paris and Bologna came too late, however, to do anything about the decline in biblical theology and the rise of the questions and commentaries on the *Sentences.*

Biblical and systematic theology, scriptural commentary and commentary on the *Sentences,* parted ways not only in Paris but also in Oxford. The Dominican *magister* Richard Fishacre († 1248) in the prologue to his commentary on the *Sentences* clearly distinguishes between the moral-tropological scriptural exegesis of a Grosseteste and speculative theology with its questions taken from sacred Scripture but collected in the book of sentences. The questions are still referred back to sacred Scripture, but the independent value of the sentences as a systematic work of theology is recognized. Therefore reading the *Sentences* should by no means be neglected, since this study deals *"de questionibus circa fidem difficilibus"* ["with difficult questions about the faith"].[27] Even such a thorough Scripture commentator as Bacon's contemporary and confrere Thomas Docking († after 1269), who taught between 1260 and 1265, lectured on the *Sentences.*[28]

In Paris it was in fact the mendicants who, unlike the *magistri* from the secular clergy, followed the Victorine school and first revived lecturing on sacred Scripture, which led to the scriptural commentaries of Thomas Aquinas and Bonaventure. We should mention here especially the postilla to the Gospels by the Dominican Hugh of St. Cher (ca. 1235). He clearly distances himself from the mutual critiques of the *"moralistae"* and the *"quaestionistae"* and combines the best of both traditions: for him theology is both scrip-

25. Corrected text: Little, "Franciscan School," 808–9; see also Tshibangu, *Théologie,* 122–36; Bérubé, "Dialog," 100–110; Antolić-Piper, "Begründung."

26. Roger Bacon, *Opus Minus,* ed. J. S. Brewer (London, 1859), 330, 349; Bacon, *Opus Tertium,* 84.

27. Richard Fishacre, *In Sent., prol.,* ed. Long, in "Science," 96–97; see also Niederbacher and Leibold, *Theologie,* 131–87.

28. See Little, "Franciscan School," 846–50.

tural interpretation and also systematic theology, as represented by his confrere Richard Fishacre.[29] The symbolic interpretation of sacred Scripture gained new impetus, especially in the Franciscan tradition. On the other hand the general acceptance of the pagan, Aristotelian worldview in the faculty of arts posed serious problems for the theologian, too, who looked to the actual wording of Scripture. Aristotelian categories (esp. the doctrine of the four causes) make their way into exegesis.[30]

The attempt to strike a balance between theology as scriptural interpretation and as a systematic science is evident also at an influential position in the works of Thomas Aquinas, in the first question of his *Summa Theologiae.* After discussing theology as *"sacra doctrina"* along the lines of the Aristotelian concept of science, in articles 9 and 10 he poses apparently unmediated questions about the character of *"sacra Scriptura"* and about the validity of its metaphorical language and of the manifold sense of Scripture.[31] Yet the relation between Scripture and systematic theology has plainly changed. Whereas Roger Bacon claims that systematic questions must be traced back to the text of Scripture, Thomas attempts a systematic justification of the language and interpretation of sacred Scripture. He succeeds by assuming that God is generally the *Auctor* of Scripture, who determines that the *res* [things] designated by the words are also supposed to function in turn as signs for a further meaning. Thus for Thomas the words or sentences do not have various meanings, but rather the *res* are read as signs.[32] The spiritual sense of Scripture is therefore not just the product of interpretation but is rather built into the literal sense *(in una littera)* thanks to God's comprehensive knowledge, although the *intentio auctoris* (i.e., God's intention) initially concerns the literal sense.[33] This accomplishes three things:

1. Scripture and theology remain interrelated. Scriptural exegesis must allow itself to be justified systematically, however.
2. Literal exegesis is clearly restricted in its significance (e.g., as opposed to the Victorine school).
3. Spiritual exegesis (probably also as a result of the experience of the confusion surrounding Joachim of Fiore [ca. 1130–1202]) is deprived of its arbitrariness and acquires a certain ontological character. The *res* [things]

29. See Smalley, *Study,* 269–70: Niederbacher and Leibold, *Theologie,* 37–78.
30. On Hugh of St. Cher and Guerricus of St. Quentin: Smalley, *Study,* 295–98.
31. Thomas Aquinas, *S.Th.* I q.1 a.9 f., ed. Marietti (Turin-Rome, 1952), 8–9.
32. For Bonaventure's similar position, see also Leinsle, *Res et signum.*
33. *S.Th.* I q1 a10 i.c. (9).

as such in Scripture have further meanings that are determined by the author (God), not by the exegete.

2 Aristotle as a challenge to theology

At the same time that theology was being incorporated into the university, a difference of opinion arose within theology which was to be decisive for the thirteenth century: should theologians accept or reject the philosophy of Aristotle (which had been translated since the mid-twelfth century) and of his Arabic commentators?[34]

2.1 A new scientific model

Aristotle posed an initial theoretical challenge for theology as a science. Whereas in the twelfth century theology had still been guided essentially by Augustine and Boethius, the general acceptance of the *Posterior Analytics* in the teaching of logic meant that now theology was confronted with a scientific ideal that until then had been foreign to it, and many of its elements must have appeared at first to be incompatible with theology understood as the interpretation of Scripture. On the other hand, only the proof of the strictly scientific character of theology could secure its place at the university. Therefore the Aristotelian concept of science had to be adopted, if possible, or else surpassed. The self-reflection and self-assurance of theology that we could observe already in Praepositinus finds expression now in a special introductory or theoretical doctrine of theology.[35]

Aristotle's *Posterior Analytics* can be regarded as a fundamental document in the western understanding of science.[36] Its concept of science, however, is initially applicable only to mathematics and the natural sciences. Ἐπιστήμη *(scientia)* is certain, proven knowledge that is based on experience and for its method allows only a logically precise procedure of proof by means of syllogisms. Knowledge in the strict sense is not just knowledge of "The Fact That" (something is true), which can be gained through experience also, but rather the knowledge of the Why (of the causes): *scientia ex causis.* Moreover, knowledge refers to being, not to becoming or doing,

34. See Van Steenberghen, *Philosophie,* 149–66; Grabmann, *Forschungen;* Van Steenberghen "Aristoteles."

35. See esp. Köpf, *Anfänge;* Dreyer, *More mathematicorum;* Langer, "Aristoteles."

36. See Aristoteles, *Analytica Posteriora;* English translation in *The Basic Works of Aristotle,* ed. Richard McKeon (New York: Modern Library, 2001), 110–86.

and therefore has for Aristotle a theoretical and not a poietic character like τέχνη *(ars)*.[37]

The following elements of the Aristotelian concept of science are of decisive importance to thirteenth- and fourteenth-century theology for its self-understanding as a science in the context of the university:

1. The *object* of science *(subjectum scientiae)*. Every science is concerned with a class of things as its object; it presupposes the existence and definition of this object and inquires into its qualities, which should be proved to the extent possible from the definition. If theology wants to show that it is a science, it has to explain what its central object is (e.g., God), how its existence can be established (the theoretical problem of the "proofs of God's existence") and how its qualities can be identified.
2. The *proof* as a logical method. A proof is a "syllogism that produces knowledge."[38] Theology as a science that proves is therefore subject to the logical testing of the validity of its proofs. Such a syllogism proves something, however, only if it is obtained from necessary and true premises.
3. The *problem of [first] principles* therefore becomes just as central for theology as the problem of its object. The principles of the proof should be prior to and more evident than the conclusions derived from them.[39] In twelfth-century theology, metaphysical or theological axioms were sometimes assumed as principles of theology, but usually articles of faith served that purpose. The latter, however, are grasped only by faith and therefore do not satisfy the conditions for Aristotelian principles of proof.[40] Since Aristotle assigns the understanding of principles to another cognitive faculty, the νοῦς *(intellectus)*, the object of knowledge *(scientia)* is ultimately the conclusion that is proved.
4. The requirement that the principles of the proof be *necessary*. The conclusion is based on necessary premises.[41] Theology, considered as the exposition of God's historical salvific acts, as they are recorded in its central *textus*, sacred Scripture, was hitherto unfamiliar with such strict necessity, which on the other hand could jeopardize God's freedom.
5. The requirement that the principles and the known propositions be *general*. Our modern understanding of the humanities and social sciences notwithstanding, in Aristotle's view individual historical facts are not the

37. See Aristoteles, *An. post.* B 19, 100 a 6; *Met.* A 1, 891 a 28.
38. Aristoteles, *An. post.* A 2, 71 b 17.
39. Ibid., 71 b 19.
40. See Lang, *Prinzipienlehre.*
41. Aristoteles, *An. post.* A 4, 73 a 24.

object of knowledge and science: *de singulari non est scientia.*[42] Theology, however, deals with historical, free, unique acts of God. If it is to be a science in the Aristotelian sense, it must demonstrate that its object and its propositions are general.

6. The distinction between *theoretical* and *practical* science. If one argues for the scientific character of theology, one must explain whether it is a theoretical science in the Aristotelian sense, that is, restricted to the knowledge of the object's essence and the proof of its attributes, or a practical science, and therefore related to human activity and its goal. With reference to precisely this question, various authors, orders, and schools will manifest profoundly different concepts of theology and its status: for at this juncture is decided also the significance of theology beyond the university for religious, ecclesial, and political life.[43]
7. The *certainty* of theological statements. Proven knowledge in the most strict sense is attained when any further question about what is known has been ruled out.[44] Theological truths do not appear to have this objective certainty, independently of their subjective certainty, that is, the believer's degree of conviction. For they, like their premises, are based on faith. Moreover, God's freedom must be taken into account, since theological topics ultimately depend on it.

2.2 A pagan view of the world and man

Whereas the ideal of science set forth in the *Posterior Analytics* presented a formal challenge to theology, the latter compelled medieval scholars to grapple with the contents of Aristotle's writings on natural philosophy (*Libri naturales,* including *De anima*) as they were more widely circulated. They had already been translated in part by Gerard of Cremona († 1187) from the Arabic. Here the theologian who believes in creation and thinks largely along Augustinian lines encounters an explanation of the world and of man that not only knows nothing about revelation, but seems to contradict it in some of its central tenets. The question then arises: Can this pagan knowledge be integrated as a component of philosophical education that is still understood as a propaedeutic to theology, or even be carried over into theology? Doesn't that simply mean baptizing the pagan Aristotle? The old formula that philosophy is the *ancilla* [handmaid] of theology presup-

42. Ibid., B 21, 67 a 27.
43. See Krebs, *Theologie und Wissenschaft.*
44. See Heim, *Gewissheitsproblem.*

posed a philosophy restricted to instrumental logical disciplines. Could this formula still be applied to an independent, comprehensive pagan interpretation of the world, as found in Aristotle's works, or did scholars have to redefine the relationship [between theology and philosophy]?

The theologians in Paris and Oxford only gradually became aware of the problems posed by Aristotle's works on natural philosophy. In particular the following teachings of the Stagirite had to be viewed as incompatible with Christianity:

1. *The eternity of the world.* Calcidius and Boethius were acquainted with this as an opinion of Plato (*Timaeus* 28 A–38 C); the question as to the truth of this thesis became pressing, however, partly because Aristotle's interpretation of the world in his works of natural science proved to be far superior to the previous explanation, even in the view of thirteenth-century theologians. If the thesis of the eternity of the world, time and movement is a necessary component of this natural science, then from the theological perspective it is false because it contradicts revelation.[45] If one were to attribute to it a truth in the sphere of natural explanation (philosophy) but not in the sphere of theology, this would give the impression of a double truth: what is true in philosophy can be false in theology.[46] Philip the Chancellor († 1236) already dealt with this expressly in his influential *Summa de bono.* For him creation implies a temporal beginning. Therefore Aristotle cannot teach a strict eternity *(aeternum)* but only an unlimited temporal duration *(perpetuum)* of the world.[47] Alexander of Hales, on the other hand, sees no contradiction between the Stagirite's thesis, which is to be interpreted purely in terms of natural science, and the wording of the Bible, since Aristotle only means to say that space, time, and movement came into being at the same time.[48] For Robert Grosseteste, who adheres strictly to the text of the Stagirite, this conciliatory attitude of Alexander is mere nonsense and an attempt to make a Catholic out of the heretic Aristotle. The real compromise was achieved by Thomas Aquinas, who managed to show that an eternal creation is theologically and philosophically possible.[49]

45. See Dales, *Discussions.*
46. See Dales, "Origins."
47. *Philippi Cancellarii Summa de Bono,* ed. N. Wicki (Bern, 1985), I, 49.
48. See Dales, *Discussions,* 66–70.
49. Robert Grosseteste, *Hexaemeron* 1, 8, 2–4, R. C. Dales—S. Gieben, eds. (London, 1983),

2. The *denial of the Ideas.* This did not contradict Scripture as much as it questioned the great authority of the theological tradition: Augustine. Anyone who denies the Ideas as the thoughts of God destroys also the ontological basis for the symbolic interpretation of the world, as cultivated especially in Franciscan circles. He implicitly denies at the same time, for example in Bonaventure's view, God's plan for his world, and thus Divine Providence, and consigns everything to mere fate or chance.[50]
3. A lack of clarity with respect to the *individuality of the intellectual soul.* Even in Aristotle's work the status of the νοῦς (*anima intellectiva, intellectus agens* = intellectual soul, agent intellect) vis-à-vis the biological constitution of man is not explained fully. Then there is an epistemological problem: According to the Stagirite and his Arabic commentators, something that is singular and transitory cannot know anything that is generally valid and necessary. Therefore the intellect itself must be thought of as universal and eternal, interpreted ontologically as a spiritual substance (intelligence) outside of the human individual. It is merely active in various subjects. This interpretation is theologically unacceptable, because it would mean that the human individual was no longer constituted by a unique, personal, and immortal intellectual soul and was thus released from eternal reward or punishment, which would make morality arbitrary. There were facile attempts at harmonization even in this regard; William of Auvergne (ca. 1180–1249), for instance, simply applies Aristotle's statements about the agent intellect of the human race to God, in connection with the Neoplatonic interpretation of Avicenna (ca. 980–1037).[51] Here again Thomas Aquinas, in grappling with a heterodox variety of Aristotelianism (Siger of Brabant [† 1284], Boethius of Dacia [† before 1284]), was the one to provide the crucial clarification by showing that an individual intellect corresponds more closely to the Aristotelian approach than the previous interpretation.[52] Even then the epistemological problem could not be resolved in purely Aristotelian terms, but outright conflict with previous theological doctrine was avoided.

58–61; Thomas Aquinas, *De aeternitate mundi contra murmurantes,* in *Opuscula philosophica* (Turin: Marietti, 1954), 103–8.

50. Bonaventura, *Collationes in Hexaemeron,* vis. I coll.3, 2–5, ed. F. Delorme (Quaracchi, 1934), 91–92; see also Leinsle, *Res et signum,* 74.

51. See Van Steenberghen, *Philosophie,* 339–50, 154; Bazán, "Conception."

52. Thomas Aquinas, *De unitate intellectus* in *Opuscula philosophica* (Turin: Marietti, 1954), 59–90.

The three problematic areas mentioned above were not just incidental skirmishes. They were central to the conflict between an independent, purely natural interpretation of the world that knows nothing of revelation, and a theology based on the authority of revelation and its doctrinal tradition. At stake was the correct (= true) interpretation of the world, man and knowledge from the perspective of Christian truth. On the other hand, scholars also saw the great advantages of Aristotelian physics and especially metaphysics for the interpretation of theological truths (e.g., the teaching about the matter and form of the sacraments). The new paradigm of science as a way of explaining the world prevailed in *sacra doctrina* as well, despite resistance and obvious difficulties in harmonizing it with the truths of revelation.

2.3 The influence of non-Christian syntheses

Along with the entire philosophy of the pagan Aristotle, the thought of Arabic and Jewish philosophers made its way into educational world of the Middle Ages, which until then had been essentially Christian. Although the syntheses of philosophy and revealed theology created in Arab-Jewish cultural circles and especially in Spain had no immediate influence as models, they had to be reckoned with, in view of the Crusades and the efforts of Frederick II (1194–1250).[53] Here again it was not the theology of Islam that was initially the object of the discussion, but rather its philosophy, especially in the figures of Avicenna (Ibn Sina, † 1037) and Averroës (Ibn Rushd, † 1198).

Avicenna, who significantly was first translated into Latin by Jews, contributed to the Middle Ages not only a wealth of knowledge in the natural sciences and medicine but also a metaphysics which, although partly Aristotelian, was nevertheless deeply dyed in Neoplatonism, with God as the *"dator formarum"* ["Giver of forms"] at the summit. This metaphysics could be more easily integrated into the previous way of thinking than Aristotle's "first philosophy" or Averroës' naturalistic system. Avicenna's influence, even in matters of style, can be detected also in a not exactly revolutionary theologian like William of Auvergne, but likewise in the works of Albert the Great and Thomas Aquinas.[54] Avicenna became very important even after the 1277 condemnation of so-called Averroist teachings; for now Averroës could be supplanted so to speak by Avicenna, who thanks to his Neopla-

53. Concerning the background of Islamic-Christian relations see esp. Southern, *Western Views;* Daniel, *Arabs.*

54. See Gilson, "Avicenne."

tonic implications could also be harmonized with Augustine's doctrine of the ideas, as attempted for instance by Henry of Ghent.[55] Finally, Avicenna had a decisive influence on Duns Scotus (ca. 1265–1308), so that E. Gilson prefers to speak of the time after 1277 as a second *aetas Avicenniana* [age of Avicenna], following the first one which lasted until the massive influx of commentaries by Averroës. Avicenna supplied valuable elements for theology: his teaching about intellects can be combined with the doctrine on the angels; God as the *"dator formarum"* seems closer to the Christian understanding of God than the "unmoved mover" of Aristotle; yet Avicenna makes God subject to a strict necessity to diffuse himself, which is difficult to reconcile with God's freedom in creation. Moreover, even William of Auvergne saw the incompatibility of the Islamic notion of blessedness with the Christian idea, whereas he plainly accepted the independent existence of the *intellectus agens* [agent intellect] along with Avicenna.[56]

Integrating Averroës into the Christian intellectual heritage proved to be more difficult, if not impossible. For he is by design a strict Aristotelian, so that in his case all the difficulties in accepting the Stagirite are increased. Tellingly, his treatise on the agreement between religion and philosophy was not translated into Latin. It taught a priority of philosophy, even in matters of faith, which led in the Islamic world to a conflict that can be viewed as a parallel to the twelfth- and thirteenth-century disputes in Christian lands.[57] For Thomas Aquinas, nevertheless, Averroës became the *Commentator* pure and simple, even though he did not follow him at every point.[58] Instead Thomas would be concerned, especially in the critical point about the individuality or generic unity of the human intellect as a whole, with establishing an Aristotelianism that would be compatible with the Christian faith and opposed to the influence of the Averroës commentary on *De anima* and its recipients in the faculty of arts.

Accepting Jewish sources must have seemed easier to the medieval theologian than integrating Islamic thought. We have already observed the influence of Jewish exegesis, for instance in the work of Andrew of St. Victor. Loris Sturlese has pointed out a possible mutual influence of Jewish and Christian

55. Heinrich von Gent, *Summa quaestionum ordinariarum* a.22 q.5 (printed edition Paris, 1520; reprinted New York: St. Bonaventure, 1953), f.134v D; a.25 q.3 (f.156r S); see also Emery, "Image of God."

56. See Roger Bacon, *Opus maius* II, 5, ed. J. H. Bridges (reprinted Frankfurt 1964), II, 45–48; Gilson, "Avicenne," 98–103; and for a list of discrepancies between William and Avicenna (119).

57. Averroës, *Traité décisif sur l'accord de la religion et de la philosophie* (Paris: L. Gauthier, 1983).

58. See Vansteenkiste, "Tommaso d'Aquino."

schools in the Rhineland.[59] Especially significant for the thirteenth century was the philosophical-theological synthesis of Moses Maimonides (1138–1204), who like Averroës was originally from Córdoba. His program, presented in the *Guide for the Doubtful* (*Dux dubitantium*, ca. 1190), corresponds to a thirteenth-century need resulting from the separation of philosophy and theology. In it Rabbi Moses tries to show not only that is there no contradiction between them but on the contrary that the Bible itself contains the true (Aristotelian-Arabic) philosophy. This can be discovered through allegorical interpretation, which is customary in the Latin-speaking world as well. In the Jewish world itself, Maimonides' teaching led initially to a bitter controversy over the correctness of this interpretation of the Bible as opposed to the previous literal exegesis.[60] For Maimonides' synthesis can be read in two ways, and both have the force to disrupt Jewish as well as Christian theology: in this synthesis philosophy is substantiated by the Bible (a position taken again by the strict biblicism of seventeenth-century Calvinism),[61] but on the other hand the Word of revelation is measured against the truth of Arabic-Aristotelian philosophy, which is assumed. Thus even the individual practical precepts of the Old Testament Law are now set on a rational, philosophical foundation. The controversy surrounding Maimonides therefore becomes a concern of Christian theology and the Church as well. The study of Maimonides' books, which was sometimes banned by the Jewish authorities, could become a danger for Christianity also. Thus the intervention of the tribunal of the Inquisition in 1232 led to a book-burning in Montpellier. This was followed in 1242 by a burning of the Talmud in Paris. The equation of Arabic-Aristotelian philosophy with the Bible (or the biblical substantiation thereof) resulted in a theological legitimation, from a Christian perspective, of the fundamental errors of Aristotelianism; according to William of Auvergne, the Jews became heretics because after their dispersal in the Arab world they accepted Arabic philosophy, including the doctrine that the world is eternal.[62]

2.4 The Church's reaction: The prohibition of Aristotle

The influx of pagan and Islamic thought, first into philosophy and later into theology, presented a major challenge to Christianity, as we can see

59. Sturlese, *Philosophie*, 86–95, 265–76.

60. See Greive, "Maimonideische Kontroverse."

61. See, for example, Johann Heinrich Alsted, *Triumphus Bibliorum sacrorum* (Frankfurt, 1625).

62. William of Auvergne, *De legibus* in *Guilelmi Alverni Opera omnia* (Paris, 1674; reprinted Frankfurt, 1963), I, 24b.

from the reaction of the official Church, manifested in the repeated prohibition of Aristotle in Paris.[63] As always with ecclesiastical condemnations, an occasion was required. This had been provided in 1210 at a provincial synod presided over by Archbishop Peter of Corbeil (ca. 1150–1222) through the condemnation of Amaury of Bène († 1206) and David of Dinant († after 1206) along with Amaury's disciples.[64] The ruling that David's *quaternuli* [notebooks] should be handed over to the bishop to be burned was accompanied by a prohibition (applying to Paris only) against reading *"libri de naturali philosophia"* and *"commenta"* under pain of excommunication.[65] The reason, of course, was the teaching of David of Dinant about nature, which relied on Aristotle. Clearly, prohibiting the "reading" (that is, the *lectio,* both in public and in private) of Aristotle's writings on natural philosophy was an attempt not only to treat the symptoms but to strike at the root of the evil. The *"commenta,"* of course, are primarily the Arabic commentaries of Avicenna; Averroës had not yet been translated. Precisely because these writings were already being "read," if not within the framework of theological studies then at least in the *artes,* it was known that the Aristotelian teaching was dangerous and incompatible with Church doctrine. The expanded version of the prohibition, which Chancellor Robert of Courson included in the statutes of the university in 1215, shows that initially it applied only to the masters and students of the arts. Here the prohibition is expressly extended to the *Metaphysics* also, which in 1210 could very well be classified among the *"libri de naturali philosophia"* as opposed to *"philosophia moralis."* Next textbooks on the subject *(summae de eisdem)* were forbidden, specifically the teachings of David of Dinant, Amaury of Bène, and Maurice of Spain (Mauritius Hispanus).[66] Thus Aristotle's natural philosophy and metaphysics were banned from the university. Private reading (not *lectio*) of the works was not ruled out. Moreover the prohibition was a local one; it did not apply in Oxford, for example, where in later years intensive translation activity (under the direction of Robert Grosseteste) and a thorough discussion of Aristotle's natural philosophy could be conducted.

The faculty of theology in Paris, thinking along the lines of Petrus Comestor or Praepositinus of Cremona, regarded these prohibitions be-

63. See esp. Grabmann, *Divieti.*

64. On these proceedings against the "sects" which were obviously connected with the teachings of the *Cathari,* see Fichtenau, *Ketzer,* 280–83; Lambert, *Heresy,* 99–100.

65. CUP I n.11 (I, 70); see also Van Steenberghen, *Philosophie,* 90–100.

66. CUP I n.20 (I, 78–79).

nevolently, especially since Peter of Corbeil and Robert of Courçon themselves had once been *magistri* in Paris.[67] Certainly at this point in time the influence of Aristotle in the theological faculty was still insignificant. *"Tranquillitas scholarum"* ["calm in the schools"], the express purpose of Robert of Courson's statute, was plainly agreeable to the theologians, who were mostly conservative and pastorally minded.[68] The picture becomes clearer only in the letter of Gregory IX (1227–1241) to the theological faculty dated July 7, 1228.[69] Written in a homiletic style strewn with quotations from Scripture, the letter contains a clear warning against having anything at all to do with philosophy. Philosophy must remain instead the handmaid, or indeed, as Jerome puts it, the captive slave girl of theology. The *"theologicus intellectus"* ["theological mind"], however, has the dominant role of the man in the house of the sciences. He is stationed over all the faculties and is responsible for disciplining them and guiding them along the right path. Therefore, a disordered inclination to philosophy should be equated with adultery and idolatry. Then the pope speaks plainly: In Paris many masters of theology have left the path of the ancients [the Church Fathers] in interpreting the *"celestis pagina"* [i.e., sacred Scripture] and given themselves over to "profane innovations," namely the *"doctrina philosophica naturalium,"* not for the benefit of their students, but rather to prove their own erudition. This inverts the order of instruction: the slave girl forces the mistress to serve; only leaves are offered to the students but no fruit with which to satisfy their hunger; this drink does not quench their thirst. Therefore the Pope exhorts the *magistri* of the theological faculty to have done with this madness *(vesania)* and in the future to teach only theology strictly speaking (= *sacra pagina*) without the addition of philosophical fables. Now Aristotle is not mentioned by name here, but the philosophy of the day was precisely the Stagirite's. James of Vitry (1180–1254), at any rate, understood the pope well: "Since theological books suffice for a Christian, it is not fitting to busy oneself all too much with the *'libri naturales.'*"[70] Therefore in 1230 there was already among the theologians in Paris a trend in favor of Aristotle which included him at least to some extent in theology, as we can observe in the works of William of Auvergne and (less often) in the writings of William of Auxerre.

67. See Grabmann, *Divieti* 64–65.
68. See also J. Châtillon, "Mouvement théologique."
69. CUP I n.59 (I, 114–16); Grabmann, *Divieti*, 72–75.
70. See Van Steenberghen, *Philosophie*, 102.

The pope—probably influenced by William of Auxerre, who in 1230 was staying in Rome—could not maintain the strictly negative attitude. Yet only very slowly did the conviction gain acceptance that at least several points of Aristotelian philosophy could be put to use profitably for theology as well.[71] The letter *"Parens scientiarum"* dated April 13, 1231, does not permit the forbidden books of Aristotle for the faculty of the arts but proposes that they be reviewed and expurgated. A commission headed by William of Auxerre was appointed but because of his death did not begin its work. The theologians, on the other hand, were enjoined not to conduct themselves as philosophers, to allow neither vernacular nor Hebrew expressions and to debate only those questions that can be decided *"per libros theologicos et sanctorum tractatus"* ("by theological books and the treatises of the saints").[72] Innocent IV (1243–1254) extended the Parisian prohibition of Aristotle, as formulated by Gregory IX, to Toulouse as well on September 22, 1245.[73] Urban IV (1261–1264) renewed it for Paris as late as January 19, 1263, long after Aristotle had in fact legitimately gained admission to the university lectures.[74] A new wave of translations included in particular the commentaries of Averroës, which became known in Paris from around the year 1230.[75]

2.5 Theological truth and the truths of the natural sciences

The writings of Averroës, in connection with Aristotle's writings on natural philosophy, which from 1252 *(De anima)* or 1255 became an official course of lectures in the faculty of the arts,[76] presented now for theology a serious challenge which determined the climate and the literary output of the leading theologians of the day. Albert the Great and Thomas Aquinas, neither of whom was ever a professional philosopher, wrote their commentaries on Aristotle. On that account Albert had to put up with being rebuked for uncultured dilettantism by Roger Bacon.[77] In his series of lectures to the Franciscan convent, Bonaventure tried to salvage the old order of philosophy and theology. There was a theological concern in this inten-

71. See the letter of Gregory IX dated April 23, 1231: CUP I n.87 (I, 143–44): *quaedam utilia et inutilia.*

72. CUP I n. 79 (I, 138); see also Grabmann, *Divieti,* 95–101.

73. CUP I n. 149 (I, 185–86).

74. CUP I n. 384 (I, 427–28).

75. See Van Steenberghen, *Philosophie,* 110–16.

76. CUP I n. 201, 246 (I, 227–30, 277–79).

77. Roger Bacon, *Opus Minus,* 327–28.

sive discussion of Aristotle's philosophy: to make this new understanding of the world and man compatible with Christian revelation and thus to prevent the break up of philosophy and theology and the danger of a heterodox Aristotelianism.[78]

At the faculty of the arts, where scholars did not have to have these theological misgivings, a heterodox Aristotelianism took shape principally in the figures of Siger of Brabant and Boethius of Dacia. At first there were the familiar difficulties with regard to the eternity of the world and the species-wide unity of the human intellect, which were theologically offensive.[79] Yet more was at stake: The question about a philosophical (= natural scientific) truth that was independent of revelation and theology had yet to be resolved. To theologians it could appear that an independent truth of philosophy was being set up in opposition to the truth of revelation, *"quasi sint due contrarie veritates"* ["as though there were two contrary truths"].[80] At any rate, the methods used by the masters of arts to explain the relation between philosophical and theological truth claims had been developed by the theologians themselves. Alexander of Hales had already conceded that Aristotle settled questions only according to the principles of natural science and knew nothing about creation as a supernatural divine intervention. His philosophical doctrine, therefore, is not absolutely true *(non simpliciter),* but rather should be interpreted in terms of the state of the author's knowledge.[81] One could fall back on this position and derive Aristotle's opinion from his sources and presuppositions. As a philosopher one can dispense with the question about the relation between Aristotle's and Averroës' teaching and the truth of revelation, but the theologian cannot.[82] Significantly, Alexander's distinction was not derived from Averroës, who recognizes only one truth, philosophical truth, but rather from Moses Maimonides, who uses it as Catholic theology does to reconcile the biblical and[83] Aristotelian worldviews.

78. See Van Steenberghen, *Philosophie,* 335–87.

79. See Wéber, "Discussions"; Zimmermann, "Mundus est aeternus."

80. Thus Etienne Tempier in his ruling dated March 7, 1277: CUP I n. 473 (I, 543).

81. Dales, "Origins," 172, following the Paris B.N. Ms. lat. 16406, fol.7vb. On similar opinions expressed by Albert the Great, see Sturlese, *Philosophie,* 332–50.

82. Thus Siger of Brabant, *De anima intellectiva* c.7, in Siger de Brabant, *Quaestiones in tertium de Anima, De anima intellectiva, De aeternitate mundi,* ed. B. Bazan [Philosophes Médiévaux 13] (Louvain-Paris, 1973), 101.7–9: *"quaerendo intentionem philosophorum in hoc magis quam veritatem,* cum philosophice procedamus" ("examining in this matter the intention of philosophers rather than the truth, *since we are proceeding philosophically"*].

83. Moses Maimonides, *Dux dubitantium* 2.15 (Paris, 1520) f. 48v; see also Dales, "Origins," 173.

This distinction between the author's intention *(intentio auctoris)* relative to the state of his knowledge and the truth of an assertion is now applied by the masters of arts to redefine the relation between philosophy (science) and theology. Boethius of Dacia formulates the typical argument. The *naturalis* (i.e., the philosopher who proceeds according to the principles of natural science) knows no truths of revelation, for example *creatio ex nihilo* [creation from nothing]. It is not found among his principles and work methods. He can affirm or deny everything that he affirms or denies only *"ex causis et principiis naturalibus"* ["on the basis of natural causes and principles"]. If we heed this foundation, it follows that a thesis in natural science cannot be accepted as absolutely true; rather, if it contradicts the simple truth of revelation, it is false *"absolute accepta"* ["taken absolutely"], even though it is methodologically correct and has been derived logically from the limited principles of natural science. Therefore the truth of revelation, correctly interpreted, does not contradict natural science (philosophy), rightly understood. For the *"christianus subtiliter intelligens"* ["Christian who understands subtly"] recognizes that the truth of revelation is a matter of faith, whereas a thesis in natural science has been derived methodically from the corresponding principles. And so he can keep both: *"salvat fidem et philosophiam neutram corripiendo."* ["He saves faith and philosophy, while wresting neither."] Theologians and those in authority in the Church, however, who do not understand such difficult things, should listen to the wise man and abide by the law of Christ with the obedience of faith, knowing meanwhile that faith is not knowledge *(scientia)*.[84]

This stance taken by Boethius also shows, however, that philosophy had transformed its understanding of itself in its dealings with theology. Faith in the *"lex Christi"* [law of Christ] is not knowledge. Knowledge, however, is restricted to proofs derived from premises; it is determined by logical validity and the value of the premises. What happens, though, when theology itself now claims to achieve, out of the *"lex Christi"* that is grasped through the obedience of faith, a form of knowledge *(scientia)* in the absolute sense, indeed, claims to be a science in the Aristotelian sense? The theoretical problem is intensified in everyday practice. Boethius' short work, *De summo bono sive de vita philosophi* presents a philosophical ethics that is by no means anti-Christian yet is acquainted with an independent,

84. Boethius of Dacia, *De aeternitate mundi,* ed. Géza Sajó (Berlin, 1964), 45–62; see also Dales, "Origins," 177–78.

this-worldly happiness in the philosopher's ideal way of life, which is clearly set apart from the eternal happiness *"quam in futura vita per fidem expectamus"* ["which we look for in the next life by faith"].[85] The "god of the philosophers" who is loved and honored here is the *"primum principium"* ["first principle"] and *"summum bonum"* ["supreme good"]. Love for this God is manifested *"secundum rectam rationem naturae et secundum rectam rationem intellectualem"* ["according to the right reason of nature (i.e., as required by natural law) and according to intellectual right reason"].[86] All of this is elaborated as a purely philosophical ideal, along with the *"sola recta delectatio"* ["sole proper delight"] in contemplating the Supreme Good: *"Haec est vita philosophi, quam quicumque non habuerit, non habet rectam vitam."* ["This is the philosopher's life; anyone who does not have it does not have an upright life."][87] Faith and knowledge, theological hope for the afterlife and the philosophical formation of this world have plainly diverged.

2.6 The condemnations of 1270 and 1277

The most vigorous theological reaction of the Church authorities to the appearance of a heterodox philosophy occurred in the condemnations of 1270 and 1277. While both had a purely local character, they were nevertheless of fundamental importance. Each ruling was preceded by an intensive debate at the theological faculty.[88] The thirteen propositions[89] condemned on December 12, 1270, by Bishop Étienne Tempier († 1279) were to a great extent the same as the errors that Bonaventure had combatted in the series of sermons that he gave in 1267 and 1268: unity of intellect, eternity of the world, denial of the bodily resurrection, denial of Providence, fatalism.[90] At least four of the condemned propositions were clearly aimed at Siger of Brabant; yet the radical current of thought at the faculty of the arts could not be restricted to him and his followers.

85. M. Grabmann, ed., "Die Opuscula *de summo bono sive de vita philosophi* und *de sompniis* des Boethius von Dacien," in Grabmann, *Mittelalterliches Geistesleben,* vol. 2 (Munich, 1936), 200–24, citation at 211.7.

86. Ibid., 216.6–12.

87. Ibid., 216.15–17.

88. See Van Steenberghen, *Philosophie,* 442–462; or the anthology edited by Flasch, *Aufklärung im Mittelalter? Kritisch zur Überbewertung der Verurteilung von 1277,* for example, Bianchi, "Turning Point." Leppin, *Theologie,* 118 f. suggests the designation "consistent Aristotelianism" as opposed to the expression "heterodox Aristotelianism" introduced by Van Steenbergen. But that might make the representatives of the Theological Faculty look like "inconsistent" Aristotelians.

89. CUP I n. 432 (I, 486–87).

90. Bonaventura, Collationes de decem praeceptis (1267) (Op. V, 4505–32); Collationes de donis Spiritus sancti (1268) (Op. V, 455–503).

Whereas we can understand the condemnation in 1270 to a great extent as a listing of the theologically incompatible philosophical teachings of the new Aristotelianism, the 219 propositions condemned on March 7, 1277, with the help of a commission including several high-ranking theologians had a more fundamental character. The later ruling had been preceded by serious conflicts with the theological faculty and in the faculty of the arts itself. Moreover the condemnation took place explicitly at the behest of Pope John XXI (1276–1277), who on April 28 would demand an investigation of the theological faculty as well.[91] Heresy was already suspected there, too. Thus the condemnation of 1277 could not simply be taken as a reaction *of* the theologians to the masters of arts, especially since theologians like Thomas Aquinas (exactly three years before his death) and Ægidius Romanus (1243/47–1316) were affected by the condemnation and the associated burden of excommunication. Granted, the prologue accuses the masters of arts of overstepping boundaries as a matter of principle. The masters of arts now faced the very same charge that had been leveled at the theologians in 1228: they were meddling in matters that did not concern them.[92] Symptomatic of the climate of mistrust was the university-wide decree of September 2, 1276, forbidding lectures and disputations *"in locis privatis"* and secret assemblies. The only exceptions were the departments of logic and grammar, which were generally not suspect.[93]

An examination of the sources for the 1277 list of errors shows that these formulas applied only in a very qualified sense to the teachings of the *magistri* Siger of Brabant and Boethius of Dacia and sometimes condemned propositions about the relation of philosophy to theology that were quite true. Since the excommunication of the teachers and hearers of these propositions naturally presupposes a literal interpretation [of the Bible], this caused great uncertainty in theological teaching as well. Beside the well-known "errors" of Aristotle and the condemned teachings of Thomas Aquinas (the possibility of an eternal world, the individuation, unity and essential form of man, localization of spiritual substances, etc.), other condemned propositions that seriously affected the self-understanding and development of theology concerned the relation between reason and faith, philosophy and theology, divine omnipotence and natural causes, divine and human knowledge. The epis-

91. See Van Steenberghen, *Philosophie,* 354; De Libera, "Philosophie et censure."

92. See CUP I n.59 (I, 114–16); n. 473 (I, 543): *"proprie facultatis limites excedentes"* ["going beyond the limits of their own faculty"].

93. CUP I n. 468 (I, 538–39).

temological status of the individual philosophical sentence was not made explicit; instead it was assumed that they were all asserted as equally true. Theologically, however, they are false. Thus Étienne Tempier must have had the impression that the notorious "double truth" was being proposed, as he explains in his prologue. Therefore it was not the so-called "Averroists" but rather the Bishop himself who was actually the author of the "doctrine of the double truth."[94]

Besides those propositions, however, there were fundamental attacks on the position of theology at the university in the first place. These characterize the climate in which theology had to fight for its scientific status: Theological discourse in based on human fables (152). Theological knowledge does not broaden our knowledge (153). Consequently theology does not convey any knowledge at all and it therefore not a science. There are fables and false statements in the Christian law (= sacred Scripture, theology) as there are elsewhere (174). The Christian law impedes the acquisition of knowledge (175). There is no higher state of human existence than the free pursuit of philosophy (40). Philosophers are the sole *"sapientes mundi"* ("wise men of the world," see 1 Cor 1:20) (154). In deciding a question with certainty one must not be content with authorities (150).[95]

Of particularly great significance for the theological development of the fourteenth century were the condemnations of the theses concerning God's causality, which for the most part were inspired by Avicenna:[96] The first cause has no knowledge of future contingencies, because something contingent in the future cannot be classified as being and is singular, whereas God recognizes nothing singular (42). The first principle of being cannot be the cause of the complex variety of creatures on earth without the mediation of other causes (43). A multiplicity of effects cannot proceed from the first efficient cause (44). God brings forth necessarily that which comes forth from him immediately (58). God can bring about the effect of a secondary cause only with its cooperation (63). Intelligible substances participate in the creation of things (73).[97] The controversy over these condemned theses would lead to a broader discussion about the power of God with the distinction

94. See Dales, "Origins," 179.

95. See Flasch, ed., *Aufklärung*, 137–38, 215–18, 229–30. For a discussion see esp. De Libera, "Philosophie et censure"; Bianchi, "Turning Point"; Boulnois, "Chisame," and other essays in Aertsen and Speer, eds., *Was ist Philosophie im Mittelalter?* esp. 371–434.

96. See Bannach, *Lehre*, 96–111.

97. See Flasch, ed., *Aufklärung*, 139–43, 155, 158, 165.

already present in the *Summa Halensis* between his absolute power and his ordered power (i.e., that which is freely bound by the existing course of the world and by salvation history).[98] God's freedom with regard to the causal explanation of the world, however, leads also to questioning the value of the rational explanation of the world (and of theological self-assurance) against the backdrop of a divine will that is independent of all secondary causes and this-worldly facts (and thus explanations). This means that there are clear theological reservations about the philosophical claim to truth; the truth-claim of theology, however, which must struggle for its own scientific character, and the certainty of the believer are subject to the proviso of God's will, which could also be quite different. The theoretical scientific self-assurance of theology as a university discipline therefore necessarily appeared to be the pressing need of the hour.

3 The scientific character of theology

Theology's controversial encounter with the new ideal of science and its position at the university created a new theological treatise: the introduction to theology and its epistemological teaching.[99] It can be found in individual questions, series of questions, parts of monographs, but especially in the introductions to summas and commentaries on the *Sentences*. They manifest the self-understanding of a theology poised between its responsibility to the *sacra pagina* and the claim to be a science in the Aristotelian sense.

3.1 Faith and argument: William of Auxerre

The so-called *Summa aurea* or "Golden Summa" of William of Auxerre († 1231) was probably completed during the 1220s (after 1215, before 1229). In the prologue it offers us an initial introduction to theology, although not in the Aristotelian sense. It does identify well the point of departure for the discussion.[100] The very first *quaestio* of the prologue formulates a funda-

98. Alexander of Hales, *Summa theologica*, p. 1 inq. 1 tr. 4 q. 1 c. 2 (I, 207); q. 2 c. 2–3 (I, 219–22); q. 3 c. 2 a. 1 (I, 233–34); see also William J. Courtenay, art. "Potentia absoluta / ordinata" *HWP* VII, cols. 1157–62; Courtenay, *Capacity*, 68–74.

99. See Köpf, *Anfänge*, 67–69; Grabmann, *Erkenntnislehre;* Chenu, *Théologie comme science;* Kraml, *Rede von Gott;* Niederbacher and Leibold, eds., *Theologie.*

100. *Magistri Guillelmi Altissiodorensis Summa Aurea,* ed. J. Ribaillier, vol. 1 (Spicilegium Bonaventurianum 16) (Paris-Grottaferrata, 1980); see in the same series *Introduction générale* (Spicilegium Bonaventurianum 20) (Paris-Grottaferrata, 1987), 3–16; see also Niederbacher and Leibold, eds., *Theologie,* 13–35.

mental attack on theology. Starting from the "definition of faith" in Hebrews 11:1, where faith itself is described as an *"argumentum,"* it must seem perverse that the *magistri* try to support the faith with arguments from reason. For faith itself is *"probans non probatum"* [something that proves but is not proved], an argument, not a conclusion that would require proof. A science of faith in the strict sense would thus be an oxymoron.[101] The solution offered by William follows the earlier teaching of Praepositinus. Faith relies in three ways on *ratio:* among believers faith is strengthened and increased by it; it defends the faith against heretics; finally, simple folk may be moved to believe by rational arguments. William by no means subscribes to an Aristotelian explanation of theological science; instead he adheres to the traditional understanding of faith and theology exemplified by Augustine and Anselm of Canterbury. Faith is an illumination by God and therefore affects *intellegere* [understanding]: The more enlightened a soul is, the more clearly she sees also that the matter in question is in fact as she believes it to be, but also how and why it is so: *"quod est intelligere"* ["which is to understand"].[102] Therefore William also agrees with Simon of Tournai (ca. 1130–1201), who considers the connotation of *"argumentum"* in Aristotle to be incompatible with the linguistic usage of the Bible: in Aristotle the argument is a reason *(ratio)* for believing a dubious thing; for Christians, on the other hand, the argument is faith itself, which creates its own reasons *(ratio).*[103] Theological progress (in persons) is therefore, as Augustine says, possible only as progress in faith, not as a deductive extension of knowledge from a first principle. Instead the first principle and the first truth is God himself, upon whom one must rely in making the ascent of faith.[104]

In the second *quaestio* William emphasizes, as Peter Lombard had done, that arguments drawn from reason must be suitable; this is not the case with reasons that are related only to *"res naturales"* ["natural things"]. The heretics' blunder consists precisely of the fact that they simply applied such arguments to God and thereby arrived at their errors (Arius and Sabellius being the prime examples).[105] William generally agrees with this: all heresies ultimately can be traced back to a hasty transference of purely natural circumstances to God, that is, to an unwarranted natural-philosophical

101. William of Auxerre, *Summa aurea,* l.1 prol.1 (15, 1–10); see also Beumer, "Theologie als intellectus fidei."

102. William of Auxerre, *Summa aurea,* l.1 prol.1 (16.35–37).

103. Ibid., (16.39–41).

104. Ibid., (18.80–84).

105. Ibid., prol. 2 (18.1–19, 37).

or metaphysical line of argument in theology. Therefore in his own theology he tries to do entirely without the *"propriae rationes rerum naturalium"* ["proper reasons of natural things"]. Instead in his theological pursuit he intends to stick exclusively with reasons that are theological or suited to the matter at hand.[106] By design, therefore, William is already practicing that sort of abstinence with regard to teachings from other disciplines, namely, Aristotelian natural philosophy, which Gregory IX so urgently recommended to the theologians of Paris in 1228. From the perspective of William's understanding of faith, in any case, theology cannot become an Aristotelian science.

3.2 Between Bible and science: The early Dominicans

The biblical, evangelical impulse of the mendicant way of life and their theology would necessarily be expressed also in their systematic reflection on theology itself. The earliest introduction to theology by a Dominican has been preserved in the theological summa of the first Dominican *magister* in Paris, Roland of Cremona, which was probably written in the 1230s.[107] He was clearly influenced by William of Auxerre yet on the other hand presupposes the Aristotelian concept of science. He still understands theology as *divina scriptura,* although for the first time he now regards the central object and scientific character of this activity as problematic, with reference to the Aristotelian framing of the methodological questions.[108] In a quotation from the *Posterior Analytics* Roland takes as his foundation Aristotle's strict, experientially based concept of science.[109] This already makes it clear that biblical theology in itself is not yet science in the strict sense. Rather it surpasses mere science—as understood in the tradition of Hugh of St. Victor—and constitutes wisdom *(sapientia),* the goal of all other sciences.[110] Theology therefore has the status of mistress in relation to the other sciences and *artes,* and employs them comprehensively.[111] Although theology is not strictly speaking a science, one can examine it according to all the elements of an Aristotelian science: object, principles, and proof. Its central object, viewed in terms of the Bible and salvation history, is *"Christus inte-*

106. Ibid., (20.56–71).

107. See Filthaut, *Roland von Cremona;* Köpf, *Anfänge,* 54–55.

108. Roland of Cremona, *Summa,* prol. q.2 (unpublished): see also Köpf, *Anfänge,* 276; Grabmann, *Erkenntnislehre,* 189.

109. See Roland, *Summa* prol.q.2, cited in Köpf, *Anfänge,* 152, n. 105.

110. Ibid., cited in Köpf, *Anfänge,* 219, n. 325.

111. See Köpf, *Anfänge,* 241, 244.

ger" ["the whole Christ"], which includes God, man and the whole Church from the beginning until the end of time, and even the damned (*in imagine* [as creatures made in the divine image]).[112] The articles of faith cannot be the principles of demonstration for theology in the Aristotelian sense, because they lack the requisite self-evident character. Moreover according to Hebrews 11:1 the articles of faith themselves are arguments that cannot exist without faith. In any case it is possible to draw further conclusions from the articles of faith using the scientific method. This still presupposes personal faith, however.[113] The articles of faith themselves, though, are not syllogistically derived from a preexisting faith, but rather are the content of faith that is believed. In *"fides formata,"* the faith that is realized (in works as well), the objective and the subjective or affective elements of faith coincide, and the faith becomes a thematic *"argumentum."* Without this faith, which assumes the role of the foundation for science that is played in the Aristotelian concept by experience, there is no theology.[114]

We are indebted for Richard Fishacre († 1248) for the first commentary on the *Sentences* by a Dominican at Oxford.[115] His introduction to theology in the prologue of his commentary uses the Aristotelian four causes as an outline.[116] Under the heading *causa finalis* he inquires into the necessity and usefulness of theology. Here already, as with Roland of Cremona, the concept of science defined in the *Posterior Analytics* is taken as a basis, yet it is immediately replaced by the fundamental division of all knowledge into *scientia deorsum* (natural, worldly knowledge) and *sapientia de sursum* (God-given wisdom in the three books of life, Scripture, and creation). Theology (regarded as *sacra scriptura*), however, is necessary because God cannot be known adequately from nature alone. This is also the reason for the priority of theology over the natural sciences; for the useful knowledge that can be learned in them is found in sacred Scripture too, along with much more that cannot be found in the natural sciences. Therefore the other sciences are still *"pedissequae et ancillae"* ["women in waiting and maidservants"]; scholars—unlike many theologians of his day—should not bother too much

112. Roland of Cremona, *Summa,* prol. q.2, cited in Köpf, *Anfänge,* 100–1, n. 93.

113. Ibid., cited in Köpf, *Anfänge,* 141, n. 60–62; see also *Summa* l.3, CIV, 5, ed. A. Cortesi (Bergamo, 1962), 321; CV, 1.322.

114. Ibid., prol. q.2, cited in Köpf, *Anfänge,* 198–99, n. 220.

115. See Pelster, "Richard Fishacre"; Long and O'Carroll, *Fishacre,* 15–48; Niederbacher and Leibold, *Theologie,* 131–87.

116. Long, ed., "Science," 79–98; see the more detailed discussion in: Grabmann, *Erkenntnislehre,* 205–15; Niederbacher and Leibold, *Theologie,* 165–84.

about them so as not to awaken the suspicion of an adulterous relationship with a hired maid.[117] Clearly we see here the aftereffects of the warning by Gregory IX to theologians not to busy themselves with (natural) philosophy. The efficient cause of sacred Scripture and theology is God. Therefore it is *"verissima, ordinatissima et certissima"* ["most true, highly ordered and quite certain"]. Its truth, method and certainty, then, are dependent in principle, not on the Aristotelian theory of science and a procedure of demonstration, but rather on the truth and veracity of God.[118] Therefore *"scientia vel scriptura"* (= theology) knows no syllogistic method of proof; it is based in principle not on human arguments from reason but rather on the authority of the author, that is, God. This very argument demonstrates the equation of sacred Scripture and theology, which is not yet regarded as problematic. In this discipline, moreover, there is no transition from what is known to what is less known; instead, everything that is taught is equally certain, since God's authority guarantees the entire contents of Scripture. This is immediately turned into an appeal to the moral sense of the theologians: *"Quod si tantus est huius sapientiae auctor, quales debent esse auditores!"* ["Now if the Author of this wisdom is so great, what should the students be like!"][119] The *materia* of theology is initially described very comprehensively and skillfully in the three simple elements of *"natura suprema, media et infima"* ["highest, middle and lowest nature"], namely God, rational creatures and bodies, and the structures compose of those elements, the Church and man, which are both incorporated again into Christ. The object of theology, therefore, cannot be so easily defined as Roland does. The indivisible fundamental element is God himself; the *"maxime compositum"* ["most composite element"], in contrast, is Christ, whereas the actual *subjectum* is the union of the two higher elements: God and the rational creature, that is, the Church or God's salvific history with mankind.[120] In man, however, there are two powers: the *virtus motiva* and the *virtus apprehensiva,* the affective faculty of will and theoretical understanding. Theology, being aligned with both, is neither a purely theoretical nor a purely practical discipline, but necessarily concerns the knowledge of God as the highest truth, insofar as that is possible on earth, and union with the highest good. Now the theoretical part is reserved for the discussion of more difficult questions about

117. Fishacre, *In Sent.,* prol., ed. Long, "Science," 85–87; see also CUP I n.59 (I, 114–16).
118. Fishacre, *In Sent.,* prol., ed. Long, "Science," 87–89.
119. Ibid., 89–90.
120. Ibid., 91–96; see also Köpf, *Anfänge,* 101–2; Niederbacher and Leibold, *Theolgie,* 175–77.

the articles of faith, that is, in the historical context of lectures on the *Sentences*. The moral, practical part, on the other hand, is treated in the interpretation of sacred Scripture. Both parts refer, nevertheless, to Scripture as the foundation of theology as a whole; for speculative theology, too, is present "indistinctly" in Scripture, but is elaborated by the *"magistri moderni"* in disputations for methodological reasons. The questions in the Lombard's *Sentences* are expressly declared to be excerpts from the Bible; this legitimizes systematic theology biblically.[121] Along the lines of the Augustinian moral preparation for the speculative investigation of the faith, the moral interpretation of sacred Scripture must precede the lectures on the *Sentences.* Neither one is an Aristotelian science, however; instead, the two together convey a knowledge that, according to the self-understanding of the theologian, surpasses all Aristotelian scientific theory.

Clearly dependent on Richard Fishacre is Robert Kilwardby († 1279), whose commentary on the *Sentences* dates to the 1250s (after 1256).[122] Taking Proverbs 9:1 as his point of departure, he develops his introdution to theology in several questions; the basic understanding of theology as wisdom is present, while at the same time it is investigated again according to the four causes. In the very first sentence, however, Kilwardby distinguishes more clearly than Fishacre between theological teaching and *sacra scriptura.*[123] The problematic relation between the *Sentences* and the Bible is resolved in such a way that God naturally remains the *auctor* of Scripture, while the Lombard is only the *"compilator vel promulgator"* of the sacred text. The fact that the *Sentences* are derived from Scripture is already taken for granted.[124] Question 12, which is decisive for the question of scientific character, lists all the reasons why the Aristotelian concept of science appears to be inapplicable to theology (viewed here as *scriptura*): generality, necessity, knowledge of causes, evidence. In order to resolve the question, Kilwardby distinguishes in principle between two kinds of knowledge: the one comes from divine inspiration and is obtained through the study of a book; the other comes from human ingenuity and is conveyed *"viva voce."*

121. Fishacre, *In Sent.*, prol., ed. Long, "Science," 96–98.

122. Robert Kilwardby, *Quaestiones in Librum Primum Sententiarum,* J. Schneider, ed. (Bayrische Akademie der Wissenschaften, Publication #13 of the Kommittee für die Herausgabe ungedruckter Texte aus der mittelalterlichen Geisteswelt [Committee for the printing of unpublished texts from the medieval intellectual world]) (Munich, 1986); see also Grabmann, *Erkenntnislehre,* 215–26.

123. Kilwardby, *I Sent* q.1 (3.1–3).

124. Ibid., 3.15–16.

Theology presupposes the first mode of knowledge. Only within this framework can one meaningfully discuss theology as a science.[125] Furthermore one should distinguish between theoretical and practical science *(scientia speculativa, activa)*. The fact that theology does not come under the heading of theoretical science is not discussed further here at all. Theology as a whole has to do with man's actions, more specifically with the perfect redemption of man. The theoretical part of theology is aimed at this as well; as contemplation it is subordinate to the commandment of love of God and is called *sapientia* [wisdom], while the practical part is defined by the commandment of love of neighbor and is called *scientia*. In theological terms, all other objects of contemplation or faith, however, become *scibilia* ["knowable things," suitable topics for scientific investigation] inasmuch as they are ordered to this goal.[126]

In keeping with the way of life of the early mendicant orders, there was a very decisive adherence to the practical orientation of theology as a whole. The Aristotelian concept of science, however, was not in keeping with theological tradition. First of all, Aristoteles is unacquainted with a science based on divine inspiration. The philosophical concept of science is therefore not applicable to *sacra scriptura*, and furthermore it does not even cover all manmade sciences, but in the strict sense only the theoretical sciences, principally mathematics.[127] Therefore theology (as sacred Scripture) does not produce a habit of knowledge in the sense of knowledge about a conclusion that has been proven, but rather first generates faith in all those things which are simply accepted *"sine ratiocinatione"* ["without argumentation"] on the evidence of Scripture. This faith, however, surpasses the purely natural knowledge *(scientia)* of the philosophers, because it is founded upon love for the first truth. If *ratio* is added to faith, the result is not science but again the Augustinian *intellectus* or *intelligentia*, insight into the faith. We can speak here about knowledge *(scientia)* only in the Augustinian sense as the common habit of faith and contemplation, and likewise about wisdom.[128] Theological knowledge is therefore in principle insight into the faith, gained from the practice of living out the faith and serving it, but not from science in the Aristotelian sense.

125. Ibid., q. 12, 30.45–49; see also Kraml, *Rede von Gott*, 93–103.
126. Kilwardby, *I Sent* q. 12.30.31–44.
127. Ibid., 30.50–31.73.
128. Ibid., q. 13.33.1–34.34.

3.3 Salvation history or metaphysics: The *Summa Halensis*

Alexander of Hales († 1245) figures in the Parisian tradition as the founder of lectures on the *Sentences* and at the same time as the first Franciscan *magister* (starting in 1236). His *Glossa in quatuor libros Sententiarum,* which dates to around 1223–1227, still does not provide a detailed theoretical justification of theology as a science, but rather a treatment of the *materia* of the book of sentences.[129] The entire contents of the systematic theology are derived from Exodus 3: the doctrine about God in book 1 from Exodus 3:14–15, and the contents of the remaining books from Exodus 3:7–8. Theology is therefore still understood essentially in terms of salvation history: God reveals himself in his merciful care for his oppressed people and leads it to the land of milk and honey. Thus theology sets out from the doctrine about God and leads via the teaching about the fall, repentance, and redemption to the Church and her sacraments and to eternal happiness with its gifts of grace.[130]

In contrast, the so-called *Summa Halensis,* which should be regarded as a collaborative work of the early Parisian Franciscan school, presents a detailed scientific theory of theology.[131] The first chapter of question 1 immediately inquires into the scientific character of systematic theology *(doctrina theologiae,* not *sacra scriptura).*[132] The answer proceeds not so much from the *Posterior Analytics* as from the concept of science in the Aristotelian *Metaphysics.* As Aristotle did, the *Summa* distinguishes between knowledge about causes and knowledge about what is caused (which depends on the former). The first type is a knowledge for its own sake, especially the knowledge about the *"causa causarum"* ["cause of causes"].[133] This *scientia,* however, is theology, which thereby is defined in the genuine sense as metaphysics and *sapientia,* which agrees well with the introductory quotation from Boethius and his view of theology.[134] Although the concept of science and wisdom found in the *Metaphysics* is applied at first to theology,

129. Alexander of Hales, *Glossa in quatuor libros Sententiarum Petri Lombardi* I, Introitus (Bibliotheca Franciscana Scholastica Medii Aevi 12) (Quaracchi, 1951), 1–4; see also Osborne, "Alexander of Hales," 9.

130. See Kraml, *Rede von Gott,* 90–92.

131. (*Summa Halensis* =) Alexander of Hales, *Summa theologica,* I (Quaracchi, 1924). On the question of authenticity and sources, see *Summa theologica,* IV, Prolegomena; Pergamo, *De Quaestionibus;* Osborne, "Alexander of Hales," 5–18; Niederbacher and Leibold, *Theologie,* 110–12.

132. *Summa Hal.* I Tr. int. q.1 c.1 (I, 1–4); see also Gössmann, *Metaphysik,* 15–36; Niederbacher and Leibold, *Theologie,* 77–130.

133. See Aristoteles, Met. I, 1–2.

134. *Summa Hal.* Tr. int. q.1 c.1 (I, 1); see also *Supra* 1.1.4.

it is nevertheless rendered more specific by the affective and practical orientation that distinguishes it from pure metaphysics. This affective, practical orientation constitutes the real sapiential ("relishing, tasting") character of theology, whereas metaphysics (as *theologia philosophorum,* the theology of the philosophers) is only wisdom as the perfection of knowledge and thus of the habit of knowing. The other sciences, however, which deal only with subordinate causes, are only *scientiae,* not *sapientia.*[135]

It is remarkable that the answer given by the *Summa* does not go at all into the foundation of theology in sacred Scripture. Only in the response to the objections against applying the Aristotelian concept of science (now from the *Posterior Analytics*) to theology does it bother to mention Scripture. The insufficient generality of the contents of sacred Scripture is immediately rejected as a reason for the inapplicability of the concept of science. Whereas secular history recounts the individual fact only as such, in Scripture the individual historical fact has a universal meaning. Through historical facts, general acts and conditions are indicated for the instruction of men and the contemplation of the divine mysteries. Since what is singular in Scripture designates something universal, the concept of science is therefore applicable to it. The universalization of what is manifested in salvation history ought therefore to guarantee the scientific character of theology in its biblical foundation as well.[136] Moreover, the *Summa* now demonstrates (just as desperately) that Scripture contains not only singular but general propositions (of a moral kind), for example, Proverbs 1:7 or 1 Timothy 1:5, so that the *"universale in praedicando"* ["the universal in preaching"] is present here just like the *"universale in exemplando"* [". . . in providing examples"] on the basis of its prophetic meaning, while the *"universale in significando"* [". . . in giving signs, i.e., warning"] is found in the general meaning of salvation history. Through the metaphysical attribution of the facts of salvation history to God, who is the universal cause of creation, or to Christ who is the universal cause of redemption, theology can furthermore lay claim to the *"universale in causando"* ["the universal in causing"], so that in its biblical foundation, too, theology can now claim to be an Aristotelian science par excellence, as *sapientia* in the sense explained in the *Metaphysics* I,1.[137]

135. Ibid., q.1 c.1 sol. (I, 2a). For a further development of the teaching about the practical or sapiential character of theology, see Amorós, "Teologia"; Niederbacher and Leibold, *Theologie,* 116–20.

136. *Summa Hal.* Tr. int. q.1 c.1 ad 1 (I, 2–3); see also Gössmann, *Metaphysik,* 18–19; Niederbacher and Leibold, *Theologie,* 128.

137. *Summa Hal.* Tr. int. q.1 c.1 ad 2 (I, 3).

The discussion of the object and method of theology shows how difficult it is to balance this concept of theology as a science with biblical thinking about salvation history. Depending on the perspective, the object of theology is considered to be the work of redemption, Christ or God *(divina substantia),* so that theology can then be defined in a handy formula as *"scientia de substantia divina cognoscenda per Christum in opere reparationis"* ["the science of the divine substance which is to be known through Christ in the work of reparation"].[138] The *Summa* strikes a balance here between the definition of theology as *sapientia* as understood in the *Metaphysics (substantia divina),* the Christocentrism of a Roland of Cremona and the definition of theology in terms of salvation history along the lines of Hugh of St. Victor. In the methodological treatise, finally, the current schemata from the theory of science must be entirely abandoned. The *"modus sacrae Scripturae"* [the "method of sacred Scripture"] does not follow the rules of an art or a science. The reason for this, however, lies in the divine wisdom, which through the Scriptures informs man about what is important for his salvation. Ultimately theology is defined as *knowledge about salvation* on the basis of divine instruction and thus exempt from the laws of methodology.[139] It is moreover an affective, practical discipline, to which the methods of the theoretical sciences—namely definition, division, and syllogism—are not applicable. Instead we find methods that are suited to the *"affectus pietatis"* ["devotion of piety"], namely precept, example, admonition, revelation, prayer. The *"pietas"* in question here, however, is *"cultus Dei"* ["the worship of God"].[140] In a Franciscan way, therefore, theology appears to be related here again to piety and reverence for God, thus embedded in Franciscan religious life.

This affective element is expressed also in the discussion of the specifically theological certainty in comparison with the other sciences. Weighty objections arise to a certainty that would be equivalent to that of the sciences: the certainty of mere belief as opposed to *intellectus* [understanding], insufficient perspicuity of the principles, the metaphorical and equivocal style of Scripture. The *Summa* makes a fundamental distinction between affective and intellectual certainty. Theology leads to greater affective [i.e., subjective] certainty than experience; on the other hand it lags behind empirical

138. Ibid., q.1 c.3 sol. (I, 6); see also Gössmann, *Metaphysik,* 25–26; Niederbacher and Leibold, *Theologie,* 120–22.

139. *Summa Hal.* q.1 c.4 a.1 sol. (I, 8a); see also Gössmann, *Metaphysik,* 27–31; Niederbacher and Leibold, *Theologie,* 122–27.

140. *Summa Hal.* q.1 c.4 a.1 ad 2 (I, 8b).

evidence [*Anschauungs-Evidenz*] in intellectual certainty, since it is based on faith alone.[141] Therefore even in its principles theology is different from the other sciences, namely the theoretical sciences. The latter are founded on self-evident, true principles; theological principles, in contrast, have two components: truth and goodness, and thus a theoretical and a practical element. They are *"principia veritatis ut bonitatis"* ["principles of Truth considered as the Good"]. With regard to theoretical [speculative] truth they are less evident than the principles of other sciences. With regard to practical goodness, however, they are acknowledged to have the status of *"principia per se nota"* ["self-evident principles"], namely, for moral conduct.[142]

Theology is described here with an unmistakably practical emphasis, yet it is not just a moral philosophy; its supernatural element becomes apparent in its divine origin: It is *"a Deo et de Deo et ductiva ad Deum"* ["from God and about God and leads to God"].[143] Now the other sciences come from God *(a Deo),* too, but they are not conveyed in the same manner, through divine inspiration as a gift of grace, which is why it is possible to say formulaically that theology *(doctrina sacra)* comes from the Holy Spirit. The truth in it is therefore a *"bonum gratuitum"* ["a gratuitous good," i.e., a grace], and this is precisely the basis for its *practical* certainty also, which consequently should not be measured according to the standards of human science. It is not concerned about God *(de Deo)* only in the metaphysical sense, but rather in terms of the Triune God in his salvific work. It leads to God *(ad Deum)* through the principles of fear and love, based on faith in God's mercy and justice.

Since theology (again in the sense of sacred Scripture) thus conveys a practical certainty based on inspiration and a knowledge of the same sort, the question arises as to the validity and necessity of theoretical attention to the scientific status of theology itself. A certain discrepancy in the *Summa Halensis* cannot be overlooked: the scientific character of theology is initially proved along Boethian lines with a concept of theology as understood in the *Metaphysics,* while the Christian character of this theology and its unique status and independence from all other sciences is supposed to be explained then by a markedly affective, practical concept of theology founded on sacred Scripture. The latter sort of theology, however, hardly corresponds to the scientific concept from the *Metaphysics* and is largely exempt

141. Ibid., a.2 sol., ad 1 (I, 9).

142. Ibid., ad 2 (I, 9b).

143. Ibid., q.1 c.2 ad ob. (I, 5b).

from the methodological claims of the theory of science. This "immunity" is not so difficult to defend, inasmuch as the Franciscan theologians hark back to the sapiential theology of the monastic and Victorine circles and understand theology as *sapientia* [wisdom] and thus as something which in principle surpasses every *scientia* [science, knowledge]. The fault lines in the attempted equilibrium are all too plain.

3.4 Presuppositions and goal of theological science: Albert the Great

Composed around the year 1245, the commentary on the *Sentences* by Albertus Magnus (ca. 1200–1280) contains no question specifically devoted to the problem of the scientific character of theology.[144] Instead it is assumed in the very first article. This article inquires as to the object of theology, now understood however from an unmistakably Aristotelian perspective on science. As described by the *Posterior Analytics,* science presupposes its object. Theology, in contrast, appears to have to define and prove its object first. Doesn't that contradict its scientific character?[145] In the answer the scientific character of theology is explicitly affirmed: It is the highest science. Its object is presupposed as *"materia de qua"* ["the matter about which"], yet it is investigated in the science itself out of didactic considerations, especially when the definition of the object is obscure, such as the statement by Peter Lombard that according to Augustine *"res et signa"* ["things and signs"] are the object of theology. They are its object, not absolutely, but rather with regard to the goal of theology, which again is markedly practical: to share in eternal blessedness, whereby even the Augustinian distinction between *uti* and *frui* [to use and to enjoy] is brought in. Either the things and signs themselves effect blessedness or they are useful, that is, dispose the soul to it.[146]

In the Aristotelian sense, however, the subject of a science is the central object; the object's properties, considered as *passiones* [i.e., the ninth Category], and its differences are proved through the principles proper to the science. Besides the problem of the object, this now poses the problem of principles: Starting from what principles does theology prove its propositions? In this sense the question about the object alludes to the fundamen-

144. For the philosophical background, see Sturlese, *Philosophie,* 224–388.

145. Albertus Magnus, *I Sent* d.1 a.1, in *Opera omnia,* ed. A. Borgnet, vol. 25 (Paris, 1893), 15; see also Senner, "Wissenschaftstheorie"; Burger, "Bedeutung."

146. Albertus Magnus, *I Sent* d.1 a.2 sol. (16).

tal presuppositions of theology as a science. Albert presents them using the traditional term of *credibile* [something that can be believed]. This, however, includes the *praeambula* or fundamental axioms that are logically prior to the individual articles of faith, for example:

1. God is truthful.
2. God exists.
3. The Holy Spirit is the author of sacred Scripture.
4. Sacred Scripture is infallible.

Only then do the twelve or fourteen articles of faith follow, along with several basic moral truths, for example: Fornication is a mortal sin. In contrast to the *praeambula,* these are the genuine premises of theology from which everything else in theology is proved. Albert has thereby clarified the later distinctions among fundamental-theological, dogmatic and moral-theological contents within the framework of theological science. The fundamental axioms are not immediately the premises of theological reasoning but rather the presuppositions thereof.[147] Their justification is therefore not within the scope of the genuinely scientific exposition of theology. At *III Sent.* d.24 a.8, in any case, Albert distinguishes between *"suppositiones et dignitates,"* that is, the underlying axioms that are implied in the articles of faith, and the articles of faith themselves, which are derived as *theoremata* from the principles. Finally, the consequences for moral conduct are corollaries.[148] In this passage, therefore, the articles of faith themselves have become propositions derived from axioms, whereas at *I Sent.* d.1 a.2 they appear together with the moral principles as premises: *"de istis enim probatur omne quod probatur in Sacra Scriptura."* ["For from them is proved everything that is proved in Sacred Scripture."][149]

Specifically, at any rate, the matter of theology is God as its most eminent and central object, from which it also takes its name. Yet theology does not consider God in himself *(absolute tantum)* but rather as the Alpha and the Omega, *"principium et finis,"* whereby Albert has at the same time struck a balance between the two concepts of theology (as science, as salvation history) in his treatment of creation *(principium)* and the arrangements for arriving at the goal (virtues, gifts of the Holy Spirit, sacraments).

147. See Lang, "Bedeutung."

148. Albertus Magnus, *III Sent* d.24 a.8 sol. (Ed. Paris. 28, 465); see also Senner, "Wissenschaftstheorie," 327–28; on the Augustinian tradition, see Fuchs, *Zeichen,* 33–48.

149. Albertus Magnus, *I Sent.* d.1 a.2 sol. (Ed. Paris. 16b).

Albert also poses the question about the unity of theology, expressly along the lines of the Aristotelian theory of science.[150] Here unity is guaranteed by the generic unity of the object *(unius generis subjecti scientia)*. Albert does not see such a unity in theology, since on the one hand God is the object in several sciences (e.g., in metaphysics also), while on the other hand theology contains much heterogeneous material: the lives of the patriarchs and the status of the angels, creation, moral instructions, etc. Like the early Dominicans and Franciscans, nevertheless, Albert sees theology as a practical science, directed toward the one *"finis beatificans"* ["beatific end"]. Theology investigates how the *"beatificabile"* ("thing that can be beatified," i.e., man) can reach this goal by means of the *"dispositiones beatificantes"* ["beatifying arrangements"] that assist him as means or free him from obstacles, which are the *"res hujus mundi"* ["things of this world"]. Theology can therefore treat of all things; it is a universal science, but with an unequivocally practical-affective character, directed toward the goal of eternal blessedness. The things of this world, however, are means to this end. Theology is thereby implicitly defined as a practical science. Even the historical facts of sacred Scripture and its contents are not the object of theology *"secundum se"* ["in and of themselves"] but rather only as means with regard to this goal. Thus the study of sacred Scripture is fruitful only from this overall theological perspective: it combines the scientific-theoretical element with the traditional ascetical element of *"lectio divina."* Here too Albert's thought is informed by the Dominican way of life. On the other hand, the problem of the insufficient universality of biblical facts is thereby resolved. They are general examples in a practical science, the purpose of which is defined as follows: *"ut boni fiamus"* ["that we may become good"].[151]

The question explicitly asked in article 4, whether theology is a theoretical or a practical science, thus seems to be answered already in principle. Remarkable in any case is the biblical foundation on which the question is decided: Titus 1:1–2, which speaks about the *"agnitio veritatis quae secundum pietatem est, in spem vitae aeternae"* ["knowledge of the truth which accords with piety, in the hope of eternal life"]. *"Secundum pietatem"* is explained by the Gloss as "in accordance with the Christian religion." The foundation of theology is still practical religion, the practice of worshipping God within the context of living out a Christian life. Even "Scholastic" theology, ac-

150. Ibid., d.1 a.3 (17).
151. Ibid., d.1 a.3 ad2 (18).

cording to Albert, cannot be separated from it. In this way the knowledge of the truth in the secular sciences *(in liberalibus artibus)* is different from the knowledge of theological truth. Theological truth, however, is always *"veritas secundum pietatem"* ["truth which accords with godliness"]. There are two aspects to this: first, reverence for God in himself and in the members of the Body of Christ and everything that serves that purpose. This is the objective, practical orientation of theology. Its distinctive feature however, in Albert's view, comes from the *"finis intentionis"* ["end which is intended"], namely substantial union, including the intellect and will, with God as the *"finis beatificans."* Through its consistent orientation to this goal theology becomes an *affective science of salvation.* Theological truths are not merely rational truths; they are oriented to moral conduct and affective behavior. Within the sciences of natural philosophy there is no such orientation. Consequently this establishes both the distinctiveness and the necessity of theology as an autonomous science.[152]

The traditional concept of *"sapientia"* can also be applied to this affective science, certainly with arguments drawn from *Metaphysics* I.1: it is knowledge about the highest objects and to the highest degree, namely, about God and according to the principles of the faith. The latter rank higher than the principles of reason, so that there can be no problem at all with regard to the self-evident character of the principles.[153] Theology in the metaphysical sense, moreover, is the only free science *(gratia sui),* because here the object of knowledge is sought at the same time for its own sake: God, to whom all aspire through this *"scientia beatificans."* Albert clearly opposes a purely moral, practical theology without any affective orientation: *"Ut boni fiamus,"* personal ethical improvement, is only a subordinate goal; the final goal of theology remains the *"veritas affectiva beatificans"* ["the affective truth that beatifies"]. An increase of theoretical knowledge is at first not even mentioned.[154] Therefore theology does not exist in order to further our knowledge about "theological subjects" or truths, but rather to lead us to blessedness by improving our lives.

The method of theology therefore is guided by the goal: being an admonition and encouragement of the faithful, it employs the methods of scriptural interpretation according to the fourfold sense of Scripture.[155] In

152. Ibid.; see also Rohner, "De natura Theologiae."
153. Albertus Magnus, *I Sent.* d.1 a.4 ad 1 (19a).
154. Ibid., ad 3–4 (19).
155. Ibid., a.5 (19–20).

the debate that has been institutionalized in the book of *Sentences,* there is a need, of course, for argument so as to prove the truth and to expose error. Three grounds for proof are mentioned: authority, natural reason, and analogies. The rather succinct impression given by the short article shows clearly that the controversy over the Bible and the *Sentences* plays no role here. Scientific character, in the strict sense of a procedure of proof *(scientia istius libri),* nevertheless, is attributed only to lectures on the *Sentences* and consequently to systematic theology.

Albert makes it clear that the Aristotelian concept of science offers theology many useful clarifications, especially with regard to its unique nature and the status of its fundamental principles. As an affective science of salvation, however, theology is still bound up with faith and the living out of religion. Its preeminence is thus demonstrated only theologically, and not in terms of the theory of science.

3.5 Theology as science and wisdom in Christ: Bonaventure

Bonaventure (1217/18–1274) does not pose the question as to the scientific character of theology explicitly in his commentary on the *Sentences.*[156] He inquires instead about the object and goal of the theological enterprise, more precisely of the book of *Sentences,* which is equated with theology. His concept of science is still relatively vague. Theology and faith, however, are clearly distinguished according to their respective objects: The object of faith *(credibile)* is in itself a primary truth to which the believer assents; this is to be distinguished from the *"doctrina sacrae Scripturae"* ["teaching of sacred Scripture"], which is endowed with the highest divine authority; finally, in a third step beyond faith and authority, there is also the *"ratio probabilitatis"* ["reason of formal proof"], and this gives rise to the object of (systematic) theology or the collection of *Sentences.* For here it is a matter of setting forth *"rationes probantes fidem nostram"* ["reasons proving our faith"].[157] Faith, sacred Scripture, and systematic theology are precisely distinguished. Systematic theology comes about through the addition of plausible, probable reasonable arguments. Is that enough to guarantee its scientific character?

The question can be answered only in view of the practical, affective character of theology. Science, then, is understood in principle to be a *"hab-*

156. Bonaventura, *I Sent.* prooem. q.1–4 (Op.I, 6–15); see also Tavard, *Transiency;* Kraml, *Rede von Gott,* 107–12; Niederbacher and Leibold, *Theologie,* 189–233.

157. Bonaventura, *I Sent.* prooem. q.1 ad 5–6 (I, 8b).

itus directivus" of the intellect. It is therefore a guiding authority, either a theoretical, speculative one for the intellect per se, or a practical, moral one with regard to man's ethical perfection, or finally the union of theoretical and practical knowledge *(sapientia)* for affective action. Bonaventure sees this *sapientia* embodied in theology, but with a clear preponderance of the practical element: theology is in the first place not theoretical but practical knowledge with one purpose: *"ut boni fiamus."* The two are combined, however, in the devotion that is formed by faith. Theological truths, for example, the fact that Christ died for us, are different from the theorems of geometry, for example, because of their affective orientation.[158] As was already the case in the *Summa Halensis,* so too here the sapiential character of theology is emphasized with a markedly affective and practical orientation. The method, in contrast, is defined as *"modus ratiocinativus sive inquisitivus"* ["an argumentative or investigative method"]: reasoning, argumentation and *quaestio* thus define *systematic* theology; for unlike the *Summa Halensis,* Bonaventure is not inquiring about the method of the sort of theology that is identified with sacred Scripture, but rather about the method of a commentary on the *Sentences* as the basis for systematic theology.[159] The relation between the *Sentences* and the Bible, however, is resolved now according to the Aristotelian model of subaltern sciences.[160] With regard to their certainty and their method, the *Sentences* are "subaltern" or subordinate to the authority of scriptural as understood in faith. The rational, scientific method of systematic theology therefore remains nonetheless connected with the authority and certainty of sacred Scripture, but not to the [particular] method of its exposition.[161]

This sapiential understanding of theology also dominates the sermon *Unus est magister vester Christus* (ca. 1257), which may have been intended for the *inceptio* ceremony.[162] In a way that is still nonpolemical as compared with his later work, the Franciscan *magister* presents his view of theology. In keeping with the Scripture verse Matthew 23:10 on which it is based, the Christocentrism of theology is clearly elaborated. To a great extent Bonaventure's procedure is still the compilation of various passages from the Church Fathers; Augustine is by far the one most often cited. Bonaventure

158. Ibid., q.3 sol. (I, 13).
159. Ibid., q.2 sol. (I, 10–11).
160. See Köpf, *Anfänge,* 145–46.
161. Bonaventura, *I Sent.* prooem. q.2 ad 4 (I, 11); for the concept of theology as distinct from *sacra scriptura* see also Donneaud, "Sens."
162. Edition by Russo, *Metodologia,* 99–133.

takes his program for theology from Hugh of St. Victor and is thus in good Franciscan company. Theology is geared on the one hand to the human effort for certain knowledge *(cognitio certitudinalis)* but on the other hand to living the faith in the three-step process of *pietas, ratio,* and *veritas.*[163] *Pietas* corresponds to faith, *ratio* to proof and consequently science, whereas truth corresponds to contemplation. As a science, therefore, theology as a whole has a mediating function; it is only a part—albeit an important one—of the path leading from faith to the comprehension of the truth. Scientific knowledge is ordered to the spiritual gift of understanding; faith, however, is ordered to virtue, and contemplation to blessedness. The knowledge sought in scientific theology is a *"cognitio collativa"* ["comparative knowledge"] and consists therefore increasingly in the compilation and comparison of authorities and arguments.[164] The theology which in the Augustinian tradition is viewed as insight into the faith is based on revelation and authority, mediated or confirmed by Christ. Without enlightenment by Christ, no one can penetrate the *"sacramenta fidei"* ["mysteries of faith"] (as Hugh of St. Victor understands that expression), and thus be a theologian in the true sense of the word.[165] The nonbelieving theologian, as we find later in the case of Ockham, is for Bonaventure still unthinkable. Christ, however, is also the center of Scripture, *"fundamentum totius fidei christianae"* ["the foundation of all Christian faith"], of the teaching of the apostles and prophets, of the Old and New Testaments.[166]

Bonaventure now significantly incorporates Aristotelian material into his elaboration of the second step, the knowledge of reason, without deviating from his basic perspective. He lists the following requirements for scientific knowledge: unchanging truth on the part of what is known, infallible certainty on the part of the knower. According to the *Posterior Analytics* I,2, however, necessity and certainty are found in the knowledge of causes. Nevertheless, even in this Aristotelian interpretation of science, Christ is still the *"magister cognitionis"* ["Master of knowledge"], for unchangeable truth cannot be found in the realm of created truth. That is also why the Aristotelian interpretation is immediately supplemented and rendered harmless by Augustine's doctrine of the eternal truth about us. Indeed, according to Augustine only the being of things *"in ratione aeterna"* ["in their eternal form/aspect"] is unchangeable, that is, in the Word, in Christ. He alone is

163. Bonaventura, *Serm. theol.* IV, 1 (ed. Russo 100.8–12).

164. Ibid., (100.12–19).

165. Ibid., n.2–3 (100.21–102.44).

166. Ibid., n.5 (102.65–72).

the medium of knowledge that makes things *"perfecte scibiles"* ["perfectly knowable"].[167] Natural, Aristotelian knowledge is therefore never a complete, perfect knowledge of things. It is just as incapable of leading to the certainty that is required for science. Certainty can be found only in the *"sapientia increata"* ["Uncreated Wisdom"], Christ. Thereby Bonaventure manages also to introduce long passages from the Augustinian theory of illumination into his teaching about science. For without enlightenment by Christ, the created intellect does not even arrive at sure knowledge of any thing; how then could it ever attain certainty about theological truths?[168] Natural knowledge is therefore deficient knowledge. It must in principle be surpassed and requires a theological foundation. Theology proves therefore to be the authority that legitimizes the "natural" sciences as well.[169]

Scientific theology in turn, however, is only one part of the way to wisdom, which is to be attained in contemplation. This too is at all points connected with Christ in his divinity and humanity.[170] The way to wisdom, however, has only one order and one author who must be "read" here. The order leads from faith via *ratio* to contemplation; the *sancti* (the saints, but in the technical sense the Church Fathers), who are contrasted with the *philosophi* (the pagan philosophers), knew this way. The latter are accused of ignorance of the correct method, since they disregarded the foundation of faith, relied on reason alone and thus were completely unable to attain contemplation. Philosophy is therefore in principle a deficient mode of knowledge. This is already a denial of a philosophy that is emancipated from theology; it was later formulated even more forcefully starting in 1267 in the fight against the heterodox currents within the faculty of the arts, in several series of lectures: *Collationes de decem praeceptis* (1267), *Collationes de donis Spiritus sancti* (1268) and so on until the *Collationes in Hexaemeron* (1273). For philosophy does not know the *"doctor et auctor"* Christ, the *"director et adjutor nostrae intelligentiae"* ["guide and help of our intellect"], whose specific direction is necessary for knowledge of the truth.[171] God's cooperation in the knowledge of reason involves on the one hand the effort to know and on the other hand the certainty of the object. Natural, *a posteriori* knowledge retains its rights, though; it must however be combined in an Augus-

167. Ibid., n.6–7 (106.77–96).

168. Ibid., n. 9–8 (108.113–112.157).

169. See Hattrup, *Ekstatik der Geschichte.*

170. Bonaventura, *Serm. theol.* IV, 11 (ed. Russo 112.158–65).

171. Ibid., 16 (118.235–39); on Bonaventure's development, see esp. Ratzinger, *The Theology of History in St. Bonaventure* (Chicago: Franciscan Herald Press, 1971, 1989).

tinian way with the *"lex aeterna"* ["eternal law"]. As far as the natural foundation of our knowledge in experience is concerned, Aristotle was perfectly correct. Bonaventure can accept also his critique of Plato's doctrine of ideas as the only certain knowledge: We need to reject not the ideas but rather Plato's disdain for the sensible world. In order to establish the *"via sapientiae"* ["way of wisdom"] in the eternal ideas, Plato abolishes the *"via scientiae"* in creaturely categories. In contrast, Aristotle is accused of the converse: disdaining the ideas so as to make experiential science alone possible. But each philosopher has received a special discourse: Plato that of wisdom, and Aristotle that of science. Plato looks predominantly upward, Aristotle—downward. Augustine, on the other hand, received both discourses at the same time from the Holy Spirit. That is why he is the most eminent interpreter of sacred Scripture, and therefore the theologian par excellence. To an even more eminent degree Paul and Moses unite science and wisdom, whereas Christ, as the *"principalis magister et doctor"* has them to the highest degree possible.[172] Theology must therefore combine Aristotelian knowledge and Platonic wisdom in the spirit of Augustine, in order to understand Paul and Moses and to be instructed by Christ.

This happens when the honor due to a *magister* is shown to Christ by imitating him in practice, when one listens to him in humble faith, when he is the authority who decides one's *quaestio,* which must not spring from *curiositas* or disbelief but proceeds from a willingness to learn, as in the case of Nicodemus. The object of these questions, however, is the entire field of knowledge, of practical conduct and ethical decision-making.[173] The theologian therefore is just the *"ministerialis doctor"* ["learned official"] who must align his teaching with Christ's, that is, with the *"scientia veritatis fidei"* ["science of the truth of the faith"].[174] With Franciscan optimism (which in light of the actual situation at the university could easily strike us as naïve), Bonaventure finally points out that all *"doctores christianae legis"* ["doctors of the Christian law"] strive after all for the bond of love and consequently must reach an agreement in their *sententiae* as well. Dissenting opinions and sentences brought into theology from outside originate only in the presumption of the *magister* and therefore do not belong to theology in the Franciscan sense. Rather, excessive reliance on sense knowledge, discrep-

172. Bonaventura, *Serm. theol.* IV, 18–19 (ed. Russo 120.258–124.300).

173. Ibid., 21–23 (124.312–126.340).

174. Ibid., 24 (128.356–60).

ancies among sentences and the despair of finding the truth are obstacles on the way to truth, which have been overcome in principle by Christ.[175] Bonaventure, of course, is setting up an ideal of theological science and wisdom, which even in his time must have seemed outmoded in view of the developments at the university, although he accepts Aristotle in part and thereby immunizes him theologically and incorporates his understanding of science in the overall scheme of an Augustinian-Franciscan synthesis.

3.6 A proof of scientific character? Thomas Aquinas

In contrast the Bonaventure's Franciscan synthesis, Thomas Aquinas (1225–1274) firmly aligned himself, even in his early commentary on the *Sentences* (1254–56), with the Aristotelian concept of science.[176] According to the latter, it should be proved that theology *(sacra doctrina)* is a science; Thomas was obviously aware of the difficulties standing in the way of his endeavor in his day. Sometime before the year 1259 he took up the topic again in his *Expositio super librum Boethii De Trinitate* and finally in abbreviated form for beginners in question 1 of the *Summa Theologiae.*[177] What strikes the reader initially is that Thomas is explicitly grappling with the necessity of an autonomous theology alongside the disciplines of philosophy and the natural sciences.[178] The necessity is substantiated by man's supernatural goal, the vision of God. As in the writings of Thomas' teacher, Albert the Great, theology is therefore understood here as *"manuductio"* ["guidance"] to man's eternal destination, but certainly not as the mere satisfaction of intellectual needs concerning *"res divinae"* ["the things of God"]. Man receives this guidance not only from creatures, as in philosophy, but directly from divine inspiration. Thomas now uses this as an argument for the preeminence of theology and for its claim to rule the other sciences. What was traditionally described by the image of the *"ancilla," "pedissequa,"* or *"famula"* ["handmaid," "woman in waiting," or "servant girl"] becomes in Thomas' treatment a model of dominion: the other sciences are vassals to theology, which for its part is proved to be the sovereign in the kingdom of the sciences. The relationship is explained in terms of the Aristotelian mod-

175. Ibid., 26–28 (130.381–132.410).

176. On the dating and textual criticism, see Oliva, *Débuts;* see also Niederbacher and Leibold, *Theologie,* 235–89.

177. See Kraml, *Rede von Gott,* 112–17; Grabmann, *Erkenntnislehre,* 101–85; Neumann, *Gegenstand.*

178. Thomas Aquinas, *I Sent.* prol. q.1 (edited by Oliva, *Débuts,* 310–14); *S.th.* I q.1 a.1 (I, 2–3); see also Niederbacher and Leibold, *Theologie,* 235–89.

el of subaltern sciences, justified here, of course, by the respective purposes of the sciences.[179] The other sciences are destined to be auxiliary sciences to theology, just as the apothecary's art *(pigmentaria)* is an auxiliary science to medicine: The physician orders the apothecary and employs his services for his own purposes. This subordination out of practical considerations is described in the *Summa Theologiae* as a relation between the military and politics (the *bonum exercitus,* the good of the army, is aimed at the *bonum civitatis,* the good of the state) and is accompanied by an additional theoretical reason: the object of theology (God) and its degree of certainty account for its preeminence over all theoretical sciences.[180]

This claim, however, makes the certification of the scientific character of theology unalterable. The singularity of biblical facts causes little trouble. They are generalized in the traditional manner as *"exempla operandorum"* ["examples of works to be performed"] as in a practical science.[181] On the other hand, the problem of principles and certainty takes on a more difficult form, especially since science is defined as *"cognitio certitudinalis"* ["knowledge characterized by certitude"]. This very quality, however, is explained here solely by a reference to the *"lumen fidei"* ["light of faith"] that unbelievers do not have.[182] Theology itself cannot substantiate the articles of faith scientifically, just as no science in the Aristotelian sense can prove its own fundamental axioms. But that would seem to make theology in principle a science that owes its existence solely to a special illumination (of faith). As such, can it be recognized as general knowledge?

Thomas finds the way out of the theoretical problem by applying once again the model of subaltern sciences. While it is not possible for us to verify the articles of our faith, nevertheless they are verified in the knowledge of God. This corresponds to the model of subaltern sciences: The higher sciences proceed from self-evident principles and derive from them conclusions that are then used by the lower sciences, with faith in the reliability of the higher sciences, as premises for their own conclusions.[183] Thomas is fond of using the example of optics, which presupposes geometry with re-

179. On the scheme of subaltern sciences, see: Köpf, *Anfänge,* 145–49; Niederbacher and Leibold, *Theologie,* 277–80; for the perspective that regards them as *"famulantes et praeambulae,"* see Thomas Aquinas, *In De Trin.* q.2 a.3 ad 7 (ed. B. Decker, *Studien und Texte zur Geistesgeschichte des Mittelalters* 4 [Leiden, 1965], 97.6–7).

180. Thomas Aquinas, *S.Th.* I q.1 a.5 i.c. (I, 5).

181. Thomas Aquinas, *I Sent* prol. a.3 ad 2.1 (ed. Oliva, *Débuts,* 322).

182. Ibid., ad 2.2-A and 2.2-B (322–324); for the findings of text- and literary criticism (re revisions), see also Oliva, *Débuts,* 139–85.

183. Thomas Aquinas, *III Sent* d.24 a.2 sol.3 (III, 770).

gard to the definition of a line and applies geometric knowledge to its particular case, the visible line. In a similar way theology assumes the articles of faith as premises. These, however, are not self-evident principles, but rather are presupposed as theorems of the *scientia Dei* [science of God], believed, and used as premises in proving theological conclusions.[184]

This solution, however, has its problems as well, which become evident in the commentary on Boethius.[185] Theology, considered as the *"scientia de divinis"* [science of divine things] must be further subdivided into *human (nostra)* theology and *divine* theology *(theologia Dei et beatorum).* "Theology" becomes, like "science," an equivocal or analogous expression, and the rules for its use must still be established. Human theology is connected with experience and takes creatures as its point of departure. In this context God is known only *a posteriori,* not as he is in himself. We possess no knowledge of God's essence, as is actually presupposed for an Aristotelian *demonstratio potissima* [best sort of proof].[186] Now such knowledge is assumed only for God himself and for those who have been perfected and are enjoying eternal happiness (i.e., the vision of God). Human, *a posteriori* theology is viewed here, of course, not as the theology of revelation but as metaphysics. The theology of revelation, in contrast, appears as an imperfect participation in and assimilation of the knowledge of God through faith. Therefore we have to distinguish among three kinds of theology, each with its own mode of knowledge:

1. metaphysics as *"scientia divinorum ex parte nostra"* ["the science of divine things from our perspective"].
2. the knowledge of God and of the saints (*ex natura ipsorum:* by their own nature).
3. the theology of revelation as a participation in (2) through faith.

The difference between the second and third kinds of theology, however, lies also in the fact that (2) is intuitive, while (3) is discursive knowledge. The Aristotelian model of subaltern sciences, however, holds for two sciences with discursive knowledge; for something that is a theorem (i.e., a derived proposition) in the superior science is used in the subaltern science as a premise. In (2), however, everything is self-evident, so that there is no

184. Thomas Aquinas, *S.Th.* I q.1 a.2 i.c. (I, 3).

185. Thomas Aquinas, *In De Trin.* q.2 a.3 resp. (ed. Decker 86–87); see also Jenkins, *Knowledge,* 56–76.

186. See Aertsen, "Von Gott."

need to distinguish between principles and conclusions. It seems dubious, therefore, that the term *"scientia"* can be applied in the strict sense to (2).[187] The things which constitute the knowledge of God are known to the theologian of the third kind only in faith. From these contents of faith he can derive further conclusions through scientific methods. Obviously in this passage Thomas is trying to highlight the preeminence of revealed theology with regard to philosophy (including metaphysics), and he does this by deriving its principles from a higher source.[188] This proof of the scientific character of revealed theology adds little to that form of theology itself except further problems: if the principles are grasped only in faith, pointing out that they are evident in the knowledge of God and of the saints is of little relevance to the theologian or his status at the university.

Explaining revealed theology as participation in the "theology" of God and the saints, however, settles the question as to the theoretical or practical character of our theology. Although it seems at first that theology, with its orientation to man's final end in the commentary on the *Sentences,* can be defined in affective terms, as it had been in the writings of Albert the Great, this immediately changes in Thomas' treatise when he examines the contents of this end or goal.[189] This, of course, is not to dispute the fact that theology has practical elements as well, which are aimed at right conduct. Its final goal, however, in terms of which the character of the whole science is defined, is the *"contemplatio primae veritatis in patria"* ["contemplation of the first truth in (our heavenly) homeland"], and therefore precisely that perfect "theology" that we do not have here. This latter kind, however, is by nature purely theoretical, speculative. The affective element of beatitude found in Albert the Great is missing here. That is why all of theology, too, is primarily a speculative, theoretical science. Theology is no longer primarily concerned now with rules for the Christian life on the way to eternal happiness, but rather with the theoretical consideration of the "first truth" of God and of the true propositions derived from it.[190] This first truth, nevertheless, is still incorporated into Christian life as a partial realization of man's goal, on the basis of good works, whereby the practical implications of theology are brought in as well.[191]

187. Thomas Aquinas, *In De Trin.* q.2 a.3 ad 5 (89.5–14).

188. Ibid., resp. n.3 (87.21–23).

189. Thomas Aquinas, *I Sent.* prol. a.3 resp. (ed. Oliva, *Débuts,* 320–21); see also Friederichs, *Theologie.*

190. A critique of this view is found in Kraml, *Rede von Gott,* 114–16.

191. Thomas Aquinas, *I Sent.* prol. a.3 ad 1 (ed. Oliva, *Débuts,* 322).

This theoretical, scientific definition of theology also has consequences for its methodology. The separation of Bible from the *Sentences,* each with a different method, which Albert the Great had still advocated, has been surpassed already in the commentary on the *Sentences.*[192] The unity of theology is underscored also by the fact that the [various] modes of theological discourse are justified for individual parts or steps: revelation or prayer for the principles (by the Revealer or the receiver, respectively), narrative for corroboration; similes and metaphors to guide the listener; argumentation to refute errors (only on the basis of the literal sense); precepts, examples, and tropological interpretation for moral teaching; *"quaestiones sacrae scripturae,"* though, for the *"contemplatio veritatis"* that is the final end of theology as a whole. That goal can be reached, however, only through the argumentative method, which naturally includes allegory and anagogy: exegesis and sentences are fused in a unified theology that tries to assert itself as science.

3.7 The Franciscan reaction: William de la Mare

The doctrine about the science of theology in the commentary on the *Sentences* (ca. 1270) by William de la Mare, who is better known as the author of the *Correctorium fratri Thomae,* can be read to some extent as the Franciscan reaction to the Thomist "proof" of the scientific character of theology in the Aristotelian sense. William served as *magister regens* [full professor] in Paris in 1274/75.[193] His concept of science is clearly and logically formulated. *Scientia* in the sense of a scientific discipline is a collection of true propositions, or more precisely of true statements, since only statements have a definite truth value.[194] In contrast, a law *(lex)* is a collection of precepts and prohibitions that are not true or false but rather good or bad, just or unjust, to be observed or not. We must decide between the two, *scientia* and *lex,* with regard to theology: is it a science of theoretical, true, proven propositions or does it have a normative, prescriptive character for everyday life? The Franciscan is inclined toward the second solution, but is also aware of the burden of tradition, in which the *"sancti doctores"* ["holy

192. Ibid., a.5 resp. (329–31).

193. Guillelmus de la Mare, *Scriptum in primum librum Sententiarum,* ed. H. Kraml (Bayrische Akademie der Wissenschaften; Veröffentlichung der Kommittee für die Herausgabe ungedruckter Texte aus der mittelalterlichen Geisteswelt 15), esp. 29*–83*; concerning the few certain dates in William's life, see de la Mare, 13*; see also Kraml, *Rede von Gott,* 117–26; Niederbacher and Leibold, *Theologie,* 191–324.

194. William de la Mare, *I Sent.* q.1 sol. (12.27–13.38); on the continuance of this understanding of science in the writings of Ockham, see Leinsle, "Einheit der Wissenschaft nach Wilhelm von Ockham."

doctors"] knew of no clear distinction between descriptive and normative sentences and therefore did not use the terms *"lex"* and *"scientia"* correctly. For after all, from the law we derive a practical knowledge of what to do; besides, the law too contains many statements, yet that is not the primary intention of the law, but rather a means of convincing people to accept or observe the law. Their presence does not turn the law into a collection of descriptive statements. Only in the sense of this confused linguistic usage of tradition does William acknowledge that theology has a scientific character. In the proper sense, however, it is a normative, practical collection of instructions about how to act, and consequently *lex.* Above and beyond the equation of theology and sacred Scripture, theology is thus shown to be the epitome of the *"vetus et nova lex"* ["Old and New Law"].[195]

For this reason William maintains that the scientific character of theology can be demonstrated in an exclusively biblical way as well, by showing the inferential procedure of proof in Scripture. Generally Paul is referred to for this purpose, and then individual passages such as Isaiah 53:7, Matthew 5:3, and the other Beatitudes are interpreted as syllogistic arguments. There is the possibility of proofs even in statements of faith; by no means do all of them have the same faith-character based on authority; rather, we should distinguish between faith on the basis of the certainty of the matters themselves and faith on the basis of authority. In the first case there are gradations in our knowledge that allow for a syllogistic procedure in which the premises must be better known than the conclusion. In the second case, which actually corresponds to the legal character of Scripture, this is not the case, insofar as faith only is being considered here. If faith, however, is accompanied by the spiritual gifts of understanding and knowledge [*Wissenschaft*] based on merit, then clearly we recognize gradations in our knowledge about the articles of faith also, so that here too a syllogistic procedure becomes possible.[196] This presupposes, however, not a science obtained by human effort, but rather the infused gifts of grace that are called knowledge and understanding, and it consequently eludes human effort and cannot be deemed a general proof of the scientific character of theology.

This is precisely what constitutes for William the difference between theology and the secular sciences. Theology (considered as *sacra scriptura* and hence as *lex*) is accepted in faith based on the authority of the speak-

195. For the sources of this interpretation see Sileo, *Teoria della scienza teologica* II, 131–64.
196. William de la Mare, *I Sent.* q.1 sol. (13.39–64).

er. Only from faith does understanding then follow. In the other sciences, however, belief follows understanding. William maintains that both can be admitted, that theology is therefore a law and also a science; his conclusion should be interpreted in this sense: its scientific character should be viewed only within the framework of its legal character. It does not produce a new or a natural wisdom that is independent of the act of faith—not even when it proceeds syllogistically.[197] In clear contrast to the *Summa Halensis,* the universality of the science is seen now in the moral application of individual events as examples, and furthermore William denies that universality is necessary in order for theology to have a scientific character. For it is precisely the business of the law to incite people to do good by presenting individual good deeds and to discourage them from doing evil by decreeing singular punishments. If theology is understood in this moral, prescriptive sense, then universality is not required of its statements.[198]

The limited scientific character of theology within the framework of its legal character results also in a solution to the question of whether it is a theoretical or a practical science. Here Thomas is referred to directly, and his solution is immediately rejected as null and void: *"Sed hoc nihil est."* For here Thomas is arguing not in terms of the immediate goal of science, but rather from its more remote final end, the contemplation of God's truth in beatitude. Since our whole life and quest for knowledge is aimed at that, however, this would make all sciences theoretical, so that there would be no practical sciences at all. In any case one cannot define the meaning and task of theology as Thomas tried to do.[199] Science as a human activity must be defined in terms of its immediate goal, not from the final end of human life as a whole. Now William is unequivocally taking the legal character of theology as his point of departure. Law, however, is a collection of precepts of a practical nature, concerned with man's conduct. Therefore if we can speak about a scientific character of theology, then it must be within the framework of this understanding. Consequently theology should be addressed unequivocally as a practical science. Only in a subordinate clause does William mention the possible difference between the legal character of sacred Scripture and the allegedly systematic, theoretical scientific character of the book of *Sentences.* The *Sentences* are justified in principle only as an explanation of sacred Scripture *(expositoria)* and thus of the law: systematic theol-

197. Ibid. (14.65–71).

198. Ibid., ad 1 (14.72–87).

199. Ibid., q.2 sol. (15.21–24).

ogy is still an exposition of the law and thus dependent upon the practical character of the law itself.[200]

Of course William does not deny that theology as a practical exposition of law contains theoretical parts in the form of statements. This pertains especially to the doctrine about the One, Triune God. Yet this is a common feature of the practical sciences: Not everything that is treated in them deals directly with human activity. Thus in medicine one must know a lot about the human body and the humors, but that does not make medicine a merely theoretical science. Aristotle himself in his *Ethics* deals with the faculties of the soul as a prerequisite for his teaching on human action and the virtues. The important thing is that even the theoretical parts be related to human action. Thus the teaching about God in theology is not a theoretical science (or, in Thomistic terms, a participation in the beatific vision) about what God is like in and of himself; it is taught, rather, with a view to man's activity in worshipping God, in believing and hoping.[201] On the one hand, therefore, theology has a direct connection to life, and on the other hand, as a practical science with theoretical elements, it is in good company with medicine and ethics, at the university as well. Consequently there is no need to reformulate it as a theoretical science in order to assure it of a place there.

Through this practical character, scriptural theology is also clearly distinguished from any sort of metaphysics in the Aristotelian sense. Any blurring of the boundaries, such as we find in the *Summa Halensis,* is rejected at the outset. Metaphysics as a purely human theology on the basis of natural arguments from reason is theoretical or speculative; scriptural theology as *lex* [law], in contrast, is based on divine revelation and is of a practical nature. Although metaphysics determines that [natural] theology is the highest science and *"sui gratia,"* because it is directed only to knowledge for its own sake, these definitions are not applicable to [scriptural] theology. For no law is given for its own sake or merely for the sake of knowledge, but rather with a view to human activity. Finally, the connection with man's final end, described by Thomas as the contemplation of God, takes nothing away from the practical character of theology. For at issue, after all, is not a theory of contemplation *(scire contemplari),* but rather the act of contemplation itself. Therefore this end, again, is not an increase of theoretical knowledge but rather an activity.[202] Therefore even Thomas would have had to define

200. Ibid. (15.25–28).

201. Ibid., ad 1 (16.29–38).

202. Ibid., ad 2–4 (16.39–51).

theology, correctly understood, as a practical science, had he grasped the fact that *"contemplari"* describes a human act. Its immediate object is therefore what it prescribes: the right worship of God *(cultus divinus).*[203] The object of the Bible and the *Sentences,* however, is the same; for the *Sentences* are only the explanation of the law. A purely speculative-theoretical theology is thus just as impossible as Thomas' thesis about the primarily theoretical character of this science.[204] Once again school and life, "Scholastic" theology and a Christian-Franciscan way of life are connected to each other in theology's understanding of itself: theology is the explanation of revelation (understood normatively) with a view to human activity in right worship.

3.8 Immunization through "enlightenment": Henry of Ghent

Another possible alternative to the Thomistic theory of subaltern sciences, besides the *"lex"* concept of William de la Mare, is the Augustinian theory of theology that Henry of Ghent (ca. 1217–1293) develops in the very extensive questions in his *Summa* dealing with the theory of science.[205] In his view, too, proving the scientific character of theology is still a problem, yet he tries to accomplish it by other means than his predecessors used. From Augustine he borrows the fundamental view of knowledge as enlightenment *(illustratio, illuminatio);* for only sensory knowledge can be traced back to purely natural factors; God participates in all knowledge beyond that, guaranteeing by his illumination the truth and the certainty of the knowledge. Knowledge of truth is possible for man, therefore, only if God in his freedom concurs in it.[206] In general, however, we can rely on the fact that the course of the world is so ordered that man can recognize the truth on the basis of the natural faculties with which he is endowed.[207] The divine light itself, however, in which he knows the other truths, eludes knowledge in this world.[208]

Now theology is based on a knowledge of faith that surpasses human nature with respect not only to man's capacity to know but also to its object.[209] Theology consists of an understanding of faith, as Augustine and

203. Ibid., q.3 a.1 sol. (24.258–25.280); concerning the discussion of the object of theology, see de la Mare, "Einleitung" [Introduction], 51*–66*.

204. Ibid., q.3 a.2 sol. (27.344–28.364).

205. See Beumer, "Erleuchteter Glaube"; Kann, "Skepsis"; Speer, "Sapientia nostra," 260–66.

206. Henry of Ghent, *Summa quaestionum ordinariarum,* P.I a.1 q.2 (facsimile reprint of the 1520 Paris edition, New York: St. Bonaventure, 1953), I f. 7r I.

207. Ibid. (I f. 7v M).

208. Ibid., I a.1 q.3 (I f. 8v–10v).

209. Ibid., I a.3 q.4 ad 2 (I f. 29v R).

Anselm had defined it, but in a scientific manner: it should become *"intelligentia fidei"* and therefore presupposes the faith at all points.[210] It unfolds in a three-step process:

1. The believing theologian assents to the truths that he derives immediately from sacred Scripture. These serve as premises of the further scientific development.
2. From these premises he deduces further truths that are hidden in them *"sub primis scibilibus"* ["beneath the first knowable truths"] and are not explained immediately by the wording of Scripture.
3. As a theologian he tries to examine rationally all the truths that he previously adhered to only in faith.[211]

A definition of theology as a science on the basis of its method alone therefore falls short, because it does not include the decisive step (3). This step cannot be taken with faith and natural reason alone, but rather presupposes a special enlightenment in which the revealed truths of the faith become intelligible [*einsichtig*]. The light of faith allows one to recognize only *the fact that* the truths of the faith are true and it corresponds therefore to knowledge of a given; the step to real insight into the coherence of what is believed presupposes an illumination by grace that is somewhere between faith and the beatific vision.[212] Moreover, the syllogistic derivation of further articles of faith from the initial truths of the faith is likewise possible only on the basis of this supernatural, gratuitous enlightenment.[213] The work of theology is properly speaking an activity that owes its existence to a twofold grace: the grace of faith and the special illumination that enables one to understand the faith. The mere application of the Aristotelian, methodological concept of science to theology therefore falls too short.

The solution proposed by Henry [of Ghent] with regard to the scientific character of theology harks back to Bonaventure's principle of the transition from *credibilia* [believable things] to *intelligibilia* [intelligible things]. At the same time Henry distinguishes between a broad concept of science and a narrow one. In the broader sense every certain knowledge of a truth should be treated as *scientia.*[214] In this sense also the objects grasped by

210. Ibid., I a.13 q.3 (I f. 91r); q.6 (I f. 94r–95r).
211. Ibid., a.13 q.8 (I f. 98v); see also Finkenzeller, *Offenbarung*, 175–76.
212. Henry of Ghent, *Summa* I a.13 q.4–7 (I f. 92v–97v).
213. Ibid., I a.6 q.1 ad 1. (I f. 42v).
214. Ibid., sol. (I f. 42v).

faith are known; theology, therefore, in the form of steps (1) and (2), should be treated as science, even though a comprehension of the truths of faith through contemplation or insight is not present. For the strict concept of science Henry significantly does not accept the syllogistic method of Aristotle but rather Avicenna's demand that the thing be self-evident. Certainty must not depend on the authority of another, as is the case with faith. Such self-evidence is not present in mere statements of faith. Unlike the *"res naturales"* of the natural sciences, they can only potentially be made intelligible. Yet the intelligibility of faith statements is due precisely to the *"lumen medium"* ["mediating light"] in which they acquire the necessary evident character. Thereby theology in itself becomes the most certain of all sciences. For it deals with the most certain things with the highest possible reliability [*Sicherheit*] and greatest evidence for the knower, at least for a man[215]—woman is expressly excluded from the pursuit of theology—upon whom that spiritual *"lumen intellectuale"* has shined. Thus even the strict concept of science as Avicenna understood it is now applicable to theology.[216] The scientific character in this sense is of course guaranteed supernaturally by a gratuitous and free intervention of God.

Thomas' theory of subaltern sciences, in Henry's opinion, endangers the very scientific character of theology. He accuses the theory of oversimplification and ignorance of what "subalternation" really means according to Aristotle. The knowledge of God is not a discursive knowledge in which the principles of our theology can be known with respect to their "why and wherefore." Subalternation comes about not with respect to the degree in which known propositions are known, but rather and solely in the distinction between *scientia quia* [knowledge that] and *scientia propter quid* [knowledge of causes]. Thomas' doctrine does not prove any subalternation but rather that divine knowledge should be treated as wisdom in the highest degree and as the first norm of all human knowing.[217]

The very method of theology described by Henry makes it clear that he understands theological knowledge as a real extension of knowledge which is not just aimed at practical life or the attainment of the final goal. Here in his argumentation he proceeds along lines that are to some extent quite similar to those of Thomas Aquinas, and he even strengthens the ar-

215. See Beumer, "Stellung Heinrichs von Gent."
216. Henry of Ghent, *Summa* I a.7 q.2 sol. (I f.49v); see also Porro, "Statuto," 501–3.
217. Ibid., I a.7 q.5 sol. (I f. 53v); see also Grabmann, *Erkenntnislehre,* 306–13.

guments for interpreting theology as a theoretical science. For all practical moral effort, in Augustine's view, is supposed merely to purify the mind for the theoretical contemplation of the truth *(speculatio veri)*.[218] This theoretical activity, however, begins with faith and is meant to lead to the best understanding thereof that is possible in this life, so as then to end in eternal contemplation. Therefore what William de la Mare determined to be the final goal of theology, *cultus divinus* [divine worship], is here only a preparation for the real task of theological endeavor, corresponding in the ascent toward God to the stage of purification, whereas the stage of illumination is logically attributed to theology. Theology therefore does not have a twofold goal either, as for instance Thomas, Bonaventure, and Albert the Great assumed, but rather a single one: theoretical knowledge. To it all practical knowledge is ordered. The toil and effort of work is undertaken in theology not for the sake of a practical moral goal, but rather *"propter quietem speculationis"* ["for the sake of the repose of speculation"]. Any practical parts of theology should be interpreted in terms of this theoretical goal and thus classified within the framework of theology as a theoretical science. Yet precisely as a theoretical science theology is normative for all practical knowledge; for in Henry's writings, too, it consists of drawing near to God, who in his purely theoretical knowledge knows and directs everything that is to be done by man. Henry explicitly rejects the understanding of sacred Scripture and thus of theology as *"lex"* ["law"] found in the writings of William de la Mare. Theology is indeed God's law, but by that very fact it is not a practical rule like human law, but rather consists—harking back to Boethius' concept of rule—of theoretical rules *(ex regulis speculativis)* and is therefore of a purely theoretical nature.[219] The theoretical character of theology is thus shifted back into sacred Scripture itself, even at the risk of prompting later commentators to discover a contradiction in the expression *"regula speculativa."*[220]

The question as to the agreement of the other sciences with the truth of theology can be regarded as a theological reaction to the accusation of teaching a "double truth" in the 1277 condemnation.[221] The first thing to note is that specific truths of the faith are beyond natural knowledge, for example, the virgin birth and the resurrection. Any contradiction between

218. Henry of Ghent, *Summa* I a.8 q.3 sol. (I f. 65v); see also Leone, "Zum Status."
219. Ibid., ad 2 (I f. 65v); see also *IST*, ch. 1.1.4 and 2.8.
220. See Köpf, *Anfänge*, 207–8.
221. Henry of Ghent, *Summa* I a.7 q.13 (I f. 62r–63r).

theological truth and the truth of natural knowledge is ruled out as a matter of principle. It is possible, of course, for a theological truth to be false according to the personal judgment of a philosopher. In that case, nevertheless, the underlying problem is only an error of the philosopher, who considers false anything that surpasses his ability to know. In themselves, however, philosophical and theological truth cannot contradict; instead philosophical truth is claimed as a guide and preliminary step to theology. Therefore a theologian who out of ignorance of philosophy considers to be false many things that have in fact been proved true philosophically is rash *(temerarius)*. Truth that has been proved philosophically, however, in no way diminishes the status of theology, since the latter owes its scientific character not to any human effort but rather to divine enlightenment.

3.9 Augustinian or Aristotelian science? Ægidius Romanus

The period of theoretical discussion about theology as a science following Thomas Aquinas and already in the debate with Henry of Ghent is characterized by the commentary on the *Sentences* (book I, ca. 1276/77) by the Augustine Recollect Ægidius Romanus († 1316), who was a *magister* in Paris from about 1285 until 1292 and while he was still alive was declared the most important theological authority in his order.[222] Like Henry, he favors Augustine over Aristoteles, without however denying Thomistic influences, especially in his acceptance of the theory of subalternation.[223] He understands theology as *sapientia,* and the scientific character of theology, in his view, is situated within that framework. Insofar as theology regards its objects principally as *divina* [the things of God], it is wisdom; it can be addressed as science only to the extent that it considers its objects *"ut humana"* ["as human matters"], because science for Ægidius is in principle restricted to human effort and the corresponding objects. This distinction is derived from Augustine, not from Aristotle.[224] Of prime importance for the scientific character of theology, therefore, is not so much Aristotle as Augustine. On the other hand, in order to clarify the problem of first principles, the Thomistic theory of subalternation is brought in, again of course in a way combining Augustinian and Aristotelian arguments that is typical

222. See Prassel, *Theologieverständnis.*

223. See Beumer, "Augustinismus"; Egenter, "Vernunft."

224. Ægidius Romanus, *In Primum Librum Sententiarum,* prol. p.2 princ. 1 q.1 (Venice, 1521; reprinted Frankfurt, 1968), f. 6vb.

of Ægidius: The scientific character of theology is maintained according to Augustine, *De Trinitate* XIII, 9. But in order to prove that it is scientific in the Aristotelian sense as well, the obviousness of its principles in a higher science must be established, since they exist in our theology only as articles of faith. A higher science, however, exists only in the knowledge of God and of the saints. Therefore theology (but not "our theology") is a subaltern science to the knowledge of God and the knowledge of the saints.[225] On the other hand, none of the usual modes of subalternation between the natural sciences applies to this instance of subalternation. In principle Ægidius recognizes, not just one (like Henry of Ghent), but three ways of subalternation:

1. Subordinate service to a higher science that has a higher-ranking object.
2. Subordination of "knowing that" to "knowing why." Henry of Ghent had recognized this as the sole model of subalternation. The example of geometry and optics cited by Thomas comes under this mode of subalternation. Ægidius immediately concedes that the term is used equivocally.
3. Two sciences deal with the same object, but the superior in a more precise way than the subordinate science.[226]

Consequently, in the proper sense only the ambiguous mode (2) remains as a real model of subalternation. Yet neither this nor any other mode is applicable in the strict sense to theology. Points of comparison can be found with all three models of subalternation, yet subalternation can no longer serve as a proof of scientific character.[227] It is referred to, however, to clarify the degree of certainty of theological statements. One can give reasons for this certainty in three ways:

1. on the part of the object,
2. through an appropriate light of knowledge, or
3. in relation to the knower.[228]

A science that deals with principles has a higher degree of certainty; theology, though, deals with God, the original principle; therefore it is (in itself) the most certain of all sciences. Moreover it relies not only on the natural light of knowledge (natural understanding) but, as Henry of Ghent also says, on a supernatural light. This is completely unknown to the Phi-

225. Ibid., a.2 (f.4va).
226. Ibid., a.1 (f.4ra); see also Prassel, *Theologieverständnis,* 40–47.
227. Ibid., a.2 (f.4va.).
228. Ibid., princ. 2 q.2 (7rab).

losopher (Aristotle). He assumed that one could attain certainty only by the light of the natural intellect. Therefore theological certainty is not derived from the same source as philosophical-scientific certainty, and by the same token it eludes philosophical discussion. The certainty of faith, however, is the highest degree of certainty, at least considered as the believer's *"certitudo adhaesionis"* ["certitude of adherence"]. In contrast, the situation is less than ideal with *"certitudo speculationis,"* the objective certainty of the propositions derived from what is believed, since it is based on faith, which cannot claim the evident character of objective knowledge.

As to the question about the aim of theology, Ægidius (unlike Henry of Ghent) subscribes to the solution of Albert the Great, which again has a strongly Augustinian orientation. In his opinion there is nothing at all wrong about attributing more than one aim to theology (still considered as *sacra pagina*), and does not try to make it an absolutely theoretical or merely a practical science.[229] An initial aim of theology, for Ægidius, is good conduct. On the other hand, however, he also acknowledges that Scripture deals *"de summe speculabilibus"* ["with things capable in the highest degree of being the objects of speculation"]. Above all, however, love is sought in theology; the various subordinate aims are ordered to it; for upon it depend the Law and the Prophets. The chief aim of sacred Scripture, therefore, is to lead man to love of God and love of neighbor. A science, however, is defined in terms of its chief aim. Love *(charitas),* however, is a virtue of the will [*Affekt*], not of the intellect. Therefore, first of all, the purely theoretical-intellectual interpretation of theology by Henry of Ghent must be rejected. But neither is theology a practical-moral science that could be subordinated to the *"intellectus practicus"* ["practical intellect"]. It is, rather, as in the works of Albert the Great, a *"scientia affectiva"* ["affective science"] and therefore more wisdom than mere science. Only within the context of this affective understanding of theology can one ask and answer the question as to the predominance of the theoretical or the practical element in it. In this regard Ægidius now gives priority to Thomas, inasmuch as he assumes that the vision of God is the principal feature of beatitude and orders all our knowledge to it, but especially theology. Therefore it still has a more strongly theoretical than practical character. Thomas' optimism, in thinking that he could make an Aristotelian science out of theology and ensure its certainty by arguments from the theory of science, had vanished at any rate by the end of the thirteenth century.

229. Ibid., princ. 4 q.1 (7vb–8ra).

4 Theological Controversy and Church Reform

The scientific theology of the fourteenth and fifteenth centuries—a period often deprecated as the decline of "late Scholasticism"—is characterized on the one hand by the logically precise analysis of theological truths and of their presuppositions, and on the other hand by the transition of theology from the lecture hall to a position of social and ecclesial influence in its effort to bring about reform in the Church. Within academic theology during those uncertain times, the question about the foundation and the certainty of theological statements and thus of our knowledge of salvation became the foremost theological and existentially pressing problem.

1 Scholastic theology amid societal upheaval

Whereas thirteenth-century theology had been concerned primarily with its position at the university and with proving its scientific character, in the fourteenth and fifteenth centuries the differences between the theological schools came to the fore with the utmost clarity, because of refined logical techniques, among other reasons. The reason why theology did not become bogged down in the "Scholastic" squabbles between the various schools was its involvement in the societal and ecclesiastical situation of the late medieval period, which was characterized by societal upheavals, the rise of the territorial state, heretical movements, and the Western Schism and reform councils.[1]

1.1 The development of academic study

Paris and Oxford, the centers of theological life in the thirteenth century, continued to set the tone in the fourteenth; especially after the con-

1. See esp. Obermann, *Herbst.*

demnations of 1277, Oxford gained preeminence.[2] Now the decisive philosophical and theological innovations generally came from England, such as those connected with the names Duns Scotus (ca. 1265–1308) and William of Ockham (ca. 1285–1347). They were welcomed in Paris with vehement controversy. Oxford, however, was also the source of John Wycliffe's theses concerning theology and church polity, which fell on more fertile soil at the new University of Prague.

Paris, however, rose to the occasion of the ecclesiastical controversies of the late Middle Ages and became the most important ecclesiastical advisory authority; debated questions that were to be officially decided by the pope and the Curia were referred to *magistri* in Paris for a provisional theological decision *(doctrinalis determinatio praevia)*.[3] Prime examples were the Immaculate Conception of Mary (1387), the theoretical debate about poverty and the controversy with the Franciscan groups (especially the Fraticelli) inspired by the teachings of Joachim of Fiore.[4] Luther, too, would appeal to the university against the pope. The Western Schism (1378) at first had a debilitating effect on theology at the University of Paris but on the whole strengthened its position; all but a minority of the Parisian *magistri* professed obedience to Avignon, while at the same time the university became the seedbed of anti-papal tendencies that favored a national Church.[5] Yet the decisive models for overcoming the schism were supposed to come from Paris (of all places), where initially the *"via cessionis"* ["way of resignation"] without a general council was the preferred solution. However, Peter of Ailly (1352–1420) and John Gerson (1363–1429), the leading figures in the reform movement in Pisa and Constance, were Parisian theologians, too.[6]

The theological university scene, nevertheless, was drastically changed by the founding of new universities in the fourteenth and fifteenth centuries. In the territory of the Holy Roman Empire alone, nineteen university foundations were registered between 1347 (Prague) and 1502 (Wittenberg).[7] Sometimes in implementing the plan of the founder (emperor, prince, city, bishop) there were considerable delays before instruction actually began. During the Western Schism the obedience [i.e., confessional allegiance] in

2. See Leff, *Paris and Oxford;* Courtenay, "Parisian Faculty of Theology."
3. Rashdall, *Universities* 1:549–50, with reference to Jean Gerson.
4. See Leff, *Heresy* 1:51–258; Lambert, *Heresy,* 189–214.
5. See esp. Swanson, *Universities.*
6. See Rashdall, *Universities,* 1:549–83.
7. Ibid., 3:211–288: Prague (1347/48), Vienna (1363), Erfurt (1379), Heidelberg (1385), Co-

a given place could be strengthened by the foundation of universities.[8] The sheer abundance of localities for university teaching, which in many cases had been preceded by cloister or city schools, and in Cologne even by a Dominican *studium generale* [general house of studies],[9] produced a kind of theological awakening which cannot be reconciled with notions about a decadent "late Scholasticism." Naturally, new ideas were more easily admitted at new universities than at old ones, where hard and fast traditions already prevailed. The new universities at least claimed to be, like Paris, transregional institutions, but at the same time there was an unmistakable tendency to nationalize and regionalize even theological instruction. This was most clearly evident in the founding of the University of Leipzig (1409) by the emigration of the German professors and students from the University of Prague. The University of Greifswald owed its establishment to the pronouncement of the interdict against Rostock (1437).

The exchange of professors and the traveling of itinerant students, however, kept academic life from becoming too provincial while again resulting in relations and rivalries between universities that were often quite distant.[10] The theology at the new universities was sometimes influenced also by the religious orders, for example, in Erfurt and Wittenberg by the Augustine Recollects, in Tübingen by the Benedictine Abbey at Blaubeuren [*Brüder vom gemeinsamen Leben*]. The communities of canons regular at cathedrals [*Prälatenklöster*] now sent their most gifted men to the new universities and thus brought university theology back to their own cathedral schools where they trained their confreres; there is little evidence that university theology influenced the education of the lower clergy in the late Middle Ages.[11] In this respect as well, Scholastic theology in the late Middle Ages, situated in the midst of the ecclesial and social tensions of an urban culture, was many-layered, more complex and less easily characterized than in the thirteenth-century controversies that played out essentially between Dominicans, Franciscans, and secular clergy.

Formally, the focal point in theological instruction in the fourteenth and fifteenth centuries was still the course of lectures on the *Sentences*, which in

logne (1388), Würzburg (1402), Leipzig (1409), Rostock (1419), Louvain/Leuven (1425), Trier (1454), Greifswald (1456), Freiburg im Breisgau (1455/56), Basel (1459), Ingolstadt (1459), Mainz (1476), Tübingen (1476/77), Frankfurt an der Oder (1500/06), Wittenberg (1502).

8. See Swanson, *Universities*, 216–17: List of universities approved by the popes from 1374–1418.

9. See Sturlese, *Philosophie*, 324–26.

10. See, for example, Uiblein, "Beziehungen"; Gabriel, "Via Antiqua."

11. See Oediger, *Bildung*.

many respects however was changing. First we should distinguish between the cursory *"lectura textualis"* [textual reading] of the *baccaleureus* [bachelor] and the work of the *magister* [master], which has been preserved most often in the form of questions pertaining to the *Sentences.* Both forms of instruction dispense to a large extent with the Lombard's text. Instead an abridged version was taken as the textual basis, sometimes even in the *"lectura."*[12] At any rate, questions are already incorporated in the introductory lectures at important passages. In contrast, the *Quaestiones in Libros Sententiarum* dispense with all reference to the text and now systematically discuss the individual questions that are important in a given context without regard for completeness. Thus Heinrich Totting of Oyta (ca. 1330–1397) discusses ten questions on book 1 of the *Sentences* but only one apiece for the rest. That alone shows the overemphasis given here to the philosophical problems of the doctrine about God. In contrast to the simple form of the *quaestio* in Thomas' writings, its structure had already changed in the works of Henry of Ghent (ca. 1217–1293) and even more markedly from Ockham on. The general arguments pro and con carry much less weight than the extensive discussion (sometimes subdivided into *quaestiunculae*) of the contemporary *opiniones,* citing and sometimes refuting the arguments that support them.[13]

Just as scholars often were acquainted with the Lombard's text only from abridgments, the university teachers themselves likewise wrote abbreviations of important commentaries on the *Sentences,* especially at the new universities, which were not yet endowed with libraries. So, for example, an abbreviation of the commentary on the *Sentences* by the Franciscan Adam Woodham (or Goddam, ca. 1298–1358) is attributed to Heinrich Totting of Oyta.[14] The Scholastic masterpiece of Gabriel Biel (ca. 1410–1495) was his *Collectorium,* which closely follows Ockham's commentary on the *Sentences,* while of course borrowing also from other authors for the purpose of revision.[15]

The explanation of Scripture, which was per se still the province of the *magister,* was carried out in a twofold course, like the lectures on the *Sentences:* first the *"lectura textualis,"* the cursory reading by the *baccalaureus,* and then the exposition by the *magister,* which was usually restricted to just one book or a few chapters; the text again became merely the occasion for an independent

12. Thus Heinrich Totting of Oyta used the abbreviation *"Quoniam velut quattuor flumina paradisi"* attributed to Hugh of St. Cher; see also Lang, *Heinrich Totting,* 50–53.

13. See Rentsch, "Kultur der quaestio," 88–89.

14. Lang, *Heinrich Totting,* 54–61.

15. Gabriel Biel, *Collectorium circa quattuor libros Sententiarum,* praef., ed. W. Werbeck/U. Hofmann (Tübingen, 1973), 1:6–7.

discussion of questions. Heinrich of Langenstein (1325–1397) during his thirteen years of teaching in Vienna did not get past the first three chapters of the book of Genesis.[16] Francis of Retz († 1421) took the Proverbs as his text and within that context discussed all the current theological questions; Heinrich Totting did the same with the Psalms (1–50). Thus, for example, at Psalm 21 Christological questions are considered (the separation of Christ's divinity from his body and soul at his death) as well as the permissibility of casting lots and of praying to God for temporal goods, but also whether the priest must refuse Communion to a sinner even if his sin is not publicly known.[17] In the following period these questions were not infrequently detached from the commentary and handed down independently in manuscripts.

This practice of abbreviating older works leads us also to the first commentaries on the *Summa Theologiae* and the *Summa contra Gentiles* by Thomas Aquinas.[18] Outside of the Dominican Order, however, the works of Aquinas did not yet belong to the official literary canon in the faculty of theology. Even in the order they served as a doctrinal plumb line rather than as the basis for instruction. We find a collection of questions on the *S.Th.* for university use in the *Compendium Summae Theologiae* by Heinrich of Gorkum († 1431 as a professor in Cologne).[19] As Gabriel Biel does with Ockham, Heinrich of Gorkum presents questions that correspond thematically but not textually to the contents of the *S.Th.* His student Johannes Tinctoris († 1496) wrote the first non-Dominican commentary on the *S.Th.*, which he probably compiled as part of a teaching assignment. From Cologne the interpretation of Thomas by *magistri* traveled to Vienna, where the Dominican Leonhard Huntpichler († 1478) expounded the *S.Th.* for the first time; in 1490 we find lectures on it in Freiburg and Rostock, while the great commentaries of Cardinal Cajetan date from 1497 on. In Paris Peter Crockaert, O.P. († 1514) was the first to lecture on Thomas in 1507. His student Francisco de Vitoria (1483/93–1546) brought this practice to Salamanca and thus inaugurated the Thomist commentaries of Spanish Scholasticism in the early modern period.[20] We owe an early commentary on the *Summa contra Gentiles* to the Viennese Dominican Johannes Werd († 1510).[21]

16. Lang, *Heinrich Totting,* 80.

17. Ibid., 93.

18. See Grabmann, "Hilfsmittel des Thomasstudiums," 424–89.

19. See Höhn, "Köln."

20. Ibid., 655. For a list of commentaries on the *S.Th.*, see Mitschelich, *Kommentatoren.*

21. I. W. Frank, "Der Wiener Dominikaner Johannes Werd († 1510) als Verfasser von Thomaskommentaren," in Eckert, ed., *Thomas von Aquino,* 609–40.

The societal and ecclesiastical situation in the late Middle Ages, along with the new perspective on the pastoral dimension of theology, caused the professors to take positions also on practical questions of pastoral care and Church polity in the form of their own disputations, sermons, treatises and more pastorally oriented commentaries on parts of the liturgy (e.g., Gabriel Biel's commentary on the canon [of the Mass], commentaries on the Our Father, the Magnificat, etc., and Heinrich Totting's *Advisamenta* against abuses in the Diocese of Passau). Particularly important, of course, were the treatises on the theoretical debate about poverty and on ending the Western Schism and the efforts to bring about reform in the Church,[22] which led to the so-called reform theology of the fifteenth century.

1.2 Formation of schools and the dispute about the two ways

The opponents of Scholastic philosophy in the early modern period were fond of characterizing it as *"philosophia sectaria"* because it was said to be slavishly bound up with a particular doctrinal tendency or "school."[23] The historical phenomenon of the formation of more or less fixed doctrinal traditions, often independent of localities but usually connected with religious communities, takes us back to the condemnations of 1277. Since both Avicenna and Averroës, both Aristotle and Thomas Aquinas were affected by them, now the Franciscans especially sought to consolidate their position by turning decidedly to Augustine.[24] This was already becoming clear in William de la Mare's concept of theology, but also in the works of the secular priest Henry of Ghent and the Augustinian friar Ægidius Romanus. Besides the antagonism between religious orders [*Ordensgegensatz*], another important factor in the development of the late Scholastic schools was the difference between the doctrinal traditions at Paris and Oxford, as we encounter it in the critique by Roger Bacon. Thus it was the Dominican Robert Kilwardby who in 1277 as Archbishop of Canterbury pronounced the first ruling that pertained to Oxford, condemning sixteen propositions of Thomistic philosophy; his arguments were taken up again by the Franciscan John Peckham (ca. 1230–1291) in 1284 and 1286.[25] The decisive moment for the first phase in the formation of schools, however, was the so-called

22. See, for example, Prügl, *Ekklesiologie;* Prügl, *Antonio de Cannara.*

23. See, for example, Albrecht, *Eklektik,* 184–85.

24. Van Steenberghen, *Philosophie,* 464–69, summarizes this reliance under the general name of "Neo-Augustinianism."

25. Ibid., 457–58.

Correctorium debate. The first and most important *Correctorium fratris Thomas* by William de la Mare (1277/79) was recognized by the general chapter of the Franciscan Order in 1282 as the norm for the correct interpretation of Thomas' works. It was forbidden to read Thomas without this compilation of corrections. Dominican scholars described it as a *corruptorium* and tried to refute it in various *Correctoria corruptorii* [corrections of the corruption].[26] The fact that this and later debates did not discuss the overall context but rather individual sentences (particularly in this instance the unity or multiplicity of the Forms, the possible eternity of creation, the relation between intellect and will) gives the impression of typically "Scholastic" controversies among schools of thought, contributing to the image of late Scholasticism as analytical quibbling over individual sentences and words.

The condemnations of 1277 prevented the Dominicans at first from elaborating Thomas' teachings further; yet the students and followers of Thomas were being formed in Paris (Bernard of Trilia [ca. 1240–1292]), Oxford (Richard of Knapwell [† after 1286], Robert of Oxford [† before 1300]), Germany (John of Sterngassen [† after 1327]) and Italy (Hannibaldus de Hannibaldis [† 1272], Remigius of Florence [1235–1319]) in the controversy with the Franciscans. The general chapters of the Dominicans in 1278 and 1286 committed the order to the *"doctrina venerabilis fratris Thomae"* ["teaching of Venerable Friar Thomas"]. Of course we find no towering figures in these early Thomistic schools.[27] On the other hand Thomism was not so binding upon the Dominican Order that could there be no exceptions. The Oxford Dominicans especially manifest a line of thinking in Crathorn—who, records show, was at Oxford from 1330 to 1332—and (even more clearly) in Robert Holcot († 1349) that is connected to Ockham and modern linguistic criticism, albeit with different emphases, which naturally led in turn to controversies within the same Dominican school at the university.[28]

The decisive stimuli for early fourteenth-century theology, but also for new controversies among the schools, would come from Franciscan England in the figures of John Duns Scotus and William of Ockham. In each case we are dealing with the formation of a new school, which is already evident in the extant work of these authors. The students modified the work

26. On the *Correctorium* debate, see Roensch, *Early Thomistic School.*

27. See Van Steenberghen, *Philosophie,* 469–71; Grabmann, "Italienische Thomistenschule"; Grabmann, "Forschungen"; Grabmann, "Einzelgestalten."

28. See Hoffmann, *Die "Conferentiae";* Hoffmann, *Methode;* Hoffmann, *Crathorn;* Hoffmann, *Ockham-Rezeption.*

of their master and attributed their own subsequent developments of the teaching to the authority of the *"Doctor subtilis"* or the *"Venerabilis Inceptor,"* respectively.[29] The hypothetical text-critical reconstruction of the Oxford *Scriptum super libros Sententiarum* of Duns Scotus attempted by V. Richter and his school is therefore an important step toward understanding the further development of the Scotist school in England and France. The parts published so far clearly show on the one hand Scotus' ties to the Franciscan school with its praxis-oriented theology and its ongoing debate with Henry of Ghent, but on the other hand, also differences that very soon appeared especially among his Parisian students.[30] Yet these very controversies testify to how profoundly he changed theology at the turn of the fourteenth century during his short life and in his few authentic works. Scotist schools formed on the one hand in Franciscan circles in France and England (John of Bassoles [† 1347], Francis of Meyronnes [1288–1328]), but soon in Spain and Italy also.[31]

Unlike Duns Scotus, William of Ockham, the *"Venerabilis Inceptor"* [venerable Founder] of the *"Nominales"* ["Nominalists"] was not only opposed academically to his contemporaries who viewed universals in realistic terms, but also became involved, after his flight from Avignon, in the political conflict between Emperor Louis of Bavaria and the pope.[32] Both in his *ordinatio* [introductory list of topics] to the First Book of Sentences and also in the list of his philosophical and polemical writings there is much later material, extending even to the central question about universals.[33] In both cases, with Scotus and Ockham, we are dealing with a relatively short teaching career, the literary expression of which we owe to a great extent to the first students. Ockham's linguistic-critical solution to the problem of universals and science must have appeared to be the "destruction" of the metaphysical foundation of theology both to Thomists and to the Franciscans who had an Augustinian orientation.[34] The battle of the united *Reales* (Realists, i.e., Thomists, Scotists, Augustinians) against the *Nominales* [Nominalists] was

29. See esp. Richter, *Studien;* Richter and Leibold, *Unterwegs.*

30. See Richter, "Duns Scotus' Text zur Univozität"; anthology of texts: Johannes Duns Scotus, *Über die Erkennbarkeit Gottes. Texte zur Philosophie und Theologie,* edited and German translation by Hans Kraml, Gerhard Leibold, Vladimír Richter (Hamburg, 2000).

31. See Vázquez Janeiro, "Rutas e hitos"; de Castro, "Bibliographía"; Manrangon, "Le origini."

32. Concerning the problem of the political writings, see also Richter, "Unterwegs . . . Ockham," 143–46; Kraml and Leibold, *Wilhelm von Ockham,* 77–88.

33. See Richter, "Zu Ockhams Entwicklung"; Richter, "Aus der Nominalismus-Forschung."

34. An initial impression is provided by the critique by Walter Chatton († ca. 1344), Walter

therefore waged not only *disputando* [in formal disputations], but also with academic and ecclesiastical prohibitions, for example, the Parisian Nominalist Statute of 1340.[35]

The effort of the orders to determine their theological bent quasi-officially was further evidenced by the Augustine Recollects, who could point to [Ægidius] Romanus as their first eminent theologian in Paris. The general chapter in 1287 prescribed acceptance of the *"opiniones, positiones et sententiae"* of Ægidius for the entire order; this precept was incorporated in mitigated form in the 1290 statutes.[36] Here, however, as in the other schools founded by religious Orders, the model was not followed slavishly; there was still some intellectual independence despite all the attachment to Ægidius and the marked reliance on Augustine. This is evident in the influential figures of James of Viterbo († 1307/08), Hermann of Schildesche (ca. 1290–1357), Alphons Vargas Toletanus (ca. 1300–1366) and Hugolin of Orvieto (ca. 1300–1373), but especially in the works of Gregory of Rimini († 1358), who for his part would become the point of departure for a *"via Gregorii"* that extended as far as Johannes von Staupitz († 1524) and the young Luther.[37] The Augustinian school remained the most important strain of Augustinian thought in the late Middle Ages, especially in their doctrine on grace. Precisely in its adherence to Ægidius, however, it also incorporated Thomistic-Aristotelian thinking, whereas Gregory of Rimini and his school were closer to the basic positions of Ockham (conceptualism, *potentia dei absoluta* [the absolute power of God]), while adhering to Augustinian teachings on grace and predestination. The most important localities for Augustinian teaching careers beside Paris were Oxford, Bologna, Prague, Erfurt, and finally, in the case of Staupitz and Luther, Wittenberg.

The development of the schools associated with religious Orders clearly shows that they were strongly influenced by the two "ways" of philosophy and theology in the late Middle Ages: the *"via antiqua"* of the Realists and the *"via moderna"* of the Nominalists; the latter were especially important at fifteenth-century German universities. When both methods were ensconced to different degrees at the same university, this led not infrequently to an open conflict, to a "dispute about the two ways" [*"Wegestreit"*].[38]

Burley († ca. 1345) and John Lutterells († 1335) *Libellus contra doctrinam Guilelmi Occam*. See Hoffmann, *Johannes Lutterell;* Hoffmann, *Ockham-Rezeption.*

35. See Paqué, *Pariser Nominalistenstatut.*

36. See esp. Zumkeller, "Augustinerschule."

37. See Oberman, ed., *Gregor von Rimini.*

38. See Zimmermann, ed., *Antiqui und Moderni* in its entirety.

However, this heading conceals rather than reveals the actual differences at the individual universities and among the particular groups.[39] There was still no mention of a *"via moderna"* during the controversies in Paris in 1340; there the decisive debate came about from 1466 on. On March 1, 1474, at the instigation of the Realists, the basic books of the Nominalists or *Terministae* were forbidden by King Louis XI (Ockham, John of Mirecourt [Sent. 1344/45], Gregory of Rimini, Pierre d'Ailly, Adam Woodham et alii). In contrast, Averroës, Albert the Great, Thomas Aquinas, Ægidius Romanus, Alexander of Hales, Duns Scotus, and Bonaventure were recognized as the founding authors of the Realists.[40] The fact that Albert the Great is the first to be mentioned after the "Commentator," indicates the continuing strength of the *Albertistae,* who were able to become established in Paris after 1403, especially among the Dominicans when they were allowed to return after having been expelled from the university in 1387 on account of their adherence to the doctrine of the Immaculate Conception. The ban on Nominalist books and studies was not revoked until 1481/82. The de facto exclusion of one school of thought in Paris resulted in the migration of many Nominalists back to universities within the territory of the Holy Roman Empire.[41]

The universities in imperial territory were usually characterized by the (temporary) predominance of one school of thought. We might mention Cologne as the main center of the Albertist *via antiqua.* Major tensions beginning in 1425 eventually led each party to petition the Elector to ban the other. Here, too, *"via antiqua"* or *"via moderna"* is just a collective name, especially in the faculty of theology, which actually comprised Thomists, Ægidians, Scotists, and Albertists (all of them *Reales*) and Nominalists with their own colleges.[42] From Cologne the *"via antiqua"* came to Heidelberg also, which until then had been predominantly Nominalist; in 1452 the earlier school of thought received the same official protection as the more modern one, and in 1453 it was able to open its own residential college [*Burse*]. Here, too, the debate manifested itself, among other ways, in disturbances during the lectures of the "Realist" *magistri.* In Freiburg the *via antiqua* bore the marks of Scotism in particular. In 1484 both ways were officially established; this had less to do with philosophical reasons than with competition from the new University of Tübingen, where both ways

39. Gilbert, "Ockham, Wyclif."
40. Ehrle, *Sentenzenkommentar Peters von Candida,* 311–13.
41. For particulars, see Gabriel, "Via antiqua."
42. Ibid., 467.

were being taught. Tübingen showed great tolerance not only for the two ways but also for the new humanism (Reuchlin, Melanchthon), which was regarded precisely as a means of overcoming the old dualism.[43] The humanistic approaches joined forces here significantly with the *via antiqua.* Elements common to the various schools of thought at Tübingen were a high regard for John Gerson and an Augustinian orientation, especially through the master of the *moderni,* Gabriel Biel, who was among the proponents of the *devotio moderna.*[44] The quarrel between the schools of thought was more severe in Ingolstadt, where in 1477/78 plans to divide the university were considered and the conflict lasted until the official abolition of both ways in 1518/19. Whereas Erfurt was regarded in the fifteenth century as an essentially Nominalist university, the two ways were described in Wittenberg in 1502 not in the conventional manner but as "Thomists" and "Scotists," with an additional third school of thought, the *"via Gregorii"* (Gregory of Rimini) that was professed especially by the Augustine Recollects.[45] The classical opposition of *Nominales* and *Reales* was thought to have been resolved already in principle.

In fact the "dispute about the ways" manifested also a certain institutional and terminological ossification at the universities in the second half of the fifteenth century, in particular vis-à-vis the really "modern" movements—humanism and the new philosophy of the Italian Renaissance, which at first came from outside the university. After all, it was possible to study at a university only by enrolling in one of the two "ways" (which had their own burses, colleges, etc.). Along with the generally recognized fundamentals in theology came then the doctrinal traditions of the respective school with its standard manuals. Their prohibition in Paris was therefore tantamount to the prohibition of the school in question. The linguistic-logical analyses of the *via moderna* with its formalism seemed to contemporaries, at any rate, more backward and "Scholastic" than the openness of "realist" metaphysics to humanistic concerns. Thus it was possible for the proponents of the *via antiqua* to regard themselves as more modern and broadminded than the adherents of the *via moderna,* which placed the main emphasis on the individual science and the tradition of logic cultivated since Ockham and John Buridan († after 1358). In Cologne dangerous innovations were attributed

43. See the detailed discussion in Oberman, *Werden und Wertung,* 4–140.

44. See Oberman, *Spätscholastik.*

45. See Gabriel, "Via antiqua," 476–81; Knuuttila, "Trutfetter."

to the *via antiqua* in 1425. In Heidelberg it appeared quite plainly as a reform movement in opposition to the *via moderna,* and the students demonstrated against it because they wanted to stay with the old doctrinal habits of the *moderni.*[46] These facts clearly testify that the "dispute about the ways" had nothing to do with modernity or conservatism above and beyond the contrasting doctrines about universals.

A decisive catalyst for fifteenth-century theology, however, was the revival of Augustinian theology, in particular of its anti-Pelagian doctrine of grace; in the fourteenth century Thomas Bradwardine († 1349) and Gregory of Rimini provided important impetus to this development. Bradwardine's return to Augustine to argue against the *Pelagiani moderni* went on to influence Wycliffe, although we can hardly speak about a special *"via Bradwardini."*[47] In a way typical of theology on the eve of the Reformation, both theologians interpreted Augustine's anti-Pelagianism so as to counteract the late Medieval pious practices that suggested justification by works, but also to refute the speculation of "Nominalist" theology about power [*Macht*] and grace in terms of an "assurance of salvation" or, in the writings of Johann von Staupitz, even of a "claim to salvation." The edition of Augustine's works (Basel 1506) organized by Johannes Amerbach (ca. 1443–1513) then made the thought of this Father of the Church accessible almost in its entirety.[48]

1.3 Theology, Church and society: Wycliffe and Hus

If one regards late Scholastic theology merely as an academic endeavor in the quarrel among "ways" and schools of thought, its societal relevance seems insignificant. On the other hand, the decisive Church-state conflicts of the fourteenth and fifteenth centuries were brought about by university theologians: John Wycliffe (ca. 1330–1384) in Oxford and Jan Hus (1370/71–1415) in Prague. The path from the professor's podium to societal change and Church reform had plainly become shorter than in the twelfth or thirteenth century. For both theologians, however, academic, "Scholastic" doctrine was the foundation of the ecclesial and social consequences and of their conflict with the ecclesiastical authorities.

John Wycliffe spent most of his life in the schools of Oxford (until 1381), first as a philosopher (*baccalaureus* 1356, *magister artium* 1360), then from

46. See Gössmann, *Antiqui und Moderni,* 108–16.

47. See Oberman, "Tuus sum, salvum me fac," 350; for a critique thereof, see Schulze, "Via Gregorii," 22–24.

48. See Oberman, *Werden und Wertung,* 82–140.

1372 on as *magister actu regens* of theology.[49] The influential elements of his theology were:

1. The blatant *realism* of his metaphysics with regard to *universals* and the resulting rejection of Nominalist philosophy, which is clearly expressed both in his *Summa de Ente* and in the treatise *De Ydeis.* God's perfect knowledge implies the real existence of the ideas of things in his mind, but likewise the necessity of the individual fact.[50]
2. A strict *scriptural principle* which attributes directly to statements in sacred Scripture the character of necessary and eternal truth *(absoluta necessitas),* to an even higher degree than in mathematical statements, and thus contrasts with the nominalist distinction between a truth *"secundum intentionem auctoris"* ["according to the author's intention"] and a truth *"secundum virtutem sermonis"* ["according to the force of the utterance"].[51]
3. Reliance on *Augustine's anti-Pelagian teaching about grace,* as transmitted by Thomas Bradwardine, including his teaching about predestination.[52] Bradwardine's *Causa Dei* (1344) is the decisive attack against the allegedly "Pelagian" tendencies of Ockham and his contemporaries (Holcot, Woodham) in their teaching about free will and merit (that a *meritum de congruo* is possible even for a sinner).
4. Augustine's *concept of the Church* in *De civitate Dei* [*The City of God*], with his distinction between the visible Church and the heavenly, true Church, which consists exclusively of those who are predestined for salvation *(praesciti).* For its part, predestination cannot be ruined even by an individual's mortal sin. Nor can the multitude of the damned *(corpus diaboli)* be changed through human agency.[53]

In the academic life of his times Wycliffe's theology appeared as a resolute challenge to "modern" trends on the part of a "fundamentalist" reactionary. His program, indeed, rejected those critical elements of the "modern" theology that had become widely accepted: a linguistic-critical rejection of realism about universals, a critical examination of the truth of theological sentences, man's free will vis-à-vis God's free will in his contingent dis-

49. See Leff, *Heresy,* 2:494–558; Robson, *Wyclif;* Lambert, *Heresy,* 225–42.
50. Concerning the treatise *De Ydeis,* see Robson, *Wyclif,* 171–95.
51. Ibid., 164.
52. See Leff, *Bradwardine;* Leppin, *Theologie,* 148–51.
53. See Leff, *Heresy,* 516–46.

positions of grace. Taken together, however, these theoretical-Scholastic elements of Wycliffe's theology did not yet necessarily result in that thrust which later led to his condemnation (1377; 1381/82; 1407 and 1411) and his association with the revolutionary social movement of the Lollards. His condemnation and departure from Oxford in 1381 also had another immediately theological, Scholastic cause: his rejection of the doctrine of transubstantiation as a contradiction to the teaching of the early Church.[54]

The combination of the scriptural principle and the Augustinian understanding of the Church, however, produced those teachings that brought Wycliffe into conflict with Church teaching and practice. Once again it was actually a conservative program of reform that incorporated Franciscan initiatives and a vision of life in the early Church, especially in its rejection of worldly property and secular power *(De civili dominio)*. His spiritual understanding of the Church led him to reject the hierarchy, precisely with respect to the Western Schism: God alone elects the pope from the Church of the predestined and for it; who that is cannot be known without a special revelation. In the Schism, ultimately, both popes appeared as Antichrist.[55] In this understanding of the Church, of course, the power to bind and loose belongs to God alone, and not to the pope or the priests. Whereas the Nominalists had guaranteed some role for secondary causes in the work of salvation (albeit one that could be dispensed with at any time), they are completely ruled out here: just as God's knowledge is absolutely necessary, so too is his action; anything above and beyond the revelation in sacred Scripture must be dismissed, even if a precept or an article of faith were pronounced by an angel.[56] It is quite a different matter, though, with the office of the king, which is divinely established. Yet even the king, who by virtue of his office is *"vicarius dei"* ["God's vicar"], is in principle *"frater noster"* ["our brother"].[57] Although it is not very consistent with his theological approach, Wycliffe also concedes to the king far-reaching rights over the visible Church, including the right to confiscate Church property and to convert church buildings into fortresses.

His step from the professorial chair at Oxford to the heretical move-

54. Wycliffe, *De eucharistia*, ed. J. Loshert (1886), in John Wyclif, *Latin Works* (New York, reprinted 1966), vol. 12; see also Leff, *Heresy*, 549–57; Lambert, *Heresy*, 243–83.

55. Wyclif, *De potestate pape*, ed. J. Loshert (1907), in *Latin Works*, 19:185; see also Leff, *Heresy*, 530–33.

56. Wyclif, *De potestate*, in *Latin Works*, 19:259.

57. Wyclif, *De officio regis*, ed. A. W. Pollard/C. Sayle (1887), in *Latin Works*, 4:4.

ment of the Lollards was based on the fact that both rejected papal authority and the contemporary Church with its secular power and property. The transformation of Wycliffe's theology into political agitation was manifested for the first time in the Farmers' Uprising of 1381; consequently, of course, one could now suspect that Wycliffe's influence was behind all disturbances.[58] The controversies of the Lollards at Oxford (Blackfriars 1382) concerned what was still in part a university movement, which was supposed to be quelled once again according to academic custom by the condemnation of Wycliffe's followers and their expulsion from the university. The popularization of Wycliffe's teachings in Lollard circles led on the one hand to their reformulation as brief theses for the purpose of easier comprehensibility and on the other hand to the production of works ascribed to their theological forefather.[59]

Less genuinely philosophical in his mindset yet in agreement with Wycliffe's realism was the *magister* from Prague, Jan Hus, whose condemnation and burning at the stake by the Council of Constance would lead to the most radical disturbances of the fifteenth century.[60] Hus's influential teacher Stanislaus of Znaim († 1413) had already tried to reconcile Wycliffe with official Church doctrine.[61] In his academic theology, Hus himself presents the picture of a none-too-independent theologian of the *via antiqua,* especially in his Commentary on the *Sentences* (1407–1409).[62] Typical here of the later Wycliffe, of course, is his concept of Church as *"universitas praedestinatorum"* ["the company of the predestined"]. A predestined soul, however, is someone who really lives a Christian life; therefore the true Church is the communion of real Christians, of good Christians. As in Wycliffe, the catalyst of the Hussite movement was found here in its spiritualized concept of Church. Furthermore Hus, too, had an understanding of the Eucharist that was rather unclear yet deviated from the doctrine of transubstantiation.[63] Wycliffe had had a much greater influence on Hus's teachers, Stanislaus of

58. Concerning the Lollards, see: Leff, *Heresy,* 559–605; Lambert, *Heresy,* 243–83.

59. See Leff, *Heresy,* 574–77; especially the 25 articles of 1388.

60. See Herold, *Pražká Univerzita;* for a critical review of the ideological interpretations of Wycliffe's influence on the "early bourgeois revolution" in the case of Hus and afterwards, see: Sousedík, "Wyclif und Böhmen," with bibliography. On Hus and the situation in Bohemia, see also Lambert, *Heresy,* 284–348; Seibt, ed., *Jan Hus.*

61. Stanislaus de Znoyma, *De gracia et peccato,* ed. Zuzanna Silagiová (Fontes Latini Bohemorum 1) (Prague, 1997), Introduction xxvi–xxvii.

62. Magistri Joannis Hus, *Super IV libros Sententiarum* in *Opera omnia,* ed. W. Flajšhans/M. Komínková (Prague, 1903–1907), vol. II. See esp. De Vooght, *Hérésie,* 60–84.

63. See Sousedík, "Huss"; Kolesnyk, "Hussens Eucharistiebegriff."

Znaim and Stephan Páleč (ca. 1370–1424), who were therefore accused in Rome in 1407/08 and forced to recant.[64] While the university theologian Jan Hus was to a great extent orthodox in his teaching, above all what mattered for the Hussite Reformation was his preaching, but also the tensions between the German majority and the Czech minority at the university. After the attempt by King Wenceslaus to crush the German majority, these tensions led in 1409 to the departure of the German professors and students for Leipzig. This left Jan Hus and Jerome of Prague († 1416) as the representatives of the now-Czech faculty of theology.[65]

In his preaching ministry at "Bethlehem" (as opposed to his university sermons, even in the vernacular), Hus aligned himself with the moralizing reformer's theology of Konrad of Waldhausen (ca. 1325–1369, in Prague from 1360 on) and Jan Milič of Kremsier (ca. 1325–1374), both of whom were not so much theologians as clergymen concerned about practical reform in the Church.[66] It was precisely their abandonment of the Scholastic distinctions in their teaching about sin and grace and their black-and-white depiction of issues, for example, with regard to God's judgment of sinners, which produced the effect that a reform sermon ought to have. The luxury, greed, and simony of Church rulers were standard themes. Hus's spiritualist concept of the Church was evident here especially in the contrast between the real Church (*universitas* of good Christians = the predestined) and the existing, corrupt institutional Church, with a marked devaluation of ecclesiastical institutions and human laws in favor of immediate contact with Christ, who is Life, by his grace and by obedience to God's Word. Thus the established Church during the Great Schism necessarily appeared not as a way of salvation but as an obstacle to it.

Hus's conflict with the Church was, after all, of a more practical than genuinely theological nature. This is clearly evident in his treatise *De Ecclesia* from the year 1413 and the polemical works that followed, aimed now directly at the practices of the antipope John XXIII (reigned 1410–1415).[67] Here too his theology, insofar as it concerns the forgiveness of sins and ecclesial obedience, is still thoroughly Catholic. Given the contemporary situation, however, even such a theology must have seemed provocative when

64. See Leff, *Heresy,* 625–26; Hrdlička, "Hus und Páleč."

65. Ibid., 608–20.

66. On their sermons, see De Vooght, *Hérésie,* 72–84.

67. *Magistri Joannis Hus Tractatus de Ecclesia,* ed. S. Harrison Thomson (Cambridge, Mass., 1956); see also Holeček, "Hussens Kirchenverständnis."

it called abuses by their names. Despite the adherence to the sacrament of Penance and the spiritual power of the keys, it was an indictment of their misuse by the ruling clergy: They took from the Gospel only what served their position of authority and personal comfort, while they were unwilling to undertake the fundamental *"ministerium caritativum"* ["charitable ministry"]. In chapter 11, for example, and elsewhere the words of Scripture are constantly played off against the abuses in the contemporary Church:

> Every passage of Scripture, especially from the Gospel, that seems to them to mean that they ought to live in wealth and pleasure, to be attached to the world and to suffer no humiliation for Christ, they will repeat over and over again, proclaim at the top of their lungs and interpret at great length. Every passage, however, that admonishes them to imitate Christ and his poverty, meekness, humility, long-suffering, chastity, zeal and patience, they suppress, gloss it as they see fit or explicitly dismiss it as unnecessary for salvation.[68]

This excerpt shows that Hus is taking aim at Scholastically trained clerics, who have mastered the technique of glossing uncomfortable passages of Scripture as well as logic; for the devil, *"sophista pessimus"* ["the worst Sophist"] leads them astray to this false conclusion: that Christ gave this authority (the power of the keys) to Peter and the other Apostles; therefore to us; consequently we can do what we want. They erroneously consider it equally self-evident that they will attain blessedness and rule with Christ when he comes again. These "powers of darkness" are contrasted with the true believers who possess the *"potestas predestinacionis"* ["power of predestination"]; therefore the *"veraces christicole"* ["true worshippers of Christ"] must, if need be, resist the power of the institutional Church when it tries to keep them by force or deceit from imitating Christ.[69] Resistance is not offered here to God's command but only to the abuse of authority, especially by simoniac priests; Hus goes on to prove in great detail that they are the real heretics. In doing so Hus also expressly vindicates the opinion of Stephan Páleč and Stanislaus of Znaim *"de clero pestifero"* ["concerning the pestilential clergy"].[70] The very fact that the treatise *De ecclesia* proceeds by the logical argumentation of a formal debate shows that Hus's plea for a reform of the Church cannot be separated from his academic activity; on the contrary, Church reform has become here the object of academic theology, which of course has left the narrow confines of the lecture hall; for this treatise was read aloud not at the

68. Ibid. (91); see also Liguš, "Schriftbegriff."
69. Ibid. (92).
70. Ibid. (95).

university but rather in "Bethlehem." This combination of academic and reformational activity anticipates Luther, who in 1520 after reading *De ecclesia* declared: *"Breviter: sumus omnes Hussitae. Denique Paulus et Augustinus ad verbum sunt Hussitae."* ["In short: we are all Hussites. Finally Paul and Augustine, read literally, are Hussites."][71]

1.4 Toward a biblical and affective theology: John Gerson

The Great Schism, the decline of ecclesiastical life, political conflicts, the controversies among the schools of thought, and the sterility of academic theology formed the background for the reform theology of the Parisian professor and chancellor John Gerson (1363–1429), who through his influence that transcended all allegiance to particular schools became the "Church Father of the fifteenth century."[72] After the usual baccalaureate years (1388–1392), Gerson was authorized to teach theology in 1392. As early as April 13, 1395, he was appointed chancellor of the University of Paris, a position which he formally held, in addition to numerous other offices and benefices, until his death.[73] Gerson continued to fulfill the professorial duty of interpreting sacred Scripture, yet his lectures on the Gospel of Mark are not exegesis but rather the treatment of current questions on the basis of individual (and often partial) verses from the Bible.[74] Even the titles of the individual lectures show his fondness for contemporary problems of morality and asceticism: for example, *De comparatione vitae contemplativae ad activam* [On comparing the contemplative to the active life]; *De non esu carnium* [On abstaining from meat]; *Super victu et pompa praelatorum* [On the prelates' way of life and pomp]; *De vita spirituali animae* [On the spiritual life of the soul]; *Contra curiositatem studentium* [Against studying for curiosity's sake]; *De desiderio et fuga episcopatus* [On desiring and fleeing the episcopate]; *De theologia mystica* [On mystical theology].

Gerson was clearly aware of the deficiencies of the academic theology of his day. In a letter dated April 1, 1400 to Peter of Ailly he regards the standard set by the theological faculty in Paris as the nucleus of Church reform. Yet only useless questions are being discussed there, which like husks unprofitably burden the stomach of the memory.[75] All their attention is focused on

71. WA Br 2.52.24–25; see also Oberman, "Hus und Luther."

72. See Oberman, *Werden und Wertung*, 56–71; Burger, *Aedificatio.*

73. Biographical information in Burger, *Aedificatio*, 24–26; Roth, *Discretio spirituum*, 61–75.

74. Ibid., 35–40, with its critique of the plan of the edition by P. Glorieux: Jean Gerson. *Oeuvres complètes* III (Paris, 1962).

75. Ed. Glorieux, 2:26, 31 (29 April 1400).

the *Prolegomena* to book 1 of the *Sentences,* where speculative philosophical problems are discussed, whereas the actual teaching about the faith in books 2–4 is scarcely elaborated. The accusation that Roger Bacon had leveled in the thirteenth century against lecturing on the *Sentences* returns now in different circumstances: Theologians are no longer occupied with their own field: *"solida veritas, moralia, biblia,"* and this makes them the laughing-stock of the other faculties. The controversies among the schools (especially over the superfluous formalities of the Scotists) and the lifestyles of individual faculty members contribute little to their reputations.[76] Instead of such useless activity, Gerson assigns a pastoral duty to academic theology: instructing simple believers and solving the moral problems of the day ought to be the most urgent goals of the faculty. To that end he recommends the literary genre of short treatises on the most important points of religion, especially the commandments: theological education of the people instead of academic controversies! On the other hand Gerson also encourages the cataloguing of forbidden or scandalous opinions by inquisitors. The chancellor must make sure that no one who advocates such teachings receives an authorization to teach.[77] The academic independence of university theology, with its special terminology, methods and rules that put off outsiders, should be pruned for the sake of a simple, pastoral and ecclesial theology.

For Gerson the abiding foundation of theology is sacred Scripture in its literal sense. In his lecture on Mark 3:29 entitled *De sensu Litterali Sacrae Scripturae*[78] he formulates this in twelve conclusions of a theological critique of language and method:

1. The literal sense of sacred Scripture is always true.
2. It should be explained according to the rules of grammar, figures of speech and rhetorical tropes not (as the Nominalists do) according to the laws of Scholastic logic.
3. It should be judged according to the decisions that the Church has made under the inspiration and with the guidance of the Holy Spirit, not at one's own discretion.
4. Sacred Scripture, especially in moral matters, makes use of indefinite instead of general expressions. Such propositions must be verified in at least one definite case.

76. Ibid., 2:26–27; see also *Contra curiositatem studentium* II (Glorieux, 3:242).
77. Ed. Glorieux, 2:28.
78. Ed. Glorieux, 3:333–40.

5. A theological proposition that is correct in the logical sense must be disavowed if it is false in the literal sense, offensive or morally doubtful.
6. The literal sense was first revealed through Christ and the Apostles, illustrated by miracles, corroborated by martyrs, explained and defended (along with the conclusions drawn from it) by the Church Fathers and defined by the Councils. Appropriate punishments have been prescribed by the ecclesiastical authorities for transgressions of these norms.
7. If the literal sense is attacked when it has already been defined by the Church, one should therefore proceed against the challengers not with academic disputations *(curiosis ratiocinationibus)* but rather with the appropriate punishments.
8. If the literal sense has been defined by decrees, decretals or at councils, it is just as much a part of theology and sacred Scripture as the Apostles Creed.
9. Although the literal sense is sufficiently clear in Scripture itself or has been explained by the work of scholars, it can be proclaimed *"compendiose"* ["summarily"] in a few articles separately (e.g., as a profession of faith), especially in view of the uneducated and differences of opinion.
10. The literal sense is interpreted reasonably in theological houses of study [affiliated with Generalates of religious orders], in other dioceses or by means of consultation with a *concilium* [advisory council] of local theologians.
11. Anyone who denies an interpretation that has been defined as biblical by the bishop (or the bishop together with a *concilium doctorum*) should be punished and obliged to recant.
12. If someone maintains that the literal sense is not true and proceeds to oppose it in word and deed, this gives rise to the urgent suspicion of heresy, more precisely, of incorrigibility and obstinacy in an error of intellect and will.

The impression of purely positive ecclesiality given by this list should be viewed within the context of the goal that Gerson is trying to attain with this decidedly biblical and ecclesial alignment of theology as a whole.[79] Theology should again serve the purpose of human life, eternal salvation, for man aspires to God as his natural center and place of rest. This is where certainty can be found with regard to Scholastic disputes and the insecurity of theological knowledge.[80] Therefore theology must immediately become a bib-

79. See Burrows, *Gerson,* 102–25.
80. Gerson, *De consolatione,* ed. Glorieux, 9:196; see also Grosse, *Heilsungewissheit.*

lical, affective, mystical theology in which theory and practice are united. The first requirement for that is repentance, a key word as Gerson interprets Mark 1:15 on the one hand *Contra curiositatem studentium* [against merely speculative theology] and on the other hand *De theologia mystica speculative conscripta* [in terms of systematic mystical theology].[81] The path therefore leads away from "Scholastic mischief" to an experiential theology. For Gerson, however, such a *theologia mystica* is the object of doctrine (*speculative conscripta,* rationally ordered and put into writing). Mysticism is rendered systematic, schematic and thus teachable: this gives rise to a "spiritual theology" *(doctrina de mystica theologia),* a theory of mystical experience.

Mystical theology intends to address precisely those faculties in man that are not satisfied by purely intellectual Scholastic theology: the heart [*den Affekt*], which is supposed to come to the experiential knowledge of God through repentance.[82] Another prerequisite for theology is an appropriate moral attitude: Only the *"boni et devoti"* ["the good and the devout"] can know God in this way; in contrast, morally corrupt theologians, whom Gerson also takes into account, remain at the level of *"theologia ratiocinativa,"* where they can indeed know very much; yet even the demons believe and tremble (James 2:19). Unlike Scholastic theology, mystical theology does not rely on previous philosophical training; it is itself a kind of philosophy, but one that is also for simple people and the ignorant.[83] Gerson found models for a mystical theology especially in the writings of Pseudo-Dionysius, about which he wrote commentaries.[84] Through the purification and activation of all the faculties of the soul that have been weakened by sin, the whole man should be involved in aspiring to God, and not just the intellect, as Gerson explains by pointedly contrasting the two kinds of theology and noting ten differences between them. They are already distinguished by their respective objects: Speculative theology aims for the True, mystical theology—for the Good. In principle mystical theology can reach its goal without speculative theology, but not vice versa; for the goal of theology as a whole involves the will and not merely the intellect. The mere Scholastic, however, lacks both experience of any kind and the instruments with which to reach this goal. Speculative theology does not produce calming certainty

81. Ed. Glorieux 3:224–92; *De mystica theologia,* ed. A. Combes (Lugano, 1958), see also Quinto, *Scholastica,* 114–28.

82. Gerson, *De myst. theol.* c.6, ed. Combes 70.6–8.

83. Ibid., p.1, ed. Combes 8.11 f.; see also Burger, *Aedificatio,* 129–43; Burrows, *Gerson,* 143–48.

84. See A. Combes, *Jean Gerson Commentateur Dionysien: Les "Notulae super quaedam verba Dionysii de Caelesti Hierarchia"* (Paris, 1973); Quinto, *Scholastica,* 114–28.

but rather intellectual unrest. It does not lead to sure results. This unrest, however, can be traced back ultimately to an insufficiency of the will: the sea of sensual desires. Only mystical theology leads away from these to *terra firma,* the shores of eternity.[85] The Bible, the Church's Magisterium and religious experience are the main pillars of this largely conservative reform program that is offered as an alternative to a Scholasticism that is perceived as sterile and starry-eyed, concerned with *quaestiones* that are no longer the questions of the day.[86]

1.5 University theology and spiritual direction for aristocratic ladies: Vienna

John Gerson was not alone in opting for a biblical, pastoral theology. At that same time a trend originating in Paris, a conciliatory *via moderna,* became popular in Vienna; the associated moral-theological, ascetical, and catechetical works, some of them in German translations, were circulated in monastic circles (especially among adherents of the Melk Reform), and also among canons regular and sometimes even among the laity. It was supported by theologians, some of whom belonged to the university while others were employed at the court of the Duke: Heinrich of Langenstein (1325–1397), Nicholas of Dinkelsbühl[87] (ca. 1360–1433) and their students Thomas Peuntner (ca. 1390–1439) and Nikolaus Kempf (1397–1497).[88] We find pastoral and moral-theological problems as well as opinions on current questions in the works of Heinrich Totting of Oyta also (ca. 1330–1397), who after studying and teaching in Erfurt, Prague, and Paris (1337–1381) taught in Vienna with Heinrich of Langenstein from 1383 to 1397.[89] Both scholars owe much to university theology for their methodology and framing of questions. Their discussions—at times precise but other times prolix—range from the principles of theology to the temptations of the devil.

A remarkable foundation for a biblically and ecclesiastically oriented

85. Gerson, *De myst. theol.* p.6, ed. Combes, 73–87.

86. See Hübener, "Konservativismus."

87. See R. Damerau, *Der Galaterbriefkommentar des Nikolaus von Dinkelsbühl* (Giessen, 1968); Damerau, *Die Quästionen des Nikolaus von Dinkelsbühl zum Galaterbriefkommentar* (Giessen, 1970). Idem, *Der Herrengebetskommentar des Nikolaus von Dinkelsbühl* (Giessen, 1971) (vols. 7, 9, and 10 in the series: Studien zu den Grundlagen der Reformation).

88. See Rupprich, *Wiener Schrifttum;* Th. Hohmann, *Heinrichs von Langenstein 'Unterscheidung der Geister': Lateinisch und deutsch: Texte und Untersuchungen zur Übersetzungsliteratur aus der Wiener Schule* (Munich, 1977), 257–76. Concerning the diffusion and significance of the Viennese "pious literature," see also Drossbach, "Innovation."

89. See Lang, *Heinrich Totting,* 37–43, 99–115.

school of theology, which avoids the extremes of the Nominalist and Realist positions, is the introduction to theology that Heinrich Totting summarizes in twelve axioms or principles in his *Quaestiones super libros Sententiarum,* which belong to the period that he spent in Prague or Vienna (before 1388):[90]

1. It can reasonably be assumed that there is only one God.
2. God is supreme wisdom, which cannot be deceived, and supreme truth, which cannot deceive.
3. Everything that God has revealed is true; that is, if something has been revealed by God, it is true.
4. God is the free First Cause, upon whose generous goodness creatures depend for their entire being and goodness.
5. To God is due all respect and submission on the part of his creatures, the *cultus latriae* [the worship of adoration].
6. Since in God all perfection and goodness are joined in the highest possible unity, the *cultus latriae* is due to him alone.
7. There is one Church, that is, one assembly of mortal men who possess the true worship of God.
8. A Church or assembly of men possesses the most salvific worship of God.
9. The law of the Christian Church teaches most truthfully the most salvific divine worship owed by mortal men.
10. Considering the law of the Christian Church and its most pure wisdom, the rationality and dignity of her divine worship, her miraculous beginning, her constant endurance and the merits of Christians, any human being with normal judgment must arrive at the conclusion that all the books presented by the Church as godly according to her law or as composed by divine revelation are to be held firmly as such.
11. All the canonical books of the OT and NT are to be considered divine or composed by divine revelation.
12. All the truths of sacred Scripture from which other theological truths can be inferred causally, on the basis of properties or intrinsic relationships, are the essential principles of our theology.

A decisive figure for the organizational development and theological approach of the early University of Vienna, moreover, was Heinrich of Langenstein (1325–1397), who was a master of theology in Paris from 1376 on and

90. Clm 18364; cited by Lang, *Wege der Glaubensbegründung,* 231–35; on its influence, see 225–37.

taught in Vienna in 1383/84.[91] Besides his activities at the university and in ecclesiastical politics during the Western Schism, there is a decidedly pastoral emphasis in his writings. The biblical foundation for his theology is evident in his Viennese Commentary on Genesis (chapters 1–3 only) and his work *De idiomate hebraico,* which underscores the importance of the biblical languages for the study of theology. Heinrich himself had learned Hebrew in Paris and Vienna from baptized Jews. In his theology Heinrich brings to bear an eclectic variation of the *via moderna* which borrows especially from Gregory of Rimini and thereby, like Heinrich Totting, avoids objectionable or radical theses.[92]

Heinrich's pastoral and ascetical writings, however, were the most widely circulated.[93] He gave the secular priests in his benefice of Grossrussbach precise instructions about how to teach catechism to the children in the parish. Above all they should teach them the correct wording and understanding of the Our Father, the Hail Mary, and the Creed (in German).[94] Earlier in 1380, Langenstein himself had given a "*Lectura super Pater noster*" in Paris.[95] Other works by Heinrich that were translated into German included his treatise "On the discernment of spirits" (the Latin text of which has been lost) and his "*Quaestio* on the temptations of the devil and helps against them." The latter had a long and influential textual tradition.[96] This very *quaestio* is well suited to illustrate the step from university to pastoral theology and from the Latin original to the German translation. The question is situated, moreover, within the context of the late Medieval belief in the devil and demons, although it by no means supports it. The main source for the *quaestio* on temptations is *De virtutibus* by William of Auvergne, whose outline is still applied here. Quantifying the temptations and remedies was a favorite schema of the period. Thus Gerson describes fifty-eight temptations of the devil in *De diversis diaboli tentationibus* alone.[97] Langenstein's *quaestio,* however, proves to be a university lesson, not pastoral

91. About his life see Kreuzer, *Heinrich von Langenstein.*—Heinrich von Langenstein, *Der Sentenzenkommentar,* ed. R. Damerau (Studien zu den Grundlagen der Reformation 15–18) (Marburg, 1979/80).

92. See Lang, *Christologie.*

93. Heinrich von Langenstein, *Erchantnuzz der sund,* ed. R. Rudolf. (Texte des späten Mittelalters und der frühen Neuzeit 22) (Berlin, 1969). The authenticity of this work is disputed because of its vocabulary by Wiesinger, "Autorschaft."

94. Clm 17645, fol. 125va–126r; see also Kreuzer, *Heinrich von Langenstein,* 146.

95. See Kreuzer, *Heinrich von Langenstein,* 105.

96. Synoptic edition: Hohmann, *Langenstein;* see also Hämmerl, *Welt,* 151–62.

97. Ed. Glorieux, 7:343–60; see also Grosse, *Heilsungewissheit,* 8–44.

instruction: "*Quaestio magistralis de temptatione diaboli.*"[98] The translation, which presumably was done by a clerical courtier for a lady at the ducal court,[99] already deviates from the original Latin *quaestio* in the fact that it does not adopt its precise formulation of the question or the main arguments. The questions are still framed in a purely scientific, theological manner: Can a man on the earthly pilgrimage be led astray by the devil through deceit and cunning? Even the general distinctions among temptations (*temptatio probativa/pulsativa,* [i.e., a temptation that tests/impels one] to perform or omit an action) and their subdivisions are missing. On the other hand the translation expands on the text, sometimes with citations from Augustine, but also with rather colorful comparisons that have no place in a Scholastic *quaestio.*[100] The translation begins immediately with the four aims of the devil's temptations: mortal sin, schism and heresy, error in human sciences, superstition. The quantifying continues: The devil, presented as *magister* of antitheology, tries to prove his conclusions contrary to ours, and he opposes the Ten Commandments with the seven capital sins and the twelve (or fourteen) articles of faith with his own theses, resulting in either nineteen or twenty-one conclusions.[101] The basic framework of the *quaestio* is provided however by the seven temptations of the devil according to William of Auvergne:

1. Wearing the sinner down or tormenting him with a [particular] sin,
2. The unusual or marvelous character of the object,
3. Temptation to change one's state of life,
4. Counsel to seek goods that are unattainable for human weakness,
5. Counsel to run a risk for the sake of a supposed good,
6. Recommendation of a vice under the guise of virtue,
7. Complete peace and the cessation of temptations 1 through 6.[102]

98. Vienna, Schottenstift Codex 128 fol. 204va; Cod. 326, 300v; on the question of authorship, see also Hohmann, *Langenstein,* 151–57.

99. Cf., Hohmann, 157–58; inferred from Schottenstift Codex III, 4–7 (181/183): "*dye ich hye durich dye sunder lieb, dye ich hab zu ewrem ewigen hayll, wirdigew fraw, vmb dye lieb, dy ir mir habt erczaigt, yn dewczsch hab geschriben, das ir euch dester pas chündt halten gegen dem selbem.*" ["which (instruction), for the love of sinners that I have unto your eternal salvation, Honorable Lady, and for the sake of the love that you have shown me, I have written in German, so that you may all the more suitably be informed and armed against it (i.e., temptation)."]

100. For example, Schottenstift Codex III, 45–85 (185–87): Just as the fisherman lures the fish from their spawning place so as to catch them in his net, so the Devil lures men from their state in life (laymen, priests, bishops).

101. Hohmann, *Langenstein,* 178.17–20.

102. Ibid., 180–94.

Finally, besides the threefold remedy that every virtue offers against temptations, namely in considering the value of the virtue itself *(proprio gladio),* in contrasting it with the vice *(gladio alieno)* and in fleeing from the missiles of the Evil One, sixteen remedies taken from William of Auvergne are listed.[103] This produces an impressive and easily remembered outline of good and evil with which to apply Scholastic teaching to the needs of practical spiritual direction.

1.6 Scholastic criticism of *devotio moderna* and Reform theology

One force for renewal within the Church that also affected the operations of academic theology in the fifteenth century was *devotio moderna.*[104] In the person and original intention of Geert Groote (1340–1384), who studied in Paris himself (M.A. 1358), we must at any rate describe this movement initially as anti-Scholastic. He was mainly concerned about a reform of Christian life according to an ideal of the early Church. University theology and its fashions were castigated in the harshest possible words.[105] This rejection of academic science appears also under Groote's name in the *Conclusa et proposita non vota* [Resolutions and intentions not vowed], which not only reject the study of the *artes* and profane sciences, but also repudiate the mainspring of late Scholastic theology: disputation.

Item: avoid and abhor all public disputation which is quarrelsome for the sake of triumphing or excelling, as all disputations of theologians and artists in Paris are; indeed, do not even go to them for the sake of learning, because they are obviously contrary to silence [i.e., recollection], give rise to lawsuits and disagreements and are vain and forever impertinent and usually superstitious, beastly, devilish and worldly, so that the teaching is often harmful and always useless. Vain also is the waste of time. . . . Item: you should never study in order to earn the title of Doctor of Theology. . . . Item: generally speaking it is of the flesh, and they think carnally. Item: you would be distracted in many respects from your neighbor's salvation. Likewise from prayer, from purity of heart and seclusion [i.e., detachment from the world]. Item: you must then attend many idle lessons and have dealings with a lot of people, among whom a man becomes defiled and dissipated.[106]

103. Ibid., 189–214.

104. Anthology of texts: *Geert Groote, Thomas von Kempen und die Devotio moderna,* ed. H. N. Janowski (Olten-Freiburg, 1978); on the problems of defining and delimiting the movement, see also Derwich and Straub, eds., *Neue Frömmigkeit;* Gerwing, "Devotio moderna."

105. See Klinkenberg, "Devotio moderna," esp. 402–5, discussing Ep. 9 dating from 1381.

106. *Beschlüsse und Vorsätze,* no. 14.16, ed. Janowski, *Geert Grote,* 50.

This attitude, which in many respects recalls the Gregorian Reform of the twelfth century, would give way, however, in the fifteenth-century movement of *devotio moderna* to a more moderate position which—while primarily concerned about the religious welfare of pupils and students—eventually no longer excluded even university studies or teaching by its members. This late phase becomes evident especially in the *via moderna* of the new University of Tübingen with Gabriel Biel, Wendelin Steinbach († 1519), and Peter Braun († 1553), all three of whom belonged to the Brothers of the Common Life according to the monastic reform of the Windesheimer Congregation (*"Fraterherren"*). The anti-Scholastic impulse of the early period continued in their attempt to overcome the boundaries between schools without giving up their own membership in a school and in their reliance on the Church Fathers (especially Jerome) and John Gerson, who became the "fifteenth-century Father of the Church."[107] Thus in this movement, most importantly in the figure of Gabriel Biel, university theology, the clerical lifestyle and pastoral commitment (not accidentally along Augustinian lines) were once again united in a way of life. Deliberately included in this synthesis was the enthusiasm of the Italian humanists for antiquity and the revival of its literature and philosophy. Within this spirituality, new forms of theological presentation could develop, such as Biel's commentary on the canon of the Mass or Johannes Altenstaig's (ca. 1480–after 1525) glossary, *Vocabularius theologiae* (1517).

Even apart from the movement itself, *devotio moderna* strongly influenced many theologians who distanced themselves from the conventional forms of academic theology and demanded a reform of the Church and of clerical studies that would be clearly oriented to sacred Scripture. Especially worth noting in this regard are Johannes Pupper of Goch († 1475), Johannes Ruchrath of Wesel (ca. 1425–1481) and Wessel Gansfort (ca. 1419–1489).[108] In his *Epistola de scripture sacre dignitate,* Johannes of Goch contrasts the fundamental authority of *"canonica scriptura"* with *"aliorum scripta, praesertim Scholasticorum et Philosophorum"* ["the writings of others, especially Scholastics and Philosophers"].[109] *"Scholastici"* here are the disciples of the prevailing theological schools, for whom the authority of Thomas Aquinas, for example, is more important than sacred Scripture. To build upon

107. See Oberman, *Werden und Wertung,* 56–71.

108. Anthology of texts: G. A. Benrath, ed., *Reformtheologen des 15. Jahrhunderts* (Texte zur Kirchen- und Theologiegeschichte 7) (Gütersloh, 1968).

109. Text found in Benrath, ed., *Reformtheologen,* 10–19.

such weak authorities, which can easily be disputed and overturned by others and consequently only produce dissension, is a sign of an extreme lack of understanding and furthermore contradicts the unanimity of the early Church. The Bible versus Scholastic theology, the unity of the early Church versus Scholastic squabbles—so the battle lines were drawn now. The writings of contemporaries, especially of the Mendicant Orders, generate even more doubts by listing many *opiniones.* Their arguments are of philosophical origin, springing from the darkness of Aristotle, who knew nothing about the light of Sacred Scripture. The pagan Aristotle thus becomes the ancestor and forefather of "Scholastic" theology as a whole. In view of the knowledge of salvation found in sacred Scripture, philosophical knowledge proves to be inadequate and false, the "wisdom of the world" which is countered in Christ by the folly of the cross. Therefore when theologians rely on Aristotle instead of on sacred Scripture, they are fundamentally in error: what is required is a scriptural principle instead of philosophy as the basis for theology.[110]

Outside of sacred Scripture, which alone can lay claim to infallible authority and faith without doubt, there is a gradated hierarchy of authorities. Next in rank after Scripture come the Church Fathers, insofar as they agree with it. Their doctrine is to be accepted *"fideli devotione"* ["with faithful devotion"]. The teachings of the *"doctores moderni,"* however, especially the mendicants, are mere opinions. They are based on philosophical arguments and therefore have no firm foundation; they muddle the mind instead of enlightening it and serve vanity more than the truth. In a dispute among opinions, however, one must decide according to the degree of probability. Whenever a proof from Scripture is lacking, it is completely arbitrary whether Thomas, Albert the Great or Duns Scotus said something. The contemporary practice is contrasted with the example of the Church Fathers (Jerome and Augustine), who as a matter of principle presented their teachings as opinions only and never tried to attribute to them the authority of the canonical books. Given the multiplicity of theological opinions and schools, the question about theological truth and about the possibility of ascertaining it was bound to reappear. The Scholastic theology of the late Middle Ages is therefore a wrong way that is in need of reform. No wonder Luther in his *Epistula gratulatoria* applauds Johannes of Goch's indictment of the "billy goat" Aristotle and expresses the hope that soon there will be

110. See Schüssler, *Primat der Heiligen Schrift.*

no more Thomists, Albertists, Scotists, and Ockhamists left on earth, but only simple children of God and true Christians.[111]

2 Theological certainty in an uncertain age?

A fundamental problem of late Medieval theology, which also manifested in varying degrees its development, was the search for certainty. Within theology itself the question was raised as to the status and truth of theological statements and the possibility of substantiating them; theologians also investigated the existential question as to the knowledge of God and of his salvific will for the individual sinful human being in view of the fundamental freedom of God and the gratuitousness of grace.[112]

2.1 Human action in the knowledge of God: Duns Scotus

The most powerful impetus for the elaboration of the problem of certainty in fourteenth- and fifteenth-century theology came from the short life and the few authentic works of the *"Doctor subtilis,"* John Duns Scotus (ca. 1265/66–1308). These, moreover, sometimes have to be reconstructed by distinguishing the actual text from the materials that were superimposed by his students.[113] In the Franciscan tradition that was shaped especially by William de la Mare, Scotus sees theology as a whole in relation to human action. Acts, however, are performed for a purpose, which the acting person must know and aspire to. The necessary requirement for that is a definite, sure knowledge both of the end and also of the means to that end. Uncertainty with reference to one's final end ultimately makes action just as impossible as ignorance with regard to the means. The acting person therefore must know:

1. how the end is to be attained;
2. what means are necessary for that end;
3. whether those means are sufficient to attain the end.

Therefore theology is necessary, above and beyond philosophy, as a teaching about *the supernatural end of human action,* eternal blessedness, which God bestows by a freely given grace, contingently, not by necessity,

111. Text: Benrath, ed., *Reformtheologen,* 9–10.

112. See in general: Perler, *Wahrheitsbegriff;* Lang, *Glaubensbegründung;* Dettloff, *Entwicklung;* Grosse, *Heilsungewissheit,* 35–44.

113. See esp. Richter, *Studien,* 11–16.

but rather out of a free acceptance of merits. No knowledge about that end can come from natural understanding. Theology owes its existence to God's revelatory action, which produces in us a knowledge—albeit an obscure one—of supernatural truths (e.g., *"Deus est trinus,"* "God is Three").[114] Precisely in view of God's freedom, however, this must suffice to obtain certainty about the supernatural end of human action and about the means of attaining this end. Thus already in the first *quaestio* of the Oxford lectures on the *Sentences* in 1300/01, Scotus dismisses the (Aristotelian-Arabic) philosophy that supposes that it can reckon God's action of necessity and calculate human action accordingly.

The basis for understanding theology, according to Duns Scotus, is therefore not a theoretical insight into its object, God, but rather man's action (praxis), which Scotus, like Aristotle, clearly distinguishes from the intellect; this earned his approach the label of "voluntarism," as opposed to the "intellectualism" of Thomas Aquinas. Theology is practical knowledge *(cognitio practica),* which unlike the intellect is directed toward something outside of itself: the deed, the activity. Because of this (possible) relation to an object, it is defined as practical knowledge. Human action in the precise sense, however, logically and ontologically presupposes the intellect and is thereby distinguished from vegetative and sensory processes (behaviors). Action is based on an act of free will, a choice *(electio).* This is governed by the norm of rightness, that is, conformity with *"ratio recta"* ["right reason"], and it can therefore be judged ethically. For that purpose, however, the human act needs a guideline, a *"directio,"* at least with respect to the moral quality of the circumstances of the act. Theology, therefore, as a theory of action and ends, has to teach three things and thus provide the needed *"directio":*

1. Under what conditions is it possible to strive for the supernatural end of human action?
2. What conditions must the acts toward that end fulfill?
3. What conditions must the means to that end satisfy?

Theology therefore is neither a theoretical science, as Henry of Ghent claims, nor is it according to the view of Thomas Aquinas a theoretical-practical science, but rather it is thoroughly related to praxis. For man's end,

114. Duns Scotus, *In I Sent.,* prol. q.1 (edition consulted: Johannes Duns Scotus, Über die Erkennbarkeit Gottes. Texte zur Philosophie und Theologie, lateinisch-deutsch, hg. u. übers. von Hans Kraml, Gerhard Leibold, Vladimir Richter, Hamburg 2000, 4–20; as interpreted by Richter, "Textstudien," 439–45; see also Leibold, "Kontroverse."

beatitude (*fruitio Dei,* the enjoyment of God) is after all the end of activity, not of theoretical knowledge.[115]

Our theological knowledge therefore is subject to a twofold arrangement, the individual elements of which would not infrequently be played off against each other in subsequent periods:

1. This knowledge is partial and not comprehensive, obscure and not clear, in accordance with the free, contingent revelation of God.
2. It is nevertheless sufficient for practical action with regard to man's supernatural end.

The question of theological certainty and truth is therefore, to Duns Scotus' way of thinking, an immediately practical and existential question: How can theology provide the certainty that I must presuppose if my life is to be meaningful with respect to its ultimate success or failure? Duns Scotus still succeeds in considering both partial aspects at the same time. This is evident especially in the question about the object *(subjectum)* of theology. The central object of a science is that which cannot be attributed to something else, the thing in terms of which virtually all the propositions of that science can be asserted. Perfect theological knowledge, by its very nature, is possessed by God alone, for only God knows himself perfectly. In this knowledge of God all theological truths are virtually contained and verified. Theological knowledge therefore has as its central object God, not in some relation or other to his work (e.g., as Creator or Redeemer), but not in the philosophical-metaphysical definition of him as *ens* [Being] or *ens infinitum,* either, but rather in his nature [*Wesen*], in which all of these relations are included (as theological truths).[116]

If theological knowledge is to attain the certainty required for action and at the same time declare in accordance with the truth what it is possible for us to say about God, then it must be proved in the first place that an unequivocal discourse about God is possible. God's existence and action must be recognizable for us and describable in precise language.[117] This is the theoretical-scientific background for the doctrine of the univocal character of being, which is inseparably connected with Scotus' name. It is aimed

115. Duns Scotus, *In I Sent.,* prol. q.3 (Scotus, *Erkennbarkeit,* 28–43); see also the interpretation by Richter, "Duns Scotus' Text zur Theologie," 465–75.

116. Duns Scotus, prol. q.2 (Scotus, *Erkennbarkeit,* 20–28); see also the interpretation by Richter, "Textstudien," 445–49.

117. On the problem of proving the existence of God, see Richter, *Studien,* 30–78.

especially against Henry of Ghent, whose opinion Scotus summarizes in three conclusions:[118]

1. God cannot be known *"per se"* but only *"per accidens,"* that is, only his attributes can be known.
2. God can be known *"in universali,"* that is, in a general concept that can be predicated about several things, but only by an analogous concept, not by strict, univocal predication.
3. God cannot be known *"in particulari,"* in his proper individuality, because a creature is only a *"peregrina similitudo"* ["passing, distant likeness"] of God and allows us to infer only some of God's attributes.

Duns Scotus sees that as an invalidation of any precise theological knowledge and of its claim to truth. His critique takes language, the proposition, as its point of departure. Attributes (e.g., *"sapiens"*) are predicated of a subject and therefore presuppose some knowledge about what the subject is (*quidditative,* "with respect to its what-ness"). This is true also for knowledge about God, if theological discourse is to obey the rules of grammar. As Henry of Ghent correctly observes, our knowledge does not arrive at an understanding of God's nature, of how he is in himself, but for other reasons than Henry supposes. God is knowable in this way for himself alone; for all others he is knowable only as a freely chosen object of cognition. Here, at any rate, the creature's likeness to God is no reason to assume that it provides particularly accurate or inaccurate knowledge about him.

That requires, rather, that a concept be constituted in such a way that one can predicate univocally with it, so that it becomes possible to formulate propositions with truth value and thus to construct correct syllogisms (without *quaternio terminorum,* a set of four terms yielding no real conclusion).[119] This is not the case, however, with a merely analogous concept, but only with a univocal concept. In order to form such a concept about God it suffices that the predication be unambiguous and that it be possible to as-

118. See Richter, "Univozität"; about Henry of Ghent, see also Aertsen, "Von Gott kann man nichts erkennen," 30–36.

119. Duns Scotus, *In I Sent.* dist.3 q. 1 (Duns Scotus, *Erkennbarkeit,* 98, 5–10): *"Conceptum univocum dico qui ita est unus quod eius unitas sufficit ad contradictionem, affirmando et negando ipsum de eodem. Sufficit etiam pro medio syllogistico ut extrema unita in medio sic uno sine fallacia aequivocationis concludantur inter se uniri."* ["I call univocal a concept which is 'one' is such a way that its unity suffices to formulate a contradiction by affirming and denying it about the same thing. It suffices also as a syllogistic middle term or mean, so that we may conclude that the extremes which are united in the mean that is 'one' in this way are united to each other without any fallacy of equivocation."]

sign a precise content to the concept, although that by no means solves all further questions. Of course, the predication as such (and consequently the concept) cannot be certain and dubious at the same time. It suffices, therefore, to speak about God as *ens* [being], without yet having determined whether this *ens* is finite or infinite. Only on this basis will a philosophical discussion about God be meaningful, because there is a common object of discourse, whereas the analogy of concepts in Henry of Ghent eliminates precise, common discourse and consequently abolishes theology as a science. Someone might just as well claim that "man" cannot be predicated in the same way of Socrates and Plato, that there are instead two concepts here, which appear to be one because of their great similarity. With that, however, all univocal predication, the foundation of scientific discourse, is abolished. We must take as the epistemological source of theology not just any vague (ontological) similarity, but rather the successful predication that is presupposed by human speech acts. This guarantees that our theology, though partial, is nevertheless sufficient to make our actions ultimately meaningful.

2.2 Assuring human statements about God: Francis of Meyronnes

The stimulus that Duns Scotus provided for fourteenth-century theology was further developed in many different areas of theology by his students. One example of this was the work of Francis of Meyronnes, OFM (1288–1328), a representative of the Franciscan theology of the following generation. He lectured on the *Sentences* as a *baccalaureus* in Paris in 1320/21 and in 1323 became a *magister;* he was already Provincial Minister of Provence in 1324 when he was called to Avignon to work in the papal Curia, where he served, among other capacities, as arbitraror in the dispute over religious poverty and in the proceedings against Ockham.[120] We are dealing in this case as well with a relatively short teaching career and successive redactions of his commentary on the *Sentences;* the final one, the so-called *Conflatus,* is extant in a relatively early print edition. Here in particular, however, additional texts that do not date back to the original lectures on the *Sentences* were obviously incorporated.[121]

120. See esp. Möhle, *Formalitas,* 25–27; also Roth, *Franz von Mayronis;* in places corrected by: Rossmann, *Hierarchie.*

121. Edition used: Franciscus de Mayronis, *In Libros Sententiarum, Quodlibeta, Tractatus Formalitatum, De Primo Principio, Terminorum Theologicalium Declarationes, De Univocatione* (Venice,

Francis also illustrates quite clearly the debate among the Parisian schools: Dominican Thomists against Franciscan Scotists along with eclectics and a few independent theologians like Peter Aureol (ca. 1280–1322). This debate can be followed literarily in the *Disputatio collativa* by Petrus Rogerii [Pierre Roger], OSB (1292–1352, later Clement VI), which he conducted with Francis of Meyronnes in 1320/21 as a *baccalaureus* in Paris.[122] The disputed points may seem "typically Scholastic" to the modern reader: Whether the principle of contradiction can be established in theology; whether the divine essence *de potentia dei absoluta* can be contemplated without the Divine Persons; whether a real distinction can be made between the creaturely status by which a creature is dependent on God and the creature itself; whether in the order of origin an angel was created by the Father earlier than by the Son; whether in God there is only a *"signum a quo"* (["sign from which"] Petrus Rogerii) or a *"signum in quo"* (["sign in which"] Francis of Meyronnes), etc. The language and style of the disputations also produce the impression of sterile "Scholasticism," especially due to the fourfold division of all decisions and conclusions, which is sometimes carried out quite strictly.[123]

The real concern and the theological importance of such controversies becomes clear only when on reflects on the "linguistic turn" taken by theology since Duns Scotus. It is not by chance that the *Conflatus* begins with a long exposition of the principle of contradiction as a principle of ambivalence in theology.[124] With this principle Scotus had laid the foundation for univocal predication about God. Every predication is true or false, never both at the same time. Thus unambiguous predication and bivalent [*zweiwertige*] logic are set forth as the basis for theology as a whole. Theological propositions have definite truth value, even our statements about God; for the principle of contradiction is equally valid for God and creatures. Our theological statements can be rendered certain only if contradictions are inadmissible in God as well. According to the underlying realistic semantics, however, univocal predication and the validity of the principle of contradiction in statements about God presuppose "something" (ontologically) about which contradictory statements (with reference) are possible. Contradictory statements

1520; reprinted Frankfurt, 1966). Concerning the problems of literary criticism: Rossmann, "Sentenzenkommentare"; Möhle, *Formalitas*, 29–41.

122. Ed. J. Barbet, *François de Meyronnes—Pierre Roger, Disputatio (1320–1321)* (Textes philosophiques du moyen-âge 9) (Paris, 1961); see also Rossmann, "Sentenzenkommentare," 140–65.

123. See Rossmann, "Sentenzenkommentare," 220–27.

124. Franciscus de Mayronis, *Conflatus*, prol. q.1 (2^r–4^r); see also Roth, *Franz von Mayronis*, 297–369; Möhle, *Formalitas*, 42–73.

presuppose distinctions: one thing and another thing, same and different, example and counterexample. Corresponding to our distinctions in statements about God, therefore, there must be actual distinctions in the nature of God, if theological discourse is to be assured semantically (and thus ontologically). This becomes especially urgent in the doctrine of the Trinity: multiplicity of Persons—oneness of nature; communication [i.e., sharing = *Mitteilung*] of the essence—non-communication of the Persons, etc. A real distinction is ruled out, since that would imply a division in God; a mere[ly notional] distinction on the part of man does not assure predication along the lines of a "realistic" semantics. Consequently an additional sort of distinction must be assumed (*"ex natura rei,"* "resulting from the nature of the thing"), which does not signify a real division yet does guarantee a semantic-ontological correspondence with our distinctions and thus a univocal reference of our theological discourse. This is the origin of the so-called formal distinction, which is already found in the writings of Duns Scotus and became a point of dispute with the Thomists and Nominalists. The application of this potential solution in Francis of Meyronnes is initially restricted to the relation between relational statements (concerning properties or persons) and absolute statements (about the essence or nature), and also between essential attributes and the substantiality [*Wesenheit*] of God himself. These signify different *"formalitates,"* not different things, but not just moments or aspects of an intellectual/notional subdivision, either. Now of course it is possible to make further statements about such *"formalitates."* The attributes ascribed to them cannot in turn signify real qualities or distinctions, but only corresponding modifications (in disjunct pairs) of the formalities; they are therefore only *"modi intrinseci"* ["inner modalities"] that do not change the nature of the formalities: finitude—infinitude, reality—possibility, necessity—contingency, existence, reality, and *haecceitas* (individuality).[125]

The importance of the principle of contradiction in theology is also evident on another level: with regard to God's freedom and sovereignty, which Francis staunchly defended as a good Scotist, most clearly in a *quaestio* from Codex Vaticanus lat. 901 that was probably submitted as an opinion in the Ockham trial.[126] God's sovereignty is explicitly compared to the universal sovereignty of the Pope, which Francis emphatically advocated while a member of the Curia in Avignon, despite their divergent opinions in the

125. *Conflatus* l.1 d.33 q.3 (101^rv); ibid. q.5 (103^rv); see also Roth, *Franz von Mayronis,* 319–25; detailed discussion in Möhle, *Formalitas,* 74–113, 286–336.

126. Text: Rossmann, *Hierarchie,* 251–57.

debate about poverty.[127] He attributes to both a *potentia absoluta* [absolute power] that is not connected with existing laws (even its own), but rather is itself the cause of its freely willed laws.[128] In view of this absolute sovereignty of God, the question arises concerning the validity of human theological statements, but by the same token concerning the meritoriousness of human contingent action with respect to man's final end. The factual order of creation and redemption is contingent; it springs from a sovereign, free-will decision of God, who consequently complies with it in his *potentia ordinata* [ordered power], although in and of himself he would not be compelled to do so. Finally, which statements can then derive their permanent validity [*Bestand haben*] not only from God's nature but also to his creative and redemptive acts, independent of God's dispositions? Thus God could have saved mankind, for example, even without the death of Christ.[129] Can we then *in theologicis* [in theological matters] rely on those arguments that are valid in our lawfully ordered reality: for example, that guilt has punishment as a consequence, and merit results in reward? Francis discusses this question explicitly in three respects: with regard to the principles of nature, of moral action and of supernatural merit. From a purely causal perspective, there is no necessary connection between the state of grace and acceptance by God, in the sense that there would be no contradiction if the consequence failed to materialize. From the moral perspective, the absolute sovereign can determine the price of a thing with complete freedom; thus God, who is free per se, determines what is necessary in order to obtain eternal happiness. Therefore at any time he can also change, increase or diminish the price: thus eternal happiness must not depend on the presence of supernatural gifts of grace, much less on merits. In and of himself, God can grant it even without these prerequisites or refuse it when they are present. It is remarkable, in any case, that the question of whether man is accepted or rejected in God's sight is discussed according to the rules of a bill of sale, albeit in order to show forth the mercy of God, who can supply eternal happiness even below the agreed-upon "selling price."[130] The *Conflatus* accepts as a possible "consideration" or service by man in return even a morally bad act *(actus vitiosus),* which naturally would then be not only morally good but even meritorious. Thus God in and of himself *(de potentia absoluta)* can

127. Ibid., 106–31.
128. Franciscus de Mayronis, *IV Sent.* d.25 q.4 (213^{r}); see also Rossmann, *Hierarchie,* 245.
129. Ibid., 252.
130. Rossmann, *Hierarchie,* 253–54.

determine that everyone who blasphemes God is admitted to eternal life, and everyone who praises God is damned; in the same way he could damn all the righteous and save all sinners.[131]

The sole supporting principle of this discussion proves to be the principle of contradiction, rigorously interpreted to mean a simultaneous contradiction that cancels out everything positive. Even God cannot do something that involves such a contradiction.[132] On the other hand, everything else is subject to his will and thus contingent. As in the writings of Duns Scotus, however, the first rule of everything contingent is the divine will. He freely establishes the norms of how it comes about.[133] This expressly revokes all the *"rationes necessariae"* of Anselm of Canterbury in theology. The only reason that can be given for all contingent (salvific) action of God is his will; to inquire further makes no sense, especially since all theological reasons are only reasons *quoad nos* [with respect to us], even with recourse to the prudence [*Klugheit*] of God, whose will is certainly regarded as being guided by his intellect. In and of himself *(de potentia absoluta),* God could act quite differently. Theological reasons for God's actions are therefore mere reasons of convenience.[134] Univocal statements about God's nature are therefore ultimately juxtaposed with [*stehen . . . gegenüber*] unconfirmed statements about his actions.

2.3 Axiomatic metaphysics as the foundation of theology: Meister Eckhart

The image of the Dominican Meister Eckhart (ca. 1260–1328) is defined and encumbered more by his German-language treatises and sermons than by his Scholastic Latin works from the periods when he taught in Paris (1293/94, 1302/03, 1311–13).[135] In 1293/94 he lectured on the *Sentences.*[136] The questions that come up during his teaching career as *magister* show how strong a proponent Eckhart was of the Thomistic, Neoplatonic tradi-

131. See *Conflatus* I d.17 (73^{rv}); see also Dettloff, *Entwicklung,* 173.

132. See *Conflatus* I d.43/44 q.4 (125^{r}): *"Utrum deus possit facere quicquid non includit contradictionem"* ["Whether God can do whatever does not involve a contradiction"]; see also Möhle, *Formalitas,* 71–73.

133. *Conflatus* I d.45 q.1 (129^{v}–130^{r}).

134. See Rossmann, *Hierarchie,* 259–63.

135. Introduction to his life and work: Ruh, *Meister Eckhart.*

136. So far only the *Collatio in libros Sententiarum* has been edited: Meister Eckhart, *Die lateinischen Werke,* 5:1–26.—The dating of the work to 1293 is according to Ruh, contrary to J. Koch, who still dates it to 1297–1300, when Eckhart was already Prior in Erfurt and Vicar of Thüringen.

tion of his order.[137] That scholastic tradition was at the same time important for Eckhart's early view of God.[138] It inquires into the identity of being and knowing in God, which leads then directly to the controversies between Thomists and Scotists over the doctrine of distinctions [in God], and on the other hand also underscores the Thomistic emphasis on God's knowledge rather than his action. Eckhart's thesis is that the indistinguishability here is real and possibly notional and intellectual as well; as his first argument he immediately cites two passages from Thomas.[139] In keeping with the *Liber de causis,* God's *intelligere* [understanding] is even depicted as the foundation of his being: God does not know because he is, but rather is because he knows, whereby *"esse"* is understood in principle as creaturely being.[140] This is confirmed by John 1:1, which does not say, *"In principio erat esse"* (or *ens*) ["In the beginning was being"], but rather *"In principio erat verbum"* ["... the Word"]. *"Verbum,"* however, connotes truth and thus knowledge. In the dialectical interaction with these concepts in this Neoplatonic interpretation of being and knowing, everything that belongs to the intellect becomes *non-ens* [nonbeing], of course, because in that way nothing is said about its being realized outside of the intellect. If God is only intellect, however, and as such the cause of all being, then in God there is neither existence nor being (that is, considered as something created and definite).[141] The game of affirmation and negation that Eckhart is playing here is supposed to show forth the radical otherness of God even within the framework of the Thomistic analogy of being and can consequently be interpreted as the exact antithesis of Scotist univocality. Formally speaking *(formaliter),* God is not being *(ens)* but rather something higher of another sort, namely, the cause of all being and *"puritas essendi"* ["purity of being"], a being of an altogether different kind than creaturely being.[142] Compared with the linguistic, logical presuppositions and methods of a Duns Scotus, Eckhart's *quaestiones* appear quite modest. Their importance lies rather in their Neoplatonic, dialectic development of Thomistic metaphysics and of its thinking about the analogy of being.

The *Opus tripartitum,* Eckhart's principal work in Latin, which dates at least in part from his second stint as *magister* in Paris, has been preserved

137. Meister Eckhart, *Quaestiones Parisienses,* in *Lateinische Werke,* 5:27–83.
138. See Imbach, *Deus est intelligere.*
139. Meister Eckhart, *Quaestiones Parisienses* q.1 n.1 (37, 4–7): S. Th. I q.26 a.2; ScG I, 45.
140. Ibid., n.4 (40.5–41.14).
141. Ibid., n.8 (44.10–45.5); see also Manstetten, *Esse est Deus,* 305–44.
142. Meister Eckhart, *Quaestiones Parisienses* q.1 n.12 (47.14–48.8).

essentially only in its overall plan and in the *Opus Expositionum* (Scriptural exegeses). No longer extant is the set of metaphysical axioms and thus the foundation of the entire work, the *Opus propositionum,* and the Scholastic elaboration in the *Opus quaestionum.* The immediate effect that it had was negligible; its influence was of considerable importance only on Nicholas Cusanus (1401–1464). The academic world, especially in Paris, was occupied with other trends in the years 1311–1313 and afterward, so that the idiosyncratic *Summa* of the *magister* from Thüringen was not very influential. Meister Eckhart explains the purpose of the work and its method in the prologue to his exegesis of the Gospel of John:

> In interpreting this Word [John 1:1] and the sayings that follow it, the author intends, as in all his works, to explain the doctrines of the holy Christian faith and of the Scriptures of both Testaments *with the help of the natural arguments of philosophers.* . . . Furthermore this work proposes to show how the truth of the principles, conclusions and peculiarities evident in nature for him "who has ears to hear" (Matthew 13:43) is clearly suggested precisely in the words of Sacred Scripture, which are interpreted with the help of these natural truths.[143]

Eckhart's exegesis is therefore not a conventional Scriptural commentary, but rather a demonstration of the exact agreement of biblical revelation and natural, metaphysical reason. He proceeds in a way that obviously shows no signs yet of the divergence of philosophy and theology, faith and rational insight since 1277 and aligns itself with the Albertine-Thomistic tradition of his order. The entire *Opus tripartitum* thus tries to meet the needs of the *"fratres studiosi"* ["student friars"] and to set down in a kind of *summa* everything that seems worth noting about doctrinal statements, *quaestiones,* and scriptural exegesis.[144] The *Summa Theologiae* of Thomas Aquinas serves as the model for the *Opus quaestionum,* but Eckhart is striving here for brevity rather than completeness.[145] Eckhart is quite conscious of the novelty and boldness of his metaphysical theology and conceptual dialectics. He is counting on the fact that much "will appear at first glance atrocious, dubious or false"; yet that should only lead to a more precise, in-depth study, so as to arrive finally at an insight into the agreement of Scripture, authority and arguments from reason.[146] Eckhart specifies the precise connections

143. Meister Eckhart, *Expositio Sancti Evangelii secundum Iohannem,* prooem. n.2 f. (*Lat. Werke* 3:4.4–6, 14–17); German translation, i.e., the cited work is a Latin-German edition.
144. Meister Eckhart, *Prologus generalis in Opus Tripartitum* n.2 (*Lat. Werke* 1:148.5–149.2).
145. Ibid., n.5 (1:151.2–6).
146. Ibid., n.7 (1:152.3–7).

among metaphysical axioms, *quaestio* and scriptural exegesis in the first article of each part: In the *Opus propositionum* it is the statement, *"Esse est Deus"* ["God is being"]; in the *Opus quaestionum*—the question *"Utrum Deus sit"* ["Does God exist?"], and in the area of scriptural exegesis—Genesis 1:1. The metaphysical foundation of scriptural exegesis is thus clearly underscored. The fundamental propositions of metaphysics remain the norm for the interpretation of Scripture.[147]

Against the background of the first Parisian *quaestio* it must appear at first to be a rupture in Meister Eckhart's teaching when already in the prologue to the *Opus tripartitum* he repeatedly and decidedly insists on the fundamental proposition: *"Esse est Deus."*[148] In the first *quaestio* he had still used *"ens"* and *"esse"* primarily for creaturely things and assigned preeminence to *intelligere.* Yet even in that work he already speaks about God as *"puritas essendi"* ["purity of being"]. Now, within the framework of Christian Neoplatonic metaphysics, this becomes the prevailing point of view, without which one can neither prove the existence of God nor carry out Eckhart's program of a metaphysical interpretation of Scripture. Methodologically little has changed since the first *quaestiones.* We no longer encounter disputations pro and con but rather theses that are proved by multiple arguments (the shorter arguments being enumerated). In neo-Platonic conceptual dialectics, in each case the (abstract) fundamental concept is sought first, the concrete thing is then derived from it and the negative contrary concept is formed as well: being/an existing thing/nothingness, unity/one/many, truth/a truth/a falsehood, goodness/a good/an evil; the pattern is not followed through consistently, however.[149] The "purity of being" [*or:* "Pure being"] has now become *"esse"* ["being"] itself as the fundamental definition of the biblical, Christian, and metaphysical God, whose identity is fundamental for Eckhart. *"Esse"* or *"ens"* in the absolute sense should be distinguished from *"ens hoc et hoc"* ["this or that being"]: with that, God's logical otherness is just noted by means of another predicate, as Eckhart will go on to show with the remaining transcendentals.[150] Then, through the corresponding negative concepts, everything that is not *ens* in the proper sense appears as nothing: *"praeter esse et sine esse omnia sunt nihil, etiam facta."* ["Aside from and without being, all things, even those that are made,

147. Ibid., n.11 (1:156.11–14).
148. Ibid., n. 12 (1:156.15); see also Tabula Prologorum n.1 (1:11–12).
149. Ibid., n.4 (1:150.1–151.1); for a philosophical exposition see esp. Schirpenbach, *Wirklichkeit.*
150. Meister Eckhart, *Prologus in Opus propositionum* n.1–15 (1:166–76).

are nothing."][151] Already in the Neoplatonic *Liber de causis,* the wealth of the origin is contrasted with the paltriness or "the nothingness" of anything else: This provides the metaphysical basis of the mystical longing for God, but also of the personal *"Entwerdung"* ["un-becoming, being unmade"] that occurs by emptying oneself and recognizing one's own nonbeing in comparison with God's being.[152] The costs of such metaphysical-theological speculation, however, follow close behind: natural causation and metaphysical participation in being go their separate ways, but the same is true also of the explanation of nature and metaphysical-theological speculation. Explanation by natural causes has become theologically dispensable, since the being, unity, truth, and goodness of things depend not on natural causes but directly on God.[153]

On this foundation Eckhart constructed a theology and a mysticism that even in his day gave offense by the dialectical and (especially in the German works) misleading way in which they were formulated. On the one hand his theology emphasizes the absolute preeminence of God, not in his will and his power, as in the thought of Scotus and his school, but rather in his being; on the other hand, through direct ontological participation in God's being, a close association becomes possible, overcoming of the chasm between the "nothingness" of the creature and the "Being" of God in the no longer analogous but univocal ontological relation of God, the Son of God as image *(imago)* and "what is divine in the soul."[154] Immediate contact with God and intellectual certain are to be gained along this speculative path, which proves to be dangerous, however, as demonstrated by the trial and posthumous condemnation of Eckhart in the Bull *"In agro dominico"* by John XXII (1316–1334) dated March 27, 1329.[155]

2.4 What can we know? William of Ockham

Like Duns Scotus, William of Ockham (1285–1347) provided important stimuli for the development of fourteenth- and fifteenth-century theology during a relatively short teaching career (Oxford, ca. 1317–1324), especially in his consistent application of logical linguistic criticism to the assertions of theology.[156] The theoretical equipment developed in logic and physics to

151. Ibid., n. 22 (1:178.16–17).
152. Ibid., n. 21 (1:178, 10–15).
153. Ibid., n. 24 (1:180.6–181.2); n.25 (1:182.3–6).
154. Idem, *In Joh* n. 23–24 (3:19–20); see also Ruh, *Meister Eckhart,* 78–86.
155. See Ruh, *Meister Eckhart,* 168–87, with bibliography on the Eckhard trial: 204–5.
156. For the certain dates and authentic works see esp. Richter, "Unterwegs . . . Ockham"; Kraml and Leibold, *Wilhelm von Ockham,* 6–13, 89–101.

discuss the requirements of a science is immediately brought to bear on theology in the prologue of his *Scriptum in I Sent.*, where he inquires about the evidence of theological truths in the very first *quaestio.*[157] Theological truths are in principle statements, propositions; for we do not know things (except in an intuitive understanding) but really only propositions. "Knowledge" is used propositionally. Theological truths in the strict sense are the truths necessary to obtain eternal happiness, whereby Ockham immediately aligns himself with the practical orientation of Franciscan theology. Among these theological truths are those which can be known by natural reason as well (God exists, God is wise, good, etc.), but also purely supernatural truths (Trinity, Incarnation). The question as to the evidence of theological truths in general is more far-reaching than the question of their scientific character that was formulated in the thirteenth century: How do we go from the knowledge of the terms of a proposition (insofar as they are referential) to an insight into the truth of the proposition? This question arises not only with necessary, scientific statements, but also with contingent propositions based on immediate intuitive knowledge, for example, *"Socrates est albus"* ["Socrates is white"]. If I don't have Socrates right in front of me, this proposition does not have the necessary evidence for me. Ockham inquires therefore into the epistemological status of supernatural theological statements for man, who has no intuitive insight into the truth of God: What then, if anything, can we know in theology?[158] Ockham answers the question in one of his typically complex replies, with a discussion of each of the objections and opinions, so that question 1 expands to fill seventy-two pages of the critical edition:

1. With regard to theological statements, a human being places an act of perception *(apprehensio)* and of judgment or assent *(judicium)* that it is true. The judgment is partially dependent on one's experience with these matters *(habitus).*
2. The act of judgment presupposes knowledge of the terms of the proposition (in their significance).
3. Sensory perception alone does not cause the act of judgment (assent to the truth); there must be additional intellectual (propositional) knowledge.

157. On this whole subject, see Guelluy, *Philosophie;* Leff, *William of Ockham,* 320–98; Leppin, *Geglaubte Wahrheit.*

158. William of Ockham, *I Sent.* prol. q.1, in Guillelmi de Ockham, *Opera theologica* I, ed. G. Gál/S. Brown (New York: St. Bonaventure, 1967), 5–7.

4. With respect to the same object, intuitive and abstract knowledge is possible for man. The two should be separated from each other, even in the case where God is the object.
5. Man on his earthly pilgrimage can have an abstract knowledge of God. In contingent matters, however, abstract knowledge does not convey complete certainty about existence or nonexistence, since it does not directly presuppose them. The ultimate foundation of certainty remains the immediate, intuitive knowledge of the terms insofar as they are referential.
6. Normally we human beings on our earthly pilgrimage have no intuitive knowledge of God, yet such knowledge is possible *de potentia dei absoluta* [by God's absolute power]. It is independent of abstract knowledge. In this way *homo viator* [man the wayfarer] can arrive at a distinct knowledge of God, which nonetheless does not remove all doubts.
7. *De potentia absoluta* God can grant to man on his earthly pilgrimage an evident knowledge of many theological truths, but not of others, especially not of contingent and future statements: "God has assumed flesh," "There will be a resurrection of the dead," "The holy soul will come to share in eternal happiness." Evident knowledge of statements about salvation history and of those derived from it is therefore ruled out.[159]

The certainty of a theology of salvation history in its fundamental statements therefore rests at most upon an abstract knowledge (and assent), which cannot remove the decisive doubt as to whether that is really the case. Recourse to a certainty of faith, however, is meaningless for the *certainty of theology,* since Ockham explicitly separates theology and faith. The theologian can be a believer, but need not be: the figure of the personally nonbelieving or heretical theologian appears.[160] The question then arises: What additional knowledge does a human being acquire through the knowledge of theological truths? Can theology broaden his knowledge? In the case of a believer, his faith *(fides adquisita)* is surely deepened thereby. In the case of a non-believer or a heretic, however, theological knowledge contributes nothing at all to his faith. Every student of theology, of course, acquires knowledge about many things that do not belong to other sciences. At the very least he learns them simply in the way of comprehension (*actus apprehensivus,* for example, hearing and learning by heart), regardless of whether they are technical terms, articles of faith or scientifically proved

159. Ibid., q.1 (1:15–51).
160. Ibid., q.7 (1:196–99).

conclusions. Thus equipped, the theologian can do everything that there is to do in theology: preach, teach, reaffirm, etc., except believe. Nothing more is required for theology than to learn theological truths and to master the techniques of logic. Nevertheless, as a whole it cannot be described either as knowledge in the strict sense nor as a science in the Aristotelian sense, because assent to the truths of faith is possible only in faith. Faith and evident knowledge, however, cannot be united. Yet theology can contain statements that are proved rigorously and thus can be regarded as scientific; for science ["knowledge of a thing"] in the strict sense refers to the individual demonstrated conclusion; only in the sense of an orderly classification can physics as a whole, for example, be regarded as science.[161] Much less can theology as a whole claim the honorary title of wisdom, since evidence is indispensable for that. Nevertheless, if a theologian had a knowledge that enabled him to defend and confirm the faith with evidence, he would possess wisdom. In the natural course of things, however, that is impossible. Scientific technique cannot disguise the fundamental uncertainty of theology, due to its lack of evidence, or the uncertainty of the theologian with respect to the presuppositions of his faith. Therefore a careful examination of the degree of evidence of the individual theological statement is required.

This examination becomes urgent in the case of statements that affect man's life insofar as it is ordered to its final goal, especially with regard to God's freedom and the contingency of his salvific work, which in his absolute power could have been different from what was in fact decreed *de potentia ordinata.*[162] When, for instance, are my actions justified in God's sight; when am I (as sinner) accepted by God?[163] In theses that sounded harsh to his contemporaries, namely the Oxford Chancellor John Lutterell († 1335), who initiated his trial in Avignon (1324),[164] Ockham expounds the nonnecessity of all created causes (or forms) for acceptance by God: God in and of himself is free to grant eternal life to whomever and for whatever reason he wills; his will (love, hatred) alone decides, not some necessary dispositions *(forma, habitus, caritas)* on the part of the human being. The presence of grace and meritorious acts, therefore, says nothing per se about whether a human being is accepted by God and destined for eternal life.

161. See Leinsle, "Einheit der Wissenschaft."

162. See Bannach, *Lehre;* Schröcker, *Verhältnis,* 25–87.

163. William of Ockham, *I Sent.* d.17 q.1 (*Op. theol.* 3:440–466); see also Dettloff, *Entwicklung,* 253–90.

164. See Hoffmann, *Johannes Lutterell.*

Ockham certainly does, however, maintain that they, along with the sacraments (baptism), are in fact necessary *de potentia ordinata* [by virtue of God's ordinances].[165] There is clearly a discrepancy between this factual necessity in the contingent order of salvation and the absolutely free will of God. A question like this can, however, be resolved and understood in human terms on the basis of the principle of contradiction. Thus, formally speaking, it is not a contradiction to say "Act X is meritorious" and "Act X is not informed by a supernatural *habitus*," because the reason for the first statement is not some natural or supernatural *habitus* (e.g., virtue, grace, faith). The meritoriousness of our actions is therefore not based on our good qualities or on some other created cause (e.g., habitual grace) but solely on God's actual, voluntary and free bestowal of grace: the acceptance of my actions as merit with respect to eternal life. In his action, God in and of himself is free and not dependent on created causes. Therefore in and of himself he can also reject an act performed with the help of grace and accept a purely natural act as meritorious. In principle, therefore, meritorious action does not exceed human potential.[166] As human acts, both kinds of acts are within the realm of human possibility, but with respect to their meritoriousness and consequently their value in God's sight, both are left to God's discretion. Two divergent practical consequences result from this teaching:

1. the effort and obligation to do something for one's own salvation: late medieval devotion to works and the multiplication of pious practices;
2. the fundamental uncertainty as to whether everything that I do is sufficient for my salvation in God's sight or contributes anything at all, and thus the existential uncertainty: "What must I do to inherit eternal life?" (Mark 10:17).

Given God's freedom and the contingency of the order of salvation, theology, being uncertain knowledge without definitive evidence, cannot answer the question unequivocally in a way that would remove all doubts. From the perspective of the theory of science, and also existentially, theological optimism is not justified.

165. Ockham, *I Sent.* d. 17 q.1 (3:452.6–13); see also Dettloff, *Entwicklung*, 263.

166. Ockham, *I Sent.* d.17 q.2 (3:471–72); this would then be misunderstood as "Pelagianism"; see also Leppin, *Theologie*, 142–43.

2.5 Propositional logic of the faith: Robert Holcot

The current of theological linguistic criticism inaugurated by Ockham soon burst through the hard and fast boundaries between schools of thought and crossed over to other religious orders. Previously the Dominican Durand of Saint Pourçain (ca. 1275–1334) had already turned aside from the Thomism of his order.[167] In the Dominican Order we find Ockhamistic thought critically accepted in the work of Robert Holcot († 1349), who lectured on the *Sentences* in Oxford from 1330–1332 and in 1334 became a master of theology. Holcot combined an academic career with pastoral work (preaching), which lends color particularly to his scriptural commentaries.[168]

As Francis of Meyronnes and Ockham did before him, Holcot poses the question: What logic is satisfied by statements of faith and of theology, if certain knowledge generally cannot be obtained in theology? Therefore Holcot clearly distinguishes between scientific-Aristotelian logic and a *"logica fidei,"* which nevertheless should not be dismissed as "irrationalism" or "fideism"; for Holcot intends thereby to assure the rationality of assent given in faith to an unproved truth and to remove it from the realm of a sheer willful decision with regard to eternal life.[169] To do that, he must first distinguish between the natural act of faith and the supernatural act of faith proceeding from the habit or virtue of faith. The natural act of faith is not a matter of sheer will, but rather depends on the degree of insight into the unproved statement that is supposed to be believed; for the truths of faith, strictly speaking, are for Holcot not *"supra rationem"* ["transcending reason"] but rather *"contra rationem"* ["contrary to reason"]: they are opposed to conventional Aristotelian logic.[170] This however does not exempt the assent of faith from investigating the object of faith and reasoning intellectually about it.[171] In his *Conferentiae,* Holcot once again expressly delineates his understanding of the act of faith in contrast to the opinion of Crathorn and the Franciscan Walter of Chatton († ca. 1344).[172] Here he refers to the per-

167. See Dettloff, *Entwicklung,* 107–28.

168. See esp. Hoffmann, *Methode;* Hoffmann, *Ockham-Rezeption,* 85–94; Smalley, *English Friars,* 133–202; on the Scriptural commentaries, see Smalley, "Robert Holcot."

169. Robert Holcot, *I Sent.* q.1 (*Opus quaestionum ac determinationum super libros Sententiarum,* Lyon, 1497, a II rb 19–34); see also Hoffmann, *Methode,* 33.

170. See Lang, *Glaubensbegründung,* 159–65; corrected by Hoffmann, *Methode,* 175–77.

171. Holcot *I Sent.* q.1 a.6 (f. a V rb 47–va 11); see also Hoffmann, *Methode,* 179–82; citation at 179, n. 36.

172. Holcot, *Conferentiae* a.2 (Ed. Hoffmann, *Conferentiae,* 82–104).

sonal experience of every human being: If two contradictory propositions seem equally dubious to me, I need additional knowledge that will provide me with sufficient certainty to assent to one of the two. If on the other hand the truth of a statement is established, for the "intellectualist" Holcot assent is no longer a matter of the will but rather a necessity of reason. However, a doubtful proposition never becomes true or certain through an act of will.[173]

In principle, however, the object of faith consists of propositions, statements, and not the (ontological) things or matters *(res significatae)* designated by the propositions.[174] Faith is therefore just as propositional as knowledge:

> By the object of faith I mean only that which is designated as being believed, and by the object of cognition I mean only that which is designated as being known. And because strictly speaking no thing that exists outside the mind is designated as being known—for example, I do not know the stone, but rather the fact that the stone is heavy; so it is known by me that the stone is heavy; and the verb "is known," as well as the participles "known" or "believed," are predicated not of something simple but rather of a complex that is variously formulated—this is why we say that only the complex is the object of the act of faith.[175]

The act of assenting to faith occurs with reference not to a *"res"* [thing] outside the mind, but rather to a proposition whose terms, however, signify (in personal supposition) and thus stand for the thing and do not just have a purely grammatical or logical meaning. The truth of the proposition is for Holcot the *"res significata,"* not an intentional or mental object *(complexum significatum),* as Crathorn and Gregory of Rimini claim.[176] The material truth of faith statements and theological propositions is consequently assured with regard to their extension. It is dependent on the use of the terms in the proposition as signifiers, that is, they are true if the terms really do designate what they mean, and consequently a corresponding *res* outside the mind can be produced for which they stand. This is not the case, for example, in Anselm's proof of the existence of God; here it would be necessary first to prove that *"istud quo majus cogitari nequit"* ["that thing than which nothing greater can be thought"] can be used as a signifier [i.e., with

173. Ibid., a.2 (91.2–18).

174. See Hoffmann, *Methode,* 211–16 (with literary-critical emendations of the incunabulum text); see also Perler, *Wahrheitsbegriff.*

175. Translated from the German version by Hoffmann, *Methode,* 216; see also Hoffmann, "Satz," 300.

176. See Crathorn, *I Sent* q.2, ed. Hoffmann, *Crathorn,* 152–205; Holcot, *Conferentiae* a.1 (67–82).

a real, objective referent].[177] The verification of theological statements now becomes the decisive problem. This cannot be accomplished by means of a proof that immediately entails knowledge, but rather is a matter of faith and its own logic. That is why "God is," meaning the result of a philosophical proof, is something different from a faith statement; the philosophical proof does not attain the object of the Catholic faith, since the concept "god" for the philosopher or the pagan is different from the Catholic's concept. We are dealing therefore with an equivocation which rules out all proof and indeed requires a special "logic of faith" in order to assure theological statements.[178]

This logic is required precisely in those situations where statements about God necessarily involve an appraisal of his freedom or man's freedom, that is, with (future) contingent statements—another point disputed by Holcot and Crathorn.[179] Statements about the future have no definite truth-value; contingent statements are not demonstrable. If we maintain both God's freedom and his omniscience, then statements about future contingent matters are necessarily either true or false, as statements, but not at the same time nor successively. Consequently, in view of the freedom of God and of man, there must be statements which are true and yet in another respect false, for example, "Socrates (*or* this man) will go to heaven." For that depends both on God's freedom and also on the freedom of that man. But what is true today cannot be false tomorrow, except for predictions of contingent events which as future statements are falsified by the actual occurrence, for example, "The soul of the Antichrist will be created," or "The day of judgment will take place." Once the event takes place, the statement in its future form can no longer be made and is thus false. Now since such contingent future statements can be the object of revelation, Holcot accepts, for purely logical reasons, the possibility that such statements can be falsified even when they are found in the Bible, and therefore admits the possibility of a faith in statements that are possibly false, even in the case of the *"anima Christi."* This leads to "objectionable" theological formulations: "God can deceive. The soul of Christ was capable of being deceived. Sacred Scripture can be false. A false faith can be meritorious."[180]

177. Holcot, *Quodlibet;* cited in Hoffmann, "Satz," 302, nn 23–24.

178. Holcot, *I Sent* q.4 (f. d VII vb 7–14); see also Hoffmann, "Satz," 302–3.

179. See Hoffmann, *Methode,* 36–40, 279–379.

180. Holcot, *II Sent.* a.2 a.9 (f. h VI vb 22–39; h VI vb 55–VII ra 10); vgl. Hoffmann, *Methode,* 37, 392.

In his theology Holcot maintains the freedom of man with at least the same intensity as God's freedom, starting with the question about the freedom of the act of faith. Just as theology has individual propositions as its object, so too, man's behavior is to be observed and judged in individual acts. The vocabulary used reflects this: Holcot no longer speaks primarily about the [faculty of] will *(voluntas)* but rather about the individual act of will *(velle)* and its (propositional) object. There is a remarkably strong emphasis on man's natural powers and rational arguments, which is why Thomas Bradwardine numbers Holcot among the *"Pelagiani moderni."*[181] Precisely in ethical questions, however, these rational arguments are aimed at a More or Less, for example, in Holcot's hypothesis that there is a natural love of God:

> Anything that the human intellect can consider supremely lovable, [man] can also love above all things, and this by his natural powers, because he is completely and utterly master of his voluntary decisions. . . . God should be loved above all things. God should be loved more than Plato, than Socrates, etc., because He is better (and consequently more lovable) than Plato, than Socrates, etc.[182]

Furthermore, man by his natural powers can will that God (and not something else) should be God.[183] Thereby, however, he places an act of supreme benevolence toward God. Holcot agrees with Bradwardine, though, in a purely logical way, that God can also be the efficient cause of man's sinful acts, and of the act of faith, too, which then however would no longer be an act of assent. Holcot, in any case, restricts this causality to God's *"voluntas beneplaciti"* ["permissive will"] and thus rejects any direct command of sin by God *("voluntas signi")*.[184] The technique used in the discussion here, as always, is propositional logic, with all its possibilities for analyzing fallacies, especially through the perennial distinction between the proper and improper use of language *(modus loquendi* vs. *forma loquendi),* so as to guarantee theological statements in their truth value as well.[185] The latter are still dependent on Scripture but likewise on the logical proof of their truth or credibility.

181. See Leff, *Bradwardine.*

182. Holcot *I Sent.* q.4 (fol. d III ra48–rb28); see also Hoffmann, *Methode,* 58–59.

183. Luther would later argue for precisely the opposite thesis.

184. Holcot, *II Sent.* q.1 (fol. f VIII ra1–b18); see also Hoffmann, *Methode,* 40–44; on Ockham see also Schröcker, *Verhältnis,* 126–42.

185. See Hoffmann, *Methode,* 71–77 (applied also to the example of Eucharistic doctrine: transubstantiation or annihilation).

2.6 What can we do? Gregory of Rimini

The question as to the meritoriousness of our actions *ex puris naturalibus* [by our unaided natural faculties] that had been raised by Duns Scotus, Ockham, and their students, among others, was answered by the Augustine Recollect Gregory of Rimini († 1358) in his revival of Augustine's anti-Pelagian teaching on grace.[186] His predecessor in this endeavor in the *via antiqua* was Thomas Bradwardine († 1349). Gregory, however, followed the *via moderna.* He lectured on the *Sentences* in Paris in 1343–1344 and was promoted to the degree of *magister* as early as 1345, contrary to the regulations of his order.[187] His *quaestiones* on *II Sent.* d. 26–29, which are crucial for this debate, are overloaded to an otherwise unusual extent with citations from Augustine, along with passages from Pelagius. Gregory intends thereby to secure his teaching historically as well. His opponents, the *"Pelagiani moderni,"* are Duns Scotus, Ockham and Adam Woodham. To them can be attributed historically, at worst, a kind of Semipelagianism—a term that was not yet available in the fourteenth century, though. In Gregory's writings they appear as "super-Pelagians" who err more seriously than Pelagius himself by attributing too much to our powers and too little to God's grace.[188]

That is the crux of the debate: With respect to a God who is omnipotent and free, what can man do by his own power? Can he comply at all with God's will? What happens to man's autonomy and self-assertiveness (freedom) vis-à-vis this God? Gregory conducts his debate with his opponents by means of citations from Augustine,[189] but he is basically addressing the problem of "modern," late medieval man, who realizes that in his subjectivity he is confronted with God's action. To a great extent Gregory agrees with Ockham in the nominalist presuppositions of his teaching on human action and grace, and its pointedness follows as a consequence precisely from this: In this regard we cannot observe man in his habitual disposition, but rather his individual actual deed. Likewise God's actual *"auxilium speciale"* ["special assistance"] is necessary for these individual acts; God's *"influentia generalis"* on man's life is of as little use here as an habitual grace.[190]

186. See Burger, "Augustinschüler."

187. See Marcolino, "Augustinertheologe."

188. Gregory of Rimini, *II Sent.* d.26–28 q.1 a.2, in Gregorii Ariminensis OESA *Lectura super Primum et Secundum Sententiarum,* A. D. Trapp and V. Marcolino, eds. (Spätmittelalter und Reformation 6–12), vol. VI (Berlin-New York: 1980), 59.34–35; see also the Foreword, vol. VI, vi–vii.

189. For a list of the citations from the anti-Pelagian writings in *II Sent.* d. 26–29, see Burger, "Auxilium speciale," 225.

190. Gregory of Rimini, *II Sent.* d.26–28 a.1, a.3 (6:77, 7–12); see also Burger, "Auxilium speciale," 220–22.

Gregory's *quaestiones,* which sometimes are quite elaborate with multiple subdivisions,[191] are remarkable in the first place for their precise framing of the questions. The description of man's condition (before or after the fall) is assumed; at issue is the kind of influence that God chooses to exercise upon human action:

d.26–28 q. 1: "Whether man in his present condition—assuming God's general influence—can perform any morally good act by his free will and his natural endowments without the special help of God's grace."

d.26–28 q. 2: "Whether man in his present condition can avoid any sin whatsoever by his natural powers without the special help of God's grace."

d.29 q. un.: "Whether man before he committed sin was capable, by his free will and the powers of his nature, without further help from God, to accomplish any morally good or truly righteous or virtuous act."

One expects precise questions to have equally precise answers, which Gregory does give in his conclusions and proves in separate steps:

1. No human being in his condition after the Fall—under the effect of God's general influence—can *accomplish* any morally good act without the special help of God.
2. No human being in his condition after the Fall—under the effect of God's general influence—can *discern adequately,* without God's special help in matters of morality, what should be willed or not willed, what should be done or avoided.
3. No human being in his condition after the Fall—given the operation of God's general influence—can will or act accordingly without God's special help, not even if he had the adequate discernment described in (2).[192]
4. No sinful, free human being in the present state can avoid any actual sin whatsoever without God's special help.
5. No sinful, free human being in the present state can or could avoid even one of his sins without God's special help.[193]
6. No human being habitually possessing *gratia gratum faciens* [i.e., in the state of sanctifying grace] (therefore a *justus* in the technical sense) can avoid any actual sin whatsoever without God's special help.
7. No human being habitually possessing *gratia gratum faciens* can avoid even one of his sins without God's special help.[194]

191. See Burger, "Auxilium speciale," 201–5.

192. Gregory of Rimini, *II Sent.* d.26–29 q.1 a.1 (6:24.10–19).

193. Ibid., q.2 a.1 (6:88.25–89, 10).

194. Ibid., a.2 (102.3–5; 104.8–9).

8. Before the Fall, the first man, Adam, was not capable of performing any good act by his own powers without the help of God's general influence.
9. By his natural powers alone, supported by God's general influence, Adam before the Fall was not capable of performing any morally good or truly virtuous act; rather, he needed additional special help from God, above and beyond the conditions mentioned previously.
10. Before he had committed sin, Adam was able, by his free will and natural powers and with the additional help of grace (over and above God's general influence) to perform a morally good act without the further special help of God.[195]

The picture that Gregory draws of the ability, will and action of a human being after the fall presupposes at all points the necessity of the exercise of God's influence through actual grace in the special case. As a matter of principle, a human being after the fall is incapable of withstanding a temptation without the special help of God's grace, but also of fulfilling God's commands; indeed, in principle he is no more capable of willing the good than the devil.[196] To begin with, a morally good act requires that one comply with God's commands for God's sake and not for some other purpose. This presupposes loving God for his own sake; this is no longer possible after the fall, unless God himself bestows this ability upon man anew. According to Augustine, however, every act that does not originate in this way from the love of God for his own sake is morally bad. Therefore among the pagans, too, there are no morally good acts performed by natural powers.[197]

The moral quality of an act should be strictly distinguished from its meritoriousness and acceptance unto eternal life, which is discussed in *I Sent.* d.17 q.1.[198] A moral act becomes meritorious only through God's acceptance of it unto eternal life; he does this freely as a matter of principle, however, most importantly *de potentia dei absoluta,* as Gregory maintains in three conclusions:

1. *De potentia dei absoluta* someone can be in God's grace and accepted without the habit of infused charity (the love of God).
2. On the other hand someone who does have this *habitus* may not be accepted by God for eternal life.

195. *II Sent* d.29 q. un. a.1 (116.18–20; 117.18–21; 130.12–15).
196. *II Sent.* d.26–28 q.1 a.1 (25.1–2; 26.8–12; 28.13–14).
197. See Burger, "Auxilium speciale," 207–11.
198. Gregory of Rimini, *I Sent.* d.17 q.1 (2:215–249); see also Dettloff, *Entwicklung,* 313–21.

3. A human being can love God meritoriously without this habit of grace; for the sole basis of the meritoriousness is God's acceptance.[199]

Thus to infer that a morally good act, which itself becomes good only through the help of a special grace of God, is automatically meritorious (valuable with respect to eternal salvation) is *per se* an invalid conclusion. The acuity of Gregory's logical argument is evident precisely in his reasons for the second thesis: the habitual love of God *(caritas)* and eternal happiness are two created entities which *in and of themselves* are not so necessarily connected that one could not exist without the other. Therefore it is logically conceivable, and furthermore possible *de potentia absoluta,* that God might not accept for eternal life a human being who possesses the habitual love of God, or might take the state of happiness away from him after a time and leave him with the *caritas* alone.[200] God is free, in principle, to give one of those gifts without the other; and both are gifts, not merited by man. For no act by a human being, whether performed for the love of God or without it, is meritorious in and of itself in such a way that God would have to accept it as valuable unto eternal life. It is rather a *"gratuita ordinatio divina"* ["gratuitous divine decree"], which is based on his free will.[201] We can abide by this decree, however, trusting that God does not change what he has freely ordained. What can we do, then? By our natural powers, we can only sin, but with the help of God's special grace we can do good deeds, act meritoriously through his free acceptance thereof, and attain eternal life. Gregory's solution, modeled on Augustine's anti-Pelagianism, would become important for Luther, who praised Gregory as the one who had dared in Paris *"Augustinum producere et Sophistis opponere in hac materia"* ["to promote Augustine and to oppose the Sophists in this matter"].[202]

2.7 God's knowledge and human freedom: Marsilius of Inghen

Whereas man's knowledge is rendered uncertain with regard to divine freedom, on the other hand the question arises: what about God's knowledge with regard to human freedom? What do we know theologically about God's knowledge concerning the free, contingent, future actions of man? The question of *futura contingentia,*[203] which was the subject of a lively discussion

199. *I Sent.* d.17 q.1 a.2 (2:222, 5–10); see also Dettloff, *Entwicklung,* 317.

200. *I Sent.* d.17 q.1 a.1 (2:234.23–235.21). 201. Ibid. (245.24–31).

202. WA Br 12.387.16–20.

203. For the debates at the University of Louvain/Leuven, see Baudry, *Querelle des futurs contingents;* for a history of the problem: Craig, *Problem of Divine Foreknowing;* Schwamm, *Vorherwissen.*

in the fourteenth and fifteenth centuries and was thoroughly debated even in difficult university disputations, is in modern dress the question as to absolute knowledge even of future and contingent things: How will the course of the world continue? As an example of the medieval discussion, which was carried on not only at the universities but also by every *"muliercula vel etiam laica persona"* ["common woman or even lay person"],[204] we present here Marsilius of Inghen (ca. 1330–1396), a professor in Paris and Heidelberg, who studied in Paris (theology beginning in 1366) together with Geert Groote, the founder of *devotio moderna,* and kept in contact with Heinrich Totting of Oyta. From 1386 on he taught the *artes* at the new University of Heidelberg, and he held the office of rector there from 1386–1392 and in 1396. Not until 1396 was he promoted in Heidelberg to the degree of doctor of theology, but he died that same year.[205] His *Quaestiones super Quattuor libros Sententiarum,* which were influenced by Ockham, Adam Woodham and Gregory of Rimini, were composed in Heidelberg in the years 1392–1394 and grapple with the problem in a logically precise manner. Every *quaestio* is subdivided according to its premises *(suppositiones)* and conclusions, which in turn are proved individually with many arguments.[206]

Even his way of framing the questions is oriented to the propositional understanding of truth: Can the following propositions be true simultaneously, or are they contradictory?

I. Divine foreknowledge infallibly knows everything beforehand.
II. There are consequences that are produced contingently and freely.[207]

Marsilius maintains both presuppositions in faith, both God's comprehensive foreknowledge and also the contingency of future, freely willed events. Accordingly, the first proposition is proved very briefly in article 1:[208]

1. God knows in advance everything in the future.
2. God's foreknowledge is absolutely infallible with regard to future events.
3. Although most contingent future events depend on a created, free will, they are infallibly known by God in advance.

204. Marsilius of Inghen, *I Sent.* q. 40; ed. Hoenen, *Marsilius van Inghen,* 2:71.

205. See Hoenen, *Marsilius of Inghen,* 7–11.

206. Ibid., 19–22; on the sources see also Santos Noya, "Auctoritates theologicae."—Published works: *Questiones Marsilii super quattuor libros sententiarum* (Strasbourg, 1501; reprinted Frankfurt, 1966).

207. Marsilius van Inghen, *I Sent.* q. 40 (ed. Hoenen, 2:61–113).

208. Ibid., a.1 (2:73–74).

But now what is the relation between this comprehensive foreknowledge of God and the contingency of created things and the freedom of human will that are emphasized at all points by Ockham?[209] God's knowledge, however, being knowledge, is propositional. It refers to circumstances as the referential objects of propositions *(complexe enuntiabile),* not to things.[210] There must be contingent future circumstances, if theological discourse about sin is to retain its meaning; for sin is in principle a free human act. The prime example is the Antichrist (a future figure), according to Daniel 11:36–37 and 2 Thessalonians 2:4. Now given that he will demand to be worshiped as God, there are in principle three possible ways of explaining this:

1. The Antichrist acts freely, and this action is sin.
2. The Antichrist acts out of necessity and therefore does not sin. If God then punishes him with eternal damnation, however, he is acting unjustly.
3. The Antichrist acts out of necessity and necessarily sins; he is damned justly *"ex natura rerum"* ["by the nature of things"]. This answer (given by Robert Holcot), however, makes God the *"principalis actor"* of sin and is therefore just as unacceptable as (2).

Therefore only possibility (1) is theologically acceptable, and this results in a typical formulation of contingent future statements and of divine knowledge about them:

(a) The Antichrist will sin at a point in time *a,* and
(b) The Antichrist is capable of not sinning at the same time *a.*
These two propositions are combined as:
(a–b) The Antichrist will sin *contingently* at the point in time *a.*
(c) God knows infallibly that the Antichrist will sin at the point in time *a.*[211]

God's foreknowledge and the contingent future are therefore not contradictory, as one might assume. God's knowledge implies also the mode in which circumstances come to be, and thus also the contingency of future circumstances. Yet Marsilius goes beyond that by making this knowledge of God to be itself a contingent knowledge, and thus declares the mode of what is known to be a mode of the knowledge: God himself does not know necessarily, but rather only contingently what I will do in the future; but if

209. See Perler, "Notwendigkeit und Kontingenz"; Beckmann, "Weltkontingenz."
210. See Hoenen, *Marsilius of Inghen,* 217–18.
211. Marsilius van Inghen, *I Sent.* q.40 a.2 (ed. Hoenen 2:75–82).

he knows it contingently, then also temporally. Therefore it is possible that at a point in time *a* he did not know it. God's knowledge is therefore not a knowledge about eternal, unchangeable ideas and their necessary consequences in the world, as Marsilius maintains, clearly criticizing the *via antiqua* (Thomas Bradwardine). The room for human freedom is therefore expanded, so that even God's knowledge is thereby restricted, at least in its mode. Truth, considered in purely logical terms, implies not necessity but rather facticity: The proposition "God knows (from all eternity) that *p* will be the case at time *t*" does not imply the *necessary* occurrence of *p* at *t*. Consequently, *p* can also not occur. God, however, could never have *known* this latter proposition also, that *p* will not occur at *t*. Similarly, Marsilius attempts to find a way out of the dilemma between the immutability of God's foreknowledge and the mutability of the future, again by tranferring the mode of what is known to the mode of the knowledge. He plainly criticizes our temporal notions of God's foreknowledge as a procedure that is already concluded and past. Instead one must speak about it in the present tense: God knows (simultaneously) that *p;* this is compatible, however, with the proposition: God did not know in advance that *p,* since in his knowledge it is not determined in what way God himself or the human being will freely decide. Therefore we should not think about the truth of the future according to the model of historical truth. Statements about the past are true or false in a *determinate* way. Statements whose truth-value still depends on the influence of other potential circumstances are true only *indeterminately.*[212] Thus not all truth should be interpreted according to the model of factual truth.

Furthermore God's nonknowledge with regard to *futura continentia* refers only to the *scientia visionis,* the immediate, intuitive knowledge of reality, not to the *"notitia simplicis notitiae vel apprehensionis"* ["the knowledge of simple cognizance or apprehension"] in which God knows all possible circumstances. Thus it goes without saying that he knows that a contingent future circumstance is *possible.* Thus in God there is simultaneously [1] necessary cognizance [*Kenntnis*] of everything that is possible and [2] contingent knowledge [*Erkenntnis*] of individual contingent events, dependent on the free decision of the creature.[213] A causal connection between foreknowledge and freedom, however, is ruled out entirely. Knowledge exerts

212. See Hoenen, *Marsilius of Inghen,* 322–23.
213. Marsilius of Inghen, *I Sent.* q.40 a.2 (ed. Hoenen 2:82–83).

no causal influence on the occurrence or non-occurrence of the known circumstance. In keeping with this fundamental decision, individual formulations related to this set of problems are discussed semantically, along the lines of theological linguistic criticism, as to their truth or admissibility *in theologicis* [in theological discourse].[214]

Marsilius settles the last part of the *quaestio* only with an explicit proviso: the simultaneous possibility of the infallible and all-encompassing foreknowledge of God and a contingent future is for him incomprehensible and utterly inexplicable. Nevertheless he will attempt it haltingly *(balbutiendo)*.[215] The reason that they are reconcilable appears to be the quantitative immensity of God. Another decisive factor is the realistic and at the same time voluntaristic understanding of the divine ideas as the cognitive form, original image and possible choices of the artist as he executes his work.[216] God's knowledge comprises everything possible, but his realizing will is selective. The foundation of this willing is not his knowledge about the mere possibility, but rather God's positive disposition *(scientia dispositionis, beneplaciti)*. The latter, however, can as a matter of principle extend only to what is good. The problem of theodicy can therefore be charged only to the account of man, whom God with his utmost skill created as a free being. Corresponding to the *"immensitas"* of God's power there is an immense knowledge, in which God, notwithstanding human freedom, eternally knows also the circumstances of the creature's free-will decision. This knowledge of present and future circumstances is itself contingent.

Understanding must ultimately bow to faith, see through inadequate temporal notions and in any case rule out a temporal change of God in his knowledge.[217] In view of God's immensity and the autonomy of freedom and its power to shape the future, human theorizing about God's knowledge, which has grown clever through linguistic and epistemological criticism, has no suitable expression left except stammering.

2.8 How do I find a gracious God? Gabriel Biel

The anti-Pelagian doctrine in the writings of Gregory of Rimini, Ockham's theory which relativizes God's free dispositions and secondary causes as opposed to the first cause, and Marsilius' more modest knowledge and

214. Ibid., 2:84–92.
215. Ibid., 2:92.
216. *I Sent.* q.1 a.1 (ed. Strasbourg f.3vb); see also Hoenen, *Marsilius of Inghen,* 153–54.
217. Marsilius of Inghen, *I Sent.* q.40 a.2 (ed. Hoenen 98–99).

discourse about divine things, taken together as a whole, form the background of the late Medieval search for theological certainty about one's own salvation.[218] The most important figure connecting Ockham to Luther, besides Gregory of Rimini, was Gabriel Biel (ca. 1410–1495), in whom we see at the same time a combination of *devotio moderna* and university theology in Tübingen.[219] The question, "What must I do to inherit eternal life?" (Mark 10:17), or "How do I go about finding a gracious God?" is for Biel, from the perspective of fallen man who nevertheless is not deprived of his freedom, initially—*de potentia ordinata*—a question of the right disposition, and therefore an utterly practical, moral question. Here the rudimentary level of our knowledge about God and his will should be borne in mind.[220] The decisive thing is that the human being should first do what he can *(facere quod in se est)* so as to present himself disposed to receive grace. This formula, however, states neither the measure nor the specific substance of what the human being has to do.[221] This disposition therefore cannot be equated with a natural morality; that is, not every human being who acts morally is thereby already disposed to grace; rather, he must do his best according to his knowledge. He does this, negatively speaking, by removing every obstacle to grace, and positively by striving *(bonus motus)* after God as his origin and destination. God, *de potentia ordinata,* accepts such a double act in his generosity as a prerequisite for grace.[222]

The pagan or unbeliever attains [this necessary] disposition by following his reason and yearning with all his heart for greater enlightenment in his knowledge of truth, justice and the good. The believer, in contrast, knows more about God and has the *regula fidei* [rule of faith], by which he must abide primarily. He knows, even if he is in the state of mortal sin and possesses only a *fides informis* [unformed faith], that God in his justice punishes sinners and in his mercy leads the elect to salvation. Therefore believers are obliged to have a loathing for sin and to obey God and his commandments. The moral obligation is a *prerequisite* for grace: I must, in certain cases, do something difficult in order to obtain in the first place the grace that enables me to act meritoriously as a Christian. On the other hand, God in his *ordi-*

218. See Grosse, *Heilsungewissheit,* 35–44.

219. See esp. Oberman, Herbst passim; Grane, *Contra Gabrielem;* concerning the *Vita Crusius,* see *Gabriel Biel.*

220. On the prehistory [of this problem] in high Scholasticism, see also Hamm, *Promissio.*

221. Gabriel Biel, *II Sent.* d.27 q.un. concl.4, in: *Collectorium circa quattuor libros Sententiarum,* ed. W. Werbeck—U. Hofmann (Tübingen, 1984), 2:517–18. See Grane, *Contra Gabrielem,* 214–22.

222. Biel, *II Sent.* d. 27 q.un. concl.4 (2.517.3–10).

natio has bound himself to do his part: He has obliged himself to give his grace to everyone who has done his best.[223] A human being can therefore—*de potentia ordinata*—depend on this and also rely on his God and make claims upon him within certain limits, yet he can never be sure that he himself has already done his best. For he has to love God above all things and purely for God's sake. Gabriel Biel considers such a love as possible *ex puris naturalibus,* thus even without grace. At any rate we never know precisely whether the extent of our love of God has met the standard *"super omnia"* and thus is already sufficient as a disposition, according to which God in his justice *must* give us grace. Indeed, the exact quantity of the "price" of grace is known to God alone. We just know that in the case of a sufficient disposition, God *"certissime"* ["most certainly"] bestows grace, but ultimately we never know whether our actions are really sufficient.[224]

In any case we may still have a *cognitio conjecturalis,* that is, be able to surmise our situation from fallible signs. Biel cites Alexander of Hales in listing such indications that we possess grace: light, joy, and peace (see Psalm 4:6–8). He then adds further symptoms mentioned by John Gerson and other authors. Symptoms, however, can be ambiguous and are not sufficiently evident (apart from a special revelation) to guarantee certain knowledge. They can likewise be due to demonic deception. The same goes for the knowledge that one does not want to resist grace through a mortal sin and [therefore] wishes to receive the sacrament of Penance. For Biel, however, the absolution of the priest is only the sign (proclamation) of the forgiveness by God that has already taken place through perfect contrition. For this, however, the minimal requirement assumed by Duns Scotus—removal of the obstacles (mortal sins)—does not suffice; it must be accompanied, rather, by the love of God *"propter deum, super omnia"* ["above all things, for God's sake"].[225]

But how can a human being love God in this way, without first being enabled to do so by grace? Explicitly citing Duns Scotus, Ockham, and Peter of Ailly, Biel explains this ability *ex puris naturalibus* [by man's natural, unaided powers] in terms of free will and the dependence of the individual act of will upon *recta ratio* [right reason]. To love God above all things is a precept of practical reason.[226] Every degree of the *bonum* [good] presented

223. Ibid. (2.518.29–55).
224. Ibid., a.3 dub.5 (2.524–26).
225. Ibid. See also Oberman, *Herbst,* 139–49.
226. Biel, *III Sent.* d.27 q.un a.3 dub.2 (3.503–7).

by reason must be attainable for the will; otherwise the will would not really be free. Furthermore love in the highest degree is possible with respect to creatures also; it is likewise possible, then, with respect to the Creator. Otherwise the will could bow only to an erroneous dictate of practical reason but not to a correct one. *De potentia ordinata* [because God has so ordained it], such an act of love for God can then continue only together with grace and infused *caritas.* For the love of God for his own sake and above all things is the final disposition to grace, which is granted at the same moment. Simultaneity, nevertheless, is not causal dependency: The grace is not the cause of the disposition to grace; the latter must instead proceed from a different cause, and therefore *ex puris naturalibus.*[227]

On the other hand, the meritoriousness of such an act—that is, its salvific significance with respect to eternal life—is a different matter.[228] The only act meritorious in God's sight is one that occurs with the assistance of grace. Anything else would be the Pelagianism that Gregory of Rimini battled. Grace and the human act, however, are two different entities. Therefore God *de potentia absoluta* is not compelled to give grace to someone who in every respect is disposed to receive it, nor to recognize that person's act as meritorious.[229] Therefore there could be a human act that was morally perfect in every respect, which nevertheless would not be meritorious. It is therefore impossible, at least *de potentia absoluta,* to make an inference from the moral perfection of human acts to their value for eternal salvation. Furthermore, the initial choosing of a morally perfect act is not meritorious, for this occurs temporally before grace as a disposition to it. Only the further execution of the act can be meritorious, since it alone stands under the influence of grace.[230]

A human being can, however, comply with the logic of grace and sin: if someone has performed such an act of love for God by his natural capacity, then he cannot have committed a mortal sin, as long as the act continues to be the object of his willing. Here it becomes clear that grace and the human act are connected almost as if by a natural law: the act of love for God (as the disposition) and the bestowal of grace are bound up with each other. Grace and mortal sin cannot exist together; therefore neither can the final disposi-

227. Ibid. (3:505.61–506.3).

228. See Dettloff, *Entwicklung,* 353–61.

229. On the doctrine of *potentia absoluta* in the writings of Biel see also Schrama, *Gabriel Biel,* 53–55; on the accusation of (semi-)Pelagianism see: Metz, *Gabriel Biel,* 395–98.

230. Biel, *III Sent.* d.27 q.un. a.3 dub.2 (506.5–21).

tion to receive grace coexist with mortal sin. All other human action, however, is logically consistent with the individual act of willing an all-surpassing love of God for his own sake.[231]

This security is certain, nevertheless, only for a human being who himself stands in the salvific order of grace. In contrast—as Peter of Ailly noted, again in fending off "Pelagianism"—man *sub lege* (under the law, i.e., in sin, outside of the order of redemption) can never *de potentia ordinata* properly fulfill the command to love God by his natural powers and consequently can never act meritoriously. He can, indeed, produce exactly the same act as a human being in the state of grace, but not in a way corresponding to the lawgiver's intention. Consequently he has neither fulfilled the law of love for God, nor done something meritorious. Instead he has not even acted rightly, in the precise sense of the word, if we define "to act rightly" with Peter of Ailly to mean "to act according to God's law." Certainly, though, he can act morally. Natural morality, moral-theological rectitude and the value of an act in God's sight should therefore be strictly distinguished.[232]

In his mitigated view, however, Gabriel Biel also avoids a rigoristic interpretation of grace that regards every human act that does not occur with the assistance of grace as a (mortal) sin. The divine law, the Decalogue, does not oblige one to act constantly upon the intention of all-surpassing love for God, but rather corresponds to *recta ratio.* To follow the latter cannot be a mortal sin. Otherwise God's law would lead the human being to ruin and would not be the way to the kingdom of God. Moreover, at every moment in which a human being did not have charity, he would be transgressing the law, even if he acted according to the Commandments. Therefore there is a sort of act which, while fulfilling the law *ad litteram* [to the letter], is not meritorious because it is not motivated by love for God; it is consequently worthless for eternal life.[233] It is therefore not permissible to conclude from the moral quality of one's own acts to one's own eternal salvation. We have only misleading signs, however, that we are in a state of grace. This leaves us with a *"certitudo conjecturalis"* (conjectural certainty) and the moral effort to go at least as far as the obligation of *facere quod in se est* [doing whatever we can], which is to be fulfilled *de potentia ordinata.* For with that we can conclude that God in turn will bestow his gift on the basis of his justice.

231. Ibid. (506.23–507.39).
232. Ibid. (507.41–62).
233. *III Sent.* d. 37 q.un. a.3 dub.1 (III, 639–641).

5 Humanist and Reformation Theology

Humanism and the Reformation are generally considered to have been opponents of late Scholastic theology or else the victory over it.[1] To some extent, however, their roots and development lay in university theology as well.[2] They led to a reform of theological studies, which had decisive consequences not only for Protestant teaching but also for Catholic instruction in the early modern period. Within the parameters of this introduction, therefore, we will disregard the dogmatic and controversial theological problems[3] and focus primarily on the Reformers' concept of theology and that of their Catholic dialogue partners with regard to a "paradigm shift" in theology.

1 University, humanism, and Reformation

The reconfiguration of theology during the Reformation cannot be viewed in isolation from the reform of Church, university, and theology that was already demanded in so-called reform theology since the days of John Gerson.[4] Moreover the debate between the "two ways" was overcome as humanism turned to *bonae litterae* [classical literature], at the universities also.

1.1 *Reformatio studii:* Wish and reality

The humanist movement, in all its complexity, was initially a phenomenon outside the university, which set itself up in deliberate contrast to aca-

1. One of the first to overcome this assessment, in the case of humanism, was Ritter, "Bedeutung."

2. See esp. Oberman, *Werden,* passim; on the concept of humanism: Oppermann, ed., *Humanismus;* Kristeller, "Humanismus und Renaissance"; also Bejczy, *Erasmus,* 62–103; Quinto, *Scholastica,* 129–40.

3. For those topics see, in general, *HDThG,* vol. 2 and *HDG;* also Jung and Walter, *Theologen des 16. Jahrhunderts.*

4. See *IST,* ch. 4.1.4–4.1.6.

demic life in the late Scholastic period, with its established structures that had become particularly rigid during the fifteenth-century debate about the two ways. Possibly the Italian universities were an exception, most of all Padua, which became a stimulating center for philosophical development, in German-speaking regions as well.[5]

The contrast between the humanist movement and the prevailing Scholasticism can be summarized in the following points:

1. *A departure from the Scholastic method* of disputation and its foundation in late Scholastic logic. This was said to be based less on Aristotle's writings on logic than on the *logica modernorum* [logic of the moderns] with their *sophismata* [sophistries, quibbles], and *insolubilia* [interminably debated questions].[6]
2. *A turn to new sources. "Ad fontes!"* now no longer meant consulting only the Scholastic authorities, but rather Plato, the authentic Aristotle, the Stoics, Cicero and the poets, and in theology—the Church Fathers, especially Augustine and Jerome. Their thought was no longer summarized in just a few sentences; now the art of printing books made it available in its full context in exemplary editions.[7]
3. *The promotion of language studies.* The *"vir trilinguis"* ["trilingual man"], the ideal educated man *(eruditus),* had to master Latin, Greek, and Hebrew. The linguistic elegance of the ancient writers and humanist authors was contrasted with the "barbaric" Latin of the Scholastics with their wretched *termini technici.* Disputation was not infrequently replaced by rhetorical declamation.

Thus the rejection of Scholasticism was for the most part based on literary and methodological reasons (especially in the writings of Lorenzo Valla [1405/07–1457]), whereas other Italian humanists, led by Giovanni Pico della Mirandola (1463–1494), accepted much of the medieval intellectual heritage.[8]

The reception of these humanist demands in the universities met with material and organizational difficulties north of the Alps. Often they came into conflict with the old rights of the professors of the arts to provide the sole authoritative preparation for study in the higher faculties and to teach

5. See esp. Kristeller, "Humanism and Scholasticism," 553–83; Schmitt, *Aristotelian Tradition.*
6. See esp. Lawn, *Rise and Decline,* 107–26.
7. See Baron, "Der erste Druck."
8. See Kölmel, "Scholasticus literator."

the only authoritative methodology. Accordingly, the *studia humanitatis* at first did not find a proper place at the universities; they were usually situated outside the system of faculties: for example, the short-lived *Collegium poetarum et mathematicorum* founded by the emperor in Vienna in 1502, but also the more permanent *Collegium trilingue* in Louvain (1519), and various humanistic lectures in Tübingen and Ingolstadt. Only in Wittenberg were the humanist departments successfully incorporated into the faculty of the arts, even before Melanchthon's reform of the university.[9] The widely travelled humanist lecturers or poets, moreover, usually could not prove their qualifications by an appropriate university education. This resulted in difficulties with the students' societies and academic stipends.

University reform along humanist lines, as it was carried out in Erfurt and Leipzig (1519), Rostock (1520), Greifswald (1521), Heidelberg (1522), and Tübingen (1525), by its very nature affected the faculty of the arts initially.[10] Precisely through this change in preparatory studies, however, it had considerable consequences for theology. This is illustrated by the inaugural discourse of the twenty-one-year-old Melanchthon at the University of Wittenberg, *De corrigendis adolescentiae studiis* [On revising secondary studies] on August 29, 1518, which is supported not so much by Reformation as by humanist principles.[11] The humanist propaedeutic, which was an education in speaking and judging, consisted of subjects that are still called "humanities," (languages, poets, rhetoricians, history), along with a philosophy that was restricted to natural science and ethics. The humanist *"ad fontes"* [return to the sources], however, applied also to theology: the Greek and Hebrew languages made those sources accessible. Instead of so many "cold" (= Scholastic) glosses, concordances, and dissensions [*Diskordanzen*], the *res* [matter] itself was supposed to become clear from a reading of the text, so that one could "savor Christ" *(Christum sapere).*[12] The humanist student was to have Homer in one hand and Paul in the other, but above all the courage to taste the subject in the ancient texts themselves: *"Sapere audete!"* ["Dare to taste!"].[13] In reducing the study of theology to the Bible and the Church Fathers and eliminating lectures on the *Sentences,*[14] Melanchthon

9. See Boehm, "Bildungsbewegung"; de Vocht, *History.*

10. See Benrath, "Universität."

11. CR 11.15–25; see also Stempel, *Melanchthons pädagogisches Wirken;* Wriedt, "Begründung," 169–82; Scheible, *Melanchthon,* 31–32.

12. CR 11.23.

13. CR 11.25.

14. For the Protestant critique of the *Sentences,* see also Valentini, "Il primo commentario prot-

was in agreement with Luther, but not in many questions concerning the propaedeutic study.[15]

The troubles, disturbances, and wars of the Reformation period were by no means conducive to a fruitful development of university studies. A marked decrease in the number of students was the result.[16] *"Evangelici non student,"* ["Evangelicals (i.e., Lutherans) don't study,"] complained the aging Erasmus about the lack of students.[17] Settling down to the new situation was a slow process, with respect to confessional lines of demarcation as well. In 1527 the first Protestant university was newly founded in Marburg. Remarkably, two professorial chairs exclusively for biblical studies were provided for the theological faculty, whereas the faculty of the arts was set up with ten professors (for Hebrew, Greek, rhetoric, and history, among other subjects).[18] Melanchthon's plan for the university and its curriculum, including a return to Aristotle (starting in 1537), the reintroduction of disputations and the granting of doctoral degrees (1533), while it did not lead to a "rescholasticizing" of Protestant theology, did incorporate certain elements of "Scholastic" academic life, informed by a humanistic spirit, however. The reformation of the other universities of Protestant princes was usually carried out according to Melanchthon's plans. The new universities were "from the very beginning destined for the training of officials, pastors, and teachers of the given territory."[19]

In the territories that remained Catholic, the humanistic reform of the universities usually occurred in connection with the partial or complete takeover thereof by the Jesuits, as was the case in Ingolstadt, at the *Collegium Sancti Hieronymi* founded in 1549 in Dillingen (which became a university in 1552 and was Jesuit from 1563 on) and in Würzburg (1575/82). According to the Jesuits' *Ratio studiorum* [Plan of Studies] (1599), the *"humaniora"* ("more humane subjects," i.e., the humanities) belonged to the gymnasium

---

estante." The author in question is Lambert Danaeus (1530–1595), *In Petri Lombardi librum primum Sententiarum Commentarius triplex* (Geneva, 1580).

15. See Luther, *Briefwechsel* [*Correspondence*] I, 170 (9 May 1518): *"ut rursum Bibliae et S. Patrum purissima studia revocentur"* ["so that unadulterated studies of the Bible and the Church Fathers might be reinstated"].

16. See the statistics on numbers of university students in Oberman, *Werden,* 432–33.

17. *Opus epistolarum Desiderii Erasmi Roterodami,* ed. P. S. Allen (Oxford, 1906–1958), vol. VII, ep. 2006, 16–17; vol. IX, ep. 2446, 53–54;—vgl. Oelrich, *Der späte Erasmus,* 105–17.

18. See Benrath, "Universität," 70.

19. Ibid., 70, 73–74: the university reforms: Basel (1532), Tübingen (1536), Leipzig (1539–1543), Greifswald and Copenhagen (1539), Frankfurt an der Oder (1540), Königsberg (newly founded 1544), Jena (newly founded 1548), Heidelberg (1557/58), Rostock (1564), Helmstedt (newly founded 1576); concerning the curriculum, see also Scheible, "Aristoteles."

or secondary school and not really to the faculty of the arts [at the university], which was reserved instead for a philosophical course of studies.[20]

1.2 Biblical-humanist reform of theology: Erasmus of Rotterdam

The theology of the Reformers, especially of Melanchthon and Calvin, in its peculiar humanistic, anti-Scholastic character was profoundly influenced by the reform of theology that Erasmus of Rotterdam (1466–1536) strove to bring about. Erasmus' ideas were set down most importantly in his essays that served as "Introductions" to the new 1516 edition of the New Testament *(Paraclesis, Methodus,* and *Apologia)* and in the 1518 *Ratio seu Compendium verae Theologiae,* a more extensive treatment that developed out of the *Methodus.*[21] The turn away from Scholastic theology to a biblical, practical *"philosophia Christi"* was for Erasmus a fundamental option, although it did not lead to an all-inclusive condemnation:

> I think that no one should consider himself to be a Christian if he disputes in thorny and tiresomely muddled terms about "instances," "relations," "quiddities," and "formalities"; he should instead hold and profess what Christ taught and showed us. Not that I would condemn the efforts of those who have exercised the strength of their talent in subtleties of this sort—and not without renown—nor that I would wish to offend someone, but I would think—and truly, I hope that I am not deceived—that that pure and unadulterated philosophy of Christ cannot be drawn successfully from any other place than from the books of the Gospels, from the Letters of the Apostles, in which someone who is philosophizing piously, by praying rather than by arguing, more intent on changing his life than on arming himself, will certainly find that there is nothing that is so important for man's happiness or for any duty of this life whatsoever that is not handed down, treated and settled therein.[22]

In this humanistic invitation to theology as *"philosophia Christi"* all the elements of the Erasmian reform of theology are already mentioned:

1. Theology is not an academic science but rather is accessible to all Christians: *"Nulli non licet esse theologum."* ["No one is forbidden to be a theologian."][23]

20. See Schubert, "Typologie," 85–99; Boehm, "Bildungsbewegung," 342–45: Leinsle, *Dilinganae Disputationes,* 86–91.

21. Published together in a Latin-German edition by G. Winkler: *Erasmus von Rotterdam, Ausgewählte Schriften,* gen. ed. W. Welzig, vol. 3 (Darmstadt, 1967); see also Winkler, *Erasmus von Rotterdam;* Hoffmann, *Erkenntnis;* Bejczy, *Erasmus,* 134–50.

22. Erasmus, *Paraclesis* (ed. Winkler, 27).

23. Ibid., 22.

2. The *"philosophia Christi"* consists first and foremost of following what Christ taught; it is an *"illiterata philosophia"* of simple people, which can however change the world.[24]
3. Christian philosophy, in contrast to pagan philosophy, offers something decidedly new; traces of its truth are to be found nevertheless even in the ancient authors, who consequently ought to be read.[25]
4. Theology as "Christian philosophy" is generally related to man in his concrete societal status and his striving for happiness, which should be attained by putting into practice Christ's instructions (*"pie philosophari"* ["philosophizing piously"]).[26]
5. The central object of theology is Christ, as we encounter him in the NT writings. The study of sacred Scripture is therefore the real subject matter of the "old and true theology."
6. The essential preparatory training for scientific theology is therefore philological and humanistic, not dialectical and Scholastic. Nevertheless, exegesis presupposes some knowledge of systematic (dogmatic) theology, which cannot be derived from Scripture inductively.[27]

By no means does Erasmus, in his conciliatory approach, intend to condemn Scholastic theology and its great masters without distinction. Its fundamental problem, however, appears to be its overemphasis on human authorities, especially those belonging to the individual schools of thought, as opposed to the authority of Scripture. Only in the latter is Erasmus willing to worship what he does not understand![28] Erasmus sees a further defect of Scholastic theology in the useless questions that overrun dogmatic theology and the casuistry that stifles moral theology, which contradicts his ideal of simple *pietas.*[29] Theology as such is not to blame for this, but rather the fact that it is overloaded with Aristotelian philosophy and logic. In regard to Scholastic *quaestiones,* Erasmus recommends, if need be, academic *epoché,* the refusal to give a positive or negative judgment, and by way of example he enumerates several late Scholastic *quaestiones* of this sort:

What sense would it make for me to torment myself over whether God could create man to be *anamárteton,* that is, incapable of sin? Whether God would be one and undivided if another God distinct from himself existed? . . . Or whether the propo-

24. Ibid., 18.
25. Ibid., 22–24.
26. Elaborated more extensively in the *Ratio* in terms of the three *circuli* of Christian society: see also Winkler, *Erasmus,* 149–59.
27. See Hoffmann, *Erkenntnis,* 73–100; Krüger, *Humanistische Evangelienauslegung.*
28. Erasmus, *Paraclesis* (ed. Winkler, 32–34).
29. Erasmus, *Ratio* (ed. Winkler, 204–8).

sition "God is a beetle" is possible in the same manner as "God is man"? Whether the capacity to beget in the Father is something absolute or is a quality, a property of the Father. . . . Whether Christ's soul was endowed with the fullness of grace that can be bestowed upon a creature. Whether Christ's soul knows in the Logos everything that the Logos himself knows. Whether Christ's soul mourned at the moment of his conception. Whether the fire that punished the damned is of the same kind as in our world.[30]

Humanist theology, in contrast, is based on Scripture and the Church Fathers; instead of Scholastic guild erudition it offers profitable training in how to live, instead of disputation—simple faith, and instead of curiosity—piety.[31] Teaching this is the essential matter of the second introductory essay, *Methodus,* which immediately establishes its credentials as a continuation of what Augustine intended in *De doctrina christiana.*[32] For like a good Augustinian, Erasmus attaches great importance to the moral qualities of the person who occupies himself with theology. The propaedeutic consists in the *artes* and in the knowledge of the biblical languages, Greek and Hebrew. Like *devotio moderna,* Erasmus advocates an affective theology: *"professio theologica magis constat affectibus quam argutiis"* ["the theological profession depends more on one's dispositions than on subtleties"].[33] *"Affectus"* here means "not only feelings, but the evaluative reaction of the whole man to the difficult but desirable *philosophia Christi* that he encounters in the images and figures of Scripture."[34] This requires a literary and rhetorical education, the pursuit of the Muses to which Augustine had already urged the young Licentius.[35] The entire Aristotelian-Scholastic philosophy, on the other hand, is unnecessary, since it has no basis in Scripture. Erasmus is sure, at any rate, that he is in agreement with Augustine in the fundamentally Neoplatonic orientation of his systematic thought.[36] Ancient philosophy, however, should be replaced by the *"philosophia Christi."* In comparison to the elite, subtle theology of the universities, this new paradigm of "simple," humanist lay theology will necessarily seem to be quite plebeian: *"nos plebeium instituimus theologum";*[37] on the other hand it enables someone who is not academically trained to be a theologian.

30. Erasmus, *Ratio* (ed. Winkler, 470–73).
31. Ibid., 474–83.
32. Erasmus, *Methodus* (ed. Winkler, 38); see also Winkler, *Erasmus,* 65–91.
33. Erasmus, *Methodus* (ed. Winkler, 50).
34. Winkler, *Erasmus,* 86.
35. Erasmus, *Methodus* (ed. Winkler, 50–51); see also Augustinus, *De ord.* I, 8.23 (CCh SL 29. 100.34–45).
36. See esp. Krüger, *Evangelienauslegung,* 29–46.
37. Erasmus, *Methodus* (ed. Winkler 54–55).

This theology however is by no means an "uneducated" theology of the sort that the late Erasmus would deplore among the Protestants.[38] Rather, it requires a new, "encyclopedic" education in sacred Scripture, which Erasmus strikingly calls the *"circulus et orbis Christi"* ["orbit and sphere of Christ"] and contrasts with the previous *"circulus et orbis doctrinae"* [". . . of doctrine"].[39] First a *Summa* should be procured for the *"tirunculus"* [young beginner]—not of Scholastic theology, but rather of the *"dogmata Christi in summam redacta"* ["doctrines of Christ gathered into a *summa*"]: the foundational pillars of all further instruction, as they are to be found in the Gospels and Letters of the Apostles. This *Summa* consists above all in the teaching about the new people of God instituted by Christ and about their moral qualities.[40] Only then can one study the life of Christ in detail, again with a view to the *"pietatis doctrina"* ["teaching of piety"], incorporating multiple senses of Scripture, which Erasmus retains as a good, patristic approach.[41]

Assuming as a matter of principle that Scripture per se is clear and easily understood, the commentaries of the Church Father, first and foremost of Origen, can be consulted so as to save work; in contrast to the Scholastic method, however, Scripture should be studied in its own context, and not from the *summulae,* sermons and compendia of the Scholastics.[42] The humanist rallying cry, *"ad fontes!"* becomes a personal return to the *"philosophia Christi"* in Scripture. The library of the Scholastics is replaced by a new library: "Why don't you make your heart into a library of Christ, from which you can take new things and old as though from a storeroom, as the need arises?"[43] The undefeated debater in Scholastic armor who has memorized his Duns Scotus is not the one to ask now, but rather the pious theologian who is guided by the word of God, that is, who has proved by his life that he is a Christian and yet is educated, *"qui pure Christum docet"* ["who teaches Christ and Him alone"].[44]

1.3 University theology and Reformation: *Disputatio*

The Wittenberg Reformation, unlike the South German and Swiss Reformation, started out at a university and was articulated during its initial

38. See Oelrich, *Erasmus,* 105–17.

39. For a definition of encyclopedic education, see Henningsen, "Enzyclopädie"; Henningsen, "Orbis Doctrinae."

40. Erasmus, *Methodus* (ed. Winkler, 58–60).

41. Ibid., (ed. Winkler, 60); see also Krüger, *Evangelienauslegung.*

42. Erasmus, *Methodus* (ed. Winkler, 62–70).

43. Ibid. (ed. Winkler, 69).

44. Ibid. (ed. Winkler, 74–76).

phase using the methods of academic debate: in theses, *assertiones* or *disputationes.*[45] The disputations at Heidelberg (1518) and Leipzig (1519) in particular should be mentioned as landmarks. The method of debating, however, had changed in the fifteenth century. Now individual theses *(propositiones)* are presented, which must then be proved or refuted *(probatio),* whereby of course particular attention must be given to the question of admissible authorities *(auctoritas, ratio).* With regard to the textual tradition of the disputations, in principle we are acquainted with three types: only the theses (or else the *conclusiones*) of many disputations have come down to us,[46] for many we have also the steps of the proofs *(probationes, resolutiones),* and for still others there are more or less detailed protocols or transcripts.[47] When a thesis was assigned for academic disputation, it was initially assumed to be demonstrable in principle, but not an already proven truth *("disputabilia, non asserta").*[48] As long as the disputation continues, the truth of the theses is still a matter of debate, and agreement with one's opponent is just as possible as a refutation of his theses. The thesis becomes an *assertio* with a claim to truth and personal conviction only through the *probatio:* "Correct assertion is the combination of [1] a subject matter that has been qualified by good probation with [2] a forceful [truth-]claim, whereby the matter establishes the claim, but the claim affirms the matter."[49]

Disputation, of course, is in the first place a university affair among scholars *(coram universitate),* as Luther originally had in mind even with the theses on indulgences; yet precisely here the step is taken to the public or ecclesial forum *(coram publico, coram ecclesia),* before which the further debates were usually carried on.[50]

In Luther's polemics, the following are initially admitted as authorities for proof (in individual cases they should be applied critically, and occasionally they make competing claims):

45. See esp. Kerlen, *Assertio.*

46. For example, Luther's *Disputatio contra scholasticam theologiam* (1517) in 97 theses (WA I, 224–28).

47. See Hanspeter Marti, Art. "Disputation," in Gert Ueding, ed., *Historisches Wörterbuch der Rhetorik,* vol. II (Tübingen, 1994), cols. 886–80. So, for example, the *Disputatio pro declaratione virtutis indulgentiarum* in 95 theses concerning indulgences (WA I, 233–38) and the *resolutiones* (WA I, 530–628); the Heidelberg disputation (1518) with theses and *probationes* (WA I, 353–74); the Leipzig disputation (1519) in a detailed protocol (WA II, 254–383) and separate *resolutiones* by Luther (WA II, 391–435).

48. See WA Br 1.140.70–72.

49. Kerlen, *Assertio,* 22; see also Luther, *De servo arbitrio: "Non contuli, sed asserui, et assero"* ["I did not discuss/contend, but rather I asserted and do assert"] (WA 18.787.11–12).

50. Ibid., 79–82.

1. Sacred Scripture,
2. Tradition,
   a) *traditio theologiae* [the tradition of theology] (the Fathers of the Church, but only with qualifications, since here we often find only *opiniones*),
   b) *traditio ecclesiae* [Church Tradition] (decrees and definitions of the Universal Church),
3. Church (*doctores, opinio communis,* the Pope, the Council in a conditional and restricted sense, depending on the particular case),
4. experience and reasonable judgment (only about preliminary, hypothetical statements).[51]

Luther accuses his opponents precisely of a lack of proof for their theses, wrong evaluation of their authorities, or else mere dependence on a school of thought and violations of the rules of disputation: In a *petitio principii* [an instance of begging the question], only positive authorities are admitted for the alleged "proof" of the thesis that has already been assumed to be true.[52]

As of 1520, however, as a result of the development of the reform movement and the intervention of the pope, Luther's tenets *(assertiones)* no longer appear to be merely debatable: They are to be accepted in faith, whereas further debate about the details is possible.[53] Now Scripture becomes central as the probative authority: Where there is no scriptural proof, there has been no *probatio* of the theses, but only the defense of an opinion.[54] For Luther himself, disputation had no longer seemed advisable as a means of discussion with his opponents, in view of the extreme divergence of their evidence, questions, and methods, and also of the refusal of the theologians in Cologne and Louvain to debate; only with his followers could he continue to debate, since with them there was a fundamental consensus about principles and methods. Consequently the [very idea of a] nonpartisan panel of judges appointed over the disputing parties to decide victory or defeat had become illusory.[55] With that, of course, the Reformation had also ceased to be a university exchange modeled on the academic quest for truth.

The Reformation in southern Germany and Switzerland, too, was ac-

51. Ibid., 22–33.

52. Ibid., 34–44.

53. WA 6.598.17–20.23; 609.10–15.

54. WA 6.508.19–20: *"Nam quod sine scripturis assertitur aut revelatione probata, opinari licet, credi non est necesse."* ["For that which is asserted without Scriptural references or a proven revelation can be held as an opinion but need not be believed."]

55. See Kerlen, *Assertio,* 128–81.

quainted with disputations, but they were of a different character than the academic exercises of the Wittenberg theologians. This becomes clear with the so-called "first Zurich disputation" dated 29 January 1523.[56] As Huldrych Zwingli (1484–1531) imagined it, this was supposed to be a "para-academic" disputation of theses over which he would preside, much like the ones that had taken place that same year at the University of Basel and in Solothurn. The Minor Council [*Der Kleine Rat*] that initiated the proceedings, however, evidently was planning a cross-examination of the two religious parties.[57] The council therefore had civic and political considerations (keeping the peace) uppermost in mind. Theologians from the University of Tübingen were admitted as representatives of the bishop of Constance: "With a number of scholars, as we deem appropriate, we will listen attentively, and according to their findings from Sacred Scripture and in keeping with the truth, we will let each one go home again, some of them with the command to cease their proclamation, so that everyone does not keep preaching from the pulpit whatever seems right to him, without a proper foundation in Sacred Scripture."[58] The Council clearly regarded itself as a judge in a disputation for the purpose of conducting a *probatio* of questionable theological teachings, using Scripture as the standard. Yet the delegation from Constance came not to dispute but rather to make a [canonical] visitation; the session of the Major Council [*Grossen Rates*] therefore proceeded not as a disputation, but rather as a hearing, in which the accusation of heresy was not leveled against Zwingli, however. Johannes Fabri (1478–1541), the bishop's representative, for his part wanted an academic disputation and not a discussion in the Council, since he had no mandate for the latter and had to reject uneducated laymen as judges.

What was already evident in Zurich would become clearer in the settlement of disputations through [inter]religious dialogues [*Religionsgespräche*]: a new role for theologians in the development of the Reformation.[59] Then there was the failure of the plan for a national council, as it had been proposed in Nuremberg. At this juncture the idea of a gathering of theologians to serve as a judicial authority to evaluate the teachings from Wittenberg appeared already as an alternative. The town clerk in Nuremberg, Lazarus Spengler (1479–1534) suggested on March 27, 1524, that "several pious, Christian, learned and intelligent men in the [Holy Roman] Empire or in Christendom" should be commissioned "to confer about the main points of these

56. See Oberman, *Werden*, 241–66.
57. Ibid., 246.
58. CR 88.467.11–17.
59. See Honnée, "Religionsverhandlungen."

matters, to consider them in light of Sacred Scripture and to decide them."[60] Thus Luther's model of disputation (*assertio* + *probatio* from Scripture) was still influential. Optimally, in order to prepare for a national council, the theologians should convene in the vicinity of a university so as to draft a compendium of Christian doctrine, of all the articles of the faith "established in Scripture," by which "the common man would have to be governed."[61] The representatives of the traditional beliefs, too, for their part, submitted a plan for a commission of theologians.[62] The important decisions, however, were made now, not in the national council, but rather in sessions of the Imperial Diet, which at any rate was originally planned, as far as Speyer was concerned, as a *"nacional versamlung"* ["national assembly"] including theological experts.[63] Finally, provisions were made in Speyer (1526) for an evenly balanced panel with six or eight theologians from each side; now, however, they were no longer supposed to test theses against Scripture (and thus to conduct a disputation in the academic sense), but rather to bring about a consensus in matters of religion on the basis of Scripture:

> In order to waste less time in the aforementioned council and to prevent great and unnecessary expenses, it was considered useful and good to assign meanwhile six or eight excellent, learned, pious and brave men from both sides, to be lodged at imperial expense in a [suitably] located town agreeable to all; these men should take up all controversial matters and articles and with the utmost diligence venture to settle them according to the Gospel, true Scripture and God's word; and any matters in which they reach agreement, they should forward in a timely fashion to the abovementioned council, together with the articles about which they could not agree, and they should make known to the Christian Diet their opinions, and thereafter take further action as needed.[64]

Thus the element from the practice of theology at the university that remained a constant in the Reformation process was not really the disputation, but rather the test of the scriptural character of theological doctrines, the *probatio.* Scripture—instead of the many Scholastic authorities and ways—was recognized as the sole authority for this test, which both religious parties could in fact agree upon.

60. RTA VI, 492, no. 107. On Spengler see Grimm, *Lazarus Spengler.*

61. RTA IV, 202–3.

62. G. Pfeilschifter, *Acta Reformationis Catholicae Ecclesiam Germaniae Concernantia Saeculi XVI. Die Reformverhandlungen des deutschen Episkopats von 1520 bis 1570,* vol. I (Regensburg, 1959), no. 50.

63. RTA VII, 1142.14–17; see also Honnée, "Religionsverhandlungen," 25–27.

64. Friedensburg, *Reichstag zu Speyer,* 557.

2 Approach to theology in Reformed Christianity

The self-assurance of Reformation theology and its determination to distance itself from the schools of late Scholasticism are evident in a new methodological and substantial concept of systematic theology. We can observe this in the new comprehensive presentations that now replace the reading of the *Sentences.*

2.1 *"Contra scholasticam theologiam":* Martin Luther

Martin Luther's (1483–1546) first explicit altercation with Scholastic theology was the *Disputatio contra scholasticam theologiam* [Disputation against Scholastic Theology] dated September 4, 1517.[65] In the printed version, some of the "Scholastics" against whom he inveighs are named: Besides general opinions *(contra dictum commune, contra scholasticos)* and philosophers *(contra philosophos)* they are Duns Scotus, William of Ockham, Peter of Ailly, and Gabriel Biel. For Luther, therefore, these thinkers essentially represent "Scholastic" theology. We do not find here a critical discussion of Thomism, as we do in Karlstadt's theses of April 26, 1517, which contain objections to Capreolus, among others.[66]

Luther's critique is substantially defined by the incompatibility of his Pauline picture of God and man, informed by the anti-Pelagian Augustine, with the prevailing Aristotelian Scholasticism. Thus he begins his theses with the Augustinian view that without grace man can neither know nor will the good (theses 1–4), which is immediately contrasted with the teachings of the Scholastics, especially Biel, about man's natural capacity (theses 5–36). Luther finds the basis for this false teaching in Aristotle's ethics and a purely philosophical view of man, which makes him the free master of his actions and tries to attain justice through moral behavior (theses 37–40, *Contra philosophos*). Almost the entire *Ethics* of Aristotle is therefore set aside as the enemy of grace, especially his doctrine of happiness, which contradicts the Catholic doctrine (theses 41–42, *Contra Scholasticos, Contra Morales*). Therefore the theologian must be liberated from Aristotle, as it is stated in theses 42 and 43:

65. WA I, 224–28; see esp. Grane, *Contra Gabrielem; idem, Modus loquendi theologicus,* 130–38; Lohse, *Luthers Theologie,* 114–15; Quinto, *Scholastica,* 208–15.

66. See *Karlstadt und Augustin: Der Kommentar des Andreas Bodenstein von Karlstadt zu Augustins Schrift "De spiritu et littera,"* introduction and text by E. Kähler (Hallische Monographien 19) (Halle, 1952), 8*–37*.

"43. It is an error to say: Without Aristotle one does not become a theologian. Contrary to common opinion.

"44. Indeed, no one can become a theologian unless he becomes one without Aristotle."[67]

The rejection of Aristotle is nevertheless not limited to the *Ethics,* but extends to the *Logic* also, whereby the *"logica fidei"* of Peter of Ailly is rejected in particular (theses 45–49), and indeed to Aristotle's work as a whole, which like darkness is driven away by the light of theology—this includes even the doctrine of universals in the *Isagoge* by Porphyry (theses 50–53). Consequently, once the philosophy of Aristotle and thus the core curriculum of the faculty of arts is withdrawn as a propaedeutic to theology, then the genuine relation between grace, the law and human will can be set forth according to Paul and Augustine and against Biel and Peter of Ailly (theses 54–98).

This formal and substantial rejection of Scholastic theology is intensified in the Heidelberg disputation (April 26, 1518). Already in the *resolutiones* to the theses on indulgences (1518) Luther contrasts the *theologus crucis* [theologian of the cross] and the *theologus gloriae* [. . . of glory] (thesis 58) and sees in the latter the Scholastic theologian, who on the basis of natural, Aristotelian ethics knows about the goal of his striving, that is, about good and evil, yet does not know the crucified and hidden God, but only the glorified, omnipresent God who is supposed to be known from visible things (see Romans 1:19–20).[68] The rejection of Scholastic theology is therefore no longer articulated merely in terms of the theology of grace and ethics, but also with regard to knowledge about God in general. In Heidelberg Luther sets out immediately from his view of the relation between the law and grace, an approach that then allows him to critique earlier theology precisely as a *"theologia gloriae."*[69] In particular Luther objects to the teaching, found in the writings of Gerson and Biel, among others, of *"facere quod in se est"* ["doing whatever one can"] as a prerequisite for grace. Instead, a human being must abandon hope in himself and acknowledge his nothingness so as to desire grace (thesis 18). A natural, metaphysical knowledge of God, which tries to derive God's attributes from creatures, does not lead to wisdom, but rather is dismissed as foolishness according to [his reading of] Romans 1:22 (thesis 19). Instead, the only access to knowledge of God is the

67. WA I, 226.14–16.
68. WA I, 613–14; see also Lohse, *Luthers Theologie,* 122–25; Lohse, "Luthers Selbstverständnis."
69. WA I, 353–56.

cross. By this way, however, God's metaphysical attributes (power, divinity, wisdom, justice, goodness) are not known, but rather the *"posteriora et visibilia Dei"* ["the subsequent and visible things of God"], namely his humanity, weakness, and folly (thesis 20). The Scholastic *theologia gloriae* is therefore a false, mendacious theology that views what is genuinely good *(bonum crucis)* as only bad, and what is really bad (*malum operis,* the evil of work) as good (thesis 21). Scholastic theologians therefore appear as "enemies of the cross of Christ" (Philippians 3:18). Only by a previous acknowledgment of one's own nothingness does one arrive at true theology. But one does not learn this in the philosophy of Aristotle, which Luther here criticizes philosophically as well (theses 29–40). Instead, being puffed up, blind, and rigid are the moral consequences of Scholastic theology (thesis 22). The remedy for this is radical: obliterating it and turning to the folly of the cross. Luther's deliberately paradoxical formulation of this "theology of humility"[70] must have struck his contemporaries as the clearest possible rejection of the prevailing Scholastic theology: "The theology that Luther opposed consists not only in a false doctrine, but in an approach that is false from the outset, which cannot lead to theology but only to a pseudo-theology."[71]

What, then, should theology look like—the true, correct, pure theology that Luther has in mind—as opposed to the one devised by the "swinish theologians" who are asleep and at best produce a *"theologia diabolica"* that the devil has no cause to fear?[72] Unlike the humanists Erasmus and Melanchthon, Luther expressly and frequently uses the terms *"theologia"* and *"theologus"* so as to make clear thereby his own claim: "Theology is tantamount to God's word. The theologian is the one who speaks God's word."[73] In inquiring as to the central object of this theology (the subject of the science), Luther plainly turns aside from all Scholastic definitions. The [proper] object is not God or Christ, but rather fallen, lost man and the justifying and saving God.[74] Everything beyond this definition that is taught de facto in theology does not belong to it but rather is error and *"vanitas."* Knowledge about man and knowledge about God belong together in theology, but only in that mutual relation which is now decisive: *fallen* man and the

70. See Grane, *Modus loquendi theologicus,* 146–51.

71. Ibid., 151.

72. See WA 56.274.14; WA 39.1.19, 17; WA 7.218.18–21; see also Ebeling, *Lutherstudien,* vol. II.3.18–19.

73. WA 41.11.10.

74. WA 40.2.327.11–328.3: *"ut proprie sit subjectum Theologiae homo reus et perditus et deus justificans vel salvator."*

God who *justifies.* Therefore only theology and not philosophy defines man correctly and fully.[75] This relation becomes the distinguishing characteristic of theology, which at all points has a practical orientation. In his *Table Talks* (1531), Luther wants to send speculative theology as a whole to the devil, in the strict sense.[76]

The question as to the scientific character of theology, as understood in the Aristotelian-Scholastic theory of science, has become quite superfluous after the elimination of Aristotle from theology. Luther's theology, too, would have difficulty asserting its scientific, academic status, as the reactions of Karlstadt (ca. 1480–1541) and Jodok Trutfetter († 1519) show.[77] Luther insists on the clear and simple meaning of Scripture, on its relation to experience and on the distinctions between the letter and the spirit, the Law and the Gospel, which affect all theological interpretation.[78] Theology is usually understood as *sapientia,* and as such it stands in opposition to the "human wisdom" of philosophy, as Luther characterizes it in thesis 1 of the *Disputatio de homine* dated January 14, 1535.[79] Unlike philosophy, theological wisdom is brought about by the Holy Spirit, hidden in revelation and in principle is infinite with respect to life.[80] Moreover, as practical theology it is founded on experience and not on abstract metaphysical speculation: *"Sola . . . experientia facit theologum."*[81]

In this Scripture- and experience-based theology, reason naturally does not have the same place as in late Scholastic university theology. *Ratio,* if it is to become fruitful for theology, is reason enlightened by faith and the Holy Spirit, not presumptuous natural reason.[82] Nevertheless Luther still has reservations about it; it remains "a dangerous thing, especially when it intervenes in spiritual matters."[83] For it always runs the risk of dealing arbitrarily with God's word, confusing philosophical teaching and theological truth or overestimating its own powers.[84]

75. Thus thesis 20 of the *Disputatio de homine* (1536): Ebeling, *Lutherstudien,* II, 1.19: *"Theologia vero de plenitudine sapientiae suae hominem totum et perfectum definit."* ["Theology, however, out of the fullness of its wisdom, defines the whole and perfect man."]

76. WAT 1.72.16–24.

77. See Ebeling, *Lutherstudien,* II, 3.59.

78. Thus he wrote already in the first lecture on the Psalms (1513/15): *"In Scripturis sanctis optimum est Spiritum a litera discernere, hoc enim facit vero theologum."* ["In Sacred Scriptures it is best to distinguish the Spirit from the letter; indeed, this is what makes the theologian."] (WA 55.1.1; 4.25–26).

79. Edition by Ebeling, *Lutherstudien,* II, 1.15.

80. Ibid., II, 3.

81. WAT 1.16.13, no.46 (1531).

82. WA 40.1.457.6–7; WAT 191.25–26, no. 439.

83. WA 9.187.5–7.

84. See the general discussion in Lohse, *Ratio und Fides,* esp. 113–19.

How should this new theology be implemented at the university? Luther sees very clearly that his concept tends toward a dismantling of the instructional methods previously used. And so he writes on May 9, 1518, to Trutfetter:

I simply believe that the Church cannot possibly be reformed unless canon law, decretals, Scholastic theology, philosophy and logic, as they are currently pursued, are completely stamped out and replaced with other studies; and in this firm conviction I have proceeded until now, so that I pray daily that the unadulterated studies of the Bible and of the holy Fathers [of the Church] may be revived as quickly as possible.[85]

Although Luther realizes here that he is in agreement with the humanist educational reform as well, nevertheless the impulse behind his reform and his concept of theology are different from those of Erasmus, for instance, or of the young Melanchthon. On March 11, 1518, Luther had already submitted a suggestion for a reform of the curriculum, the contents of which, however, can only be reconstructed. Humanistic language studies (Greek and Hebrew), Pliny, Quintilian, and mathematics are recommended; Aristotle and the previous textbooks of logic are abolished.[86] The abolition of Aristotelian ethics, which in Luther's view is related to theology as the wolf to the lamb[87] (i.e., threatens to devour it), and the discontinuance of Thomistic physics and logic proved, however, to be substantially more difficult. The reform of theology was supposed to be made possible in turn, therefore, by a reform of the preparatory studies.[88] Then in article 25 of his circular letter *To the Christian nobility* (1520), Luther discusses in detail the reform of the universities and of theological studies.[89] Again "the blind, pagan master Aristotle" is the one to get rid of, meaning his *Physics, Metaphysics, De anima,* and *Ethics.* On the other hand, the *Logic, Rhetoric,* and *Poetics* can stay or be summarized in short compendia; in any case all commentaries by the various schools of thought must be eliminated. In the faculty of law, canon law must be abolished entirely; in theology the reading of the *Sentences* must be replaced by the reading of Scripture. The faculty must put an end to the predominance of reading the *Sentences,* and thus of speculative theology, over exegesis. Luther recalls the original custom of reading the *Sentences* only as

85. WA Br.1.170.33–37; German translation in Grane, *Modus loquendi theologicus,* 129.
86. See Grane, *Modus loquendi theologicus,* 143; Scheible, "Aristoteles."
87. WA Br. 1.196.27–28.
88. See Grane, *Modus loquendi theologicus,* 138–46.
89. WA 6.457–62.

an introduction to the books of the Bible and notes the theology professor's title: "teacher of Sacred Scripture." Theological books should be brought in only sparingly, especially the Fathers of the Church, insofar as they provide an introduction to Scripture: "The dear Fathers wished to lead us into Scripture with their writings, and so let us use them to lead ourselves out [of the present curriculum], so that Scripture alone is our vineyard, in which we all should practice and labor."[90] Luther, however, would not be the one to bring about an organizational reform of university theology; Melanchthon accomplished this in a synthesis of Reformation and humanist trends.

2.2 The new *"Summa"*: Melanchthon's *"Loci theologici"*

In 1521 Philipp Melanchthon (1497–1560) published the first work of systematic theology of the Reformation, his *Loci communes rerum theologicarum seu Hypotyposes theologicae.*[91] In 1535 a revised edition appeared, followed in 1543/44 by a third version, which was the standard one until Melanchthon's death in 1560 and, like the earlier versions, was circulated in numerous editions.[92] The original intention, as Melanchthon presents it in the dedicatory epistle, is both pedagogical and anti-Scholastic: The main points *(loci)* of Christian doctrine should be conveyed to young students, so that they see "what they should especially inquire about in Scripture, and how horridly those masters babbled at every turn in theology, who instead of Christ's teaching presented to us Aristotelian subtleties."[93] Formally speaking, from the very beginning the *Loci* thus replaced the *Sentences* of the Lombard, which after all had also been conceived as a systematic introduction to the exegesis of sacred Scripture. Still excluded here—on both humanistic and Reformation grounds—is Aristotle's philosophy, since Melanchthon accuses both of his methodological predecessors, John Damascene and Peter Lombard, of an excess of philosophy and/or of collecting mere opinions.[94] As opposed to the "obscure and difficult disputations" and commentaries of the Scholastics, who no longer deal with Scripture at all,

90. WA 6.461, 8–10; 462.8–10.

91. Philipp Melanchthon, *Loci communes,* 1521; Latin-German edition, translated and annotated by H. G. Pöhlmann (Gütersloh, 1993).

92. For the textual history, see E. Bindseil in CR 21.59–82.230–51; 562–602. For a synopsis of the structure: Wiedenhofer, *Formalstrukturen* 1:397–98; on the little known German version of 1558 composed by Melanchthon himself, see Schilling, "Loci communes deutsch."

93. *Loci,* Dedication n. 4 (Pöhlmann 12/13); see also Wiedenhofer, *Formalstrukturen,* 1:315–26; Quinto, *Scholastica,* 215–21.

94. *Loci,* Introduction n. 2 (Pöhlmann 16–19).

the *Loci* are intended merely as a list *(nomenclatura)* of those main aspects by which the reader of Scripture can proceed systematically, or else those aspects on which the *"summa doctrinae christianae"* ["summary of Christian doctrine"] depends.[95] These were enumerated by Melanchthon in 1521 in a list, which he himself did not regard as exhaustive:

God the One and Triune, Creation, man, the faculties of man, sin, the consequences ["fruit"] of sin, vices, punishments, the Law, the promises, renewal through Christ, grace, the fruits of grace, faith, hope, charity, predestination, sacramental signs, man's states, magistrates, bishops, damnation, beatitude.[96]

Although the list still looks like a summary of the conventional treatises of systematic theology, because of a pronounced turn away from the Scholastic *"theologia gloriae"* to the Reformation *"theologia crucis,"* many highly elaborate parts of the teaching on God and the Trinity, creation and Incarnation were immediately dropped:

We should worship the mysteries of the Godhead instead of investigating them.... God Almighty, the Most-High, clothed His son in flesh so that He might lead us from meditating on His majesty to meditating on the flesh and thus on our human frailty.... Hence there is no reason why we should apply much effort to those most exalted themes: God, His Unity, the Trinity, the mystery of creation, the nature and manner of the Incarnation.[97]

Instead the theological discussion begins with the doctrine about man, his faculties, his will, so as to go on and treat in detail the topics of sin and the Law. For only when one knows the power of sin, the law and grace can one really know Christ—and not when one speculates about His two natures and the manner of the Incarnation.[98] Not until the 1535 version are the teachings on God, the Trinity, and creation actually developed, and as of 1543 they are further elaborated with philosophical trains of thought, although the biblical approach is still clearly predominant.[99] Even now the epistemological principal for the doctrine about God remains Christ, in whom the Father is known. The *"sapientia Christianorum"* ["wisdom of Christians"] is an altogether *practical* knowledge of God, which recognizes

95. *Loci,* Introduction n. 5–6 (Pöhlmann 14–15).

96. *Loci,* Introduction n. 4 (in the edition by Pöhlmann 18–19); on the problems of systematic theology, see also Köpf. "Melanchthon," 122–27.

97. *Loci,* Introduction n. 6–8 (Pöhlmann 18–21).

98. Ibid., n.12–13 (Pöhlmann 22–23).

99. CR 21.255–274.607–43; on the philosophical foundations see esp. Frank, *Theologische Philosophie.*

God by comprehending His mercy, not by a theoretical insight into His *"arcana natura."*[100]

While Melanchthon avoids the name *"theologia"* for his presentation in the *Loci,* he certainly does want to make sure that *"doctrina"* is anchored in the university curriculum.[101] His method of presenting it is therefore the one generally used in the *artes:* the most important passages *(loci)* are briefly summarized so as to make a *summa,* which at the same time indicates what is to be investigated in this science.[102] Unlike Scholastic theology, the outline of Christian "doctrine" is organized by topic: a way of ordering the main points so as to determine the principles, progress and goal of the *ars.*[103] The purpose is the concise, methodical presentation of the main matter of the *ars* in question. Theology therefore proves by its general scientific method to be a genuine *ars. Methodus,* moreover, denotes on the one hand the arrangement of the *loci,* and on the other hand the resulting *summa,* the ordered, methodical presentation of the art in question. These definitions would remain decisive for Protestant philosophy and theology well into the seventeenth century.[104]

As Melanchthon announces in the 1521 introduction, his *Loci* are supposed to replace the old summas of the Scholastics.[105] The systematic approach, however, is due to the *methodus,* whereby *"methodus,"* like *"summa,"* also denotes the work itself as a brief summary. Thus within the context of sacred Scripture, the Letter to the Romans (or the Letter to the Galatians) is the *methodus* of all Scripture or theology.[106] In either case, each letter treats everything that makes up the core or the *"summa"* or Christianity: the Law and the Gospel, sin, justification, and grace. The *Loci,* which originally in 1521 resulted from lectures on the Letter to the Romans, are now a systematic work that is for theology what the Letter to the Romans is in the context of sacred Scripture: *"mea methodus,"* an expression that is eventually used as an alternative for *"summa."*[107] For in it the central concern *("summa")* of Christianity is supposedly presented, which Melanchthon repeatedly at-

100. CR 21.255–56.
101. See Wallmann, *Theologiebegriff;* Bayer, "Theologiebegriff."
102. Even in the 1521 version: Introduction n. 1 (Pöhlmann 16–17).
103. CR 21.253.
104. See the detailed discussion in Leinsle, *Ding,* esp. 11–20.
105. Introduction n. 3 (Pöhlmann 18–19).
106. CR 1.638. 1044; 11.37–38; see also Wiedenhofer, *Formalstrukturen,* 1:391–94.
107. See CR I, 285.366.451.487.567; III, 1112: *"summa quaedam seu methodus est informanda"* ["a certain summa or method should be fashioned"]; vgl. Köpf, "Melanchthon," 117–22.

tempts to express in brief formulas, so as to expound it in a way that makes sense pedagogically: Man, who cannot find his salvation by himself, but rather owes it to justification through Christ.[108]

This method is adopted by theology from general philosophical and theoretical reflections about science that Melanchthon—in a clear return to tradition—drew again from Aristotle beginning in 1536. In the 1538 version of the *Dialectica* he explicitly recommends that students have Aristotle on hand, for he is the *"unus ac solus methodi artifex"* ["one and only framer of a method"].[109] Without Aristotle there is no science, but only a great confusion of doctrines.[110] Of course, Melanchthon does not read his Aristotle in the manner of the Scholastics, but rather as a humanist who is acquainted also with Cicero and the Stoics; moreover he eliminates the *Metaphysics,* while retaining the *Ethics* (unlike Luther).[111] This new propaedeutic, which furthermore still contains metaphysical elements (categories, the four causes) in its dialectics, creates the conditions under which theological instruction can once again become academic, although not Scholastic. This trend becomes evident also in the reintroduction of disputations alongside humanist declamations in Wittenberg from 1533 on. Melanchthon's view of philosophy and theology finds expression especially in the speech *De philosophia* dated 1536. From the humanist perspective, philosophy consists of the various *artes,* and their propaedeutic and methodological importance for theology is underscored. Indeed, for the humanist Melanchthon, the root problem consists of an *"inerudita theologia"* of the sort that was common in the initial discussions by the Reformers but could often be observed among the Scholastics as well.[112] It is "uneducated" because it lacks the correct method. It is a *"confusanea doctrina"* in which the important points are not set forth precisely, in which things that ought to be treated separately are mingled, and things that should be explained in connection with each other are pulled apart. Often contradictory statements are made; whatever sounds like the truth is immediately taken for a genuine argument. The result is a *"doctrina monstrosa"* in which nothing is methodologically consistent, which can only give rise to endless errors and disputes. A conventional knowledge of grammar and logic is not enough to remedy this sorry state of affairs; rather an *"erudita philoso-*

108. See the 17 "summa"-formulas listed in Wiedenhofer, *Formalstrukturen,* 1:392–94.
109. Ph. Melanchthon, *De dialectica libri quattuor* (Strasbourg, 1538), Dedication.
110. CR 11.349, in the *Oratio de vita Aristotelis,* dated 1537.
111. See Leinsle, *Ding,* 11–13.
112. CR 11.278–80; see also Frank, *Vernunft,* 55–57.

phia" is needed, which contains in the first place methodology and rhetoric, but also natural science and ethics.[113] For this purpose it will not suffice to carry over isolated bits of knowledge into theology; instead the science in question must be studied as a whole. The Church needs the whole *"orbis doctrinae"* ["sphere of teaching"] and therefore a new encyclopedic education so as to be able to pursue real theology. Everything else is barbarity, as one may encounter among uneducated Baptists [*Täufern*], but also among humanists who despise the real sciences.[114] Therefore theology needs a method; it finds one, however, only in Aristotle.

2.3 Summa of self-knowledge and practical knowledge about God: Calvin

The *Christianae Religionis Institutio*—the Reformed *"summa pietatis"* ["summary of religious duties"]—by John Calvin (1509–1564) underwent a development similar to that of Melanchthon's *Loci.* In the first edition (1536) it appeared as a small, slim volume made up of six chapters that was clearly dependent on Luther's little catechism. Here the presentation of the Ten Commandments, the Apostles' Creed and the Our Father is followed merely by teaching on the sacraments that is polemically opposed to the Roman doctrine and teaching about Christian freedom, ecclesiastical power, and political rule.[115] In the last authentic edition dated 1559 the work had expanded to eighty chapters, by that time systematically arranged:

Book 1: "On knowledge of God the Creator"

Book 2: "On knowledge of God the Redeemer"

Books 3–4: "In what manner we receive the grace of Christ, the kinds of fruits that it produces for us, and the sorts of effects that result from it."[116]

The fundamental concern of this extremely influential Reformed overview of theology nevertheless remained the same at all its stages. It intends, as the title already made clear in 1536, to present *"totam fere pietatis summam et quidquid est in doctrina salutis cognitu necessarium"* ["almost a complete summa of religious duties and whatever is necessary to know in the doctrine of salvation"] so as to offer a helping hand to *"pietatis studiosi"* ["students of religion"].[117] Calvin had had a humanist schooling and was profoundly

113. CR 11.280.

114. CR 11.281–38.

115. Joannis Calvini, *Opera selecta,* ed. P. Barth (= OS), vol. I (Munich, 1926; reprinted 1963), 19–238; see also van't Spijker, *Calvin,* 121–28.

116. OS vols. 3–5 (Munich, 1927; reprinted 1963).—Concerning the development, see: W. Neuser in *HDThG* 2:241–42; van't Spijker, "Calvin," 191–94.

117. OS 1:19.

influenced by Erasmus, although according to Johannes Maior (ca. 1469–1550) he was also trained in Scholastic logic at the Collège de Montaigu; for Calvin, who strictly speaking was not educated in university theology but rather in law,[118] theology as a matter of principle should be classified under the heading of the practical worship of God *(pietas)*. Scholastic, speculative theology, with which he occasionally debates in his teaching on the sacraments, is thus abolished from the outset.[119]

Calvin agrees with Augustine, however, that the *"summa sacrae doctrinae"* (again the title of theology, as it was for Thomas Aquinas!) consists of the knowledge of God and the knowledge of oneself.[120] Nominally the knowledge of God is situated within the tension between law and grace, as in the early Melanchthon; in 1536 this subject is developed very briefly and in purely biblical terms at the beginning of chapter 1, *"De lege"* (i.e., not out of the experience of the sinful and justified human being), whereas the more precise presentation is reserved for the treatment of the Creed in chapter 2.[121] Knowledge of God is prior to knowledge of oneself. It comprises here, as a prerequisite for knowledge of the law:

1. the fundamental attributes of God (hypostatized): God is infinite Wisdom, Justice, Goodness, Mercy, Truth, Power and Life;
2. God as the Creator of the universe and the consequent duty of creatures to render service and obedience;
3. God as just Judge;
4. God as the merciful and gracious One, who is ready to accept whoever comes to him in faith and trust.

Self-knowledge is in stark contrast to the knowledge of God. It shows that human beings were created in the image and likeness of God but through sin have become "children of wrath," so that we are neither willing nor able to do our duty. The Law—both the inner law (conscience) and the written law—only reveals our fallen state: "This teaching about justice clearly shows us how far away we are from the right path."[122] The law, how-

118. See Ganoczy, *Calvin;* Reuter, *Vom Scholaren;* Partee, *Calvin;* Spijker, "Calvin"; Frank, *Vernunft,* 69–74.

119. See Ganoczy, *Calvin,* 179–92; van't Spijker, "Calvin," 205–6.

120. OS 1:37: *"Summa fere sacrae doctrinae duabus his partibus constat: Dei cognitione et nostri."* See Augustinus, Soliloquia I, 2.7; on the influence of Bernard of Clairvaux: Reuter, *Vom Scholaren,* 63–65. On anthropology and self-knowedge, see Faber, *Symphonie,* 87–131.

121. OS 1:69–76.

122. OS 1:39.

ever, also leads to a correct self-evaluation in God's sight, which in turn corresponds to the steps in knowing God:

1. God is the Creator, our Lord and Father; we owe Him glorification, respect and love.
2. No one can accomplish this by his own unaided powers; therefore we are all liable to judgment and eternal death.
3. Consequently some way to salvation must be sought other than through one's own righteousness. Left to our own devices, we have nothing but despair.
4. This way is opened up for us in the forgiveness of sins in Christ.
5. With His Spirit and equipped with a new heart, we are able to keep His commandments.[123]

Therefore this knowledge of God is initially an altogether practical and personal knowledge. Calvin's theology here is consciously dependent on its ideal of *"pietas"*; indeed, the *Institutio* is supposed to be the *"summa"* of these religious duties.[124] Already in the dedicatory epistle to King Francis I (which is reprinted in all the later editions), he underscores his efforts in this work to lead people *"ad veram pietatem"* ["to true piety"] and thus to the knowledge of Christ.[125] Theological knowledge is therefore conveyed in a practical way that applies to everyday life; it does not lead to the knowledge of a superterrestrial substance, but rather to knowledge of the *living* God and of Christ.[126] This *pietas* on the one hand corresponds to our status as creatures, based on a proper acknowledgment of our duties with regard to the Creator; an even more forceful reason, though, is our status as adopted children of the Father.[127] The learned jurist Calvin is certainly thinking here in terms of Roman law. The meaning of *pietas* is summed up in the right way of fearing and loving God.[128] The *"pietatis studiosi"* ["those seeking to practice piety"] for whom Calvin originally planned his work are therefore not only students of theology. This fundamentally distinguishes his intention from that of Melanchthon's *Loci:* He does not want to write an academic introduction for the study of theology. For, as Erasmus also had said, all Christians are called to *pietas* as a lifelong endeavor: *"Tota Christia-*

123. OS 1:40.

124. See Ganoczy, *Calvin,* 220–32.

125. OS 1:21.

126. OS 1:23: *"non nostra est, sed Dei viventis et Christi eius."*

127. OS 1:76; see also Faber, *Symphonie,* 81–85: *"Geschöpfliche Wesenheit als Gehorsamakt"* ["Creaturely Essence as Act of Obedience"].

128. OS 1:52.

norum vita quaedam pietatis meditatio esse debet, quoniam in sanctificationem vocati sunt."[129] ["The whole life of Christians must be a certain preparation or training for piety, for they are called to sanctification."] In contrast, the false worship of God, which Calvin sees in idolatry, superstition and Romish customs, is held up as *"impietas"* ["impiousness, irreverence"].[130]

Calvin's approach as a Reformer leads to a demand for a new method of theological instruction, which he himself means to provide in the *Institutiones.* The Scholastics appear as the *"impii"* who are to blame for the fact that the truth of Christ, while not yet entirely vanished, is nevertheless buried under the rubble, that is to say, under an inextricable tangle of complicated theses that have no basis is Scripture.[131] The theologian should start out from *"scripturae simplicitas"* ["the simplicity of Scripture"] and should rule out all the secondary literature of the Scholastics, which Calvin—like a good Augustinian—regards as the product of *curiositas.*[132] The Scholastics take up positions either this side of Scripture or beyond it; in no instance is their doctrine in keeping with Scripture; instead it is their own intellectual construct.[133] Besides Scripture, the young Reformer—like a good humanist—approves of the Church Fathers only. They unanimously refused to mingle God's word with subtle sophistries or to make it the object of logical wrangling. If the Fathers were to come back today and listen to a disputation in so-called speculative (= Scholastic) theology, they would not be able to detect that the subject matter was God.[134]

Calvin confronts Scholastic theology with his ideal of the authentic, simple, and pure word of God. Scripture, which in itself is clear, should be interpreted plainly for simple people as an "appeal, exhortation and instruction for men." Therefore, despite his humanistic and philological schooling, he intends to follow a simple and nonscholarly method of teaching even in his scriptural exegesis, without dismissing as irrelevant, however, a thorough education in languages and the Church Fathers.[135] Comprehensibility and brevity are considered methodological norms both for scriptural

129. OS 1:224; *"meditatio"* here means training, practical effort to do something.

130. See Ganoczy, *Calvin,* 224–26; esp. OS 1:289–328: *Epistola de fugiendis impiorum illicitis sacris* [Letter on fleeing the illicit sacred rites of the impious].

131. See also Ganoczy and Scheld, *Hermeneutik.*

132. OS 1:139.

133. OS 1:144.

134. OS 1:29.

135. OS 1:21: *"Hanc mihi fuisse propositam rationem liber ipse loquitur, ad simplicem scilicet rudemque docendi formam appositus."* ["The book itself testifies that this was my intended plan: namely (to write a book) suitable as a model for teaching the simple uneducated man."] See Ganoczy and Scheld, *Hermeneutik,* 182–87.

interpretation and for the separate systematic presentation of the faith in the *Institutiones.* Exegesis and systematic theology are methodologically separate but serve the same ideal and complement one another.[136] They are adapted to "God's pedagogy" in Scripture instead of giving an arbitrary or speculative interpretation of Scripture, as though the word of God were a plaything or a wax nose that can be twisted in any direction.[137] Partial obscurities should be illuminated through analogies; otherwise, though, one's point of departure should be the simple and clear sense of Scripture as the norm for theology also: "The rule for thinking and speaking is to be derived from Scripture; all thoughts and words should be very precisely aligned with it."[138]

3 The Catholic understanding of theology

The Catholic understanding of theology during the Reformation period also experienced the tension between Scholasticism and humanism, but in addition it was diametrically opposed to substantial elements of Reformation theology. This is evident in the works of the two most important dialogue partners of the Reformers: Dr. Johannes Eck and Cardinal Cajetan.

3.1 Humanist reform of Scholasticism and controversy: Johannes Eck

The most important German opponent of Luther, Dr. Johannes Eck (Johannes Maier von Egg an der Günz, 1486–1543), was by no means a Scholastic of the old school.[139] Already as a celebrated teacher in Tübingen he was an adherent of the *via moderna,* yet he sought to improve Ockhamist logic by opening it up to humanist methods of interpretation and a new linguistic culture.[140] In 1510 he was appointed professor in Ingolstadt. He was initially on friendly terms with both Luther and the humanists. In his first theological work, *Chrysopassus praedestinationis* (1514), he exhibited at least a distinct affinity to the Reformation doctrine of grace and justification.[141]

136. See, for example, OS 3:6, 24–28 (Introduction to the Inst. 1539); see also Ganoczy and Scheld, *Hermeneutik,* 122–23.

137. *Johannis Calvini Opera quae supersunt omnia,* ed. G. Baum, E. Cunitz, E. Reuss, 59 vols. (Braunschweig, 1863–1900), 6:268; 9:533 et passim; see also Ganoczy and Scheld, *Hermeneutik,* 114–15.

138. OS 1:73.

139. See Iserloh, *Johannes Eck;* Smolinsky, "Johannes Eck."

140. See Seifert, *Logik.*

141. See Greving, *Johann Eck.*

Unlike Erasmus and the Reformers, Eck was also concerned about refining and simplifying Scholasticism in theology. Thus in the dog days [midsummer] of 1542 he was still lecturing: a short explanation of the first book of the *Sentences,* in which he discussed the introductory theoretical questions about science in a few pages.[142] In contrast to the existential, anthropological approach of Reformation theology, Eck's definition of theology adopts the Scholastic tradition in summary form: "Theology is the science that deals with God, His perfections, attributes and relations, and also with creatures insofar as they are considered in relation to God."[143] According to the *methodus definitiva et divisa* [method of definition and division], the individual expressions in the definition are then explained and/or illustrated. The relation of creatures to God is inherently twofold: creation and sanctification [*Beseligung*]. The *subjectum theologiae* [subject of theology] in the primary and perfect sense is therefore God, but secondarily also the creature, especially man, since he can acquire grace and attain justification. A clear, concise distinction is made between natural and supernatural theology—the latter based on inspired Scripture—or between acquired and infused theology. The theology of God, who is the *"theologotatos,"* in other words, theology *"in se"* ["in itself"] without regard to man's status in salvation history, is clearly separated from *"theologia in nobis"* ["theology in or among us"] or theology as it is believed according to man's status at a given time as opposed to the *"theologia in se,"* which is known. *"More philosophorum loquendo"* ["speaking in the manner of philosophers"], Eck adopts as his criterion for the subject of a science the Scotist definition, namely that it should contain virtually the truths of that science. The object of theology consists of sacred Scripture and the valid conclusions that are drawn logically from it. Theology is—in keeping with the *via moderna*—partly practical, partly affective, depending on the propositions that it contains. Thus *"pater genuit filium"* ["The Father begot the Son"] is a theoretical proposition, even when something about appropriate divine worship is inferred from it.[144]

Although Eck's instructional method in his lectures on the *Sentences* is consistently that of definition and division, in his *Enchiridion locorum communium adversus Lutherum et alios hostes ecclesiae* ["Handbook of common-

142. *In Primum Librum Sententiarum Annotatiunculae D. Johanne Eckio Praelectore Anno ab Christo nato 1542, per dies caniculares, quos alioqui a studiis gravioribus feriari solebat,* ed. W. L. More, Jr. (Studies in Medieval and Reformation Thought 13) (Leiden, 1976), 15–17.

143. Ibid., In prol. (15.7–10): *"Theologia est scientia quae de Deo, eius perfectionibus, attributis et relationibus tractat, aut etiam de creaturis secundum quod in Deum referentur."*

144. Eck, *I Sent.* prol. (15–17).

places contrary to Luther and other enemies of the Church"] (First printing 1525, successively enlarged until 1543) he has recourse to the common repertoire of Scholasticism as refined by humanism.[145] Unlike Melanchthon's *Loci,* Eck does not try to give an overview of theology, but rather a summary of the main points of controversy between the religious parties, which are treated according to a scheme of *propositio* (sometimes called *axioma* also) and its *probatio* [proof] from established passages from Scripture and the Fathers. The basic scheme is often that of a disputation as well: *propositio—probatio—objectiones—solutiones.*[146] Even at the methodological level, therefore, Eck's *loci* [citations, passages]—Zwingli's influential observation notwithstanding—is not a Catholic imitation of Melanchthon's;[147] rather, Eck is posing the question as to the order, relative weight, and authoritative proof of the theological theses that are to be discussed controversially. The following topics are situated at the head of the *loci:* Church—Council—papal primacy—Scripture. Then come: faith and works, the sacraments and ecclesiastical rites and customs. The *probatio* of the central propositions (e.g., the veneration of the saints, chapter 15) follows the pattern: Scripture—*ratio—auctoritates sanctorum* (the Fathers)—*ecclesiae consuetudo* [custom of the Church] in broadly developed chapters. The practical purpose of this controversial-theological presentation is underscored by references to thematically related sermons by Eck.[148] The practical significance of the *loci* is set forth even more plainly in the foreword to the shorter German edition of 1530: in connection with the "simple" humanist theology, they are meant to serve as an abridgment of Scholastic theology.[149] Here Eck has "briefly drawn up and compiled in this little handbook the foundation and summary idea [of theology], first and foremost the most important sayings of Holy Divine Scripture, so that everyone—even somebody with little understanding—might be able to gain insight quickly into any matter that may arise and to find at hand [i.e., conveniently] the chief passages from Scripture, and sometimes also the authority of the holy divine doc-

145. Johannes Eck, *Enchiridion locorum communium adversus Lutherum et alios hostes ecclesiae* (1525–1543), ed. P. Fraenkel (CCath 34) (Münster, 1979). On the history of its composition, see Minnich, "Origins."

146. For example, *Enchiridion* c. 1 prop. 4 (24–34).

147. See Fraenkel, *Einleitung zu Eck, Enchridion* 1*–16*; Zwingli's letter to Vadian dated 22 April 1526: CR 95.574.

148. For example, *Enchiridion,* c.5 prop.2 (92.3).

149. Johannes Eck, *Enchiridion: Handbüchlin gemainer stell unnd Artickel der jetzt schwebenden Neuwen leeren,* Faksimile-Druck der Ausgabe Augsburg 1533, ed. E. Iserloh (CCath 35) (Münster, 1980).

tors, as they have then been accepted by the Christian Churches."[150] The purely topical arrangement of the material is explained here by the character of this small reference work. Of course, because this work is destined for the "simple" Christian, a coarsening of the style can be observed, especially in the supplementary material not found in the Latin original.[151]

Topical, controversial theological debate thus replaces the discovery of truth through disputation. This is explicitly justified in the last chapter of the original version: *"Non disputandum cum haereticis"* ["One should not dispute with heretics"].[152] Earlier, chapter 26 *"De haereticis comburendis"* ["On burning heretics"] cites an objection of the heretics (specifically Luther's), that one must dispute with them and defeat them with the sword of the Spirit, that is, with the word of God, and not with fire.[153] Relying on papal condemnations, Eck adduces proof of heresy in Luther's case (Zwingli's also in the German version) by the tried and true procedure of showing that their works repeat the teachings of the old condemned heretics: "then they revive the old condemned heresies of Arius, Manes [and the Manichees], Helvidius, Vigilantius, Jovinian, Aëtius, Eutyches, Felix, Wycliffe, Hus, and other heretics; therefore one should not dispute with them."[154] The reproach that disputation was vicious, which Luther had levelled against Scholasticism and his Catholic opponents, is now turned against the heretics: they lack fundamental docility; instead they just want to defend their tenets unto death. Moreover they want to dispute, not in the presence of learned, educated individuals who are well-versed in theology, but rather (as in Zurich, for example) *"coram indoctis, vulgaribus laicis"* ["before uneducated, common lay people"], who are in no way capable of deciding such difficult questions of faith. Furthermore, Eck has recourse to the condemnations of the new doctrine by the universities (Paris, Spain, Oxford, Cambridge, Louvain/Leuven, and Cologne). Disputation, an academic method of finding the

150. Eck, *Enchiridion* 13.

151. Thus *Handbüchlin* c.12 (38); *Enchridion* 149, n. 35: *"in allen fleischlichenn wollust, wie Zwingli, Luter: betten nit, fasten nit, lesen nit mesz, hörend kaiene, kommen weder in vesper noch metten, ist jn Freytag, Quotember, Fasztag, Fasztnacht als gleich, nemmen weiber jrs gefallens und fressen der kirchen und clöster güeter. Das ist gut evangelisch. Ja, in der hell!"* ["In all carnal pleasures, as Zwingli goes, so goes Luther: they don't pray, don't fast, don't say Mass or hear (attend) any, don't come to vespers or matins, whether it's Friday, an ember day, a fast day or Shrove Tuesday, they take wives according to their fancy and consume the assets of the churches and monasteries. That's certainly the Evangelical (Protestant) way. Well, to hell with them!"]

152. *Enchiridion* c. 27 (280–85); on the biographical background, see also Minnich, "Origins."

153. Ibid., c.26 (277).

154. Eck, *Handbüchlin* c.27 (75).

truth, is therefore no longer appropriate with the innovators [*Neugläubigen*], especially since the Lutherans allegedly are only trying to win people over to their doctrine. Moreover Christian doctrine is thereby held up to ridicule by the heathens, Turks and Jews, whereas it is a major scandal for simple Christians when age-old ordinances of the Church and of the Fathers are called into question. Therefore such things should not be debated *"coram frigidis et male sentientibus laicis"* ["before dull laymen who do not think aright"].[155] Eck regards the question of probative authorities as precisely the crux of the whole problem: the supporters of the Reformation accept Scripture alone, in their own interpretation, of course, which is in turn unacceptable for Eck, with his Scholastic and humanist education:

> Besides, by design it is their stiff-necked and blockheaded [*verstopffte*] method, that they are unwilling to tolerate any other judge than Scripture; yet they tear it to pieces dismissively and find fault with it in their false interpretations and glosses, so that St. Paul [himself] has to contend with such prohibitions [*verbotten*].[156]

Only if suitable judges were present would a disputation still have any value; otherwise the topical armamentarium of the *Loci communes* remains the necessary preparation for the battle that is beginning in the Counter-Reformation.

3.2 Cajetan and the new Thomism

When the Reformation runs directly up against the living Scholastic tradition, it is not so much the *via moderna* from which Luther and Eck developed, but rather the new Thomism[157] that had grown stronger since the mid-fifteenth century as a result of the debate about the two ways; this Thomism was represented in particular by Cardinal Thomas de Vio, O.P. (1469–1534), who served as a professor in Padua, Pavia, and Rome, then as general of his order and was called Cajetan.[158] Cajetan's work was voluminous (philosophical commentaries on Aristotle and Thomas, Scriptural commentaries, treatises); especially worth noting here is his commentary on the *Summa Theologiae* of Thomas Aquinas (on the *Prima Pars*, 1507/08).[159] Unlike the influential *Defensiones theologiae Divi Thomae Aqui-*

155. Eck, *Enchiridion* c.28 (282).
156. Eck, *Handbüchlin* c.27 (145/75).
157. See Grane, *Modus loquendi theologicus*, 161–91.
158. Concerning his biography and his controversy with Luther, see Wicks, *Cajetan*.
159. Published along with the Leonine Edition of the Summa, vols. IV–XII; separately: *Thomae de Vio Caietani Commentaria in Summam Theologiam*, ed. H. Prosper, vol. 1 (Lyrae, 1892); list

natis by Johannes Capreolus, O.P. († 1444),[160] Cajetan's commentary is informed not so much by intramural Scholastic debates with the Scotists and Nominalists as by the encounter with the new philological Aristotelianism and the Averroës renaissance in Padua (Pietro Pomponazzi [† 1524]). Even stylistically it displays far more humanist elegance than Scholastic "barbarity."[161] Another ongoing feature, of course, is the debate with Scotism, which also was represented in Padua by the Franciscans. Remarkable, too, for the controversy with the Reformation, which was generally hostile to metaphysics, is the extensive incorporation of metaphysical questions in theology, whereby Cajetan deviates from Thomas, however, along the lines of "more modern" solutions.[162]

Methodologically Cajetan strives for the *"perspicuitas"* [clarity] that was so highly prized by the humanists and at the outset raises the question, whether it is not perverse to cram a work designed as a beginner's textbook (the *Summa*) with the subtleties of the various schools of thought.[163] In a pedagogically skillful way, the *"novitius"* [novice] in theology is addressed directly and alerted to the significance of conceptual distinctions for purposes of disputation, e.g., between *theologia in se* and *theologia in nobis.*[164] Cajetan's training in humanistic scholarship is evident when he distinguishes with philological precision among the senses of individual terms. The first comprehensive commentary on the whole *Summa* proceeds at each article according to the pattern:

1. *expositio formalis:* an explanation of the individual terms of the question or the conclusions, according to their various meanings;
2. *expositio et diviso textus:* a methodically arranged table of contents of the article;
3. *expositio magistralis:* discussion of Thomas' teaching (as summarized in his conclusions), in the form of objections or *dubia* and the solution thereof in individual steps of argumentation, along the lines of a *quaestio disputata.*[165]

---

of his works, x–xiii. The commentary on the *Sentences* composed in Padua is unpublished: Paris, Bibliothèque Nationale Cod. lat. 3076.

160. Johannes Capreolus, *Defensiones theologiae Divi Thomae Aquinatis,* ed. C. Paban—Th. Pègues, 7 vols. (Tours, 1900–1908); see also Grabmann, "Johannes Capreolus."

161. See Wicks, *Cajetan,* 10–19; Grabmann, "Stellung."

162. See Hegyj, *Bedeutung;* Hallensleben, *Communicatio,* 53–220.

163. Cajetan, *In I S.Th.* prol. (1a).

164. Ibid., q.1 a.1 G (7a). (For the distinction see Cajetan, *I S.Th.,* 5.38.)

165. Grabmann, "Cajetan," 607–8.

Aquinas' understanding of theology, in its basic features, is valid for the commentator as well. Yet the latter distinguishes much more precisely than Thomas does between *theologia dei* [God's knowledge of himself], the subaltern *theologia in se* [knowledge about God in himself] as a real science, and *theologia in nobis* [knowledge about God in us, his creatures]—which depending on one's status is either the theology of the blessed or *theologia viatorum* [. . . of wayfarers, i.e., in salvation history]; in either case it is only imperfectly a science and is moreover generally subordinated to God's knowledge. The discursive technique of our theology is regarded as an imperfection that is to be removed, and not as something constitutive for the intuitive and necessary theological knowledge of God.[166] Consequently the first division of the sciences cannot be into theoretical and practical sciences, but rather into infinite and finite knowledge. Only finite knowledge is theoretical or practical. Therefore theology, regarded at first in principle as the theology of God, can combine theoretical and practical knowledge. What Thomas Aquinas attempted to resolve in terms of the theory of science is now demonstrated metaphysically as a consequence of God's knowledge.[167] Our theology, however, is nothing more than an *"impressio et sigillum proprium scientiae divinae"* ["an impression and a particular seal of divine knowledge"]; for both deal with God insofar as he is God *(de Deo inquantum Deus),* but our knowledge does so in a derivative way, through a slight but genuine participation in the light of God's knowledge.[168] This provides the metaphysical proof for the speculative *"theologia gloriae"* that Luther disputed; of course the boundary between acquired and infused theology is less clearly emphasized. Our theology also grasps its formal object (*sub ratione Dei* [considered in relation to God]) only in an epistemological light that is diminished in comparison to the divine light, and therefore it does not lead to a comprehensive knowledge of all truths about God.[169] Remarkably, for his second proof for God as the *subjectum theologiae,* Cajetan uses a Scotist argument that has been accommodated to Thomas: the subject of a science contains the entire science virtually within itself. God, however, is the subject of the articles of faith, which are the principles of theology.[170] In the question about the argumentative character of theology (I q.1 a.8), Cajetan explicitly addresses the objection that Scholastic speculative theology spends too much time on philosophical arguments that are

166. Cajetan, *In I S.Th.* q.1 a.1 F–G (6b–7b).
167. Ibid., q.1 a.4 C (12b–13a).
168. Ibid., E (12a).
169. Ibid., q.1 a.7 E (18ab).
170. Ibid., G (18b–20b); see also Leinsle, "Einheit der Wissenschaft nach Johannes Duns Scotus."

foreign to theology. Cajetan acknowledges that philosophical arguments per se are foreign to theology. Yet the theologian may make use of them *"ut ministrae theologiae"* ["as maidservants of theology"], and insofar as he does this, they become genuinely theological arguments, even if only *"ministerialiter"* ["in an ancillary way"]. In particular, arguments from metaphysics and natural philosophy are needed to refute opposing positions, to resolve objections and to declare the truths that theology deals with only secondarily, for example, the existence and metaphysical attributes of God. Replying to philosophical objections purely in terms of faith, however, makes theology a laughingstock for philosophers.[171]

Luther's meeting with the papal legate, Cajetan, in Augsburg in October 1518[172] was thus the meeting of two very different intellectual paradigms and theologies as well. Cajetan's Augsburg treatises in the form of *quaestiones*—"the first major work of controversial theology against the teachings and demands of the Lutheran Reformation"—show this quite clearly.[173] Cajetan's approach in countering Luther's teachings is basically the one foreseen in his commentary on the *Summa:* rational analysis within the framework of natural reason, terminological clarification and the testing of theses against accepted probative authorities. For Cajetan, however, the latter are of different kinds (in contrast to Luther's retreat to the position of *"sola Scriptura"*):

1. *recta ratio* [right reason] as the basis for philosophical-theological argumentation;
2. the *consensus of theologians;* it is irresponsible to contradict it, especially when this is done *"sine ratione et sine auctoritate et contra communem sententiam"* ["without reason, without authority, and contrary to common opinion"];[174]
3. the *sensus ecclesiae* [mind of the Church], as a Spirit-wrought, infallible guiding principle in the transmission of revelation, in questions of faith and as an element of the Church's unity;[175]
4. the *official teaching of the Church,* above all in papal decisions and bulls.

Luther's anti-Thomistic stance, from as early as his controversy with Tetzel (ca. 1465–1519) and Prierias (1456–1523), should be seen also as a con-

171. Cajetan, In *I S.Th.* q.1 a.8 F (21b–22a).

172. See Hennig, *Cajetan und Luther;* Wicks, *Cajetan,* 43–112; Morerod, *Cajetan;* Hallensleben, *Communicatio,* 438–536; Lohse, *Theologie,* 125–34.

173. Wicks, *Cajetan,* 80–81; Cajetan, *Opuscula omnia* (Lyons, 1581), 91a–118b.

174. Cajetan, *Opuscula,* 108a.60–108b.2; see also Wicks, *Cajetan,* 86–93.

175. Cajetan, *Opuscula,* 103a.8; see also Cajetan, in *II/II S.Th.* q.1 a.1 (Leonine edition 7:8–10).

frontation between the new theological claim that he makes for his *assertiones* as opposed to Scholasticism, which because of its reliance on human authority moves in principle solely at the level of *opiniones.*[176] When Tetzel appeals to Thomas and the latter's approval by the Pope, this makes no more impression on Luther than Cajetan's insistence on the consensus among theologians. Consensus usually comes about because later scholars are only "yes-men and followers" of the opinions of our "dear cousins" [*vetter,* i.e., not quite "Fathers" = *Väter*] (Thomas, Bonaventure, Alexander of Hales).[177] Thomas should not be considered an authority when he speaks without the decisive probative authorities: Scripture, the Fathers, the canons, *rationes.*[178] The decisive debate between Luther and Cajetan in Augsburg (conducted in terms of the understanding of theology at that time) concerns the doctrine of the Church and her role with regard to Scripture: theses based (in Luther's view) on Scripture violate the norms of Scriptural interpretation, ecclesial consensus and ecclesiastical decisions that are promoted by Cajetan.[179] Luther, given his understanding of Scripture and theology, could no longer accept Cajetan's insistence that in this case the official interpretation of Scripture by the pope took precedence.[180] The discrepancy between two fundamental theological options was consequently obvious.

176. WA 1.647–48.
177. WA 1.384.
178. See Luther's polemic against Prierias: WA 1.647–72.
179. WA Br. 1.238–39.
180. See also WA 2.9–16.

6 Scholastic Theology: Early Modern Period

"Baroque Scholasticism" or the "Second Scholasticism" is the name usually applied to the period of Catholic (and in a qualified sense Protestant) theology and philosophy between humanism and the Reformation on the one hand and the Enlightenment on the other.[1] This "second" Scholasticism developed however out of the "first" of the late Middle Ages. Thus the altercations between nominalists and realists in Paris prompted Petrus Crockaert, O.P. († 1514) and his student Francisco de Vitoria (1483/93–1546) to put Thomism on a new foundation—an endeavor that we have already encountered in Cajetan. In its method and manner of framing questions, the Scholasticism of the early modern period nevertheless adopted critically the issues and solutions of its time.

1 Development and presentational forms

The Scholastic theology of the early modern period had its home in the educational institutions and universities, which in the age of confessional absolutism increasingly became "denominational institutions for the training of the next generation [of clergymen] in a given territory."[2] In addition, on the Catholic side, there were the houses of studies of the religious orders, where often only a few professors trained the clerics of their own monastery or friary.[3] In the literature of that time and place, apart from the great masters and points of debate, a large number of manuals, compendia, *systemata,* lexicons, collections of axioms, and treatises [*Thesenschriften*] of the various higher institutes and monastic schools are still anxiously awaiting an evaluation.

1. See Leinsle, *Scholastik;* Quinto, *Scholastica,* 221–37; Giacon, *Seconda Scholastica.*
2. Dreitzel, *Protestantischer Aristotelismus,* 28.
3. Described by way of a few representatives examples in Leinsle, *Studium.*

1.1 The university as a territorial and confessional institution for education

Medieval universities were associations *utriusque iuris* [having legal status in both civil and canon law] that were divided according to nationalities but were in principle international. In the post-Reformation period the territorial principle came to prevail at the universities of the Holy Roman Empire also, as it had already done in the universities founded during the fifteenth century. The territorial idea was further complicated by the confessional division: the university became a territorial, state educational institution influenced directly by the local ruler and at the same time the guarantee of the creed to which the ruler adhered. As such it was directly responsible for the training of the clergy, officials, and teachers of the territory.[4] Catholic, Lutheran, and Reformed institutions of higher education competed with each other. A change of confession by the ruler or territorial alterations often brought about a change in the university landscape. Thus after the assignment of the Reformed University of Marburg to Hessen-Darmstadt (1625), the Lutheran University of Giessen (founded 1607) was transferred to Marburg; the Calvinists who were driven from Marburg took over the *Gymnasium illustre* [a selective secondary school] in Kassel. After Marburg reverted to Hessen-Kassel (1645), another university affiliated with Reformed Christianity was founded there in 1653.[5]

The universities in France and Italy had a stronger international character while maintaining their old structures. Records from the period show that Bologna, Padua, and Perugia in particular had a significant presence [*natio*] of German students. Besides the amenities of studying south of the Alps, the more modest financial and doctrinal demands may sometimes have proved attractive. Within confessional boundaries, nevertheless, we sometimes find a remarkably international community of students and professors. Hungarian Calvinists and Bohemian or Moravian Brothers traditionally studied in Herborn, Heidelberg, and the universities in Holland, among them Johann Amos Comenius (1592–1670, 1611–1613 in Herborn). Gabriel Bethlen brought professors from Herborn to his school in Weissenburg (Alba Julia) in Transylvania.[6] The Catholic universities in the imperial

4. See Hammerstein, "Universitäten," 248.
5. See Benrath, "Universität," 71–72.
6. See Wolf, "Niederländischer Einfluss"; Schöffler, *Deutsches Geistesleben* (on Jena); Leinsle,

realm were likewise attended by "foreigners," and not just from adjoining territories—which in splintered Swabia, for example, could often mean in the very next city; instead in Dillingen we meet students from the Rhineland, from North Germany, Bohemia, Moravia, Poland, Lithuania, Italy, France, the Netherlands, and Scotland.[7] There was naturally the danger of a certain provincialism at the universities; nevertheless it was diminished by the extensive contacts with colleagues at other universities, as well as by the *peregrinatio academica* [traveling] of the students and the confessional connections of the rulers.[8] Then too, in the Catholic sphere there was the transnational organization of the Jesuit Order, which until its dissolution (1773) occupied the most professorial chairs in theology. On the other hand, the ritualized academic life led by scholars and students in the "European republic of the learned" made up the real-world background against which theology, too, could become institutionalized in its modern form as a university discipline. On the Protestant side, supervision of the universities was up to the territorial ruler or his consistory [Lutheran Church Council]. Yet the theological faculty itself became an instrument of ecclesiastical supervision in doctrinal questions—in Wittenberg as early as the 1533 statutes.[9] At the Catholic universities, questions of university supervision not infrequently led to conflicts between the local rulers (duke, prince, bishop) and the superiors of the Society of Jesus.[10]

The institutions of higher learning of the three confessions in question not only had institutional and structural features in common; they also saw the further development of the "Scholastic" instructional methods of *lectio* and *disputatio*. In this regard we must not underestimate the importance of the alignment of the Jesuit *Ratio Studiorum* [plan of studies] with the *"modus Parisiensis"* ["Parisian manner"], which compared with the *"modus Italicus"* lay greater stress on disputation.[11] *Lectio* was still the reading of a textbook, that is, Scripture, the *Loci communes* or Luther's Catechism, or in Catholic curricula the *Sentences* of Peter Lombard, or the *Summa Theo-*

Ding, 369–70 (on Johann Heinrich Alsted [1588–1638]); Leinsle, *Reformversuche*, 27–28 (Johann Heinrich Bisterfeld [ca. 1605–1655]); 40–42 (Johann Amos Comenius [1592–1670]).

7. See Leinsle, *Dilinganae Disputationes*, 17.

8. See Trunz, "Späthumanismus."

9. See Paulsen, *Geschichte*, 1:219.

10. For example, the dispute about the "foundation candle" that was supposed to be handed over to the bishop by the rector of the University of Dillingen: Specht, *Geschichte*, 140–43. On the various sorts of Jesuit participation at or administration of universities, see also Hengst, *Jesuiten*.

11. See Codina Mír, *Aux Sources;* Leinsle, *Dilinganae Disputationes*, 27–48.

logiae of Aquinas. The decisive element, however, now became the professor's dictation, although dictating lessons per se was prohibited—and not only among the Jesuits.[12] The lecture was accompanied by repetition as the "sinew of instruction," sometimes at the end of the lecture, at the beginning of the next one, or at home at the residential college with "repetitors" who were specially appointed for that purpose.[13]

Disputation was considered very important in all the confessions, despite repeated objections from humanist and Reformation circles even at Lutheran universities. Disputations were conducted in Greek and Hebrew as well.[14] Disputations were just the place to discuss current interreligious questions or controversial issues within a confession. Above and beyond the daily repetitions, we should distinguish at least the following:

1. *weekly* disputations in a smaller circle *(disputationes circulares),* in which the students disputed publicly while a professor presided,[15]
2. *monthly* disputations *(disputationes menstruae),* sometimes reduced to four per year. In Dillingen, for example, they consisted of two two-hour sessions in the morning and the afternoon and were supposed to cover no more than twelve to fifteen theses. Seven *argumentatores* (opponents) competed with five defendants.
3. ceremonial disputations *(disputationes solemnes) pro gradu* (leading to the conferral of the baccalaureate, licentiate, master's or doctor's degree), at the conclusion of a course *(disputatio finalis)* or on other important occasions.[16] At institutions of higher learning that were not authorized to confer degrees *(gymnasium illustre, lyceum)* and at monastery schools the degree disputations were omitted; graduation and occasional disputations were celebrated with eminent guests and considerable expense.[17]

1.2 Catholic theology after the Council of Trent

The Council of Trent (1546–1563) was the standard, both institutionally and thematically, for the Catholic theology of the following period. Thematically the most important decisions proved to be those concerning questions about the sources of revelation, justification, sacramental doc-

12. See Tholuck, *Das akademische Leben,* 1:88–95.
13. Ibid., 95; see also Specht, *Geschichte,* 207.
14. See Tholuck, *Akademisches Leben,* 241–46.
15. See Horn, *Disputationen,* 30–38; Marti, "Disputation."
16. See Horn, *Disputationen,* 13–30; Leinsle, *Dilinganae Disputationes,* 27–34.
17. See Leinsle, "Festdisputationen."

trine and ecclesiology.[18] They proposed, so to speak, a research program for theology, while also leaving room for it to fill out the definitions through speculation and to develop theories independently in undecided questions. Institutionally the documents that became especially important were the decree *De Reformatione* (session V, June 17, 1546) and the decree on seminaries (session XXIII, July 15, 1563). The first foresees in suitably endowed local Churches the establishment of professorial chairs of sacred Scripture or at least the appointment of a grammar teacher to instruct poor students *gratis*. The *"lectio sacrae scripturae"* is likewise prescribed, when possible, for the independent monasteries and the convents of the other religious orders. The decree on seminaries institutionalizes the education of the diocesan clergy and at the same time specifies the basic curriculum: grammar, singing, ecclesiastical chronology, and other *"bonae artes"* ["fine arts"]; then sacred Scripture, ecclesiastical books, patristic homilies, and everything pertaining to the administration of the sacraments (above all Penance) and to the celebration of the liturgy.[19] In these minimum requirements the educational program of the Middle Ages was clearly readopted, but also modified for practical and pastoral purposes.

In the years that followed, educational institutions slowly developed according to this pattern. Theology is clearly subdivided here into the study of sacred Scripture and moral theology with a view to hearing confessions. We find an application in the first lesson plans for the year 1550–1551 at the Collegium Sancti Hieronymi [College of St. Jerome] in Dillingen that had been founded in 1549 by Cardinal Otto Truchsess von Waldburg (1514–1573, one of the Council Fathers). The plans provide for two theology professors, one of whom explains the pastoral letters and then "Gospel history" (*"Evangelica historia"*), and then in 1551–1552 the first chapters of Genesis and Daniel, while the other lectures on the *Sentences* and then in the second year of the Letters of Paul. For the practical and pastoral training of those who cannot study as long on account of their age or *"per ingenium"* ["because of their natural character"], the briefest possible individual instruction (*"seorsim quam brevissime"*) is offered in all that is necessary and sufficient for the

18. See the pertinent sections of the *HDG;* for a summary from the Lutheran perspective: W. Dantine, "Das Dogma im tridentinischen Katholizismus," *HDThG* 2:411–98.

19. Fr. Diego Lainez (1512–1565) testified at the Council of Trent that the following were required in order to hear confessions: acquaintance with Latin, theological knowledge (mortal, venial sins, circumstances), canonical knowledge (reserved sins, ecclesiastical punishments): see also H. Grisar, *Iacobi Lainez secundi praepositi generalis Societatis Iesu Disputationes Tridentinae* (Innsbruck, 1886), 2:440–41.

care of souls and the administration of the sacraments. The lecturer on the *Sentences* is explicitly ordered to omit all useless questions that do not serve to edify. In this program of instruction, which is basically still humanistic, sacred Scripture and the Church Fathers are mentioned as the probative authorities in explaining the *Sentences.* There is a strong warning against quarreling, shouting, and useless questions during theological disputations, which in 1550 were scheduled for the fifteenth of each month. Instead one should modestly inquire about *"veritas Catholicae et sanae doctrinae"* ["the truth of sound, Catholic doctrine"] and accept it charitably.[20] In the initial statutes from 1557 the lectures on the *Sentences* are expressly broadened to include both Summas by Thomas Aquinas; Bonaventure and Alexander of Hales are likewise recommended. This acknowledgment of Scholastic theology still turns out to be critical, however: it must not be rejected, but anything in it that does not pertain *"ad rem,"* that is, to edification in faith, hope, and charity, should not be taught.[21]

Of far-reaching importance for the institutional theology of the post-Tridentine era was the position accorded to it in the *Ratio Studiorum* of the Jesuit Order. Ever since it took charge of the University of Coimbra (1542), followed by the founding of Messina in 1548 and the takeover of Gandia in 1547 and of the Collegium Romanum in 1549, the Jesuits increasingly set the tone for theological life in the early modern period.[22] The Constitutions from 1540 on already speak about Scholastic theology as the form of education for members of the Society of Jesus, as distinguished from *positive* theology.[23] The latter comprises "conciliar decisions, works of ecclesiastical writers, sections of canon law—excluding trial law—and moral themes or writings."[24] Thus theology is arranged in three parts:

1. Sacred Scripture,
2. Scholastic theology,
3. positive theology.

Scholastic theology is bound up with the *"doctrina Scholastica Divi Thomae"* ["Scholastic teaching of St. Thomas"], yet one should continue to

20. Specht, *Geschichte,* 606–7.

21. Ibid., 630.

22. For German-speaking lands, see Duhr, *Geschichte der Jesuiten,* 1:237–94; 2:1, 494–606.

23. *Constitutiones Societatis Iesu* IV, 6, ed. G. M. Pachtler, in *Ratio Studiorum et Institutiones Scholasticae Societatis Jesu per Germaniam olim vigentes* (reprinted Osnabrück, 1968), 1:28–29.

24. See Theiner, *Entwicklung* 106–7.; on the previous history of the distinction since Johannes Major (1469–1550) and Melchior Cano (1509.1560), see Quinto, *Scholastica,* 238–55.

read the *Sentences* also, until a special Jesuit textbook or a summa of Scholastic theology approved by the general superior is introduced as a basis for lectures.[25] At the same time the purpose of education as a whole is defined: it is to benefit the salvation of one's own soul and the souls of others.[26] Moreover *"scholasticus"* acquires an additional, special meaning in the Jesuit Order: It designates the Jesuit who is being trained in philosophy and theology.

Unlike the existing traditions of the Franciscans (Scotists) and Dominicans (Thomists), the new order brought with it no particular theology. Selecting theological opinions and orientations from tradition therefore posed a considerable problem. The selection was made in principle according to their probability (justifiability).[27] The adherence to Thomas Aquinas was not servile. Not everything that he taught was to be adopted, nor were all other opinions to be rejected: in 1578 the Jesuits in Cologne defined their position with regard to Thomas as *"neque omnia, neque sola."*[28] Furthermore every age has its current problems which not only broaden theology but also lend it a new form, so to speak. The methodological consciousness of the modern era therefore prompted the streamlining and systematization of Scholastic theology: The Jesuits in Cologne classified the material in Thomas' works under eight headings after the pattern of the *Loci theologici:*

1. Principles of theology,
2. Doctrine about God,
3. *De homine* (On man: creation and anthropology),
4. *De justitia* (morality),
5. Christology,
6. Sacramental theology,
7. *De Caeremoniis* [concerning rituals],
8. *De consummatione* (eschatology).

The drafts and proposals leading up to the *Ratio Studiorum* of 1599 list—sometimes in long catalogues—those questions from the *Summa Theologiae* that are to be treated elsewhere or not at all.[29] With regard to the selection of *opiniones,* we find similar lists with binding and nonbinding *sententiae* by Thomas.[30] The definitive *Ratio Studiorum* of 1599 immediately underscores

25. *Const. SJ* IV, 14 (Pachtler 1:58–59).
26. Ibid. IV, 5 (Pachtler 1:25).
27. See Leinsle, *Delectus opinionum;* collection of sources: MPSI.
28. *Synopsis locorum theologicorum in certas classes distributa* (Pachtler 1:244–47).
29. MPSI 5:275–77.
30. MPSI 5:2–40.

in the *Regulae Professoris Scholasticae Theologiae* the requirements for a theology professor: *"orthodoxa fides"* and *"pietas,"* whereby orthodox belief is viewed as serving religious piety. Thomas Aquinas is to be regarded as the *"Doctor proprius"* ["special Doctor"] of Scholastic theology, and he should be followed, but not as the Thomists do or even more slavishly, but rather with a free and judicious reliance [*Anschluss*], which also allows deviations in favor of a *"sententia magis communis"* or *"magis recepta"* [a more common or more generally accepted opinion], as is explicitly prescribed for the question of the Immaculate Conception. In controversial questions that Thomas did not decide or discuss, one may choose a position freely. As a matter of principle, however, even here one's teaching must be aligned with the faith of the Church and the *"receptae traditiones"* ["generally accepted traditions"] and one should avoid everything that is detrimental to genuine piety. The document explicitly warns against discarding traditional reasons of fittingness or suitability [*convenientia*] and devising new "proofs," unless these are based on sure and solid principles. It also emphasizes conformity to local doctrinal traditions, even if that means renouncing many opinions, as a demand of prudent love of neighbor. It foresees that two or three professors will teach Scholastic theology. After a three-year preparatory study of (Aristotelian) philosophy, the study of theology lasts four more years. Excluded from this purely Scholastic, speculative theology are all questions of exegesis, apologetics, philosophy, and casuistry *(casus conscientiae)*. After 1599, therefore the business of the Scholastic theologian is to comment on Thomas. The method follows that of the thirteenth-century commentaries on the *Sententiae:* explanation of the text while indicating the *ratio* [rationale, reason for proceeding in a certain order] and then after each article, as needed, a more precise explanation of the matter through *quaestiones.* Under no circumstances should the professor merely present different *sententiae;* instead, where applicable, he should defend Aquinas' teaching.[31] The freedom of opinion that was thereby guaranteed led to various currents of thought within the Jesuit Order itself. Faced with new difficulties, the General Superior Claudius Aquaviva (1543–1615) had to insist emphatically in 1611 and 1613 on the solidity and uniformity of doctrine in its central points.[32] After the 9th General Congregation in 1649/50, General Superior Francesco Piccolomini (1582–1651) presented once again, as guidelines for theology professors,

31. MPSI 5:380.
32. MPSI 7:657–64; see also Leinsle, *Dilinganae Disputationes,* 59–60.

an extensive list of required questions *"juxta ordinem Summae Angelici Doctoris"* ["according to the plan of the Angelic Doctor's *Summa*"], and likewise a series of forbidden *sententiae.*[33]

The new regulations by the Council of Trent for the study of theology were implemented by the other religious orders also to the best of their ability. Whereas the mendicant orders already had their general and provincial houses of studies, now the abbeys were called to institute courses of study. Sometimes a monastic congregation chose to have a *studium commune,* which could be hosted by different houses in turn, as, for example, in the Bavarian Benedictine Congregation (1687–1769). Residential colleges for religious orders were established in university cities, for instance the Collegium Norbertinum of the Premonstratensians, founded 1628 in Prague.[34] The University of Salzburg, which was run by the Benedictines (1622),[35] became the most important non-Jesuit institution of higher learning in the Catholic territories of the Holy Roman Empire. Usually the only religious sent to the universities and central colleges were those who had been assigned to serve afterward in the administration of their community or to teach at their own house of studies. Generally they brought back to their own monastery the philosophical or theological current that they had studied at the university.[36] In the monastic schools, too, courses in Scholastic theology (usually three years) could be clearly distinguished from courses in positive theology (moral theology, casuistry, usually two years). Often the entire community was included in a course on positive theology, which also served as continuing education for the priests who had pastoral duties, whereas Scholastic theology had an influence on the clergy in the surrounding areas through the major disputations.[37] The immediate basis for the lectures, which were usually dictated in this setting too, was not so much the works of Aquinas as the current textbooks or *cursus* that were being used more and more often at the universities. Of course abridgment often leads also to a certain coarsening or simplification of what is taught; on the other hand, the meeting of the various teaching traditions in one place helped to guarantee a lively exchange among the schools of thought. These expanded courses of study in the monasteries (which were conscious of their own locality and state in life) were precisely what made Scholastic theology ap-

33. Pachtler 3:77–101; on the development see: Hellyer, "Construction," 24–30.

34. See Kuchařova, "Kolej."

35. See Bauer, *Metaphysik,* 1–30.

36. See Leinsle, *Studium,* 146–57.

37. Ibid., 95–97; Leinsle, *Disputationen.*

pear to be not just an academic affair but a fundamental element in Catholic education and culture during the early modern period, more so than during the Middle Ages.

1.3 Scholastic and positive theology

The Jesuit plan of studies institutionalized for the following period the divergence of speculative (= Scholastic) and positive theology that had already been clear in the petitions and draft versions that led up to it.[38] Then too there was the division into *cursus major (academicus)* and *cursus minor (seminaristicus).* Only the former, which consists essentially of Scholastic theology, qualifies the student for academic degrees; the latter serves as practical training for future pastors. It does without Scholastic theology and instead teaches the *casus conscientiae* [casuistry for the confessional]. Those who attended lectures in the *cursus minor* were therefore described as *"casistae"* (also as "casuists") or "positivists." Whereas in the *cursus major* moral theology was expounded in a speculative manner following the *Secunda pars* of the *Summa* by Thomas Aquinas, the practical course was concerned with solving cases of conscience on the basis of general principles by applying them to the individual case. In the Jesuit Order, too, the *casus* were read at first outside the course of academic studies. Those who attended the lectures were clerics, sometimes laymen also, so that in Barcelona in 1557 the course had to be relocated to the principal church in the city because of the large crowd.[39] Even here, besides the lectures, the courses offered practical exercises in solving hypothetical "cases," which were often quite complicated. Finally, in the 1586 draft version of the plan of studies, the *cursus minor* was supplemented with lectures on apologetics and sacred Scripture which were to be attended by those enrolled in the *cursus major* as well. In addition, on many days the [conciliar] *Catechismus Romanus* was explained. The education provided by the *cursus minor* as a whole was described in these terms in Dillingen from 1609 on: *"Institutio sacerdotum ex Divinis et Ecclesiasticis Canonibus deprompta"* ["The Instruction of priests, derived from Divine Laws and Ecclesiastical Canons"], which already indicates the close connection between moral-theological and canonical casuistry.[40] Apologet-

38. See Theiner, *Entwicklung,* 57–250; Quinto, *Scholastica,* 238–95; little attention is paid to the development during the early modern period in Tshibanghu, *Théologie positive* (only Melchior Cano is mentioned: 186–210).

39. Theiner, *Entwicklung,* 121.

40. On casuistry see Leites, ed., *Conscience.*

ics was understood as controversy with heretics (usually Protestants) over those points of Catholic doctrine that they attacked. Here, too, the method was no longer that of Scholastic commentary but rather of the positive presentation and apologetic refutation of false doctrines, often in connection with an explanation of the catechism.[41] Often the professor of sacred Scripture or a professor of Scholastic theology was one of the dignitaries in charge of the debates.[42]

The decision as to which of the two courses a student should attend was connected with the results of his philosophy examinations. If a student did not display above-average speculative talent, he could not be admitted to the *cursus major.* Merely average capacity was described as understanding what was heard and read, and the ability to answer, although without any special distinction in debating.[43] This could easily give the impression that the less gifted students were better suited (or good enough) for pastoral ministry, while the Scholastic theologians lacked the requisite practical skills. In order to prevent that misfortune, the 1591 plan of studies provides for the establishment of a chair of moral theology in the *cursus major* also; in 1599, however, this was modified according to the custom in each individual province.

The 1599 *"Regulae Professoris Casuum Conscientiae"* ["Rules for a Professor of Casuistry"] immediately focus on educating "capable pastors or ministers of the Sacraments." Therefore the subjects taught are: sacraments, ecclesiastical punishments, the duties of various states of life, and the Decalogue, whereby contracts are to be treated also under the seventh commandment. Less important matters are only to be discussed briefly: depositions, demotions, magic, etc. Theological matters that have nothing to do with casuistry should be omitted entirely; those that offer something of a foundation for cases in moral theology should be noted briefly as definitions: for example, what a sacramental character is, the difference between mortal sin and venial sin, consent, etc. Expressly forbidden is the *"apparatus scholasticus,"* that is, the usual method of disputation while quoting as many opinions and arguments as possible. Moral theology works instead with *dubitationes* [moral uncertainties] and *conclusiones.* Authorities should be cited sparingly; general laws or rules should be illustrated by a few particular cases (around three). Casuistic conferences, which serve as practical exercises, should be

41. A still indispensable study of the history of apologetics is, Werner, *Apologetische Literatur.*
42. This was the custom in Dillingen: Specht, *Geschichte,* 203.
43. See Theiner, *Entwicklung,* 212, 417.

clearly distinguished from Scholastic disputations. The "proof" of one's own solution is carried out according to the principle of probability: one should recognize also a certain probability in the rejected *sententia* according to the reasons and authorities adduced in its favor.[44]

Out of this principle of probability developed "the most Jesuitical of moral systems," *probabilism.*[45] In its simplest form this approach, which goes back to Bartholomew Medina, O.P., is intended to facilitate moral judgment of the individual specific act, and therefore it works to a great extent casuistically. In the individual case, however, one is often in doubt as to which opinion to take as the basis for one's action. The more certain or safer *(tutior)* opinion then is the one which, if followed, enables the individual with greater certainty to avoid breaking a law. On the other hand, the degree of probability of an opinion depends on intrinsic reasons and on the authority of the expert in the matter. The certainty and the probability of an opinion can therefore differ in degree. For example, if there is doubt as to whether a particular act is commanded or optional, or whether it is forbidden or permissible, according to probabilism one may morally follow the less certain opinion, even if it is less probable (justifiable) [provided that there *are* solid probable reasons for that opinion]. Probabilism with its subdivisions, which have often been opposed and condemned as "laxism," dominated moral theology—not just of the Jesuits—and practical decision-making against the opposition of *tutiorism* (one should follow the more certain opinion in every case, even if a less certain opinion is more probable) and *probabiliorism* (one may follow a less certain opinion only if it is more probable than the contrary opinion).[46] Sometimes probabilists reply to the accusation of laxism by painting probabiliorism as a form of Jansenism. The political consequences of the moral system are displayed, not least, in its justification of the alliance between France and the Turks. Within the Jesuit Order itself the Superior General Thyrsus Gonzalez (1624–1705) took steps against radical, vulgarized probabilism, which caused a reaction that went so far as a plan to depose him.[47] Since the students of casuistry must have seemed less gifted than the "Scholastics" anyway, the spread of a practical probabilism or laxism was quite possible. Thus many considered as probable anything that could be found in a book with an ecclesiastical *imprimatur.*

44. Pachtler, 2:322–29.
45. See Otte, "Probabilismus"; Schmitz, "Probabilismus."
46. See Döllinger and Reusch, *Moralstreitigkeiten,* 1:23–25; Otte, "Probabilismus," 284–92.
47. Döllinger and Reusch, *Moralstreitigkeiten,* 1:28–60, 120–272; de Francescini, "Thomisme."

In the systems of tutiorism, probabiliorism, equiprobabilism (if two opinions have the same probability, one may follow the less certain), and probabilism, moral theology gave rise to its own subtleties and vehement controversies. The systematic organization of moral theology in textbooks usually displayed the elements present in the *Ratio studiorum* or its precursors in varying arrangements.[48] Because of the exclusion of the speculative parts of theology, all that remained was a set of principles of human action as the foundation for a practical treatment of the virtues, commandments, sins, sacraments, and ecclesiastical punishments. While the great textbooks by Enrique Henriquez (1536–1608; *Summa theologiae moralis,* Salamanca 1591), Johannes Azor (1536–1603; *Institutiones morales,* Rome 1600–1611), Thomas Sanchez (1550–1610), or Paul Laymann (1574–1635; *Theologia moralis,* Munich 1625) display considerable theological depth, in the *Medulla theologiae moralis* (1650) by Hermann Busenbaum, S.J. (1600–1668), which by 1776 had run to more than 200 editions, theological thinking degenerates into Decalogue morality and casuistry for confessors listing individual doubtful cases—a manual that can be used as a pastoral reference work. But this was the work that became the standard equipment for the pastoral clergy who were often educated exclusively in moral theology.[49] In seven books Busenbaum discusses:

1. Basic principles (rules of human action: conscience and law),
2. Precepts of the theological virtues (faith, hope, charity),
3. The Ten Commandments and the precepts of the Church,
4. Duties of one' state of life,
5. Sins,
6. Sacraments,
7. Ecclesiastical punishments and irregularities.

Within and outside of the Jesuit Order, however, there were also attempts to develop a speculative, more in-depth moral theology and thus to overcome the rigid separation of Scholastic and positive theology. The distinguished Jesuit Cardinal Juan de Lugo (1583–1660), for example, was at home in both fields.[50] On the Thomistic side we should mention above all the *Ethica Supernaturalis Salisburgensis* (1718) by the Salzburg profes-

48. See Theiner, *Entwicklung,* 130–39, 251–325.
49. See Leinsle, article "Medulla theologiae moralis," *HThW,* 949.
50. See Olivares, "Juan de Lugo" and other essays in *ATG* 47 (1984); Knebel, *Wille.*

sor, Fr. Ludwig Babenstuber (1660–1727), a Benedictine from Ettal.[51] As indicated by the title, Babenstuber intends to follow the arrangement and method that is customary at the University of Salzburg. He expounds moral theology in eight treatises: conscience, human acts, laws, ecclesiastical punishments and irregularities, Ten Commandments, ecclesiastical commandments (fasting and tithing), civil law and justice (property, restitution and contracts), sacraments. At that time a real connection between Scholastic and positive theology of the kind that Eusebius Amort would later create with his *Theologia eclectica moralis et scholastica* (Augsburg-Würzburg 1752),[52] did not yet seem to be considered desirable.

1.4 The development of schools of Catholic theology

One characteristic of the "Second Scholasticism" also in Catholic theology was the continuation or new development of philosophical-theological orientations in connection with important theologians of the Middle Ages.[53] The parting of the "ways" in philosophy still occurs sometimes, as in late Scholasticism, but not so much between realists and nominalists as between Thomists and Scotists, which proved to be the most viable medieval schools.[54] Now individual philosophical and theological teachings were developed much more vigorously as "hallmarks" of the individual schools and were debated controversially. Exclusive federations of religious orders and the traditions of a given monastic house or university faculty reinforced the impression of rigid theological "schools," which often had unmistakable local coloring. The honor shown to these medieval "forefathers" sometimes took on characteristics of the Baroque veneration of the "domestic saints" of a monastery, city, or country.

Of the medieval schools, Thomism was the first to experience a revival.[55] The declaration of Thomas Aquinas as Doctor of the Church in 1567 by the Dominican Pope Pius V (1566–1572) and the dominant role of Thomistic thought at the Council of Trent did more than was necessary to assure for

51. L. Babenstuber, *Ethica Supernaturalis Salisburgensis sive Cursus Theologiae Moralis* (Augsburg, 1718). Babenstuber explicitly describes himself as a "*Theologiae, tum moralis, tum scholasticae, necnon Sacrae Scripturae Professor*" ["professor of both moral and Scholastic theology, as well as Sacred Scripture"].

52. See below, 6.4.3.

53. In general, see Grabmann, *Geschichte der katholischen Theologie*, 147–205. Werner, *Geschichte der katholischen Theologie*.

54. See Jansen, "Scholastische Philosophie."

55. See Jansen, "Thomisten."

him the recognition of theologians. Besides the Dominican Order, which was traditionally oriented to Thomas, the Discalced Carmelites (O.C.D.) became especially zealous defenders of the teachings of the "Angelic Doctor," whom they were obliged to study by the statutes of their order.[56] The Universities of Salamanca and Alcalà became the center of Thomism in Spain, which we can see in the great work of philosophical commentary (on Aristotle) of the *Complutenses* (Alcalà) and in the *Cursus theologicus Salmanticensis* (1631–1704). Francisco de Vitoria, O.P. († 1546) had already brought the renewed Thomism to Salamanca from Paris. From there it went into the Old and the New World through his students, the Tridentine conciliar theologian Domingo de Soto, O.P. († 1560), the Oxford professor Pedro de Soto († 1563), who also taught in Dillingen, and Melchior Cano († 1560, consecrated bishop of the Canary Islands 1552). The Superior General Philippus a SS. Trinitate, O.C.D. (Esprit Julien, 1603–1671), author of an influential *Summa theologiae thomisticae* (5 vols., 1653) and a *Summa theologiae mysticae* (1656), was for a time professor at his order's house of studies in Goa. The figures of Dominicus Báñez († 1604) and Bartholomaeus Medina († 1581) lent particular weight to Salamancan Thomism in the controversy *de auxiliis,* concerning the action of grace in conjunction with human freedom [*Gnadenhilfen*]. The *Cursus theologicus* by the Portuguese Johannes a S. Thoma (Juan Poinsot, † 1644) acquired downright canonical importance. Thomism (initially of an Italian but later of a Spanish cast) found a permanent home north of the Alps in the Benedictine University of Salzburg, which in turn radiated it to the monasteries and houses of studies of the Benedictines, Cistercians, Augustinian Canons Regular, and Premonstratensians.[57]

The theology of the Scotists flourished a second time in the various branches of the Franciscan family.[58] Here too there was a tendency toward a common discipline for the order. The 1633 General Chapter of the Friars Minor in Toledo prescribed Scotism, as opposed to the earlier possibility of choosing between the great friar-theologians, and commissioned a new edition of the works of the *Doctor subtilis.* This was organized by the historian of the order, Luke Wadding († 1657), at the Irish Franciscan College of Saint Isidore in Rome (1639). Immediately the various branches of

56. See Merl, *Theologia Salmanticensis,* 23–25.
57. See Bauer, *Metaphysik;* Leinsle, "Thomismus."
58. Concerning their philosophy see B. Jansen, "Skotisten."

Franciscans (especially the *Fratres de Observantia* and the Conventuals) set about commenting on the works of Scotus and developing courses in philosophy and theology *"ad mentem Doctoris subtilis"* ["according to the mind of the Subtle Doctor"], while the Capuchins adhered more closely to Bonaventure. Particularly influential would be the philosophical and theological course of the Irishman John Punch (Poncius, † 1660), Wadding's collaborator at S. Isodoro, and the theological works of Bartolomeo Mastri (1602–1678), who together with Bonaventura Belluti (1603–1676) was in charge of the standard course in philosophy *"ad mentem Scoti"* (which sometimes diverged from that of Friar Punch).[59] In France, where Thomists (e.g., Jean-Baptiste Gonet [1616–1681]) and Scotists (e.g., Bartholomeus Durandus [† 1720]) protected themselves in their battle against each other with theological shields *(clypeus theologiae thomisticae* or *scotisticae),* we should mention the Conventual Franciscan Sebastian Dupasquier with his *Summa theologiae scotisticae,* which he followed up with a summa on Scotist philosophy. Prague became an important center of Scotist theology, since the "subtle doctrine" was taught in three places there: the Collegium Ferdinandeum (1621) in St. James, the ancient convent of the Friars Minor in the old city, the general house of studies of the Observant Friars at St. Mary of the Snows (1627) and the College of the Irish (Hibernian) Observant Friars (1629). Furthermore the Hibernians and the Observants taught at the Archdiocesan Seminary (1635).[60] One theologically important work of Prague Scotism was the four-part *Schola theologica Scotistarum seu Cursus theologiae completus ad mentem J. D. Scoti* (Prague, 1675–1681) by the Observant Friar Bernhard Sannig (1634–1704), to whom we are indebted also for the *Scholae Philosophiae Scotistarum* (Prague, 1684/85).[61] Blasius Antonius de Comitibus a Mediolano (1634–1685) of the Friars Minor published in 1686/88 a Scotist commentary on the first book of *Sentences.*[62] In 1740 the conservative Scotist Narcissus Lang edited what was probably the last commentary on the *Sentences* to be written in Bohemia.[63]

Nevertheless, as with the regional situation, the major schools of thought were joined by smaller schools promoted by the religious orders. Besides Au-

59. See Forlivesi, *Scotistarum Princeps.*

60. Sousedík, "Scotismus"; Sousedík, *Filosofie,* 216–26; Pařez and Kuchařová, *Hyberni.*

61. See Jansen, "Scotisten," 152–54.

62. Blasius Antonius de Comitibus a Mediolano, *Theologiae scholasticae in primum librum Sententiarum ad mentem J. D. Scoti pars prima* (Vetero-Pragae, 1686); *pars secunda* (Vetero-Pragae, 1688).

63. Narcissus Lang, *Liber primus Sententiarum . . . per quaestiones proponi solitas ad mentem J. D. Scoti* (Prague, 1740).

gustine, Ægidius Romanus continued to be the leading figure of the schools of the Augustine Recollects, whereas the Italian Servites discovered a patron in Henry of Ghent with his form of Augustinianism, while some of the Carmelites (O. Carm.) adopted the approach of John Baconthorp († 1346).[64]

The new orders and Congregations had the advantage of not being restrained by Scholastic traditions. The Jesuits in particular managed to profit from this in their free, eclectic and critical adoption of Thomas.[65] The contrast to the strict Thomism of the Spaniards became an almost irreconcilable ideological opposition, partly through the debate *de auxiliis,* about the manner in which grace helps human freedom [*Gnadenhilfen*] (Molina's *scientia media* or the Thomistic *praedeterminatio physica*). Moreover a series of important Jesuit theologians of the early period (Franciscus Toletus [1532/33–1555], Gregory of Valencia [1549–1603], Francisco Suárez [1548–1617], Gabriel Vázquez [1549–1607], and Diego Ruiz de Montoya [1562–1632]) had studied in Salamanca. One can speak of a separate "Jesuit school," however, only with respect to certain standard teachings; in other teachings the members of the Society of Jesus differed widely, despite the influence of the *"Doctor eximius"* Francisco Suárez, so that repeated decrees and prohibitions were required in order to produce a unified doctrine in the order.[66] Sometimes in the Jesuit Order we also observe nominalist thinking, for example, in Pedro Hurtado de Mendoza (1592–1651) and Francisco de Oviedo (1602–1651), but above all in the works of the Prague professor Rodrigo de Arriaga (1592–1667).[67] For the German Jesuit schools the most important Scholastics were Gregory of Valencia, a professor in Ingolstadt and Dillingen, with his *Theologicorum Commentariorum libri IV* (Dillingen 1602/03) and his student Adam Tanner (1572–1632) with his four-volume *Theologia scholastica.* Influential for both moral theology and Scholastic (speculative) theology were Christoph Haunold (1610–1689) and Paul Laymann (1574–1635).

The opposition and rivalry of the various schools of thought contributed on the one hand to the liveliness of Catholic theology in the early modern period, but on the other hand they also led to a "Scholastic" self-sufficiency, in which the great figures of the past were almost invested with the nimbus of infallibility; not infrequently it led also to sterile polemics in which one often finds the same arguments over the course of a hundred years. The question

64. See Jansen, "Scholastische Philosophie"; Leinsle, *Scholastik,* 55.

65. Leinsle, *Delectus opinionum;* Leinsle, *Dilinganae Disputationes,* 48–63.

66. See esp. the *Ordinationes* collected in Pachtler, *Ratio studiorum,* vol. III.

67. See Caruso, *Hurtado de Mendoza;* Saxlová and Sousedík, eds., *Arriaga.*

as to what authority one should follow in doctrine, but especially in practical life, led directly to the debate over probabilism, but also to a theologically reasoned skepticism of the type advocated by Premonstratensian Abbot of Strahov, Hieronymus Hirnhaim (1637–1679) in his work, *De typho generis humani* (Prague 1676), which was placed on the Index.[68]

1.5 Presentational forms

In keeping with the narrower concept of Scholastic theology in the Catholic world in this period, as opposed to the Middle Ages, we will discuss only those presentational forms that developed directly from doctrine and disputation. The explication of the *Sentences* [*Sentenzenlesung*] (usually in the form of a commentary with *quaestiones*) continues in the early modern period, especially at the non-Thomistic schools, whereas the Jesuits very early on (in 1571 in Dillingen) went over to commenting on the *Summa Theologiae* of Aquinas.[69] We distinguish complete commentaries on all the parts of the *Summa* from the more common works on individual parts, especially on the *Secunda* (which serves as a basis for speculative moral theology).[70]

In keeping with the instructions from the order about teaching method, the most voluminous Jesuit commentaries on the *Summa* are often miscellaneous in character. Thus Suárez offers a remarkably short commentary on the individual articles from Aquinas, only to follow up the *quaestio* with an extremely broad discussion of the debatable matters in the form of a *disputatio.* This is subdivided into several *sections.* The commentary and twenty-five disputations on the first nine questions of part 3, for example, make up an entire volume in the edition by Vivès.[71] Disputation 4 alone on the suitability and necessity of the Incarnation is discussed in twelve sections on 145 pages in terminology that is more precise at each step according to the restricted *status quaestionis:*

Sect. 1. Whether it was necessary or fitting that God should restore fallen man.

Sect. 2. Whether it was necessary or fitting that God should become man in order to restore the human race.

Sect. 3. Whether Christ's works had sufficient value and efficacy to atone *de condigno* for the sins of men.

68. See Leinsle, "Hieronymus Hirnhaim"; Sousedík, *Filosofie,* 235–42.

69. *Lektionskatalog* [Course catalogue] Dillingen 1571: *Studienbibliothek Dillingen* XV γ 134.

70. Listing in Mitschelich, *Kommentatoren.*

71. F. Suárez, *Opera omnia,* vol. 17 (Paris, 1877), 675.

Sect. 4. Whether Christ's works had infinite value and infinite efficacy for atonement.

Sect. 5. Whether Christ's atonement was a matter of justice in the true and proper sense.

Sect. 6. Whether all the laws of perfect justice were observed in Christ's atonement.

Sect. 7. Whether man by his own powers can suffice to redeem other human beings in terms of perfect justice.

Sect. 8. Whether man solely by his own powers can make satisfaction for his own mortal sin in such a way that he is sanctified by his actions and freed from sin.

Sect. 9. Whether man solely by his own powers can make perfect satisfaction for his own mortal sin and reach a settlement, so that according to the laws of perfect justice he attains the forgiveness of sins and divine favor.

Sect. 10. Whether man can make satisfaction for his own mortal sin at least in an imperfect manner.

Sect. 11. Whether man solely by his own powers can make satisfaction to God at least for venial sins.

Sect. 12. Whether man solely by his own powers, at least as a member of Christ, can make satisfaction to God for his sins according to the rules of perfect justice.

The systematic elaboration and arrangement of the *Sentences* or of the commentaries on the *Summa* led to a systematic presentation in the *cursus theologici* [theological courses] that were divided by treatise; these were sometimes the collaborative work of a local school and codified the theology of a school even in the title. They were usually preceded by similar philosophical courses as a propaedeutic.[72] We should mention, for example, the *Theologia Universitatis Coloniensis* [Theology of the University of Cologne] (1638), the Thomist *Theologia scholastica Salisburgensis* [Salzburg] (1695) by Fr. Paulus Mezger (1637–1702), the *Cursus theologicus S. Galli* (1670), down to the *Theologia Wirceburgensis* [Würzburg] (1766–1771).[73]

No doubt the *Cursus theologicus Salmanticensis* of the Discalced Carmelites from San Elia in Salamanca came to be the most important course of a religious community; work on it continued for almost one hundred years. In the Parisian edition of 1879/80 it alone comprises twenty volumes. It was decided to publish it (without indicating the authors) in 1616/17; the first volume was printed in 1631, while the last volume of the course (which like the *Summa* of Aquinas was not completed) appeared in 1712.[74] The course

72. Blum, *Philosophenphilosophie*, 158–81.

73. On the last-mentioned see Lesch, *Neuorientierung*, 121–36.

74. See Merl, *Theologia Salmanticensis.*

in theology is related from the very beginning to the philosophy course of the *Complutenses.* It goes without saying that such monumental works are intended primarily for those who teach at other schools of the order, as is evident from the original plan of Fr. Antonius a Matre Dei (1583–1637). Originally planned in six volumes, the work was to have a clear structure which, while omitting many questions, highlights those *quaestiones* from the *Summa* that were in fact treated in theological instruction:

1. *De Deo Uno* [On the One God],
2. *De Deo Trino et Creatore* [On God, Triune and Creator],
3. *De ultimo fine et mediis perveniendi ad eum* [On (man's) final end and the means of attaining it],
4. *De Virtutibus* [On Virtues],
5. *De Incarnatione* [On the Incarnation],
6. *De Sacramentis* [On the Sacraments].[75]

As the plan was carried out, however, there was an overriding tendency to make each of the twenty-four treatises independent. Thus Fr. Antonius a Matre Dei alone worked for twenty years on the questions dealing with God and the angels. Furthermore in the moral theology and sacramental theology a two-track system of *theologia scholastica* and *theologia positiva* becomes evident. Fr. Johannes ab Annuntiatione (1633–1701) asks whether it still makes any sense to dispute the sacraments "in the Scholastic manner" [*"scholastice"*], since they are treated anyway in the *Cursus Moralis* in the way that is necessary for the practical training of the confreres.[76] The specific intramural purpose of the work becomes clear in the introduction of a special treatise *De Statu Religioso* in a place where Thomas has only one *quaestio* (II/II q. 184).

While the major *cursus* were intended primarily for instructors, we find alongside them many smaller compendia (often in octavo) and individual dogmatic treatises, which not infrequently were the immediate subject of disputation. Despite the bibliographical inclusion of a work under the name of the *praeses* [head, director], one should determine in each individual case whether one is dealing with his work or a student exercise or a collaborative work.[77] Since the individual treatises of a professor were defended several

75. Ibid., 47–48.

76. *Cursus Theologicus Salmanticensis,* ed. V. Palmé (Paris, 1879), 1:56; see also Merl, *Theologia Salmanticensis,* 49.

77. See Horn, *Disputationen,* 51–72; Leinlse, *Dilinganae Disputationes,* 39–45.

times a year or over several years, a more or less complete *cursus* could develop from that, also. Thus, for example, Jakob Bidermann, S.J. (1578–1639), who is famous more for his dramas than for his philosophy and theology, has left us from the heyday of the University of Dillingen a series of little treatises which were submitted for disputation.[78] Often a treatise was given to several defendants, each of whom had to publish it with a different title page at the expense of the patron to whom it was dedicated.[79] Because of the consequences of the Thirty Years War (troubles, plague, dwindling enrollment, poverty) there was a considerable decrease in the number of such disputations in most places. In Dillingen, for example, there were still eight in 1622, and in 1623 as many as nine theological disputations with individual written theses, but in 1641 we find only one; the years 1645, 1647, and 1649–1655 mark a complete break in the production of this academic literary genre. At the beginning of the eighteenth century, the number of individual extensive theses diminished, whereas in Salzburg and in the monasteries, for example, the students zealously continued to dispute.[80]

One requirement for obtaining a licentiate in theology was a disputation *ex universa theologia;* the theses selected often provided an overview of the professor's teaching, for example the *Controversiae Scholasticae ex universa Theologia selecta* (1657) of the Salzburg professor and later Abbot of Einsiedeln, Augustinus Reding (1625–1692).[81] In fifty-one controversies from all three parts of the *Summa* by Aquinas the main themes of Salzburg Thomism are set forth, mainly in a polemic against the Jesuits, whereby the Trinity, for example, is treated very briefly since it offered little occasion for actual debates. In the sacramental theology, on the other hand, the influence of the moral theological treatment is noticeable: the *quaestio* style is for the most part abandoned. Instead there is a positive presentation of Thomistic teaching.

Particularly in the case of the theses *ex universa theologia* for the licentiate, a special literary form developed in the Catholic world: the graphically

78. May 1620: *Theses theologicae* (24 pp.); May 1621: *Sponsalia* (51 pp.); June 1621: *Matrimonii impedimenta* (60 pp.); June 1621: *Poenitentiae sacramentum* (84 pp.); April 1622: *Censurae* (91 pp.); June 1622: *Irregularitas* (54 pp.); Jan. 1623: *Suffragia* (62 pp.); April 1623: *Praedestinatio* (38 pp.) June 1623: *Iesu Christi status triplex, mortalis, immortalis, sacramentalis* (40 pp.; for his doctorate); June 1624: *Conscientia* (78 pp.); Nov. 1624: *Prolusiones theologicae* (227 pp.); once for his doctorate, a second time with another defendant for his licentiate); Feb. 1625: *Eleemosyna* (43 pp.); May 1625: *Gratia* (63 pp.); see also Sommervogel, *Bibliothèque,* 1:1148–50.

79. See Leinsle, *Dilinganae Disputationes,* 37.

80. See Leinsle, *Studium.*

81. On Reding: Mittermüller, *Beiträge,* 19–21.

designed thesis page, which has been of interest mainly to art historians.[82] Originally only the theses gathered from the defendant (often from earlier pages) were posted on a display for vespers (on the afternoon before the graduation).[83] Especially when the patrons ("Maecenas") were very wealthy, at promotions in the presence of the prince-bishop, duke, or *"sub auspiciis Imperatoris"* ["under the Emperor's auspices"], the thesis pages were designed as an exercise in Baroque symbolism with increasingly extravagant (often emblematic) copperplate engravings *"cum emblemate."* In Augsburg a thriving business in printing thesis pages developed. These served initially as a poster to announce the disputation and as a printed invitation for special guests, but later as the "program" for those in attendance, and finally as "trophies for the defendants and dedication pages for the patrons"; as early as the seventeenth century, however, they also became collector's items.[84] Thesis pages, like the frontispieces of published theses, were also reused with different material. The text, which was only a small portion anyway, was eliminated, for example, by pasting something else over it. The philosophical or theological content of the thesis, which could very well be omitted completely in the presentation copy, was frequently reduced to a list of propositions that were printed, often in tiny type, in a box or at the bottom margin of the page, which sometimes was composed of several sheets of paper. The gift copies for the patrons sometimes had to be printed on silk.[85] When a graphically designed thesis page did not satisfy the Baroque need for ostentation, the candidates had large *thesis pictures* painted, sometimes also as the basis for the engraving. Only the beginning of the Enlightenment would interfere with the disproportion between the Baroque packaging and the meager contents of the thesis pages.[86]

2 The "Scholasticism" of Protestant orthodoxy

In the late sixteenth and early seventeenth century the Protestant institutions of higher learning, too, were characterized by an academic de-

82. See esp. Appuhn-Radtke, *Thesenblatt.*

83. See Leinsle, *Dilinganae Disputationes,* 27–34.

84. See Appuhn-Radtke, *Thesenblatt,* 28–29.

85. See Leinsle, *Studium,* 217–18.

86. See Specht, *Geschichte,* 197–98: Decree of the Prince-Bishop for Dillingen 1745; in a similar way Prince-Bishop Friedrich Karl von Schönborn (1729–1746) opposed the *"Augsburger Bilder"* ["Augsburg-style pictures"] in Würzburg. In Bamberg they were forbidden in 1780 because of the expense: see also Appuhn-Radtke, *Thesenblatt,* 18.

velopment of Reformation doctrine, which meanwhile had been defined as a creed. During the period of so-called Protestant Orthodoxy between Melanchthon's or Calvin's death (1560 or 1564) and the new teaching [*"Neologie"*] under the banner of the Enlightenment, theology developed as a methodical, creedal, systematic doctrine that was to be communicated didactically.[87] This Protestant "Scholasticism" nevertheless exhibited a markedly different character from that of medieval and early modern Catholic Scholasticism.

2.1 From creed to theological system

The development of Protestant systematic theologies is not accidentally connected with the doctrinal debates within Protestantism.[88] The latter were not immediately resolved in a theological system, but rather in creedal formulas with a claim to validity (and their acceptance in a territory). Within the sphere of the Lutheran Reformation this status belonged to the Formula of Concord (1577), which should be regarded on the one hand as a compromise among the various trends in Swabian and Saxon theology, and on the other hand as a definition distinguishing Lutheranism from Calvinist and crypto-Calvinist teachings.[89] Here the regional *"corpora doctrinae"* ["collections of doctrine"] and creedal documents were combined into a "summary, unanimous understanding and form containing the general summary teaching professed by the churches that adhere to the true Christian religion."[90] It was the duty of the civil-ecclesiastical authority, however, to ensure the acceptance of the Formula of Concord by supervising schools and censoring printed matter—all this with a view to the salvation of the subjects' souls.[91] Now, however, the authority of the Reformers and their theology (especially Luther's) had less significance than the Formula of Concord in the central questions of original sin, free will, justification,

87. See *HDThG* 2:306–52; 3:71–96; older literature: Ritschl, *Dogmengeschichte;* Althaus, *Prinzipien;* Heppe, *Dogmatik.*

88. Overview in *HDThG* 2:102–38, 272–85.

89. Edition: *BSLK* 1967[6], 735–1110; see also *HDThG* 3:138–64.

90. *BSLK* 833, 9–16.

91. Ibid., 743, 42–49: *"damit in unseren Landen und Gebieten denselben darin eingeführten und je länger je mehr einschleichenden falschen verführerischen Lehren gesteuret und unsere Untertanen auf rechter Bahn der einmal erkannten und bekannten göttlichen Wahrheit erhalten und nicht davon abgeführet werden möchten."* ["so as to curb in our lands and territories those same false and seductive teachings which have been introduced and which insinuate themselves more with each passing day, and to keep our subjects on the right path of divine truth once it has been recognized and professed, so that they may not be led astray from it."]

works, law and Gospel, the Last Supper, Christology, predestination, and church customs.

The Formula of Concord aimed at uniformity, even though it was by no means generally accepted;[92] the regional creeds of the Swiss and Calvinist Reformation (e.g., the *Confessio Helvetica posterior* of Heinrich Bullinger [1504–1575]) had nothing equivalent to offer.[93] Although it was usually allied with the *Confessio Augustana* [Augsburg Confession] and Melanchthon's theology, Reformed theology came to oppose Lutheranism overtly as a result of the second debate about the Last Supper and the formation of regional confessions; it exhibited a more markedly regional character in the individual schools (Bern, Geneva, Herborn, Heidelberg, Samur, Sedan, Leiden, Groningen, Franeker, etc.).[94]

Both the Formula of Concord and the later creedal documents of the Reformed Christians (and also the Heidelberg Catechism by Zacharias Ursinus [1534–1583]) exhibited pronounced systematic tendencies. Nevertheless they still required a systematic theological interpretation. This is not possible without an appropriate method and philosophy. Unlike Catholic Scholasticism, Protestant Scholasticism could not have recourse to a ready-made method but had to derive one—in a more or less deliberate way—from contemporary philosophizing, which produced a plethora of treatises *De methodo* [on methodology].[95] The following were offered as such:

1. The relatively simple topical outline of *Melanchthon* and his school, which restricted its understanding of philosophy to logic, ethics, and physics and thus could readily be assimilated to theology. Following Melanchthon's example, the results were more or less systematically arranged collections of *loci* or *propositiones* (axiomatic theology).
2. The dialectic of *Peter Ramus* (1515–1572) which was accepted especially by Reformed Protestants and ran to 103 extant editions between 1581 and 1610 in the imperial realm alone.[96] Originally quite antimetaphysical, Ramus placed methodology at the center in the 1572 edition and outlined a universal *method of definition and arrangement* based on conceptual logic

92. In Denmark it was forbidden under pain of death to propagate it; it was rejected by England and important German territories.

93. See *BSRK*.

94. On the development of Reformed doctrine: *HDThG* 2:165–306; see also H. Leube, *Kalvinismus und Luthertum im Zeitalter der Orthodoxie* (Leipzig, 1928; reprinted Aalen, 1966).

95. See Leinsle, *Methodologie,* 150–52.

96. See Ong, *Ramus,* 298; Bruyère, *Méthode;* Schmidt-Biggemann, *Topica universalis,* 47–48.

[*begriffslogischer Natur*]. This often resulted in *tabular* representations of theology or of the sciences (e.g., Johann Heinrich Alsted [1588–1638], Johannes Scharf [1595–1660]). The reception of Ramism in the school of Melanchthon led to the development of the Philippo-Ramism that was typical in the German schools before 1600, which was then combined with Aristotelian elements in the *methodus definitiva* of Johannes Hülsemann (1602–1661) and Johann Adam Scherzer (1628–1683).

3. The *Aristotelian* methodology and theory of science in the *Posterior Analytics,* revived most notably by the Aristotelian movement in Padua (Jacopo Zabarella [1533–1589], Francesco Piccolomini [1520–1604]).[97] Unlike the Ramist arrangement, the *methodus* here is essentially deduction, argumentation, and syllogistic proof according to the rules of the *Posterior Analytics.* All theoretical sciences are bound up with the synthetic-deductive method, while all practical sciences rely on the analytic method (goal—means for attaining it).

In principle philosophy and theology can be pursued using all three methods. The choice of one method is therefore often connected with the local academic tradition *("philosophia recepta").* Continuing the tradition of Catholic Scholasticism, or arguing with it, could be done most easily, of course, with Aristotelian methodology and philosophy. Moreover Melanchthon and the later Ramus describe their methodologies as Aristotelian. If one includes Aristotle in the theology curriculum, however, at least as a preparation, then soon there is one subject that one can no longer exclude: the *Metaphysics.*[98] Thus, for various reasons (intraconfessional disputes, polemics with the Catholics, the humanist return to the complete works of Aristotle, the methodological requirement of a First Philosophy), metaphysics was reintroduced around 1600 in Protestant institutions of higher learning.[99] Scholars dealt with it at least humanistically and philologically, even though—as in Altdorf—they refused to accept the Scholastic-Jesuit metaphysics of Suárez and Benedictus Pereira (1535–1610). The methodical development of metaphysics, nevertheless, as argued by Lutherans Cornelius Martini (1567/68–1621) in Helmstedt, Jakob Martini (1570–1649) in Wittenberg and Christoph Scheibler (1589–1655) in Giessen, and among the Reformers by the controversial Clemens Timpler (1563/4–1626) in Burgsteinfurt and Johann Heinrich

97. See Randall, *School of Padua;* Poppi, *Dottrina della scienza.*
98. See Leinsle, *Methodologie,* 152–61; Sparn, *Wiederkehr der Metaphysik,* passim.
99. See Leinsle, *Ding,* passim.

Alsted (1588–1638) in Herborn,[100] became a decisive factor in Protestant Orthodoxy. The return of metaphysics was accompanied, however, by vehement polemics from the theologians who were guided by Luther's rejection of the discipline, most plainly in the debate of Cornelius Martini with Daniel Hofmann (1538–1621).[101] A modified and theologically corrected acceptance of metaphysical theories in theology is evident especially in the teaching about God, Christology, and the Last Supper.[102]

The methodical-metaphysical thinking of Protestant Orthodoxy was articulated in a theology that was forced by its abandonment of medieval Scholasticism and its new Reformation perspective to discover its own systematic form of presentation in the first place. *"Methodus," "Syntagma,"* or *"Systema"* are therefore frequently selected as titles for the academic presentation of theology in the compendia designed for university students (although sometimes they were used for practical training and personal edification).[103] There was no science without method.

Therefore deliberate methodological considerations were brought to bear in theology among the Protestants less emphatically than in the *cursus* [courses] and commentaries of Catholic Scholasticism—thanks also to the Philippist or Ramist logic that had prevailed for over a half century instead of the *Metaphysics.* The choice of method was decided—to put it in Aristotelian terms—by the theoretical or practical character of the theology. Above and beyond the confessional boundaries between Lutherans and Reformed Christians, we can observe synthetic and analytic methods of presentation—often in hybrid forms, which correspond to the theoretical-practical character of theology.

2.2 Concept of theology in early Lutheran Orthodoxy: Johann Gerhard

The step from the Reformation to a well-reasoned theological system became especially evident in the masterpiece of Johann Gerhard (1582–1637), a professor at Jena: the *Loci theologici* (1610–1625), which was as influential as it was monumental. Not until he had completed that work, however, did Gerhard supply a theoretical consideration on the science of theology in

100. See Freedman, *European Academic Philosophy.*

101. See Petersen, *Geschichte,* 259–338.

102. See esp. Sparn, *Wiederkehr;* Althaus, *Prinzipien;* Bizer, *Frühorthodoxie;* Ratschow, *Lutherische Dogmatik,* part 2.

103. On the concept of system, see: Ritschl, *System;* examples in Bizer's "Introduction" to Heppe, *Dogmatik,* xli–lxiii.

the *Prooemium de Natura Theologiae* to his 1625 *Exegesis.*[104] All the more significant in view of the avoidance of the word *"theologia"* in Melanchthon's *Loci,*[105] here for the first time in Lutheranism we find a comprehensive reflection on theology as such.

The structure of the work follows the usual *loci*-scheme.[106] Citing Julius Caesar Scaliger (1484–1558), Gerhard adopts the method of humanist Aristotelianism.[107] It combines philology and the synthetic technique with a strongly topical admixture, inasmuch as a nominal definition is sought first in the *Onomatologia,* while a real definition is given only at the conclusion of the whole discussion of the subject of a *locus,* in the *Pragmatologia.* The onomatology [nomenclature] is stereotypically treated according to etymologies, homonyms, and synonyms; the pragmatology follows a pattern of topical questions: *an sit, quid sit, principia, causae, adjuncta, opposita* [whether it is, what it is, principles, causes, circumstances, opposites]. Subdivisions are often marked for instructional purposes; occasionally, however, one also finds a syllogistic treatment of a question, especially in an argument with opponents and heretics.

This method is applied to define the concept of theology also. In the onomatology the etymology of the word *"theologia"* is discussed first, with direct references to Aquinas and Albert the Great, and the absence of the expression in Scripture is noted, for there only its *concreta* [specific truths] and components are given.[108] The *Homonymia* then notes the breadth of the linguistic usage (in profane writers, in philosophical theology, and metaphysics) and restricts it. Most importantly, three areas in which to apply the word are discussed:

1. to the Christian faith and religion as a whole. In this sense even simple believers are theologians on the basis of their knowledge of the faith.
2. to the service of ecclesiastical preaching. In this way all "servants of the word" are *theologi.*
3. to the more precise knowledge of the divine mysteries for the purpose of consolidating divine truth and mightily destroying false statements about

104. Johannes Gerhard, *Loci theologici,* ed. E. Preuss, vol. I (Berlin, 1863); see esp.: Wallmann, *Theologiebegriff;* Schröder, *Christologie;* Kirste, *Zeugnis.*

105. In contrast to Scholastic theology, Melanchthon usually replaces the term with *"doctrina"* or *"Ecclesiastica doctrina,"* e.g., CR 1:399–400.

106. See "Schema" in Schröder, *Christologie,* 45.

107. On Scaliger: Leinsle, *Ding,* 78–87.

108. Gerhard, *Loci,* prooem. §§1–3 (1:1); see also Wallmann, *Theologiebegriff,* 30–33.

it. This is the kind of theology that is actually scientific (accentuated here as being systematic and polemical).[109]

The *Synonymia* is developed with the aid of the Rabbis, Scripture, and the Fathers, from which the most important testimonials for the status and importance of theology are also taken.[110] The *Pragmatologia* opens with the question as to the existence of theology *(an sit),* which is not insignificant for the Lutheran tradition in view of Melanchthon's silence and Luther's rejection of Scholastic theology. The fact that there is such a thing as theology is proved in a typical mixture from Scripture and philosophical (especially Stoic) views:

1. from revelation as the efficient cause and principle of theology,
2. from the nature of God as *"summum bonum communicativum et diffusivum"* ["the supreme good which communicates and diffuses itself"], which thus makes revelation possible in the first place,
3. from the end of creation: the knowledge of God,
4. from the natural endowment of man (a Stoic or Neoplatonic idea), the natural and universal views of humankind *(koinai ennoiai),* along with the obligation to worship God,
5. and consequently from the *consensus gentium* [consensus of the nations] (another Stoic idea).[111]

The question of defining the nature of theology is answered synthetically by reviewing Scholastic and contemporary opinions.[112] As the *genus proximum* there is a choice between the Aristotelian *habitus* of science (according to Thomas, with his arguments) and wisdom. If one wants to squeeze theology into that framework, it can most readily be defined as wisdom, but more accurately as *habitus* νέος δότος [newly given habit], that is, a habit granted by God and not (just) obtained through learning and practice.[113] Gerhard sees clearly that theology can be grasped but inadequately with the five Aristotelian *habitus* and has a different source than that of the natural sciences. With the Franciscan tradition he maintains the at least indirectly practical character of theology.[114]

109. Gerhard, *Loci,* prooem. §4 (1:1–2); see also Wallmann, *Theologiebegriff,* 33–45.

110. Gerhard, *Loci,* prooem. §§5–6 (1:2); on the inclusion of the rabbis, see also Steiger, "Kirchenvater," 59–61.

111. Ibid., §7 (1:2).

112. Ibid., §§8–31 (1:2–8).

113. From Aristoteles, *Eth. Nik.* A 10, 1099 b 12; see also Wallmann, *Theologiebegriff,* 71–75.

114. The practical character is strongly emphasized by Steiger, *Johann Gerhard,* 27–45.

The "division" of theology takes place whenever possible by way of dichotomy, as required by the later tabular presentations.[115] Luther's distinction between true and false theology is not a division, however, but rather an equivocal use of language, since false theology (divided into *vulgaris* and *philosophica*) cannot be considered as theology in the proper sense. True theology can be observed in God (Ἀρχήτυπος), in Christ as the Head of the Church (ἔκτυπος [the figure stamped out according to the pattern], *theologia unionis*) and in rational creatures as its members. Here, according to the subject's status in salvation history, we should distinguish between the theology of the saints who have already attained the beatific vision (whether angels or men, *theologia comprehensorum*) and that of believers who are still on the way *(theologia viatorum)*. The latter *(theologia revelationis et viae)* is either natural or supernatural. Natural theology, which Gerhard has already presupposed in his proof of the existence of theology, is either innate in the form of the κοιναὶ ἔννοιαι of universal human principles, or else acquired. These principles are on the one hand of a theoretical nature, insofar as they convince man of God's existence, goodness and justice, but on the other hand of a practical nature, insofar as they oblige him to worship God. Acquired natural theology originates in the contemplation of creatures; a distinction must be made according to its status in salvation history (unlike innate natural theology, which is the same throughout history). Before the fall it was substantially more complete than now, when according to the Lutheran understanding only feeble vestiges of man's likeness to God remain. Supernatural theology is found in an extraordinary manner in those to whom revelation was entrusted (prophets, apostles), but ordinarily it is acquired through the Lutheran triad of prayer, careful meditation while reading and hearing Scripture, and testing by temptation *(oratio, meditatio, tentatio)*.[116] Despite the overall practical orientation it can be divided into theoretical and practical theology.

Supernatural theology is at all points a theology of revelation, founded upon the God who reveals himself as the chief efficient cause and upon the (internal and external) Word of God as the instrumental cause. Its adequate epistemological principle [*or* principle of knowledge] is therefore revelation, which is given definitively in sacred Scripture. In contrast, Thomas and Capreolus notwithstanding, the articles of faith are not principles of theol-

115. See, for example, the division of J. Fr. König in Ratschow, *Dogmatik,* 1:32–33.

116. Summarized from Luther WA 50, 658, 29–659, 4; see also Wallmann, *Theologiebegriff,* 74–75.

ogy, but rather are themselves based on Scripture, which is proved in detail from the attributes of principles according to the *Posterior Analytics.*[117] In no instance is human reason a second principle alongside revelation. The recognition or adoption of natural truths in theology takes place purely on the basis of the principles of revelation theology, which is to say, from Scripture. Therefore theological conclusions are unassailable, that is, not open to criticism by philosophical reasoning. The theological truths that make up the proper subject matter of theological instruction are consequently the principles and conclusions derived from the revealed Word, their proper epistemological principle [principle of knowledge]. Since theology ought to serve the purpose of the glorification of God and the salvation of man, and since its object, after the glorification of God, is man in need of redemption, the method suited to it is actually that of the practical sciences, after the model of medicine: The first matter to be treated is the original endowment and the fall of man, then the means to attain the goal. In the concluding definition the concept of theology is summarized: "Theology (considered systematically and abstractly) is a doctrine built up from the Word of God, through which men are instructed in the true faith and in a pious life unto eternal life. Considered as a *habitus* and concretely, theology is a God-given habit, bestowed on man through the Word by the Holy Spirit, which enables him, instructed through the illumination of his mind, to affirm affectively with his heart what he has grasped with his understanding upon recognizing the divine mysteries and to carry it out in deed unto his salvation, but also to instruct others about these divine mysteries and the way to salvation and to defend this heavenly truth against corruption and gainsayers, so that men might be led by the true faith and good works to the kingdom of heaven."[118]

2.3 Anti-Scholastic "Scholasticism": Abraham Calov

The self-confidence of Lutheran orthodoxy *"in Alma Cathedra Lutheri"* ["in the dear professorial chair of Luther"], the battle against all deviant doctrines, in particular the syncretism of the Helmstadt scholar Georg Calixt (1586–1656),[119] and a thorough systematic development of philosophy, understood encyclopedically, are combined in the "Lutheran pope," the

117. Gerhard, *Loci* §§18–21 (1:4–5).
118. Ibid., § 31 (I, 8).
119. See Henke, *Georg Calixtus;* Merkt, *Das patristische Prinzip,* 37–85.

Wittenberg professor Abraham Calov (1612–1686).[120] Even the dedication of his *Systema Locorum Theologicorum* (1655) to Elector Johann Georg of Saxony (1634–1686) shows the complete self-assurance of Wittenberg theology as *"Zion Saxonica"* [i.e., the Saxon mother of all true believers, see Psalm 87:5]: this theology is founded on the *"sacrae institutiones"* of Scripture and is therefore, in biblical terms, *"typus doctrinae, forma sanorum verborum, depositum sacrum"* ["the pattern of doctrine, the formula of sound words, the sacred deposit"], the treasure of the kingdom of heaven, the pearl of great price, the tree of the knowledge of good and evil, indeed the tree of life, the spring of salvation, spiritual paradise, and divine beehive.[121] Calov situates his theological work in the tradition of the Church Fathers and humanist theology (with references to Jakob Faber Stapulensis [ca. 1450–1536] and Jodok Clichtovaeus [ca. 1472–1543]) and distances himself from medieval Scholasticism, which is envisaged with its summas and commentaries on the *Sentences.* After that darkness, Luther appears as a light-bearer, thanks to whom theology was subsequently restored again to its genuine and ancient *"modus tractandi"* ["method of treating matters"] by Melanchthon, Ægidius Hunnius (1550–1603), and Leonhard Hutter (1563–1616). Through the influence of this reform of theology, much was reformed among the Catholics also, even among the early Jesuits; yet the old Scholasticism, with its deficient knowledge of languages and its useless questions was still prevalent to a great extent. In contrast to mere allegiance to a school as epitomized in the *Summa Angelica* [of Aquinas], *Seraphica* [of Bonaventure] or *Subtilis* [of Scotus], the Reformation scriptural principle states: *"Nobis Summa plusquam Seraphica est Scriptura sacra, et Doctor unicus Christus"* ["Our more-than-seraphic Summa is Sacred Scripture, and our only Doctor is Christ"].[122] Calov does not reject entirely, however, the Scholastic theology of the Catholic tradition, but rather recommends a *"moderatum Scholasticorum Theologorum studium"* ["guided study of the Scholastic Theologians"] with regard to the controversies. He can get along with a definition of Scholastic theology in the sense of systematic theology along the lines of Peter Lombard and Melchior Cano.[123] On the contrary, one should not share

120. See Leinsle, *Ding,* 411–33; Tholuck, *Geist,* 185–211; Leube, *Kalvinismus,* 232–330; on his philosophy, see Sparn, "Schulphilosophie," 375–78.

121. A. Calov, *Systema Locorum Theologicorum e Sacra potissimum Scriptura et antiquitate, nec non adversariorum confessione, Doctrinam, Praxin et Controversiarum fidei tum veterum tum imprimis recentiorum pertractationem luculentam exhibens* (Wittenberg, 1655), Widmung (vol. I, Wid. 4–7).

122. Ibid. (I, Wid. 7–23).

123. Ibid., Proleg. c.1 s.2 q.15 (1:75–81): *Utrum Theologiae scholasticae auctoritas sine fidei dis-*

Cano's praise for those who compiled sentences, summulas and quodlibets. Together with the humanist critics, to whom Calov refers individually, one should reject in particular the method of the Scholastics. *"Theologia Patristica et Scholastica"* in this sense, as an historical discipline, forms only an unimportant addition to *Theologia acroamatica* (scientific theology).[124]

In another sense Calov himself professes a *theologia scholastica,* namely, as one part of theology as a whole as it was clearly subdivided by Johann Gerhard. This is defined as a practical habit of knowledge derived from divine revelation; it deals with the true religion through which fallen man is to be led through faith to eternal salvation.[125] It should be subdivided into *theologia catechetica* (catechetical instruction) and *acroamatica* (scientific theology). The latter is divided into *scholastica* and *ecclesiastica,* whereby Scholastic theology in turn falls under the headings of *exegetica* and *didactica,* and the latter is further subdivided into polemic theology (controversies) and systematic theology *(loci communes).* Ecclesiastical, or in the special sense, "practical" theology, on the other hand, consists of ascetical doctrine, homiletics, and casuistry. Theology is therefore at least partially an academic discipline and therefore precisely in its systematic part requires an academic method so as to attain its end of σωματοποίησις, the formation of *"unum corpus fidei"* ["one body of faith"].[126] Calov creates one by alternating *theoremata didactica,* doctrines or precepts, which are then explained in detail (s. 1), and *quaestiones* (usually current controversies, s. 2), with a very clear structure in each case (gainsayers or opponents—proofs of the thesis while citing probative authorities exactly).

If we survey only the questions (seventeen in chapter 1 and twenty-one in chapter 2) in the theory of theology, which runs to 267 pages, we can speak at any rate about a certain re-Scholasticizing of Lutheran theology. Thus, for example, in opposition to all supporters of absolute predestination there is a discussion of whether the *theologia paradisiaca* was based purely on the Law or already on the Gospel, and what headings it consisted of. In the seventeen *loci communes* of paradise theology, according to

crimine contemni, eiusque accuratiori Theologiae carere non possit? [Can the authority of Scholastic theology be disregarded without imperilling the faith, and can one do without its more accurate theology?] According to Cano a *"scholasticus theologus"* is someone *"qui de deo, rebus divinis, apte prudenter, docte literis institutisque sacris ratiocinetur"* ["who reasons fittingly, prudently and learnedly about God and divine things by means of Sacred Scriptures and precepts"].

124. Ibid., s.1 (1:12–14).

125. Ibid. (1:1).

126. Ibid. (1:11–13).

Calov, not a trace of the Gospel is to be found.[127] The philosopher Calov pays particular attention, naturally, to the relation between philosophy and theology.[128] Luther's teaching about the double truth, reiterated by Daniel Hofmann, applies in Calov's opinion only to propositions which necessarily seem absurd to pure philosophy, such as *"Verbum caro factum est"* ["the Word was made flesh"], and to the misuse of philosophy. Philosophy can by no means be rejected as contradictory to theology, as beastly, earthly, impure, and demonic (as the fanatics and *theosophi* claim). This is proved by Romans 1:19–20; Romans 2:14 and from the common origin of philosophy and theology in God, whose gifts they are, as even Melanchthon teaches. Philosophy, moreover, leads us to the knowledge of God; the individual disciplines thereof (physics, astronomy, music, arithmetic, geometry, architecture, and practical philosophy) are praised in Scripture. Augustine underscores the usefulness of philosophy for theology, especially in logic, methodology, physics, and ethics, and it is recommended by the Church Fathers. If, however, philosophy is to be learned from sacred Scripture, as the *"novelli prophetae"* ["new prophets"] say, then how can it be carnal and demonic? The only thing to be rejected is the misuse of philosophy, but by no means the *"notitia naturalis"* ["natural knowledge"], which still exists in man's sinful state as a small vestige of his likeness to God. Apparent contradictions are easy to resolve by making distinctions. Philosophy, nevertheless, should remain within its limits as a matter of principle. Calov strictly rules out a mixture of philosophical and theological subjects.

Calov, a trained mathematician, was characteristically a systematic thinker. Now the topical organization of the *Loci* no longer sufficed; a *system* of *loci* had to be devised instead. Even more than in his 1655 *Systema* this becomes evident in the *Theologia positiva*[129] that he composed for his son

127. Ibid., s.2 q.3 (1:22–26). The *loci* are: *de Deo, de creatione, de imagine Dei, de angelis, de providentia divina, de revelationibus Dei, de lege, de cultu et invocatione Dei, de sabbati sanctificatione, de peccato et poena peccati, de Ecclesia et omnium hominum sanctorum cognitione, de Ministerio Ecclesiastico (Adam übertragen mit Ehe- und Zeugungsauftrag), de Magisterio Politico (Herrschaft über Geschöpfe, Vorrang des Mannes vor der Frau), de Conjugio, de Morte tum corporali, tum aeterna, de Fine huius vitae, de vita aeterna.* [on God, on creation, on the image of God, on the angels, on divine providence, on God's revelations, on the Law, on the worship and invocation of God, on keeping the Sabbath holy, on sin and the punishment thereof, on the Church and the knowledge of all holy men, on ecclesiastical ministry (Adam is charged with the duty of marriage and procreation), on political authority (dominion over creatures, the precedence of man over woman), on marriage, on death—both physical and eternal, on the end or goal of this life, on eternal life.]

128. Ibid., q.14 (1:67–75).

129. A. Calov, *Theologia positiva, per definitiones, causas, affectiones, et distinctiones, locos Theo-*

Abraham († 1685). In the Protestant tradition, as opposed to the Catholic, *"theologia positiva,"* a translation of "θεολογία θετική," designates the simple presentation of theology in the form of theses with short proofs, dispensing with *quaestiones* and controversies.[130] Like Ariadne's thread in the labyrinth, it serves in the first place as a guide through the bewildering complexity of Scriptural exegesis and thereby fulfills the original purpose of systematic theology (e.g., in Peter Lombard). Thus Calov offers here the outline of a *Systema* in 1,135 paragraphs printed on 610 octavo pages. The structure in itself follows the analytical method that is obligatory for practical sciences: the end and the means for attaining it. Actually, though, this schema is combined with a model from the theory of science which tries to explain the entire structure of theology in terms of its definition (end—subject—means). After the prolegomena about theology, religion, revelation, sacred Scripture, and the articles of faith, the end or goal of theology is presented (part 1): God and the blessed enjoyment of him (the latter topic, of course, is not treated, but creation and providence instead). The subject of theology (part 2) is subdivided into indirect (angels) and direct (man), resulting in *angelognosia* and *anthropologia* (including sin, works, law, and Gospel). Then part 3 deals with the causes and means of salvation, namely (sect. 1) the divine economy of salvation (Christology, soteriology), the Church (*Ecclesiometria,* sect. 2), the means of salvation from God's perspective (word and sacrament, sect. 3) and from man's (*soteropoiia,* sect. 4, in chapters that are often very short: call to the Church, illumination, rebirth, conversion, justification, justifying faith, repentance, mystical union with the faithful and with Christ, anointing by the Spirit, sanctification, glorification, sin against the Holy Spirit, election, reprobation, the cross as the identification papers or passport of the elect), divine legislation (*divina nomothesia* in the Decalogue, sect. 5), and eschatology (sect. 6, in eight articles).

This structure clearly shows the intention to proceed reflectively, methodically and systematically, which collides, however, with the theological material. Whereas most of the third part, *"de causis et mediis salutis"* can be explained in terms of the analytical structure, even this arrangement would allow for alternative ways of including certain individual doctrines, for ex-

logicos universos, succincte, justoque ordine proponens: Ceu Compendium Systematis Theologici (Wittenberg, 1682).

130. Ibid., Dedication: *"Theologia positiva, qua thesin et dicta probantia sibi familiarem reddiderit, solidum fundamentum iacturum universae Theologiae."* ["With positive theology, whereby the reader will become acquainted with the thesis and the proofs, he will lay the foundation of universal theology."]

ample, Law and Gospel *(nomothesia)* and eschatology. The arrangement of the *soteropoiia* still clearly betrays the topical origin of the individual *loci.* The *theologia positiva* also shows, however, the tendency of Protestant "Scholastic" theology, which had again become academic, to produce smaller and smaller mnemonically organized textbooks for memorization and reference in school.[131]

2.4 Theology in one sentence: Johann Adam Scherzer

The trend toward the academic textbook took complete possession of theology in the writings of Johann Adam Scherzer (1628–1683), a philosopher and theologian from Leipzig.[132] Scherzer, like his teacher, Johannes Hülsemann, was a proponent of the so-called *methodus definitiva,* whereby one sets out from a definition and then explains all of its components in the *exegesis.* Since the definition in question was real, the hope was to give thereby a complete explanation of the matter. In his *Systema Theologiae*[133] the "Calov of Leipzig" presents theology as a whole in 29 definitions, still in the arrangement of the *loci,* but this is the only possible systematic order, because it was used even by God in his catechetical instruction of the Jews and pagans. The definitional method provides familiarity with the matter, leads to the discovery of truth and moreover greatly aids the memory; it makes all the lines, so to speak, reach out synthetically from the midpoint and come back to it again analytically. The exegesis should if at all possible prove orthodox teaching conclusively from Scripture against all errors; Scherzer is just as concerned about the purity of this teaching as Calov. The execution is also stereotypical: The individual phrases of the definitions (which can run to three quarters of a page)[134] are elucidated in paragraphs and the *errores* are listed, whereby Scherzer understands error in a broader sense than heresy. Theology thus becomes at the same time a polemical defense against all deviant doctrines: *"Sententiam orthodoxam plane proponimus, adversam reprobamus."*[135] For the task of theology consists also of a three-step process: *"tradere Thesin et Dialysin atque Elenchum"* ["to relate the thesis, the

131. For similar trends in Wittenberg philosophy, see: Leinsle, *Ding,* 288–92 (C. Bartholinus [1585–1629]), 337–51 (J. Scharf [1595–1660]).

132. See Leinsle, *Reformversuche,* 20–26; Sparn, "Schulphilosophie," 520–22.

133. J. A. Scherzer, *Systema Theologiae, XXIX Definitionibus absolutum* (1680); edition consulted: (Leipzig-Frankfurt, 1691), 872 pp. in quarto.

134. For example, the definition of Christ, loc.8 (172–175).

135. Ibid., Praefatio. ["We propose the orthodox opinion plainly and condemn the opposing one."]

explication and the refutation"], which is proved from 1 Corinthians 3:11 and 2 Timothy 3:16. Theology is accordingly divided into *theologia positiva seu didactica* (considered here as identical, since the theology that employs theses is the scientific form), the *hermeneutica seu exegetica* and the *polemica seu elenchtica.*[136] Metaphysics is now completely incorporated into theology, as evident especially in Christology, and also in the treatment of the *status exinanitionis* [state of self-emptying, *kenosis*], in which the manner of the Logos' presence and the manner of his dominion over the universe are discussed thoroughly.[137]

Scherzer's polemics were no less formidable than those of his prototype in Wittenberg, as is proved by his controversial writings on the occasion of the conversion of Johannes Scheffler (Angelus Silesius [1624–1677]) 1664/65,[138] his *Bibliotheca Pontificia* (1677), the *Collegium Anti-Socinianum* (1672), the *Anti-Bellarminus* (1681), and the *Disputationes Anti-Calvinianae* (1681). He prefers to debate with the Jesuits (especially those at the University of Dillingen), whereas on the other hand in his very popular *Vade mecum sive Manuale Philosophicum* (1654), which was studied by Gottfried Wilhelm Leibniz (1646–1716) and Christian Wolff (1679–1754), he simply adopts the *distinctiones philosophicae* of the Dillingen Jesuit Georg Reeb (1594–1662).[139] In the final *locus* of the *Systema* he proves in detail from the attributes of the Antichrist, contrary to Adam Tanner and Lorenz Forer, that only the Roman pope should be regarded as the Antichrist.[140]

This academic contraction of orthodoxy according to the definitional method reaches its climax, however, in Scherzer's *Breviculus theologicus,* in which he summarizes all of theology in one sentence (with numerous parentheses and a sprinkling of Greek terms) in eleven duodecimo pages. This sentence is previously elucidated in 158 paragraphs over the course of 245 pages.[141] This method places Scherzer himself in the tradition of the early Scholastic summas, which tried to present a *"verbum abbreviatum"* as the core of sacred Scripture and at the same time to provide a summa of the-

136. Ibid., Proleg. §16 (4).

137. Ibid., loc.8 §25 (221–39).

138. See Reichert, *Johannes Scheffler.*

139. Johann Adam Scherzer, *Vade mecum sive Manuale philosophicum,* reprinting of the 1675 Leipzig edition, edited with an introduction by Stephan Meier-Oeser (Stuttgart–Bad Cannstatt, 1996); see also Leinsle, *Reformversuche,* 21–22; Leinsle, *Dilinganae Disputationes,* 73–79.

140. Scherzer, *Systema Theologiae,* loc. 28 (843–72).

141. Scherzer, *Breviculus theologicus, Unica Positione generali, Systema Theologiae exhibens* (1675). Edition consulted: (Leipzig, 1687). German edition: *Kurzer Weg und Handgriff durch einen Hauptsatz den Kern Heiliger Schrifft zu fassen* (Leipzig, 1677); new edition 1732.

ology. All forty-three *loci* of theology are supposed to be contained in this sentence, which is composed as a comprehensive definition of *"theologia."* In the explanations the previously listed opponents are noted only by abbreviations in the margins.

The revealed theology of human beings on their pilgrim way (the only kind of theology treated here) is accordingly the wisdom which hands down, explains and defends the true religion for the honor of God and the salvation of mankind (loc. 1, *de theologia*); it does so on the basis of sacred Scripture. The latter consists of the Law and the Gospel; it is worthy of belief both in light of God's truthfulness and also on its own merits; it is one, true, good and thus *catholica* (loc. 2, *de Scriptura*). It is revealed by God. He is indefinable, pure spirit, everlasting, immortal, immense, omnipresent, uniquely eternal, without temporal duration, omniscient, omnipotent, supremely good; in accordance with his stern and equally merciful will he imparts himself to all, but punishes with the necessary severity. He alone therefore is to be honored in religion (loc. 3, *de Deo*). He is by nature one in three Persons (loc. 4, *de Trinitate*). The Father begets the Son, who is truly God, of the same nature as the Father; of the ever-Virgin Mary he became the God-Man, fully God and fully man in the hypostatic union (and he is consequently the Son of God according to his human nature also) with the communication of the *idiomata.* He exercises a threefold ministry; for he is anointed by the Holy Spirit with immeasurable riches to be the prophet of the Good News, the sole and sinless priest of the New Testament, and king. Thus he is mediator between the two natures, and through the obedience of his life and death he makes satisfaction and is thereby for us the one universal Savior and Redeemer. He divests himself of everything, even unto death. Although during the three days of his death the natural bond between his soul and his body is broken, the latter was not a cadaver, nor did Christ cease to exist during that time. After the revival of his humanity by his own power and his exaltation, he is the future judge of the living and the dead (loc. 5, *de Christo*). The Holy Spirit proceeds as the Third Divine Person from the Father and the Son (loc. 6, *de Spiritu Sancto*). The whole Trinity, however, is the Creator of the universe, that is, of heaven and earth (loc. 7, *de creatione*), of the angels (some of whom were confirmed in their original goodness after the voluntary fall of the others; loc. 8, *de angelis*) and of men, the first of whom was Adam (loc. 9, *de homine*). Man and woman in their original state were perfect, immortal, and supremely happy (loc. 10, *de imagine Dei*); they fell however through their own fault and are now subject to sin from conception and without exception (not even Mary; loc. 11, *de lapsu et peccato*), completely dead to what is spiritual (loc. 12, *de servo arbitrio*). They can be reborn therefore only through an external cause (loc. 13, *de regeneratione*) and restored through the Word and the two salvific sacraments (the efficacy of which depends solely on God's command and not on the intention or holiness of the minister; loc. 14, *de sacramentis in genere*), namely, Baptism by water (loc. 15, *de Baptismo*) and the Eucharist (loc. 16, *de Eucharistia*), in the Church under Christ as the sole Head, who can have no substitute or vicar (loc. 17, *de Ecclesia*). After previously applying the pedagogy addressed to the natural light of reason through the Word (i.e., through *gratia sufficiens* or *efficax,* which however is not irresistible), God calls all men to the Church (loc. 18, *de vocatione*) as penitents (loc. 19, *de poenitentia*) through the forgiveness of sins (loc. 20, *de absolutione*). Instead of these sins, the active and passive justice of Christ is imputed to men, who are justified through faith alone without works (loc. 21, *de justificatione*); they become holy, however, by living in consideration of God, their neighbor and themselves (loc. 22, *de bonis operibus*), without giving scandal (loc. 23, *de scandalo*), [and thus] finally are found to be true to that faith which is the sole object of predestination in man (loc. 25, *de praedestinatione*) and the purpose of providence (loc. 26, *de providentia*), and after this earthly life (loc. 26, *de termino vitae*) die in that faith (loc. 27, *de morte*). The reprobate, however, on account of their unbelief, will be punished at the end of their lives in hell with the devils for eternity, deprived of the vision of God, and the glory of the blessed (loc. 28, *de damnatis et inferno*); anyone who departs with genuine trust in Christ comes immediately to heaven into the presence of God and will rejoice with the blessed (loc. 29, *de statu piorum post mortem*). After the resurrection of the numerically [but not qualitatively] identical bodies [of the departed], regardless of their sex or state of life (loc. 30, *de resurrectione*), and after the Last Judgment of the damned (without the thousand-year reign of the Chiliasts; loc. 31, *de extremo judicio*) and the end of the world (loc. 32, *de consummation saeculi*), they will receive again, in glorified form, their former bodies and in them they will behold God in perfect, ineffable, eternal beatitude (loc. 33, *de glorificatione et vita aeterna*). According to divine law, all men are equal, notwithstanding their hierarchical position (loc. 34, *de tribus Hierarchiis*): whether they are legitimately called and ordained ministers of the Church or their hearers (loc. 35, *de ministerio ecclesiastico*), whether they are the political authorities established by God or their subjects (loc. 36, *de magistrate politico*), whether they are tradesmen (loc. 37, *de statu oeconomico*), single, or married, that is, united with one another by a humanly indissoluble bond, or their children, servants or maids (loc. 38, *de coelibatu et conjugio*), or finally even the universal enemy, the Antichrist (loc. 39, *de Antichristo*), all heretics (loc. 40, *de Haeresi*), schismatics (loc. 41, *de Schismate*), apostates (loc. 42, *de Apostasia*), those who are unwilling to profess allegiance to any religion *(neutrales)* or, like the syncretists, those who try to abolish the differences between the confessions (loc. 43, *de Syncretismo*).[142]

With that, in Scherzer's view, he has completely described theology, but also the world of God's creation until Judgment Day and mankind in all possible ecclesiastical and secular manifestations. Theology thus makes an encyclopedic claim, which is reminiscent of Johann Amos Comenius' *Orbis pictus.* On the other hand theology itself has become the framework of an ontologized Bible that is squeezed into the *loci* of orthodoxy; since there is no way to amplify it further, all that remains is to defend it.

2.5 Theology within the framework of the encyclopedia: Johann Heinrich Alsted

Among the Reformed Christians, Johann Heinrich Alsted (1588–1638), a philosopher and theologian at Herborn and Weissenburg (Alba Julia, Transylvania), explicitly acknowledges a *"theologia scholastica."*[143] However the *"methodus scholastica"* found in his works, which were esteemed in England and Havard, was no longer that of the Middle Ages but rather the academic, didactic presentation of a discipline in terms of *praecepta* (theses) and *regulae* (rules) with short explanations of each. Alsted, who was considerably influenced by Ramism and Lullism, incorporated theology in this form into his encyclopedia of all sciences (1630).[144]

Being a Reformed Christian, Alsted regards sacred Scripture as the basis of the entire encyclopedia in his "biblical encyclopedia," *Triumphus Bibliorum Sacrorum* (1625). In this work he tries on the one hand—in the tradition of *philosophia sacra*—to supply arguments from Scripture in support of philosophy as a whole (even its foundational disciplines), and on

142. Scherzer, *Breviculus* L3v–L8v.

143. J. H. Alsted, *Theologia scholastica didactica exhibens locos communes theologicos Methodo scholastica* (Hanau, 1618); Alsted, *Methodus sacrosanctae theologiae* (Hanau, 1623); Alsted, Compendium *theologiae* (Hanau, 1624); see also Leinsle, *Ding*, 369–393; Schmidt-Biggemann, *Topica*, 100–139. On his influence in England see also Clouse, *Influence;* Klein and Kramer, eds., *Alsted.*

144. J. H. Alsted, *Encyclopaedia* (Herborn, 1630), vol. 5 (reprinted Stuttgart–Bad Cannstatt, 1992, vol. 3).

the other hand to bring Scripture itself into the proper order of the *loci communes* and thus to create a *"systema methodicum."*[145] The program itself shows the intention to devise a method and system, even with regard to sacred Scripture, the importance of which is acknowledged. Indeed, Scripture supplies factual knowledge, method or at least examples for the individual sciences in the encyclopedia.[146] Theology, too, is situated within this encyclopedic framework; for the encyclopedia is understood here as the summary of the four faculties—which are founded on Scripture.[147] Theology itself is defined as *"facultas ad summum bonum perveniendi"* ["the means for attaining the supreme good"]. Its parts are: positive ("biblical" theology in the form of theses without explanations), natural, catechetical, didactic, polemical theology, casuistry, prophetic theology (= pastoral theology), and acroamatic theology (= moral theology).[148]

This whole field of theology is an encyclopedic science and is therefore treated according to the stereotypical encyclopedic (= scientific) method. Alsted is not acquainted with a separate *theologia scholastica* as the Catholics understood it, but rather with a *Scholastic* encyclopedic discipline as the final part of practical philosophy (after politics): *"de felicitate scholastica obtinenda,"* that is, "On the successful establishment and administration of schools."[149] The methodical rules of academic instruction and presentation (if possible in tabular form) that apply to all sciences are provided, though, by the Ramist-topical methodology of logic.[150] The arrangement of the material in tables through successive dichotomies, however, presupposes a reflection on the intrinsic correlation of the parts of theology and of the *loci* with one another.

In the 1630 Encyclopedia Alsted also adopts Bartholomäus Keckermann's definition of theology as *prudentia* (a practical *habitus*) and defines it as *"summa hujus vitae sapientia et prudentia perveniendi ad vitam aeternam"* ["the supreme wisdom of this life and the practical knowledge of how to attain eternal life"].[151] Like all disciplines (even *Tabacologia*), it is to be di-

145. Alsted, *Triumphus Bibliorum Sacrorum Seu Encyclopaedia Biblica* (Frankfurt, 1625), "Mens authoris in hoc opera" (2r); see also Leinsle, "Lehet," 248–51.

146. Alsted, *Triumphus,* Praef. (5v).

147. Ibid., *Technologia sacra* n. 3 (10); with references to 1 Kings 4:29–33; 2 Timothy 3:16; Exodus 21; Genesis 50:2; Colossians 4:14; Ezra 3:2–3.; Sirach 43:2–6.

148. Ibid., n. 7 (13); elaborated on 286–413.

149. Alsted, *Encyclopaedia* 4:1505–49.

150. See Leinsle, *Ding,* 382–83.

151. Alsted, *Encyclopaedia,* Theol. s.1 c.1 (5:1555); on Keckermann's concept of theology, see also Frank, *Vernunft,* 186–204.

vided first into general and special parts. The general part teaches what is necessary for man to know, believe and do in order to reach the goal mentioned in the definition. According to the epistemological principle, theology is either natural or supernatural. The natural type is based on the natural light of reason (with innate principles) and, on the other hand, on the book of nature (world and man). Its goal is the necessary knowledge about the existence and supremacy of God as well as about the obligation to worship God and to love one's fellow man. Now all this can readily be known, independently of revelation, from the nature of reason, man and the world. Natural theology therefore remains for Alsted the basis of revelation theology also.[152]

Initially this is conveyed catechetically in the *Theologia catechetica* as a compendium of the Christian religion which, modeled on the Hessian Catechism of 1607,[153] consists of five chapters: Creed, Ten Commandments, Our Father, Baptism, and Lord's Supper. For this theology, too, a special *modus docendi scholasticus* [academic method of teaching] with three catechism classes is envisaged besides the *modus domesticus* and *ecclesiasticus* [home and church methods].[154] Corresponding exactly to catechetics in its structure is casuistry, which of course deals with the cases of conscience and doubts arising from catechesis.[155] Besides catechetical instruction there is the ecclesiastical form in preaching and church institutions [*Einrichtungen*]. This is the object of *theologia prophetica,* the teaching of the prophetic, that is, pastoral ministry in the Church. It consists of instructional preaching *(rhetorica ecclesiastica)* and *politia ecclesiastica,* teaching about church polity with regard to persons and things.[156] Moral theology (in its noncasuistic form), finally, has the goal of forming morals that are worthy of a Christian. After the pattern of practical philosophy it is subdivided into individual ethics, economics [household management] and politics, and it presents its teaching about the duties of all states of life (including that of the *status scholasticus* with the duties of tutors, professors, and students) in the form of rules that can be memorized easily.[157]

The really systematic theology, however, is the *theologia didactica.* This is the system of forty-six *loci theologici* which have now been subdivided di-

152. Alsted, *Encyclopaedia,* Theol. s.1 c.1 (5:1555–65).
153. *BSRK* 822–33.
154. Alsted, *Encyclopaedia,* Theol. s.2 c.1 (5:1565–66); *Theologia Catechetica*: 5:1565–74.
155. Alsted, *Encyclopaedia,* Theol. s.5 (5:1662–74).
156. Ibid., s.6 (5:1674–84).
157. Ibid., s.7 (5:1684–90).

chotomously.[158] Although he had still included it in 1625, Alsted now dispenses with the *theologia positiva,* which contains principles taken directly out of Scripture. Instead he incorporates the positive theology into the didactic, but distinguishes carefully between *regulae positivae,* which require simple assent, and *regulae didacticae,* which serve to elucidate, to confirm, or to refute false doctrines.[159] Thus in loc. 1 *(de sacra scriptura)* we find the following positive rules:

1. Scripture is inspired by God.
2. It is a light, that is, clear [in itself, perspicuous] and a guiding principle of faith and living.
3. It is complete.
4. It is to be read by all Christians.
5. It is read with different results, however, by the pious and the godless.

In Alsted's writings also, didactic theology as a whole can be summarized dichotomously in a comprehensive definition:[160] It deals with sacred Scripture as the principle of all dogmas (loc. 1) and with the dogmas contained therein, namely, God (loc. 2) and his works and deeds (loc. 3). The latter are either eternal—in general his decrees (loc. 4), but in particular his providence (loc. 5) and predestination (loc. 6)—or else temporal in their fulfillment. The fulfillment of providence consists of creation (loc. 7) and his governance of the universe (loc. 8), specifically of non-rational (loc. 9) and of rational nature (loc. 10), that is, of the angels (loc. 11) and of men. Before the fall this concerns the image and likeness of God (loc. 12) and the natural covenant (loc. 13); after the fall, however, it concerns free will (loc. 14), sin (loc. 15) and the limitation thereof through the law in general (loc. 16), but in particular through marriage (loc. 17), political authority (loc. 18), and school (loc. 19). In this life predestination is exercised with regard to the angels (loc. 20) and men under the covenant of grace, which should be considered according to its form (loc. 21) and its foundation, the mediator Christ (loc. 22). The [practical] application [*Anwendung*] of the covenant of grace is proclaimed by the Gospel (loc. 23) in the Church as an assembly (loc. 24) under a leadership that consists chiefly and most profoundly of the administration of God's gifts of grace, the most important of which is vocation (loc. 25)—with the operation of repentance (loc. 26), faith (loc. 27) and holiness (loc. 28)—jus-

158. Ibid., s.3 (5:1575–1638).
159. Ibid., s.3 loc.1 (5:1575–76).
160. Ibid., table (5:1636).

tification (loc. 29) and sanctification in general (loc. 30), and in particular (loc. 31). From these proceed further gifts of grace, namely adoption (loc. 32), Christian freedom (loc. 33), and perseverance (loc. 34). *Loci* 35–37, which are elaborated dichotomously, discuss the further gifts of grace for this life, the external hierarchy and the enemies of the Church. The covenant of grace is sealed by the sacraments (loc. 38) of the OT (loc. 39) and the NT, namely, Baptism (loc. 40) and the Lord's Supper (loc. 41). The fulfillment [*Ausübung*] of predestination after this life consists generally in the Second Coming of Christ (loc. 42), the resurrection of the body (loc. 43), and the Last Judgment (loc. 44), but in particular in eternal life (loc. 45) or else in eternal death (loc. 46). In polemical theology (controversial theology), which really ought to be named irenic theology after its goal, the unity of the churches, this impressive but rather dry system is to be defended against Catholics and Lutherans in its relevant points, which are listed according to Johannes Haller (1523–1575).[161]

2.6 Reformed "Cartesian Scholasticism": Christoph Wittich

The turn away from the subjection of Protestant orthodoxy to Aristotelian philosophy and toward Cartesian philosophy occurs most clearly in the Reformed institutions of higher education in the Netherlands. This was also the place of origin for the form of academic theology that is described as "Cartesian Scholasticism."[162] One of its most outstanding representatives is Christoph Wittich (1625–1687), a professor in Nijmegen and Leiden,[163] who was influenced both by the covenant theology of Johannes Cocceius (1603–1669) and by Cartesianism. Strenuously opposed by his teacher in Groningen, Samuel Maresius (1599–1673), whose textbook he commented on in his lectures, and by Gisbert Voetius (1589–1676),[164] in his *Theologia pacifica* he justifies at length the use of Cartesian philosophy in theology.[165] Wittich's Cartesianism is a comprehensive system of philosophy which includes the foundations of knowledge in the truth-criterion of the clear and distinct perception, or "idea," but also the cosmology of the *Principia phi-*

161. Ibid., s.4 (5:1639–62).

162. See Dibon, *L'enseignement;* Thijssen-Schoute, *Nederlands Cartesianisme;* Bohatec, *Cartesianische Scholastik;* Goudriaan, *Philosophische Gotteserkenntnis.*

163. See Althaus, *Prinzipien,* 108–25.

164. See Heppe-Bizer, *Dogmatik,* lxi–lxiii; Goudriaan, *Gotteserkenntnis.*

165. J. Wittich, *Theologia pacifica in qua varia problemata Theologica inter Reformatos Theologos agitari solita ventilantur, simul Usus Philosophiae Cartesianae in diversis Theologiae partibus demonstratur, et ad Dissertationem Celeberrimi Viri, Samuelis Maresii, De abusu Philosophiae Cartesianae in rebus Theologicis et fidei, modeste respondetur* (Leiden, 1671); edition consulted: Leiden, 1675.

losophiae and the dualistic metaphysics and psychology of Descartes' *Meditationes.* On the other hand we find here already a markedly ontologized Cartesianism of the sort that Johannes Clauberg (1622–1665), a colleague of Wittich in Herborn for a short time, had developed.[166]

In responding to Maresius' accusation that he mingles philosophy and theology, Wittich argues from the basis of the new philosophy. By no means should creaturely categories be imported into theology, for instance into the treatise on God, which was precisely the danger of Aristotelian philosophy. Therefore the turn to Cartesianism is "in the first place not a revolution" in the fundamental relation between philosophy and theology.[167] The Aristotelian-Ramist philosophy that is still in vogue in some places is unusable, however, since it only makes logical concepts available but offers no factual knowledge, favoring prejudices instead on the basis of sensorial experience.[168] On the contrary, the Cartesian truth-criterion of clarity and distinctness must also find an application in theology, specifically with regard to its foundation: revelation. Whatever is not clearly and distinctly recognized as being revealed by God cannot be accepted as such. Just as Descartes ultimately has to have recourse to God's truthfulness, so too must Wittich at this juncture.[169] At any rate, this makes a philosophical criterion decide what is to be accepted as revealed truth. This (theologically founded) criterion of revelation, however, is not an autonomous faculty of reason that accepts only what it can understand independently. Instead Wittich is explicitly emphasizing that one must also accept in faith that which our limited reason cannot comprehend, if it is certain as revealed truth. This acceptance in faith occurs then—occasionally contrary to the Cartesian truth-criterion of clear, distinct perception—on the basis of divine authority, which is more deserving of faith than our intellect.[170] In addition to the external revelation of Scripture, however, there is also the internal revelation through *recta ratio.* The degree of certainty is the same in both cases. We have certainty about our own saving faith not only by indirect but also by direct knowledge.[171] Certified faith in revelation is combined in Wittich's writings with a marked emphasis on God's free will in revealing himself and bestowing grace. This results in a theological critique of human prejudices, especially since our errors are dependent on the will, for affirming and de-

166. See Leinsle, *Reformversuche,* 88–105; Verbeek, ed., *Johannes Clauberg.*
167. Althaus, *Prinzipien,* 111; 111–120.
168. Wittich, *Theol. pacif.* c.1 (1–13).
169. Ibid., c.3 (20–28).
170. Ibid., c.4 (28–31).
171. Ibid., c.11 (93–94).

nying are acts of the will. Voluntarism in his teaching about salvation and grace allows Wittich here, too, to remain within the framework of his Reformed confession and to counter the accusation of Pelagianism or Semi-pelagianism.[172]

Clearly Wittich's Cartesian principles affect the cosmology that he presents according to the scheme of Descartes' *Principia;* for sacred Scripture does not offer us sufficient evidence for a consistent cosmology. But when revelation is not unequivocal, philosophy can and must come to its aid.[173] Cartesian cosmology, of course, follows natural laws, but these are assumed at least hypothetically to be ordered by God's will. Speculations about moon-dwellers cannot be decided based on Scripture any more than the question of whether all the works on a given day of creation took place in a single moment or in succession. Philosophically, in contrast, it can be shown that an instantaneous creation of all the works of a day is self-contradictory.[174] An indefinite extension of the world according to Cartesian principles contradicts neither reason nor revelation; yet even an infinite world—despite Maresius' objections—would be within God's infinite power.[175] Cartesian mechanics, which dispense with final causes, is interpreted theologically within the framework of a revealed faith of fallen human reason: we may not investigate ends and decrees that God has not revealed to us. In Romans 9:20 and Romans 11:33–36 we are explicitly warned against doing so. A clear distinction should be made between the usefulness (function) of a thing and God's objective.[176]

Dualist metaphysics and psychology are cited at great length in Wittich's teaching about God and anthropology (including the doctrine of the *passiones animae).*[177] The most important ideas that the theologian borrows from Cartesian philosophy, however, are the true nature of the mind, the priority of will over reason and the exact relation between knowledge and will in desire. Wittich considers a disregard for the clear distinction between *res cogitans* [the thinking thing] and *res extensa* [the extended object] as the root of many heresies and errors. Without this distinction one cannot even defend rationally the immortality of the soul.[178] In contrast to traditional Scholasticism, however, Cartesianism cannot recognize subsistence that is

172. Ibid., c.5 (31–41).
173. Ibid., c.2 (13–20); see also Althaus, *Prinzipien,* 120–22.
174. Wittich, *Theol. pacif.* c.7 (47–59).
175. Ibid., c.8 (59–74).
176. Ibid., c.9 (75–83).
177. Ibid., c.6 (41–47).
178. Ibid., c.10 (83–93).

really distinct. In Wittich's view, nevertheless, this is an advantage in demonstrating the subsistence of the *anima separata* [separated soul]. It is more difficult to harmonize the non-spatial nature of the soul with this idea: one can attribute a place to it only as an operative principle (in the body or outside of it), but not to the soul per se; the same is true of angels, pure spirits who act purely through their will and are essentially *res cogitantes* [things that think].[179]

Cartesian philosophy, moreover, can counter any sort of empiricism; for the axiom, "there is nothing in the intellect that was not previously in the senses," is just not true, as our knowledge of God sufficiently demonstrates.[180] This knowledge is innate—a theory which can readily be combined with the Philippo-Ramist tradition of the κοιναὶ ἔννοιαι In any case God is a substance, especially since substance, according to Descartes, is not combined with accidents but only with *modi.* Consequently God's attributes must be pondered anew in regard to their compatibility with Cartesian philosophy. As in man, so too in God the will is the predominant faculty. God's will is therefore the cause of all that is true and good and of all reality, of uncreated possibilities also. Thus God is the first truth and the cause of all truth in the world. On the other hand God's power is limitless; hence what is contradictory for our way of thinking and rightly rejected as absurd is not necessarily so for God. Wittich logically rejects a divine ubiquity in the strict sense, since it contains spatial notions (even with reference to imaginary spaces) and cannot be predicated before creation; it is better to speak of God's presence everywhere *(omnipraesentia)* with regard to his operation, his power and his nature.[181] The optimal principle dominates throughout the treatise on God's decrees: *"Deus semper facit id quod est optimum."*[182] ["God always does what is best."]

Finally, in the Christology and the soteriology, the Cartesian denial of absolute accidents, of the real distinction between essence and potencies, and between essence and existence, becomes problematic. The Hypostatic Union is therefore understood along the lines of the human body-soul composite. The Incarnation occurs at the moment when Christ's soul is united with his body.[183] With remarkable intensity Wittich applies to Christologi-

179. Ibid., c.12–13 (113–163). The manner of their movement is discussed at length.
180. Ibid., c.11 (93–113); see also Goudriaan, *Gotteserkenntnis,* 202–30.
181. Wittich, *Theol. pacif.* c.14–15. (163–94).
182. Ibid., c.16 (194–95); see also Knebel, "Necessitas moralis ad optimum"; Ramelow, *Gott.*
183. Wittich, *Theol. pac.* c.16 (194–216).

cal and soteriological questions a sort of linguistic criticism and exegetical procedure that also dominates his interpretation of controversial passages in the final chapters of his work.[184] The "Scholastic" inquiries of Reformed orthodoxy are rethought here on the basis of a new philosophy, which certainly does not answer all the questions in the usual way yet despite its unique character as a dualistic, voluntaristic metaphysics does not shatter the fundamental theoretical framework of "scholastic" Protestant theology.

3 God and modern man: The debate about grace

No debate within the Catholic world preoccupied Scholastic theology of the early modern period as long or as intensely as the so-called debate about grace (more precisely: about the means of grace) between the Jesuits who followed Luis de Molina (1535–1600), on the one hand, and the strict Thomists on the other, who belonged chiefly to the ranks of the Dominicans (Dominicus Bañez), Discalced Carmelites, and Benedictines.[185] From the theoretical scientific perspective, this is a case of two competing theoretical systems, which through a papal decision dated August 28, 1607, both received at least "the right to hospitality [i.e., a courteous hearing], liberty of action and the freedom to make propaganda" in the Church.[186] Substantially it is a question of nothing less than the status and efficacy of God vis-à-vis the modern consciousness of man's freedom. With regard to ecclesiastical politics, for a time there was reason to fear a schism, which is why the leading courts of Europe were involved in the debate also. The debate acquired interdenominational significance through the fact that Calvinist orthodoxy adopted the Thomist doctrine of predestination, while Lutheran orthodoxy took up the Molinist position.[187] The decisive theoretical outlines will be presented here not in terms of their origin and development but by way of examples at the level of Scholastic discussion.

3.1 Man as a free instrument of God: Francisco Suárez

To define God's efficacy vis-à-vis man while acknowledging the nature and freedom of the latter—as opposed to the Lutheran thesis of *"servum ar-*

184. Ibid., c.17–21 (217– ff.).

185. See *HDG* III, 5b, 93–108; Stegmüller, *Molinismus;* Werner, *Scholastik* IV/2 (Vienna, 1887), 70–94.

186. Stegmüller, *Molinismus,* 63*. The Jesuits of Salamanca celebrated the decision with festivities including a bullfight: *HDG* III, 5b, 104.

187. See W. Hübener, "Praedeterminatio physica," *HWPh* 7:1216–25; crucial corrections in

bitrium" ["servile or slavish will"]—means to find a theory that can explain the supernatural operation and the natural freedom or at least preserve them. Such a theory is provided by the *"Doctor Eximius"* ["Extraordinary Doctor"], Francisco Suárez (1548–1617) in his assumption that there is a *potentia oboedientialis activa*[188] [active obediential potency], a thesis that he first published in his 1590 commentary on part III of Thomas' *Summa*. This largely metaphysical theory is discussed within the context of the treatise on the Incarnation as part of the question: What proper power or potency enables Christ's humanity to operate miraculously as the instrument of the divine Logos (s. 5)? The question is generalized in section 6: Whether there is in created things some *"vis activa oboedientialis"* ["active obediential power"] that enables them to be raised to the status of God's instruments. The theory of a *"potentia oboedientialis"*[189] was influential from Augustine via Thomas down to Karl Rahner; to accept it is to declare that creatures are created in such a way that they are enabled, above and beyond their natural operations and their capabilities, to obey the will of God in supernatural operations [*Wirkungen*] also. This ability is generally recognized among theologians as a passive ability to obey, yet this is not sufficient for Suarez, precisely in the case of human beings who act freely. Since every operation has to correspond to a like potency, and since supernatural activities (e.g., believing) are real activities of a human being, we must assume that there is not only a purely passive potency but rather a *potentia oboedientialis activa* in things, by which they can achieve supernatural operations, not by their own power, of course (that would be crude Pelagianism), but rather merely as God's instruments. The instrumentality of freely acting creatures is nevertheless taken seriously also, insofar as a suitable cooperation on the part of the instrument—one that surpasses the general constitution of creatures as God's instruments in producing natural operations—must correspond to the effect.[190] In principle this active obediential power extends to all possible supernatural operations of God, that is, to everything that does not involve a contradiction and is thus possible for God.

Suárez is aware that he is introducing a new theory, which therefore

---

Sparn, "Subjekte," 173–79: the connection in Protestantism concerns mainly the doctrine of predestination and not the teaching about grace.

188. F. Suárez, *De Incarnatione,* disp. 31 s.5–6, in *Opera omnia* (Paris, 1877), 18:103–152; on the development of Suárez' teaching on grace: Stegmüller, *Gnadenlehre.*

189. See O. Wanke in *HWPh* 7:1166, where, however, he does not discuss the *potentia oboedientialis activa* in the writings of Suárez.

190. Suárez, *De Incarn.* disp.31 s.5 n.7 (18:105–106b).

has to be discussed according to all the criteria for developing a theological theory:

1. It is free from contradiction. It is not logically inconsistent that God designed creatures in that way.
2. It has a certain degree of probability and credibility based on reasonable arguments and authorities.
3. It resolves the questions related to the matter without excessive difficulties.

Being a genuine metaphysician, Suárez regards the active instrumentality of creatures as something already present in the complete concept of created being. This instrumentality does not become active, however, without the *agens principale*, just as a tool cannot work by itself.[191] Furthermore it does not mean a directly active ability to do something independently, but rather only a more remote condition which makes the creature not *potens* ["able," in the sense of having both power and mastery] but rather *capax* [capable] of being elevated by God to a supernatural mode of operation.[192] Like any new theory, this one also faces formidable objections, which Suárez meticulously lists and ultimately refutes. Particularly weighty is the accusation that it involves a subtle Pelagianism and a confusion of the natural and the supernatural orders, since the theory assumes a natural endowment of man to accomplish what is supernatural and thus appears to deny the absolute necessity of grace for any good work.[193] Suárez initially carries out the positive proof of the new theory starting from metaphysical principles that are acknowledged by his opponents also:

1. Action presupposes in its cause a power to act.
2. The power to act as an instrument is not a special, superadded quality in God's instruments over and above their ontological endowment.
3. The power to act as God's instrument is not a movement transferred to the instrument.[194]

Based on these premises, Suárez defines what the "elevation" of the creature to an instrument of God actually involves. It is not purely a matter of terminology, nor is it a mere subordination to God's will; rather it signifies the elaboration of a creaturely endowment to a higher or nobler status.

191. Ibid., s.5 n.8 (106b–107a).
192. Ibid., s.5 n.9 (107a).
193. Ibid., s.6 n.4 (108a).
194. Ibid., s.6 n.10–17 (110b–114b).

Therefore it presupposes something that is elevated and an *"agens superius"* ["higher agent"] that brings about this elevation with a superior natural [*physischer*] efficacy. Here again there are three possibilities:

1. The entire operative power is imparted to the thing through the addition of an inner form: for example, the warming of water.
2. Through the addition of an inner form a potency, which by itself is insufficient, is rendered capable of operating (e.g., understanding and will through grace to perform supernatural works).
3. The operative power is perfected through union with an external cause and is thus enabled to perform an operation for which the thing by itself is incapable and unsuited. This is precisely the case with elevation to the status of an instrument of God; it presupposes however a *"vis activa et intrinseca"* ["an active, intrinsic power"] on the part of the thing being elevated.[195]

Suárez defends himself vigorously against the suspicion of Pelagianism yet at the same time admits that his theory includes within the creaturely endowment of man a causal element which is partially responsible for supernatural operations. By themselves, however, creatures cannot produce such effects (as instruments), but rather only with a kind of supernatural help, the nature of which is left unspecified.[196] Indeed, the precise manner of this supernatural help is the subject of the debate *"de auxiliis."* The foundation of cooperation with God *(fundamentum cooperationis),* however, must exist in nature. For Suárez this is in no way Pelagianism but rather the safeguarding of human freedom against Luther's view.[197] In order for a created entity to be capable of being taken up by God as an instrument in the full sense, therefore, we must assume that there is within it, by virtue of its ontological endowment, an activity oriented toward this instrumental operation. Before its elevation to the status of an instrument, nevertheless, this is only a fundamental, rather remote disposition to "obedience" vis-à-vis God's action.[198] The creature is by no means purely passive with regard to this elevation to instrumental status; this happens, rather, through

195. Ibid., s.6 n.31–32 (121b).

196. Ibid., s.6 n.43 (124a): *"ita etiam de fide certum, cum supernaturali auxilio (quicquid illud sit) posse illos efficere."* ["Thus as an article of faith also it is certain that with supernatural help (whatever it may be) they can produce effects" i.e., of a supernatural nature.]

197. Ibid., s.6 n.44 (124a–125a).

198. Ibid., s.6 n.45 (125ab).

a cooperation of superior and subordinate causes, in which the causality of the instrumental cause is fully preserved as well. Nor can we conclude from the designation of this potency as an "obediential power" that it is purely passive; rather we ourselves experience *("veluti experimento")* the capability *(capaces)* to perform supernatural acts (e.g., believing, loving, etc.).[199]

The natural faculties of the soul are in no way sufficient to perform these supernatural acts; nevertheless, on the basis of their active obediential power they can be enabled to do so as God's instruments. Since living and instrumental action are just as compatible as instrumental and free action (for freedom here means only the freedom to omit an act or to choose the contrary act), Suárez sees the best theological definition of man in his role as a living, free instrument *(instrumentum liberum, vitale)* of God. The best possible way to explain this definition, however (and to ensure his own theory), is to assume a faculty, in itself free, which on the one hand can accept the power that is elevated to instrumental status and can thus produce a corresponding supernatural act (e.g., of faith), but on the other hand can also refuse it by its own power or place a contrary act (e.g., of disbelief).[200]

3.2 Natural morality or the effect of grace? Gabriel Vázquez

The tension between Augustinianism and the modern consciousness of freedom is exemplified in the treatise on grace by Suárez' opponent and successor at the Collegium Romanum, Gabriel Vázquez, S.J. (1549–1607).[201] In his commentaries and disputations on the *Summa* of Thomas Aquinas, which are very clear and written in good Latin, he poses the question, as *quaestio* 190 on the *Prima Secundae* (I-II, first printing 1605), whether we require help through the grace of God, mediated by Christ, to perform individual morally good works.[202] In other words, can there be for a human being in Christ a natural morality? It is valid [*Es gilt*] to debate this question *ad utramque partem* [from either side].

Proponents of late medieval Augustinianism and Luther were not the only ones to dispute the possibility of independent, naturally moral action. The question was debated among the *Scholastici* as well, as Vázquez makes

199. Ibid., s.6 n.55 (129ab).

200. Ibid., s.6 n.98–99 (146b–147b).

201. See *HDG* III, 5b, 101; on Vázquez generally: Werner, *Scholastik*, 95–160; Stegmüller, "Prädestinationslehre"; Knebel, *Wille*, 573.

202. Edition consulted: G. Vázquez, *Commentariorum ac Disputationum in Primam Secundae Sancti Thomae Tomus secundus* (Lyon, 1631), 321b–356b.

clear in his thorough treatment of the *status quaestionis* with a long list of authorities. Not at issue here is God's general concurrence *(concursus generalis)* in the work of his creatures. For many theologians (from Bonaventure to Cajetan and Johannes Maior) this is already enough to enable man to act morally, at least in minor matters, that is, with regard to the ethical-natural value of the deed, for example, helping the poor, because it is good for natural-ethical reasons.[203] On the other hand an even longer list of Scholastics (from Albert the Great to Pedro de Soto) denies the possibility of naturally perfect moral action without the help of grace. This is the opinion of Thomas Aquinas as well, whose teaching corresponds to the interpretation of Capreolus, but not of Cajetan. This understanding of the matter is confirmed by Scripture, the councils, and papal doctrinal decisions, the testimony of the Church Fathers before Augustine and the entire *"Augustini schola."*[204] Finally four explanations of the arguments of the second *sententia* are rejected: *"gratia"* is meant here, according to Vázquez, not just in the Pelagian sense of the grace of creation or in the sense of God's general concurrence *(auxilium generale)*; the necessity of special helps of grace mediated by Christ is not restricted just to works of love of God or to those that are important for eternal life. Instead the Fathers of the Church try to show that without the help of grace we cannot think, will or accomplish anything that is of significance for true justice and piety, or that relates to God and eternal life.[205]

Vázques adduces proof for the necessity of special helps of grace for any individual morally good work from the reasons that he used in his earlier teaching that not even the smallest temptation can be overcome without such a special help of grace:

1. It is useful for us to *ask* (repeatedly) for the help of God's grace for individual good works.
2. We *thank* God for every good deed that he in his providence allows us to succeed in doing.
3. *Reductio ad absurdum:* If man could act morally by his own unaided power, he could at least incipiently perform works of mercy and thereby induce God to forgive sin or to grant grace. This position is at least Semipelagian.

203. Ibid., c.1 (321b–23a).

204. Ibid., c.2–6 (323b–28b) with a detailed discussion of Thomas (c.3) and four (not genuinely anti-Pelagian) passages from Augustine (c.6). The decision of the *Concilium Palaestinum* is reprinted verbatim in the appendix (661).

205. Ibid., c.7–9 (330b–37a).

4. Argument by way of analogy: Since man cannot overcome any temptation against the moral law by natural morality, he is just as incapable of acting morally thereby.[206]

Nevertheless Vázquez, despite his sympathy for Augustinianism, is unwilling to take up a radical position. He resolves the controversy by asserting that both positions are probable and by reconciling them. A natural moral act is possible in the individual case without the special supernatural help of graces mediated by Christ. Such an act, however, does not attain comprehensive, perfect goodness without the special help of a grace mediated by Christ. The help in this case, however, is not of the supernatural but rather of the natural order: it consists of God's protection and guidance of things through natural causes. Vázquez guarantees his teaching historically as well: He presented it as early as 1580 in Alcalà in his treatise *De gratia* and again in 1586 at the Collegium Romanum in his treatise *De praedestinatione,* and finally it was approved by Cardinal Robert Bellarmine. Consequently three things are to be demonstrated:

1. In every good work we find the help of a grace that is different from the creaturely endowment and general influence with which God as the First Cause cooperates with the working of secondary causes.
2. This help is in some way necessary for the work to be an *"opus studiosum"* with moral value.
3. This helping grace is mediated by Christ.[207]

Human freedom, to which Vázquez is thoroughly committed, must not cancel out this helping grace in the natural order, but what then does that grace consist of, or what does it accomplish? Again Vázquez in a very clear train of thought starts with generally acknowledged facts from the theory of human acts, so as to prove his opinion on the basis of them:

1. We are free (decisional freedom).
2. Our will can freely decide to go either way.
3. In every case the movement of the will presupposes thought.
4. The fact that the will is guided (applied) to this later (good) thought rather than to that (bad) first thought, must be explained through an external influence.

206. Ibid., c.10–11 (339b–43a).
207. Ibid., c.12 (343b).

5. Therefore every time the will is prompted by thought to choose good freely, it receives a special helping grace from God, different from the grace of creation.

Insofar as we are creatures [*Schöpfungsmässig*] we are not more prone to think about good than about evil. The application of grace can occur either directly by God or through secondary causes: yet even in the latter case it is to be attributed to God. The application of grace in the individual case thus does not necessarily cancel out the natural course of the world; rather the causal order of the world is so designed by God that through it an act of thought that prompts the will to a good work occasionally can occur. But in this case, too, God is to be acknowledged as the cause of the *bona cogitatio* [good thought].[208]

The helping grace consists therefore precisely in the causation of a good thought as a proportional occasion for a voluntary decision for the good. In the subsequent discussion this theorem of Vázquez was then also referred to under the heading of *cogitatio congrua.* This *cogitatio congrua* which is necessary for a good act does not abolish man's freedom. For the will does not necessarily follow the thought, as everyone knows from experience; the thought is only a *conditio sine qua non* of willing. Consequently what God brings about through his helping grace, and what is required from our perspective for a comprehensive morally good act, is precisely that *cogitatio congrua* about which God already knows that our will is going to follow it. This connection between thought and voluntary decision is then indeed necessary, but not in the sense of causally determined dependence *(necessitas antecedens),* but rather in view of God's knowledge about the human being's ensuing free voluntary decision *(necessitas consequens).*[209] The further problems concerning God's knowledge about our free decisions would be discussed in Jesuit Scholasticism under the rubric of *scientia media.*[210] The helping grace of the *cogitatio congrua,* moreover, considered in itself, does not work infallibly, since it can be obstructed by many other influences. We ask God precisely for this *cogitatio congrua* when we pray for the grace to do a good deed; we thank him for it.

Vázquez adduces the proof that this special helping grace is mediated by Christ from Augustine and the African Fathers of the Church. The meri-

208. Ibid. (344a).
209. Ibid. (344b).
210. See Knebel, "Scientia media"; Sparn, "Subjekte von Freiheit," 169–79. See below 6.3.4!

torious character of the morally good act with respect to eternal life (in the case of the Christian) is also based on its derivation from Christ. Not only deeds that are informed by infused virtues are meritorious, but also deeds informed by acquired virtues. According to Augustine, however, a *cogitatio congrua* can be found even among heathens and unbelievers and those in the state of sin; for it consists precisely in the fact that the natural light of reason is thereby induced to grasp the thought of that morally good act which the will by its free decision then intends to perform. The fact that the help is greater for those in the state of grace is based on new circumstances, not on a greater helping grace per se. Finally, the last *conclusio* is again quite Augustinian and far removed from all suspicion of Pelagianism: every morally good act that we perform originates from the grace of Christ, that is, with respect to its meritoriousness: Christ by his sufferings merited for us all those good works that we have.[211]

Above and beyond his resolution of the matter, Vázquez offers here a good example of the development of a theological theory about religious accomplishments in the everyday world. The solution is found, not through metaphysics, but through the theory of the human act, in the prerequisite of a corresponding thought for the act of will. However, this solution makes a clarification of God's knowledge about man's free-will decisions indispensable.

3.3 God's decision and man's freedom: Bartolomeo Mastri

The question as to the compatibility of God's free decision *(decretum)* with man's occupied the adherents of all schools of thought. The Scotists, who usually viewed the innovations of the Jesuits negatively, will be represented here by the commentary on the *Sentences* by the Conventual Franciscan Bartolomeo Mastri (1678).[212] "Mastrius" discusses only a few controversial questions and therein exhibits a marked consciousness of his school.[213]

How can man be free if God always knows his decision already and determines the outcome himself? This question concerns on the one hand God's knowledge about *futura contingentia,* which had been discussed at such great

211. Vázquez, *Comm.* II/II q.190 c.12 (344b–47a).

212. Edition consulted: B. Mastrius, *Disputationes theologicae in Librum Primum Sententiarum* (Venice, 1698). Concerning his philosophy, see also Jansen, "Skotisten," 48–51; on his life and work: Forlivesi, *Scotistarum Princeps.*

213. Book I: disp.1 *de nativitate theologiae* [on the origin of theology]; disp.2 *de divinis attributis;* disp.3 *de divino intellectu;* disp.4 *de divina voluntate;* disp.5 *de divina praedestinatione et reprobatione;* disp.6 *de visione beatifica;* disp.7 *de Sanctissima Trinitate;* see also Forlivesi, *Scotistarum Princeps,* 230–52, 393–98.

length in late Scholasticism, and on the other hand the status of God's decisions with relation to man's. It is debated by Mastrius chiefly in his treatment of divine intellect, whereby the discussion of all the *opiniones* of the other school takes up considerable space.[214] Thus he rejects the following opinions about divine knowledge of *futura contingentia:*

1. Cajetan: God knows them through the real presence in eternity.
2. Bañez: God knows them in the disposition of their immediate cause, that is, the created free will, which under the given circumstances will infallibly produce a corresponding effect.
3. Capreolus: God knows them in his ideas.
4. Miguel de Palacios: God knows them in the efficacy of his foreknowledge as Universal Cause.[215]
5. Jesuit theory *("schola libera"):* He knows them in themselves, presupposing the infinite perfection of the divine intellect.
6. Arriaga: God knows them through the *scientia media.* This innovation of the *"Neutrales"* (= the Jesuits who are neither Thomists nor Scotists) is rejected as contradicting the opinion of Scotus, although it is accepted by other Scotists (Philippus Faber [† 1630], Johannes Poncius [† 1660]).[216]
7. Thomistic theory: God knows them through his decision that precedes the free decision of man *(decretum antecedens).*[217]

His rejection of the Thomistic thesis about God's antecedent decree and the physical predetermination *(praedeterminatio physica)* of the human act of will shows how seriously human freedom is taken in the Scotist school. At best, God's decision could be called antecedent in the sense of a *prioritas a quo* [priority from which], inasmuch as God's decree includes at least virtually the free decision of the human being; the latter, however, does not depend causally on the former; instead God decides not before but rather with the created free will, in such a way that God of his own volition decides that what will occur is precisely that which the free will of the human being decides of its own volition. Therefore, in Scotist terms, one should not speak of an antecedent but rather of an accompanying decree *(decretum concomitans)* of God.[218] The relation between the two decisions is not a causal

214. Mastrius, *I Sent.* disp.3 q.3 f. (126b–187a); see also Anfray, "Prescience," 556–86.
215. On Palacios (Palatius) see: Hurter, *Nomenclator,* 3:143.
216. See 6.3.4.; Anfray, "Prescience," 580–83.
217. Mastrius, *I Sent.* disp.3 q.3 a.1–7 (126b–52b); see also Anfray, "Prescience," 583–86.
218. Mastrius, *I Sent.* disp.3 q.3 a.8 (153ab); see also Anfray, "Prescience," 586–91.

dependency but rather a mere simultaneity. With his *sententia,* which is authenticated directly from Duns Scotus, Mastrius intends to take a middle position between Thomists and *"Neutrales,"* who in their hypothesis of the *scientia media* regard God's knowledge as being dependent on man's free decision and therefore advocate a *decretum sequens* [subsequent decree] rather than a *decretum concomitans.* The logical difference between a temporal human decision and an eternal divine decision should also find linguistic expression. Therefore we should say: from all eternity God has concomitantly (thus simultaneously) defined the future free decisions of the created will. This accompanying decree of God is at the same time the suitable medium of God's knowledge about our future free decisions.[219]

The proof of the Scotist teaching initially proceeds *a posteriori* from the assignment of human perfections to God (the simultaneity of identical decisions in two subjects), then *a priori* from the (typically Scotist) virtual presence of all things contained in God: God as the First Cause virtually contains within himself the powers of all secondary causes and can cause all the effects of the secondary causes with or without them; in the same way he contains virtually within himself as the *"primum intelligens et intelligibile"* ["first intelligent subject and intelligible object"] all possible objects of understanding; likewise as the *primum liberum* [first free subject] he contains within himself virtually all possible free decisions of creatures. Therefore he can not only determine in advance all his own decisions, but also all those which he voluntarily allows to occur at a particular future moment through the action of secondary causes, in such a manner that they agree exactly with his eternal decree. In this case freedom is not abolished, since the self-determination of the created will to its corresponding effect continues to exist.[220]

God's foreknowledge is not the cause of the future existence of creaturely decisions. It is therefore not antecedent either, but rather logically simultaneous with *(concomitans)* or even logically later than (as the Jesuits maintained) the human being's free decision. Therefore we cannot speak about an external necessity, but only about an inferential necessity, comparable to

219. Mastrius, *I Sent.* disp.3 q.3 a.8 (153b): *"Dicemus itaque in hoc sensu Deum ab aeterno concomitanter determinasse eventus liberos a creata voluntate futuros, et tale decretum esse sufficiens, ac idoneum medium ad eos certo cognoscendos, etiam quatenus libere eventuros."* ["And so in this sense we will say that God from all eternity concomitantly determined future free decisions made by a created will, and that this decree is sufficient and the suitable medium in which to know them with certainty, even insofar as they will occur freely."]

220. Ibid. (155b).

the inference from the (natural) sign (smoke) to the object (fire): With this sort of necessity one could conclude the future occurrence of an event from an acquaintance with God's foreknowledge.[221] Mastrius advocates this basic position (along with the Thomists against the Jesuits) also with regard to future free conditional decisions (*futura contingentia conditionata).* Statements about them acquire their definite truth only through corresponding conditional decrees of God.[222]

The Scotist Mastrius explicitly acknowledges his allegiance to a school: this linguistic usage should be accepted *"in schola nostra"* because it is reasonable (proof) and at the same time agrees with the teaching of Duns Scotus (authority).[223]

3.4 God's knowledge dependent on free human beings: Rodrigo de Arriaga

This teaching about divine and human decrees, in the opinion of the Jesuits, did not completely solve the problem of God's knowledge about future contingent developments in the world.[224] Moreover it does not guarantee man's freedom over against divine knowledge to the extent desired. The "totem of Jesuit Scholasticism" from Molina on, therefore, was the doctrine of the *scientia media,* that is, the assumption "that God knows in advance the 'use' that would be made by the free will in every imaginable hypothesis."[225] This knowledge was called *media* originally because, as necessary knowledge about conditional contingent matters, it occupies a middle position between the *scientia simplicis intelligentiae* with which God knows himself and the *scientia visionis* with which God knows possible and real things and, in the opinion of many Jesuits, also *futura contingentia absoluta* [absolute future contingencies].[226] This theory tries to reconcile three theological facts:

1. the infallibility of divine foreknowledge;
2. the inevitability of the divine predestinating will;
3. the freedom of human will.[227]

221. Ibid., a.10 (162a–64a).
222. Ibid., q.4 a.3 (170b–71b).
223. Ibid., q.3 a.8 (157b).
224. See Knebel, "Necessitas moralis."
225. Knebel, "Scientia media," 281, 264; concerning the discourse, see also Knebel, *Wille;* Reinhardt, *Pedro Luis;* Lurz, *Adam Tanner.*
226. See, for example, Georg Hermann, *De Deo sciente* (Ingolstadt, 1737); the history of the *scientia media* was recorded quite early by G. de Henao, S.J., *Scientia media historice propugnata* (Salamanca, 1665; also: Dillingen, 1687).
227. Knebel, "Scientia media," 291.

One resolute and sharp-witted proponent of the comprehensive *scientia-media*-discourse was the Prague professor Rodrigo de Arriaga, S.J. (1592–1667). He immediately makes it clear that the entire doctrine of predestination and grace depends in practice on this question.[228] In the nominalist thought of Arriaga, the *scientia media* is the medium by which God knows the truth of future conditional statements. Arriaga distinguishes, moreover, four types of conditional statements:

1. necessary implication: When fire is applied to tow, it burns.
2. non-necessary consequence: If a poor man asks for alms, I will give it to him.
3. disparate: If the Turk sleeps [i.e., does not attack our country], then I will be learned [i.e., will take advantage of peaceful conditions to complete my education].
4. impossible: If the chimera [a mythical she-monster] were endowed with reason and a poor man asked her for alms, his request would be granted.[229]

Now the object of the *scientia media* is precisely case (2), with its free condition and non-necessary consequence: How does God know whether a poor man will ever ask me for alms, and how I will react then? As a "Scriptural proof" for God's knowledge about such matters, usually 1 Samuel 23:10–12 and Matthew 11:21–23 are cited. Arriaga refers also, however, to the common idiom which replies to questions that begin, "What would happen if . . ." by saying "God knows."[230]

The *scientia media* does in fact become theologically relevant in the question about helping graces: How does God know whether I at a future point in time will cooperate with the helping grace once it is granted? The Thomist and Scotist solutions do not satisfy Arriaga, especially since he interprets the Scotist decree *(volitio efficax)* [effective will] as antecedent—thus abolishing freedom—and not as concomitant. Moreover God would have to know in turn about these, his conditional decisions. But Arriaga regards as incred-

228. R. de Arriaga, *Disputationes theologicae in Primam Partem D. Thomae* (Antwerpen, 1643) l.1 disp.21: De scientia media, seu conditionata (215–224); 215a: *"Vix ulla praesenti saeculo celebrior quaestio in scholis agitur; quam sit haec, utpote a qua pendet tota fere materia de praedestinatione et gratia Dei."* ["Scarcely any question more famous than this one is discussed academically in the present age, inasmuch as on it depends almost the entire subject of predestination and the grace of God."] On Arriaga see also Sousedík, "Obra filosófica"; Sousedík, *Filosofie*, 100–38; Saxlová / Sousedík, *Arriaga.* On the doctrine of the *scientia media* see Sparn, "Subjekte von Freiheit."

229. Arriaga, *Disp. theol.* l.1 disp. 21 s.1 (215a–16a).

230. Ibid., s.2 (216a–17a).

ible also the theory, favored at the Collegium Romanum and at Ingolstadt, of a "total decree" of God, that God already has in his knowledge all possible (counterfactual) courses of world events, in their infinite permutations, dependent upon his will with which he has already decided them once and for all: "If I had wanted to create a different world, I would at the same time have wanted exactly the same number of leaves, fleas, and drops of water to exist in it; nevertheless if the course of world events were different, then I would want a different exact number of these things to exist."[231] The conjecture involving all hypothetically possible courses of world events results, according to Arriaga, in a contradiction. Moreover, the inhabitants of Bethsaida (Matthew 11:21) could have said then, "Why don't you have an effective will *(volitio efficax)* for our salvation; then we would have converted." On the other hand, it is an untenable objection against the *scientia media* or *cogitatio congrua* to say that God gave them no appropriate helping grace. Arriaga allows Christ himself to reply to that: "I give to you as I give to everyone. It is within your power to make this calling into a *congrua*." Therefore God knows *futura conditionata* also, not as outcomes depending on his free-will decisions, but rather in a purely logical way in themselves.[232]

This *scientia media directa* with which God knows our conditional free decisions should be distinguished from the *scientia media reflexa* with which God knows in advance how he himself would act if he knew that the free will [of a creature] were to react thus and so (e.g., to a specific helping grace). A further distinction should be made between affirmative and negative *scientia media reflexa:*

a) affirmative: If I saw that Judas would not correspond to helping grace A (= *scientia media directa* of the rejection that occurred in fact), I would still give it to him.
b) negative: If I saw that Peter would not correspond to helping grace A (= *scientia media directa* of his acceptance), I would not give it to him.[233]

God's knowledge about his own hypothetically possible acts does not abolish God's freedom, as Arriaga demonstrates through a thought-experiment which he invites the reader to make: Knowledge at point A in time does not abolish my freedom at point B, for at point B in time I may have

231. Ibid., s.3 (217a–18b); see also Knebel, "Necessitas," 16–19; Sparn, "Subjekte von Freiheit," 181.
232. Arriaga, *Disp. theol.* l.1 disp. 21 s.4 (218a).
233. See Knebel, "Scientia media," 288; discussed in detail, e.g., in Hermann, *De Deo sciente,* q.7 (283–359).

forgotten what I knew at point A. Thus at any later point in time I act *as though* I had forgotten that I already knew at an earlier time how I would act. That means that I am still free. In retrospect then I can say: I acted exactly in accordance with my foreknowledge.[234]

Nor is man's freedom impaired through this knowledge about future conditional statements. This is because the actual accomplishment of the matter in question (e.g., Peter's conversion) remains within the scope of man's freedom. Thus there is no *scientia media* of the conversion of a specific man (Peter):

a) if that man does not exist, or
b) if he does not correspond to the helping grace.

According to Arriaga, therefore, the man could say to himself at the moment when he exercises his freedom: "I can cause God to have no *scientia media* of my conversion. If I do not correspond to the helping grace that he has granted, then I cause God from all eternity to have no knowledge about my cooperation (as a *futuritio absoluta*). Therefore God's knowledge (exclusively in this regard) is in my power."[235]

Nevertheless God, too, remains free in bestowing his helping graces and in his predestinating will. Before predestination, Peter and Judas are in principle the same. If God knows through his *scientia media,* for example, that Peter and Judas will correspond to four helping graces but will reject four others, then according to his predestinating decision he will give to Peter one of the four that he corresponds to, but to Judas one that he rejects. One might object that then there could be a person who would accept or reject *(creatura rebellis)* all of them, and therefore would have to be saved or damned; Arriaga counters by making a simple distinction: that is indeed metaphysically (logically) possible, but not morally. Besides, God could then still create only the one who accepts all the helping graces, but not the other one. A human being is still free with respect to a helping grace insofar as he makes that help, without which he cannot be saved *(auxilium efficax)* effective through his action. A helping grace therefore does not work independently of or antecedent to the human being's actual deed.[236]

234. Arriaga, *Disp. theol.* l.1 disp. 21 s.4 (219ab); see also Sparn, "Subjekte von Freiheit," 182–184. The fact that the doctrine of *scientia media* also led to *"florida ingeniorum exercitamenta, seu lusus"* ["extravagant exercises or games of ingenuity"] is noted already by, Henao, *Scientia media,* 396b.

235. Arriaga, *Disp. theol.* l.1 disp. 21 s.5 (221a).

236. Arriaga, *Disp. theol.* l.1 disp. 21 s.6 a.2 (222ab); see also Knebel, *Wille,* 186–87.

The truth or falsity of disparate conditional statements without a causal connection is also known by God. In contrast, Arriaga (unlike Pedro de Arrúbal [1559–1608]) is cautious about impossible conditional statements: "If the chimera were free and were prompted by a helping grace of this sort, she would correspond to it." Such knowledge has no discernible purpose; knowledge about individual propositions could be multiplied uselessly in this way: "If this water atom were an angel, would it then be Michael or Gabriel or some other one among all possible angels?" Such speculations, while they show the logical possibilities of the calculus and the ultimate ramifications of a fruitful theory, bring into disrepute the legitimate concern of the *scientia media* in the doctrine about creation, predestination and grace.[237]

3.5 Thomistic opposition to the *scientia media:* Jean-Baptiste Gonet

Well into the New Scholasticism of the nineteenth century, the *Clypeus theologiae Thomisticae* (1659–1669) by the Dominican Jean-Baptiste Gonet (1616–1681)[238] was an influential Thomistic defense against theological innovations, especially by the Jesuits. In sometimes militant language this work singles out the *scientia media* as the chief point of contention and tries to destroy it root and branch.[239] For more than sixty years, he says, the debate has raged over whether the infallible knowledge of *futura conditionata* in God is established before and independently of the decree with which God predetermines conditional-future events (so say the Jesuits) or after the decree and in it. The differences between the two opinions are clearly set forth:

1. The *scientia media* is independent from and prior to God's actual decree; in contrast the *scientia conditionatorum* [knowledge of conditional things] that is assumed by the Thomists is later than the decree and founded on it.

237. Ibid., s.7 (223a–24a); on the great achievements in the field of probability theory, see also Knebel, *Wille*, passim.

238. Edition consulted: J. B. Gonet, *Clypeus theologiae Thomisticae contra novos eius impugnatores*, (Cologne, 1671).

239. Ibid., p.1 tr.3 disp.6 (1:285b–362a); military [*sic*] terminology, e.g., a.5 *"Variis argumentis [...] expungitur scientia media"* (296b) ["*Scientia media* is canceled by various arguments ..." (the unlikely emendation *expugnatur* would mean "overcome, taken by storm")]; a.5 § 5 *"Praecluditur aditus solitae evasioni Adversariorum"* (300b) ["This blocks off access to the usual evasion of our Adversaries"]; a.6 *"Absurdis et inconvenientibus exploditur scientia media"* (309a) ["*Scientia media* is hissed off the stage / scared away (not 'exploded') by absurdities and inconsistencies"]; a.7 *"Convelluntur fundamenta scientiae mediae"* (318a) ["The foundations of *scientia media* are overthrown"].

2. The *scientia media* is a natural and necessary knowledge, as far as the knowing subject (God) is concerned, yet free as far as the object of knowledge (free will) is concerned, whereas the Thomistic *scientia conditionatorum* is subjectively free as well, since it is independent from God's free decision.
3. The *scientia media* is speculative and determined by its object; the Thomistic *scientia conditionatorum* is *"eminenter speculativa et practica"* ["eminently speculative and practical"] at the same time and as such is itself the measure and guiding principle for the object.[240]

The innovation of the Jesuits is rejected in the first place according to the established scheme through a threefold proof from authority: It is not a new theory but rather in principle an old error which was already championed by the Pelagians and Semipelagians. It contradicts the teaching of Thomas Aquinas and moreover was rejected by Augustine.[241] Gonet goes on to oppose the new doctrine with individual *rational arguments* (in each case noting the foundation):

1. God knows creatures only in his essence and his omnipotence, consequently only in dependence on his decree.
2. Divine knowledge is never determined by its object, like the *scientia media,* but rather is itself the measure and guiding principle of things.
3. The *scientia media* lacks the epistemological medium necessary for every sort of knowledge.
4. The definition of the *scientia media* is contradictory, since before God's voluntary decision to transform possible things into reality there are no hypothetical future events to know even for the divine intellect.
5. The *scientia media* offers God no guidance in his decisions; it is useless for the infallible knowledge of the *futura absoluta.* Moreover it contradicts the absoluteness of God in his decisions. Besides that, its results in the metaphysical possibility of human beings who cannot be saved *de potentia absoluta* and cannot be predestined to salvation (cf. Arriaga).
6. As the decisions of the Universities of Salamanca, Alcalà, Douay, and Louvain show, the *scientia media* is not qualified to harmonize human freedom, divine predestination and actual grace. Augustine did it better without the hypothesis of the *scientia media.* The new hypothesis reflects instead the Semipelagian teaching of Faustus of Milève.

240. Ibid., a.1 n.5 (286b–87a).

241. Ibid., a.2–4 (287a–96a).

7. Further arguments are quoted from Fr. Vincent Baron, O.P. (1604–1674): The truth of the *futura conditionata* depends on the transition from pure possibility to the status of futurity. The latter is dependent solely upon God's decree as its ultimate cause. Proponents of the *scientia media* are blamed for confusing hypothetical and absolute judgments. It is absurd to say on a sunny day, "If the sun were shining, I would see it," or while praying the breviary, "If I had a breviary, I would pray it." Finally the proponents of the new theory destroy it themselves, because they either dispute the truth of hypothetical future statements or must abolish the freedom and contingency of human decision-making.[242]

In his next attack Gonet intends to show that the new theory leads to absurd *consequences* that are unacceptable to theologians, whereby he complies at least formally with the papal decision of 1607, which declared that Molinism must not be disparaged as Pelagianism. In fact, however, he condemns the new theory all the more harshly:

1. The theory of the *scientia media* seems to favor the doctrine of Semipelagianism, that there is in us [human beings] a beginning of faith *(initia fidei)* and of good will by our natural powers, not by grace. Since the Jesuits, unlike the Thomists, assume only a moral but not a physical efficacy of grace *(gratia excitans),* it is not possible to know in advance the occasioning of a supernatural determination of the will as a beginning of faith and justification. The moral efficacy consists only in showing the moral goodness, which attracts the will and invites it to consent. This comes about then, however, by the human being's own power.
2. Similarly, the *scientia media* seems to support the Semipelagian doctrine of predestination *post praevisa merita* [after merits have been foreseen], since the *scientia media* knows about the human being's merits before God's decree.
3. The *scientia media* abolishes the prime causality of God. This can be preserved in the case of *futura conditionata* only by assuming a decree of God's will—which is absolute from God's perspective and conditional from the perspective of the object—to grant existence to the futuribles *(futuribilia)* upon the occurrence of the appropriate condition. According to Gonet, however, the *scientia media* excludes precisely such absolute decrees.

242. Ibid., a.5 (296b–309a).

4. The *scientia media* furthermore abolishes God's status as *free* First Cause. The created free will—understood along the lines of Thomistic metaphysics—is free only through its participation in the free First Cause *(primum liberum)*. This is no longer the case in the *scientia media* theory, since then the human being's will is ultimately what first determines the indefinite decree of God. Therefore God is no longer the *"primum eligens et primum determinans"* [the first to choose and the first to determine], either.
5. The *scientia media* abolishes God's sovereign authority *(supremum dominium)* over our will. Now this authority is understood as the right to use and employ it according to his decree. Therefore if God must know before his own decision the possible free decision of the created will, he is no longer Lord over our will like a king, but only the master of our graces, like a mayor or like a husband with respect to his wife.
6. The *scientia media* thus impairs God's omnipotence and destroys the efficacy of grace.
7. It acknowledges only a blind, unknowing, vague and indefinite cooperation of God with free causes, as when fishermen simply cast their net without knowing what sort of fish they want in the first place.
8. It falsely imputes to God a confused and indefinite manner of knowing our hypothetical future acts of will.
9. It only appears to preserve freedom; in fact, however, it completely abolishes it. The proponents of the new theory, after all, assume a definite truth of the *futura conditionata*. Since they take away God's freedom with regard to his decree, they also abolish creaturely freedom—this being understood again within the framework of metaphysical participation. By annihilating the *primum liberum* (first Free Cause), they annihilate also their own freedom. Moreover they assume a hypothetical future existence *(futuritio)* of things independently of a divine decree.
10. It makes God into the author of sin, obscures the glory of God's holiness and seems to present a danger for the salvation of men. After all, God's cooperation (which is per se indifferent) in man's free decision extends—when viewed causally—to a good deed and to a bad deed as well. Thus Judas' betrayal would be just as much an *"opus Dei"* ["work of God"] as the conversion of Paul.[243]

It becomes clear in these theses, which are followed by the destruction of the foundations of the *scientia media* in Scripture and the Church

243. Ibid., a.6 (309a–18a).

Fathers,[244] that the battle being waged here is not over terminology, but rather between a medieval, metaphysical view of the world and man and an epistemological solution of the question based on the theory of the human act [*handlungstheoretischen Lösung*]: Is God still the metaphysical free First Cause, the Lord of all creation who disposes all things, or is there in a free human being a realm which is exempt from his immediate intervention, at least conditionally?

3.6 Causal-metaphysical predetermination of the will: Ludwig Babenstuber

The Thomistic metaphysical view of the cooperation of free will and the divine First Cause is labeled *"praedeterminatio physica"*—according to Dominicus Bañez and Francisco Zumel, a term supposedly invented by the Jesuits.[245] Its home was initially the Dominican school in Salamanca; however it was zealously defended also in the Thomism of the Discalced Carmelites and the Benedictines.[246] One center north of the Alps was the University of Salzburg.[247] The theory of *praedeterminatio* or (in the case of secondary causes that are not free) *praemotio physica* was regarded as a metaphysical theory; this is demonstrated by the fact that it was presented, for example, by Fr. Ludwig Babenstuber (1660–1727) within the framework of his *Philosophia thomistica Salisburgensis* and was also defended in theological disputations, sometimes as a dialogue between Thomists and Molinists against Jesuit opponents (among others Fr. Johann Christoph Rassler in Ingolstadt and Fr. Ludwig Simonzin in Dillingen).[248]

Babenstuber is very precise in analyzing agreement with and dissent from the "More Recent Thinkers" *(Recentiores)*, a party to which the Scotists also belong in this case. Agreement consists in the position that every action of a creature must depend somehow upon the First Cause, that any

244. Ibid., a.7 (318a–30b).

245. See W. Hübener, "Praedeterminatio physica," *HWPh* 7:1216–25.

246. See Stegmüller, *Francisco de Vitoria;* Stiglmayr, *Verstossung.*

247. L. Babenstuber, *Vindiciae praedeterminationis physicae recenter impugnatae,* P.1 (Salzburg, 1707), Praef. (1): *"antiquissima sententia, quam nostra Universitas hactenus constantissime tenuit et quam iudico verissimam"* ["a very ancient opinion which our University has constantly held until now and which I judge to be quite true"]; see also the detailed discussion in Bauer, *Metaphysik,* 488–586.

248. L. Babenstuber, *Philosophia thomistica Salisburgensis,* l.2 Phys. disp.5 (Augsburg, 1706), 234–74; Babenstuber, *Vindiciae praed.;* Babenstuber, *Vindiciae vindiciarum physicae praedeterminationis* (Salzburg, 1712); see also J. Chr. Rassler, *Controversia theologica de physica praedeterminatione* (Ingolstadt, 1697); L. Simonzin, *Libertas creata,* (Dillingen, 1711). See Altermatt, *Zum Problem der physischen Prämotion;* Bauer, *Metaphysik,* 502–8.

cooperation of God occurs simultaneously, that at least an antecedent moral assistance of God is required for a morally good act *(concursus moralis)*, and that the self-determination of the free will to act must be preserved. Beyond that, however, the Thomists make additional demands in their maximal theory (which is disputed by the Jesuits):

1. God's actual cooperation consists not just of an immediate influence on the action by means of the secondary cause, but of an immediate influence on the secondary cause itself. This influence (in the sense in which the word is used in physics) is really and physically received by the secondary cause.
2. This influence is a real movement in the sense of Aristotelian physics; by itself and with metaphysical infallibility it is what brings about in the first place the necessary or free action of the secondary cause, and therefore it possesses a natural priority with regard to this action.
3. If God's cooperation is merely moral, which the Jesuits assume to be the case, God so to speak places his omnipotence in the hand of his creature.[249]

While the *praedeterminatio moralis* of the Jesuits signifies only the preparation of the object, the opportunities or the motives as an invitation to action, the *praemotio* or *praedeterminatio physica* is by definition

1. real physical movement that
2. proceeds from God alone,
3. is transferred to the creaturely cause,
4. possesses natural priority over the operation of the secondary cause,
5. establishes the secondary cause as a real principle of action in the first place, and
6. effectively applies it to an operation corresponding to its nature.[250]

This metaphysical theory, therefore, is about nothing less than the actual (physical) influence of God as the universal First Cause, through which influence he works with the secondary causes subordinate to him and at the same time preserves their freedom.[251] Besides the authority of Aristotle and

249. Babenstuber, *Philosophia* l.2 Phys. disp.5 a.2 §1 n.1 (243a); see also Bauer, *Metaphysik*, 540–49.

250. Babenstuber, *Philosophia* l.2 Phys. disp.5 a.2 §1 n.2 (243a): "*physica et realis motio a solo deo procedens, causae creatae transeunter impressa, prioritate naturae praecedens ipsius operationem, eandemque causam constituens in ratione principii actualis et efficaciter applicans ad operandum conformiter naturae ipsius*"; see also Bauer, *Metaphysik*, 561–62.

251. Babenstuber, *Philosophia* l.2 Phys. disp.5 a.2 §1 n.5 (243b).

Thomas, rational arguments in particular are brought to bear here. Babenstuber presents five arguments that recur again and again in the Thomistic teaching tradition, which are connected in part to the argumentation of the *quinque viae* [five ways, i.e., of proving the existence of God] and thus underscore the central position of the theory of physical predetermination in the Thomistic view of God and creation:

1. The Aristotelian subordination of secondary causes to the First Cause (cf. *via II*) is inconceivable without *praemotio physica.*[252]
2. Every secondary mover is moved by a first mover (cf. *via I*). The movement of the second by the first is precisely this *praemotio physica.*[253]
3. Denial of the *praemotio physica* makes the secondary cause the first mover: a consequence which is manifestly false and absurd to a metaphysician.[254]
4. The created free will is indifferent as to whether it will decide this way or that; for freedom *(libertas a necessitate)* is plainly defined as indifference or the freedom to decide between contrary actions.[255] It therefore requires a determination from outside by the First Cause, which is the only thing that can move the created will internally. This determination, which is causally antecedent to the free action, is the *praedeterminatio physica.*[256]
5. In order to act, the creature must first be so organized by its *actus primus* (ontological constitution) as to function as an *actus secundus* (actual principle of action). The constitutive factor is the *praemotio physica.* Consequently there must be such a thing (i.e., it exists in keeping with the theory). The *praemotio physica* is furthermore the causal principle of action *(actus secundus causalis),* which immediately enables the secondary cause to perform real actions *(actus secundus formalis).*[257]

Contrary to the objections of the Jesuits and Scotists that the antecedent determination by God abolishes man's freedom, Babenstuber sees in it

252. Ibid., §2 n.10 (246b); see also Bauer, *Metaphysik,* 508–16.

253. Babenstuber, *Philosophia* l.2 Phys. disp.5 a.2 §2 n.17 (249b).

254. Ibid., §2 n.19 (250b).

255. Ibid., §4 n.35 (257b): *"libertas a necessitate, quae sola huc pertinet, definitur a Thomistis, quod sit dominium sui actus ad opposita; vel, facultas voluntatis et rationis ad utrumlibet."* ["Freedom from necessity, which is the only kind that pertains to this matter, is defined by the Thomists as power over one's act with regard to opposing alternatives; or the ability of will and reason to choose whichever one wants."]

256. Ibid., §2 n.22 (252a).

257. Ibid., §2 n.26–27 (253a–54a).

with Thomas the very thing that makes freedom possible.[258] The decisive argument reads:

Every free action of a created will depends immediately on God with regard to all its perfection, formal constitution and mode of action. Consequently God causes every free action of a created will with regard to all its perfection, formal constitution and mode of action. He can cause these, however, only through physical predetermination of the created will to this free action; for only in the physical predetermination can . . . the influence of the First Cause and also the application of the free second cause to the action be preserved at the same time as its essential subordination to and dependence on the First Cause.[259]

The *praedeterminatio* is constitutive not only for the ability but also for the action itself. Without it, man does not possess the full capacity to place an act; for this is precisely what empowers him to act in the first place and thereby frees him to exercise freedom. The mere capability *(potentia proxima expedita)* to place the contrary act, however, is not abolished by the physical predetermination, for example, to love God or hate him. For the contrary act, however, God gives only the ontological capacity in the sphere of the *actus primus* (mere ability), whereas for the predetermined act he gives the real action *(actus secundus)* along with the ability.[260] The freedom imparted in the *praedeterminatio physica* is real, positive liberation to act and is not comparable with the simple application of fire to combustible material (physical *applicatio*) or the mere lack of chains as freedom to go.[261] Creaturely freedom in this Thomistic sense is always a freedom that is granted and caused, not just man's self-determination in his actions. A self-determination of man (as a secondary cause) presupposes, rather, the determination by the First Cause and is made possible by it. The necessity with which the *praedeterminatio physica* works is only the conditional necessity of a consequence that is subsequently observed [*festgestellte*]; this is of course infallible. The fundamental ontological freedom to act otherwise does continue to exist; the contrary act, however, is not compatible with the circumstances of the agent that were created by the *praemotio physica.* Consequently for the contrary act a corresponding *praemotio* would again be required.[262] This theory does not

258. Ibid., §4 n.40 (259b) citing *Summa Th.* I q.38 a1 ad3 and I-II q.10 a.4. i.c; see also Bauer, *Metaphysik,* 573–83.

259. Babenstuber, *Philosophia* l.2 Phys. disp.5 a.2 §4 n.40 (259b).

260. Babenstuber, *Vindiciae praed.* p.1 §2 n.20 (14ab).

261. Ibid., §3 n.38 (28b–29a).

262. Ibid., §4 n.64 (45a): *"a quo determinetur, ut determinet etiam se ipsum"* ["by which it is determined, so that it might determine itself also"]. Ibid., §5 (73b).

make God the author of sin, as is repeatedly objected, since God causes only the material action but not the formal wickedness.[263]

The Thomistic theory of the *praedeterminatio physica*—a defense against modern Deism and an autonomous self-determination of man—is the logically consistent attempt to join God and creature to each other once again through the metaphysical clamps of participation, dependence and the essential ordering of causes. It can convince people, however, only as long as the world view of Aristotelian-Thomistic metaphysics remains alive.

4 The difficult assimilation of the new

The Scholastic theology of the early modern period was by no means unaffected by the revolutionary changes and new theories in the natural sciences and philosophy. It assimilated the new ideas, nevertheless, in its own characteristic way. On the other hand, the inventions and discoveries of the early modern period, most of which were made outside of the universities, were either accepted or rejected within the framework of academic training and became widely influential, or not, accordingly.[264] We will illustrate this acceptance and rejection of new findings with several individual examples.

4.1 Caramuel and the Galileo case

One of the most independent theologians and philosophers on the fringe of Scholasticism was the Cistercian Abbot of Emmaus, General Vicar of Prague and later Bishop of Vigevano, Juan Caramuel Lobkowitz (1606–1682).[265] Besides his logical and philosophical works we should mention here in particular his *Theologia moralis fundamentalis.*[266] Even in its structure it departs from the well-known presentations, and in many places, especially in the chapters on terminology, it shows the strong Lullist and topical influences on this theologian, who was dubbed *"princeps laxistarum"* ["the leader of the laxists"] by Alphonsus Liguori.[267] Book 1 presents in axiomatic

263. Babenstuber, *Philosophia* l.2 Phys. disp.5 a.2 §5 (272a–273a); see also Bauer, *Metaphysik,* 583–86.

264. See Leinsle, *Ding,* 2–4.

265. On his life and work see, Pastine, *Juan Caramuel;* Velarde Lombraña, *Juan Caramuel;* Sousedík, *Filosofie,* 185–210; Jacob Schmutz, art. "Caramuel y Lobkowitz, Juan," in *BBKL* 17:224–32.

266. Caramuel, *Theologia moralis fundamentalis,* (Frankfurt, 1651); this discussion cites the corrected four-volume 4th edition (Lyon, 1675/6); on this subject see Fleming, *Defending probabilism.*

267. Caramuel, *Theologia moralis fundamentalis,* Prologus De mente Authoris, Moralium Opinionum nexu et Theologicorum nominum significatione [Prologue on the Author's intention, the center of moral opinions and the significance of theological terms] (1:1–5), with its explana-

form the universal principles of moral theology, of both a speculative and a practical sort. The speculative foundations are those that refer to the human mind and are said to provide it with certainty (ch. 1): grace and freedom, whereby Caramuel rejects both the *scientia media* and the *praedeterminatio physica* in the strict sense;[268] first truth and first truthfulness, that is, God and his revelation; the certainty and infallibility of the Roman Church; the veracity of the pope; the College of Cardinals and the Rota; the definitions of the universities;[269] the alleged and actual authority of scholars;[270] the opinions of contemporaries; the authority of demons (with a reference to the *Daemonis Logica* or his course on philosophy), sensory experience, and probable opinions. The practical foundations are based on divine or human authority and legislation, and laws are treated according to the Aristotelian scheme of categories. Book 2 then presents the Decalogue, book 3—sacramental doctrine, based on a sacramental grammar (with its own chapter *De Orthographia divina*), mathematics, dialectic and physics. Finally, book 4 presents a *Dialexis de non certitudine.*

The struggle for certainty and the binding character of ecclesiastical theological decisions acquire downright explosive force in light of the Copernican worldview. Caramuel discusses the question in connection with the authority of the College of Cardinals, for hitherto only they had rejected the cosmology of Copernicus and Galileo. Their decision has a solely practical significance; they cannot declare a formal heresy if it was not previously determined to be one.[271] The teaching that the earth moves about the sun was a probable opinion before the condemnation, but no longer is now. In fact, however, what is at issue according to Caramuel is not a question of astronomy but rather the admissibility of a metaphorical interpretation of Scripture. Once this is admitted in the case of astronomy, it can also gain a foothold in sacramental doctrine (as the heretics claim). We should there-

tions of: *Deus, Trinitas, homoousios, ens secundum dici, ens morale, ens virtuale, libertas, dubium negativum, probabilitas.*

268. Ibid., l.1 c.1 fund.1 (1:55–56). Concerning Caramuel's position in the debate on grace, which in itself is Molinist, see also Armogathe, "Probabilisme," 36, 39; on his hypothesis of a *praedeterminatio infallibilitans* see Velarde Lombraña, *Juan Caramuel*, 41–42.

269. He considers the most important ones to be Salamanca, Alcalà, Paris, Louvain/Leuven, Douay, Cologne, Ingolstadt, Mainz, Würzburg, and Prague. Whatever they teach that has not been condemned has a claim to probability.

270. With a harsh polemic aimed at worthless or purchased academic degrees, according to the proverb: *"Maneat eius argentum apud nos, asinusque Laureatus revertatur ad patriam"* ["Let his money stay with us, and let the ass with the Degree return to his fatherland"] (1:120a); on the authorities of extrinsic probability see also Leinsle, "Servatius de Lairuelz," 288–92.

271. Caramuel, *Theologia moralis fundamentalis* l.1 c.1 fund.5 (1:104b).

fore, says Caramuel, be grateful to the cardinals that they warded off this possible misuse of Scripture by their condemnation of Copernicus. For in interpreting Scripture there is a general obligation to follow the literal sense, as long as this is not contradictory, thus forcing us to seek a metaphorical or moral interpretation.[272] This new theory, nevertheless, is not formally heretical, since it has not been condemned as such by the pope.[273] Nothing about this has changed even through the Galileo affair: There is no permission to defend the heliocentric system.[274] On purely rational grounds the Copernican system is at least possible, since one cannot demonstrate that God could not have created a world in which this system is valid. Caramuel himself simply wishes to abide by the Church's decision, especially since both systems have their difficulties, and so he affirms that the earth is motionless and rejects the contrary opinion as heretical and condemned by sacred Scripture.[275]

With the condemnation of Galileo, Caramuel considers the systems of David Origanus (1558–1628; professor in Frankfurt an der Oder) and Christian Longomontanus (1562–1647, professor in Copenhagen) as being repudiated also.[276] A physical proof of heliocentrism is impossible. All the ingenious endeavors by the mathematicians to find one are therefore fruitless effort and useless torment for the reader. Yet even if—*per impossibile*—a proof were someday found, Caramuel could reject it as the impossible and absurd consequence of an impossible premise, especially since the earth's rest and the sun's movement have been proved through the discovery of sunspots by the Jesuit Christoph Scheiner (1573–1650). For Caramuel a contrary proof against a valid proof is impossible as a matter of pure logic.[277] Fidelity to the positive ecclesiastical decision is thus legitimized theologically, scientifically, and logically.

4.2 Cartesian teaching on the Eucharist: Robert Desgabets

The limits of conventional theological system-building became clear to many seventeenth- and eighteenth-century authors in the case of the Thomis-

272. Ibid. (109b).

273. Ibid. (105b–6a).

274. Ibid., Caramuel addressed an inquiry to Rome in this regard and received from Cardinal Chigi (later Alexander VII) the reply: *"Imo hac de causa, et ob hunc librum Galilaeus carceratus fuit, et coactus retractare suam sententiam."* ["Indeed, for this reason and on account of this book Galileo was imprisoned and compelled to retract his opinion."]

275. Ibid. (107a).

276. Ibid. (108ab).

277. Ibid. (110a); on the discussion see also Leinsle, *Dilinganae Disputationes,* 265–69.

tic doctrine of transubstantiation. Already in trying to apply Aristotelian physics consistently, difficulties arise as to how accidents are supposed to exist without their substance. No wonder Caramuel cites a theologian friend of his who compares his difficulties with the old cosmology to those involved in the teaching on the Eucharist.[278] From Descartes to Leibniz we find various attempts to apply a new scientific paradigm to the Eucharist.[279] Thus Emmanuel Maignan (1601–1676) and the Salzburg professor Fr. Fructuosus Scheidsach († 1749) try to do so by applying the atomist or corpuscular theory.[280] Dom Robert Desgabets (1610–1678), a Benedictine of the Congregation of Saint-Vanne, was a relatively consistent Cartesian and at the same time a theologian, although the publication of his theological works was banned.[281]

Desgabets' fundamental concern is to establish a new "harmony [i.e., a systematic reconciliation] of the divine and human sciences" on the basis of Cartesian philosophy.[282] It is constructed out of several *"vérités plus simples qui sont comme les fondaments de notre harmonie"* ["more simple truths which are so to speak the foundations of our harmony"].[283] These pertain on the one hand to the divine perfections, and on the other hand to the three simple created substances: body (= matter), angel, and spiritual soul. These simple substances are imperishable.[284] Everything else besides these simple substances is only a modification of these simple substances (*êtres modaux,* modal beings).[285] The world is infinite in its extension; there is no vacuum or empty space in the strict sense *(vide philosophique);* such a thing would be a contradiction in terms.[286]

The application of these Cartesian principles to the doctrine of the Eucharist, intended originally only as a supplement to the Thomistic or nominalist understanding, came about over the course of a long, lively debate with his contemporaries, principally Claude Clerselier (1614–1684), but also Antoine

278. Caramuel, *Theologia moralis fundamentalis* l.1 c.1 fund.5 (106b).

279. See Armogathe, *Theologia Cartesiana.*

280. See Bauer, *Metaphysik,* 347–48; Scheidsach published under a pseudonym as Carpophorus del Giudice, *Tractatus de accidentibus absolutis sive Sacro-Sanctum Eucharistiae Sacramentum in principiis Philosophiae Peripateticae impugnatum, et ex placitis Philosophiae Corpusculariae propugnatum* (Paderborn, 1718).

281. His philosophical works were edited by G. Rodis-Lewis and J. Beaude: Robert Desgabets, *Œuvres philosophiques inédits* (Analecta Cartesiana) (Amsterdam, 1983–). See Beaude, "Desgabets"; Beaude, "Cartésianisme"; concerning his influence on German Protestant Scholastic philosophy via his former confrere Johannes Sperlette (1661–1740), see: Leinsle, *Reformversuche,* 113–26.

282. Desgabets, "Préface particulière," *Œuvres phil.* I, 1–14.

283. Ibid. (I, 1.26–27).

284. Ibid. (I, 6.14–23); see also Rodis-Lewis, "Quelques échos."

285. Desgabets, "Préface particulière": (I, 7.37–8.32).

286. Ibid. (I, 9.22–50).

Arnauld (1612–1694) and Pierre Nicole (1625–1695) of Port Royal, through which Desgabets was drawn by Port Royal into the debate about Jansenism.[287] Desgabets maintains that the Thomistic theory of transubstantiation cannot be reconciled with the principle that substances are imperishable; the existence of a body at two places (natural and sacramental existence), another "invention of the Scholastics," causes considerable difficulties for natural reason. If one starts from the Cartesian axiom that God does not want to deceive us, either in revelation or in the realm of reason, then another solution must be found.[288] Desgabets sees this in Cartesian physics, according to which every body is extended and consequently impenetrable. The same particle of matter, moreover, can be in only one place at a particular point in time.

According to this theory, no transformation of substance occurs in the Eucharist, but only a new combination of substances. Since the spiritual soul and body are separate simple substances in man and thus in Christ also, the Eucharist can be explained initially by a *"conjonction substantielle perfective"* between what is really substantial in the substance of bread and Christ's soul. The substance of bread vanishes, but what is substantial in it informs the substance of the Body of Christ through union with his soul. There is also, as a second line of union, the hypostatic union between Christ's humanity (with body and soul) and the Second Person of the Trinity. Just as the union of embryo and spiritual soul make a human being out of the *"animal merum"* ["mere (i.e., purely irrational) animal"], so, too, the union of the bread's substantiality with the soul of Christ is what makes the sacramental Body of Christ.[289] Desgabets confirms his first attempt through his reading of John Damascene and Durandus of Troarn (1005/20–1088) and describes his theory as *"transélémentation,"* or more precisely as *"trans-subsistentiation"* and defines it as

> a perfective substantial change by which the bread, as a thing with extension, becomes the body of a God-man as a result of its miraculous union to his soul and divinity, in keeping with the fundamental and general maxim: *forma dat esse rei* [form gives being to a thing].[290]

Desgabets is aware that he has thus preserved the mystery of the Eucharist with regard to the efficacy of the sacrament, but that he has removed the dif-

287. See Lemaire, *Cartésianisme,* 99–133.

288. See Armogathe, *Theologia cartesiana,* 91–92.

289. Ibid., 94–96 with newly compiled documentation.

290. Desgabets, *Explication familière,* MS Epinal 43, 69; cited in Arbogathe, *Theologia Cartesiana,* 98.

ficulty of separated, absolute accidents with his new theory. With logical consistency, Desgabets answers in the negative the classical question of whether during the time between Christ's death and his resurrection a transubstantiation would have resulted from an attempted consecration, claiming that his answer is probable, because during that time Christ's soul did not inform a body. The Blood of Christ, on the other hand, is not immediately informed by the soul but rather by an inner movement.[291] Desgabets explicitly submits to the teaching of the Council of Trent, which remains open with regard to the interpretive paradigm. Nevertheless his theory was exposed to vehement attacks from theologians and was denounced to the king and the archbishop of Paris as a teaching that was harmful to the *"Respublica Scholastica."*[292]

4.3 Eclectic theology: Eusebius Amort

The very title of the comprehensive presentation of theology published in 1752 by a canon from Pollingen, Eusebius Amort (1692–1775),[293] for the new seminary of the Diocese of Augsburg in Pfaffenhausen offers a striking innovation: *Theologia eclectica, moralis et scholastica.*[294] Not only are casuistic moral theology and speculative (= Scholastic) theology combined here; even in the title, as is often the case, an allusion is made to the eclecticism of Enlightenment philosophy (albeit around forty to sixty years late). Amort intends to defend a theology that "is free from the ready-made opinions of the individual schools, takes a middle position between rigidity and laxity, and is purged of useless questions."[295] The fact that Amort harks back to the Church Fathers via the Scholastics allows him to reestablish communication with humanistic theology.[296]

In his dedication to Pope Benedict XIV (1740–1758), to whom he submitted the work for revision and then dedicated it,[297] Amort makes his in-

291. See Arbogathe, *Theologia Cartesiana,* 100–3.

292. See Lemaire, *Cartésiansme,* 99–100, 127–33.

293. On his life and work see also Precht-Nussbaum, *Zwischen Augsburg und Rom;* Schaffner, *Eusebius Amort,* 9–67; Rückert, *Eusebius Amort.*

294. E. Amort, *Theologia eclectica, moralis et scholastica, Sub Auspiciis SS. D. N. Benedicti XIV. ad mentem SS. Patrum et Theologorum insignium, praesertim veterum conscripta* (Augsburg-Würzburg, 1752). The octavo edition was consulted; see also Precht-Nussbaum, *Zwischen Augsburg und Rom,* 505–10.

295. See Albrecht, *Eklektik,* 583: "Amort is therefore not thinking about a selection"; for a contrary view see Precht-Nussbaum, *Zwischen Augsburg und Rom,* 631–38.

296. For a detailed discussion of Amort's sources, see: Schaffner, *Amort,* 178–86. The patristic orientation can be found already in the commission from the bishop; see also Precht-Nussbaum, *Zwischen Augsburg und Rom,* 503–5.

297. The revisions are printed before the work but not made in the text itself. Most of them

tention clear: speculative theology should be taught in a lasting connection with practical theology. Superfluous controversies and *quaestiones* should be removed and only those questions retained which are necessary to elucidate the truths of the faith and to provide a new foundation for moral theology, given the prevailing laxism.[298] In the *Praefatio* he defines *theologia eclectica* as a theology that follows the Enlightenment critique of prejudice, free from outmoded reliance on the *opiniones* of individual theological schools or religious orders, midway between (Jansenist) rigorism and (probabilistic) laxism, purged of useless questions, with a thoroughly practical (moral-theological) orientation, apart from a few speculative-dogmatic treatises.[299] Amort draws his historical justification from the "golden rule" that Cardinal Otto Truchsess von Waldburg had established in 1557 in the humanist spirit in the first Statutes of the University of Dillingen.[300] Medieval and early modern theology derives its legitimacy essentially insofar as it transmits the principles of the Church Fathers.

Methodologically, as in his earlier *Philosophia Pollingana,* Amort professes a refined *"methodus scholastica."*[301] Its advantage lies essentially in precise terminology and expositional brevity. It manages to impress the individual controversies on the memory clearly and distinctly through definition, division, axioms, postulates, conclusions and proofs and offers the reader the greatest possible assurance, since it draws the individual conclusion directly from a few premises. However Amort clearly resists the geometric method and also the long argumentation of the Wolffian school.[302] Then, too, the individual questions have a very clear structure: *notanda* (presuppositions)—*dico* (conclusion)—*probatur* (proof through authority and reason)—*solvuntur objectiones* (objections and their solution).

In its plan, the *Theologia eclectica* does show an effort to combine positive and Scholastic theology, but also certain fissures.[303] The teaching on God and the angels is followed by the moral theological treatises on human

involve only elaboration in Scholastic terminology for the sake of precision and clarity. On the objections see also Precht-Nussbaum, *Zwischen Augsburg und Rom,* 408–510.

298. Amort, *Theol. ecl.,* Dedication (I, a4v–a5r).

299. Ibid., Praef. (I, b2r): *"Theologiam Eclecticam, a praejudicatis Scholarum particularium opinationibus liberam, inter rigores et laxitatem mediam; ab inutilibus quaestionibus emundatam, et si in paucos Tractatus Speculativos vel Dogmaticos, ad explananda mysteria fidei necessarios, excipias, per omnia Moralem ac Practicam"*; see also Albrecht, *Eklektik,* 583.

300. Amort, *Theol. ecl.* Praef. (I, b2r); see also Specht, *Geschichte,* 630.

301. Amort, *Philosophia Pollingana* (Augsburg, 1730), 8–10; see also Schaffner, *Amort,* 168–77; Precht-Nussbaum, *Zwischen Augsburg und Rom,* 167–77.

302. Amort, *Theol. ecl.,* Praef. (I, b2r).

303. See Schaffner, *Amort,* 186–207.

acts, virtues, law and justice, sins, and only then the doctrine of original sin and grace, the Incarnation and the sacraments, and after that, in connection with the sacrament of Penance, the teaching about the laws (Commandments and Precepts of the Church), contracts and the seven capital sins. In an appendix Amort presents constitutions and declarations by Benedict XIV and a systematic listing of condemned propositions. Thus the remnants of Scholastic (= speculative) theology in this work are essentially the dogmatic treatises on God, angels, original sin, grace, and Incarnation, while the teaching on the sacraments belongs both to speculative and to positive theology.

If we look, for example, at the teaching about God's knowledge and will, then Amort's eclecticism is plainly evident in the elements from the Jesuit theory of the *scientia media,* which was familiar to him from his studies in Ingolstadt, and from the *praedeterminatio physica* of the Thomists.[304] A decree that predetermines free future action is rejected as well as the Scotist *decretum condeterminans.* Instead a good meaning is attributed to the *praedeterminatio physica* as Gonet and the doctors from Salamanca interpreted it, which results in a reciprocal priority of decree and free action. On the other hand Amort recognizes also the *scientia media,* provided that it is explained correctly: *"Datus scientia media, si recte explicetur."*[305]

Remarkable also is the extensive discussion of demonology within the context of the treatise on the angels.[306] A separate realm of demons is rejected, as is the efficacy of stones, plants, and others against demons. At best their realm has a democratic structure, in which the power of the superiors consists only of persuasion. The influence of demons on men always depends on a special permission by God. The generation of insects and other complete living things by demons is impossible, but on the other hand they can, according to Amort, exercise an indirect influence, for example, on hens' eggs. The enlightened canon from Pollingen and court theologian of the Prince-Bishop of Augsburg, in his battle against Baroque superstition and the craving for miracles, was obviously trying to maintain here too a theological middle way between rationalistic Enlightenment and the popular faith with which he had to deal on a daily basis.[307]

304. Amort, *Theol. ecl.,* Tr. de Deo disp.5 De scientia Dei (I, 341–445).

305. Ibid., disp.5 q.3–4 (I, 368–425).

306. *Theol. ecl.,* De Angelis disp.4: De imperio. Potestate et operationibus Daemonum (II, 357–414).

307. See Precht-Nussbaum, *Zwischen Augsburg und Rom,* 520–88.

7 Prospect: Enlightenment and New Scholasticism

Many factors contributed to the abandonment of the research and teaching program of Scholastic theology in the eighteenth century. The most important ones with respect to the history of theology were the following:

1. Already in the seventeenth century we note a *critique* of Scholastic theology *within the Church,* chiefly in Protestantism where, after all, it had to be established on a new basis. In the name of Christian life and piety this critique was aimed at a pursuit of theology that had been reduced to Scholastic *quaestiones,* the defense of orthodoxy, and interconfessional polemics, all of which was then carried over into preaching. This critique was developed further in Pietism.[1] In addition there were forms of irenic theology (syncretism) and efforts to unite the churches, in which the fixed doctrinal distinctions in the Scholastic tradition receded into the background. In the Catholic world, especially in France, an independent existential-spiritual theology developed alongside the Scholastic tradition, both within and outside of Jansenism, which was articulated in treatises, sermons, and ascetical writings (Francis de Sales [1572–1622], Port Royal, Jean-Baptiste Bossuet [1664–1743], Fénélon [1651–1715]).
2. The *historical criticism* of Scholastic philosophy and theology likewise goes back to the seventeenth century (Christian Dreier [1610–1688], Jakob Thomasius [1622–1684]).[2] The application of historical-philological methods to Scripture and dogma became theologically important in biblical criticism (Hermann Samuel Reimarus [1694–1768], Johann Salomo Semler [1725–1791]), Church history, and the history of dogma. In contrast, the program of Scholastic theology was essentially ahistorical and metaphysically oriented. Historical scholarship was incorporated into the Protestant

1. See Schleiff, *Selbstkritik,* 12–44.
2. See Leinsle, *Reformversuche,* 127–49.

Neologie [new doctrine] and also, in the Catholic world, into the research of the Maurists and the Bollandists into the primary sources, although among Catholics it did not drive out the Scholastic paradigm of theology.[3]

3. Another decisive factor was the *philosophical critique* by the secular, usually antimetaphysical and sometimes materialistic Enlightenment philosophy, especially in France. It was relatively easy to adapt Christian Wolff's Scholastic system [of philosophy], which had a new methodology but was traditional in its metaphysical orientation, for the purposes of theology.[4] Institutionally, the philosophical *cursus* used previously was replaced—definitively after the Jesuit Order was dissolved in 1773—by the textbooks of Enlightenment philosophy.[5] The philosophy of Kant, German Idealism and early Romanticism, when adapted theologically, produced another kind of theology of the sort that would appear in the nineteenth century (Anton Günther [1783–1863], the Tübingen School).[6] The justification of such theology was radically called into question by the Church in the so-called crisis of Modernism.[7]

The abandonment of the old program did not take place abruptly, however. Nor were defenders of the old method lacking, and many suggestions for reform were eventually realized in the eighteenth-century university reforms.[8] Thus the Viennese professor Petrus Gazzaniga, O.P. (1723–1799), whose works were sometimes obligatory in the realm of the Habsburg dominions during the period of Josephism, defended a moderate use of the Scholastic method in systematic theology.[9] It had to be supplemented, however, by philological and historical studies. In this he showed himself to be the disciple of Abbot Stephan Rautenstrauch (1734–1785), who led the Maria-Theresian and Josephist reform of theological studies.[10] Both scholars relied on the small but fundamental treatise *De recto et perverso usu Theologiae scholasticae* by the later Prince-Abbot of Sankt Blasien, Martin Gerbert (1720–1793).[11]

3. See Merkt, *Das patristische Prinzip,* 196–213.

4. See Schäfer, *Kirche und Vernunft,* 103–51.

5. In Ingolstadt, for example, the works of the (Protestant) professor from Göttingen, Johann Heinrich Georg Feder (1740–1821).

6. See the essays in Coreth, Neidl, and Pfligersdorffer, eds., *Christliche Philosophie,* 1:86–419.

7. See esp. Weiss, *Modernismus.*

8. Concerning Würzburg, see, for example, Lesch, *Neuorientierung.*

9. See Wehofer, "Gazzaniga."

10. See Menzel, *Abt Stephan Rautenstrauch.*

11. M. Gerbert, *De recto et perverso usu Theologiae scholasticae* (Sankt Blasien, 1758); see also Deissler, *Fürstabt Martin Gerbert.*

Harking back to the critique of Scholasticism by John Gerson and the humanists, while employing also the methodology of Francis Bacon (1561–1626), Gerbert tried again—following in Mabillon's footsteps—to combine theological reform with monastic life. Although Fr. François Vavasseur, S.J. (1605–1681) cited as advantages of the Scholastic method its orderliness, concision and clarity, the ecclesiastical reliability and certainty of its opinions and *sententiae,* as well as the penetration and force of its arguments, in Gerbert's opinion this was only partially true.[12] They are outweighed by disadvantages: repugnant, artificial terminology (he points to Caramuel's *leptotatos* as the prime example), unnecessary controversies over mere words in matters about which we know nothing in the first place (e.g., about the beatific vision and the nature of the light of glory), the multiplication of useless questions, excessive use of reason while neglecting study of the sources, too much philosophy and logic while neglecting the auxiliary sciences, but above all the mere insistence on the dictated text of the teacher. Useless Scholastic questions are detrimental to monastic life, according to the Spanish Thomist and Benedictine Cardinal Joseph Saënz d'Aguirre (1630–1699). They deal with matters that are either clear anyway or else entirely incomprehensible; they not infrequently offend against piety and good morals. They treat subjects in the wrong place (e.g., the introductory questions about the theory of science) or are humanly insoluble.[13] Not only does this Scholasticism fail to promote morality as it should; Gerbert sees harmful consequences also and especially for theology and the Church as well as for the theologian himself. As a result of the obscurity of Scholastic terminology, most mysteries of the faith cannot be explained correctly to the faithful. They are consequently deprived of the fruits of faith and knowledge. The most talented, however, are frightened off from the study of theology; on the other hand, the only ones who do put on the harness are the ones who debate the best and can shout the loudest. Moreover, because of the poor organization of the courses, after completing their studies theologians, priests, and religious have no interest whatsoever in continuing education in theology, since "it always deals with the same subjects."[14]

Now the reform of theology, which Gerbert views in biblical terms as the restoration of the Lord's vineyard, is not to be achieved by discarding Scholastic theology as a whole, but rather by making its alleged advantages

12. Gerbert, *De usu* c.2 §1 (12).
13. Ibid., c.3–11 (24–103).
14. Ibid., c.12–14 (104–22).

useful as features of a systematic theology. Instead of quibbles over terminology and introductory questions, an appropriate lexicon should be made available. Jean Mabillon (1632–1707) and Johannes Maldonato, S.J. (1534–1583) recommend the elimination of all questions that are unrelated to progress in the spiritual and moral life, proceed from mere curiosity and the endeavor to prove even the most obscure points of theology, or are utterly superfluous. Nevertheless such questions—and here Augustine is cited as an authority—can be allowed occasionally as an exercise.[15] In contrast to the Scholastic but also rationalist optimism about reason, Gerbert would like to see a more modest, self-critical approach to theology by fallen human reason. A moderate employment of logic is certainly required, but not the thoroughgoing syllogistic organization of theology (for instance the Wolffian method). Above all, when just beginning the course of studies one should not debate and imagine that one can settle everything. One should be just as cautious in dealing with philosophy as a whole, even though theology cannot do without its concepts. Mabillon considers logic, parts of physics, and metaphysics to be necessary; yet the faith of the simple people *(fides popularis)* manages without metaphysics and is no less pure on that account. Instead of the restriction to a single author in most schools, *"polymathia"* is required; should the occasion arise, one should also refrain from making one's own judgment. Theology, moreover, should be combined with monastic training and should not be attempted in a "proletarian" fashion *("proletarie")*.[16]

Within theology itself, the most important thing is to abolish the separation of Scholastic and positive theology (in the Catholic sense). Gerbert blames this separation for the increasing idleness of Scholastic theology, since all the important subjects are already treated more simply in positive theology: *loci,* controversies, dogmas and Scripture. Moreover moral theology, freed from mere casuistry, should be joined with spiritual or mystical theology. The latter, however, is related to dogmatic theology as well: "devotional duties" *("officia pietatis")* cannot be separated from Church doctrine, as has happened sometimes in Pietism. The lecture on systematic theology, furthermore, must be accompanied by information about historical sources, yet should not be replaced by it. (Gerbert sometimes appears to be prone to this danger in his own textbooks.) What is required instead is solid sys-

15. Ibid., c.15–17 (123–44).
16. Ibid., c.18–21 (144–76).

tematic theology, in which the best parts of the Scholastic method should be employed. To that end the preparatory study of languages, philosophy, and historical criticism is indispensable. Gerbert thinks that this is best accomplished in monastic schools, since the dispute over legal ownership between systematic and positive theology continues at the universities.[17]

The reaction to the Enlightenment agenda, nevertheless, led also to a hardening of the Scholasticism that was still in existence and to a new reliance on its authors. Thus it was no accident that the incipient Neoscholasticism in Italy, represented by Salvatore Roselli (1772–1847) and Vincenzo Buzzetti (1777–1824) harked back to the *Philosophia juxta inconcussa tutissimaque D. Thomae dogmata* by the Dominican Antoine Goudin (1639–1695), which was already apologetic and conservative in its approach, and the theological works of Gonet.[18] The transition from post-Tridentine Scholasticism to Neoscholasticism was thus made more smoothly in the Italian Thomistic tradition than north of the Alps.

In Germany, on the other hand, most theologians reacted negatively to the "new" or "repristinated" Scholasticism that was invading from Italy and France. Characteristic of this was the 1823 study by Tübingen professor Johann Baptist Hirscher (1788–1865), *Über das Verhältniss des Evangeliums zu der theologischen Scholastik der neuesten Zeit im katholischen Deutschland* [*On the relation of the Gospel to recent theological Scholasticism in Catholic Germany*]. With a view to catechesis, in responding to a catechetical work from France that was inspired by Scholasticism, Hirscher developed a fundamental discussion of the theological justification of "Scholasticism in the broader sense." The latter is accused of failing to set forth Christian doctrine as an organically ordered whole; "instead of depicting the economy of God's institutions for the building of his kingdom as a great, coherent, wise, and grace-filled work, it arranges a set of dogmas alongside one another without connecting them to the whole of a salvific order."[19] It therefore lacks the appropriate system and—given the identification of Scholastic with systematic theology—it is a contradiction in terms. Yet the system presupposed by Hirscher is precisely that of the economy of salvation, not the system of metaphysically interconnected propositions. The Scholastic theologian

17. Ibid., c.22–23 (176–204).

18. Goudin's work was reprinted four times between 1851 and 1886. See Schmidinger, "Überblick zur Neuscholastik," 196; Schmidinger, "Streit um die Anfänge," 72–82.

19. J. B. Hirscher, *Über das Verhältniss des Evangeliums zu der theologischen Scholastik der neuesten Zeit im katholischen Deutschland* (Tübingen, 1823; reprinted Frankfurt am Main, 1967), 2.

is likewise reproached for disregarding the economy of salvation and overloading and distorting "his lectures with useless questions, human reveries, arbitrary speculations, and strange, unfounded statements." From the catechetical perspective, Christianity is thereby restricted to a mere collection of dogmas, commandments, and prohibitions. At the same time this Neoscholasticism is trying "emphatically in Catholic Germany to retake possession of its place, which for a time has been rather deserted." Therefore it is "an indisputable and holy duty to oppose it quite earnestly"; for it claims "to present the Catholic concept of doctrine, if not exclusively, then at least eminently" and therefore demands "that one should make use of it when instructing Catholic youth in the Christian faith."[20]

The battle lines delineated here became fixed as a result of Church politics: the term "Neoscholasticism" was used pointedly in Ultramontane circles and by those associated with papal interests in Germany and in the "Third Scholasticism" in France.[21] Unlike the lively Scholasticism of the early modern period, the early Neoscholasticism characteristically understood its object to be not so much Scholastic education [*Schulbetrieb*] as an idealized or ideological return to the Middle Ages, especially to the Thomistic tradition, with an emphasis on ecclesiality and a clear rejection of modern philosophy:

1. "True" Catholic theology can be developed only by returning to the form of theology that is considered classic, especially that of the thirteenth century. The interpretation of early Scholasticism as the preparation, and late Scholasticism as the abolition of the high Scholastic synthesis of faith and knowledge, theology, and philosophy in Thomas Aquinas depends on this judgment.
2. Not only theology but also philosophy as its mere handmaid is subject to the Magisterium of the Church in everything. The philosophy that agrees with the Magisterium, being the "perennial philosophy" (*"philosophia perennis"*), becomes the ahistorical norm of philosophy and the only permissible auxiliary of theology.
3. Secular or Protestant modern theology does not satisfy this requirement and is therefore rejected as an "anti-Christian revolution" (J. Maritain).
4. A mistrust of nature (including natural science) prevails theologically. The natural and the supernatural orders ("nature" and grace) are strictly separated.[22]

20. Ibid., 5.
21. See Gilbert, "Die dritte Scholastik."
22. See Schmidinger, "Scholastik," 48–50.

As a result of the adjustment to the dogma of papal infallibility and the encyclical *Aeterni Patris* by Leo XIII (1878–1903), on August 4, 1879, Neoscholasticism, too, became a firm Church doctrine.[23] Deviations from it were condemned under suspicion of "Modernism."[24] Catholic education in philosophy and theology was often uncoupled from scientific development or else noted the findings of the [natural and historical] sciences only as innovations to be rejected. Both the reputation and the pursuit of Scholastic philosophy and theology have suffered well into the twentieth century as a result of the narrowing of Scholasticism in practice to Neoscholasticism. On the other hand we cannot overlook the accomplishments of research, inspired by Neoscholasticism, into the sources of medieval philosophy and theology, specifically in the standard editions of Thomas Aquinas, Bonaventure, and Duns Scotus that were begun (even though they were in need of revision).[25] Unlike Scholastic and Neoscholastic theology, which to a large extent is ahistorical in its thinking, historical research into Scholastic theology sees in it a program—which gradually gained acceptance through many ruptures and conflicts—of academically imparted systematic theology that is closely connected with philosophy; it sees its advantages and disadvantages, its expressions that reflect former times, but also what it has to offer by way of methods and inquiries that should be taken seriously.

23. See Aubert, "Die Enzyklika 'Aeterni Patris'"; Quinto, *Scholastica,* 408–11.
24. See Weiss, *Modernismus.*
25. See Kluxen, "Die geschichtliche Erforschung."

Bibliography

Aertsen, Jan A. "'Von Gott kann man nichts erkennen, außer dass er ist' (Satz 215 der Pariser Verurteilung): Die Debatte über die (Un-)möglichkeit einer Gotteserkenntnis *quid est*." In *Nach der Verurteilung*. Edited by Aertsen, et al., 2001, 22–37.

———, and Andreas Speer, eds. *Was ist Philosophie im Mittelalter? Akten des X. Internationalen Kongresses für mitteralterliche Philosophie der Socitété Internationale pour l'Étude de la Philosophie Médiévale, 25. bis 30. August 1997 in Erfurt*. Miscellanea Mediaevalia 26. Berlin: Walter de Gruyter, 1998.

———, et al., eds. *Nach der Verurteilung von 1277: Philosophie und Theologie an der Universität von Paris im letzten Viertel des 13. Jahrhunderts: Studien und Texte*. Miscellanea Mediaevalia 28. Berlin: Walter de Gruyter, 2001.

Albrecht, Michael. *Eklektik: Eine Begriffsgeschichte mit Hinweisen auf die Philosophie- und Wissenschaftsgeschichte*. Quaestiones 5. Stuttgart-Bad Cannstatt, 1993.

Altermatt, Augustinus. *Zum Problem der physischen Prämotion: Die Prämotionslehre nach dem Salzburger Philosophen P. Ludwig Babenstuber OSB*. Diss., Fribourg, 1931.

Althaus, Paul. *Die Prinzipien der deutschen reformierten Dogmatik im Zeitalter der aristotelischen Scholastik*. Leipzig, 1914.

Amorós, León. "La teologia como ciencia practica en la escuela franciscana en los tiempos que preceden a Escoto." *AHD* 9 (1934): 261–303.

Anfray, Jean-Pascal. "Prescience divine, décrets concomitants et liberté humaine d'après Bartolomeo Mastri." In *Rem in seipsa cernere: Saggi sul pensiero filosofico di Bartolomeo Mastri (1602–1673)*. Edited by Marco Forlivesi. Subsidia Mediaevalia Patavina 8. Padua, 2004, 556–92.

Angelini, Giuseppe. *L'Ortodossia e la Grammatica: Analisi di struttura e deduzione storica della Teologia Trinitaria di Prepositino*. Rome, 1972.

Angenendt, Arnold. *Geschichte der Religiosität im Mittelalter*. Darmstadt, 1997.

Antolić-Piper, Pia A. "Zur Begründung der Theologie im Horizont von Philosophie, Heiliger Schrift und Weisheit bei Roger Bacon OFM." In *What is "Theology?"* Edited by Olszewski, 2007, 673–94.

Appuhn-Radtke, Sibylle. *Das Thesenblatt im Hochbarock: Studien zu einer graphischen Gattung am Beispiel der Werke Bartholomäus Kilians*. Weissenhorn, 1988.

Armogathe, Jean-Robert. *Theologia Cartesiana: L'explication physique de l'Eucharistie chez Descartes et Desgabets*. Archives internationales d'histoire des idées 84. The Hague, 1977.

———. "Probabilisme et Libre-Arbitre: la théologie morale de Caramuel y Lobkowitz." In *Le meraviglie del probabile. Juan Caramuel 1606–1682: Atti del Convegno internazio-*

nale di studi, Vigevano 29–31 ottobre 1982. Edited by Paolo Pissavino. Vigevano, 1990, 35–40.

Ashworth, E. Jennifer. *Language and Logic in the Post-Medieval Period.* Synthese 12. Boston, 1971.

Aubert, Roger. "Die Enzyklika 'Aeterni Patris' und die weiteren päpstlichen Stellungnahmen zur christlichen Philosophie." In *Christliche Philosophie.* Edited by Coreth, Neidl, and Pfligersdorffer, 1988, 2:310–32.

Baeumker, Clemens. "Die christliche Philosophie des Mittelalters." In *Die Kultur der Gegenwart: Ihre Entwicklung und ihre Ziele.* Edited by Paul Hinneberg. Leipzig, 1913, 339–43.

Baldwin, John W. *Masters, Princes and Merchants: The Social Views of Peter the Chanter and His Circle.* 2 vols. Princeton, N.J., 1970.

Baltzer, Otto. *Die Sentenzen des Petrus Lombardus: Ihre Quellen und ihre dogmengeschichtliche Bedeutung.* Leipzig, 1902. Reprint, Aalen, 1972.

Bannach, Klaus. *Die Lehre von der doppelten Macht Gottes bei Wilhelm von Ockham.* VIEG 75. Wiesbaden, 1975.

Baron, Frank. "Der erste Druck einer Schrift Augustins: Ein Beitrag zur Geschichte des frühen Buchdrucks und des Humanismus." *HJ* 91 (1971): 108–18.

Bataillon, Louis-Jaques. *La prédication au XIIIe siècle en France et Italie: Études et documents.* Aldershot-Brookfield, 1993.

———. "Sermons rédigés, sermons réportés (XIIIe siècle)." *Prédication* 3:69–86.

———. "Les instruments de travail des prédicateurs au XIIIe siècle." *Prédication* 4:197–209.

———. "Intermédiaires entre les traités de morale pratique et les sermons: les *distinctiones* bibliques alphabétiques." *Prédication* 6: 213–26.

———. "Les crises de l'Université de Paris d'après les sermons universitaires." *Prédication* 8: 155–69.

———. "L'emploi du langage philosophique dans les sermons du treizième siècle." *Prédication* 9: 983–91.

———. "*Similitudines* et *exempla* dans les sermons du XIIIe siècle." *Prédication* 10: 191–205.

———. "Les images dans les sermons du XIIIe siècle." *Prédication* 11: 327–95.

———. "La predicazione dei religiosi mendicanti del secolo XIII nell' Italia centrale." *Prédication* 12: 691–94.

Baudry, Léon. *La querelle des futurs contingents (Louvain 1465–1475).* Études de Philosophie Médiévale 38. Paris, 1950.

Bauer, Emmanuel J. *Thomistische Metaphysik an der alten Benediktineruniversität Salzburg: Darstellung und Interpretation einer philosophischen Schule des 17./18. Jahrhunderts.* Salzburger Theologische Studien 1. Innsbruck/Vienna, 1996.

Bayer, Oswald. "Melanchthons Theologiebegriff." In *Der Theologe Melanchthon.* Edited by Frank, 2000, 25–47.

Bazán, B. Carlos. "Conception of the Agent Intellect and the Limits of Metaphysics." In *Nach der Verurteilung.* Edited by Aertsen, et al., 2001, 178–210.

Beaude, Joseph. "Desgabets et son œuvre." *Revue de synthèse* 35 (1974): 7–17.

———. "Cartésianisme et anticartésianisme de Desgabets." *Studia Cartesiana* 1 (1979): 1–24.

Beckmann, Jan P. "Weltkontingenz und menschliche Vernunft bei Wilhelm von Ockham."

In *L'homme et son univers au moyen âge*. Edited by Christian Wenin. Louvain-la-Neuve, 1986, 445–57.

Beinert, Wolfgang. *Die Lehre von der Kirche nach den Schriften des Rupert von Deutz, Honorius Augustodunensis und Gerhoch von Reichersberg. BGPhThMA,* n.s., 13. Münster, 1973.

Bejczy, István. *Erasmus and the Middle Ages: The Historical Consciousness of a Christian Humanist.* Brill's Studies in Intellectual History 106. Leiden, 2001.

Benrath, Gustav Adolf. "Die deutsche evangelische Universität der Reformationszeit." In *Universität und Gelehrtenstand.* Edited by Rössler and Franz, 1970, 63–83.

Benson, Robert Louis, and Gilles Constable. *Renaissance and Renewal in the Twelfth Century.* Oxford, 1982.

Berg, Dieter. *Armut und Wissenschaft: Beiträge zur Geschichte des Studienwesens der Bettelorden im 13. Jahrhundert.* Geschichte und Gesellschaft 15. Düsseldorf, 1977.

Bériou, N. "Les sermons latins après 1200." In *Sermon.* Edited by Kienzle, 2000, 363–447.

Berndt, Rainer. "Hugo von St. Viktor. Theologie als Schriftauslegung." In *Theologen.* Edited by Köpf, 2002, 96–112.

———. *André de Saint Victor († 1175): Exégète et théologien.* Bibliotheca Victorina 2. Paris, 1991.

Bertola, Eremengildo. "La 'Glossa ordinaria' biblica ed i suoi problemi." *RThAM* 54 (1978): 34–78.

Bérubé, Camille. "Der 'Dialog' S. Bonaventura—Roger Bacon." In *Roger Bacon in der Diskussion.* Edited by Florian Uhl. Frankfurt, 2001, 67–135.

Beumer, Johannes. "Die Theologie als intellectus fidei: Dargestellt an Hand der Lehre des Wilhelm von Auxerre und Petrus von Tarantasia." *Scholastik* 17 (1942): 32–41.

———. "Erleuchteter Glaube: Die Theorie Heinrichs von Gent und ihr Fortleben in der Spätscholastik." *FStud* 37 (1955): 129–60.

———. "Die Stellung Heinrichs von Gent zum theologischen Studium der Frau." *Scholastik* 32 (1957): 81–85.

———. "Augustinismus und Thomismus in der theologischen Prinzipienlehre des Aegidius Romanus." *Scholastik* 32 (1957): 542–60.

Beyer, Michael, and Günther Wartenberg, eds. *Humanismus und Wittenberger Reformation: Festgabe anlässlich des 500. Geburtstages des Praeceptor Germaniae Philipp Melanchthon am 16. Februar 1997.* Leipzig, 1996.

Bianchi, Laura. "1277: A Turning Point in Medieval Philosophy?" In *Was ist Philosophie im Mittelalter?* Edited by Aertsen and Speer, 1998, 90–110.

Bizer, Ernst. *Frühorthodoxie und Rationalismus.* Theologische Studien 71. Zürich, 1963.

Bliemetzrieder, Franz. *Anselm von Laons systematische Sentenzen. BGPhMA* 18/2, 3. Münster, 1919.

———. "Autour de l'œuvre théologique d'Anselme de Laon." *RThAM* 1 (1929): 435–83.

Blum, Paul Richard. *Philosophenphilosophie und Schulphilosophie: Typen des Philosophierens in der Neuzeit.* StudLeib Sonderheft 27. Stuttgart, 1998.

Boehm, Laetitia. "Humanistische Bildungsbewegung und mittelalterliche Universitätsverfassung: Aspekte zur frühneuzeitlichen Reformgeschichte der deutschen Universitäten." In *Universités.* Edited by Paquet and Ijsewijn, 1978, 315–46.

Bohatec, Josef. *Die cartesianische Scholastik in der Philosophie und reformierten Dogmatik des 17. Jahrhunderts.* Leipzig, 1912. Reprint, Hildesheim, 1966.

Borgolte, Michael. "'Selbstverständnis' und 'Mentalitäten': Bewußtsein, Verhalten und

Handeln mittelalterlicher Menschen im Verständnis moderner Historiker." *Archiv für Kulturgeschichte* 79 (1997): 189–210.

Boulnois, Olivier. "Le chiasme: La philosophie selon les théologiens et la théologie selon les artistes, de 1267 à 1300." In *Was ist Philosophie im Mittelalter?* Edited by Aertsen and Speer, 1998, 595–607.

Bruyère, Nelly. *Méthode et Dialectique dans l'œuvre de La Ramée.* De Pétrarque à Descartes 45. Paris, 1984.

Burger, Christoph. *Aedificatio, Fructus, Utilitas: Johannes Gerson als Professor der Theologie und Kanzler der Universität Paris.* Beiträge zur Historischen Theologie 70. Tübingen, 1986.

———. "Der Augustinschüler gegen die modernen Pelagianer: Das 'auxilium speciale dei' in der Gnadenlehre Gregors von Rimini." In *Gregor von Rimini.* Edited by Oberman, 1981, 195–240.

Burger, Maria. "Die Bedeutung der Aristotelesrezeption für das Verständnis der Theologie als Wissenschaft bei Albertus Magnus." In *Albertus Magnus und die Anfänger der Aristoteles-Rezeption im lateinischen Mittelalter: Von Richardus Rufus bis zu Franciscus de Mayronis.* Edited by Honnefelder, Ludger, et al. Subsidia Albertina 1. Münster, 2005, 281–306.

Burrows, Mark Steven. *Jean Gerson and* De Consolatione Theologiae *(1418): The Consolation of a Biblical and Reforming Theology for a Disordered Age.* Beiträge zur Historischen Theologie 78. Tübingen, 1991.

Cantin, André. "'Ratio' et 'auctoritas' dans la première phase de la controverse eucharistique entre Bérenger et Lanfranc." *RÉAug* 20 (1974): 155–86.

———. "La 'raison' dans le 'De sacra coena' de Bérenger de Tours." *RechAug* 12 (1977): 174–211.

Caruso, Ester. *Pedro Hurtado de Mendoza e la rinascita del nominalismo nella Scolastica del Seicento.* Pubblicazioni del "Centro si Studi del Pensiero Filosofico del Cinquecento e del Seicento in relazione ai problemi della scienza" del Consiglio Nazionale delle Ricerche. Università degli Studi di Milano. Serie I, 13. Florence, 1979.

Castro, Manuel de. "Bibliographía de franciscanos escotistas españoles." In *Homo et Mundus: Acta Quinti Congressus Scotistici Internationalis, Salamanticae, 21–26 septembris 1981.* Edited by Camille Bérubé. Studia Scholastico-Scotistica 8. Rome, 1984, 437–58.

Cazier, Pierre. "Le *Livre des règles* de Tyconius: Sa transmission du *De doctrina christiana* aux *Sentences* d'Isidore de Séville." *RÉAug* 19 (1973): 241–61.

———. *Isidore de Séville et la naissance de l'Espagne catholique.* Théologie historique 96. Paris, 1994.

Charland, Thomas-Marie. *Artes Praedicandi: Contribution à l'histoire de la rhétorique au moyen âge.* Publications de l'Institut d'Études Médiévales d'Ottawa 7. Paris, 1936.

Châtillon, François. "Vocabulaire et prosodie du distique attributé à Augustine de Dacie sur les quatre sens de l'écriture." In *L'Homme devant Dieu. Festschrift H. de Lubac.* Lyon, 1964, 2:17–28.

Châtillon, Jean. "Le mouvement théologique dans la France de Philippe August." In *D'Isidore de Séville à Saint Thomas d'Aquin.* Vol. IX. London, 1985, 881–902.

Chenu, Marie-Dominique. "Théologie symbolique et exégèse scolastique aux XIIe et XIIIe siècles." In *Melanges Joseph de Ghellinck S.J.* Gembloux, 1951, 2:509–26.

———. *La Théologie comme science au XIIIe siècle.* Bibliothèque Thomiste 33. Paris, 1957.

———. *La théologie au douzième siècle.* Paris, 1966.

———. "Un essai de méthode théologique au XIIe siècle." *MS* 35 (1973): 258–67.

Claus, A. *Ho Scholastikós.* Diss., University of Cologne, 1962.

Cloes, Henri. "La systématisation théologique pendant la première moitié du XIIe siècle." *EThL* 34 (1958): 277–329.

Clouse, Robert Gordon. *The Influence of John Henry Alsted on English Millenarian Thought in the Seventeenth Century.* Ann Arbor, 1963.

Codina Mír, Gabriel. *Aux Sources de la pédagogie des Jésuites: Le "Modus Parisiensis."* Bibliotheca Instituti Historici S.I. 28. Rome, 1968.

Colish, Marcia L. *Peter Lombard.* 2 vols. Brill's Studies in Intellectual History 41. Leiden, 1994.

Coreth, Emerich, Walter M. Neidl, and Georg Pfligersdorffer, eds. *Christliche Philosophie im katholischen Denken des 19. und 20. Jahrhunderts.* Vol. 2, *Rückgriff auf scholastisches Erbe.* Graz, 1988.

Cottiaux, Jean. "La conception de la théologie chez Abélard." *RHE* 28 (1932): 247–95, 533–51, 788–828.

Courtenay, William J. *Capacity and Volition: A History of the Distinction of Absolute and Ordained Power.* Quodlibet 8. Bergamo, 1990.

———. "The Paris Faculty of Theology in the Late Thirteenth and Early Fourteenth Centuries." In *Nach der Verurteilung.* Edited by Aertson, et al., 233–47.

Craig, William Lane. *The Problem of Divine Foreknowing and Future Contingents from Aristotle to Suarez.* Brill's Studies in Intellectual History 7. Leiden, 1988.

Crusius, Irene. "Gabriel Biel—eine Karriere zwischen vita contemplativa und vita activa." In *Gabriel Biel und die Brüder vom gemeinsamen Leben: Beiträge aus Anlass des 500. Todestages des Tübinger Theologen.* Edited by Ulrich Köpf and Sönke Lorenz. Contubernium 47. Stuttgart, 1998, 1–23.

Dales, Richard C. "The Origins of the Doctrine of the Double Truth." *Viator* 15 (1984): 169–79.

———. *Medieval Discussions of the Eternity of the World.* Brill's Studies in Intellectual History 18. Leiden, 1990.

Dalfen, Ch. *Die Stellung des Erasmus von Rotterdam zur scholastischen Methode.* Osnabrück, 1936.

Daniel, Norman. *The Arabs and Medieval Europe.* London, 1975.

Davy, Marie-Madelaine. *Les sermons univeritaires Parisiens de 1230–1231.* Études de philosophie médiévale 15. Paris, 1931.

Deissler, Alfons. *Fürstabt Martin Gerbert von St. Blasien und die theologische Methode.* SMGB Erg.H. 15. Munich, 1940.

Derwich, Marek, and Martial Staub, eds. *Die "Neue Frömmigkeit." in Europa im Spätmittelalter.* Veröffentlichungen des Max-Planck-Instituts für Geschichte 205. Göttingen, 2004.

Dettloff, Werner. *Die Entwicklung der Akzeptations- und Verdienstlehre von Duns Scotus bis Luther. BGPhThMA* 40, no. 2. Münster, 1963.

Dibon, Paul A. G. *L'enseignement philosophique dans les Universités Néerlandaises à l'époque pré-cartésienne.* Diss., Leiden, 1954.

Dohmen, Christoph. "Vom vielfachen Schriftsinn—Möglichkeiten und Grenzen neuerer Zugänge zu biblischen Texten." In *Neue Formen der Schriftauslegung?* QuD 140. Edited by Thomas Sternberg. Freiburg, 1992, 13–74.

Döllinger, Ignaz v., and Franz Heinrich Reusch. *Geschichte der Moralstreitigkeiten in der römisch-katholischen Kirche seit dem sechzehnten Jahrhundert.* 2 vols. Nördlingen, 1889.

Donneaud, H. "Le sens du mot 'theologia' chez Bonaventure." *RThom* 102 (2002): 273–95.
Doucet, Vincent. *Commentaires sur les Sentences.* Quaracchi, 1954.
Dreitzel, Horst. *Protestantischer Aristotelismus und absoluter Staat: Die "Politica" des Henning Arnisaeus (ca. 1575–1636).* VIEG 55. Wiesbaden, 1970.
Dreyer, Mechthild. *More mathematicorum: Rezeption und Transformation der antiken Gestalten wissenschaftlichen Wissens im 12. Jahrhundert. BGPhThMA*, n.s., 47. Münster, 1996.
Drossbach, Gisela. "Innovation und Inquisition: Literaturproduktion in Wien um 1400." In *What Is "Theology?"* Edited by Olszewski, 2007, 487–506.
Duchrow, Ulrich. *Sprachverständnis und biblisches Hören bei Augustin.* Hermeneutische Untersuchungen zur Theologie 5. Tübingen, 1965.
Duhr, Bernhard. *Geschichte der Jesuiten in den Ländern deutscher Zunge.* Vols. 1–2. Freiburg im Breisgau, 1913/1928.
Ebeling, Gerhard. *Lutherstudien.* 3 vols. Tübingen, 1971–89.
Eckert, Willehad Paul, ed. *Thomas von Aquino. Interpretation und Rezeption.* Walberberger Studien, Phil. Reihe 5. Mainz, 1974.
Egenter, Richard. "Vernunft und Glaubenswahrheit im Aufbau der theologischen Wissenschaft nach Aegidius Romanus." In *Philosophia perennis: Abhandlungen zu ihrer Vergangenheit und Gegenwart.* Festschrift J. Geyser. Regensburg, 1930, 1:195–208.
Ehrle, Franz. *Der Sentenzenkommentar Peters von Candida, des Pisaner Papstes Alexanders V.* FStud Beih. 9. Münster, 1925.
Elswijk, H. C. van. *Gilbert Porreta: Sa vie, son œuvre, sa pensée.* SSL 33. Leuven, 1966.
Emery, Kent, Jr. "The Image of God Deep in the Mind: The Continuity of Cognition According to Henry of Ghent." In *Nach der Verurteilung.* Edited by Aertsen, et al., 2001, 59–124.
Enders, Markus. "Zur Bedeutung des Ausdrucks *theologia* im 12. Jahrhundert und seinen antiken Quellen." In *What Is "Theology"?* Edited by Olszewski, 2007, 19–37.
Ernst, Stephan. *Gewissheit des Glaubens: Der Glaubenstraktat Hugos von St. Viktor als Zugang zu seiner theologischen Systematik. BGPhThMA*, n.s., 30. Münster, 1987.
Evans, Gillian R. "Boethian and Euclidean Axiomatic Method in the Theology of the Later Twelfth Century." *Archives Internationales d'histoire des Sciences* 105 (1980): 36–52.
———. *Old Arts and New Theology: The Beginning of Theology as an Academic Discipline.* Oxford, 1980.
———. "Zachary of Besançon and the Bible Contradictions." *AnPraem* 58 (1982): 319–23.
———. *Philosophy and Theology in the Middle Ages.* London, 1993.
———, ed. *The Medieval Theologians.* Oxford, 2001.
Eynde, Damien van den. "Les *Magistri* du Commentaire 'Unum ex Quattuor' du Zacharias Chrysopolitanus." *Antonianum* 23 (1948): 1–32, 181–222.
Faber, Eva-Maria. *Symphonie von Gott und Mensch: Die responsorische Struktur und Vermittlung in der Theologie Johannes Calvins.* Neukirchen-Vluyn, 1999.
Ferrarino, Pietro. "Quadruvium (Quadrivio dei sei arti?—La caverna platonica)." In *Atti del Congresso Internazionale di Studi Varroniani, Rieti Settembre 1974.* Rieti, 1976, 2:359–64.
Fichtenau, Heinrich. *Ketzer und Professoren: Häresie und Vernunftglaube im Hochmittelalter.* Munich, 1992.
Filthaut, Ephrem. *Roland von Cremona O.P. und die Anfänge der Scholastik im Predigerorden: Ein Beitrag zur Geistesgeschichte der älteren Dominikaner.* Vechta i.O., 1936.

Finkenzeller, Josef. *Offenbarung und Theologie nach der Lehre des Johannes Duns Skotus: Eine historische und systematische Untersuchung. BGPhThMA* 38, no. 5. Münster, 1960.

Flasch, Kurt. *Geschichte der Philosophie in Text und Darstellung.* Vol. 2, *Mittelalter.* Stuttgart, 1982.

———. *Einführung in die Philosophie des Mittelalters.* Darmstadt, 1987.

———, ed. *Aufklärung im Mittelalter? Die Verurteilung von 1277: Das Dokument des Bischofs von Paris.* Excerpta classica 6. Mainz, 1989.

Fleming, Julia A. *Defending Probabilism: The Moral Theology of Juan Caramuel.* Washington, D.C., 2006.

Fontaine, Jacques. *Isidore de Seville et la culture classique dans l'Espagne wisigothique.* Paris, 1983.

Forlivesi, Marco. *Scotistarum Princeps: Bartolomeo Mastri (1602–1673) e il suo tempo.* Fonti e Studi Francescani 11. Padua, 2002.

Francescini, Sylvio Hermann de. "Le thomisme au secours du jansénisme dans la querelle de la grace: Vrais et faux thomistes au temps de la Bulle *Unigenitus.*" *RThom* 115 (2007): 375–418.

Frank, Günter. *Die theologische Philosophie Philipp Melanchthons (1497–1560).* Erfurter Theologische Studien 67. Hildesheim, 1995.

———. *Die Vernunft des Gottesgedankens: Religionsphilosophische Studien zur frühen Neuzeit.* Quaestiones 13. Stuttgart, 2003.

———, ed. *Der Theologe Melanchthon.* Melanchthon-Schriften der Stadt Bretten 5. Stuttgart, 2000.

Frank, Isnard W. "Der Wiener Dominikaner Johannes Werd († 1510) als Verfasser von Thomaskommentaren." In *Thomas von Aquino.* Edited by Eckert, 609–40.

Freedman, Joseph S. *European Academic Philosophy in the Late Sixteenth and Early Seventeenth Centuries: The Life, Significance and Philosophy of Clemens Timpler (1563/4–1624).* Studien und Materialien zur Geschichte der Philosophie 27. 2 vols. Hildesheim, 1988.

Friedensburg, Walter. *Der Reichstag zu Speyer 1526 im Zusammenhang der politischen und kirchlichen Entwicklung Deutschlands im Reformationszeitalter.* Historische Untersuchungen 5. Berlin, 1887. Reprint, Nieuwskoop, 1970.

Friederichs, Josef. *Die Theologie als spekulative und praktische Wissenschaft nach Bonaventura und Thomas von Aquin.* Bonn, 1940.

Fuchs, Michael. *Zeichen und Wissen: Das Verhältnis der Zeichentheorie zur Theorie des Wissens und der Wissenschaften im dreizehnten Jahrhundert. BGPhThMA,* n.s., 51. Münster, 1999.

Gabriel, Astrik Ladislaus. "The Conflict between the Chancellor and the University of Masters and Students at Paris during the Middle Ages." In *Auseinandersetzungen an der Pariser Universität im XIII. Jahrhundert.* Edited by Zimmerman, 1976, 106–54.

———. "'Via Antiqua' and 'Via Moderna' and the Migration of Paris Students and Masters to the German Universities in the Fifteenth Century." In *Antiqui und Moderni.* Edited by Zimmerman, 1971, 439–83.

Ganoczy, Alexandre. *Le jeune Calvin: Genèse et évolution de sa vocation réformatrice.* VIEG 40. Wiesbaden, 1966.

———, and Stefan Scheld. *Die Hermeneutik Calvins: Geistesgeschichtliche Voraussetzungen und Grundzüge.* VIEG 114. Wiesbaden, 1983.

Geerlings, Wilhelm. "Les Commentaires patristiques latins." In *Commentaire.* Edited by Goulet-Cazé, 199–211.

Gemeinhardt, Peter. "Die theologische Methode Anselms von Canterbury in seiner *Epistola de incarnatione Verbi.*" In *What Is "Theology."* Edited by Olszewski, 2007, 39–57.
Gerwing, Manfred. "Die sogenannte Devotio moderna." In *Jan Hus.* Edited by Seibt, 49–58.
Geyer, Bernhard. "Der Begriff der scholastischen Theologie." In *Synthesen in der Philosophie der Gegenwart: Festgabe A. Dyroff.* Edited by Erich Feldmann. Bonn, 1926, 112–25.
———. "Facultas theologica. Eine bedeutungsgeschichtliche Untersuchung." *ZKG* 75 (1964): 133–45.
Ghellinck, Joseph de. *Le mouvement théologique du XIIe siècle.* Brügge, 1948.
Giacon, Carlo. *La seconda scolastica.* 3 vols. Milan, 1944–1950.
Gibson, M. "The Case of Berengar of Tours." *Studies in Church History* 7 (1971): 61–68.
Gilbert, Paul. "Die dritte Scholastik in Frankreich." In *Christliche Philosophie.* Edited by Coreth, Neidl, and Pfligersdorffer, 1988, 2:412–36.
———. "Ockham, Wyclif and the 'Via moderna.'" In *Antiqui und Moderni.* Edited by Zimmerman, 1971, 85–125.
Gilson, Etienne. "Avicenne en Occident au moyen âge." *AHD* 44 (1969): 89–94.
Glorieux, Palémon. *La littérature quodlibétique de 1260 à 1320.* Bibliothèque Thomiste 5. Le Saulchoir, 1925.
———. *Répertoire des Maîtres en Théologie de Paris au XIIIe siècle.* 2 vols. Paris, 1933/34.
———. "Les *Deflorationes* de Werner de Saint-Blaise." In *Mélanges Joseph de Ghellinck, S.J.* Gembloux, 1951, 2:699–721.
———. "Les années 1242–1247 à la Faculté de Théologie de Paris." *RThAM* 29 (1962): 234–49.
———. "L'enseignement au moyen âge: Techniques et méthodes en usage à la Faculté de Théologie de Paris, au XIIIe siècle." *AHD* 43 (1968): 65–186.
———. "Le conflit de 1252–1257 à la lumière du Mémoire de Guillaume de Saint-Amour." *RThAM* 24 (1975): 364–72.
Glorieux, Pierre. "La Somme 'Quoniam homines' d'Alain de Lille." *RThAM* 17 (1950): 29–45.
Gössmann, Elisabeth. *Metaphysik und Heilsgeschichte: Eine theologische Untersuchung der Summa Halensis. Alexander von Hales.* München, 1964.
———. *Antiqui und Moderni im Mittelalter: Eine geschichtliche Standortbestimmung.* Veröffentlichungen d. Grabmann-Institutes 23. Paderborn, 1974.
Goudriaan, Aza. *Philosophische Gotteserkenntnis bei Suárez und Descartes im Zusammenhang mit der niederländischen reformierten Theologie und Philosophie des 17. Jahrhunderts.* Brill's Studies in Intellectual History 98. Leiden, 1999.
Goulet-Cazé, Marie-Odile, ed. *Le Commentaire entre traditon et innovation: Actes du colloque international de l'Institut des Traditions textuelles.* Paris et Villejuif, 22–25 septembre 1999. Paris, 2000.
Grabmann, Martin. *Geschichte der scholastischen Methode.* 2 vols. Freiburg im Breisgau, 1909/11.
———. *Forschungen über die lateinischen Aristotelesübersetzungen des XIII. Jahrhunderts.* *BGPhMA* 17, nos. 5–6. Münster, 1916.
———. *Geschichte der katholischen Theologie seit dem Ausgang der Väterzeit.* Freiburg, 1933.
———. *Mittelalterliches Geistesleben.* Munich, 1936.
———. "Aristoteles im Werturteil des Mittelalters." In *Mittelalterliches Geistesleben,* 1936, 2:62–102.

———. "Die italienische Thomistenschule des XIII. und beginnenden XIV. Jahrhunderts." In *Mittelalterliches Geistesleben,* 1936, 1:322–91.

———. "Die Opuscula *de summo bono sive de vita philosophi* und *de sompniis* des Boethius von Dacien." In *Mittelalterliches Geistesleben,* 1936, 2:200–24.

———. "Die Stellung des Kardinals Cajetan in der Geschichte des Thomismus und der Thomistenschule." In *Mittelaterliches Geistesleben,* 1936, 2:602–13.

———. "Einzelgestalten aus der mittelalterlichen Dominikaner- und Thomistenschule." In *Mittelalterliches Geistesleben,* 1936, 2:512–612.

———. "Forschungen zur Geschichte der ältesten deutschen Thomistenschule des Dominikanerordens." In *Mittelalterliches Geistesleben,* 1936, 1:392–431.

———. "Hilfsmittel des Thomasstudiums aus alter Zeit (Abbreviationes, Concordantiae, Tabulae)." In *Mittelalterliches Geistesleben,* 1936, 2:424–89.

———. "Johannes Capreolus O.P., der 'Princeps Thomistarum' († 1444) und seine Stellung in der Geschichte der Thomistenschule." In *Mittelalterliches Geistesleben,* 1936, 3:370–410.

———. *I divieti ecclesiastici di Aristotele sotto Innocenzo III e Gregorio IX*. Miscellanea Historiae Pontificiae 5. Rome, 1941.

———. *Die theologische Erkenntnis- und Einleitungslehre des hl. Thomas von Aquin auf Grund seiner Schrift "In Boethium de Trinitate."* Thomistische Studien 4. Fribourg, 1948.

———. "Methoden und Hilfsmittel des Aristotelesstudiums im Mittelalter." In *Gesammelte Akademieabhandlungen.* Paderborn, 1975, 1447–637.

Grane, Leif. *Contra Gabrielem: Luthers Auseinandersetzung mit Gabriel Biel in der* Disputatio Contra Scholasticam Theologiam *1517*. Acta Theologica Danica 4. Gyldendal, 1962.

———. *Modus loquendi theologicus: Luthers Kampf um die Erneuerung der Theologie (1515–1518)*. Acta Theologica Danica 12. Leiden, 1975.

Grauwen, Wilfried Marcel. *Norbert aartsbischop van Maagdenburg (1124–1134)*. Verhandelingen van de Koninklijke Academie voor Wetenschappen, Letteren en Schone Kunsten van België. Klasse der Letteren. Jaargang XL. Nr. 86. Brussels, 1978.

Green-Pedersen, Niels J. *The Tradition of the Topics in the Middle Ages: The Commentaries on Aristotle's and Boethius' "Topics."* Munich, 1984.

Greive, Hermann. "Die Maimonideische Kontroverse und die Auseinandersetzungen in der lateinischen Scholastik." In *Auseinandersetzungen.* Edited by Zimmerman, 1976, 170–80.

Greving, Joseph. *Johann Eck als junger Gelehrter: Eine literar- und dogmengeschichtliche Untersuchung über seinen* Chrysopassus praedestinationis *aus dem Jahre 1514*. RGST 1. Münster, 1906.

Grillmeier, Aloys. "Vom Symbolum zur Summa." In *Kirche und Über-lieferung (Festschrift Geiselmann).* Johannes Betz—Heinrich Fries. Freiburg, 1950, 119–69.

———. "Fulgentius von Ruspe, De Fide ad Petrum und die Summa Sententiarum: Eine Studie zum Werden der frühscholastischen Systematik." *Scholastik* 34 (1959): 526–65.

Grimm, Herold J. *Lazarus Spengler, a Lay Leader of the Reformation.* Columbus, Oh., 1978.

Grosse, Sven. *Heilsungewissheit und Scrupulositas im späten Mittelalter: Studien zu Johannes Gerson und Gattungen der Frömmigkeitstheologie seiner Zeit.* Beiträge zur Historischen Theologie 85. Tübingen, 1994.

Grundmann, Heribert. *Religiöse Bewegungen im Mittelalter.* Historische Studien 267. Berlin, 1935. Reprint, Hildesheim, 1977.

Guelluy, Robert. *Philosophie et théologie chez Guillaume d'Ockham.* Louvain, 1947.

Hackett, Jeremiah. "Roger Bacon: His Life, Career and Works." In *Roger Bacon and the*

Sciences: Commemorative Essays. Studien und Texte zur Geistesgeschichte des Mittelalters 57. Leiden, 1997, 9–24.

Hageneder, Othmar. "Der Häresiebegriff der Juristen des 12. und 13. Jahrhunderts." In *Concept.* Edited by Lourdaux and Verhelst, 41–103.

Hallensleben, Barbara. *Communicatio: Anthropologie und Gnadenlehre bei Thomas de Vio Cajetan.* Reformationsgeschichtliche Studien und Texte 123. Münster, 1985.

Hamm, Berndt. *Promissio, Pactum, Ordinatio. Freiheit und Selbstbindung Gottes in der scholastischen Gnadenlehre.* Beiträge zur historischen Theologie 54. Tübingen, 1977.

Hämmerl, Alfons. *Die Welt—Symbol Gottes oder eigenständige Wirklichkeit? Verachtung und Hochschätzung der Welt bei Heinrich von Langenstein († 1397).* Studien zur Geschichte der katholischen Moraltheologie 31. Regensburg, 1994.

Hammerstein, Notker. "Universitäten des Heiligen Römischen Reiches Deutscher Nation als Ort der Philosophie des Barock." *StudLeib* 13 (1981): 242–67.

Häring, Nikolaus M. "The Commentary of Gilbert of Poitiers on Boethius' de hebdomadibus." *Traditio* 9 (1953): 177–211.

———. *The Commentaries on Boethius by Thierry of Chartres and His School.* Pontificial Institute of Mediaeval Studies, Studies and Texts 20. Toronto, 1971.

———. *Die Zwettler Summe. MGPhThMA,* n.s., 15. Münster, 1977.

———. "Commentary and Hermeneutics." In *Renaissance.* Edited by Benson and Constable. Oxford, 1982, 173–200.

Hattrup, Dieter. *Ekstatik der Geschichte: Die Entwicklung der christologischen Erkenntnistheorie Bonaventuras.* Paderborner theologische Studien 23. Paderborn, 1993.

Heffernan, Thomas J. *Sacred Biography: Saints and their Biographers in the Midde Ages.* New York, 1988.

Hegyj, Johannes. *Die Bedeutung des Seins bei den klassischen Kommentatoren des heiligen Thomas von Aquin, Capreolus—Silvester von Ferrara—Cajetan.* Pullacher philosophische Forschungen 4. Pullach, 1959.

Heim, Karl. *Das Gewissheitsproblem in der systematischen Theologie bis zu Schleiermacher.* Leipzig, 1911.

Hellgardt, Ernst. *Zum Problem symbolbestimmter und formalästhetischer Zahlenkomposition in mittelalterlicher Literatur: Mit Studien zum Quadrivium und zur Vorgeschichte des mittelalterlichen Zahlendenkens.* Münchener Texte und Untersuchungen zur deutschen Literatur des Mittelalters 45. Munich, 1973.

———. "Victorinisch-zisterziensische Zahlenallegorese." *Beiträge zur Geschichte der deutschen Sprache und Literatur* 98 (1976): 331–50.

Hellyer, Marcus. "The Construction of the *Ordinatio pro studiis superioribus* of 1651." *AHSI* 72 (2003): 3–43.

Hengst, Karl. *Jesuiten an Universitäten und Jesuitenuniversitäten: Zur Geschichte der Universitäten in der Oberdeutschen und Rheinischen Provinz der Gesellschaft Jesu im Zeitalter der konfessionellen Auseinandersetzung.* Quellen und Forschungen auf dem Gebiet der Geschichte, n.s., 2. Paderborn, 1981.

Henke, Ernt Ludwig Theodor. *Georg Calixtus und seine Zeit.* 2 vols. Halle, 1853/60.

Hennig, Gerhard. *Cajetan und Luther: Ein historischer Beitrag zur Begegnung von Thomismus und Reformation.* Arbeiten zur Theologie II, no. 7. Stuttgart, 1966.

Henningsen, Jürgen. "'Enzyclopädie': Zur Sprach- und Deutungsgeschichte eines pädagogischen Begriffs." *ABG* 10 (1966): 271–363.

———. "Orbis Doctrinae: Encyclopaedia." *ABG* 11 (1967): 241–45.

Heppe, Heinrich. *Die Dogmatik der evangelisch-reformierten Kirche.* Neukirchen, 1958.
Herold, Vilém. *Pražka Univerzita a Wyclif: Wyclifovo učení o ideách a geneze husitkého revolučního myšlení.* Prague, 1985.
Hödl, Ludwig. "Die confessio Berengarii von 1059: Eine Arbeit zum frühscholastischen Eucharistietraktat." *Scholastik* 37 (1962): 370–94.
Hoenen, Maarten J. F. M. *Marsilius van Inghen († 1396) over het goddelijke weten: Zijn plaats in de ontwickkeling van de opvattingen over hat goddelijke weten ca. 1255–1396.* Diss., Nijmegen, 1989.
———. *Marsilius of Inghen: Divine Knowledge in Late Medieval Thought.* Studies in the History of Christian Thought 50. Leiden, 1993.
Hoffmann, Fritz. *Die Schriften des Oxforder Kanzlers Johannes Lutterell.* Leipzig, 1959.
———. *Die theologische Methode des Oxforder Dominikanerlehrers Robert Holcot.* *BGPhThMA*, n.s., 5. Münster, 1972.
———. *Crathorn: Quästionen zum ersten Sentenzenbuch.* *BGPhThMA*, n.s., 29. Münster, 1988.
———. *Die "Conferentiae" des Robert Holcot OP und die akademischen Auseinandersetzungen an der Universität Oxford 1330–1332.* *BGPhThMA*, n.s., 36. Münster, 1993.
———. *Ockham-Rezeption und Ockham-Kritik im Jahrzehnt nach Wilhelm von Ockham in Oxford 1322–1332.* *BGPhThMA*, n.s., 50. Münster, 1998.
———. "Der Satz als Zeichen der theologischen Aussage bei Holcot, Crathorn und Gregor von Rimini." In *Repraesentatio.* Edited by Zimmerman, 1971, 296–313.
Hoffmann, Manfred. *Erkenntnis und Verwirklichung der wahren Theologie nach Erasmus von Rotterdam.* Beiträge zur Historischen Theologie 44. Tübingen, 1972.
Höhn, Erich. "Köln als Ort der ersten Kommentare zur 'Summa Theologiae' des Thomas von Aquin." In *Thomas von Aquino.* Edited by Eckert, 641–55.
Holeček, František J. "Hussens Kirchverständnis." In *Jan Hus.* Edited by Seibt, 183–91.
Holopainen, Toivo J. *Dialectic and Theology in the Eleventh Century.* Studien und Texte zur Geistesgeschichte des Mittelalters 54. Leiden, 1996.
Holtz, Louis. "Le rôle des commentaires d'auteurs classiques dans l'émergence d'une mis en page associant texte et commentaire (Moyen âge occidental)." In *Commentaire.* Edited by Goulet-Cazé, 103–17.
Honnée, Eugène. "Die Religionsverhandlungen der Reichstage von Nürnberg (1524), Speyer (1526) und Augsburg (1530) und die Entstehung der Idee eines Religionsgesprächs." *Nederlands archief voor kerkgeschiedenis* 73 (1993): 1–30.
Horn, Ewald. *Die Disputationen und Promotionen an den Deutschen Universitäten vornehmlich seit dem 16. Jahrhundert.* Zentralblatt für Bibliothekswesen, Beih. 11. Leipzig, 1893. Reprint, Wiesbaden, 1968.
Hrdlička, Jaroslav. "Hus und Páleč." In *Jan Hus.* Edited by Seibt, 103–6.
Hübener, Wolfgang. "Der theologisch-philosophische Konservativismus des Jean Gerson." In *Antiqui und Moderni.* Edited by Zimmerman, 1971, 171–200.
Hurter, Hugo. *Nomenclator literarius theologiae catholicae.* 6 vols. Innsbruck, 1903–1913.
Imbach, Ruedi. *Deus est intelligere: Das Verhältnis von Sein und Denken in seiner Bedeutung für das Gottesverständnis bei Thomas von Aquin und in den Pariser Quaestionen Meister Eckharts.* Studia Friburgensia, n.s., 53. Fribourg, 1976.
Iserloh, Erwin. *Johannes Eck (1486–1543): Scholastiker, Humanist, Kontroverstheologe.* Katholisches Leben und Kirchenreform im Zeitalter der Glaubensspaltung 41. Münster, 1981.

Jansen, Bernhard. "Zur Philosophie der Skotisten des 17. Jahrunderts." *FStud* 23 (1936): 28–58, 150–75.

———. "Die scholastische Philosophie des 17. Jahrhunderts." *PhJ* 50 (1937): 401–44.

———. "Zur Phänomenologie der Philosophie der Thomisten des 17. und 18. Jahrhunderts." *Scholastik* 13 (1938): 49–71.

Jenkins, John I. *Knowledge and Faith in Thomas Aquinas.* Cambridge, 1997.

Jolivet, Jean. *Godescalc d'Orbais et la Trinité: La méthode de théologie à l'époque carolingienne.* Paris, 1958.

———. *Arts du langage et théologie chez Abélard.* Études de philosophie médiévale 57. Paris, 1969.

Jung, Martin H., and Peter Walter, eds. *Theologen des 16. Jahrhunderts. Humanismus—Reformation—Katholische Erneuerung: Eine Einführung.* Darmstadt, 2002.

Kann, Christoph. "Skepsis, Wahrheit, Illumination. Bemerkungen zur Erkenntnistheorie Heinrichs von Gent." In *Nach der Verurteilung.* Edited by Aertsen, et al., 2001, 38–58.

Kantorowicz, Hermann. "The Quaestiones disputatae of the glossators." *Revue d'histoire du droit* 16 (1937/38): 1–67.

Kerlen, Dietrich, Assertio. *Die Entwicklung von Luthers theologischem Anspruch und der Streit mit Erasmus von Rotterdam.* VIEG 78. Wiesbaden, 1976.

Kessler, Eckhard, Charled H. Lohr, and Walter Sparn, eds. *Aristotelismus und Renaissance: In memoriam Charles B. Schmitt.* Wolfenbütteler Forschungen 40. Wiesbaden, 1988.

Kienzle, Beverly Mayne, ed. *The Sermon. Typologie des sources du Moyen âge occidental,* fasc. 81–83. Turnhout, 2000.

Kienzler, Klaus. *Glauben und Denken bei Anselm von Canterbury.* Freiburg im Breisgau, 1981.

Kirste, Reinhard. *Das Zeugnis des Geistes und das Zeugnis der Schrift: Das* testimonium spiritus sancti internum *als hermeneutisch-polemischer Zentralbegriff bei Johann Gerhard in der Auseinandersetzung mit Robert Bellarmins Schriftverständnis.* Göttinger theologische Arbeiten 6. Göttingen, 1976.

Klein, Jürgen, and Johannes Kramer, eds. *J. H. Alsted: Herborns calvinistische Theologie und Wissenschaft im Spiegel der englischen Kulturreform des frühen 17. Jahrhunderts.* Aspekte der englischen Geistes- und Kulturgeschichte 16. Frankfurt, 1988.

Klinkenberg, Hans Martin. "Die Devotio moderna unter dem Thema 'Antiqui—Moderni' betrachtet." In *Antiqui und Moderni.* Edited by Zimmerman, 1971, 394–419.

Kluxen, Wolfgang. "Thomas von Aquin." In *Grundprobleme der großen Philosophen.* Edited by Josef Speck. Göttingen, 1972, 177–220.

———. "Die geschichtliche Erforschung der mittelalterlichen Philosophie und die Neuscholastik." In *Christliche Philosophie.* Edited by Coreth, Neidl, and Pfligersdorffer, 1988, 2:362–89.

Knebel, Sven K. "Necessitas moralis ad optimum: Zum historischen Hintergrund der Wahl der besten aller möglichen Welten." *StudLeib* 23 (1991): 3–24.

———. "Scientia media: Ein diskursarchäologischer Leitfaden durch das 17. Jahrhundert." *ABG* 34 (1991): 262–94.

Knuuttila, Simo. "Trutfetter: Usingen and Erfurtian Ockhamism." In *Was ist Philosophie im Mittelalter?* Edited by Aertson and Speer, 818–23.

Kobusch, Theo. "Grammatica speculativa (12.–14. Jahrhundert)." In *Klassiker der Sprachphilosophie: Von Platon bis Noam Chomsky.* Edited by Borsche and Tilman. Munich, 1996, 77–93.

———. *Christliche Philosophie: Die Entdeckung der Subjektivität.* Darmstadt, 2006.

Koch, Josef. *Artes liberales: Von der antiken Bildung zur Wissenschaft des Mittelalters.* Studien und Texte zur Geistesgeschichte des Mittelalters 5. Leiden, 1959.

———. "Von der Bildung der Antike zur Wissenschaft des Mittelalters." In *Kleine Schriften.* Edited by Josef Koch. Rome, 1973, 115–32.

Köhn, Rolf. "Monastisches Bildungsideal und weltgeistliches Wissenschaftsdenken: Zur Vorgeschichte des Mendikantenstreites an der Universität Paris." In *Auseinandersetzungen.* Edited by Zimmerman, 1976, 1–37.

Kolesnyk, Alexander. "Hussens Eucharistiebegriff." In *Jan Hus.* Edited by Seibt, 193–202.

Kölmel, Wilhelm. "'Scholasticus literator': Die Humanisten und ihr Verhältnis zur Scholastik." *HJ* 93 (1973): 301–35.

Köpf, Ulrich. *Die Anfänge der theologischen Wissenschaftstheorie im 13. Jahrhundert.* Beiträge zur historischen Theologie 49. Tübingen, 1974.

———. "Melanchthon als systematischer Theologie neben Luther." In *Der Theologe Melanchthon.* Edited by Frank, 2000, 103–27.

———, ed. *Theologen des Mittelalters: Eine Einführung.* Darmstadt, 2002.

Kraml, Hans. *Die Rede von Gott, sprachkritisch rekonstruiert aus Sentenzenkommentaren* Innsbrucker theologische Studien 13. Innsbruck, 1984.

———, and Gerhard Leibold, *Wilhelm von Ockham.* Zugänge zum Denken des Mittelalters 1. Münster, 2003.

Krebs, Engelbert. *Theologie und Wissenschaft nach der Lehre der Hochscholastik. BGPhMA* 11, nos. 3–4. Münster, 1912.

Kreuzer, Georg. *Heinrich von Langenstein: Studien zur Biographie und zu den Schismatraktaten unter besonderer Berücksichtigung der* Epistola pacis *und der* Epistola concilii pacis. Quellen und Forschungen aus dem Gebiet der Geschichte, n.s., 6. Paderborn, 1987.

Kristeller, Paul Oskar. "Humanism and Scholasticism in the Italian Renaissance." In *Studies in Renaissance Thought and Letters.* Rome, 1956, 553–83.

———. Humanismus und Renaissance, German translation by E. Kessler. 2 vols. Munich, 1974/76.

Krüger, Friedhelm. *Humanistische Evangelienauslegung: Desiderius Erasmus von Rotterdam als Ausleger der Evangelien in seinen Paraphrasen.* Beiträge zur Historischen Theologie 68. Tübingen, 1968.

Kuchařova, Hedvika. "Premonstrátska kolej Norbertinum v Praze (1637–1785)." *Bibliotheca Strahoviensis* 3 (1997): 15–57.

Lacroix, B. "Hugues de Saint-Victor et les conditions du savoir au moyen âge." In *An Etienne Gilson Tribute.* Edited by Charles J. O'Neill. Milwaukee, 1959, 118–34.

Lambert, Malcom. *Medieval Heresy: Popular Movements from the Gregorian Reform to the Reformation.* Oxford, 1992.

Lambert, Michel. "Nouveaux éléments pour une étude de l'authenticité Boécienne des Opuscula Sacra." In *Boèce ou la chaîne des savoirs: Actes du Colloque International de la Fondation Singer-Polignac, présidée par Monsieur Éduard Bonnefous, Paris, 8–12 juin 1990.* Edited by Alain Galonnier. Philosophes Médiévaux 44. Louvain-la-Neuve, 2003, 171–91.

Lamboij, H. Th. M., and J. A. Mol, eds. *Vitae Abbatum Orti Sancte Marie: Vijf abtenlevens van het klooster Mariëngaarde in Friesland.* Hilversum, 2001.

Landgraf, Arthur M. "Drei Zweige der Pseudo-Poitiers Glosse zu den Sentenzen des Lombarden." *RThAM* 9 (1937): 167–204.

———. "Sentenzenglossen des beginnenden 13. Jahrhunderts." *RThAM* 10 (1938): 36–55.

———. "Zum Begriff der Scholastik." *CollFr* 11 (1941): 487–90.

———. *Einführung in die Geschichte der theologischen Literatur der Frühscholastik unter dem Gesichtspunkt der Schulenbildung.* Regensburg, 1948.

———. *Dogmengeschichte der Frühscholastik.* 4 vols. Regensburg, 1956.

Lang, Albert. *Die Loci theologici des Melchior Cano und die Methode des dogmatischen Beweises.* Munich, 1925.

———. *Die Wege der Glaubensbegründung bei den Scholastikern des 14. Jahrhunderts. BGPhMA* 30, nos. 1–2. Münster, 1930.

———. *Heinrich Totting von Oyta: Ein Beitrag zur Entstehungsgeschichte der ersten deutschen Universitäten und zur Problemgeschichte der Spätscholastik. BGPhThMA* 33, no. 4/5. Münster, 1937, 50–53.

———. "Die Bedeutung Alberts des Großen für die Aufrollung der fundamentaltheologischen Frage." In *Studia Albertina: Festschrift B. Geyer. BGPhThMA* Sup. IV. Münster, 1952, 343–73.

———. *Die theologische Prinzipienlehre der mittelalterlichen Scholastik.* Freiburg, 1964.

Lang, Justin. *Die Christologie bei Heinrich von Langenstein: Eine dogmenhistorische Untersuchung.* Freiburger Theologische Studien 85. Freiburg, 1966.

Langer, Otto. "Aristoteles und die Folgen: Zur Rezeption der aristotelischen Logik und Wissenschaftstheorie im 12. und 13. Jahrhundert." *FZPhTh* 53 (2006): 559–88.

Lawn, Brian. *The Rise and Decline of the Scholastic "Quaestio Disputata": With Special Emphasis on Its Use in the Teaching of Medicine and Science.* Education and Society in the Middle Ages and Renaissance 2. Leiden, 1993.

Leclercq, Jean. "Le genre épistolaire au moyen âge." *RMAL* 2 (1946): 63–70.

———. "Drogon et Saint Bernard." *RBen* 63 (1963): 116–31.

———. *Wissenschaft und Gottverlangen.* Düsseldorf, 1963.

———. "The Renewal of Theology." In *Renaissance.* Edited by Benson and Constable. Oxford, 1982, 68–87.

Leff, Gordon. *Bradwardine and the Pelagians: A Study of His "De causa Dei" and Its Opponents.* Cambridge, 1957.

———. *Heresy in the Later Middle Ages: The Relation of Heterodoxy to Dissent c. 1250–c. 1450.* Manchester, 1967.

———. *Paris and Oxford Universities in the Thirteenth and Fourteenth Centuries: An Institutional and Intellectual History.* New York, 1968.

———. *William of Ockham: The Metamorphosis of Scholastic Discourse.* Manchester, 1975.

Leibold, Gerhard. "Die Kontroverse zwischen den Philosophen und Theologen in der ersten Quaestio des Prologs der 'Ordinatio' von Johannes Duns Scotus." In *Was ist Philosophie im Mittelalter?* Edited by Aertson and Speer, 629–36.

Leinsle, Ulrich G. *Res et signum: Das Verständnis zeichenhafter Wirklichkeit in der Theologie Bonaventuras.* Veröffentlichungen des Grabmann-Institutes 26. Munich, 1976.

———. *Vivianus von Prémontré: Ein Gegner Abaelards in der Lehre von der Freiheit.* Bibliotheca Analectorum Praemonstratensium 13. Averbode, 1978.

———. "Abt Hieronymus Hirnhaim: Zur Wissenschaftskritik des 17. Jahrhunderts." *AnPraem* 55 (1979): 171–95.

———. "Die Einheit der Wissenschaft nach Johannes Duns Scotus." *WiWei* 43 (1979): 157–76.

———. "Die Einheit der Wissenschaft nach Wilhelm von Ockham." *WiWei* 43 (1980): 107–29.

———. "Die Hugo von St. Viktor zugeschriebenen Texte 'De libero arbitrio' und Vivianus von Prémontré." *AnPraem* 57 (1981): 183–95.

———. "Aristoteles und die 'Moderni' in der Vita Siardi." *AnPraem* 58 (1982): 210–24.

———. *Das Ding und die Methode: Methodische Konstitution und Gegenstand der frühen protestantischen Metaphysik*. Augsburg, 1985.

———. *Reformversuche protestantischer Metaphysik im Zeitalter des Rationalismus*. Augsburg, 1988.

———. "Von der Weltordnung zur Lebensordnung: Aufgabe und Grenzen der Philosophie nach Augustinus' Dialog 'De Ordine.'" *ThPQ* 137 (1989): 369–77.

———. "Benediktinischer Thomismus bei den Prämonstratensern." *AnPraem* 74 (1998): 177–203.

———. *Studium im Kloster: Das philosophisch-theologische Hausstudium des Stiftes Schlägl 1633–1783*. Bibliotheca Analectorum Praemonstratensium 20. Averbode, 2000.

———. "'Charitati militare': Der klösterliche Kampf um den Frieden nach Adamus Scotus († 1212)." *AnPraem* 79 (2003): 5–24.

———. "Festdisputationen in Prälatenklöstern." In *Solemnitas: Barocke Festkultur in Oberpfälzer Klöstern, Beiträge des 1. Symposions des Kultur- und Begegnungszentrums Abtei Waldsassen vom 25. bis 27. Oktober 2002*. Edited by Manfred Knedlik and Georg Schott. Veröffentlichungen Kultur- und Begegnungszentrums Abtei Waldsassen 1. Kallmünz, 2003, 101–13.

———. "Lehet-e filozófiát alapozni a Bibliára? (Philosophie aus der Bibel?)" *Vigilia* 70 (2005): 246–57.

———. *Dilinganae Disputationes: Der Lehrinhalt der gedruckten Disputationen an der Philosophischen Fakultät der Universität Dillingen 1555–1648*. Jesuitica 11. Regensburg, 2006.

———. "Servatius de Lairuelz und Juan Caramuel Lobkowitz OCist: Zwei Auslegungen der Augustinus-Regel." *AnPraem* 82 (2006): 283–320.

———. "Die Scholastik der Neuzeit bis zur Aufklärung." In *Christliche Philosophie*. Edited by Coreth, et al., 1988, 2:54–69.

———. "Methodologie und Metaphysik bei den deutschen Lutheranern um 1600." In *Aristotelismus und Renaissance*. Edited by Kessler, et al., 1988, 149–62.

Leites, Edmund, ed. *Conscience and Casuistry in Early Modern Europe*. Cambridge, 1988.

Lemaire, Paul. *Le Cartésianisme chez les Bénédictins: Dom Robert Desgabets: Son Système, son influence et son école*. Diss., Grenoble-Paris, 1901.

Leone, Marialucrezia. "Zum Status der Theologie bei Heinrich von Gent—Ist sie eine praktische oder theoretische Wissenschaft." In *What is "Theology?"* Edited by Olszewski, 2007, 195–224.

Leppin, Volker. *Geglaubte Wahrheit: Das Theologieverständnis Wilhelms von Ockham*. FKDG 63. Göttingen, 1995.

———. *Theologie im Mittelalter*. Kirchengeschichte in Einzeldarstellungen I/11. Leipzig, 2007.

Lesch, Karl Josef. *Neuorientierung der Theologie im 18. Jahrhundert in Würzburg und Bamberg*. Forschungen zur Fränkischen Kirchen- und Theologiegeschichte 1. Würzburg, 1978.

Leube, Hans. *Kalvinismus und Luthertum im Zeitalter der Orthodoxie*. Leipzig, 1928. Reprint, Aalen, 1966.

Libera, Alain de. "Philosophie et censure: Remarques sur la crise universitaire parisienne de 1270–1277." In *Was ist Philosophie im Mittelalter?* Edited by Aertsen and Speer, 1998, 71–89.

Liguš, Ján. "Hussens Schriftbegriff in seinen Predigten." In *Jan Hus.* Edited by Seibt, 127–38.

Little, A. G. "The Franciscan School at Oxford in the Thirteenth Century." *AFrH* 19 (1926): 803–74.

Lohse, Bernhard. *Ratio und Fides: Eine Untersuchung über die ratio in der Theologie Luthers.* Forschungen zur Kirchen- und Dogmengeschichte 8. Göttingen, 1957.

———. "Luthers Selbstverständnis in seinem frühen Romkonflikt und die Vorgeschichte des Begriffs 'Theologia Crucis': Untersucht anhand des Briefwechsels zwischen 1517 und 1519/20." In *Humanismus.* Edited by Beyer and Wartenberg, 15–31.

———. *Luthers Theologie in ihrer historischen Entwicklung und in ihrem systematischen Zusammenhang.* Göttingen, 1995.

Long, R. James. "The Science of Theology according to Richard Fishacre: Edition of the Prologue to his *Commentary on the Sentences.*" *MS* 34 (1972): 71–98.

———, and Maura O'Caroll. *The Life and Works of Richard Fishacre OP: Prolegomena to the Edition of his Commentary on the Sentences.* Bayerische Akademie der Wissenschaften, Veröffentlichungen der Kommission für die Herausgabe ungedruckter Texte aus der mittelalterlichen Geisteswelt 21. Munich, 1999.

Lottin, Odon. "Le premier commentaire connu des Sentences de Pierre Lombard." *RThAM* 11 (1939): 64–71.

———. *Psychologie et Morale aux XII*[e] *et XIII*[e] *siècles.* 6 vols. Louvain, 1942–1960.

Lourdaux, Willem, and Daniel Verhelst, eds. *The Concept of Hersesy in the Middle Ages (11th–13th C.) Proceedings of the International Conference, Louvain May 13–16, 1973.* Mediaevalia Lovaniensia I, 4. Leuven, 1976.

Lubac, Henri de. "A propos de la formule 'Diversi, non adversi.'" *RSR* 40 (1951/52): 27–40.

———. *Exégèse médiévale: Les quatre sens de l'écriture.* Paris, 1959–1964. English translation by Mark Sebanc (vol. 1) and E. M. Macierowski (vol. 2). *Medieval Exegesis.* Grand Rapids, Mich.: Eerdmans, 1998, 2000.

Luscombe, David E. *The School of Peter Abelard: The Influence of Abelard's Thought in the Early Scholastic Period.* Cambridge, 1969.

Lurz, Wilhelm. *Adam Tanner und die Gnadenstreitigkeiten des 17. Jahrhunderts: Ein Beitrag zur Geschichte des Molinismus.* Breslauer Studien zur historischen Theologie 21. Breslau, 1932.

Lütcke, Karl-Heinrich. *"Auctoritas" bei Augustin.* Tübinger Beiträge zur Altertumswissenschaft 44. Stuttgart, 1968.

Madiski, George. "The Scholastic Method in Medieval Education: An Inquiry into Its Origins in Law and Theology." *Speculum* 49 (1974): 640–61.

Mandonnet, Pierre. *Siger de Brabant et l'averroisme latin au XIII*[e] *siècle.* Fribourg, 1899.

Manrangon, Paolo. "Le origini e le fonti dello scotismo padovano." In *Regnum Hominis et Regnum Dei: Acta Quarti Congressus Scotistici Internationalis: Patavii, 24–29 septembris 1976,* vol. II. Edited by Camille Bérubé. Studia Scholastico-Scotistica 7. Rome, 1978, 11–52.

Manser, Gallus. "Die mittelalterliche Scholastik nach ihrem Umfange und Charakter." *HPBL* 139 (1907): 317–39; 407–31.

Manstetten, Rainer. *Esse est Deus: Meister Eckharts christologische Versöhnung von Philosophie und Religion und ihre Ursprünge in der Tradition des Abendlandes.* Freiburg, 1992.

Marcolino, Venício. "Der Augustinertheologe an der Universität Paris." In *Gregor von Rimini.* Edited by Oberman, 1981, 127–94.

Marenbon, John. *From the Circle of Alcuin to the School of Auxerre: Logic, Theology and Philosophy in the Early Middle Ages.* Cambridge, 1981.

Marrou, Henri-Irénée. *Augustinus und das Ende der antiken Bildung.* Paderborn, 1981.

Menzel, Beda Franz. *Abt Stephan Rautenstrauch von Břevnov-Braunau: Herkunft, Umwelt und Wirkungskreis.* Veröffentlichungen des Königsteiner Instituts für Kirchen- und Geistesgeschichte der Sudentenländer 5. Königstein, 1969.

Merkt, Andreas. *Das patristische Prinzip: Eine Studie zur theologischen Bedeutung der Kirchenväter.* Supplements to Vigiliae Christianae 58. Leiden, 2001

Merl, Otho. *Theologia Salmanticensis: Untersuchung über Entstehung, Lehrrichtung und Quellen des theologischen Kurses der spanischen Karmeliten.* Regensburg, 1947.

Metz, Detlef. *Gabriel Biel und die Mystik.* Contubernium 55. Stuttgart, 2001.

Meyer, Heinz, and Rudolf Suntrup. *Lexikon der mittelalterlichen Zahlenbedeutungen.* Münsterische Mittelalter-Schriften 56. Munich, 1987.

Micaelli, Claudio. *Studi sui trattati teologici di Boezio.* Naples, 1988.

———. *Dio nel pensiero di Boezio.* Storie e testi 4. Naples, 1995.

Miethke, Jürgen. "Papst, Ortsbischof und Universität von Paris in den Pariser Theologenprozessen des 13. Jahrhunderts." In *Auseinandersetzungen.* Edited by Zimmerman, 1976, 52–94.

———. "Theologenprozesse in der ersten Phase ihrer institutionellen Ausbildung: Die Verfahren gegen Peter Abaelard und Gilbert von Poitiers." *Viator* 6 (1975): 87–116.

Minnich, N. H. "On the Origins of Eck's 'Enchirdion.'" In *Johannes Eck (1486–1543) im Streit der Jahrhunderte.* Edited by Erwin Iserloh. RGST 127. Münster, 1988, 37–73.

Mitschelich, Antonius. *Kommentatoren zur Summa Theologiae des hl. Thomas von Aquin.* Graz, 1924. Reprint, Hildesheim, 1981.

Mittermüller, Rupert. *Beiträge zu einer Geschichte der ehemaligen Benedictiner-Universität in Salzburg.* Salzburg, 1889.

Möhle, Hannes. *Formalitas und modus intrinsecus: Die Entwicklung der scotischen Metaphysik bei Franciscus de Mayronis. BGPhThMA*, n.s., 70. Münster, 2007.

Moore, Philip S. *The Works of Peter of Poitiers, Master in Theology and Chancellor of Paris (1193–1205).* Publications in Medieval Studies 1. Notre Dame, Ind., 1936.

Morerod, Charles. *Cajetan et Luther en 1518.* 2 vols. Fribourg, 1994.

Neumann, Siegfried. *Gegenstand und Methode der theoretischen Wissenschaften nach Thomas von Aquin aufgrund der Expositio super librum Boethii De Trinitate. BGPhThMA* 41, no. 2. Münster, 1965.

Niederbacher, Bruno, and Gerhard Leibold, eds. *Theologie als Wissenschaft im Mittelalter: Eine Einführung.* Münster, 2006.

Nielsen, Lauge O. *Theology and Philosophy in the Twelfth Century: A Study of Gilbert Porreta's Thinking and the Theological Exposition of the Doctrine of Incarnation during the Period 1130–1180.* Acta Theologica Danica 15. Leiden, 1982.

———. "Peter Abelard and Gilbert of Poitiers." In *Medieval Theologians.* Edited by Evans, 102–28.

Niggli, Ursula. "Philosophischer Scharfsinn in der theologischen Kritik." In *Peter Abaelard: Leben—Werk—Wirkung.* Edited by Niggli. Forschungen zur Europäischen Geistesgeschichte 4. Freiburg im Breisgau, 2003, 235–65.

Oberman, Heiko Augustinus. *Der Herbst der mittelalterlichen Theologie.* Zürich, 1965.

———. "Tuus sum, salvum me fac: Augustinréveil zwischen Renaissance und Reformation." In *Scientia Augustiniana: Festschrift A. Zumkeller OSA*. Cassiciacum 30. Würzburg, 1975.

———. *Werden und Wertung der Reformation: Vom Wegestreit zum Glaubenskampf*. Tübingen, 1977.

———. "Hus und Luther: Der Antichrist und die zweite reformatorische Entdeckung." In *Jan Hus*. Edited by Seibt, 319–46.

———, ed. *Gregor von Rimini: Werk und Wirkung bis zur Reformation*. Spätmittelalter und Reformation 20. Berlin, 1981.

Oediger, Friedrich Wilhelm. *Über die Bildung der Geistlichen im späten Mittelalter*. Leiden, 1953.

Oelrich, Karl Heinz. *Der späte Erasmus und die Reformation*. RGST 86. Münster, 1961.

Oliva, Adriano. *Les debuts de l'enseignement de Thomas d'Aquin et sa conception de la sacra doctrina, avec l'édition du prologue de son Commentaire des Sentences*. Bibliothèque Thomiste 58. Paris, 2006.

Olivares, Estanislao. "Juan de Lugo (1583–1660): Datos biográficos, sus escritos, estudios sobre su doctrina y bibliografía." *ATG* 47 (1984): 5–129.

Olszewski, Miko ai, ed. *What Is "Theology" in the Middle Ages? Religious Cultures of Europe (11th–15th Centuries) as Reflected in Their Self-Understanding*. Archa Verbi, Subsisdia 1. Münster, 2007.

Ong, Walter J. *Ramus: Method and the Decay of Dialogue: From the Art of Discourse to the Art of Reason*. Cambridge, Mass., 1958.

Oppermann, Hans, ed. *Humanismus*. Wege der Forschung 17. Darmstadt, 1970.

Osborne, Kenan B. "Alexander of Hales: Precursor and Promotor of Franciscan Theology." In *The History of Franciscan Theology*. Edited by Osborne. St. Bonaventure, N.Y., 1994, 1–38.

Ott, Ludwig. *Untersuchungen zur theologischen Briefliteratur der Frühscholastik unter besonderer Berücksichtigung des Viktorinerkreises. BGPhThMA* 34. Münster, 1937.

Otte, Gerhard. "Der Probabilismus: Eine Theorie an der Grenze zwischen Theologie und Jurisprudenz." In *La seconda scolastica nella formazione del diritto privato moderno: Incontro di studio Firenze 16–18 ottobre 1972*. Edited by Paolo Grossi. Per la storia del pensiero giuridico moderno 1. Milan, 1973, 283–302.

Otten, Willemien. "Carolingian Theology." In *Medieval Theologians*. Edited by Evans, 65–82.

Paqué, Ruprecht. *Das Pariser Nominalistenstatut: Zur Entwicklung des Realitätsbegriffs der neuzeitlichen Naturwissenschaft: Occam, Buridan und Petrus Hispanus, Nikolaus von Autrecourt und Gregor von Rimini*. Quellen und Studien zur Geschichte der Philosophie 14. Berlin, 1970.

Paquet, Jacques, and Joseph Ijsewijn, eds. *Les Universités à la fin du moyen âge: Actes du Congrès international de Louvain 26–30 mai 1975*. Louvain, 1978.

Pařez, Jan, and Hedvika Kuchařova. *Hyberni v Praze: Éireannaigh i bPrág: Déjiny františkánké kolej Neposkvrněného početí Panny Marie v Praze (1629.1786)*. Prague, 2001.

Partee, Charles. *Calvin and Classical Philosophy*. Studies in the History of Christian Thought 14. Leiden, 1977.

Pastine, Dino. *Juan Caramuel: Probabilismo ed Enciclopedia*. Florence, 1976.

Paulsen, Friedrich. *Geschichte des gelehrten Unterrichts auf den deutschen Schulen und Universitäten vom Ausgang des Mittelalters bis zur Gegenwart*. Leipzig, 1919.

Pelster, Franz. "Die Bedeutung der Sentenzenvorlesung für die theologische Spekulation des Mittelalters: Ein Zeugnis aus der ältesten Oxforder Dominikanerschule." *Scholastik* 2 (1927): 250–55.

———. "Das Leben und die Schriften des Oxforder Dominikanerlehrers Richard Fishacre († 1248)," *ZKTh* 54 (1930): 518–53.

Pergamo, Basilius. "De Quaestionibus ineditis Fr. Odonis Rigaldi, Fr. Guilelmi de Melitona et Codicis Vat. lat. 782 circa naturam theologiae deque earum relatione ad Summam Theologicam Fr. Alexandri Halensis." *AFrH* 29 (1936): 3–54, 308–64.

Perler, Dominik. "Notwendigkeit und Kontingenz: Das Problem der 'futura contingentia' bei Wilhelm von Ockham." In *Die Philosophie im 14 und 15. Jahrhundert: In memoriam Konstanty Michalski (1879–1949)*. Edited by Olaf Pluta. Amsterdam, 1988, 39–65.

———. *Der propositionale Wahrheitsbegriff im 14. Jahrhundert.* Quellen und Studien zur Philosophie 33. Berlin, 1992.

Petersen, Peter. *Geschichte der aristotelischen Philosophie im protestantischen Deutschland.* Leipzig, 1921.

Pieper, Josef. *Scholastik: Gestalten und Probleme der mittelalterlichen Philosophie.* Munich, 1960.

Poppi, Antonino. *La dottrina della scienza in Giacomo Zabarella.* Padua, 1972.

Porro, Pasquale. "Lo statuto della *philosophia* in Enrico di Gand." In *Was ist Philosophie im Mittelalter?* Edited by Aertsen and Speer, 1998, 497–504.

Prassel, Peter. *Das Theologieverständnis des Ägidius Romanus O.E.S.A. (1243/7–1316).* Europäische Hochschulschriften XXIII, no. 201. Frankfurt, 1983.

Precht-Nussbaum, Karin. *Zwischen Augsburg und Rom: Der Pollinger Augustiner-Chorherr Eusebius Amort (1692–1775): Ein bedeutender Repräsentant katholischer Aufklärung.* Publikationen der Akademie der Augustiner-Chorherren von Windesheim 7. Paring, 2007.

Prügl, Thomas. *Die Ekklesiologie Heinrich Kalteisens OP in Auseinandersetzung mit dem Basler Konziliarismus: Mit einem Textanhang.* Veröffentlichungen des Grabmann-Institutes 40. Paderborn, 1995.

———. *Antonio de Cannara: De potestate pape supra Concilium Generale contra errores Basiliensium: Einleitung, Kommentar und Edition augewählter Abschnitte.* Veröffentlichungen des Grabmann-Institures 41. Paderborn, 1996.

Quinto, Riccardo. *"Doctor Nominatissimus" Stefano Langton († 1228) e la tradizione delle sue opere. BGPhThMA*, n.s., 39. Münster, 1994.

———. *Scholastica: Storia di un concetto.* Subsidia Mediaevalia Patavina 2. Padua, 2001.

Ramelow, Tilman. *Gott, Freiheit, Weltenwahl: Der Ursprung des Begriffs der besten aller möglichen Welten in der Metaphysik der Willenfreiheit zwischen Antonio Perez S.J. (1599–1649) und G. W. Leibniz (1646–1715).* Brill's Studies in Intellectual History 72. Leiden, 1997.

Randall, John Herman. *The School of Padua and the Emergence of Modern Science.* Padua, 1961.

Rashdall, Hastings. *The Universities of Europe in the Middle Ages.* 3 vols. 1937. Reprint, Oxford, 1987.

Ratschow, Carl Heinz. *Lutherische Dogmatik zwischen Reformation und Aufklärung.* Gütersloh, 1966.

Ratzinger. *The Theology of History in St. Bonaventure.* Chicago: Franciscan Herald Press, 1971, 1989.

Reichert, Ernst Otto. *Johannes Scheffler als Streittheologe.* Studien zu Religion, Geschichte und Geisteswissenschaft 4. Gütersloh, 1967.

Reinhardt, Karl. *Pedro Luis SJ (1538–1602) und sein Verständnis der Kontingenz, Praescienz und Praedestination.* Münster, 1965.

Rentsch, Thomas. "Kultur der quaestio: Zur literarischen Formgeschichte der Philosophie im Mittelalter." In *Literarische Formen der Philosophie.* Edited by Gottfried Gabriel and Christiane Schildknecht. Stuttgart, 1990, 73–91.

Reuter, Karl. *Vom Scholaren bis zum jungen Reformator: Studien zum Werdegang Johannes Calvins.* Neukirchen-Vluyn, 1981.

Richter, Vladimír. "Aus der Nominalismus-Forschung: Zu den kritischen Ausgaben der Sentenzenkommentare Wilhelms von Ockham und Gabriel Biels." *ZKTh* 96 (1974): 431–37.

———. *Studien zum literarischen Werk von Johannes Duns Scotus.* Bayeriche Akademie der Wissenschaften, Veröffentlichungen der Kommission für die Herausgabe ungedruckter Texte aus der mittelalterlichen Geisteswelt 14. Munich, 1988.

———. "Textstudien zum Prolog des Oxforder Sentenzenkommentars von Johannes Duns Scotus." *ZKTh* 111 (1989): 431–49.

———. "Duns Scotus' Text zur Theologie als praktischer Theologie." *CollFr* 60 (1990): 459–75.

———. "Duns Scotus' Text zur Univozität." In *Historia Philosophiae Medii Aevi: Studien zur Geschichte der Philosophie des Mittelalters.* Edited by Burkard Mojsich and Olaf Pluta. Amsterdam, 1991, 2:889–910.

———. "Zu Ockhams Entwicklung in der Universalienfrage." In *Unterwegs.* Richter and Liebold, 105–21.

———. "Unterwegs zum historischen Ockham. Historisch-literarische Bemerkungen zur Authentizität von Ockhams Schriften." In *Unterwegs.* Richter and Liebold, 137–53.

———, and Gerhard Leibold.*Unterwegs zum historischen Ockham.* Mediaevalia Oenipontana 1. Innsbruck, 1998.

Rijk, Lambert M. de. *La philosophie au moyen âge.* Leiden, 1985.

Ritschl, Otto. *System und systematische Methode in der Geschichte des wissenschaftlichen Sprachgebrauchs und der philosophischen Methodologie.* Bonn, 1905.

———. *Dogmengeschichte des Protestantismus.* 4 vols. Göttingen, 1908–1927.

Ritter, Gerhard. "Die geschichtliche Bedeutung des deutschen Humanismus." *HZ* 127 (1923): 393–453.

Robson, John Adam. *Wyclif and the Oxford Schools: The Relation of the "Summa de Ente" to Scholastic Debates at Oxford in the Later Fourteenth Century.* Cambridge, 1966.

Rodis-Lewis, Geneviève. "Quelques échos de la thèse de Desgabets sur l'indefectibilité des substances." *Studia Cartesiana* 1 (1979): 124–28.

Roensch, Frederik J. *Early Thomistic School.* Dubuque, 1964.

Rohner, Anselm. "De natura Theologiae iuxta S. Albertum Magnum." *Angelicum* 16 (1939): 3–23.

Rössler, Hellmuth, and Günther Franz, eds. *Universität und Gelehrtenstand 1400–1800: Büdinger Vorträge.* Deutsche Führungsschichten in der Neuzeit 4. Limburg, 1970.

Rossmann, Heribert. "Die Sentenzenkommentare des Franz von Meyronnes OFM." *FStud* 53 (1971): 129–227.

———. *Die Hierarchie der Welt. Gestalt und System des Franz von Meyronnes OFM mit besonderer Berücksichtigung seiner Schöpfungslehre.* Franziskanische Forschungen 23. Werl, 1972.

Roth, Bartholomäus. *Franz von Mayronis O.F.M.: Sein Leben, seine Werke, seine Lehre vom Formalunterschied in Gott.* Franziskanische Forschungen 3. Werl, 1936.

Roth, Cornelius. *Discretio spirituum: Kriterien geistlicher Unterscheidung bei Johannes Gerson.* Studien zur systematischen und spirituellen Theologie 33. Würzburg, 2001.

Roth, Dorothea. *Die mittelalterliche Predigttheorie und das Manuale Curatorum des Johann Ulrich Surgant.* Basler Beiträge zur Geschichtswissenschaft 58. Basel-Stuttgart, 1956.

Rouse, Richard H., and Mary A. Rouse. "Statim invenire: Schools, Preachers and New Attitude to the Pages." In *Renaissance.* Edited by Benson and Constable, 201–25.

Rückert, Georg. *Eusebius Amort und das bayerische Geistesleben im 18. Jahrhundert.* Beiträge zur altbayerischen Kirchengeschichte 20, 2. Munich, 1956.

Russo, Renato. *La metodologia del sapere nel Sermone di S. Bonaventura "Unus est magister vester Christus" con nuova edizione critica e traduzione italiana.* Spicilegium Bonaventurianum 22. Grottaferrata, 1982.

Ruh, Kurt. *Meister Eckhart: Theologe, Prediger, Mystiker.* 2nd rev. ed. Munich, 1989.

Rupprich, Hans. *Das Wiener Schrifttum des ausgehenden Mittelalters.* Sitzungsberichte der Österreichischen Akademie der Wissenschaften, Phil.-Hist. Klasse 228, no. 5. Vienna, 1954.

Santos Noya, Manuel. "Die 'Auctoritates theologicae' im Sentenzenkommentar des Marsilius von Inghen." In *Philosophie und Theologie des ausgehenden Mittelalters: Marsilius von Inghen und das Denken seiner Zeit.* Edited by Maarten J. E. M. Hoenen and Paul J. J. M. Bakker. Leiden, 2000, 197–210.

Saxlová, Tereza, and Stanislav Sousedík, eds. *Rodrigo de Arriaga († 1667) Philosoph und Theologe: Prag 25.–28. Juni 1996.* Prague, 1998.

Schäfer, Philipp. *Kirche und Vernunft: Die Kirche in der katholischen Theologie der Aufklärungszeit.* Münchener Theologische Studien 42. Munich, 1974.

Schaffner, Otto. *Eusebius Amort (1692–1775) als Moraltheologe.* Abhandlungen zur Moraltheologie. Paderborn, 1963.

Scheible, Heinz. "Aristoteles und die Wittenberger Universitätsreform: Zum Quellenwert von Lutherbriefen." In *Humanismus.* Edited by Beyer and Wartenberg, 123–44.

———. *Melanchthon: Eine Biographie.* Munich, 1997.

Schilling, Johannes. "Melanchthons Loci communes deutsch." In *Humanismus.* Edited by Beyer and Wartenberg, 337–52.

Schirpenbach, Meik Peter. *Wirklichkeit als Beziehung: Das strukturontologische Schema der Termini generales im Opus Tripartitum Meister Eckharts. BGPhThMA*, n.s., 66. Münster, 2004.

Schleiff, Arnold. *Selbstkritik der lutherischen Kirchen im 17. Jahrhundert.* Neue Deutsche Forschungen, Abt. Religions- und Kirchengeschichte 6. Berlin, 1937.

Schmidinger, Heinrich M. "Der Streit um die Anfänge der italienischen Neuscholastik." In *Christliche Philosophie.* Edited by Neidl, and Pfligersdorffer, 1988, 2:72–82.

———. "'Scholastik' und 'Neuscholastik'—Geschichte zweier Begriffe." In *Christliche Philosophie.* Edited by Coreth, et al., 1988, 2:23–53.

———. "Überblick zur Neuscholastik in Frankreich und Belgien." In *Christliche Philosophie.* Edited by Coreth, Neidl, and Pfligersdorffer, 1988, 2:195–205.

Schmidt, Martin Anton. "Scholastik." In *Die Kirche in ihrer Geschichte.* Vol. 2, Lieferung G. Göttingen, 1969, 67–181.

Schmidt-Biggemann, Wilhelm. *Topica universalis: Eine Modellgeschichte humanistischer und barocker Wissenschaft.* Paradeigmata 1. Hamburg, 1983.

Schmitt, Charles B. *The Aristotelian Tradition and Renaissance Universities.* London, 1984.

Schmitz, Philipp. "Probabilismus—das jesuitischste der Moralsysteme." In *Ignatianisch:*

Eigenart und Methode der Gesellschaft Jesu. Edited by Michael Sievernich and Günter Switek. Freiburg im Breisgau, 1990, 355–68.

Schneyer, Johann Baptist. *Die Unterweisung der Gemeinde über die Predigt bei scholastischen Predigten: Eine Homiletik aus scholastischen Prothemen.* Veröffentlichungen des Grabmann-Institutes, n.s., 4. Munich, 1968.

———. *Geschichte der katholischen Predigt.* Freiburg im Breisgau, 1969.

———. *Repertorium der lateinischen Sermones des Mittelalters.* 11 vols. Münster, 1969–1990.

Schöffler, Herbert. *Deutsches Geistesleben zwischen Reformation und Aufklärung.* Frankfurt, 1956[2].

Schönberger, Rolf. *Was ist Scholastik?* Philosophie und Religion 2. Hildesheim, 1991.

Schrama, Martijn. *Gabriel Biel an zijn leer over de allerheiligste Drievuldigheid volgens het eerste boek van zijn Collectorium.* Bayerische Akademie der Wissenschaften. Veröffentlichungen der Kommission für die Herausgabe ungedruckter Texte aus der mittelalterlichen Geisteswelt 9. Munich, 1981.

Schrimpf, Gangolf. *Die Axiomenschrift des Boethius (De hebdomadibus) als philosophisches Lehrbuch des Mittelalters.* Studien zur Problemgeschichte der antiken und mittelalterlichen Philosophie 2. Leiden, 1966.

———. *Das Werk des Johannes Scottus Eriugena im Rahmen des Wissenschaftsverständnisses seiner Zeit. BGPhThMA,* n.s., 23. Münster, 1982.

———. "Bausteine für einen historischen Begriff der scholastischen Philosophie." In *Philosophie im Mittelalter,* Ian P. Beckmann. Hamburg, 1987, 1–25.

Schröcker, Hubert. *Das Verhältnis der Allmacht Gottes zum Kontradiktionsprinzip nach Wilhelm von Ockham.* Veröffentlichungen des Grabmann-Institutes 49. Berlin, 2003.

Schröder, Richard. *Johann Gerhards lutherische Christologie und die aristotelische Metaphysik.* Beiträge zur Historischen Theologie 67. Tübingen, 1983.

Schubert, Ernst. "Zur Typologie gegenreformatorischer Universitätsgründungen: Jesuiten in Fulda, Würzburg und Dillingen." In *Universität und Gelehrtenstand.* Edited by Rössler and Franz, 85–105.

Schulze, Manfred. "'Via Gregorii' in Forschung und Quellen." In *Gregor von Rimini.* Edited by Oberman, 1981, 1–126.

Schüssler, Hermann. *Der Primat der Heiligen Schrift als theologisches und kanonistisches Problem im Spätmittelalter.* VIEG 86. Wiesbaden, 1977.

Schwamm, Hermann. *Das göttliche Vorherwissen bei Duns Scotus und seinen ersten Anhängern.* Philosophie und Grenzwissenschaften 5. Innsbruck, 1934.

Seibt, Ferdinand, ed. *Jan Hus: Zwischen Zeiten, Völkern, Konfessionen.* Veröffentlichungen des Collegium Carolinum 85. Munich, 1997.

Seifert, Arno. *Logik zwischen Scholastik und Humanismus: Das Kommentarwerk Johann Ecks.* Humanistische Bibliothek I, no. 31. Munich, 1978.

Senner, Walter. "Zur Wissenschaftstheorie der Theologie im Sentenzenkommentar Alberts des Grossen." In *Albertus Magnus. Doctor universalis 1280/1980.* Edited by Gerbert Meyer and Albert Zimmerman.Walberberger Studien. Phil. Reihe 6. Mainz, 1980, 323–43.

Sicard, Patrice. *Hugues de Saint-Victor et son école.* Turnhout, 1991.

Sileo, Leonardo. *Teoria della scienza teologica: Quaestio de scientia theologiae di Odone Rigaldi e altri testi inediti (1230–1250).* Rome, 1984.

Smalley, Beryl. "A Commentary on the *Hebraica* by Herbert of Bosham." *RThAM* 18 (1951): 29–63.

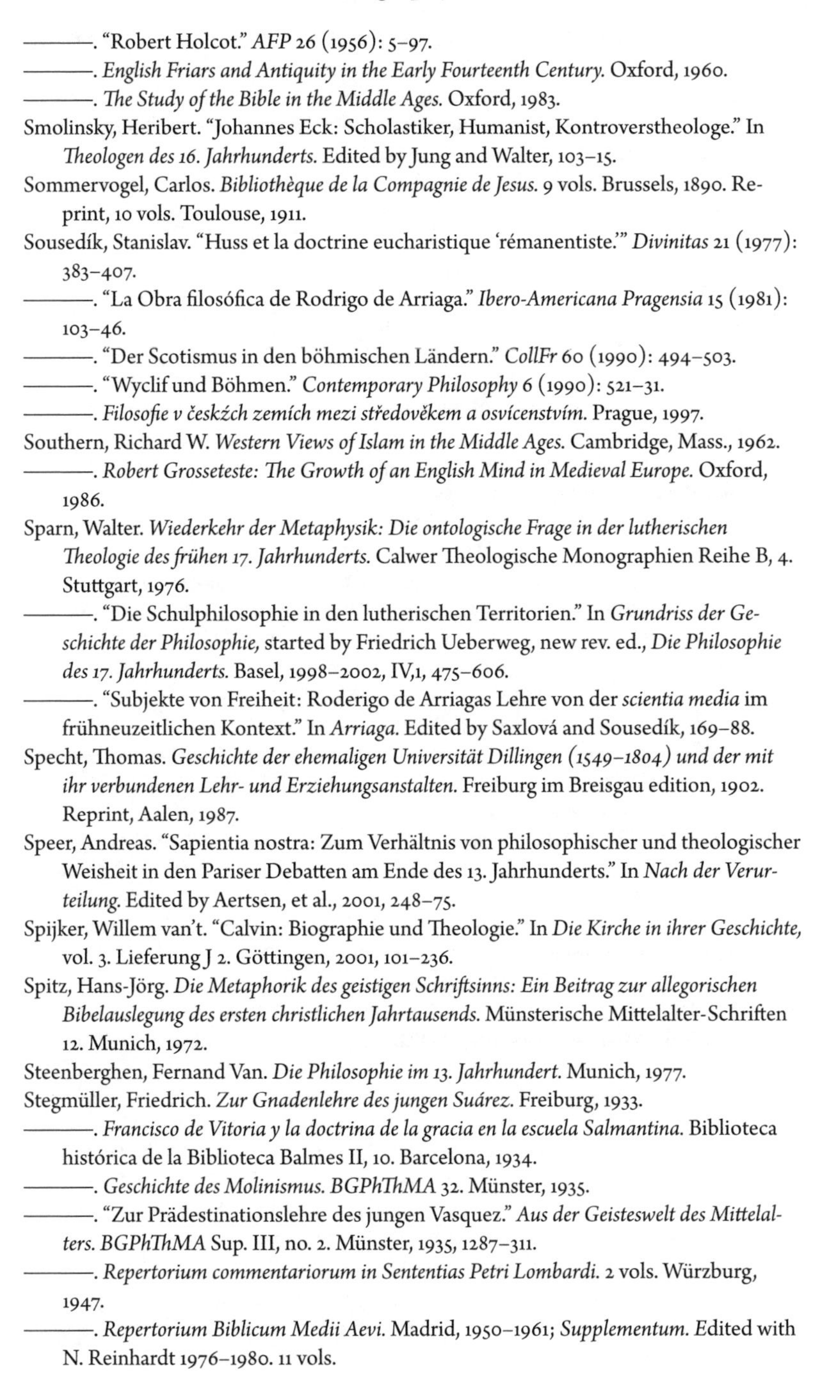

———. "Robert Holcot." *AFP* 26 (1956): 5–97.

———. *English Friars and Antiquity in the Early Fourteenth Century.* Oxford, 1960.

———. *The Study of the Bible in the Middle Ages.* Oxford, 1983.

Smolinsky, Heribert. "Johannes Eck: Scholastiker, Humanist, Kontroverstheologe." In *Theologen des 16. Jahrhunderts.* Edited by Jung and Walter, 103–15.

Sommervogel, Carlos. *Bibliothèque de la Compagnie de Jesus.* 9 vols. Brussels, 1890. Reprint, 10 vols. Toulouse, 1911.

Sousedík, Stanislav. "Huss et la doctrine eucharistique 'rémanentiste.'" *Divinitas* 21 (1977): 383–407.

———. "La Obra filosófica de Rodrigo de Arriaga." *Ibero-Americana Pragensia* 15 (1981): 103–46.

———. "Der Scotismus in den böhmischen Ländern." *CollFr* 60 (1990): 494–503.

———. "Wyclif und Böhmen." *Contemporary Philosophy* 6 (1990): 521–31.

———. *Filosofie v českźch zemích mezi středověkem a osvícenstvím.* Prague, 1997.

Southern, Richard W. *Western Views of Islam in the Middle Ages.* Cambridge, Mass., 1962.

———. *Robert Grosseteste: The Growth of an English Mind in Medieval Europe.* Oxford, 1986.

Sparn, Walter. *Wiederkehr der Metaphysik: Die ontologische Frage in der lutherischen Theologie des frühen 17. Jahrhunderts.* Calwer Theologische Monographien Reihe B, 4. Stuttgart, 1976.

———. "Die Schulphilosophie in den lutherischen Territorien." In *Grundriss der Geschichte der Philosophie,* started by Friedrich Ueberweg, new rev. ed., *Die Philosophie des 17. Jahrhunderts.* Basel, 1998–2002, IV,1, 475–606.

———. "Subjekte von Freiheit: Roderigo de Arriagas Lehre von der *scientia media* im frühneuzeitlichen Kontext." In *Arriaga.* Edited by Saxlová and Sousedík, 169–88.

Specht, Thomas. *Geschichte der ehemaligen Universität Dillingen (1549–1804) und der mit ihr verbundenen Lehr- und Erziehungsanstalten.* Freiburg im Breisgau edition, 1902. Reprint, Aalen, 1987.

Speer, Andreas. "Sapientia nostra: Zum Verhältnis von philosophischer und theologischer Weisheit in den Pariser Debatten am Ende des 13. Jahrhunderts." In *Nach der Verurteilung.* Edited by Aertsen, et al., 2001, 248–75.

Spijker, Willem van't. "Calvin: Biographie und Theologie." In *Die Kirche in ihrer Geschichte,* vol. 3. Lieferung J 2. Göttingen, 2001, 101–236.

Spitz, Hans-Jörg. *Die Metaphorik des geistigen Schriftsinns: Ein Beitrag zur allegorischen Bibelauslegung des ersten christlichen Jahrtausends.* Münsterische Mittelalter-Schriften 12. Munich, 1972.

Steenberghen, Fernand Van. *Die Philosophie im 13. Jahrhundert.* Munich, 1977.

Stegmüller, Friedrich. *Zur Gnadenlehre des jungen Suárez.* Freiburg, 1933.

———. *Francisco de Vitoria y la doctrina de la gracia en la escuela Salmantina.* Biblioteca histórica de la Biblioteca Balmes II, 10. Barcelona, 1934.

———. *Geschichte des Molinismus. BGPhThMA* 32. Münster, 1935.

———. "Zur Prädestinationslehre des jungen Vasquez." *Aus der Geisteswelt des Mittelalters. BGPhThMA* Sup. III, no. 2. Münster, 1935, 1287–311.

———. *Repertorium commentariorum in Sententias Petri Lombardi.* 2 vols. Würzburg, 1947.

———. *Repertorium Biblicum Medii Aevi.* Madrid, 1950–1961; *Supplementum.* Edited with N. Reinhardt 1976–1980. 11 vols.

Steiger, Johann Anselm. *Johann Gerhard (1582–1637): Studien zu Theologie und Frömmigkeit des Kirchenvaters der lutherischen Orthodoxie.* Doctrina et Pietas I, 1. Stuttgart, 1997.

———. "Johann Gerhard. Ein Kirchenvater der lutherischen Orthodoxie." In *Theologen des 17. und 18. Jahrhunderts: Konfessionelles Zeitalter—Pietismus—Aufklärung.* Edited by Peter Walter and Martin H. Jung. Darmstadt, 2003, 54–69.

Stempel, H. A. *Melanchthons pädagogisches Wirken.* Untersuchungen zur Kirchengeschichte 11. Bielefeld, 1979.

Stiglmayr, Emmerich. *Verstossung und Gnade: Die Universalität der hinreichenden Gnade und die strengen Thomisten des 16. und 17. Jahrhunderts.* Rome, 1964.

Stock, Brian. *The Implications of Literacy: Written Language and Models of Interpretation in the Eleventh and Twelfth Centuries.* Princeton, N.J., 1983.

Stockmeier, Peter. *Glaube und Kultur: Studien zur Begegnung von Christentum und Antike.* Düsseldorf, 1983.

Studer, Basil. *Schola Christiana: Die Theololgie zwischen Nizäa und Chalcedon.* Paderborn, 1998.

Sturlese, Loris. *Die deutsche Philosophie im Mittelalter: Von Bonifatius bis zu Albert dem Großen (748–1280).* Munich, 1993.

Swanson, Jenny. "The Glossa Ordinaria." In *Medieval Theologians.* Edited by Evans, 2001, 156–67.

Swanson, Robert N. *Universities, Academics and the Great Schism.* Cambridge, 1979.

Tavard, George H. *Transiency and Permanence: The Nature of Theology According to St. Bonaventure.* St. Bonaventure, N.Y., 1954.

Theiner, Johannes. *Die Entwicklung der Moraltheologie zur eigenständigen Disziplin.* Studien zur Geschichte der kath. Moraltheologie 17. Regensburg, 1970.

Thijssen-Schoute, C. Louise. *Nederlands Cartesianisme.* Verhandelingen der K. Ned. Akademie van Wetenschappen, Afd. Letterkunde, Nieuwe Reeks 60. Amsterdam, 1954.

Tholuck, August. *Der Geist der lutherischen Theologen Wittenbergs im Verlaufe des 17. Jahrhunderts.* Hamburg-Gotha, 1852.

———. *Das akademische Leben des siebzehnten Jahrhunderts mit besonderer Beziehung auf die protestantisch-theologischen Fakultäten Deutschlands.* Vorgeschichte des Rationalismus 1. Teil. I. Abt. [Section I]. Halle, 1853.

Trunz, Erich. "Der deutsche Späthumanismus um 1600 als Standeskultur." In *Deutsche Barockforschung: Dokumentation einer Epoche.* Edited by Richard Alewyn. Cologne, 1966, 147–81.

Tshibangu, Tharcisse. *Théologie positive et théologie speculative: Position traditionnelle et nouvelle problématique.* Publications de l'Université Lovanium de Léopoldville 14. Louvain, 1965.

Uiblein, Peter. "Zu den Beziehungen der Wiener Universität zu anderen Universitäten im Mittelalter." In *Universités.* Edited by Paquet and Ijsewijn, 1978, 169–89.

Valentini, Eugenio. "Il primo commentario protestante al 'Liber Sententiarium' di Pier Lombardo." In *Miscellanea Lombardiana.* Novara, 1957, 327–36.

Vansteenkiste, Clemente J. "S. Tommaso d'Aquino ed Averroè." *Rivista di studi orientali* 32 (1957): 585–623.

Vázquez Janeiro, Isaac. "Rutas e hitos del escotismo primitivo en España." In *Homo et Mundus: Acta Quinti Congressus Scotistici Internationalis, Salamanticae, 21–26 septembris 1981.* Edited by Camille Bérubé. Studica Scholastico-Scotistica 8. Rome, 1984, 419–36.

Velarde Lombraña, Julián. *Juan Caramuel: Vida y obra.* Oviedo, 1989.

Verbeek, Theo, ed. *Johannes Clauberg (1622–1655) and Cartesian Philosophy in the Seventeenth Century.* Archives Internationales d'histoire des idées 164. Dordrecht, 1999.

Vocht, H. de. *History of the foundation and the rise of the Collegium Trilingue Lovaniense 1517–1550.* 4 vols. Leuven, 1951–1955.

Vooght, Paul de. *L'Hérésie de Jean Huss.* Bibliothèque de la Revue d'Histoire Ecclésiastique 34 bis. Louvain, 1975.

Wallmann, Johannes. *Der Theologiebegriff bei Johann Gerhard und Georg Calixt.* Beiträge zur Historischen Theologie 30. Tübingen, 1961.

Wéber, Édouard-Henri. "Les discussions de 1270 à l'université de Paris de leur influence sur la pensée philosophique de S. Thomas d'Aquin." In *Auseinandersetzungen.* Edited by Zimmerman, 1976, 285–316.

Wehofer, Thomas M. "Der Dominikaner und Wiener Universitätsprofessor Petrus Gazzaniga über den pädagogischen Wert der scholastischen Methode des achtzehnten Jahrhunderts." *Mitteilungen der Gesellschaft für deutsche Erziehungs- und Schulgeschichte* 8 (1898): 191–97.

Weijers, Olga. *Terminologie des Universités au XIIIe siècle.* Lessico Intellettuale Europeo 39. Rome, 1987.

Weiss, Otto. *Der Modernismus in Deutschland: Ein Beitrag zur Theologiegeschichte.* Regensburg, 1995.

Weisweiler, Heinrich. *Das Schrifttum der Schule Anselms von Laon und Wilhelms von Champeaux in deutschen Bibliotheken. BGPhMA* 33, nos. 1–2. Münster, 1936.

———. "Die Arbeitsmethode Hugos von St. Viktor: Ein Beitrag zum Entstehen seines Hauptwerkes *De Sacramentis.*" *Scholastik* 20–24 (1945/49): 59–87, 232–67.

———. "Die Arbeitsweise der sogenannten Sententiae Anselmi: Ein Beitrag zum Entstehen der systematischen Werke der Theologie." *Scholastik* 34 (1959): 190–232.

———. "Wie entstanden die frühen Sententiae Berolinenses der Schule Anselms von Laon? Eine Untersuchung über die Verbindung von Patristik und Scholastik." *Scholastik* 34 (1959): 321–69.

Werner, Hans-Joachim. "'Meliores viae sophiae': Alkuins Bestimmung der Philosophie in der Schrift 'Disputatio de vera philosophia.'" In *Was ist Philosophie im Mittelalter?* Edited by Aertsen and Speer, 1998, 452–59.

Werner, Karl. *Geschichte der apologetischen und polemischen Literatur der christlichen Theologie.* 5 vols. Schaffhausen, 1861–1887.

———. *Die Scholastik des späteren Mittelalters* IV, 2. Vienna, 1887, 70–94.

———. *Geschichte der katholischen Theologie: Seit dem Trienter Concil bis zur Gegenwart.* Reprint, 1866 Munich edition, New York: Hildesheim, 1966.

Wicks, Jared. *Cajetan und die Anfänge der Reformation.* Katholisches Leben und Kirchenreform im Zeitalter der Glaubensspaltung 43. Münster, 1983.

Wiedenhofer, Siegfried. *Formalstrukturen humanistischer und reformatorischer Theologie bei Philipp Melanchthon.* Regensburger Studien zur Theologie 2. Bern, 1976.

Wiesinger, Peter. "Zur Autorschaft und Entstehung des Heinrich von Langenstein zugeschriebenen Traktats 'Erkenntnis der Sünde.'" *Zeitschrift für deutsche Philologie* 97 (1978): 42–60.

Winkler, Gerhard. *Erasmus von Rotterdam und die Einleitungsschriften zum Neuen Testament: Formale Strukturen und theologischer Sinn.* RGST 108. Münster, 1974.

Wolf, Karl. "Niederländischer Einfluss auf Nassau um 1600." *Nassauische Annalen* 58 (1938): 87–109.

Wriedt, Markus. "Die theologische Begründung der Bildungsreform bei Luther und Melanchthon." In *Humanismus.* Edited by Beyer and Wartenberg, 155–83.

Wulf, Maurice de. *Geschichte der mittelalterlichen Philosophie.* Tübingen, 1913.

Zier, Mark A. "Sermons of the Twelfth Century Schoolmasters and Canons." In *Sermon.* Edited by Kienzle, 325–62.

Zimmerman, Albert. "'Mundus est aeternus'—Zur Auslegung dieser These bei Bonaventura und Thomas von Aquin." In *Auseinandersetzungen.* Edited by Zimmerman, 1976, 317–30.

———, ed. *Der Begriff der Repraesentatio im Mittelalter.* Miscellanea Mediaevalia 8. Berlin: Walter de Gruyter, 1971.

———, ed. *Antiqui und Moderni: Traditionsbewusstsein und Fortschrittsbewusstsein im späten Mittelalter.* Miscellanea Mediaevalia 9. Berlin, 1971.

———, ed. *Die Auseinandersetzungen an der Pariser Universität im XIII. Jahrhundert.* Miscellanea Mediaevalia 10. Berlin, 1976.

Zumkeller, Adolar. "Die Augustinerschule des Mittelalters: Vertreter und philosophisch-theologische Lehre." *Analecta Augustiniana* 27 (1964): 167–262.

Index of Names

Introduction to Scholastic Theology was
designed and typeset in Arno by Kachergis
Book Design of Pittsboro, North Carolina. It
was printed on 50-pound Natural and bound
by Versa Press of East Peoria, Illinois.